Eternal Salvation

Christ Dying For Us

WILLEM J. OUWENEEL

AN EVANGELICAL INTRODUCTION TO
REFORMATIONAL THEOLOGY
VOLUME III/3

PART III: REDEMPTION:
THE CHRIST-CENTERED HEART OF THEOLOGY

AN EVANGELICAL INTRODUCTION TO REFORMATIONAL THEOLOGY

Part I: Scripture: The Revealed Source For Theology
   I/1 *The Eternal Word*: God Speaking To Us
   I/2 *The Eternal Torah*: Living Under God

Part II: God: The Personal Source Behind Theology
   II/1 *The Eternal God*: God Revealing Himself To Us
   II/2 *The Eternal Christ:* God With Us
   II/3 *The Eternal Spirit*: God Living In Us

Part III: Redemption: The Christ-Centered Heart of Theology
   III/1 *The Eternal Purpose*: Living In Christ
   III/2 *Eternal Righteousness*: Living Before God
   III/3 *Eternal Salvation*: Christ Dying For Us
   III/4 *Eternal Life*: Christ Living In Us

Part IV: Consummation: The Lived Shape of Theology
   IV/1a *The Eternal People*: God in Relation To Israel:
      Israel in the Tanakh and the New Testament
   IV/1b *The Eternal People*: God in Relation To Israel:
      Post-New Testament Israel
   IV/2 *The Eternal Covenant*: Living With God
   IV/3 *The Eternal Kingdom*: Living Under Christ

Part V: Method: The Comprehensive Foundation of Theology
   V/1 *Eternal Truth*: The Prolegomena of Theology

Eternal Salvation

Christ Dying For Us

WILLEM J. OUWENEEL

PAIDEIA PRESS

PAIDEIA
PRESS

Eternal Salvation: Christ Dying For Us

This English edition is a publication of the Reformational Publishing Project (www.reformationalpublishingproject.com) and Paideia Press (P.O. Box 500, Jordan Station, Ontario, Canada L0R 1S0). Copyright © 2022 by Paideia Press. All rights reserved. Except for brief quotations in critical publications or reviews, no part of this book may be reproduced in any manner without prior written permission from Paideia Press at the address above.

Unless otherwise indicated, Scripture quotations are from the ESV® Bible (The Holy Bible, English Standard Version®). Copyright © 2001 by Crossway, a publishing ministry of Good News Publishers. Used by permission. All rights reserved.

Scripture quotations or references marked as NKJV are taken from the New King James Version®. Copyright © 1982 by Thomas Nelson, Inc. Used by permission. All rights reserved.

Scripture quotations or references marked as NIV are taken from the Holy Bible, New International Version®, NIV®. Copyright © 1973, 1978, 1984, 2011 by Biblica, Inc.™ Used by permission of Zondervan. All rights reserved worldwide. www.zondervan.com. The "NIV" and "New International Version" are trademarks registered in the United States Patent and Trademark Office by Biblica, Inc.™

Book Design by: Paul Aurich

ISBN 978-0-88815-326-5

Printed in the United States of America

Israel is saved in the Lord
    *with an **eternal salvation:***
you shall not be confounded,
    and you shall not be ashamed
    for ever and ever.
Isaiah 45:17 (DRA)

Therefore I endure everything
    for the sake of the elect,
*that they also may obtain the **salvation***
    *that is in Christ Jesus with **eternal** glory.*
2 Timothy 2:10

And being made perfect,
    *[Jesus] became the source of **eternal salvation***
    to all who obey him.
Hebrews 5:9

[Jesus] entered once for all into the holy places,
    not by means of the blood of goats and calves
but by means of his own blood,
    *thus securing an **eternal redemption**.*
Hebrews 9:12

Table of Contents

Series Preface		i
Author's Preface		v
Abbreviations		ix
Chapter 1	A Preliminary Orientation	1
Chapter 2	The Notion of Salvation	47
Chapter 3	Salvation and God's Being	91
Chapter 4	Old Testament Sacrifices	147
Chapter 5	Special Atonement Rituals	197
Chapter 6	Special Aspects of Atonement	237
Chapter 7	The Cross of Christ	285
Chapter 8	Theological Redemption Metaphors	333
Chapter 9	Substitution and Satisfaction	381
Chapter 10	Resurrection and Reconciliation	423
Chapter 11	Some Theological Difficulties	471
Chapter 12	The Extent of Atonement	517
Chapter 13	Atonement for the Church, the World, and Israel	571
Chapter 14	Christ's Sacrifice: Healing and Deliverance	621
Bibliography		667
Scripture Index		695
Subject Index		729

Table of Contents Expanded

Series Preface		i
Author's Preface		v
Abbreviations		ix
1 A Preliminary Orientation		
1.1 Worldwide Salvation		2
1.1.1	Around the Globe	2
1.1.2	A Quest	4
1.1.3	Pathways to Salvation: Doing	7
1.1.4	Pathways to Salvation: Being	9
1.2 Christ and Salvation		11
1.2.1	Who is the Savior (Salvation Bringer)?	11
1.2.2	Person and Work of Christ	13
1.2.3	Objective and Subjective	15
1.2.4	The "Lofty Intellect"	17
1.3 What Is Salvation?		18
1.3.1	Saving Is Healing	18
1.3.2	The Trinity and Salvation	21
1.4 Aspects of Salvation		23
1.4.1	The Hamartiological Aspect	23
1.4.2	The Ecclesiological Aspect	24
1.4.3	The Pneumatological Aspect	26
1.4.4	The Nomological Aspect	27
1.4.5	The Ethical-Social Aspect	29
1.4.6	The Eschatological Aspect	31
1.4.7	The Mystical Aspect	32
1.5 The Regenerative Category of		

	Salvation	33
	1.5.1 General Introduction	33
	1.5.2 Conversion and Regeneration	35
1.6	The Theotic Category	37
	1.6.1 The New Person	37
	1.6.2 The Commandment of Love	39
1.7	The Eschatological Category	40
	1.7.1 Deliverance and Blessing	40
	1.7.2 New Testament Promises	43
2 The Notion of Salvation		47
2.1	The Old Testament Historical Books	48
	2.1.1 Salvation from Foreign Powers	48
	2.1.2 Human "Saviors"	50
2.2	The Prophetic Books	52
	2.2.1 Salvation and Justice	52
	2.2.2 Return from Babylon	53
2.3	Physical and Spiritual Powers	55
	2.3.1 The Prince of Egypt	55
	2.3.2 Other Angelic Princes	57
2.4	The New Testament Notion of Salvation	59
	2.4.1 Deliverance from the Powers	59
	2.4.2 Three Basic Terms	61
	2.4.3 Elaboration	62
2.5	The "Repulsive" Aspect of Salvation	65
	2.5.1 Living by Grace	65

	2.5.2	Grace and Humor	66
	2.5.3	Boasting in the Cross	68
	2.5.4	Saved by Blood	70
2.6	Salvation Described		72
	2.6.1	Little Attention	72
	2.6.2	The Ransom-to-Satan Model	73
	2.6.3	The Recapitulation Model	75
	2.6.4	The Sacrificial Substitution Model	76
2.7	Salvation Disowned		77
	2.7.1	The Rejection of Salvation	77
	2.7.2	Criticisms	79
2.8	Reactionary Theology		81
	2.8.1	Sola Scriptura	81
	2.8.2	Sola Fide	83
	2.8.3	Sola Cruce	85
	2.8.4	Sola Gratia	87

3 Salvation and God's Being   91

3.1	Fellowship		93
	3.1.1	God As a Communal Being	93
	3.1.2	Perichoresis	95
3.2	God Seeking Fellowship		96
	3.2.1	The Covenant God	96
	3.2.2	God Dwelling With His People	98
	3.2.3	New Testament	100
3.3.	God's Love		102
	3.3.1	Being and Attributes	102

	3.3.2	Love As God's Nature	103
	3.3.3	Trinitarian Love	105
3.4	Types of Love		106
	3.4.1	Love of Relationships	106
	3.4.2	Agapē, Eros, Philia	107
3.5	Aspects of Love		109
	3.5.1	Goodness	109
	3.5.2	Lovingkindness, Patience, Mercy	110
	3.5.3	Grace	112
3.6	God's Holiness		114
	3.6.1	Is It an Attribute?	114
	3.6.2	Attribute or Being?	115
	3.6.3	Terminology	117
3.7	God's Faithfulness		119
	3.7.1	New Testament	119
	3.7.2	Old Testament	121
	3.7.3	Faithfulness, Reason, Will	123
3.8	God's Peace		124
	3.8.1	The God of Peace	124
	3.8.2	Peace and Salvation	125
	3.8.3	Peace and the Eschaton	127
3.9	God's Bliss		128
	3.9.1	Terminology	128
	3.9.2	Happiness	130
	3.9.3	Apatheia and Other Errors	132

3.10		God's glory	133
	3.10.1	Displayed Beauty	133
	3.10.2	Glory and Light	136
	3.10.3	Glory and Salvation	138
3.11		God's Invisibility	139
	3.11.1	Mediated Vision	139
	3.11.2	Immediate Vision?	141
	3.11.3	More on the Trinity	143

4 Old Testament Sacrifices 147
  4.1 The Notion of Atonement 148
    4.1.1 Root Meaning of Atonement 148
    4.1.2 Old Testament Atonement 150
    4.1.3 "Covering, Blotting Out" 152
  4.2 Atonement Through a Sacrifice 154
    4.2.1 The Sacrificial Blood Effects Atonement 154
    4.2.2 Appeasing God? 157
    4.2.3 Other Aspects 159
  4.3 Introduction to the Atoning Sacrifices 162
    4.3.1 The Five Offerings of Leviticus 162
    4.3.2 Obligatory and Voluntary 164
    4.3.3 The Atoning Sacrifices and the New Testament 165
  4.4 The Burnt Offering 167
    4.4.1 The Old Testament Form 167

	4.4.2	The Burnt Offering and Sin	169
	4.4.3	The Laying On of Hands	171
	4.4.4	The New Testament Application	172
4.5		The Peace Offering	175
	4.5.1	The Old Testament Form	175
	4.5.2	The Eating Aspect 177	177
	4.5.3	Function and Meaning	179
4.6		The Sin Offering	182
	4.6.1	The Old Testament Form	182
	4.6.2	The Role of the Priest	183
	4.6.3	The New Testament Application	186
4.7		The Guilt Offering	189
	4.7.1	The Old Testament Form	189
	4.7.2	Various Cases	190
	4.7.3	Function and Meaning	193
5		Special Atonement Rituals	197
	5.1	Pesach	198
	5.1.1	The Institution of Pesach	198
	5.1.2	The Blood on the Doorposts	200
	5.1.3	Terminology	201
	5.2	The Spiritual Meaning of Pesach	203
	5.2.1	The Lamb in Paul's and John's	

	Writings	203
5.2.2	The Ninth Hour	204
5.3	The Day of Atonement: the Ritual	206
5.3.1	Introduction	206
5.3.2	The First Goat	207
5.3.3	The Second Goat	210
5.4	Various Sacrificial Animals	212
5.4.1	The Goat for Azazel	212
5.4.2	Other Sacrificial Animals	214
5.5	The Significance of the Day of Atonement	215
5.5.1	Satisfaction and Substitution	215
5.5.2	Cleansing of the Tabernacle	217
5.5.3	Special New Testament Aspects	219
5.6	The Law about Leprosy	221
5.6.1	The Meaning of Leprosy	221
5.6.2	The Two Birds	222
5.7	Other Atoning Rituals	224
5.7.1	The Consecration of the Priests	224
5.7.2	Purification After Childbirth	226
5.7.3	The Purification of the Person with a Discharge	228
5.7.4	The Water of Purification	230

6	Special Aspects of Atonement		237
	6.1	The Go'el	238
		6.1.1 The Lost Inheritance	238
		6.1.2 Other Forms of Redemption	239
	6.2	God As Go'el	241
		6.2.1 Introduction	241
		6.2.2 A Lost Inheritance	242
		6.2.3 Enslaved Persons	243
		6.2.4 The Abandoned, Childless Wife	245
		6.2.5 The Blood Revenge	246
	6.3	Christ As Go'el	247
		6.3.1 Introduction	247
		6.3.2 The Four Tasks of the Go'el	248
	6.4	The Place of the High Priest	250
		6.4.1 Offering As Well As Offerer	250
		6.4.2 The Two Priestly Orders	252
		6.4.3 The High Priest's Heavenly Ministry	254
	6.5	Atonement Without a Bloody Sacrifice	257
		6.5.1 Covering Over Without Punishment	257
		6.5.2 Atonement Through a Rasom	259
		6.5.3 Forms of Ransom	262
	6.6	Types in Genesis	264
		6.6.1 Adam	264

	6.6.2	Abel	266
	6.6.3	Noah	269
	6.6.4	Abraham	270
6.7	Defective Offerings		273
	6.7.1	Offering in the Right Attitude	273
	6.7.2	Love Better Than Offerings	275
	6.7.3	The True Attitude	278
	6.7.4	Forgiveness in the Old Testament	280
7	The Cross of Christ		285
7.1	Models		286
	7.1.1	A Brief Enumeration	286
	7.1.2	The Term "Model"	288
7.2	Satisfaction, Ethics, Example		289
	7.2.1	Four Classical Approaches	289
	7.2.2	Other Older Models	291
	7.2.3	Modern Models	294
7.3	Pivotal Questions		297
	7.3.1	Constitutive Versus Illustrative	297
	7.3.2	Contra the Modern Mentality?	299
	7.3.3	Gradual Revelation?	301
	7.3.4	Jesus' Own Testimony	303
7.4		Matthew and Mark	305
	7.4.1	Forsaken by God	305
	7.4.2	Guilt and Sin Offering	307

	7.4.3	Luke: the Peace Offering	309
	7.4.4	John: the Burnt Offering	311
7.5	The Seven Sayings On the Cross		313
	7.5.1	The Chiastic Structure	313
	7.5.2	Three + Four	313
7.6	The Seven Sayings		314
	7.6.1	The First Saying	314
	7.6.2	The Second Saying	316
	7.6.3	The Third Saying	319
	7.6.4	The Fourth Saying	322
	7.6.5	The Fifth Saying	324
	7.6.6	The Sixth Saying	327
	7.6.7	The Seventh Saying	329
8 Theological Metaphors for Redemption			333
8.1	Introduction		334
	8.1.1	Biological-Medical Metaphors	334
	8.1.2	Social-Economic Metaphors	336
	8.1.3	Other Metaphors for Redemption	339
8.2	Aspects and Circles		340
	8.2.1	Seven Aspects	340
	8.2.2	Four Circles	342
8.3	Christ's Work As an Act of Love		345
	8.3.1	Active Surrender	345
	8.3.2	Love and Returned Love	347
8.4	Christ's Work As an Act of Solidarity		350

		8.4.1	The Sufferings of All Humanity	350
		8.4.2	Christ in the Psalms	353
		8.4.3	The Spirit of Christ	354
	8.5	Jesus' Martyrdom		356
		8.5.1	Torturers and Tortured Ones	356
		8.5.2	Biblical Examples	358
		8.5.3	Jesus' Exemplary Death	359
	8.6	Suffering for Righteousness' Sake	362
		8.6.1	Bearing One's Cross	362
		8.6.2	Various Kinds of Suffering	364
	8.7	The Cross As Arena	366
		8.7.1	Warfare Against Satan	366
		8.7.2	Destroyed and Conquered	368
		8.7.3	Disarmed	370
	8.8	Warfare Against Death	373
		8.8.1	The Last Enemy	373
		8.8.2	The Rulers Overcome	374
		8.8.3	Old Testament Illustrations	376
9	Substitution and Satisfaction	381
	9.1	Substitution	382
		9.1.1	Introduction	382
		9.1.2	Old Testament Evidence	384
	9.2	New Testament Evidence	385
		9.2.1	Terminology	385
		9.2.2	Application of the Old Testament in the New Testament	388

	9.2.3	Conclusion	390
9.3		Expiation and Propitiation	393
	9.3.1	God's Fury Appeased?	393
	9.3.2	The Placation	395
	9.3.3	More Comments	398
9.4		Placationism versus Theopaschitism	400
	9.4.1	Propitiation and the Wrath of God	400
	9.4.2	Theopaschitism	402
	9.4.3	The Middle Way	405
9.5		Satisfaction	407
	9.5.1	Violated Justice	407
	9.5.2	Satisfied Justice	408
	9.5.3	Satisfaction and Punishment	411
9.6		Satisfaction, Love, Righteousness	413
	9.6.1	Love	413
	9.6.2	Righteousness	416
	9.6.3	The Sweet Exchange	418
10 Resurrection and Reconciliation			423
10.1		The Resurrection of Christ	425
	10.1.1	Saved by Christ's Death and Resurrection	425
	10.1.2	The View of the Heidelberg Catechism	427
	10.1.3	Theological Meaning of the Resurrection	428
10.2		Glorification	431

10.2.1	Redemptive Significance	431
10.2.2	The View of the Heidelberg Catechism	432
10.2.3	Theological Meaning of the Glorification	434
10.3	Entering (By? With?) the Blood of Christ	437
10.3.1	Hebrews 9:12	437
10.3.2	Typology	439
10.4	Is God an Enemy of Humanity?	441
10.4.1	The Sense of Reconciliation	441
10.4.2	Biblical References	444
10.5	Human Enmity	446
10.5.1	Enemies of God and Each Other	446
10.5.2	Active or Passive?	447
10.6	Mediator and Guarantor	450
10.6.1	Mediator	450
10.6.2	Guarantor	452
10.7	Who Is Reconciled to Whom?	454
10.7.1	Humans Reconciled to Humans	454
10.7.2	Humans Reconciled to God	456
10.7.3	Light from the Parables	458
10.8	Reconciliation of the World	460
10.8.1	No Universalism	460
10.8.2	A Threefold Ministry	461
10.9	The Blood, the Cross, and the Death of Christ	462

10.9.1		The Blood of Christ	462
10.9.2		The Cross of Christ	464
10.9.3		The Death of Christ	466
10.9.4		Review	467

11 Some Theological Difficulties — 471

11.1	Expiation Throughout Jesus' Entire Life?	472
11.1.1	Did Jesus Undergo the Wrath of God?	472
11.1.2	Was God's Wrath On Jesus Throughout All His Life?	474
11.1.3	Other Reformed Confessions	475
11.2	Christ's Keeping the Law	477
11.2.1	Active and Passive Obedience	477
11.2.2	No Vicarious Law-Keeping	479
11.2.3	Condition or Part?	481
11.3	Only On the Cross	482
11.3.1	Grain and Burnt Offering	482
11.3.2	Bearing On or Carrying To?	484
11.4	God's Pleasure Rested On Jesus	486
11.4.1	Pleasure or Wrath?	486
11.4.2	The Sufferings of the Cross	489
11.5	The Stripes of Pilate?	491
11.5.1	God's Stripes	491
11.5.2	"Slaughtered"	493
11.5.3	God and Humans Working Together	495
11.6	The Three Hours of Darkness	498

11.6.1	Types of Sufferings	498
11.6.2	"My God, Why . . ."	500
11.6.3	The Jewish Remnant	503
11.7	The Mystery of the Sacrifice	505
11.7.1	Why the Sacrifice?	505
11.7.2	The Atonement Message of the Gospels	506
11.7.3	Traditional Answers	508
11.8	The "Why" Remains	510
11.8.1	The Deepest Answers	510
11.8.2	God's "Own Blood"	512
11.8.3	The Two Together	513
12	The Extent of Atonement	517
12.1	Four Different Views	518
12.1.1	Summary	518
12.1.2	"All People," the "Whole World"	519
12.1.3	Between Predestination and Unlimited Atonement	521
12.2	The (Un)limitedness of Atonement	523
12.2.1	Cosmic Reconciliation	523
12.2.2	Second Corinthians 5:19	524
12.2.3	First John 2:2	526
12.2.4	Summary	529
12.3	Which Sins Atoned?	530
12.3.1	The Ambiguous Term "Unlimied"	530
12.3.2	"All" and "Many"	532

	12.3.3 Alternatives	533
12.4	Consequences For All People?	535
	12.4.1 Universalism	535
	12.4.2 Eternal Destruction	538
	12.4.3 Yet Consequences For All People	540
12.5	The Cross In the Walk of Faith	542
	12.5.1 The Cross of Christ	542
	12.5.2 The Believer's Cross	544
	12.5.3 A Double Death Sentence	547
12.6	Forgiveness	548
	12.6.1 God's Heart	548
	12.6.2 Forgiveness Is Expensive	551
	12.6.3 Four Aspects of Forgiveness	553
12.7	Conditions of Forgiveness	555
	12.7.1 Repentance, Confession, Faith	555
	12.7.2 Gratitude and Perseverance	558
	12.7.3 Forgiving Oneself and Others	559
12.8	The Consequences of Christ's Victory	561
	12.8.1 Eastern Orthodox Soteriology	561
	12.8.2 Theosis	563
	12.8.3 Redemption	566
13	**Atonement for the Church, the World, and Israel**	**571**
13.1	The Church	57

13.1.1	Collective Atonement	572
13.1.2	A New Commonwealth	575
13.2	The Gentile World	578
13.2.1	Stating the Problem	578
13.2.2	Analysis of Viewpoints	581
13.2.3	All People Enlightened?	582
13.3	Inclusivism versus Exclusivism	585
13.3.1	God's Heart For All People	585
13.3.2	Ignorance versus Rejection	587
13.4	Living in the Spirit of the Torah	589
13.4.1	Romans 2	589
13.4.2	Cornelius	591
13.4.3	Areopagus	592
13.5	The Encounter With Jesus	594
13.5.1	Saul and Paul	594
13.5.2	"Anonymous Christians"	595
13.5.3	Modern Jews	597
13.6	Conditions	598
13.6.1	Through Christ Alone	598
13.6.2	Through the Holy Spirit Alone	600
13.6.3	Through Repentance Alone	603
13.6.4	Other Religions	606
13.7	Israel	607
13.7.1	The Eschatological Yom Kippur	607
13.7.2	Israel's Penance	610
13.7.3	The Fountain for Cleansing	614

		13.7.4 The Water of Purification	616
14 Christ's Sacrifice: Healing and Deliverance			621
	14.1	Disease and Atonement	623
		14.1.1 Disease and Sin	623
		14.1.2 Jesus "Bearing" Diseases	624
	14.2	Is Healing a Part of Atonement?	627
		14.2.1 Not All Are Healed	627
		14.2.2 A Balanced View	629
	14.3	Forgiveness, But No Immortality	631
		14.3.1 Old Age Ailments	631
		14.3.2 Salvation and Disease	633
	14.4	The Place of Faith	635
		14.4.1 Faith Before the Healing	635
		14.4.2 Faith After the Healing	638
	14.5	Liberated Prisoners?	640
		14.5.1 The View	640
		14.5.2 Refutation	643
		14.5.3 Ephesians 4:8-10	645
	14.6	The Ministry of Deliverance	647
		14.6.1 "Pagan" Facets	647
		14.6.2 Converts and Bondage	649
		14.6.3 Ignorance	650
	14.7	Boundness and Possession	653
		14.7.1 Demonic Influences	653
		14.7.2 Symptoms	654
	14.8	A Way of Deliverance	657
		14.8.1 Causes of Demonic Bondage	657

14.8.2	Renouncement	659
14.9	Final Remarks	661
14.9.1	Various Metaphors	661
14.9.2	Other Metaphors	662
14.9.3	Closure	664
Bibliography		667
Scripture Index		695
Subject Index		729

Series Preface

By means of this Preface, the editor and publisher of this series wish to help the reader both understand and process the content of these volumes.

The capacities and erudition of Dr. Willem Ouweneel need no demonstration or defense from us. His voluminous work and prodigious writing stand as a testimony to his love for the Lord Jesus Christ, God's Word, and God's people.

But these volumes present ideas that will surprise some, anger others, and possibly confuse still others. Both the editor and publisher disagree with some of Dr. Ouweneel's assertions and conclusions, but this is not the place for offering our counter-arguments. That requires an altogether different venue. Nevertheless, discerning readers will legitimately wonder why this editor and publisher invested effort and resources in putting these volumes into print.

At least three reasons justify that investment. Each of them is very sensitive.

The first reason is: *self-examination*. Some of our readers may conclude that, in presenting his exegetical, doctrinal, and historical case, Dr. Ouweneel is "coloring outside the lines" of what they have come to believe. He challenges deeply and firmly held convictions and beliefs, like those associated with Israel, with the law of God, with election and reprobation, with infant baptism, with covenant theology, and with justification. At each point, his challenges call us readers to self-examination, regarding our love for Scripture, for the God of Scripture, and for the Truth revealed and incarnated personally in Jesus Christ. One of Ouweneel's challenges is for us believers in Jesus Christ who are Reformed and Presbyterian church members to recognize that there are millions, even billions, of Jesus-believers who disagree with us *and are nevertheless genuine Christians.* And they ought to be acknowledged as such.

The second reason is: *repentance.* Coming, as they do, from one who lives and teaches outside the orbit of many of our readers, Dr. Ouweneel's observations about the state of our (numerous) churches and of our (interminable) doctrinal squabbles ought to embarrass us Reformed and Presbyterian church members. Our incessant polemicizing, our cantankerous stridency, and our offenses against the unity of Christ's church seriously compromise the gospel's witness to the watching world. Brothers and sisters, we must repent of these, for the sake of the gospel, for the sake of the church's witness, and for the sake of our children.

The third reason is: *ecumenicity.* This reason may indeed strike you as strange, but one of the salutary outcomes of reading Dr. Ouweneel's arguments can be this: *not* that you surrender your commitments and convictions that are being challenged, but instead that you come to *respect* and *love* those Jesus-believers who don't share them with you. These Christians are those whose spiritual pilgrimage and gospel-guided history have not brought them to the same place on the road, but who nonetheless are walking the same road as we.

You may well be asking: How, then, is this different from advocating doctrinal relativism? If these distinctive features of Reformed confession and theology are biblical, then why is Dr. Ouweneel being given a microphone for proclaiming his criticisms and rejections of these distinctive emphases of Reformed teaching? The short answer is this: So that from this brother in Christ, this close cousin in the faith, this fellow pilgrim-soldier, we may learn how to lock arms with other Jesus-believers as we face unbelief in our day, even if we can't hold hands. So that we may learn what it means to be Jesus-believers *first*, Reformed or Presbyterian confessors *second*, and only then, *thirdly, theological advocates*.

So we leave you with this challenge: Why do you believe what you believe? What is your biblical warrant? Dr. Ouweneel presents fairly the various positions prevalent within Christianity. The reader will learn why others believe what they believe, and why they don't emphasize certain teachings in the same way that we do.

These books, then, are *not* for the faint of faith. But they *are* for those wanting to grow up and mature into the unity of faith in our Lord Jesus Christ (John 17: 20-23; Eph. 4:13).

Nelson D. Kloosterman, editor
John Hultink, publisher

Author's Preface

THIS IS THE seventh volume in a series on the "unseen, eternal" things of God (cf. 2 Cor. 4:18). This seventh and the planned eighth volume deal with soteriology, the Christian doctrine of God's redemption or salvation. Volume III/4, *Eternal Life*, will focus upon the more subjective aspects of salvation (conversion, regeneration, eternal life, and so on); justification and sanctification were already with in Volume III/2, *Eternal Righteousness*. The present volume deals with the objective aspects of salvation: the redemptive work of Christ. That is, this present volume speaks of what Christ did *for* his people, and the next will speak of what Christ did and does *with* and *in* his people.

In a certain sense, *all* systematic theology is soteriology: God is the origin of salvation, the Holy Spirit is God's instrument of salvation, Christ is the guarantee and mediator of salvation, the Torah is God's *magna carta* for the redeemed, the covenant is his alliance with the redeemed, predestination involves God's counsel with respect to salvation, the church is the incorporation of the redeemed, the kingdom of God embodies the future destination of the redeemed, and so on. I do realize, though, that by the same token all systematic theology could be called pneumatology, or Christology, or federology, or ecclesiology, or basileology, and so on. In Volume II/1, *The Eternal God* (following Vol. I/1, *The Eternal Word* and Vol. I/2, *The Eternal Torah*), I will endeavor to bring together all the various lines in the person of the Triune God.

The present volume deals largely with the sacrifice of Christ, which is explicitly an *atoning* sacrifice. That is, it is a sacrifice that is a *propitiation* for people's sins and that *reconciles* people with God. Even on the strictest conservative standpoint, atonement is not at all an easy subject. It often seems as if the most essential and fundamental Christian subjects are also the most complicated ones. Our investigation is further bothered by the fact that the doctrine of atonement is being attacked from many different sides. Thus, the subject will demand a lot from both the author and the readers. Moreover, more than in most previous volumes, the Old Testament will have to play a considerable role in our investigations. It is my thesis that the New Testament doctrine of propitiation and reconciliation cannot be understood apart a thorough study of the Sinaitic sacrificial laws.

This volume is a re-working and expansion of volume 5 of my *Evangelisch-Dogmatische Reeks (Evangelical Dogmatic Series,* published in Dutch by Medema (Heerenveen), consisting of twelve volumes in total).[1] My intention was, and is, to offer an Evangelical analysis of various subjects that traditionally have played a great role in Reformational—especially Calvinist—thinking: the law, the covenant, justification, predestination, the kingdom, the Holy Spirit, atonement, salvation, and revelation. The order of the volumes, both in Dutch and in English, is rather arbitrary, due to practical circumstances.

Bible quotations in this book are usually from the English Standard Version. However, any italics used within Bible quotations are added by the author.

---

1. Ouweneel (2009a).

Author's Preface

I thank Dr. Nelson D. Kloosterman again very warmly for his expert editorial work on the manuscript of this book. And I am again deeply thankful to my publisher, John Hultink, for his constant encouragement in this entire project.

Willem J. Ouweneel
Fall 2017

Abbreviations

Bible Versions

AMP	Amplified Bible
AMPC	Amplified Bible, Classic Edition
ASV	American Standard Version
BRG	BRG Bible
CEB	Common English Bible
CEV	Contemporary English Version
CJB	Complete Jewish Bible
DARBY	Darby Translation
DLNT	Disciples' Literal New Translation
DRA	Douay-Rheims 1899 American Edition
ERV	Easy-to-Read Version
ESV	English Standard Version
EXB	Expanded Bible
GNT	Good News Translation
GNV	1599 Geneva Bible
GW	God's Word Translation
HCSB	Holman Christian Standard Bible
ICB	International Children's Bible
ISV	International Standard Version

JUB	Jubilee Bible 2000	
KJ21	21st Century King James Version	
KJV	King James Version	
LEB	Lexham English Bible	
MEV	Modern English Version	
MSG	The Message	
NABRE	New American Bible (Revised Edition)	
NASB	New American Standard Bible	
NCV	New Century Version	
NIV	New International Version	
NLV	New Life Version	
NKJV	New King James Version	
NOG	Names of God Bible	
NRSV	New Revised Standard Version	
OJB	Orthodox Jewish Bible	
RSV/CE	Revised Standard Version/Catholic Edition	
TLB	Living Bible	
TLV	Tree of Life Version	
VOICE	The Voice	
WEB	World English Bible	
WYC	Wycliffe Bible	
YLT	Young's Literal Translation	

Other Sources

BabT — Epstein, I., ed. 1961. *The Babylonian Talmud*. London: Soncino Press.

BT — Kelly, W., ed. 1856–1920. *Bible Treasury: A Monthly Review of Prophetic and Practical Subjects*. Available at https://bibletruthpublishers.com/

Abbreviations

	bible-treasury/lpvl22465.
CD	Barth, K. 2009. *Church Dogmatics. Study Edition.* Translated by G. W. Bromiley et al. Vols. I/1–IV/1. New York, NY: T&T Clark. (Editor's Note: The original fourteen volumes have been published in the *Study Edition* as thirty-one volumes. For citation purposes, the original volume enumeration is followed by the number of the equivalent new volume: e.g., III/3=18. The sections [§] are identical in both editions. The final number[s] refer[s] to the page[s] in the new *Study Edition*. Sample citation convention: *CD* III/3=18, §51.2:130.)
COT	Commentaar op het Oude Testament
CNT	Commentaar op het Nieuwe Testament
CR	*Corpus Reformatorum.* 1st series and 2nd series. Vols. 1–87. Brunswick: Schwetschke, 1834–1900.
CW	Darby, J. N. n.d. *The Collected Writings of J. N. Darby.* Kingston-on-Thames: Stow Hill Bible and Tract Depot.
DNTT	Brown, C., ed. 1992. *The New International Dictionary of New Testament Theology.* 4 vols. Carlisle: Paternoster.
DOTT	Van Gemeren, W. A., ed. 1996. *The New International Dictionary of Old Testament Theology and Exegesis.* 4 vols. Carlisle: Paternoster.

EBC	The Expositor's Bible Commentary
EDR	Ouweneel, W. J. 2007–2013. *Evangelische Dogmatische Reeks*. 12 vols. Vaassen/Heerenveen: Medema.
EGT	Expositor's Greek Testament
KV	Korte Verklaring der Heilige Schrift
NICNT	New International Commentary on the New Testament
NICOT	New International Commentary on the Old Testament
NIDNTT	Brown, C., ed. 1992. *The New International Dictionary of New Testament Theology*. 4 vols. Carlisle: Paternoster.
NIGTC	New International Greek Testament Commentary
RC	Dennison, J. T., Jr., ed. 2008–2014. *Reformed Confessions of the 16th and 17th Centuries in English Translation*. 4 vols. Grand Rapids, MI: Reformation Heritage Books.
RD	Bavinck, H. 2002–2008. *Reformed Dogmatics*. Edited by J. Bolt. Translated by J. Vriend. 4 vols. Grand Rapids, MI: Baker Academic.
RT	Ouweneel, W. J. Forthcoming. *An Evangelical Introduction to Reformational Theology*. Edited by N. D. Kloosterman. 13 vols. Jordan Station, ON: Paideia Press.
ST	Chafer, L. S. 1983. *Systematic Theology*. 15th ed. 8 vols. Dallas, TX: Dallas Seminary Press.
TDNT	Kittel, G. et al., eds. 1964–1976. *Theo-*

	logical Dictionary of the New Testament. Translated by G. W. Bromiley. 10 vols. Grand Rapids, MI: Eerdmans.
TNTC	Tyndale New Testament Commentaries

Chapter 1
A Preliminary Orientation

I am the way,
and the truth,
and the life.
No one comes to the Father
except through me.
                                John 14:6

[T]here is salvation in no one else,
for there is no other name
under heaven given among men
by which we must be saved.
                                Acts 4:12

Summary: *"Salvation" is a very broad notion; in this chapter we make an initial foray into the field of soteriology. Around the globe we find many very different views of salvation (bliss, wholeness, etc.), and even Christians emphasize very different aspects of salvation: on the one hand, salvation consists of redemption from sin and on the other side of the spectrum, it signifies an eschatological notion. A brief survey is given. The special place of Christ and his work is underscored, against the background of the Trinity* *(which will, of course, be developed later). In fact, virtually every discipline within systematic theology has contributed to the doctrine of salvation. Three classifications are investigated somewhat more closely: the regenerative, the theotic, and the eschatological classifications.*

1.1 Worldwide Salvation
1.1.1 Around the Globe

WHEN, DURING THE SUMMER of 1973, my wife and I were in San Francisco, of course we wanted to visit Telegraph Avenue. We were hoping to see the "hippies," and the brightly dressed devotees of various Eastern religions, and we stared our eyes out. They were charming. They sang and played, they read and recited, or they were simply quietly happy. They offered us rice with saffron, but we hesitated to accept it—so deep was the cleft that separated us. Could one eat that stuff without being affected?

Since 1987 we have also been to Africa many times, where we met the adherents of animist religions—and we met Africans converted to Christianity, in whom there often was still a lot of paganism. I remember the friendly Zulu brother in the Natal countryside (South Africa), a Reformed elder, who when he had to make important decisions went to his kraal (similar to a primitive corral), among his cattle, to consult his ancestors. In various African countries, we have experienced how much more closely the natural and the supernatural world were interwoven. One of the consequences is that people are healed of diseases, and delivered from demons, so much more easily than in our Western world. Salvation seems to be grasped there more easily than in our part of the world, where the Enlightenment has created a deep cleft between the natural and the supernatural. I had similar experiences in China, India, Indonesia, and Myanmar (Burma).

Every continent knows its own experience of salvation. In many visits to the United States, we encountered Christians of both the "happy clappy" and the "frozen chosen" varieties. In Suriname we attended congregations of native Indians and Maroons, on the Russian countryside simple Russian Orthodox groups, and in Greece simple Greek Orthodox congregations. In April 2005, we were in Shanghai, where we visited (in arbitrary order) a synagogue, a mosque, a Confucian temple, a Taoist temple—in addition to one Catholic and two Protestant churches. In many Italian cities, wherever possible, I visited many churches as well as a synagogue and a mosque. And the many times I was in Jerusalem, I did the same: walking from a synagogue to a mosque, from an Armenian church to a Russian Orthodox church, and to all kinds of churches along a wide spectrum. And of course, in Haifa I visited the Baha'i shrine.

In London, during a Sunday afternoon, we were in Hyde Park to experience the "Speakers' Corner" phenomenon. Almost everyone who raised his voice there was defending either Christianity or Islam. The whole atmosphere was very religious. The Christians verbally attacked the Muslim preachers, and the Muslims the Christian preachers. A lonely Hindu tried to attract his own little audience.

Years ago I had the privilege of publicly debating a Muslim and a Hindu before a hall packed with students at Utrecht University (Netherlands). The Muslim argued, "If you become a Muslim, you do not have to sacrifice anything from your Christian faith; you will merely receive *new* blessings: the last divine prophet, and the ultimate divine revelation." The Hindu argued, "If you become a Hindu, it will be even more beautiful: you may keep Jesus, you may keep Muhammad, but in addition you receive six hundred gods! You will end up richer!" Would it be this simple? The Muslim promised me Paradise, the Hindu promised me Nirvana, the ultimate state of bliss. And I myself told both the Muslim and the Hindu, "If I would accept your religion, I would *lose* the very Christ of the Bible."

However, I must add: notice how widely Christians differ among themselves about the matter of salvation. I have encountered almost every brand of Christianity, and I have preached in dozens of denominations, even among Roman Catholics. But what different answers would many of them have given me if I had asked them about salvation! I have spoken with Mormons (in black suits) in the hot Southwest of the United States (among the Pueblo Indians). I have preached behind the Iron Curtain (i.e., before 1990) in dozens of congregations. In France I have preached at Evangelical open-air meetings, which were conducted exactly as in the time of the Huguenots. In South Africa I have preached in the heart of Soweto (near Johannesburg) among the blacks, as well as in Indian congregations, in "colored" congregations (of the descendants of black and white ancestors), and in white congregations, both in English and in Afrikaans. I have preached in Messianic-Jewish as well as in Palestinian congregations. I have preached in China for young people, in India, Indonesia, and Myanmar for small and large audiences, and of course I have preached in Europe—in nineteen different countries.

Such a widespread ministry has helped me tremendously to relativize a bit my own particular views, and to expand my understanding of salvation. The stricter a denomination is, the better it would be for young preachers in such a church to spend a couple of years on the mission field before serving a congregation in their homeland. We cannot speak of salvation within a narrow horizon. This first chapter is intended to provide support for this thesis.

1.1.2 A Quest

No matter how much these faiths and religions may differ, they all have something in common: a longing for "bliss,"[1] no matter how one might interpret this term. In the broadest sense of the word, bliss involves salvation, redemption, wholeness, perfection, well-being, prosperity, blessing, happiness, love, joy, peace, righteousness, fullness, unity, communion, and contemplation (regardless of what or whom it may be). This bliss could be enjoyed on earth or in the hereafter. This bliss may be inner and strictly personal, or collective and global, in a future Golden Age. Or both: bliss as an instant experience of the present moment, which is a foretaste of the full bliss that one day will arrive on this earth, in heaven, or on a new earth.

The English word "hail," as in "hail to the king," is related to the Dutch and German words *heil,* which themselves are related to the Dutch words *heel* (German *heil,* English *whole*) and *helen* (German *heilen,* English *to heal*). Heel/heil/whole originally meant "healthy (healed), unhurt, undamaged," and then came to mean "pure" and "happy." Those who are searching for wholeness/health begin with the concept of violation, hurt, brokenness, imperfection, as we find it in the world and in our own lives and circumstances. The collective human quest for wholeness, in whatever sense and whatever way, always begins with the insight that the world, including me, is not as ideal as it should be. Even the most secular, horizontalist quest, which tries to attain a better world through social-economic-political means, for example, begins with this conviction. It was surely due to his Jewish roots that Karl Marx portrayed a paradisal state on earth that in every respect resembled the Messianic age—but then a "Paradise" without God and the Messiah.

Incidentally, the word "Paradise" comes from Per-

---
1. In this chapter, I am using the terms "bliss," "salvation," and "wholeness" interchangeably, as three of the many renderings of the Dutch word *heil* and the German word *Heil. Bliss* is related to Dutch *blijdschap* ("joy").

sian *pardes*, which means "park" or "garden"; this loanword found its way into the Hebrew Bible (Eccl. 2:5; Song 4:13; Neh. 2:8), and into the Greek New Testament (Luke 23:43; 2 Cor. 12:3; Rev. 2:7). In some way or another, everyone's concept of bliss (secular or spiritual, present or future, natural or supernatural, earthly or heavenly) seems related to a "Paradise" of some kind, as does the Marxist view.

Some years ago, we happened to be at Stockholm during the May Day celebration, where fiery speakers addressed the crowds, and thousands of laborers sang the International Anthem of Socialism as they raised clenched fists. By coincidence we found ourselves at the tomb of the murdered Socialist prime minister Olof Palme as a long line of adorers came to lay red roses at his tomb. Seldom have I experienced more strongly how strongly Socialism and Communism exhibit religious traits, as both worldviews ardently long for Utopia, the ultimate state of bliss and wholeness, the "kingdom of humanity" on earth, in brief: Paradise. Not to mention so many more vulgar gods: the god Bacchus (alcohol, drugs), football (or whatever deified sport it may be), the goddess Lust, the god pop music, which all promise their adherents a Paradise on earth.

Conversely, others have tried to find some measure of salvation here and now by separating themselves from the evil world with all its enslaving lusts and desires. The ancient desert fathers in the fourth and fifth centuries, first and foremost Saint Anthony the Great (see §1.4.7), moved to the deserts of the Middle East; from their communities the later monasteries arose. They led a very sober life, in which they strove for detachment from all that is earthly and material. Some seem to have succeeded: they learned to bear the silence and solitude, and they devoted themselves only to prayer and meditation. This, too, is a form of salvation, though not necessarily what the Bible normally understands by it.

Until this very day, Protestants have designed their own techniques for avoiding the world, from the Amish in North America to some very strict hyper-Calvinists in the Netherlands. These people believe that it should suffice for humans to live "in a nook with a book" (Lat. *in angello cum libello;* Dutch: *in een hoekje met een boekje*), as Thomas à Kempis wrote in an autographic manuscript of his world famous *The Imitation of Christ* (Lat. *De imitatione Christi*).[2] Such separation is considered to be a modest foretaste of ultimate salvation, preparation for a blissful hereafter. If you look for (a foretaste of) Paradise today, you seem to find it either in the most pleasurable affections of the world—or in the desert (literal or spiritual) apart from the world. As one of the songs written by John N. Darby, which I've known since childhood, expresses it this way:

> This world is a wilderness wide;
> We have nothing to seek or to choose;
> We've no thought in the waste to abide;
> We've nought to regret nor to lose.

1.1.3 Pathways to Salvation: Doing

Many pathways are recommended to us for attaining salvation, regardless how it gets defined. Tokunboh Adeyemo, a man of royal descent, who for twenty-two years was the general secretary of the Association of Evangelicals in Africa (AEA), reviews some of these pathways (I am rendering them rather freely, with some additions, roughly distinguishing between "being" and "doing").[3]

(a) *Ritualism: performing the right rituals.* Salvation is attained by offering the proper sacrifices, participating in certain rites, ceremonies and religious festivals, undertaking certain pilgrimages to certain sacred places. The spiritual leadership (priesthood, or whatever it

---
2. Thomas à Kempis (2007).
3. Adeyemo (2008, 1353); see extensively, Ouweneel (1994, chapter 3).

is called), which leads the sacrificial ministry and the ceremonies, is the pivotal point around which such a system of salvation turns. This is true for Hinduism, African traditional religions, and also certain popular (not necessarily officially approved) views of Roman Catholicism. Among other things, this ritualistic experience of salvation entails "bringing the divine near" through the sacraments, particularly the Eucharist (the Lord's Supper).

(b) *Moralism: proper moral conduct.* Salvation is attained by being a good person, that is, someone who strives for the good of one's fellow human beings, trying not to hurt anyone. This moralism is found in all kinds of religions, including certain popular Christian forms, both Catholic and Protestant (traditional Protestantism and free church Evangelicalism). It is found among humanists and vegetarians as well. It occupies the central place in Jainism (an Indian religion), whose great teacher, Mahavira (d. 527 BC?), turned against the priests, the sacrifices, the gods, and thus against prayers, and taught that in the end the good is always rewarded and evil always punished.

(c) *Legalism: obedience to laws.* Here salvation is understood simply as obedience producing blessing and peace—the feeling of pleasure!—and disobedience producing curse and death. Both Judaism and Islam contain numerous commandments and ordinances, which dominate personal and collective existence, and whose observance is thought to incite the favor of the deity. Certain forms of Christianity, too, view salvation as law-keeping. A most negative example of this view of salvation is found among some hyper-Calvinists who are convinced they are reprobate, yet they pursue good works in order to receive a lighter punishment in hell (Luke 12:47-48).

To these three I add another one, not mentioned by Adeyemo:

(d) *Confessionalism: adhering to proper doctrine.* Here we are dealing with a strongly rational, if not rationalistic, view of salvation, in which salvation is found in an orthodox, often rigid dogmatism and confessionalism. This is invariably linked with sectarianism, that is, a strong divisiveness fueled by a deep conviction of one's personal rightness ("us against everyone else"). This view of salvation consists of having the true doctrine, and therefore being the true church, or at least the most biblical form of the true church. Because of rationalism, which has kept Western culture in its grip until the twentieth century, no religion is more susceptible to this dogmatism and confessionalism than Western Christianity. Faith is in danger of being reduced here to embracing a certain number of dogmas. These dogmas may all be very biblical—although this is dubious—but what gets lost is the awareness of faith as entrusting oneself to God, surrendering to him, faith as a power that can move mountains (Mark 11:23; 1 Cor. 13:2).

1.1.4 Pathways to Salvation: Being

(e) *Asceticism: quenching all covetousness.* Along this pathway salvation is attained by suppressing all lust and desire. Thus, people free themselves from *karma* (the law of positive and negative causes and the corresponding consequences), and attain Nirvana, the state of bliss. The best known and most famous pathway of suppressing one's desires is that of the Eightfold Path, taught by Siddharta Gautama (d. ca. 370 BC?), better known as the Buddha, the "Enlightened One." The doctrine of reincarnation is the expression *par excellence* of this doctrine of salvation: live well now, in view of the next life; salvation is the next, higher life that people hope to attain.

(f) *Mysticism: union with the Absolute.* Here salvation is viewed as union with Absolute Reality, or the Brahma, especially through yoga, that is, through intense concentration, deep meditation in certain prescribed body postures and controlled breathing. This view of salvation has permeated the West through the New Age movement. The divine and the cosmic are viewed as identical; thus, union with the cosmos is union with the divine, which from the beginning was and is present in humans (the divine "spark"). There is some overlapping here with extreme forms of so-called "Christian mysticism" (merging into God, ontic union with God; e.g., Jakob Boehme), and with more moderate forms of it: the passive experience of divine bliss in the silence of one's own heart, often described with the multi-valenced term "spirituality."

(g) *Hedonism: pursuing pleasure.* This is the attitude of many people in the Western world without necessarily any religious overtones. However, since the hedonism (the doctrine that pleasure is the highest good) of Epicurus (d. ca. 270 BC) (cf. Acts 17:18), this attitude has acquired not only philosophical but even religious aspects. The latter is the case especially when this attitude is connected with people's striving after the good of the neighbor, for whom they desire the same pleasure. In *every* religion there is a certain danger of hedonism if a sentiment of well-being, religious (mystical, ecstatic) experiences, and spiritual "kicks" become an aim in themselves. Much of the so-called "prosperity gospel" (God grants prosperity to all those ardently praying as well as donating) is hardly anything other than religious hedonism.

Sometimes much pleasure is derived from a strong activism, in which people pursue salvation by committing themselves with religious zeal to politics and society (see the next section for more on this). In fact, each of the salvational pathways mentioned in this section can be linked with a strong feeling of pleasure, which becomes the implicit or unconscious primary goal of salvation.

In some of these salvational pathways, there is a clear anthropological element: it is either the enterprising will ([a], [b], [c], and sometimes [g]), or reason ([d]), or feeling ([e], [f], [g]), that becomes primary.

1.2 Christ and Salvation
1.2.1 Who is the Savior (Salvation Bringer)?

In comparing these salvational views, we have not yet spoken about whether there is a human, or a group of humans, to whom salvation can be linked in a special way. Is there salvation in Moses, or at least in the pathway that he set forth? In the way of Confucius? Or of Lao Tse? Or Zoroaster (i.e., Zarathustra)? Or Socrates? Or Jesus Christ? Or Buddha? Or Muhammad? Or, in more modern terms: in the way of Karl Marx? Or of Vladimir Ilyitch Lenin? Or Mao-Zedong? Or the Bhagwan? Or the Mahareshi Mahesh Yogi? Or the Maitreya? Or, to move to a more elevated level, is there any salvation in the ancient Greek gods, who are being worshiped again by a growing multitude in Greece? Or in the ancient Germanic gods, who are being worshiped again by a growing multitude in Scandinavia? In Brahma, Vishnu or Shiva? Or in Allah? Or in the God of ancient Israel?

En route to answering this, I ask two questions: first, if people place their confidence in some great prophet, *what kind of person is this supposed prophet?* Is he, in fact, nothing but an ordinary human being, no matter how good and bright he may have been? Of none of them, not even Moses, could it be said that they are the incarnated Logos (John 1:14), God manifested in the flesh (1 Tim. 3:16). Nor is an avatar in the Hindu sense a true incarnation. Nor are "divine" prophets true incarnations. No religion knows a true God-Man except Christianity. Thus, Christian soteriology is necessarily rooted in Christology.[4] The person of Christ must be discussed before we can properly speak of the work that he has

---
4. See *RT* II/2.

accomplished.[5]

The second question has to do with this work. What have Confucius, Buddha, or Muhammad *done* for humanity? I remember a discussion with a Freemason, decades ago, who gave me his view of religion. God is on the top of a mountain, and all religions make their way to the top, each believing that *their* route is the best, or even the only way to the top. But in the end they all reach exactly the same end goal. My answer was that my view of religion differed from all the others: my religion is not one of many ways to the top, but the conviction that we, by our own strength, *cannot* reach the top, and that God in Jesus has come down from the top in order to take us there.

Confucius, Buddha, Muhammad, and all the others tell us how we have to *rethink*, or what *we* have to *do*. Think of the man who fell into a pit and could not get himself out. Confucius came by and said, "Follow my moral rules, and you will get out." Buddha said, "Follow my Eightfold Path, and you will get out." Muhammad said, "Confess Allah and his prophet, follow the five principles of Islam, and you will get out." Then Jesus came by, climbed down into the pit, and took the man out. It is a simple (if not simplistic) story, but it gives the essence: you either follow a certain recipe *to save yourself*, or you acknowledge your inability to save yourself, and throw yourself into the arms of the One who *can* save you.

Again, we cannot understand Christ's work if we do not know who Christ *is*. But the reverse is true as well: we will not understand who Christ is as the incarnate Logos, God manifested in the flesh, if we do not know for what purpose he came into the world: "I have not come to call the righteous but sinners to repentance" (Luke 5:32; cf. 19:10). "If anyone hears my words and does not keep them, I do not judge him; for I did not

---

5. See Ouweneel (2007b, §1.1.3).

come to judge the world but to save the world" (John 12:47). "[T]he Son of Man came not to be served but to serve, and to give his life as a ransom for many" (Matt. 20:28; Mark 10:45).

1.2.2 Person and Work of Christ

In the New Testament, we find several examples of Christological passages that speak in the same breath of the person and work of Christ, such as:

> [B]y him all things were created, in heaven and on earth, visible and invisible, whether thrones or dominions or rulers or authorities—all things were created through him and for him. And he is before all things, and in him all things hold together. And he is the head of the body, the church. He is the beginning, the firstborn from the dead, that in everything he might be preeminent. For in him all the fullness of God was pleased to dwell, and through him to reconcile to himself all things, whether on earth or in heaven, making peace by the blood of his cross (Col. 1:16-20)

This same Paul wrote to pastor Titus: ". . . the glory of our great God and Savior Jesus Christ, who gave himself for us to redeem us from all lawlessness and to purify for himself a people for his own possession who are zealous for good works" (Titus 2:13-14). And the apostle Peter also connected the person and work of Christ: "To those who have obtained a faith of equal standing with ours by the righteousness of our God and Savior Jesus Christ" (2 Pet. 1:1b).

We find this same connection in the Heidelberg Catechism, Lord's Day 6:

> *16. Why must he [the mediator] be a true and righteous man?*
> Because the justice of God requires (Rom. 5:15) that the same human nature which has sinned should make sat-

isfaction for sin; but one who is himself a sinner cannot satisfy for others (Isa. 53:3-5).

17. Why must he [the mediator] also be true God?

That by the power of His Godhead He might bear in His manhood the burden of God's wrath (Isa 53:8; Acts 2:24), and so obtain for (John 3:16; Acts 20:28) and restore to us righteousness and life (1 John 1:2).[6]

The person of Christ becomes manifest in his work, and, conversely, his work was possible only because he was the person he was. The two are inseparable; if we do try to separate them, we turn the confession of the person of Christ into an abstraction.[7] We must beware of a Christology that is taken exclusively in an ontological sense ("who is Jesus?"), and not in a soteriological sense ("what did Jesus do?") as well. What does it mean that Christ is truly *God* if we fail to realize that only in this way he could accomplish the work of redemption (cf. Ps. 49:7-9)? And what does it mean that Christ is truly *Man* if we fail to realize that only in this way he could become the Mediator between God and humanity (cf. 1 Tim. 2:5)? All speaking about the *person* of Christ acquires its deepest sense and meaning only from the *work* of Christ—and conversely.

It is certainly true that, if we were to limit our attention to the person of Jesus, his work would not profit us. Some people speak with great appreciation for Jesus' person and teaching but think they do not need his redemptive work. But, conversely, there is the danger that people try to construct a Christology purely on the basis of soteriological considerations, which would have no foundation in the history of Jesus.[8] Therefore, Christology is fully entitled to organize its discussion to move

---

6. Dennison (*RC* 2:273); cf. Ouweneel (2016, 44-47).
7. See Berkouwer (1954b, chapter 6); McGrath (2007, 225-26).
8. McGrath (2007, 133) refers to Wolfhart Pannenberg, who notices this danger.

from the person of Christ to his work. Scripture gives us many examples of this. In Hebrews 1:1-3, Christ is the Son, the heir of all things, the One through whom God creates and upholds all things, before he is the One who has made purification for sins. A similar sequence is found in John 1: first he is the Logos with God, then the incarnate Logos, then the Lamb of God who takes away the sin of the world (vv. 1-3, 14, 29, 35). To mention a third Bible author, it is the same with Paul in Colossians 1: it is true, he begins with redemption (vv. 13-14), but then mentions Jesus as the Son of the Father's love, the One through whom all things have been created and are held together (vv. 15-17), and through the resurrection (v. 18) he then returns to Christ's redemption (vv. 19-22).

1.2.3 Objective and Subjective

If the term "soteriology" is understood in the widest sense possible, it encompasses an immense subject. Seven of the original eighteen volumes of G. C. Berkouwer's series "Studies in Dogmatics" could be grouped under the single heading of "Soteriology," including his two volumes on hamartiology (the doctrine of sin).[9] Of the twelve chapters of H. Ridderbos' study on Paul, no fewer than five deal with soteriological topics.[10] A large number of subjects can be assigned to soteriology in the wider sense: in addition to hamartiology these include the doctrine of God's counsel, of which the most important part, election or predestination, is directly related to salvation;[11] the doctrine of the place of the law;[12] the doctrine of atonement; the doctrine of justification and sanctification;[13] the doctrines of repentance, con-

---

9. Berkouwer (1952; 1954a; 1954b; 1958; 1960; 1965; 1971).
10. Ridderbos (1975, chapters 3-7).
11. Cf. Ouweneel (*RT* III/1).
12. Cf. Ouweneel (*RT* I/2).
13. Cf. Ouweneel (*RT* III/2).

version, regeneration, eternal life, dying and rising with Christ, spiritual childhood, sonship, and heirship; and foederology (the doctrine of the covenant).[14]

These topics can all be assigned to two or possibly three categories.[15] First, there are the tenets dealing with what Christ has done *for* people through his sufferings, death, and resurrection. This is the objective aspect, which is being discussed in the present volume. Second, there are the tenets dealing with what Christ has done, and continues doing, *with* and *in* people. This is the subjective aspect; this is discussed in various volumes.[16] Third, we might distinguish what Christ does *through* the redeemed person. This also belongs to the subjective aspect; I have discussed this in an earlier volume.[17]

The objective aspect involves the unique historical event of Christ's sufferings on the cross. The subjective side is repeated daily in the many people who belong to Christ, or are going to belong to him. Among these people, we can distinguish two categories. Large parts of Protestantism have strongly emphasized, on the one hand, people's one-time conversion and regeneration (reconciliation, quickening, justification, and so on), and on the other hand, the process of continual sanctification, dying to the old nature, spiritual growth and warfare, ongoing renewal, or whatever it may be termed. The former involves *becoming* a Christian, the latter involves *being* (*living* as) a Christian. Traditionally, Reformational theology has distinguished between someone's *state* (one's *position* in Christ, which one has received once and for all at their conversion) and one's *standing* (one's spiritual condition, that is, the measure in which one *experientially* realizes their position in

---

14. Cf. Ouweneel (*RT* IV/2).
15. Cf. Chafer (*ST* 3:54).
16. Ouweneel (*RT* III/2); see also Ouweneel (*RT* III/4).
17. Ouweneel (*RT* II/3).

Christ).

Other branches of Christianity, such as the Roman Catholic and Eastern Orthodox, as well as many Kuyperian[18] groups, place less emphasis on a person's the one-time conversion, and much more on the process of a person's entire spiritual development. This is all the more important since by far most Christians were, and are, born in a Christian denomination and a Christian family, and often cannot point to a specific moment of their conversion/regeneration. Often, the specific moment that people do identify as the moment of their conversion is instead the moment when they found assurance of salvation and peace with God. We will return to all these aspects, especially in the next volume of this series.

1.2.4 The "Lofty Intellect"

One of the songs from the German folk song collection *Des Knaben Wunderhorn* ("The Youth's Magic Horn"), put to music by Gustav Mahler (ca. 1900), is called *Lob des hohen Verstandes* ("Praise of Lofty Intellect"). It is a lovely satire, in which a cuckoo and a nightingale decide to have a singing match. The cuckoo is so smart to nominate the donkey to be the referee, because he has two large ears so that he is a good hearer. The donkey brags about his "lofty intellect," and gives the award to the cuckoo, for, as he tells the nightingale, "you make me crazy with your complicated singing!" And of the cuckoo he says, "The cuckoo can be understood much more easily! He sticks to form and measure."

Occasionally this song comes to mind when theological questions are at stake. Just like the donkey, many Christians do not want to hear about complicated matters over which theologians love to rack their brains. Such Christians emphasize how simple the gospel of sal-

---

18. The term identifies sympathizers of the Dutch Calvinist theologian Abraham Kuyper.

vation really is: you are a hell-bound sinner—you cannot save yourself—Christ has paid the price for you—now you need only to believe in Christ to be saved from hell and to go to heaven. To a certain extent, this is all true. But notice, first, that this is certainly not the *full* truth about salvation, and secondly, that many Christians fail to realize that each of these claims involves many questions for thinking people.

Consider some examples. What exactly is a sinner? Why must great (non-Christian) philanthropists be called sinners? What sense does this make?[19] Why could a person not save themselves, for instance, by making amends for their mistakes? How can someone pay the price for another person?[20] What kind of price must this necessarily be? Why is there a price to be paid, anyway? Why can God not forgive without further ado? To whom is the pricee to be paid? What exactly is it to believe? How can any act of faith ever save a person?[21] And the questions continue. Indeed, the core of the gospel is quite simple—but at the same time, soteriology is an extraordinarily complex scholarly enterprise. No one is helped when this complexity is obscured in the interests of "simple" faith. Not every Christian is called to be engaged with these questions. However, such questions are not foreign to many people accustomed to asking profound questions, Christians and non-Christians alike. These people are *entitled* to the answers. The present volume intends to provide some of these answers.

1.3 What Is Salvation?
1.3.1 Saving Is Healing

No subject in the Bible is really simple. Take the sub-

---

19. Regarding these questions, see extensively, Ouweneel (2008a).
20. Interestingly, the Heidelberg Catechism (especially Lord's Day 5) painstakingly deals with some of these questions; see Ouweneel (2016, 36–43).
21. For the last two questions, see the next volume in this series.

jects dealt with so far in this series:[22] there is tremendous difference of opinion on the meaning and present applicability of the Torah (vol. 1), on the meaning and the extent of the covenant (it is the Reformed against the others here; vol. 2), on the meaning of the kingdom of God (one or two kingdoms? vol. 4[23]), on election and predestination (vol. 5), on the Holy Spirit (person or force? vol. 6). Even the question of the righteousness of God and the justification of penitent sinners is far less straightforward than many Reformed Christians seem to think (vol. 3). The same pertains to salvation, which, as we saw, includes notions like redemption, wholeness, perfection, well-being, prosperity, blessing, bliss, love, peace, joy, fullness, contemplation, and so on. This multiplicity of terms illustrates that the meaning of "salvation" cannot be caught in a simple, unequivocal description.

Recall that the Dutch and German words *heil* are related to Dutch *heel*, which is "whole, healthy, unhurt, undamaged." The German *Heil* is related to *heilen*, just as English *hail* is linked with *to heal* (the German *heil* is related to the English *healthy*). Also in the New Testament, this connection is quite common: the Greek word *sōtēria* means "salvation," and *sōtēr* means "savior," but the corresponding verb *sōzō* often means "to heal, to make healthy" (Matt. 9:22; Mark 10:52; Luke 17:19; John 11:12; Acts 4:9; 14:9; James 5:15). Concomitantly, the Greek noun *sōtēria* can also mean "healing," and *sōtēr* "healer." Old English used the word *Hæland*, related to Dutch and German *Heiland*, "Savior" or "Healer."

The root of the word is also preserved in the expression *Hail to the King*, as we find it in John 19:3 (ERV), "They kept coming up to him and saying, 'Hail to the king of the Jews!'" It means something close to "Peace/well-being/prosperity/blessing/bliss to the king."

---

22. Ouweneel (*RT* I/2–f).
23. See also Ouweneel (2017).

"Peace" (Heb. *shalom*) is the word that we find in similar greetings: "Peace to you" (1 Chron. 12:18) or "Greeting" (Ezra 4:17; 5:7; cf. Esther 10:3), where we might also expect "Hail to you" (as some Dutch translations render it). Compare the greeting *Shalom* ("Peace") in modern Israel. Compare as well the Latin (and Italian) greeting *Salve* (from *salvere*, "to save, to make sound"), which has the same basic meaning of wishing the other person well (cf. *to salute*, which also comes from *salvere*). The basic notion in all ordinary greetings is wishing the other person God's blessing; think of the Bavarian, Austrian, and German-Swiss greeting *Grüss Gott* (from *Es grüss dich Gott*, "may God greet you," i.e., "may God do you well"[24]). Even the ordinary greeting of *Good morning* originally meant: "May God grant you a good (blessed, healthy, safe, etc.) morning," just as *Goodbye* comes from "God be with you."

In Revelation 7:10 we read, "Salvation belongs to our God who sits on the throne, and to the Lamb!" Luther, followed by several older translations, took this also as a kind of greeting: "Hail to our God . . . ." Indeed, the text literally says, "Salvation *to* our God" (KJV; NASB), as if something is being offered to God. Compare with this the following shout of blessing: "Worthy is the Lamb who was slain, to *receive* power and wealth and wisdom and might and honor and glory and blessing" (Rev. 5:12; cf. 7:12.) Many translations solve the problem of Revelation 7:10 by inserting the word "belongs": "Salvation [belongs] to our God" (AMP; or, "[We owe] salvation to our God"). But it is doubtful that such a solution is necessary.

All such verses remind us of the wide array of meanings found in the Greek noun *sōtēria*, just as in the Latin words *salus/salvatio* and *salvere*.

---

24. Cf. 2 John 1:10, "do not . . . give him any greeting"; CJB: "Don't even say, '*Shalom!*', to him"; WYC, YLT: "say not to him, Hail!"; KJV: "bid him God speed [i.e., may God cause you to prosper]."

1.3.2 The Trinity and Salvation

Terms like "redemption" and "salvation" have a somewhat negative connotation because they necessarily refer to that from which a person is redeemed or saved. Indeed, in dogmatic treatises this negative aspect is sometimes emphasized too much: the saved person is no longer in prison, nor in the mouth of the lion, nor in the grip of Satan, or whatever negative metaphor one might choose. However, the term *sōtēria* tells us with equal clarity the glory that the person has now attained: no longer in prison but in the royal palace; no longer in a dungeon but in a Paradise; no longer in the mouth of the lion but in the arms of the good shepherd, no longer in the grip of devil, death, and darkness but of love, life, and light. Every soteriology should draw deep and pervasive attention to these positive aspects: wholeness, perfection, well-being, prosperity, blessing, bliss, happiness, love, joy, peace, fullness, unity, communion, and contemplation.

This concerns not only the individual but creation in its entirety, a reality that exists not only in the consummation of the ages, but already now. Therefore, Reformed dogmatician A. König rightly connected salvation with issues like environmental pollution, exhaustion of natural resources, and overpopulation.[25] I agree with making such connections, but I would examine these matters in the framework of eschatology.[26] In the present volume, we will focus on individual salvation, especially in the present age, as brought about by Jesus Christ on the cross of Calvary.

It is very important to see that the entire Trinity is involved in the work of salvation. This reminds us of the three parables in Luke 15, which may be viewed as an anticipation of the fully revealed truth of the Trinity. In the first parable, it is the good shepherd who finds the

---
25. König (2006, 204–208).
26. See Ouweneel (2012a).

lost sheep; this is the Lord Jesus, God the Son (cf. John 10). In the second parable, the femininity of the seeker[27] as well as the metaphor of the lamp seem to point to God the Holy Spirit. And in the third parable, God the Father is being clearly represented in the father of the prodigal son. It was God the Father who gave his Son for the redemption of his people (e.g., John 3:16; Rom. 8:32). It was God the Son who gave himself for poor sinners (Gal. 1:4), and he did so through God the Spirit (Heb. 9:14). All these three realities are objective. On the subjective side, we may say that the Father draws the sinner (John 6:44), that the Son seeks the lost sheep (Matt. 18:12–13), and that the Spirit regenerates hearts (John 3:5). The objective shows what God did *for* us, while the subjective shows what God did, and does, *in* us. Both can be summarized under the one term "salvation."

Millard Erickson stated that with the atonement we reach the crucial point in the Christian faith, because with it we are moving, as it were, from the objective to the subjective realities described by Christian theology.[28] This might suggest that the subjective is more important than the objective, and this cannot be Erickson's intention. Can God's work *in* us be more crucial than God's work *for* us? Or, what is even more important, can the *work* of Christ be more crucial than the *person* of Christ? With reference to Reformed theologian G. C. van Niftrik, A. F. N. Lekkerkerker also identified atonement as the "midpoint of theology."[29] More nuanced was the view of William Kelly, who called the atonement a "blessed truth," but called the person of Christ, who gave this work its divine value, more blessed.[30] The Savior himself always is and remains greater than any form of salvation.

---

27. Cf. Ouweneel (*RT* II/3, §§3.7–3.9).
28. Erickson (1998, 799).
29. Lekkerkerker (1949, 22).
30. Kelly (*BT* N9:97).

Indeed, the gift of God, or the work of Christ, cannot be more important than God or Christ himself. Perhaps it is simply wiser to not claim at all that one theological subject is more crucial than another subject. It is like being unwilling to choose what heresy is more serious: denying the deity of Christ, or denying his vicarious work of atonement. Everything is related to everything: those who think deeply about God cannot do so apart from considering what he wants to be for, with and in people, and thus apart from considering the way he restores fallen people to himself. And conversely, all of God's ways and dealings tell us something not only about what he desires with regard to humanity, but also about *himself*. In this sense, all systematic theology is truly "theo-logy," that is, doctrine of God in the broadest sense of the term. Salvation brings us not only to forgiveness, to eternal life, to heaven, to the kingdom, to Paradise, to the new earth—but it brings us to *God*: "Christ suffered once for sins, the righteous for the unrighteous, that he might bring us to God" (1 Pet. 3:18).

1.4 Aspects of Salvation
1.4.1 The Hamartiological Aspect
Let us now begin with a preliminary inventory of the various descriptions of salvation, in order to acquire some further orientation in our subject. The first description is perhaps the most popular, especially among Protestants: salvation is being saved from sin and the devil, and from God's wrath.

A typical passage is here Romans 5:8-9, "God shows his love for us in that while we were still sinners, Christ died for us. Since, therefore, we have now been justified by his blood, much more shall we be saved by him from the wrath of God." Here the emphasis lies on the sinful condition of humanity, from which humans cannot free themselves and as a consequence of which God's wrath rests upon them (cf. John 3:36, "[W]hoever does not obey the Son shall not see life, but the wrath of God remains on him"). Christ took the place of the penitent sinner on the cross, gave his blood and his life for that sinner, so that the eternal judgment can be lifted from the sinner who entrusts themselves in faith to Christ and his work.

This message occupies a central place in the teaching of the Lutherans and the Reformed, but also of the free church Evangelical doctrine of salvation. At the same time it exhibits a certain one-sidedness in its emphasis on the individual aspects of salvation. As a consequence, other aspects of salvation recede into the background, as will become apparent in following sections. But there is more: the doctrine of salvation from sin and from God's wrath has come under great pressure in recent decades, as we will see in following chapters. No wonder: what can (post-)modern humanity do with the notion of a God who "wants to see blood," a God who turns his own beloved Son into a sacrificial lamb and sends him to his death? Why does a perfect and infinite God "need" such a sacrifice? The Bible says "[W]ithout the shedding of blood there is no forgiveness of sins" (Heb. 9:22; cf. Exod. 12:13; Lev. 17:11; Luke 22:20)—but can we still believe this? How can such a manner of forgiveness ever be thought sensible?

Such questions are not new. The early Christians had difficulty explaining this to the Gentiles of their time— and modern Christians have to explain these things not only to non-Christians but also to those who have turned their backs on the church because of these supposedly barbaric teachings. No wonder, then, that these teachings will demand a lot of attention in chapters to follow.

1.4.2 The Ecclesiological Aspect

Acts 2:47 contains these remarkable words: "And the Lord added to their number day by day those who were being saved [Gk. *tous sōzomenous*]," that is, those who participated in salvation (Gk. *sōtēria*). Since Abraham, no salvation can be experienced without being received into a salvational *community*, a truth illustrated in several of Jesus' parables, especially in Luke's Gospel. The man rescued by the good Samaritan was brought to an inn, where he was welcomed and cared for (Luke 10:33-35). The poor, crippled, blind, and lame were brought together into the house of the master for the great banquet (14:12-24). The prodigal son was received not only into the arms of the father but also into a house of festivity, music, and dancing (15:11-25). No celebration occurs without a festival *company*.

In *this* specific sense of "salvational community," we can claim that outside the church, in its true meaning of "holy congregation . . . [and] an assembly of those who are saved,"[31] there is no salvation. As the Belgic Confession says, "[T]his holy congregation is an assembly of those who are saved, and outside of it there is no salvation."[32] The Latin expression *Extra ecclesia nulla salus*, "Outside the church there is no salvation," goes back to the early Christian writer Cyprian.[33] This claim cannot be made about any specific denomination, including the Roman Catholic Church; rather, it is true about the church as a whole, the body of Christ. In other words, it is impossible to be saved without at the same time becoming a member of the body of Christ (1 Cor. 12:13). There is no salvation without the salvational means of preaching, pastoral care, and the sacraments—baptism, the Lord's Supper, anointing the sick—all three of which function explicitly within the framework of the salvational community. This gives tangible form to being "together with all the saints" (Gk. *syn pasin tois hagious*, Eph. 3:18; cf. 1:15; Col. 1:4; Philem. 1:5).

---

31. Belgic Confession Art. 27; cf. Dennison (*RC* 2:440).
32. Belgic Confession Art. 28; cf. Dennison (*RC* 2:441).
33. De unitate ecclesiae 6.

It is a collective view, which is prevalent not only in the Roman Catholic Church and the Eastern Orthodox churches but also to some extent in the churches of the Reformation. The view is least present in the free church Evangelical movement, where individualism has made the greatest inroads—with all of its associated disadvantages.

1.4.3 The Pneumatological Aspect

In the pneumatological view of salvation, redemption from sin is not the contents of, but only the means to, actual salvation. Actual salvation consists in being filled with the Holy Spirit, living in the fullness of the Spirit, with all signs belonging to it: power, servitude, obedience, and dedication, empathy, worship, a life of victory, prophecy, testimony, miraculous works, and the gifts of the Spirit.[34]

This view of salvation does not link primarily to Genesis 3, the story of the Fall, which must be repaired by redemption. Rather, it links to Genesis 1, the story of creation, and the calling of humanity to display the image and likeness of God. God's primary aim in salvation is not that the problem of sin be resolved, but rather that people be "filled unto all the fullness of God" (Eph. 3:19 ASV), which is implied in being filled with the Holy Spirit (see, e.g., Acts 2:4; 4:31; 13:52; Eph. 5:18).

This emphasis on the role of the Holy Spirit in reaching the goal of salvation is predominant in the Eastern Orthodox churches, but also in the (Western) Pentecostal and Charismatic movement. In this respect, this movement is more akin to the Eastern than to the Western (Roman Catholic as well as Reformational) tradition.[35] In this Eastern tradition, the notion of *theosis*, developing the divine image in the believer by the power of the

---

34. See Ouweneel (*RT* II/3, especially chapters 11 and 12).
35. Ouweneel (*RT* II/3, §§1.1.2 and 1.5).

Holy Spirit, plays a central role.[36]

1.4.4 The Nomological Aspect

"Nomology" as a theological study is the investigation of the place and meaning of the law in the Bible.[37] For many Jews, including Messianic (i.e., Jesus-believing) Jews, the formation of the true "righteous one" (Heb. *tsaddiq*) is the highest aim of salvation. It is the highest joy of the *tsaddiq* to study the law, just as, for instance, Ezra did: "Ezra had set his heart [first] to study the Law of the LORD, and [second] to do it and [third] to teach his statutes and rules in Israel" (Ezra 7:10). This studying, doing, and teaching—in this order—arise out of pure love, without any legalism. Because the *tsaddiq* loves God they love his Torah: "[H]is delight is in the law of the LORD, and on his law he meditates day and night" (Ps. 1:2). "Oh how I love your law! It is my meditation all the day" (Ps. 119:97).

Those who truly understand the apostle Paul will grasp his claim: "[I]t is not the hearers of the law who are righteous before God, but the doers of the law who will be justified" (Rom. 2:13). Similarly, they will understand this statement of James: "[T]he one who looks into the perfect law, the law of liberty, and perseveres, being no hearer who forgets but a doer who acts, he will be blessed in his doing" (James 1:25; cf. 2:12). This is not mere theory; it was realized in a concrete way in the lives of Zechariah and Elizabeth: "[T]hey were both righteous before God, walking blamelessly in all the commandments and statutes of the Lord" (Luke 1:6).[38]

After the descent of the Holy Spirit on the Day of Pentecost the aim was still the same: Christ redeemed us "in order that the righteous requirement of the law

---

36. Ouweneel (*RT* II/3, §9.5; see also the next volume in this series).
37. See extensively, Ouweneel (*RT* I/2).
38. See extensively, Ouweneel (*RT* III/2).

might be fulfilled in us, who walk not according to the flesh but according to the Spirit" (Rom. 8:4). Later in this epistle the apostle wrote:

> Owe no one anything, except to love each other, for the one who loves another has fulfilled the law. For the commandments, "You shall not commit adultery, You shall not murder, You shall not steal, You shall not covet," and any other commandment, are summed up in this word: "You shall love your neighbor as yourself." Love does no wrong to a neighbor; therefore love is the fulfilling of the law (Rom. 13:8–10).

In yet another epistle of Paul, we read: "Bear one another's burdens, and so fulfill the law of Christ" (Gal. 6:2).

This has been the view of salvation not only of all truly godly Jews, from Sinai until the Messianic kingdom, but also of all Messianic Jews. These are Jews who retain their Jewish identity and do not wish to merge into the "church of the Gentiles." They feel at home in the church as the universal body of Christ but not in traditional churches and congregations, which have no, or hardly any, place for the Jewish identity. To go a step further: this view of the law should be central in *all* Christians' view of salvation, remembering the words of Jesus: "A new commandment I give to you, that you love one another: just as I have loved you, you also are to love one another" (John 13:34). "If you love me, you will keep my commandments.... Whoever has my commandments and keeps them, he it is who loves me. And he who loves me will be loved by my Father, and I will love him and manifest myself to him" (John 14:15, 21). "This is my commandment, that you love one another as I have loved you.... You are my friends if you do what I command you" (John 15:12, 14).

This is not the place to further analyze the identity of this "law of Christ" and its relationship to the "law of

Moses"; I have done this elsewhere.[39]

1.4.5 The Ethical-Social Aspect

The Roman Catholic theologian Karl Rahner connected salvation particularly with Matthew 25:31-46. Jesus describes the judgment of the "sheep" and the "goats," that is, of those who practice true love to neighbors and those who don't. For the sheep this judgment means entering the Messianic kingdom, or eternal life (vv. 34, 46). For the goats it means entering the eternal fire, or eternal punishment (vv. 41, 46). Rahner said of this, "*This act [of sober everyday love] is definitive as eternal life, refusing it means definitive eternal pain.*"[40] And elsewhere,

> [I]f you want to believe in Jesus, that is, want to encounter him, want your act to reach him, then you find him in the neighbor whom you really love in the act of unsentimental commonplace. . . . [The Christian] love to the neighbor—this love taken properly, radically, that is, to the very root of it—encounters really, and not in some romantic, mystical and mythological identification, the Jesus whom we confess as the Christ.[41]

In the Old Testament we read (and notice the comprehensive meaning of "salvation" in this quotation):

> Is not this the fast that I choose:
>   to loose the bonds of wickedness,
>   to undo the straps of the yoke,
> to let the oppressed go free,
>   and to break every yoke?
> Is it not to share your bread with the hungry
>   and bring the homeless poor into your house;

---

39. See Ouweneel (*RT* I/2).
40. Rahner (1971, 21).
41. Rahner (1971, 23).

> when you see the naked, to cover him,
> > and not to hide yourself from your own flesh?
> Then shall your light break forth like the dawn,
> > and your healing shall spring up speedily;
> your righteousness shall go before you;
> > the glory of the Lord shall be your rear guard.
> Then you shall call, and the Lord will answer;
> > you shall cry, and he will say, 'Here I am.'
> If you take away the yoke from your midst,
> > the pointing of the finger, and speaking wickedness,
> if you pour yourself out for the hungry
> > and satisfy the desire of the afflicted,
> then shall your light rise in the darkness
> > and your gloom be as the noonday.
> And the Lord will guide you continually
> > and satisfy your desire in scorched places
> > and make your bones strong;
> and you shall be like a watered garden,
> > like a spring of water,
> > whose waters do not fail (Isa. 58:6–11).

Especially in more liberal Christian circles, altruistic love—love for one's neighbor—as the expression of people's love toward Christ, has been given a central place. Therefore, more conservative circles have often dismissed it as the "social gospel," and as "horizontalism." That this is unfair is clear from Rahner's undoubted orthodoxy, and also from Romans 13:8–10, quoted in §1.4.4. Love is truly vertical as both the content of the law of Christ and the effect of the indwelling Holy Spirit: "God's love has been poured into our hearts through the Holy Spirit who has been given to us" (Rom. 5:5). "[T]he whole law is fulfilled in one word: 'You shall love your neighbor as yourself' . . . walk by the Spirit, and you will not gratify the desires of the flesh" (Gal. 5:14, 16). As the heart of salvation, shown in a very practical, ordinary sense, love has possibly been too neglected by some conservative Christians (see further in §1.6.2).

1.4.6 The Eschatological Aspect

Those who think of salvation in terms of the entire world often point out that "the *world*" is "saved by him" (John 3:17; cf. 12:47); Jesus is the "Savior of the *world*" (4:42; 1 John 4:14). (This meaning of "world" must not be confused with the negative one of 1 John 2:17, "the world is passing away along with its desires," and of 5:19, "the whole world lies in the power of the evil one.")

People who emphasize God's plan to save the *world* tend to view salvation as something future: salvation is ultimately realized in the Messianic kingdom of peace, righteousness, and wholeness, about which especially the Old Testament speaks so frequently. Everything featured fully in *that* kingdom exists in principle already *now*, in the kingdom in its present form: righteousness, peace, joy (Rom. 14:17), love (Col. 1:13), power (1 Cor. 4:20; Heb. 6:5), and so much more.[42] To this extent, salvation is a present possession as well. This relates also to how the relationship between the kingdom and the church is viewed.[43]

Especially in the book of Isaiah we find several passages where salvation is linked with the Messianic kingdom: "I bring near my righteousness; it is not far off, and my salvation will not delay; I will put salvation in Zion, for Israel my glory" (Isa. 46:13). "Break forth together into singing, you waste places of Jerusalem, for the Lord has comforted his people; he has redeemed Jerusalem. The Lord has bared his holy arm before the eyes of all the nations, and all the ends of the earth shall see the salvation of our God" (Isa. 52:9–10). "For Zion's sake I will not keep silent, and for Jerusalem's sake I will not be quiet, until her righteousness goes forth as brightness, and her salvation as a burning torch. The nations shall see your righteousness, and all the kings your glory, and you shall be called by a new name that

---

42. See extensively Ouweneel (*RT* IV/3).
43. Cf. Ouweneel (2010a; 2010b).

the mouth of the LORD will give. You shall be a crown of beauty in the hand of the LORD, and a royal diadem in the hand of your God" (Isa. 62:1-3; also cf. 45:8; 56:1; 60:18).

The eschatological view of salvation can be found in very different forms in every main branch of Christianity.

1.4.7 The Mystical Aspect

For many, salvation in its fullest and truest sense cannot be only redemption, blessing, bliss, peace, and righteousness, because such matters can still be very self-centered. Salvation is not like the Paradise of Islam, featuring enjoyment of all kinds of earthly and carnal pleasures but very little enjoyment of Allah. In the Bible the opposite is the case. Being in Paradise (2 Cor. 12:3; Rev. 2:7) is being *with Christ* in Paradise (Luke 23:43; cf. Rom. 6:8; Phil. 1:23); Christ is the very essence of Paradise. Being caught up to heaven means being "always with the Lord" (1 Thess. 4:17). For the believer, the greatest blessedness consists in fellowship with the Father and the Son (1 John 1:3), or as the church fathers put it, the contemplation of God (Lat. *contemplatio Dei*). This was Moses' fervent longing: "Please show me your glory" (Exod. 33:18). Jesus first prayed, ". . . that they may all be one, just as you, Father, are in me, and I in you, that they also may be in us," and then asked ". . . that they may be one even as we are one, I in them and you in me" (John 17:21-23, the enjoyment of *fellowship*, John 17:21-23). This was immediately followed by this: "Father, I desire that they also, whom you have given me, may be with me where I am, to see my glory that you have given me" (John 17:24, the practice of *contemplation*).

David confessed, "As for me, I shall behold your face in righteousness; when I awake, I shall be satisfied with your likeness" (Ps. 17:15). Jesus promised in the Beatitudes, "Blessed are the pure in heart, for they shall see God" (Matt. 5:8). The apostle Paul reminds us, "[N]ow we see in a mirror dimly, but then face to face" (1 Cor. 13:12). In a negative formulation we read, "Strive for peace with everyone, and for the holiness without which no one will see the Lord" (Heb. 12:14). Of the New Jerusalem we read, "[T]he throne of God and of the Lamb will be in it, and his servants will worship him. They will see his face, and his name will be on their foreheads" (Rev. 22:3–4).

Please note that the contemplation of God is not only an eschatological notion. It has been the aim of all mystics. Without entering here into the numerous meanings of the word "mystic" we can say that one of the greatest longings of Christian mystics has been to encounter and experience the greatness and beauty of God in absolute silence and solitude. This longing had, and has, a clearly soteriological significance. Thus, Otto Meinardus wrote about the great desert father Saint Anthony the Great (see §1.1.2), who lived in the spirit of Elijah and John the Baptist and became the father of Christian monasticism, and his name became associated with a new way of life that led to salvation.[44] It is fascinating to consider that northwestern Europe owed the gospel to Irish missionaries (often of Anglo-Saxon descent), a movement that was a child of the Egyptian church that was so strongly colored by the desert fathers.[45] To a certain extent one might say that the northwestern European church was born of Egyptian mysticism.

1.5 The Regenerative Category of Salvation
1.5.1 General Introduction

The seven descriptions of God's salvation in §1.4 are not mutually exclusive. On the contrary, each of the seven contains elements of truth that elegantly complement

---
44. Meinardus (1989, 3).
45. Meinardus (1989, 4).

one other. One reason for this is that these seven forms of salvation could be positioned along a spiritual time line, and can be distilled into three general categories.

(a) A *regenerative* category, in which salvation is linked with rebirth (Lat. *regeneratio*) (§1.5). This is the process that makes the unsaved person a saved person. It is therefore no wonder that for many Christians the focus lies here: if you are saved, you are saved; all the subsequent blessings follow from that but do not add anything to a person's salvation. There is some truth in this, but it is not the full truth. It is like saying: the baby is born, and that is enough; whatever becomes of the baby is of secondary importance.

(b) A *theotic* category, in which salvation is linked with *theosis* (a Gk. term that refers to exhibiting God's image as the result of spiritual maturation) (§1.6). For many, salvation is a much fuller concept than just regeneration and justification. They argue that the latter are just the means, not the goal. They point out, for instance, that the New Testament sometimes views salvation as a present possession (e.g., Eph. 2:5, 8), but often speaks of it as something lying in the believer's future: "Since, therefore, we *have* now been justified by his blood, much more *shall we be saved* by him from the wrath of God. For if while we were enemies we were reconciled to God by the death of his Son, much more, now that we are reconciled, *shall we be saved* by his life" (Rom. 5:9-10; cf. 13:11; 2 Cor. 1:6; Phil. 2:12; 1 Thess. 5:8-9; 1 Pet. 1:5; 2:2; 4:18). This is a future "shall" that is realized either within Christian life (this category), or in the *eschaton* (cf. the next category). (This future is certainly not realized in the well-known Christian idea that, when believers die, they "go to heaven," as if this were their real and ultimate goal; the New Testament never speaks this way.)

(c) An *eschatological* category, in which salvation is linked to the second coming of the Messiah and the establishment of his kingdom (§1.7). Some say that, in

A Preliminary Orientation

principle, we have everything we need in regeneration (category [a]), others argue that what we concretely *possess* at the present time is nothing more than the forgiveness of our sins as well as the Holy Spirit. Full salvation is not attained before we reach the *eschaton*. In the Bible, this is never called "heaven" (regardless of how this is understood), but rather it is called "the kingdom of God."

1.5.2 Conversion and Regeneration

Salvation from sin and from the wrath of God (§1.4.1) and entrance into a salvational community (§1.4.2) belong to the first category. Conversion, regeneration, and faith in Christ in the biblical sense entail redemption from sin, death, and Satan, as well as incorporation into the body of Christ, which is the salvational community. In some sense, we are dealing here with the most essential meaning of salvation. The most important Hebrew words for "salvation" (*yeshu^{c}ah, yēsha^c, moshaot, teshu^{c}ah*) are derivations of the root *y-sh-^{c}*, "to save, set free, redeem, rescue" (cf. §§1.3.1 and 2.1.1). The corresponding term in Greek, *sōtēria*, comes from the verb *sōzō*, which has the same meaning, and also means "to heal, make healthy" (§1.3.1, 2.4.3). The English terms *save, savior,* and *salvation* come from the Latin words *salvere, salvator* and *salvatio* or *salus*, respectively. The basic meaning of *salvere*, like that of Greek *sōzō*, is "to be well (healthy)."[46]

The word "salvation" (redemption, deliverance) can literally mean the deliverance from concrete, earthly powers: ". . . that we should be saved [lit., salvation, *sōtēria*] from our enemies and from the hand of all who hate us. . . . that we, being delivered [from the Greek verb *rhyomai*] from the hand of our enemies, might

---

46. Some original Germanic words in English include *hreddan* (German *retten*, Dutch *redden*) and *lousen* (German *[er]lösen*, Dutch *[ver]lossen*).

serve him without fear" (Luke 1:71, 74). By extension it can also mean the deliverance from spiritual powers, sin, death, and Satan: "And you were dead in the trespasses and sins in which you once walked, following the course of this world, following the prince of the power of the air, the spirit that is now at work in the sons of disobedience.... But God ... made us alive together with Christ—by grace you have been saved [from Gk. *sōzō*]" (Eph. 2:1–5). "[I]f while we were enemies we were reconciled to God by the death of his Son, much more, now that we are reconciled, shall we be saved [from Gk. *sōzō*] by his life" (Rom. 5:10).

The positive counterpart of this salvation *from* enemies is salvation that consists of being brought to a *safe* place ("safe" also comes from *salvere*), namely, to the church as a secure fortress against the dark powers: "I tell you, you are Peter, and on this rock [Gk. *petra*] I will build my church, and the gates of hell [better: hades] shall not prevail against it" (Matt. 16:18); "... so that *through the church* the manifold wisdom of God might now be made known to the rulers and authorities in the heavenly places" (Eph. 3:10).

In the New Testament, there is a clear distinction between the gospel of God's grace for miserable sinners (e.g., Acts 20:24; Gal. 1:6; Eph. 3:7) and the gospel of the kingdom of God (e.g., Matt. 4:23; 9:35; 24:14). The name Jesus (Heb. *yeshuʿah*, "salvation) relates more specifically with the former aspect of the gospel, as the angel said, "[Y]ou shall call his name Jesus, for he will save his people from their sins" (Matt. 1:21). The name Christ (Gk. *Christos*, "anointed") relates more directly with the latter aspect of the gospel: Jesus is the anointed King: "The kings of the earth set themselves, and the rulers were gathered together, against the Lord and against his Anointed" (Acts 4:26; cf. Ps. 2:2).

1.6 The Theotic Category
1.6.1 The New Person

Receiving the Holy Spirit (§1.4.3) is closely related to the first category (§1.5). Redemption, conversion, regeneration, and faith in Christ turn a person into a member of the body of Christ, and this also implies baptism in/with the Holy Spirit (1 Cor. 12:13). I have dealt extensively with the significance and the implications of this in a previous volume in this series.[47] There I also explained that Spirit baptism, which a person receives at the moment they receive full assurance of salvation, does not always imply being *filled* with the Spirit, experiencing the fullness of the Spirit. Often the extent of spiritual growth affects the measure in which the power of the Spirit, true servitude, obedience and dedication, true empathy, genuine worship, personally experiencing a life of victory, and enthusiastic testimony become visible in a person's life of faith—along with the presence of miraculous works and gifts of the Spirit.

Not even these things are the true goals of salvation; the goal of the disciple of Christ "is to be like his teacher" (Matt. 10:25), to "grow in the grace and knowledge of our Lord and Savior Jesus Christ" (2 Pet. 3:18), to "attain to . . . mature manhood, to the measure of the stature of the fullness of Christ" (Eph. 4:13), to be a person in whom "Christ is formed" (Gal. 4:19; MSG: "Christ's life becomes visible in your lives"). This has everything to do with what the Eastern tradition calls *theosis* (coming to resemble God, to exhibit his image).[48] Full *sōtēria* is not only being delivered *from* (the evil powers) but growing *toward* (i.e., practically realizing the image *of*) God. *Sōtēria* is then really wholeness, well-being, blessedness, becoming a whole, sound person. Although here on earth the believer still possesses the sinful nature,

---

47. See extensively, Ouweneel (*RT* II/3, especially chapters 7 and 8).
48. See Ouweneel (*RT* II/3, §9.5).

such a believer is nevertheless a "human [Gk. *anthrōpos*] in Christ" (2 Cor. 12:1), a person who is "perfect" (i.e., spiritually mature) in the sense of Philippians 3:15 (cf. Col. 1:28), a person who keeps the Lord's word (Rev. 3:8), and thus a person in whom "truly the love of God is perfected" (1 John 2:5), a "father" in Christ (vv. 13-14).

This person who is whole (healed)—the person in whom, within earthly limitations, salvation has been fully realized—is the "new person" of Ephesians 4:24 (CEV), "created after the likeness of God in true righteousness and holiness," the new person who "is being renewed in knowledge after the image of its creator" (Col. 3:10). This is the person who is "transformed by the renewal of your mind," and thus "by testing" discerns "what is the will of God, what is good and acceptable and perfect" (Rom. 12:2), "transformed into the same image from one degree of glory to another. For this comes from the Lord who is the Spirit" (2 Cor. 3:18).

This is also the person of Luke 1:6, "righteous before God, walking blamelessly in all the commandments and statutes of the Lord," and this in the fullness that is only possible since the outpouring of the Holy Spirit (§1.4.4). This is the person who loves the Torah of Christ (Gal. 6:2) because he loves Christ (John 14:15, 21). This is the person in whom "the righteous requirement of the law" is fulfilled (Rom. 8:4; cf. Gal. 5:16-18). This is the person who has been freed from all legalism, and for whom the Torah is therefore the Torah *of liberty* (James 1:25; 2:12). *This* is the true *tsaddiq*, the "righteous one," formed after the image of Christ who was and is the truest and highest *tsaddiq* (Matt. 27:19, 24; Acts 3:14; 7:52; 22:14; 1 Pet. 3:18; 1 John 2:1; possibly also James 5:6).

This is the person who one day will see the face of God, but even then will be aware that eternally one remains no more than a slave serving God (Rev. 22:3-4; cf. Luke 17:7-10). Incidentally, these two matters are related. In the Old Testament, "seeing the face of the king" means as much as standing in his service, but also being intimate with the king (cf. Esther 1:14; see also §1.7.2). These two sides remain joined together: everlasting servitude with supreme intimacy.

1.6.2 The Commandment of Love

The mature "new person" is the one who fulfills the Commandment of Love, which is the essence of the Torah (Matt. 22:36–40; John 13:34; 15:12; Rom. 13:9–10; Gal. 5:14; 6:2; James 2:8; 1 John 4:21). This new person *can* fulfill the Torah because "God's love has been poured into our hearts through the Holy Spirit who has been given to us" (Rom. 5:5). Through divine revelation, that person possesses *knowledge* of the Torah; through divine regeneration, that person possesses the *desire* to live the Torah; through the divine Spirit, that person possesses the *power* to live the Torah.

Because love is the essence of the Torah of Christ, and thus of Christian life, it is understandable that "walking in love" (Eph. 5:2) can be viewed as the highest good (§1.4.5). This goes way beyond the earthly, natural love spoken about in a horizontalist gospel. The reason is that love as the highest good is a love that cannot be severed from the new life of regeneration and from the fullness of the Holy Spirit who dwells in the believer (see again Rom. 5:5; Gal. 5:14–16).

Interestingly, Christ is present in this love in two opposite ways. First in believers themselves, for the love that flows out from them toward the neighbor is the love that Christ himself has put into believers' hearts; the first part of the fruit of the Spirit is love (Gal. 5:22; cf. Rom. 5:5). In showing love to the neighbor, it is Christ, so to speak, who flows from the believer to the neighbor. But second, believers encounter Christ in the neighbor, for Matthew 25 teaches us that, if someone loves their neighbor, they are loving Christ: "[T]he King will answer them, 'Truly, I say to you, as you did it to one of the least of these my brothers, you did it to me'" (v. 40).[49] In the neighbor the believer beholds the face of Christ. As Mother Teresa said of the miserable, "The dying, the cripple, the mental, the unwanted, the unloved, they are Jesus in disguise."[50] And: "I see Jesus in every human being. I say to myself, this is hungry Jesus, I must feed him. This is sick Jesus. This one has leprosy or gangrene; I must wash him and tend to him. I serve because I love Jesus."[51]

In such a view, salvation involves no mystical withdrawal from daily life with its sometimes unpleasant responsibilities in order to encounter Christ in silence and solitude. Rather, in the view of Mother Teresa and so many others the thing that matters is going *into* the world to seek there the poor and oppressed "brothers of the King," and to find Christ in the poor, the hungry, thirsty, homeless, naked, sick or imprisoned neighbor. Here, the believers encounters his Lord not only in the monastery, the hermit's cell, or the church service, but also in the gutter, at the sickbed, and in prison. This means not only that believers brings Christ's salvation to the poor outcasts but that they *themselves* experience salvation. In carrying Christ to the other, Christ comes to *them*. In the believer's face the neighbor may perceive and experience something of the love of Christ—but in the face of the miserable neighbor believers themselves may perceive Christ.

1.7 The Eschatological Category
1.7.1 Deliverance and Blessing

Klaus Berger once said, "Not my reconciliation with God is the main thing, but God's rule and kingdom."[52] What

---

49. Ouweneel (1994, 205).
50. http://www.servelec.net/mothertheresa.htm.
51. https://insider.pureflix.com/news/mother-teresa-each-one-of-them-is-jesus-in-disguise.
52. Berger (2004, 97).

comes first is not the personal salvation of the individual, but the collective salvation of this world. God's goal is not salvation in the present, but the fully realized salvation in the age to come.

In its full eschatological meaning, salvation is first *yeshuʿah* or *sōtēria* in the sense of deliverance "from the hand of our enemies" (Luke 1:74). As Micah puts it,

> [T]he remnant of Jacob shall be among the nations,
>   in the midst of many peoples,
> like a lion among the beasts of the forest,
>   like a young lion among the flocks of sheep,
> which, when it goes through, treads down
>   and tears in pieces, and there is none to deliver.
> Your hand shall be lifted up over your adversaries,
>   and all your enemies shall be cut off (Micah 5:8-9).

So too Zephaniah:

> Sing aloud, O daughter of Zion;
>   shout, O Israel!
> Rejoice and exult with all your heart,
>   O daughter of Jerusalem!
> The Lord has taken away the judgments against you;
>   he has cleared away your enemies.
> The King of Israel, the Lord, is in your midst;
>   you shall never again fear evil.
> On that day it shall be said to Jerusalem:
> "Fear not, O Zion; let not your hands grow weak.". . .
> Behold, at that time I will deal
>   with all your oppressors" (Zeph. 3:14-16, 19a).

Between these two sections of Zephaniah 3, we get a taste of the second, fuller, richer, definitive meaning of salvation (§1.4.6):

> "The Lord your God is in your midst,
>   a mighty one who will save;
> he will rejoice over you with gladness;
> he will quiet you by his love;
>   he will exult over you with loud singing.
> I will gather those of you who mourn for the festival, . . .
> And I will save the lame
>   and gather the outcast,
> and I will change their shame into praise
>   and renown in all the earth.
> At that time I will bring you in,
>   at the time when I gather you together;
> for I will make you renowned and praised
>   among all the peoples of the earth,
> when I restore your fortunes
>   before your eyes," says the Lord (Zeph. 3:17–20).

The deeper, more spiritual aspects of eschatological salvation come to light especially in the Hebrew notion of *shalom*, which, in addition to the basic meaning of "peace," can also mean "bliss, happiness, blessedness, well-being, wholeness, healing." In its present meaning, "peace" refers first to the "peace *with* God" that all those who have been justified by faith may enjoy (Rom. 5:1), and second to the "peace *of* God," which may characterize the practical life of faith (Phil. 4:7; cf. Col. 3:15 kjv).

In its eschatological meaning, *shalom* is described beautifully by the prophet Isaiah:

> . . . until the Spirit is poured upon us from on high,
>   and the wilderness becomes a fruitful field,
>   and the fruitful field is deemed a forest.
> Then justice will dwell in the wilderness,
>   and righteousness abide in the fruitful field.
> And the effect of righteousness will be peace,
>   and the result of righteousness, quietness and trust forever.

> My people will abide in a peaceful habitation,
>> in secure dwellings, and in quiet resting places
>> (Isa. 32:15-18).
>
> ... I will make your overseers peace
>> and your taskmasters righteousness. ...
> ... [Y]ou shall call your walls Salvation,
>> and your gates Praise.

> The sun shall be no more
>> your light by day,
> nor for brightness shall the moon
>> give you light;
> but the Lord will be your everlasting light,
>> and your God will be your glory. ...
> Your people shall all be righteous;
>> they shall possess the land forever,
> the branch of my planting, the work of my hands,
>> that I might be glorified.
> The least one shall become a clan,
>> and the smallest one a mighty nation;
> I am the Lord;
>> in its time I will hasten it (Isa. 60:17b-22).

1.7.2 New Testament Promises

In the New Testament, we find these same two eschatological aspects: deliverance from the evil powers, and positive peace and bliss:

> I consider that the sufferings of this present time are not worth comparing with the glory that is to be revealed to us. For the creation waits with eager longing for the revealing of the sons of God. For the creation was subjected to futility, not willingly, but because of him who subjected it, in hope that the creation itself will be set free from its bondage to corruption and obtain the freedom of the glory of the children of God. For we know that the whole creation has been groaning together in the pains of childbirth until now. And not only the creation, but

we ourselves, who have the firstfruits of the Spirit, groan inwardly as we wait eagerly for adoption as sons, the redemption of our bodies. For in this hope we were saved (Rom. 8:18–24).

For many people, salvation in its fullest and truest sense is not just redemption, blessing, happiness, peace, and righteousness, because these matters could still be very human-oriented (anthropocentric). Therefore, the contemplation of God (§1.4.7) also belongs to the eschatological category. In Matthew 18:10, the fact that the angels of the children "always see the face of my Father who is in heaven" perhaps means nothing more than that they serve God (see §1.6.1). But B. B. Warfield may have been right in understanding these angels (Gk. *angeloi*) to be the spirits of the dead children, who are privileged to always behold the face of their Father in heaven.[53] This fits with the use of the Greek word *angelos* in Matthew 22:30 (the risen believers are "like angels in heaven"), in Luke 20:36 (the risen believers are "equal to angels"), and in Acts 12:15 (the spirit of a [supposedly] dead person is called "his angel").[54] If this interpretation is correct, it constitutes a remarkable support for the notion of the eternal contemplation of God by the glorified righteous.

In the contemplation of God, the believer is united to God, not in the sense of a mystic-ontic union—humans always remain creatures and never become God or gods—but in the sense of perfect fellowship, communion, and intimacy. "Enoch walked with God" (Gen. 5:22, 24); "Noah walked with God" (6:9); "the LORD used to speak to Moses face to face, as a man speaks to his friend [Heb. re‘eh]" (Exod. 33:11). "The friendship [Heb. sod] of the LORD is for those who fear him" (Ps. 25:14; cf. Job 29:4). "Abraham, my friend" (Isa. 41:8, Heb. ohav,

---

53. Warfield (1970, 1:253–66); cf. Carson (1984, 401).
54. Cf. in the Jewish tradition, 2 Baruch 51:5, 12; 1 Henoch 51:4: the righteous will become angels in heaven.

"lover"; cf. 2 Chron. 20:7; James 2:23, Gk. philos, "lover"). The Hebrew word sod means "secret, mystery" (cf. "secret," i.e., "secret counsel," in Amos 3:7). Its meaning extends to refer to the secret (confidential) dimension in the fellowship of two persons; compare this word: "the upright are in his confidence [Heb. sod]" (Prov. 3:32). "We used to take sweet counsel [Heb. *sod*] together" (Ps. 55:14).

Such confidence is something believers may pursue, already today, in the power of the Spirit. As Paul explains so beautifully:

> For this reason I bow my knees before the Father . . . that according to the riches of his glory he may grant you to be strengthened with power *through his Spirit* in your inner being, so that *Christ* may dwell in your hearts through faith—that you, being rooted and grounded in *love*, may have strength to comprehend with all the saints what is the breadth and length and height and depth, and to know the *love* of Christ that surpasses knowledge, *that you may be filled with all the fullness of God* (Eph. 3:14-19; italics added).

Soteriology deals with the salvation *of* God in the sense that it is God who grants it. But, more than that, it is the salvation *of* God in the sense that he himself is its ultimate object and goal.

Chapter 2
The Notion of Salvation

Fear not, stand firm,
  and see the salvation of the LORD.
                    Exodus 14:13

Salvation belongs to the LORD;
  your blessing be on your people!
                    Psalm 3:8

[Mary] will bear a son,
  and you shall call his name Jesus,
for he will save his people
  from their sins.
                    Matthew 1:21

Summary: *The notion of salvation pervades the Old Testament (both the historical and the prophetic books): salvation from both earthly powers and the power of sin and death. Human "saviors" give us an idea of God's salvation. Both the exodus from Egypt and that from Babylon involved salvation both from earthly kings and from the angelic princes behind them. Many people long for a world of peace and righteousness but reject God's means of getting there: God's grace as well as the cross and the blood of Christ are repulsive to them. Those who do accept God's salvation* often have very different ideas of it: the ransom-to-Satan model, the recapitulation model, and the sacrificial substitution model are compared. Others accept God's salvation but reject certain traditional Reformational doctrines of salvation.

2.1 The Old Testament Historical Books
2.1.1 Salvation from Foreign Powers

AS WE HAVE SEEN, the most important Hebrew root for "salvation" is *y-sh-ᶜ*, which means "to save, deliver, redeem, rescue."[1] In the Old Testament this is especially a theological term, with YHWH as subject and his people as object. In the historical books the theme is the salvation of Israel: from Egypt, from invading neighbors, from Babylon. As soon as a redeemed people of God comes into existence, namely, at the exodus from Egypt, the term is employed: "And Moses said to the people, 'Fear not, stand firm, and see the salvation [Heb. *yeshuᶜat*] of the LORD, which he will work for you today. For the Egyptians whom you see today, you shall never see again. . . . Thus the LORD saved [Heb. *wayyosheᶜ*] Israel that day from the hand of the Egyptians, and Israel saw the Egyptians dead on the seashore. . . . The LORD is my strength and my song, and he has become my salvation [Heb. *lishuᶜah*]" (Exod. 14:13, 30; 15:2). This is the first time that God as Redeemer (Savior, Deliverer) intervened on behalf of his people, after they had cried to him for help.

At stake here was a true deliverance from the power of foreign people. This is also the case in the book of Judges (3:9, 15), where we find the deliverer (Heb. *moshiaᶜ*, from the same root *yshᶜ*) in the person of the judge (Heb. *shophet*), who delivered Israel from the power of the foreign invaders (2:16, 18; 3:31; 6:14–15, 36–37; 10:1;

---

1. See *TDNT* 7:970–89; *DOTT* 2:556–62; Pop (1999, 51–58). Other Hebrew roots are *m-l-t* (*DOTT* 2:950–54), *nts-l* (3:141–47), and *p-l-t* (3:621–26), but these do not have the theological implications that *y-sh-ᶜ* has.

The Notion of Salvation

13:5; cf. 1 Sam. 9:16; 17:47; 2 Kings 13:5; Neh. 9:27). The judge was the subject of the deliverance, though with the help and support of YHWH. There certainly was a judicial aspect in the Hebrew term *shophet* (cf. Judg. 4:4; 10:2-3; 12:7-14; 15:20; 16:31), but the salvational aspect was at least as important. The judge was the one who pronounced justice upon, or here especially, performed justice to, God's people (Heb. *sh-ph-t*; see, e.g., 1 Sam. 24:16; 2 Sam. 18:19, 31; Ps. 7:9; 10:18; 26:1; 35:24; 43:1; Isa. 1:17).

The Hebrew noun corresponding with *moshia^c* is *teshu^{c}a*, which literally means "rescue, deliverance," here with the connotation of "triumph, victory" (Judg. 15:18; 1 Sam. 11:13; 19:5; 2 Sam. 19:2; 23:10, 12; 2 Kings 5:1; 13:17). Through the judges, Israel was victorious over its enemies. This was the more remarkable because the people of Israel time and again deserved judgment, so that it was pure grace of God that he repeatedly delivered his people from the hand of their enemies. An example: David deserved the rebellion by his son Absalom (2 Sam. 12:10-12); nevertheless, God delivered him from Absalom (18:19, 31). As a contrast, compare Psalm 26:1, "Establish justice for me, LORD, because I have walked with integrity" (CEB).

Even in the face of the greatest guilt, redemption is not only a matter of divine grace but also of divine justice; I have dealt with this remarkable fact in a previous volume.[2] The main components of redemption are these: redemption is pure divine justice because God is obliged to it. This obligation is, first, due to his own covenant promises, and second, due to the vicarious sacrifices, which debouched in the sacrifice of Jesus Christ (see Judg. 6:26; 13:16, 23; 20:26; 21:4; and especially 1 Sam. 7:2-14, the sacrifice by the judge Samuel). God is righteous when he fulfills his promises, but he does need a righteous foundation for it, which he finds in the sacri-

---

2. Ouweneel (*RT* III/2).

fice, as we will see (chapter 9).

2.1.2 Human "Saviors"

God's Saviorship is practically illustrated by human saviors. Thus, Moses acted as savior for the seven daughters of Reuel (Exod. 2:17, Heb. *wayyoshi͑an*, "and he saved/rescued them"), as a portent of the salvations that God, through him, would grant his people. The Israelite king could also function as a savior of his people; thus literally in 2 Samuel 14:4 (Heb. *hoshi͑ah hammelekh*, "save, O king!" cf. 2 Kings 6:26). Just like the judges in the book of Judges, the king was the means in God's hand to prepare salvation for God's people, and subsequently a reference to *the* Man through whom God works the salvation for his people, and who thus may be called Redeemer or Savior (Luke 2:11; John 4:42; Acts 5:31; 13:23; Rom. 11:26; Phil. 3:20; 2 Tim. 1:10; Titus 1:4; 2:13; 3:6; 2 Pet. 1:1, 11; 2:20; 3:2, 18). In 2 Kings 13:5 we read, "Therefore the LORD gave Israel a savior [i.e., presumably, king Joash or Jeroboam II], so that they escaped from the hand of the Syrians, and the people of Israel lived in their homes as formerly."

Also compare the Hebrew phrase *hoshi͑ah na*, "Save, please!," which in Psalm 118:25 is said to the Messiah. Through the Aramaic form *hosha͑ na*, the expression gave rise to the Greek word *Hosanna* (Matt. 21:9, i.e., "Messiah, save us please," *or* "God, save the Messiah," like the British national anthem, "God save [here: keep] the king/queen"). The Hebrew term *hosanna* occurs in many hymns as if it were a kind of praise, whereas in fact it is a prayer. Also compare many proper names: Isaiah (Heb. *yesha͑yahu*), Hosea (Heb. *hoshe͑a*), Joshua (Heb. *yehoshu͑a*), Jeshua/Jesus (Heb. *yeshu͑a*), all from the Hebrew root *ysh͑*, "to save."

It is only a small theological step from being delivered out of the hand of physical enemies to being delivered from spiritual powers: sin, death, and devil. The

The Notion of Salvation

step is the smaller when we realize that the physical powers are allowed to hurt the people only if the latter have chosen the way of sin. Therefore, deliverance from the physical enemies is closely linked with confession of sin and walking anew in the path of righteousness: "Whoever walks in integrity will be delivered" (Prov. 28:18a). "When people are brought low and you [i.e., Job] say [to God], 'Lift them up!' then he will save [Heb. *yoshia͑*] the downcast. He will deliver [Heb. *yemallet*, from *m-l-t*] even one who is not innocent, who will be delivered [Heb. *wenimlat*, from *m-l-t*] through the cleanness of your hands" (Job 22:29–30 NIV).

There are numerous historical examples; here is one from Judges 10:

> And the people of Israel cried out to the LORD, saying, "We have sinned against you, because we have forsaken our God and have served the Baals." And the LORD said to the people of Israel, "Did I not save [Heb. *wa'oshi͑ah*] you from the Egyptians and from the Amorites, from the Ammonites and from the Philistines? The Sidonians also, and the Amalekites and the Maonites oppressed you, and you cried out to me, and I saved you out of their hand. Yet you have forsaken me and served other gods; therefore I will save [Heb. *l'hoshi͑a*] you no more. Go and cry out to the gods whom you have chosen; let them save [Heb. *yoshi͑u*] you in the time of your distress." And the people of Israel said to the LORD, "We have sinned; do to us whatever seems good to you. Only please deliver [*hatsilenu*, from *n-ts-l*] us this day." So they put away the foreign gods from among them and served the LORD, and he became impatient over the misery of Israel [NIV: he could bear Israel's misery no longer] (vv. 10–16).

Here, deliverance from the yoke of sin goes hand in hand with deliverance from the yoke of the enemies (brought upon the people because of their sins).

2.2 The Prophetic Books
2.2.1 Salvation and Justice

The Hebrew root *y-sh-ᶜ* occurs in the prophets about hundred times, more than half of which are found in Isaiah. Here, YHWH is the only One who can really save (59:16; 63:1, 5); he is called many times "Savior" (Heb. *moshiaᶜ*, 41:14; 43:3, 11, 14; 44:6, 24 etc.), and he is this in contrast with the idols (45:20; 46:7; Jer. 2:27-28; 11:12), the astrologers (Isa. 47:13), and even the king of Judah (Hos. 13:10). God is "the Mighty Warrior who saves" (Zeph. 3:17 NIV).

Here again, deliverance from the physical enemies is often placed parallel to the deliverance from the power of sin:

> Take with you words and return to the LORD; say to him, "Take away all iniquity; accept what is good, and we will pay with bulls the vows of our lips. Assyria shall not save us; we will not ride on horses; and we will say no more, 'Our God,' to the work of our hands. In you the orphan finds mercy" (Hos. 14:2-3; cf. Ps. 79:9, "Help us, O God of our salvation, for the glory of your name; deliver us, and atone for our sins, for your name's sake!").

"Zion shall be redeemed by justice, and those in her who repent, by righteousness" (Isa. 1:27). "For thus said the Lord GOD, the Holy One of Israel, 'In returning [or, repentance] and rest you shall be saved; in quietness and in trust shall be your strength.' But you were unwilling" (30:15; cf. Ps. 37:39-40, "The salvation of the righteous is from the LORD; he is their stronghold in the time of trouble. The LORD helps them and delivers them; he delivers them from the wicked and saves them, *because they take refuge in him*"; cf. 13:5; 25:5; 42:5; 65:5; 86:2). Thus, repentance is a condition for deliverance: "O Jerusalem, wash your heart from evil, that you may be saved" (Jer. 4:14).

Salvation and righteousness go hand in hand (cf. §2.1.1 on salvation and justice): "Keep justice, and do righteousness, for soon my *salvation* will come, and my *righteousness* be revealed" (Isa. 56:1; cf. Ps. 40:10; 71:15; 98:2; 119:123).

> Behold, the LORD's hand is not shortened, that it cannot save, or his ear dull, that it cannot hear; but your iniquities have made a separation between you and your God, and your sins have hidden his face from you so that he does not hear.... [W]e hope for justice, but there is none; for salvation, but it is far from us. For our transgressions are multiplied before you, and our sins testify against us; for our transgressions are with us, and we know our iniquities (Isa. 59:1-2, 11-12).

"[H]e has clothed me with the garments of salvation; he has covered me with the robe of righteousness" (Isa. 61:10).

2.2.2 Return from Babylon

Isaiah 40-54 deals with Israel's redemption from the Babylonian exile, but the spiritual redemption from the power of sin goes hand in hand with this: "I, I am he who blots out your transgressions for my own sake, and I will not remember your sins" (43:25). "I have blotted out your transgressions like a cloud and your sins like mist; return to me, for I have redeemed you" (Isa. 44:22). "Returning" (from Babylon) to the land of Israel is the same verb (Heb. *shuv*) as "returning" (penitent converting) to the Lord (cf. the way *shuv* is used in Deut. 30:1-11).

Moreover, the redemption from Babylon has an eschatological dimension: "Israel is saved by the LORD with everlasting salvation; you shall not be put to shame or confounded to all eternity" (Isa. 45:17).

And he will swallow up on this mountain the covering that is cast over all peoples, the veil that is spread over all nations. He will swallow up death forever; and the Lord God will wipe away tears from all faces, and the reproach of his people he will take away from all the earth, for the Lord has spoken. It will be said on that day, "Behold, this is our God; we have waited for him, that he might save us. This is the Lord; we have waited for him; let us be glad and rejoice in his salvation" (Isa. 25:7-9; see also 35:4-10).

The savior through whom God grants his salvation—especially Cyrus the Persian—also possesses eschatological features, as is clear from the Messianic titles that are assigned to him: *"my shepherd"* (Isa. 44:28); "Thus says the Lord to *his anointed*, to Cyrus, whose right hand I have grasped, to subdue nations before him and to loose the belts of kings, to open doors before him that gates may not be closed" (Isa. 45:1; cf. 41:2, 25); "the man of my counsel" (Isa. 46:11). It is the new "David" who, during the Messianic kingdom, will grant his people the definitive salvation (Jer. 23:5-6; 33:15-16; Ezek. 34:22-24; Zech. 9:9, 16). This will be salvation from the physical enemies but also from the power of sin:

> They shall not defile themselves anymore with their idols and their detestable things, or with any of their transgressions. But I will save them from all the backslidings in which they have sinned, and will cleanse them; and they shall be my people, and I will be their God. My servant David shall be king over them, and they shall all have one shepherd. They shall walk in my rules and be careful to obey my statutes (Ezek. 37:23-24).

This salvation will be for all the nations, as God told his Servant: "It is too light a thing that you should be my servant to raise up the tribes of Jacob and to bring back the preserved of Israel; I will make you as a light for the nations, that my *salvation* may reach to the end of the earth" (Isa. 49:6). Also compare Psalm 40:6-10, 118:24-26, and 132:16-17, where salvation is described within a Messianic context.

2.3 Physical and Spiritual Powers
2.3.1 The Prince of Egypt

The central meaning of salvation in the Old Testament is deliverance from and victory over hostile powers. This meaning is very important because, as we saw, the terminology is directly applicable to deliverance from spiritual, demonic powers, the powers of darkness. A deliverance of Israel from the hands of its neighbors goes much further than the deliverance of, for instance, the Netherlands from Nazi occupation (May 1945). Israel is *God's* people, and thus, by definition, Israel's enemies are "enemies of the LORD" (1 Sam. 30:26; 2 Sam. 12:14; Ps. 37:20; cf., e.g., Num. 32:21; Ps. 68:1, 21; 89:10, 51; Isa. 66:3, 6, 14; Nah. 1:2, 8).

The connection goes even further: the Gentile nations are under the rule of demonic powers, which they themselves call "gods." Sometimes, the Old Testament adopts this improper term (see examples below), but on other occasions more proper terms are used, such as "dragons" or "monsters" (Heb. *tanninim*, e.g., Isa. 51:9; Jer. 51:34; cf. v. 44), "lords" (Heb. *adonim*, Isa. 26:13; cf. 1 Cor. 8:5), or "princes" (rulers, Heb. *sarim*, Dan. 10:13, 20), or even "demons": "They sacrificed to demons [Heb. *sedim*] that were no gods" (Deut. 32:17). "They sacrificed their sons and their daughters to the demons" (Ps. 106:37; cf. 1 Cor. 10:19-20; Rev. 9:20).[3] Thus, the "gods" who rule over the Gentile nations are nothing but demonic powers. Each time Israel comes under the power of these heathen nations, the people also come under the power of the "gods" of these nations. This is what Israel confesses: "O LORD our God, other lords besides you

---
3. Regarding this subject see extensively, Ouweneel (Forthcoming-a).

have ruled over us," but now this has become different: ". . . your name alone we bring to remembrance" (Isa. 26:13).

Some examples clearly illustrate this, beginning with *Egypt*. When Israel was a slave people in Egypt, it suffered under the power of the Pharaoh. However, behind the Pharaoh were hidden spiritual powers; therefore, God said, "[O]n all the *gods* of Egypt I will execute judgments" (Exod. 12:12; cf. Num. 33:4). Thus, deliverance out of the hand of Egypt implied deliverance out of the hand of the "dragon" (demonic power) hidden behind Egypt. Psalm 74:13 says about the passage through the Red Sea, "You divided the sea by your might; you broke the heads of the sea monsters [Heb. *tanninim*[4]] on the waters." And the people exclaim, "Who is like you, O LORD, among the gods [Heb. *elim*, mighty ones]?" (Exod. 15:11).

Isaiah 51:9 recalls the "dragon," the demonic power behind Egypt. The prophet trusts that God will deliver his people from Babylon as he once delivered them from Egypt seven or nine centuries before. About the deliverance from Egypt he says, "Was it not you who cut Rahab in pieces, who pierced the dragon [Heb. *tannin*]?" Rahab is the spiritual power behind Egypt, as is evident from Psalm 87:4, 89:10, and Isaiah 30:7, where "Rahab" refers either to Egypt as such, or to the spiritual power behind Egypt (cf. also Ezek. 29:3, where tannin refers especially to the Pharaoh of Egypt: "Pharaoh king of Egypt, the great dragon that lies in the midst of his streams"). Concerning the statement, "[T]he horse [sing.!] and his rider he has thrown into the sea" (Exod. 15:1), a Midrash understands this to refer to the angelic prince of Egypt being thrown down, which allegedly oc-

---

4. Here possibly using a singular meaning: "sea monster" or "dragon"; cf. the plural *behemoth* (Job 40:15), which means "large beast" ("monster"); cf. also the dragon with the seven heads in Rev. 12:3.

curred before the eyes of Israel.[5]

2.3.2 Other Angelic Princes

Regarding the Babylonian empire, we clearly see that it was not the king of Babylon who was Israel's actual adversary but the spiritual power behind him was. In Jeremiah 51:34 it is "Nebuchadnezzar the king of Babylon" who has "swallowed" Israel "like a monster [Heb. *tannin*], he has filled his stomach with my [i.e., Israel's] delicacies." However, at the end of the exile it was Bel, the main god of Babylon, who had to spit out Israel: "I will punish Bel in Babylon, and take out of his mouth what he has swallowed" (v. 44). What Nebuchadnezzar swallowed, Bel had to regurgitate. What both did to Israel was one and the same thing, for the king was nothing but the earthly embodiment of his god. Here again, deliverance out of the hand of Babylon implies deliverance out of the hand of the "dragon" (demonic power) behind Babylon.

The identification of the king of a power hostile to Israel *and* the spiritual power behind this king is nowhere clearer than in Isaiah 14:12–15, where the description of Babylon's kind smoothly merges into a description of Babylon's angelic prince:

> How you are fallen from heaven, O Day Star [or, Morning Star], son of Dawn! How you are cut down to the ground, you who laid the nations low! You said in your heart, "I will ascend to heaven; above the stars of God I will set my throne on high; I will sit on the mount of assembly in the far reaches of the north; I will ascend above the heights of the clouds; I will make myself like the Most High." But you are brought down to Sheol, to the far reaches of the pit.

---

5. Mechilta 43b on Exod. 15:1.

I summarize here what I have discussed elsewhere:[6] the morning star is Venus, corresponding to the Babylonian Ishtar, goddess of sensual love. The "son of dawn" is he who is born of the dawn, the sun (god). Together, Ishtar and her consort (Bel/Nebo/Marduk) represent the demonic power behind Babylon. The prophet announces here the downfall of this pair of gods, for when the Babylonian empire collapses its gods collapse too: "Bel bows down; Nebo stoops; their idols are on beasts and livestock" (Isa. 46:1). "Babylon is taken, Bel is put to shame, Merodach [i.e., Marduk] is dismayed. Her images are put to shame, her idols are dismayed" (Jer. 50:2).

The subsequent world empires, Persia and Greece, also had their (demonic) angelic princes, and this time the word "prince" (Heb. *sar*) is explicitly used. In Daniel 10:13, an angel visiting Daniel tells him, "The [angelic] prince of the kingdom of Persia withstood me twenty-one days, but Michael, one of the chief princes, came to help me, for I was left there with the kings of Persia." And a little later (vv. 20-21): "But now I will return to fight against the [angelic] prince of Persia; and when I go out, behold, the [angelic] prince of Greece will come... there is none who contends by my side against these except Michael, your [i.e., Israel's] [angelic] prince."[7] The "princes" mentioned here are the angelic powers behind the (Medo-)Persian empire, the Greek(-Macedonian) empire, and Israel, respectively.

Notice the remarkable fact that apparently Israel has its own angelic prince: the archangel Michael. It has been presumed that this was and is the case only when Israel is in exile, because God allotted the territories of the earth to the "sons of God" (angelic princes, Deut. 32:8; for this "allotting," cf. the remarkable verses 4:19 and 29:26, where the "gods" correspond to certain celestial bodies) but he kept Israel as his heritage for himself

---

6. See Ouweneel (2004, 71-74; 2018g, §3.3).
7. Cf. Ouweneel (2004, 19-21).

(v. 9; cf. Exod. 32:34; 33:2, 14–16).

Finally, in the New Testament the angelic prince behind the Roman empire is the "dragon": "that ancient serpent, who is called the devil and Satan" (Rev. 12:9; cf. 20:2). The earthly "beast" of Revelation 13 relates to the dragon as the earthly Pharaoh related to his "god," and the earthly king Nebuchadnezzar related to his "god" Bel. I have discussed this elsewhere.[8] In all the cases mentioned, not the earthly rulers but these "celestial beings" are apparently the real authorities behind the curtain. They dominate the history of their respective kingdoms as well as the nations subjected to them (cf. the important hints in Num. 21:29; Judg. 11:24). Here again, the pivotal point is that deliverance from the power of the earthly kingdoms entails deliverance from the power of the demonic world behind these kingdoms.

2.4 The New Testament Notion of Salvation
2.4.1 Deliverance from the Powers

If we keep in mind the foregoing discussion, we can understand why the step from deliverance out of the hand of the earthly powers to deliverance out of the hand of the spiritual powers is much smaller than often thought. Behind every earthly power there is a hidden spiritual power: "For we do not wrestle against flesh and blood, but against the rulers [Gk. *pros tas archas*], against the authorities [Gk. *pros tas exousias*],[9] against the cosmic powers [Gk. *pros tous kosmokratoras*] over this present darkness, against the spiritual forces of evil [Gk. *pros ta pneumatika tēs ponērias*] in the heavenly places" (Eph.

---

8. Cf. Ouweneel (2012a, chapter 6; 2018g, chapter 5).
9. In Rom. 13:1 the "authorities" (Gk. *exousiais*) and in Titus 3:1 "rulers and authorities" (Gk. *archais exousiais*) refer primarily to earthly rulers and authorities, but in all other passages, these terms refer to spiritual rulers and authorities in the heavenly places (Rom. 8:38; Eph. 1:20–21; 3:10; Col. 1:16; 1 Pet. 3:22). According to Testament Levi 3 and 2 Henoch 20–21 these are some of highest classes of angels.

6:12).

Especially interesting is here the term "cosmic powers" (from *kosmokratōr*, "ruler over the cosmos"), a term that had been used formerly for the Greek gods. The "cosmic powers over this present darkness" are more easily understood as the "angelic princes of the present dark cosmos." There is a possible reference here to the ancient idea that each *kosmokratōr* rules over his own territory in the cosmos. Presumably, the phrase "rulers of this age/world" (Gk. *archontōn tou aionos toutou*, 1 Cor. 2:6, 8) refers to the same territorial idea (cf. §8.8.2).[10] Satan is then the ruler (Gk. *archōn*) of the world as a whole (John 12:31; 14:30; 16:11),[11] just as he is the *archōn* of the demons (Matt. 12:24) and of the power of the air (Eph. 2:2).

Thus, whether we have in view earthly or spiritual adversaries, salvation is primarily deliverance from the power of Satan: "He has delivered [Gk. *errhysato*] us from the domain [Gk. *exousias*] of darkness and transferred us to the kingdom of his beloved Son" (Col. 1:13). The Greek verb *rhuomai*, "to save, rescue,"[12] is found elsewhere: "And lead us not into temptation, but deliver us from evil" (Matt. 6:13). "And in this way all Israel will be saved [Gk. *sōthēsetai*], as it is written, 'The Deliverer [Gk. *rhyōmenos*] will come from Zion, he will banish ungodliness from Jacob'" (Rom. 11:26); "Jesus who delivers us from the wrath to come" (1 Thess. 1:10); ". . . then the Lord knows how to rescue [Gk. *rhuesthai*] the godly from trials" (2 Pet. 2:9).

For this notion of deliverance from the power of Sa-

---

10. Ouweneel (Forthcoming-a, §2.2.2).
11. Cf. Exod. Rabbah 17.4 on Exod. 12:23. I wonder wheter here the Gk. noun *kosmos* has the specific meaning of the Gk. noun *oikoumenē*, the "inhabited earth," specifically—but not always—the Roman Empire (cf. Luke 2:1; Acts 11:28; 17:6; 19:27; 24:5 NASB), given the fact that, in Rev., the dragon is the angelic prince of the Roman Empire.
12. See *TDNT* 6:998–1003.

tan recall the mission that Jesus gave the apostle Paul: he was sent to the Gentiles "to open their eyes, so that they may turn from darkness to light and from the power of Satan to God, that they may receive forgiveness of sins and a place among those who are sanctified by faith in me" (Acts 26:18).

2.4.2 Three Basic Terms

In addition to the Greek verb *sōzō* there are several other terms in the New Testament for "saving, redeeming, rescuing, delivering." Thus, in the prophecy of the priest Zechariah—still very much in Old Testament style—we find deliverance from earthly enemies and salvation from the power of sin mentioned in the same context:

> Blessed be the Lord God of Israel, for he has visited and redeemed [lit., wrought redemption (Gk. *lutrōsin*) for] his people and has raised up a horn of salvation [Gk. *sōtērias*] for us in the house of his servant David [the reference is to the Messiah] . . . , that we should be saved [lit. just one word, salvation (Gk. *sōtērian*)] from our enemies and from the hand of all who hate us; . . . to grant us that we, being delivered [Gk. *rhusthentas*] from the hand of our enemies, might serve him without fear, in holiness and righteousness before him all our days. And you, child [i.e., John the Baptist], . . . will go before the Lord, . . . to give knowledge of salvation [Gk. *sōtērias*] to his people in the forgiveness of their sins (Luke 1:68–77).

In this quotation we find, first, *sōtēria*, "salvation," from the Greek verb *sōzō*, "to save" (composite form: *diasōzō*, "to save through," "to save thoroughly," Matt. 14:36; Luke 7:3; Acts 23:24). Other cognates include *sōtēr*, "Savior," and *sōtērios*, "bringing salvation" (Titus 2:11).

The second Greek word is *lutrōsis*, from *luō*, which means "to loosen," and hence "to redeem" (Rev. 1:5). Usually the verb is *lutroō* (e.g., Luke 24:21; Titus 2:14; 1 Pet. 1:18–19) with cognates *lutron* ("ransom," Matt.

20:28; Mark 10:45; *antilutron* in 1 Tim. 2:6), *lutrōtēs* ("redeemer," Acts 7:35), and *apolutrōsis* ("redemption," Luke 21:28; Rom. 3:24; 8:23; 1 Cor. 1:30; Eph. 1:7, 14; 4:30; Col. 1:14; Heb. 11:35).

The third Greek word is the participle rhusthentas, from rhuomai, "to redeem, deliver." The participle rhuomenos means "delivering," and hence also "deliverer" (Rom. 11:26).[13]

The differences between these three word groups are of minor theological significance. They all refer to rescuing someone, or a nation, from the powers in which they were held captive.

2.4.3 Elaboration

If salvation in Luke 1:71 and Acts 7:25 means deliverance from physical enemies, elsewhere in the New Testament it means deliverance from physical dangers (Matt. 8:25; 14:30; John 12:27; Acts 27:20, 31, 34, 44; Heb. 5:7; 11:7) or from physical illnesses (Matt. 9:22; Mark 10:52; Luke 17:19; John 11:12; Acts 4:9; 14:9; James 5:15). In the latter case, salvation ("making whole") means healing ("making healthy"); Jesus says, "Your faith has saved you," or "made you well." For the rest, the spiritual meaning dominates: deliverance from the power of sin, death, and Satan. This comes to light in the name of Jesus: "She [i.e., Mary] will bear a son, and you shall call his name Jesus [Gk. *Iēsous*, Heb. *Yeshuᶜa*], for he will save [Gk. *sōsei*] his people from their sins" (Matt. 1:21). In Mark 10:26 and Luke 19:10, "to be saved" means to reach the safe and blessed realm of the kingdom of God (Mark 10:23-25), here described as "eternal life" (vv. 17, 30).

---

13. For the Gk. words *luō* en *lutroō*, see *TDNT* 4:328-37, 349-51; for *sōzō*, 7:965-1024; for *luō, lutroō, rhuomai, sōzō,* and cognates, see *DNTT* 3:177-223; see also Bromiley (1985, ad loc.). Much of what is mentioned in these articles will be dealt with below.

The Notion of Salvation

For deliverance from physical dangers, the apostle Paul prefers the Greek verb *rhuomai* (e.g., 2 Cor. 1:10); he reserves the Greek verb *sōzō* for deliverance from spiritual dangers. Sometimes he uses the word "salvation" as a synonym for conversion and regeneration (Eph. 1:13; 2:5, 8; 2 Tim. 1:9; Titus 3:5; sometimes still with a future dimension: Rom. 8:23-24; 1 Cor. 15:2), or for present deliverances (thus perhaps Phil. 1:19). However, often in Paul's letters, salvation has an eschatological significance (Rom. 13:11; 1 Cor. 3:15; 5:5; Phil. 3:20-21; 1 Thess. 5:8-9; 1 Tim. 4:16; 2 Tim. 3:15; 4:18). It is similar in 1 Peter (1:5, 9; 2:2; 4:18, but cf. 3:21) and in Hebrews (1:14; 10:25, but cf. 2:3; 6:9; 7:25). In the book of Acts we find both the present (2:40, 47) and the future aspects (15:11; neutral: 4:12; 11:14; 15:1; 16:17, 30-31; cf. John 3:17; 5:34; 10:9; 12:47). In the book of Revelation, salvation is entirely eschatological (7:10; 12:10; 19:1). That is, ultimate salvation from sin, death, and Satan coincides with the salvation from the final physical enemies and other physical perils (16:12-16; 17:12-14; 19:11-21). Ultimately, all soteriology is eschatology, and all eschatology is soteriology; in other words, soteriology/eschatology is ultimately about the breakthrough of the Messianic kingdom.

In analogy with this, God the Savior is presented as the One who delivers from all powers and leads his people into the glory and blessedness of the Messianic kingdom. In the wonderful chapter on the arrival of this kingdom, Isaiah 60, we read,

> Whereas you [i.e., Israel] have been forsaken and hated,
> with no one passing through,
> I will make you majestic forever,
> a joy from age to age.
> You shall suck the milk of nations;
> you shall nurse at the breast of kings;
> and you shall know that I, the Lord, am your Savior [Heb.

moshia^c, from *y-sh-^c*]
and your Redeemer [Heb. *go'el*; see §§6.1–6.3], the Mighty One of Jacob (vv. 15–16).

In the New Testament, God is the "Savior" (Gk. *sōtēr*, Luke 1:47; 1 Tim. 1:1; 2:3; Titus 1:3; 2:10; 3:4; Jude 1:25), and more often this is Jesus Christ (Luke 2:11; John 4:42; Acts 5:31; 13:23; Eph. 5:23; Phil. 3:20; 2 Tim. 1:10; Titus 1:4; 3:6; 2 Pet. 2:20; 3:2, 18; 1 John 4:14). Here again, the context is sometimes clearly eschatological: ". . . waiting for our blessed hope, the appearing of the glory of our great God and Savior Jesus Christ" (Titus 2:13); ". . . entrance into the eternal kingdom of our Lord and Savior Jesus Christ" (2 Pet. 1:11). All salvation comes forth from God, but Jesus Christ is the instrument through whom God realizes his salvation in this present world. In him, "the grace of God has appeared, bringing salvation for all people" (Titus 2:11). Thus, salvation is hardly linked with some notion of "going to heaven." Salvation is not so much about taking earthlings to heaven but rather about bringing heaven to earthlings.

Other relevant Greek terms include *exagorazō* ("to ransom," Gal. 3:13; 4:5; from *agorazō*, "to buy"; cf. *agora*, "market," e.g., Acts 16:19), *apallassō* ("to redeem," Heb. 2:15), and *eleutheroō* ("to deliver, set free"; derivations: *eleutheria*, "freedom, liberty"; *eleutheros*, "free").[14] Soteriologically, the latter may involve being (set) free from sin (Rom. 6:18, 22), from the law (i.e., of legalism; Rom. 7:3–4; Gal. 2:4), and from death (Rom. 6:21–22; 8:21). Christ is the One who brings this freedom about (John 8:36; Gal. 5:1); he is the Deliverer, that is, the One who sets free of sin, death, and Satan.

---

14. Regarding the various terms, see *TDNT* 1:124–28, 251 53;2:487–502; and *DNTT* 1:267–68, 715–20; 3:173.

2.5 The "Repulsive" Aspect of Salvation
2.5.1 Living by Grace

As we saw, salvation entails wholeness, peace, well-being, blessing, and bliss. Every human can imagine such a state. Many people long for a world in which this salvation will one day be completely realized, that is, a world full of peace and righteousness, joy and happiness, blessing and well-being. However, not all people understand the way in which, according to Scripture, God will actually realize this salvation. There are several aspects of salvation that are *a priori* repulsive to the "natural person" (1 Cor. 2:14); in this and the following sections we will consider three: *grace*, the *cross*, and the *blood*.

Concerning the first aspect Paul says, "[T]he grace of God has appeared, bringing salvation for all people, training us to renounce ungodliness and worldly passions, and to live self-controlled, upright, and godly lives" (Titus 2:11-12). Though many people long for a world of peace and righteousness, they do not appreciate grace as the vehicle of salvation; nor do they wish to give up "ungodliness and worldly passions." A salvation that is not brought about by people's own efforts, but in which they depend totally on God's grace, turns them off, damages their self-esteem, and wounds their longing for achievement. "For by grace you have been saved through faith. And this is not your own doing; it is the gift of God, not a result of works, so that no one may boast" (Eph. 2:8-9).

To the "natural person," who "does not accept the things of the Spirit of God," this is pure folly, because "he is not able to understand them because they are spiritually discerned" (1 Cor. 2:14). In reality, not the gospel but the "natural person" is foolish: how can we ever expect that people, who by nature are *not* peaceful and righteous, can ever bring about a world dominated by peace and righteousness? If they have failed to do so for thousands of years, how could such a world be built other than by the saving grace of God himself? Attaining peace and righteousness on this earth involves people being saved from *their own* lack of inner peace and righteousness, that is, from their own sin. How could people ever free *themselves* from sin? How could such deliverance ever be attained apart from the grace of God—grace that does not condemn (as humans deserve) but saves?

Such salvation is an ongoing process. Believers know that they not only *have been* saved by grace, but also *are being* saved by grace. In other words, grace is essential not only for *coming* to faith but also for *living* by faith, and thus for contributing to a world of peace and righteousness. Several New Testament letters, including the Revelation of John (1:4; 22:21), begin or end with a prayer of grace. The *charismata* (Rom. 12:6-8; 1 Cor. 12:8-10) are literally portions of *grace* (Gk. *charis*) in the widest sense of the word. They function in the body of Christ as a continual reference to the fact that believers live by grace. Paul had to learn that the Lord's grace was sufficient for him (2 Cor. 12:9). Even the fact that believers must endure tribulations and persecutions is evidence of God's grace (1 Pet. 2:19-20; see for the peculiar role of grace in this letter also 1:1, 10, 13; 3:7; 4:10; 5:5, 10.)

Not only being saved by grace but also continually living by the grace of God is for many unbelievers an intolerable thought. They want to handle their own business, claiming responsibility for what they do, achieving things by their own strength and wisdom. Thus, grace is one of the repulsive components of the gospel. A world of peace and righteousness—yes. But grace as the only possible way to achieve it—no, thanks.

2.5.2 Grace and Humor

For the believer it is the reverse: grace is not repulsive but joyful. Besides "grace," the Hebrew *chen* also means "graciousness"[15] (see Ps. 45:2 in the AMP versus other translations). This is probably the reason why girls are called Anna or Hannah (Heb. *Channah*, derived from *chen*; 1 Sam. 1:2; Luke 2:36): "gracious" or "lovely." The Dutch word *gein* ("fun"), derived from Yiddish *chen*, shows that there is a link between grace and humor; this is because God's grace brings joy and happiness. In Greek we find something similar: *chara* means "joy," and *charis* means "grace, loveliness." Some Protestant groups speak of God's grace in a rather sober and somber way, but in the Bible grace is always something cheerful.

Humor is not unspiritual but a special grace, which can suddenly bring light into darkness, joy into sadness. In the most troublesome times and circumstances, the Jewish *witz* (joke) flourished best. The word *witz* is related to German *wissen* ("to know") and to English *to wit* and *wisdom*. Genuine humor is often deep wisdom (cf. the English words *wit* and *witty*).[16] People who manage to tell jokes about themselves show thereby that they do not take themselves too seriously, and are thus better equipped to cope with troubling circumstances. Wit and (spiritual) wisdom are not necessarily conflicting; on the contrary, those who are never witty, and cannot appreciate wit, easily become hypocrites. Bigots rarely laugh.

In a witty way, Jesus exposed the hypocrisy of many Pharisees and scribes. They were very fussy about details of the Law but overlooked the main issues. Thus, they sifted all their wine to prevent drinking a tiny gnat—but when a camel floated around in their cup, they swallowed it with no problem (Matt. 23:24). This is both wise and witty. It is *gein* (grace as well as humor) if a person is able to speak and think like this. When

---

15. Both "grace" and "graciousness" come from the Lat. *gratia*, derived from *gratus*, "pleasant."
16. See Landmann (1962, 21-31).

hypocrites asked Jesus whether they should pay taxes to the emperor, he asked them to show him a coin for the tax. We can vividly imagine how Jesus held up the coin, which clearly showed the image of the emperor, and how the listeners burst out in laughter (Matt. 22:15–22). And they probably also smiled when he said, "[I]t is easier for a camel to go through the eye of a needle than for a rich person to enter the kingdom of God" (Luke 18:25).

Those who can laugh do not always necessarily know God's grace (cf. Eccl. 7:6, "the laughter of the fools"). But those who know God's grace have every reason to laugh. When Sarah bore a son at 90 years of age, she said, "God has made laughter for me; everyone who hears will laugh over me" (Gen. 21:6). Jesus told his disciples, "Blessed are you who weep now, for you shall laugh" (Luke 6:21). And future Israel way say,

> When the LORD restored the fortunes of [or, returned the captives to] Zion,
> we were like those who dream.
> Then our mouth was filled with laughter,
> and our tongue with shouts of joy;
> then they said among the nations,
> "The LORD has done great things for them."
> The LORD has done great things for us;
> we are glad (Ps. 126:1–3).

2.5.3 Boasting in the Cross

The Hellenistic world in the days of the apostles experienced the *pax Romana*, the peace that the Roman emperors, Augustus in particular, had achieved. However, a "peace by the blood of his [i.e., Christ's] cross" (Col. 1:20), and a peace by someone who had returned from death (Acts 17:31–32), was to them the height of foolishness. As the instrument of execution for the worst criminals, the cross embodied to the Gentile world shame and malfeasance, the very reverse of salvation: "For the

The Notion of Salvation

word of the cross is folly to those who are perishing, but to us who are being saved it is the power of God. . . . [W]e preach Christ crucified, a stumbling block to Jews and folly to Gentiles, but to those who are called, both Jews and Greeks, Christ the power of God and the wisdom of God" (1 Cor. 1:18, 23-24).

Many people who sympathize with Jesus' person and message, who want to be "friends" of Jesus, of his person and his message, are—perhaps not in their consciousness but—*de facto* "enemies of the *cross* of Christ" (Phil. 3:18). Salvation, and the cross specifically, create a sharp division between those who take refuge in Christ's work on the cross and those who may well long for salvation, but never through the cross: "[F]ar be it from me to boast except in the cross of our Lord Jesus Christ, by which [or, through whom] the world has been crucified to me, and I to the world" (Gal. 6:14). Believers view the world as crucified in Christ, that is, radically terminated in him. Conversely, the world views believers as crucified; in the world's estimation, they no longer count, they no longer exist. This is what the cross necessarily is: one's supreme glory or one's greatest shame. There is nothing in between.

After enjoying limited results at Athens, where Paul's preaching connected with the learnedness of the Stoics and Epicureans—I leave aside here the question whether this was wise on his part[17]—in Corinth he chose a different approach. This approach seemed to conflict with common sense but was nevertheless very successful:

And I, when I came to you, brothers, did not come proclaiming to you the testimony of God with lofty speech or wisdom. For I decided to know nothing among you except Jesus Christ and him crucified. And I was with you in weakness and in fear and much trembling, and my speech and my message were not in plausible words of wisdom, but in demonstration of the Spirit and of

---

17. See the discussion of this question in Fee (1987, 92).

power, so that your faith might not rest in the wisdom of men but in the power of God (1 Cor. 2:1–5).

Through the power of the Holy Spirit, the preaching of the cross, which is resisted by unbelievers, can touch even the most hardened hearts.

2.5.4 Saved by Blood

For the Gentile world during apostolic times, the gospel was just as unacceptable as it is for liberal Christians and non-Christians today: how is it conceivable that there is a God who, before granting salvation, first "wants to see blood" (see more extensively §§9.2.3 and 11.6.1)? "Indeed, under the law almost everything is purified with blood, and without the shedding of blood there is no forgiveness of sins" (Heb. 9:22; cf. Lev. 17:11, "it is the blood that makes atonement by the life"). As Jesus instituted the Lord's Supper, he said about the cup, "[T]his is my blood of the covenant, which is poured out for many for the forgiveness of sins" (Matt. 26:28). For modern people, such a claim is unacceptable, as is this "cannibalistically" sounding statement:

> [U]nless you eat the flesh of the Son of Man and drink his blood, you have no life in you. Whoever feeds on my flesh and drinks my blood has eternal life, and I will raise him up on the last day. For my flesh is true food, and my blood is true drink. Whoever feeds on my flesh and drinks my blood abides in me, and I in him (John 6:53–56).

Incidentally, there is a remarkable difference here: in verse 53, the verbs "eat" (Gk. *phagēte*) and "drink" (Gk. *piēte*) are in the aorist tense, referring to a one-time event, whereas in verses 54 and 56–58, the verbs (Gk. *trōgōn, piōn*) are in the present tense, referring to continuing or repeated events. This is quite important for exegesis: in the former case, Jesus is apparently referring to the one-time event of conversion/regeneration, that is, to how a person *receives* a share in him. In the latter case, Jesus is referring to daily "feeding" on him in faith, that is, to how a person *retains* a share in him, in Jesus' "flesh" and "blood." Whether Jesus is referring here to the Lord's Supper,[18] it is true that believers remain attached to Jesus' blood through all their lives. This is also the case with this statement, which always remains true for every penitent believer: "[I]f we walk in the light, as he is in the light, we have fellowship with one another, and the blood of Jesus his Son cleanses us from all sin" (1 John 1:7).

So-called "blood theology" (Lat. *theologia sanguinis*) is just as much a stumbling block as "cross theology" (Lat. *theologia crucis*) and "grace theology" (Lat. *theologia gratiae*). But Scripture is more than clear about this; almost every New Testament writer testifies about the significance of the blood of Christ. Believers are allowed to enter the heavenly sanctuary, and *cannot* enter in other way than "by the blood of Jesus," says Hebrews 10:19 (cf. 9:12, 22). Peter argues that all the world's gold and silver cannot bring about the salvation for humanity that only the blood of Christ, the true sacrificial Lamb, can effectuate (1 Pet. 1:18–19). In a somewhat mysterious way, John tells us about Christ who "came by water and blood" (1 John 5:6).[19]

The apostle Paul in particular is a genuine "blood theologian": Christ has been put forward by God "as a propitiation by [Gk. *en*, in the power of] his blood, to be received by [Gk. dia] faith" (Rom. 3:25). "The cup of blessing that we bless, is it not a participation in the blood of Christ?" (1 Cor. 10:16). Paul also quotes the words of Jesus himself: "This cup is the new covenant in my blood" (11:25; cf. Matt. 26:28; Mark 14:24). In him "we have redemption through his blood" (Eph. 1:7). Jesus has made peace between God and humans "by the

---

18. See extensively, Ouweneel (2010b, chapter 9).
19. See Ouweneel (*RT* II/3, §6.8.2).

blood of his cross" (Col. 1:20). Critics may criticize and reject these and many other similar Bible passages. But they cannot deny that the biblical doctrine of salvation is permeated with the notion of the blood of Christ.

2.6 Salvation Described
2.6.1 Little Attention

Historians of theology have frequently observed that the early church paid extensive attention to, and expended tremendous energy on behalf of, Christology and the doctrine of the Trinity, but devoted far less to the doctrine of the atonement.[20] The Council of Nicaea (325) dealt with the deity of Christ, the Council of Constantinople (381) with the deity of the Holy Spirit, and the Council of Chalcedon (451) with the two natures of Christ.[21] The ancient Creeds (the Apostles', the Nicene-Constantinopolitan, and the Athanasian) helped resolves these Christological and Trinitarian problems, whereas the doctrine of the atonement receives meager attention.

The Apostles' Creed says, "I believe ... in the forgiveness of sins," without indicating a proper ground for this forgiveness. Regarding Christ's work on the cross we confess, "... suffered under Pontius Pilate, was crucified, died, and was buried." In the Nicene Creed we find this clarification: "... who for us men, and for our salvation [Lat. *propter nostram salutem*], came down"—a statement that allows many interpretations. The Athanasian Creed begins with the well-known words "Whosoever wants to be saved" (Lat. *Quicunque vult salvus esse . . .*)—but this is not followed by an exhortation to repent and confess one's sins, and in faith lay one's hand on Christ's work of atonement. On the contrary, in a rather

---

20. See, e.g., Kelly (2003, 375); Brümmer (2005, 117–20); Thiselton (2015, 204–14).
21. Cf. Ouweneel (2007b, chapters 2–3), and the ninth volume of the present series.

intellectualist way salvation is made dependent on correct Trinitarian and Christological viewpoints. The *only* soteriological passage is found near the end of the Athanasian Creed: "who suffered for our salvation" (Lat. *Qui passus est pro salute nostra*), and this, too, is capable of various interpretations.

The vigorous desire of the church fathers to express themselves very precisely in Trinitarian and Christological matters was hardly met with the same vigor when it came to the doctrine of atonement. One reason for this might have been that the fathers held different views on the atonement but considered none of them so defective or heretical that they felt obliged to organize councils to formulate an orthodox view concerning the atonement, and to codify this in ecclesiastical creeds.[22]

2.6.2 The Ransom-to-Satan Model

Among the church fathers, especially three models of atonement were current and quite influential. They differ significantly in nature, but apparently the fathers did not view them as contradictory or mutually exclusive. Not until the Middle Ages did the soteriological battle explode, with Anselm of Canterbury and Peter Abelard as main figures (see further in §7.2.2).

The first of these models is called the *Ransom-to-Satan Model*.[23] This was the view of Irenaeus, Origen, Gregory of Nyssa, and some other church fathers and early Christian writers. Perhaps we should say that it was *the* view of the early church.[24] Anselm was the first or main theologian who objected to it.[25] This view entails the

---

22. Cf. Burnaby (1959, 115).
23. See Wiles (1974, 64); Bloesch (1997, 148-58); Kelly (2003, 170-74, 375-95); Brümmer (2005, 120-25); Shelton (2006, ch. 9).
24. See especially Gregory of Nyssa, *Oratio catechetica magna*; Gregory the Great, *Moralia in Iob*.
25. Van Veluw (2002, 160-61).

idea that the ransom (Gk. *[anti]lutron*) that Christ paid on the cross (Matt. 20:28; Mark 10:45; 1 Tim. 2:6; cf. 1 Pet. 1:18; Rev. 5:9) was paid to Satan for the justified claims upon humanity that Satan, through sin, was exercising. In this view what comes to the fore is not the power of sin but the power of Satan. People are imprisoned as captives of Satan, and are ransomed from captivity by Jesus Christ.

Indeed, the term "ransom" raises the theological question *to whom* this ransom could have been paid by Christ. The New Testament does not answer this question, presumably because this would imply stretching the ransom metaphor too far.[26] Could it have been paid to Satan? But what obligations did God have toward Satan? The New Testament teaches that Satan was defeated (Col. 1:15; Heb. 2:14; 1 John 3:8b), not that a prize had to been paid to him. Rather, we might say that the ransom, paid to *God*, "was to satisfy God's justice... It was a substitute for the life that the person really had a right to."[27] However, this too has its problems: must a ransom not be paid to the one in whose hands the captive is? People are in Satan's captivity, not in God's.

Apart from this question to whom Jesus paid the ransom, we find that the "dramatic" aspects of this view, entailing especially Christ's battle against, and victory over, Satan, has maintained itself in the Eastern Orthodox churches until today (see further §§8.7-8.7). If Western soteriology identifies sin as the greatest enemy, Eastern soteriology rather identifies Satan as such (Acts 26:18 mentions both, alongside each other). Incidentally, Larry Shelton distinguished these two models: the ransom model and the *Christus Victor* model (the battle model). Paying a price to a jailor is different from fight-

---

26. Cf. Grosheide (1957, 177); Ridderbos (1975, 195-97); Carson (1984, 433); Den Heyer (1997, 60-61); Van Veluw (2002, 160n110).

27. Ridderbos (1987, 373); cf. Heyns (1988, 283-84); *TDNT* 4:341-49; *DNTT* 3:195.

ing with the jailor; in the latter, the elements of warfare and victory come to expression more clearly,[28] as we will see.

2.6.3 The Recapitulation Model

The *Recapitulation Model* is the patristic view, which today is still dominant in Eastern Orthodox churches, just like the previous one. It is based on the fundamental notion of *theosis* (see §§1.6 and 12.8.2), which will be dealt with more extensively in a forthcoming volume in the present series.[29] The term does not mean that humans ontically become God but it does mean that they begin to participate in the divine life. Christ himself is called "eternal life" (1 John 5:20; cf. 1:2), but eternal life is also described as "knowing" (having fellowship with, being intimate with) the Father and the Son (John 17:3).

Of central importance is here 2 Peter 1:4, which says that believers become "partakers of the divine nature." In contrast with the two other models mentioned here, which both concentrate upon Jesus' death on the cross, *this* model views redemption as having begun with the incarnation of the Logos: the Son became what *we* are (human), in order that we would become what *he* is (divine), said church fathers Irenaeus and Athanasius ("divine" meaning here resembling God, displaying the image of God).

Whereas the Western fathers, beginning with Augustine, took their starting point in Genesis 3 and wondered how the problem of sin in human life could be solved, the Eastern fathers took their starting point in Genesis 1 and wondered how the image of God, in which humanity had been created, could be restored (recapitulated); hence the name "recapitulation" model. In a sense, the Western approach could be viewed as more negative—how do people get rid of their sins?—whereas

---

28. Shelton (2006, ch.7).
29. See Ouweneel (*RT* IV/3, §9.5).

the Eastern approach is more positive: how do people participate again in the divine world? The way of *theosis* could also be described as the being filled with the Holy Spirit[30]—a matter for which, throughout the centuries, the Western church has shown little interest, generally speaking.

2.6.4 The Sacrificial Substitution Model

The *Sacrificial Substitution Model* is the view of the early church fathers, especially of Augustine, that found most resonance among the Reformers. For many Protestants this is *de facto* the only acceptable, and sometimes the only known, view of the atonement. It is the only view that can be found in Calvin's *Institutes of the Christian Religion* and in the Reformed creeds and confessions.[31] Another example of someone who held this view is the Puritan Stephen Charnock, who published his book with the subtitle, "A Puritan's View of the Atonement,"[32] which contained only this model, concentrating on the metaphor of Christ as the true Paschal Lamb.

The main element of this model was that of substitution: for people's benefit and in their stead, Christ underwent the punishment for their sins (see §§9.1–9.3): "[U]pon *him* was the chastisement that brought us peace" (Isa. 53:5). Another element, that of satisfaction (see §9.5), was actually added by Anselm. This model dealt with what humanity in Christ did, and had to do, toward God (satisfy his justice) rather than with what God did for humanity. This was the view of the Reformers, and this one-sided approach remains influential today. It has produced various ideas that, in my view, do not pass the test of Scripture. First, it yields the idea that God must be reconciled with the sinner instead of the

---

30. Ouweneel (*RT* II/3, §9.5).
31. See especially *Institutes* 2.16; cf. Belgic Confession, Art.
21. and Heidelberg Catechism, Lord's Day 16.
32. Charnock (2002).

other way round (§§10.4-10.7). Second, connected with this is the erroneous idea that atonement involves appeasing God, satisfying the wrath of God. Third, there is the idea of the active and passive righteousness of Christ. I have dealt with this third idea in an earlier volume.[33]

On the whole, the sacrificial model enjoys its greatest popularity among Protestants, but it is not without problems. Therefore, in the twentieth century much criticism was leveled against this model, which, unfortunately, often disposed of the baby with the bathwater. In my view, the notion of the vicarious sacrifice of Christ clearly agrees with Scripture, but it must be maintained in a way that does justice to appropriate criticisms. This will be explained in the remainder of this book.

2.7 Salvation Disowned
2.7.1 The Rejection of Salvation

By now it should be clear what model I wish to follow in this book, no matter how unacceptable it may be to the natural (i.e., unregenerate) person. As G. C. Berkouwer said regarding the work of Christ: "Since only the illumination of the Holy Spirit imparts the right insight into the profound significance of Christ's work, he realize the great danger connected with human interpretation and construction. . . . Human thinking is not excluded, but it certainly is not sufficient."[34] Indeed, it concerns a matter that is "s/Spiritually discerned" (cf. 1 Cor. 2:14); "we impart this in words not taught by human wisdom but taught by the Spirit" (v. 13).

In the Gospels we find various examples of how Christ and his work were rejected. His own relatives once said, "He is out of his mind" (Mark 3:21). On another occasion many Jews said, "He has a demon, and is insane; why listen to him?" (John 10:20; cf. 7:20; 8:48,

---
33. Ouweneel (*RT* III/2, chapter 4).
34. Berkouwer (1965, 10-11).

52, "You have a demon"). When Jesus demonstrated his redemptive power by casting out evil spirits, some responded saying, "He casts out demons by Beelzebul, the prince of demons" (Luke 11:15; cf. Matt. 9:34; 12:24). It was very much the same today: if a religious phenomenon strikes people as strange, if it does not fit into people's frame of reference, they dub it occult, demonic, or simply absurd, crazy, and dangerous.

Jesus' followers fared no better. When Stephen described how Israel had always resisted God's salvation, his Jewish listeners responded by stoning him (Acts 7:50-56). When Paul and Barnabas announced God's salvation in Lystra, the pagans first wanted to sacrifice to them as if they were gods, but the Jews went to the other extreme by stoning Paul (14:19). In Philippi there was an uproar because Paul had delivered a poor woman from a spirit of divination (16:16-23). In Thessalonica and Berea, the Jews formed a mob and accused Paul because he had taught that the Messiah had to suffer, die, and rise from the dead (17:2-9, 13). When Paul brought the message of the risen Lord on the Areopagus at Athens, people ridiculed him or turned their backs to him (17:30-33). In Corinth the Jews dragged him before the judge when he preached the gospel there (18:12-17). In Ephesus there was an uproar because the way of salvation had been preached there (19:21-41). In Jerusalem a Jewish crowd erupted in anger when Paul told them that Christ had sent him to the Gentiles (22:21-22). When Paul gave his testimony before king Agrippa and governor Festus, the latter said, "Paul, you are out of your mind; your great learning is driving you out of your mind" (26:24).

This pattern has been repeated throughout church history. People need not only God's salvation, but they first need the insights (a) *that* they need this salvation because of their imprisonment in the power of sin, death, and Satan (Acts 26:18), (b) that only God can grant them this salvation (cf. Ps. 3:8), and (c) this can occur only in God's way, no matter how incomprehensible this may be to us (cf. Isa. 55:8–9), and (d) that "there is no other name under heaven given among men by which we must be saved" than the name of Jesus Christ (Acts 4:12). People can acquire these insights only by the power of the Holy Spirit through the Word of God; for the "natural person does not accept the things of the Spirit of God, for they are folly to him, and he is not able to understand them because they are spiritually discerned" (1 Cor. 2:14).

On the one hand, theologians may and must ask as many critical questions as they can, such as: Why the cross? Why blood? Why substitution? Why only Jesus? And so on. Asking such intellectual questions is their professional calling. On the other hand, we believers must accept that although theologians may shed significant light on these issues, in the end we must accept *in faith, in our hearts*, that the way of Jesus and his cross is God's way of salvation. Our ultimate objective is not theological understanding but faith in God and his Word: "[I]f you confess with your mouth that Jesus is Lord and *believe in your heart* that God raised him from the dead, you will be *saved*. For with the *heart* one believes and is justified, and with the mouth one confesses and is *saved*" (Rom. 10:9–10).

2.7.2 Criticisms

Of course, outright rejection of salvation is very different from criticizing certain points in the traditional doctrine of salvation. Yet, some forms of criticism have, for many Christians, simply amounted to a rejection of salvation as such.

This rejection is always most painful when it comes from those who were once close to Christian faith. This was true of the young Muhammad. The Koran (53:368) says "that no bearer of burdens will bear the burden of another,"³⁵ which in one interpretation means that "nobody can bear the sins of another."³⁶ Does this imply a contradiction between the Bible and the Koran? The Bible says, "Truly no man can ransom another, or give to God the price of his life, for the ransom of their life is costly and can never suffice" (Ps. 49:7-8), and: "[E]ach will have to bear his own load" (Gal. 6:5). That sounds quite similar to what the Koran says! However, in the whole of Scripture such verses form a beautiful contrast with the One who did ransom others, and did bear the load of others: "He himself bore our sins in his body on the tree" (1 Pet. 2:24). In contrast with this, in the entire Koran the idea of One dying vicariously for others is not only absent but also inconceivable.

Closer to home, I think of the well-known Dutch poet H. Marsman, who was raised a Christian. In his poem *Verzet* ("Resistance," published in 1932) he radically turned away from his Christian education; into the mouth of a dying man he put the following words: "Do not take away my last possession from me: MY sins go with me into MY grave." The statement of Dutch novelist S. Vestdijk—that it hurt his pride that someone else would have himself nailed on the cross for him—gave rise to the Good Friday article (1959) of the Dutch Reformed theology professor P. Smits, in which he wrote the following infamous words: "It also hurts my pride that somebody would have to die for my guilt. I wish to take responsibility for the consequences of my own acts. And then as far as Paul is concerned, you can count me out³⁷."³⁸The latter words he wrote after an analysis of Romans 5, in which he concluded that he could only smile about Paul's argument. In Dutch Reformed circles his article triggered an intensive discussion of atone-

---

35. https://quran.com/53.
36. Abdolah (2008, 43).
37. Dutch: geef mij portie maar aan Fikkie.
38. Smits (1959, 2); see on this Borger-Koetsier (2006, 157-62).

ment, understandably so.

Shortly afterward, the Roman Catholic *New Catechism* caused a similar uproar by discarding the notion of satisfaction (see §9.5).[39] The same thing happened in Kuyperian Reformed circles with the dissertation of Dutch theologian H. Wiersinga.[40] As we will see later, theologians like Wiersinga have leveled justified criticisms against many points of the Anselmian-Reformed doctrine of atonement, for instance, atonement viewed as satisfying God's wrath (see §§9.3 and 10.4). Therefore, in my view, much of the criticism that was heaped upon Wiersinga by conservative theologians was not at all justified. However, Wiersinga himself was an easy target because in his own criticisms of the tradition he had gone to the other extreme.

Subsequently, Dutch theologian G. H. Ter Schegget leveled similar criticism against the traditional doctrine of satisfaction.[41] But here again the refutation was easy because Ter Schegget, too, went way too far. Many other theologians could be mentioned who have lost their balance when it came to the doctrine of the atonement. Balance is desperately needed here. But the time has come to take very seriously the criticisms of theologians like Wiersinga and Ter Schegget without adopting their extreme views.

2.8 Reactionary Theology

2.8.1 *Sola Scriptura*

Several times we have seen the danger of reactionary theology. People aim their criticisms at certain dubious elements of the traditional doctrine of atonement, but in doing so they are easily led to opposite extremes. Of course, the reverse occurs as well: in reaction to a liberal approach to soteriology orthodox arguments can be just

39. New Catechism (1967).
40. Wiersinga (1971; see also 1972).
41. Ter Schegget (1999).

as one-sided. Here is one example: the four well-known *solas* of the Reformation can degenerate into reactionary theology, and thus, from a biblical viewpoint, can become imbalanced.

Consider *sola Scriptura*, Scripture alone. This is a powerful and praiseworthy confession over against the Roman Catholic appeal to authoritative ecclesiastical tradition, an authority so strong that no exegesis and dogmatics can compete with it. However, there are at least two caveats we must mention for Protestant consideration.

First, this confession threatens to become imbalanced if God's creational revelation is ignored. The Belgic Confession says in Article 2: "We know [God] by two means," not only by Scripture, but also by the creation, preservation, and government of the universe, which is before our eyes as a most elegant book, wherein all creatures, great and small, are as so many characters leading us to "see clearly the invisible things of God, even his everlasting power and divinity," as the apostle Paul says (Rom. 1:20). All which things are sufficient to convince men and leave them without excuse.[42]

When it comes to revelation, then, we could better adopt the motto of *sola natura et Scriptura*.

Second, the criticism concerning the Roman Catholic emphasis on the formal authority of tradition often implies a false estimation of human nature. I mean this: we cannot do without Scripture, but neither can we do without the secure intimacy of an authoritative *interpretation* of Scripture. The greatest theologians throughout church history, no matter how original and creative they may have been, were always part of such a community; the truth of God's Word is comprehended only "with all the saints" (Eph. 3:18), never in an individualistic way. In the Protestant circles who most strongly emphasize *sola Scriptura* the cherished creeds

---

42. Dennison (*RC* 2:425); cf. Ouweneel (1995a, 70–71).

and confessions operate functionally in the same way as tradition functions for Roman Catholic theologians (compare, e.g., for Reformed the Three Forms of Unity; for Presbyterians the Westminster Standards). This is the case despite the many acknowledgements that such creeds and confessions are "subject to Scripture" and can be altered. Something is judged to be in conflict with "Scripture and the Confession," in such a way that "the Confession"—not *de jure*, to be sure, but certainly *de facto*—has a status comparable to that of Scripture.[43] In practice, when it comes to establishing the truth of a matter, for many Protestants the motto is *sola Scriptura et Confessione*.

Such an attitude is basically un-Reformational. For soteriology, only Scripture must be our criterion, not any confessional document. When the Heidelberg Catechism (Lord's Day 23, Q/A 60) says, "God . . . grants and imputes to me the perfect satisfaction . . . , righteousness, and holiness of Christ . . . ,"[44] it is saying something that is nothing less than a human invention. Elsewhere I have tried to show that Scripture speaks very differently.[45] Later in this book, we will examine other Protestant confessional statements that, in my view, are at variance with Scripture.

2.8.2 Sola Fide

The motto of *sola fide*, "by faith alone," is a powerful and true testimony over against all those, especially the Roman Catholic Church in the days of the Reformation, who believe that people must earn or merit salvation by their own efforts. People earn or merit nothing; they are totally dependent on the grace of God, to which they entrust themselves in faith (see Acts 15:10–11; Rom. 3:20,

---

43. Reformed theologian C. Graafland (2000) has sharply exposed this state of affairs.
44. Dennison (*RC* 2:783).
45. Ouweneel (*RT* III/2, chapter 4; cf. 2016, Days 193–194).

28; 4:6; Gal. 2:16; 3:11; Eph. 2:8-9; 2 Tim. 1:9; Titus 3:5).[46] However, here again we are dealing with reactionary theology if people neglect the testimony of especially James 2, as Martin Luther indeed did:

What good is it, my brothers, if someone says he has faith but does not have works? Can that faith save him? . . . So also faith by itself, if it does not have works, is dead. . . . You see that faith was active along with his [i.e., Abraham's] works, and faith was completed by his works. . . . You see that a person is justified by works and not by faith alone (vv. 14, 17, 22, 24).

This passage is stating the very opposite of the Reformational slogan when it declares: "*not* by faith alone" (Vulgate: *non ex fide tantum*). Yet there is no contradiction at all here between Paul (especially in Rom. and Gal.) and James. The Paul who says, "by works of the law no human being will be justified in his sight" (Rom. 3:20), says in the same letter that it is "the doers of the law who will be justified" (Rom. 2:13); that "the righteous requirement of the law" is "fulfilled" in the believers (8:4); and, "the one who loves another has fulfilled the law . . . love is the fulfilling of the law" (13:8, 10). Paul is speaking about faith *versus* works as the ground for people's salvation; James, however, is speaking about true faith (expressing itself in works) and dead (false) faith (not expressing itself in works). When it comes to justification, both Paul and James could be summarized in one and the same sentence: people are justified by faith, but then "faith working through love" (Gal. 5:6)—otherwise it is not true faith at all.

You need only raise the question in a traditional Protestant context, "Is it true that people can get to heaven only if they have done good works?" Most people present will automatically answer, "No, that's not true." I have conducted this experiment several times, and the result was always the same. This is the conse-

---

46. See extensively, Ouweneel (*RT* III/2).

The Notion of Salvation

quence of reactionary theology. Yet, it is not hard to make clear that a faith that does not produce fruits is a dead (non-saving) faith. Even the converted criminal on the cross produced four-fold fruit for God (Luke 23:40-42): he acknowledged the legitimacy of the judgment he was suffering, he referred the other crucified criminal to God, he gave a good testimony of Jesus—not only of his innocence but also of his kingship—and he entrusted himself to Jesus when the latter would come into his kingdom.

A faith without fruit *is* not true biblical faith, and thus cannot save. This is why we can say that no person will get to heaven without having produced spiritual fruits (good works). This truth is self-evident—except for those who, as a consequence of the sixteenth-century Catholic-Reformational battle, have come to distort the meaning of *sola fide*. It is "by faith alone, *including* the works produced by true faith." According to *these works* God, or Christ, will deal with people when they stand before his judgment seat (Matt. 25:31-46; Rom. 2:6; 14:10-12; 2 Cor. 5:10; Rev. 2:23; 20:11-15).

2.8.3 *Sola Cruce*

In addition to *sola Scriptura*, *sola fide* and *sola gratia*, less known is *sola cruce*; yet, the expression is not totally unknown.[47] It is based on Pauline statements like this one: "[F]ar be it from me to boast except in the cross of our Lord Jesus Christ, by which the world has been crucified to me, and I to the world" (Gal. 6:14), and: "I decided to know nothing among you except Jesus Christ and him crucified" (1 Cor. 2:2). In Galatians, Paul sets forth the cross in opposition to Jewish Christian legalism, which made circumcision a condition of salvation in addition to the cross. In Corinth, he set forth the cross in opposition to Greek presumption: he embraced the shame of salvation through the cross alone, and left it to God to

---

47. I found the expression in Stauffer (1948, 24).

touch people's hearts through the cross.

At Athens, Paul had attempted to connect with the intellectual ideas of the Stoics and the Epicureans—at Corinth he had opposed all pagan wisdom:

> For *the word of the cross is folly* to those who are perishing, but to us who are being saved it is the power of God. . . . Has not God made foolish the wisdom of the world? For since, in the wisdom of God, the world did not know God through wisdom, it pleased God through the folly of what we preach to save those who believe. For Jews demand signs and Greeks seek wisdom, but we preach *Christ crucified*, a stumbling block to Jews and folly to Gentiles, but to those who are called, both Jews and Greeks, Christ the power of God and the wisdom of God (1 Cor. 1:18-24).

Yet, here again one can easily go astray. In opposition to theology and intensive Bible study, some Christians have boasted that they wish "to know nothing except Jesus Christ and him crucified." They forget the words "*among you*" in the passage: to the *Corinthians* Paul wished to speak of Jesus and the cross alone. But that did not mean that his entire theology consisted in reflection about only Jesus and the cross. Every "theology of the cross" (Lat. *theologia crucis*; cf. Luther's *Kreuzestheologie*) runs the risk of overlooking, for instance, the indispensable redemptive significance of Christ's resurrection and glorification (see §§10.1-10.2), not to mention the significance of the outpouring of the Holy Spirit and of Jesus' second coming. A one-sided theology of Good Friday pushes Easter, Ascension Day and Pentecost into the background.[48]

Here is a musical illustration of this: Johan Sebastian Bach's Easter Oratorio lasts forty minutes at most, while his Saint Matthew's Passion lasts one hundred sixty-five minutes. Bach was a Lutheran, and as such he was a typical "Good Friday Protestant."

---

48. Cf. Ouweneel (*EDR* 2:233-34).

It has been said that, in addition to *Pentecostal* Christians, Roman Catholics are especially *Christmas* Christians, the Eastern Orthodox are typically *Easter* Christians, and traditional Protestants are typically *Good Friday* Christians. But the motto of *sola cruce* should really be *sola cruce, sola resurrectione et sola glorificatione*.

2.8.4 *Sola Gratia*

The slogan of *sola gratia*, "by grace alone," is strongly emphasized in the New Testament: we "are justified by his grace as a gift, through the redemption that is in Christ Jesus" (Rom. 3:24); "if it is by grace, it is no longer on the basis of works; otherwise grace would no longer be grace" (11:6); "by grace you have been saved through faith. And this is not your own doing; it is the gift of God" (Eph. 2:5, 8). This may not be diminished in any way. However, the sovereign grace of God should never be played off against human freedom and responsibility, as happened in the unfortunate conflict between Remonstrants (Arminians) and Contra-Remonstrants (mainstream Calvinists), which reached its nadir during the Synod of Dordt (1618–1619).

In such a situation, a kind of reactionary theology will easily arise, which by definition is one-sided, and thus ultimately untrue.[49] The statement, "No one can come to me unless the Father who sent me draws him" (John 6:44), is just as true as the statement, "whoever comes to me I will never cast out" (v. 37). The statement, "work out your own salvation with fear and trembling," is just as true as the statement, "for it is God who works in you, both to will and to work for his good pleasure" (Phil. 2:12–13). The statement, "the grace of God has appeared, bringing salvation for *all* people" (Titus 2:11), is just as true as the statement, "whoever does not obey the Son shall not see life, but the wrath of God remains

---

49. See extensively, Ouweneel (*RT* III/1, especially chapters 8–14).

on him" (John 3:36). The statement, "as many as were appointed to eternal life believed" (Acts 13:48), is just as true as the statement that the apostles "spoke in such a way that a great number of both Jews and Greeks believed" (14:1).

Thus, numerous conflicts have arisen in connection with salvation in Christ, during which parties defended reactionary theology. Consider the debate about the meaning of Christ's work on the cross (was it an act of love, or a martyr's death, or spiritual warfare, or an atoning sacrifice?), the conflict over the notion of substitution, over the relationship between the wrath and the love of God (God's wrath appeased by Christ? Is there *Umstimming* [change of mood] in God? What is satisfaction to God?), the discussion about the time of atonement (throughout Jesus' entire life, or only on the cross?), the human role in providing atonement (did it involve the wounds inflicted by Pilate, or only those inflicted by God?), the intended extent of the atoning sacrifice (for all people, or only for the elect?), the debates around forgiveness, regeneration, justification, sanctification, *theosis*, and so many other subjects.

Throughout this and the next volume, we will need to steer a middle course between numerous cliffs and rocks, trying to walk a path between liberal theology and reactionary theology (so often viewed as orthodox theology).

Now Available from Paideia Press
www.paideiapress.ca

Chapter 3
Salvation and God's Being

> *... the light of the gospel of the glory of Christ,*
>   *who is the image of God ....*
> *For God, who said,*
>   *"Let light shine out of darkness,"*
> *has shone in our hearts*
>   *to give the light of the knowledge of*
>   *the glory of God*
>   *in the face of Jesus Christ.*
>   2 Corinthians 4:4, 6
>
> *... the gospel of the glory of the*
> *happy God ...*
>   1 Timothy 1:11 (MacLaren)

Summary: *Understanding salvation begins with a better grasp regarding God's being. He is a communal being (the covenant God, the God who dwells with his people). God is a loving being; love is his very nature, both in the sense of the Greek terms agapē and of philia; this also includes his being good, kind, patient, merciful, gracious, and so on. God is a holy being (an important issue because it illustrates how often divine being and attributes are confused). God* *is a faithful being (faithful to his promises but also to himself). God is the God of peace, in both present salvation and the eschaton. God is a blissful (happy) being ("blissful" and "blessed" often being confused), yet far removed from the pagan Greek notion of apatheia. God is a glorious (beautiful) being, whose glory is the ultimate goal of salvation. God is an invisible being, raising the question whether, how, and to what extent, believers will behold the glory of God in the eschaton.*

3.0 Introduction

WHEN IN DISTRESS, people can easily slip into an anthropocentric rather than a theocentric way of thinking. They believe that, since they are the *object* of salvation, everything turns around *them*—whereas the *subject* of salvation is at least as important. "Salvation belongs to the LORD" (Ps. 3:8; Jonah 2:9), it is *God's* salvation (Ps. 50:23); "see the salvation of the LORD" (Exod. 14:13); "wait quietly for the salvation of the LORD" (Lam. 3:26). All too often, soteriology begins with sinful people and *their* needs instead of beginning with the glorious, holy God and *his* "needs" (desires, longings). The criterion for salvation does not lie primarily in the need of the creature but in the being of the Creator. It is not primarily the gospel *for* the sinner but the gospel *of God* (Rom. 1:1); the gospel is not only *from* God but *about* God. Salvation is not primarily about sinners but about the "glory of the blessed God" (1 Tim. 1:11); it is "the gospel of the glory of Christ, who is the image of God . . . the knowledge of the glory of God in the face of Jesus Christ" (2 Cor. 4:4, 6).

The expression "needs (desires, longings) of God" may sound a bit strange. We sometimes hear that God ignored his own interests and acted exclusively for the benefit of sinners, giving them all they needed. But this is a rather one-sided picture. Jesus accomplished his work on the cross not only for others but also "for the joy that was set before him" (Heb. 12:2). God "predestined us to be adopted through Jesus Christ *for Himself*" (Eph. 1:5 HCSB). Christ cleanses and sanctifies his bridal church to present "*to himself* in splendor, without spot or wrinkle or any such thing, that she might be holy and without blemish" (Eph. 5:26-27). He always lives for his people (Heb. 7:25)—but it is equally true that they live *for him* (Rom. 14:8; 2 Cor. 5:15). When it comes to the two parties, the interests are not on the side of only one party, but on both sides. Salvation answers to the needs and natures of both parties.

Thus, the gospel cannot be understood only from the needs of the sinner but must be viewed also from the attributes of God. Therefore, we will devote attention in this chapter to his divine being, more specifically for the following two reasons. First, in the divine being lie the *grounds* of salvation: in God's concern ("fellowship") with his creation (§§3.1.2 and 3.2), in his love (§§3.3-3.5), in his holiness (§3.6), and in his faithfulness (§ 3.7). Second, in the divine being lie the *goals* of salvation: in God's peace (§3.8), his bliss (§3.9) and his glory (§§3.10-3.11), which he—insofar as this is granted to finite creatures—shares with redeemed people.

There is one more aspect in God's being that certainly belongs in this chapter, namely, his righteousness. But because this subject is so closely interwoven with the doctrine of justification, it has been dealt with in an earlier volume of the present series.[1]

3.1 Fellowship
3.1.1 God As a Communal Being

God loves and practices fellowship. This *communion* goes deeper than *communication*. The Word of the God communicating with humans aims to establish and further fellowship between God and humans, and between humans and humans. This fellowship is nothing less than an extension of the inter-Trinitarian fellowship:

1. Ouweneel (*RT* III/2).

"... that they all may be one, *as* You, Father, [are] in Me, and I in You; that they also may be one *in Us*, that the world may believe that You sent Me. And the glory which You gave Me I have given them, that they may be one *just as* We are one: I in them, and You in Me; that they may be made perfect in one, and that the world may know that You have sent Me, and have loved them as You have loved Me" (John 17:21-23 NKJV).

And again: "... the Word of life ... we declare to you, that you also may have fellowship with us; and truly our fellowship [is] with the Father and with His Son Jesus Christ" (1 John 1:1, 3 NKJV).

True divine attributes have belonged exclusively to God's being from all eternity. In my view, here lies the answer to the age-old question what God did before he created the world. The answer is that (a) all God's true attributes are eternal, (b) all these attributes were eternally active, (c) this eternal activity of God's attributes are his work, and (d) God therefore has been eternally at work: his personal characteristics imply immanent and eternal works of God.[2] The importance of the doctrine of the Trinity becomes clear once again,[3] for this doctrine alone is able to explain how the attributes that presuppose an "other," an "over against"—communication, fellowship, righteousness, love—could have been active from eternity. Lewis Sperry Chafer derived a rational proof for the Trinity doctrine from this, entirely in the tradition of Peter Abelard, for instance: God *must* have been manifold, otherwise he could not from eternity have been exercising communication, fellowship, righteousness, and love.[4]

God did not become a communing being for the first time after he created humanity. From eternity God was

---

2. Cf. Bavinck (*RD* 2:329-34); Chafer (*ST* 1:291-92).
3. See Ouweneel (*EDR* 2:chapter 20); see also the subsequent volume in the present series on the Trinity.
4. Chafer (*ST* 1:291-95).

One who practiced fellowship in the sense that there existed eternal fellowship between the three persons of the Godhead. From eternity he is the communicating, communing, righteous, good, loving, and faithful God in that the three persons within the Godhead were communicating with *each other*, were having fellowship with *each other*, were showing righteousness, goodness, love, and faithfulness toward *each other* (doing justice to *each other*, being good, loving, and faithful to *each other*). From eternity there was perfect fellowship, perfect righteousness, perfect love, and perfect faithfulness between the persons of the Godhead.

This point is of special importance in a time when the immanence and condescension of God are being emphasized at the expense of his transcendence. Our is a time when God being the Partner of humans, and humans being partners of God are emphasized so strongly as though God would ontologically need humans and would not be able to do without them. In so-called "process theology," God is made to depend on the world's historical process in such a way that God supposedly changes together with this process.[5] Such a view belittles God, and is unaware that God existed from eternity before he created humanity, perfect in his self-sufficiency and his Trinitarian fellowship and love. Insofar as we can say that God "needs" humans, this is because God himself has *sovereignly decided* to make himself in a certain sense dependent upon humanity.[6]

3.1.2 *Perichoresis*

Gregory of Nazianzus coined the Greek term *perichorēsis* (Lat. *circumincessio*) for the intimate fellowship between the persons of the Deity (Lat. *communio perso-*

---

5. Cf. Erickson (1998, 304–08); Wentsel (1987, 173–74); Ouweneel (*RT* III/1, §3.3.1).
6. Ouweneel (*RT* III/1, §4.1.2).

narum divinarum)[7] in such a way that they pervade or permeate one another.[8] None of them can exist or act apart from the other two. Therefore, the Council of Florence (1439) stated that, because of this fellowship, the Father is entirely in the Son and in the Spirit, the Son is entirely in the Father and in the Spirit, and the Spirit is entirely in the Father and in the Son.[9]

The term perichoresis, which involves a continual "turning around" of the three persons, as in a dance (cf. Song 6:13 EXB), is not ideal, however. The Western church has tried to express the same matter with the Latin terms *circuminsessio* (dwelling in each other; different in one letter from *circumincessio*, the actual equivalent of perichoresis), immanentia (abiding in each other), or inexistentia (existing in each other).[10]

The deeper goal of all these terms was and is to underscore the strict unity within the Trinity, and thus that God is a communal being. Only when we see that the Triune God is a being entirely characterized by communion (fellowship), first internally, then externally, will we understand why and how it is possible that God longs for fellowship with creatures. If God creates human beings in his image, after his likeness, this can only with a view to establishing fellowship with them. We will investigate this more closely in the next section.

3.2 God Seeking Fellowship
3.2.1 The Covenant God

As soon as God had created humans, he extended his

---

7. We remember that, although Gregory wrote in Greek, much of our theological terminology has been handed down to us in Latin through the Western fathers.
8. Cf. John of Damascus, *Ekdosis* I.8 and 14; see Barth (*CD* 1/1=2, §11.1:111–13, 117–18, 140–42); Ouweneel (*RT* II/3,§ 10.3.2).
9. Van Genderen and Velema (2008, 153–54).
10. Barth (*CD* 1/1=2, §11.2:77).

fellowship to them. We see this already in Genesis 1:28, where God addresses the first humans directly.[11] When Genesis 1:22 tells us that God "blessed them saying," referring to the animals, this means little more than "blessed them with the words"; it is not yet a real "addressing." But in Genesis 1:28 the subject of the sentence, God, is repeated with a new direct verb: "And God blessed them. And God said to them, ..." Here God was not addressing the animals, but he was addressing people.[12] He stretched out his hand to humans to become their *socius*, their companion, partner, friend. After the Fall of the first humans, he came to them again as the One "walking in the garden in the cool of the day" to ask Adam where he was, that is, where he was in his relationship to God, in order to restore this relationship (Gen. 3:8–9).[13]

After the Flood, God made his covenant with Noah and his offspring, and even extended it to all creatures (Gen. 9:9–17).[14] After this, he made his covenant with Abr(ah)am (Gen. 15 and 17), and renewed it with Isaac (Gen. 26) and Jacob (Gen. 35 and 46).[15] Subsequently, he made his covenant through Moses with their offspring, the people of Israel (Exod. 6:1–13; 19:5; 24:1–8), and renewed it many times.[16] He made his covenant with David and his offspring (2 Sam. 7).[17] He has walked, and is walking, with Israel to the new covenant.[18]

Thus, the fellowship-seeking God became the covenant partner of humanity. How much his *being* is involved in this is evident from the name with which he

---

11. See Ouweneel (2008a, §3.3.2).
12. Jacob (1974, ad loc.).
13. Ouweneel (2008a, §10.3.1).
14. See Ouweneel (*RT* IV/2, §2.2.3).
15. Ibid., §2.3.1.
16. Ibid., §2.4 and chapter 3.
17. Ibid., §2.3.3.
18. Ibid., §2.4.3 and chapter 6.

presented himself to this soon-to-be covenant people: YHWH, which he himself explained as follows: "I am who I am" (Heb. *ehyeh asher ehyeh*), adding to this: "Say this to the people of Israel: 'I am [Heb. *ehyeh*] has sent me to you.'" God also said to Moses, "Say this to the people of Israel: 'The LORD [Heb. YHWH], the God of your fathers, the God of Abraham, the God of Isaac, and the God of Jacob, has sent me to you'" (Exod. 3:14-15). The expression "I am" is not a statement about God's ontic status in any Hellenistic sense, as both Jews and Christians have often taken it (the both Jewish and Christian rendering "the Eternal One" is a consequence of this). Rather, it means in a very practical sense, "I am *there*," namely, for you, or: "I will be there [for you]" (cf. CJB: "*Ehyeh Asher Ehyeh* [I am/will be what I am/will be].")

In Exodus 14, God's name, YHWH, is implicitly explained as a form of the Hebrew verb *h-y-h*, "to be." In the German Tanakh translation of Jewish scholar M. Buber, this Hebrew name is rendered, *Ich bin da* ("I am there"), that is, I will always be with you and for you. It is the name that fits in with God's covenant faithfulness. God would be known to Israel in a very special way as even the patriarchs had not known him (cf. Exod. 6:2-3; although the patriarchs apparently did know the name YHWH: Gen. 15:2, 8; 16:2, 5; 18:3). This involved God's granting Israel the blessing of his immediate and continual presence among them as implied in his name YHWH, and as concretized in his dwelling on the mercy seat, between the cherubim, in the Most Holy Place (Exod. 15:17; 25:8, 21-22; 29:42-46; 40:34; Num. 7:89; 1 Sam. 4:4; 2 Sam. 6:2; 2 Kings 19:15; 1 Chron. 13:6; Ps. 80:1; 99:1; Isa. 37:16).

3.2.2 God Dwelling With His People

It was only when a redeemed *people* had been formed, that is, after the exodus from Egypt, that this communal feature of God's being fully came to light in his expressed desire to dwell in their midst. The matter of divine dwelling never arose with Adam, Enoch, Noah, Abraham, Isaac, Jacob, or Joseph. On the very first day of Israel's salvation, the people, in their jubilant hymn and through the Holy Spirit, referred to God's "holy abode," a "sanctuary" where God would dwell: "You have led in your steadfast love the people whom you have redeemed; you have guided them by your strength to your holy abode.... You will bring them in and plant them on your own mountain, the place, O LORD, which you have made for your *abode*, the *sanctuary*, O Lord, which your hands have established" (Exod. 15:13, 17).[19]

This is what the people themselves said. But after Moses had ascended Mount Sinai, the very first thing that *God* told him was that the people were to make preparations, and "let them make me a sanctuary, that I may *dwell* in their midst" (Exod. 25:1-9), that is, not only when they would arrive in the Promised Land (this was the intention in Exod. 15), but right then and there, at the foot of the mountain.

This sanctuary is known as the "tabernacle" (Heb. *mishkan*, lit. "[God's] dwelling place"; Lat. *tabernaculum* means "tent"), also known as the "tent of meeting," that is, God's abode where he would meet with his people. The very first sacrifice that was to be offered, namely, the daily burnt offering "at the entrance of the tent of meeting before the LORD," had this motive: "... where I will meet with you [plur.], to speak to you [sing.] there. There I will meet with the people of Israel, . . . I will *dwell* among the people of Israel and will be their God. And they shall know that I am the LORD their God, who brought them out of the land of Egypt that I might *dwell* among them" (Exod. 29:42-46).

God's communal being comes to expression in a special way for his people during times of distress. Salvation is God being "with us" (Heb. *Immanuel*, cf. Isa. 7:14;

---

19. Ouweneel (*RT* II/3, chapter 10).

8:8, 10; Matt. 1:23), and we being with God (cf. 1 Pet. 3:18). When Israel was in the "iron furnace" (Deut. 4:20; 1 Kings 8:51; Jer. 11:4), God "came down" to redeem them (Exod. 3:8). He himself said this while speaking to Moses from the burning bush, about which God later said that he "dwelt" (Heb. *sh-k-n*) in it (Deut. 33:16).

It is a wonderful illustration of the splendid truth of Isaiah 63:9, "In all their affliction he was afflicted [!], and the angel of his presence saved them; in his love and in his pity he redeemed them; he lifted them up and carried them all the days of old." In their affliction he personally went with them. Yes, he is even with them *in* the affliction, as the Angel of YHWH[20] was with the three friends of Daniel in the fiery furnace (Dan. 3:25, "a son of the gods"; [N]KJV even: "the Son of God"): "When you pass through the waters, *I will be with you* [cf. Mark 4:35–41]; and through the rivers, they shall not overwhelm you; when you walk through fire you shall not be burned, and the flame shall not consume you" (Isa. 43:2). "Even though I walk through the valley of the shadow of death, I will fear no evil, for *you are with me*; your rod and your staff, they comfort me" (Ps. 23:4).

3.2.3 New Testament

At this point, moving through the entire Bible to catalog the notion of God's dwelling with his people would carry us too far afield. It will suffice to note that, also in the New Testament, God's salvation for humanity realizes itself against the background of God's communal being. In the person of Jesus Christ, the Logos—who was with God, and is God—became flesh, and since then "dwelt" (Gk. *eskēnōsen*, see below) among God's people (John 1:1, 14). The *shekinah* (the glorious Presence of God—the term is related to mishkan and sh-k-n mentioned in §3.2.2) dwelt in Jesus, so that he could speak about his

---

20. Regarding this Angel, see Ouweneel (2007b, §7.3).

body as being the true temple of God (2:19-21).[21]

Since the Day of Pentecost, the church of the living God is the "house of God" (1 Tim. 3:15 [N]KJV; cf. 1 Pet. 2:5; 4:17): "Do you not know that you [plur.] are God's temple and that God's Spirit *dwells* [Gk. *oikei*, from *oikos*, "house"] in you?" (1 Cor. 3:16)."For we are the temple of the living God; as God said, '*I will make my dwelling* [one Gk. word: *enoikēsō*] among them and walk among them, and I will be their God, and they shall be my people'" (2 Cor. 6:16). "Christ Jesus ... in whom the whole structure, being joined together, grows into a holy temple in the Lord. In him you also are being built together into a *dwelling place* [Gk. *katoikētērion*] for God by the Spirit" (Eph. 2:20-22).[22] In the Old Testament, God dwelt in a physical building in the midst of a natural people—in the New Testament, God dwells in a spiritual building, and this building (Gk. *oikos*, house) *is* his spiritual people (1 Tim. 3:15; 2 Tim. 2:20-21; Heb. 3:6; 10:21; 1 Pet. 2:5; 4:17).

Of the eternal state it is said, "Behold, the dwelling place [lit., tent or tabernacle, Gk. *skēnē*][23] of God is with man. He will dwell [Gk. *skēnōsei*] with them, and they will be his people [or, peoples], and God himself will be with them as their God" (Rev. 21:3). Thus, the notion of the God practicing fellowship with, and dwelling among, humans stretches virtually from the Bible's first page to its last page. That is, from God seeking fallen humans (Gen. 3:8-9) until the God tabernacling with renewed humanity on the renewed earth. No view of salvation is biblical that fails to take into account the communal being of God. Salvation is God fellowshipping with his people, and his people fellowshipping with God.

One of the basic aspects of the Fall was the loss of

---

21. See extensively, Ouweneel (*RT* II/3, chapter 6).
22. See extensively, Ouweneel (*RT* II/3, chapter 10).
23. Notice that both "house" and "tent" are used in the New Tetament as metaphors for God's dwelling place.

this fellowship ("your iniquities have made a separation between you and your God," Isa. 59:2). Salvation involves the restoration of this fellowship, on a higher level than would have been possible without the Fall.[24] Much more could, and will, be said on what the Fall and salvation have brought about, but this communal aspect remains essential.

3.3. God's Love
3.3.1 Being and Attributes

All God's attributes are equally important, and are equally expressions of God's being. This statement conflicts with the view of Regin Prenter, for example, which was quoted approvingly by Wolfhart Pannenberg. They claimed that 1 John 4:8 and 16, "God is love," refers not merely to an attribute of God but to the being of God, which is love. That is, love is supposedly not merely one of God's many attributes but he *is* altogether love.[25] Similarly, philosopher Ludwig Feuerbach feared that, if love were viewed as a predicate and not as a subject, God would be viewed as a subject in itself, apart from his love.[26]

However, both views involve a false dilemma. God's being can never be viewed apart from his attributes; his being *is* his attributes in their unity and fullness, and his attributes *are* his being in its diversity. The underlying misconception is the traditional false distinction arising from ancient substantialism between substance and accidental properties (Lat. *substantia, accidentia*). I have tried to thoroughly refute this false dualism elsewhere.[27]

Despite the equality of God's attributes, the moral attributes stand out prominently, if only because there

---
24. Regarding this important point, see Ouweneel (2012a, §14.1).
25. Pannenberg (1991, 1:424-25).
26. See the discussion by Jüngel (1977, 430-53).
27. See Ouweneel (2007b, 293-96).

are so many of them. To this category belong God's love, goodness, his grace, mercy, patience, and lovingkindness, and in a certain sense his holiness (see §3.6). However, this multiplicity is a little misleading. First, God's love and goodness are closely related: God's love is manifested in his benevolence and beneficence (the Lat. adverbial *bene* means "good" or "well").

Second, his grace, mercy, patience, and lovingkindness mainly constitute the way God's eternal love is manifested within time toward people, particularly since the Fall.[28]

Third, where love is manifested especially in the longing to do good to the beloved party, holiness is manifested particularly in the longing to avoid and combat evil. God's love for doing well finds its counterpart in his hatred toward evil.

3.3.2 Love As God's Nature

The terms "love" along with all of its cognates, from the Hebrew root '-h-b and the Greek root *agap-*, has a strongly sensible element in it. It implies warm affection and devotion, as illustrated in Jeremiah 31:20 (NIV), "Is not Ephraim my dear son, the child in whom I delight? Though I often speak against him, I still remember him. Therefore my heart yearns [lit., my bowels yearn] for him; I have great compassion for him." More essential, though, is the element of self-surrender, an attitude that is strongly oriented toward the well-being of the neighbor—without eliminating oneself, as the important addition in Leviticus 19:18 and 34 shows: ". . . love your neighbor *as yourself*."

The extent of this love is indicated elsewhere in the Torah: "You shall love the LORD your God with all your heart and with all your soul and with all your might" (Deut. 6:5; cf. 13:3).[29] Luke 10:27 mentions four anthropic

28. Cf. Wentsel (1987, 395–408).
29. Cf. *TDNT* 1:22–23.

aspects: "You shall love the LORD your God with all your heart and with all your soul and with all your strength and with all your mind, and your neighbor as yourself." Even love in a seemingly abstract sense, "loving good" (Amos 5:15), is not loving some abstract *bonum* but actually loving to do good to others, or love for good acts performed by good people.

God is love (1 John 4:8, 16); that is, it is entirely his nature to love. This involves first and foremost the eternal love between the divine persons within the Trinity (John 17:24b; see §3.1). The Father calls Jesus "my beloved Son" (Matt. 3:17; 17:5; cf. the "beloved son" in the parable, Mark 12:6), and Jesus says, ". . . the world may know that I love the Father" (John 14:31). There is a circle of love in which divine persons dwell eternally, and into which believers are invited to abide (Gk. *menō*): "As the Father has loved me, so have I loved you. Abide in my love. If you keep my commandments, you will abide in my love, just as I have kept my Father's commandments and abide in his love" (John 15:9-10). "God is love, and whoever abides in love abides in God, and God abides in him" (1 John 4:16).

About this, P. Althaus wrote:

> . . . It means that the eternal love between Father, Son, and Spirit is the ultimate reality. God's loving is from eternity loving in himself, yet not self-love. . . . The confession of the eternal essential Trinity offers a safe boundary against all pantheism. God is eternally love. If we confess this, and reject the Trinity, then we need an eternal world as object of God's eternal love.[30]

About this love, Scripture testifies in many ways. It is God's love toward, for instance, the patriarchs (Deut. 4:37; 10:15), toward the people of Israel (7:7-8, 13; 23:5; 2 Chron. 2:11; Isa. 43:4; 63:9; Jer. 31:3; Hos. 11:1, 4; 14:5;

---

30. Althaus (1952, 694); cf. also Pannenberg (1991, 1:422-32).

Zeph. 3:17; Mal. 1:2-3), the tribe of Benjamin (Deut. 33:12), Solomon (2 Sam. 12:24-25; Neh. 13:26), Cyrus (Isa. 48:14), individual believers (the *tsaddiqim*; Ps. 127:2; 146:8; Prov. 15:9; John 14:23; 16:27; 17:23; Rom. 5:5, 8; 8:39; 2 Thess. 2:13, 16), the stranger (Deut. 10:18), and humanity in general (John 3:16; 1 John 4:9-10).

3.3.3 Trinitarian Love

As we saw, the full meaning of God's love comes to light only when we connect this with the truth of the Trinity. If God were dependent on other beings to express his love, he could not have been love from eternity. Or the most we could have said is that God possessed the potential of loving but could not yet effectively love because there was nothing or no one to love. Or we could have said that God loved only future beings. But what sense would it have made to say that God *is* love? The only remaining solution would then have been that God's love was *self*-love. However, we can hardly imagine how God's *self*-love could ever have been the moral standard for *believers'* love, which is supposed to be shown not only toward themselves but toward others as well.

No, God's eternal love is conceivable only because of the eternal love expressed by the three divine persons toward *each other*. In the same way, as we saw, from before the foundation of the world God is the communicating and communing God, the good and loving God, the faithful God. From all eternity, the persons of the Trinity enjoyed perfect fellowship, perfect righteousness, perfect love, and perfect loyalty. This is always an interesting subject in any discussion with an orthodox Jew or a Muslim: Do you believe that God is love? Do you believe that he has been love from eternity? What sense does it make to call God "love" from eternity if there was no other person to love?

As Eduard Schlink put it,

From eternity, God is not a lonely God, but at once unity and fellowship—not an isolated I but an eternal over against of I and You, and thus eternally I and We at the same time. God became the loving, speaking and glorifying One not only through the over against of his creation, but from eternity he is the Loving One, the Loved One and the One returning love—the Speaking One, the Word and the Responding One—the Glorifying One, the Glorified One and the One returning glory in the unity and fellowship of the Father, the Son and the Holy Spirit.[31]

3.4   Types of Love
3.4.1 Love of Relationships

In our temporal human relationships, we know love in many forms: parental love, matrimonial love, patriotic love, and so on. Several of these forms are used in the Bible to offer us a certain approximation of God's love.

His love is parental, viz., fatherly (Deut. 1:31; Ps. 103:13; Hos. 11:1-4; John 16:27) as well as motherly (Ps. 131:2; Isa. 49:15; 66:13; Luke 13:34).[32] First, as to the fatherly aspect: Otto Weber emphasized that the name "Father"—not so much in the sense of the eternal Father of the eternal Son but rather the Father who, beginning in the Old Testament, cares for his people—summarizes God's love, grace, mercy, faithfulness, and patience.[33] This love resists punishing a beloved child even if such discipline is indispensable for the child's education (Prov. 3:12; Hos. 11:8-9).

Second, God's love is also matrimonial, viz., like that of a bridegroom and husband toward his bride, his people (Ps. 45; Isa. 54:5-8; 61:10; 62:4-5; Ezek. 16:8; Hos. 2:15, 18-19; 3:1; cf. Song 8:6-7; in the New Testament this is the love of Christ: Eph. 5:25). This matrimonial love is also a suffering love if it is not answered (Isa. 50:1-2; Jer. 3:6-13; Hos. 2:1-12). It is remarkable that every trace of

---

31. Schlink (1986, 1037).
32. See extensively, Ouweneel (1998, §2.4.3; 2018f, §§3.7-3.9).
33. Weber (1981, 1:422).

religious eroticism is lacking in this matrimonial love: "The love of God for Israel (Deut. 7:13) is not impulse but will; the love for God and the neighbor demanded of the Israelite (Deut. 6:5; Lev. 19:18) is not intoxication but act"[34]—a view that, by the way, is valid only if we leave the traditional (Jewish and Christian) interpretation of the quite erotic Song of Solomon out of consideration.[35]

If Reformed theology claims that the relationship between God and humans is always basically covenantal, I maintain that both the parental and the matrimonial relationships far surpass these. There is certainly a covenantal element in matrimony (cf. Mal. 2:10-16), but the latter is much more than any form of contractual relationship. In parental love this is even more clearly the case: there is no contractual element at all in it. I am not denying that there is an element of love in biblical covenants (see, e.g., Deut. 7:6-16); what I am denying is that the love aspect of the relationship between God and humans can be fully reduced to the covenantal aspect.[36]

Third, even the element of patriotic love is not lacking in God. The Promised Land is *his* land (Lev. 25:23), and he loves Mount Zion (Ps. 78:68, "he chose ... Mount Zion, which he loves"), which as a poetic notion that may extend to the Holy Land in its entirety: "[T]he LORD loves the gates of Zion more than all the dwelling places of Jacob" (Ps. 87:2; cf. 132:13-14; Rev. 20:9).

3.4.2 *Agapē, Eros, Philia*

Already in the Greek world, *agapē* related "for the most part to the love of God, to the love of the higher lifting up the lower, elevating the lower above others."[37] Thus, it is a condescending love (in the good sense),

---

34. *TDNT* 1:38.
35. See my own early attempt at such an interpretation: Ouweneel (1973).
36. See extensively, Ouweneel (*RT* IV/2).
37. *TDNT* 1:37, with reference to Plotinus, *Enneads* V.1.6.

which in John takes the character of a "heavenly reality which in some sense descends from stage to stage into this world."[38] Therefore, the New Testament never uses *erōs* or its derivations, a love that selfishly "seeks in others the fulfilment of its own life's hunger."[39] The New Testament does use *philia* and its cognates, which in the ancient world signified "for the most part the inclination or solicitous love of gods for men, or friends for friends,"[40] but rarely for God's love. Some exceptions are: "[T]he Father loves [*philei*] the Son" (John 5:20); "the Father himself loves [*philei*] you" (16:27); "the goodness and loving kindness [one word: *philanthrōpia*] of God our Savior appeared" (Titus 3:4).

Thus, *agapē* with its cognates is by far the best Greek description of divine love, as are the Latin words *caritas* and *dilectio*, rather than *amor*. In philosophical and theological literature, though, *amor Dei* ("love of God") is quite common;[41] here, the word *amor* is elevated, so to speak, to the level of *caritas* (cf. in English "love" and "charity," though today the latter means something like "altruism"). This love is first in God himself, and is then reflected in the believers. It has often drawn the attention of investigators that, in the ancient world, *agapē* was originally an extremely rare word, and a weak, colorless word at that. Only through Hebrew *ahaba* (which, with its vowels, its central guttural consonant, and its final labial consonant, remarkably resembles *agapē*), in the Septuagint has the Greek *agapē* word group received its rich and deep meaning that was later adopted

---

38. *TDNT* 1:53.
39. Ibid., 1:37; see also Nygren (1930–37); Barth (*CD* 4/2=26, §68.1). In Gen. 34:3 LXX, though, *agapaō* comes close to this selfish eroticism (cf. v. 2, Shechem raped Dinah).
40. *TDNT* 1:36.
41. An older example: the *amor Dei intellectualis* in Baruch Spinoza's *Ethica,* possibly a rendering of Rabbi Abraham Abulafia's *ahaba elohit sikhlit.*

in the New Testament.[42]

Moreover, *agapē* is the love that loves because it *is* love, is unable to do anything but love, and does so voluntarily (Rom. 11:28), unreservedly, and undeservedly. It does not love primarily because of the loveliness of its object, but for reasons that it finds purely in itself (as stated about the LORD, for example, in connection with 1 Sam. 12:22, that he would not cast off his people "for his great name's sake": "he drew his reasons from himself"[43]). This love does not love what is already lovely, as does natural human love, but this love creates its own object of love.[44] As Martin Luther has expressed it so well: "For sinners are beautiful because they are lo*v*ed, *they are not loved because they are beautiful*" (Lat. *Ideo enim peccatores sunt pulchri, quia diliguntur, non ideo diliguntur, quia sunt pulchri*).[45]

3.5 Aspects of Love
3.5.1 Goodness

In his discussion of God's moral attributes, H. Bavinck chose his starting point in God's goodness because goodness can be attributed to God in an absolute sense. That is, he is good in himself, and then, secondly, good toward others, which is expressed in lovingkindness, mercy, grace, and love.[46] Yet, in Scripture God is never called "goodness" as such, but he *is* called "love" (1 John 4:8, 16). And God *is* love in himself, not only in relationship to others, for love is the essence of the relationship between divine persons.[47] Therefore I prefer to take my starting point in God's *love*, considering goodness to be

---

42. *TDNT* 1:36, 39; cf. also Brunner (1950, 200-204).
43. *TDNT* 1:36, 39; cf. also Brunner (1950, 200-204).
44. Cf. Althaus (1952, 279).
45. Luther (1883, 1:365).
46. Bavinck (*RD* 2:210-16); cf. how Trevethan (1995) assigns God's goodness to his holiness.
47. Cf. Lewis (1944, 25-26); see extensively, Lewis (1971).

one of its features.

In addition to this, I notice that speaking of God as the "highest good"(Lat. *summum bonum*),[48] "the good in itself" (Lat. *bonum in se*), or "supernatural goodness" (Lat. *bonitas metaphysica*) are expressions that emit the odor of Greek thought; we need only recall the Platonic notion of God as the idea of the good. In the Bible, God is seldom called "good" in an absolute sense (Matt. 19:17, Gk. *agathos*). Just once, the Greek word *kalos* is used for divine persons, namely, for Christ, in the expression "the good shepherd" (John 10:11, 14). This does not mean the "lovely" shepherd in any romantic, bucolic sense but the "true, genuine" shepherd in contrast to the many false ones.[49]

Bavinck spoke of God's "absolute goodness," and distinguished in it especially the elements of self-sufficiency, perfection, and blessedness.[50] Clearly, however, Scripture refers to God's goodness almost always in relationship to his creatures (Num. 10:32; 1 Chron. 16:34; 2 Chron. 5:13; Ps. 25:8; 34:8; 54:6; 65:11; 69:16; 73:1; 86:5; 100:5; 106:1; 107:1; 109:21; 118:1, 29; 119:68; 135:3; 136:1; 145:9; Jer. 33:11; Lam. 3:25; Nah. 1:7; Acts 14:17).

3.5.2 Lovingkindness, Patience, Mercy

After *goodness*, a second feature of God's love is *lovingkindness* or *steadfast love,* which is Hebrew *chesed*. The root meaning of this term is "solidarity, reliability, faithfulness, loyalty," found in many Old Testament passages (concerning God from Gen. 32:10 to Micah 7:18, 20). In the New Testament, the Greek term is *chrēstotēs*, which means "goodness, kindness, generosity" (concerning God: Rom. 2:4; 11:22; 2 Cor. 10:1; Eph. 2:7; Titus 3:4). Sev-

---

48. E.g., Augustine, De Trinitate VIII.3; Enarrationes in Psalmos 26; De doctrina christiana I.7.
49. TDNT 3:548; cf. also James 2:7: "the honorable [Gk. *kaon*] name" (of God).
50. Bavinck (*RD* 2:211).

eral of these characteristics are reflected in the believer, namely, in the "fruit of the Spirit" (Gal. 5:22-23): "love [Gk. *agapē*], joy, peace [Gk. *eirēnē*; see §3.8], patience [Gk. *makrothumia*], kindness [Gk. *chrēstotēs*], goodness [Gk. *agathōsunē*], faithfulness Gk. [*pistis*; see §3.7], gentleness, self-control."

A third feature of God's love was just mentioned (Gal. 5:22): "patience" ([N]KJV: "longsuffering"; Gk. *makrothumia*). This corresponds with Hebrew *erek apayyim*, literally, "[one's] anger elongating," being slow in getting angry ("slow to anger," Exod. 34:6; Num. 14:18; Neh. 9:17; Ps. 86:15; 103:8; 145:8; Joel 2:13; Jonah 4:2; Nah. 1:3; cf. James 1:19). The Greek term *makrothumia* literally means "being great of mind" (Rom. 2:4; 9:22; 1 Tim. 1:16; 1 Pet. 3:20; 2 Pet. 3:15).[51] This means not only that God can postpone the eruption of his anger, but also that he can delay his love for his elect (which, of course, is not patience in the usual sense of the word). See for instance Luke 18:7, "[W]ill not God give justice to his elect, who cry to him day and night? Will he delay long over them [Gk. *makrothumei ep' autois*]?"[52] Exegetical opinions regarding these final words of the verse differ widely, however.[53]

A fourth feature of God's love is *mercy* (clemency, pity, sympathy), that is, God's goodness that unfolds itself toward those who are in miserable circumstances. It is the Latin *misericordia*, in which we recognize the words "misery" and *cor*, "heart," that is, God's heart going out to the miserable.[54] Mercy is a typical feature of God's love, which presupposes a certain miserable (desperate) condition of humans and a heart of God being moved because of this condition.

It is fascinating to see how Scripture makes free use

---

51. Barth (*CD* 2/1=8, §30.3:155-70).
52. Cf. Kamphuis (1982, 29-30).
53. Cf. Geldenhuys (1983, 448); Liefeld (1984, 1000-1001).
54. Cf. Barth (*CD* 2/1=8, §30.2:115-22).

of various anthropopathisms here. The Hebrew term *rachimim* ("bowels," hence "mercy") comes from *rechem*, "womb," just like as the Greek term *splanchna*, "mercy," also literally means "bowels" (cf. Jer. 31:20 KJV, "my [= God's] bowels are troubled for" Ephraim; Hos. 11:8, "My heart recoils within me; my compassion grows warm and tender"). These terms, together with Greek *eleos* and *oiktirmos*, and their cognates, occur many times in Scripture. In view of all of this, we identify "mercy" as a less genuine attribute of God's own being than his love and his goodness, and his grace (see next section). Rather than being an attribute, mercy is a specific consequence of God's love, responding to a specific troublesome human condition.

3.5.3 Grace

Grace is a fifth feature of God's love (cf. Heb. *chen* and Gk. *charis*, and their cognates). It often presupposes people who, because of their sins, have forfeited every right to blessing. This is true, however, not just because of sin.[55] Even without sin, humans would have been dependent on God's grace or favor for every blessing, for in themselves they have no rights or claims; they earn nothing by themselves. Therefore, Paul speaks of an eternal grace of God as the total sum of all God's blessings, which does not necessarily presuppose the Fall at all:[56] God "who saved us and called us to a holy calling, not because of our works but because of his own purpose and grace, which he gave us in Christ Jesus before the ages began" (2 Tim. 1:9).

In the Garden of Eden, the first humans lived by pure grace; as a Reformed pastor wrote: "True, we cannot yet speak about [prelapsarian] Adam as living in

---

55. Cf. Barth (*CD* 2/1=8, §30.1:98–105); Ouweneel (*RT* IV/2, §3.6.1).

56. This view might be called "supralapsarian"; cf. Ouweneel (*RT* III/1, §§2.4.3 and 14.6).

Salvation and God's Being

grace by which his trespasses were forgiven. But he was called to acknowledge God in everything, and to be totally dependent on Him. Today we call this: living by grace."[57] There are many examples in the Old Testament in which God's "grace" or "favor" was *not* linked to forgiveness and redemption, such as Laban asking favor from Jacob (Gen. 30:27), Jacob asking favor from Esau (32:5), or from Joseph (47:29), Joseph asking favor from the Pharaoh (50:4). Adam in Paradise lived by the favor of God, totally apart from the problem of sin (which had not yet presented itself). The term "favor" covers such terms as benefit, benevolence, indulgence, kindness, in addition to grace.

Grace is simply the opposite of merit, and neither concept is necessarily linked with sin. People receive grace from earthly kings apart from sin (Esther 2:17; 5:8). Paul called his apostleship a gift of grace, which had nothing to do with the problem of sin (Rom. 1:5). The point is that in his grace God bestows blessings upon humans that they have not deserved. To put it more strongly: humans, fallen or not, do not deserve anything at all. Both before and after the Fall, they lived and live by grace. The only difference is that, since the Fall, God's grace also includes forgiveness and redemption. But that does not change the general rule: humans cannot live before God any other way than by grace.

It *is* true, though, that God's lovingkindness, mercy, and grace always imply a relationship with other beings, whereas they can scarcely be used to describe the eternal relationship between the divine persons within the Trinity; in this case one can perhaps speak of grace in the sense of favor or benevolence. Therefore, love and goodness truly belong to God's being, whereas lovingkindness, mercy, and grace are the consequences of God's being toward humanity, depending on its condition and needs. Thus, we do understand that, in the tra-

---

57. Van der Waal (1990, 55).

ditional view, grace did not primarily refer to a divine virtue but rather to God's benevolent actions of favor. Therefore within the discipline of theology, grace was discussed in connection not with the doctrine of God (Lat. *locus de Deo*) but with the doctrine of salvation (Lat. *locus de salute*).[58] In Roman Catholic dogmatics this is still the case.[59]

3.6 God's Holiness
3.6.1 Is It an Attribute?

If some are surprised by the fact that God's grace has often been viewed as not a virtue of God, the same is the case even more strongly with God's *holiness*.[60] Peter Lombard and Thomas Aquinas did not mention it as a divine attribute. Protestant theologians have often reckoned it to God's perfection, or to his righteousness, to his goodness, his truthfulness, his wisdom, his sovereignty and power, his majesty, or still other attributes, or they viewed it as a purely relational notion, not as an essential quality of God.[61]

In my view, it is very difficult to maintain such a view in the light of a Bible verse such as Isaiah 6:3, "Holy, holy, holy is the LORD of hosts; the whole earth is full of his glory!" Here, the seraphim praise the Lord as the Thrice Holy (the well-known *Trisagion*), and this returns in the song of the four living creatures: "Holy, holy, holy, is the Lord God Almighty, who was and is and is to come!" (Rev. 4:8). In such passages, God's holiness receives strong emphasis. Its unique significance is underscored; God is not praised in such a way with any other attribute. Therefore, it is important to stress the holiness of God precisely in connection with the love of

---

58. Bavinck (*RD* 2:214–15).
59. Cf. the comments by Althaus (1952, 280–81) and Weber (1981, 1:424–28).
60. Bavinck (*RD* 2:216).
61. Diestel (1859).

God, because the two are inseparable.⁶² In opposition to this, the Apostolic Fathers connected the love of God rather with the Stoic notion of God's general benevolence.⁶³

Rudolf Otto wrote his famous work on the divinely holy as the "fearful and fascinating [that is, repulsive as well as attractive] mystery" (Lat. *mysterium tremendum et fascinans*).⁶⁴ In agreement with this, Emil Brunner and Paul Althaus used Isaiah 6:3 and other Bible passages to show that God's holiness allegedly is not just one of many attributes of God, and also not a purely ethical attribute.⁶⁵ In this respect, they rightly opposed the overwhelming majority of Roman Catholic and Protestant dogmaticians. They viewed holiness as a feature of God's actual *being*; according to Althaus it was in this respect similar to God's glory and blessedness. Thus, the Spirit is the *Holy* Spirit, not because this is one of many attributes but because the term "holy" describes God's being. The holy is the lofty, the unfathomable, the majestic, the mysterious, the unapproachable, and all of this in a much wider sense than being morally unapproachable. God's holiness is his splendor, his brilliance, his grandeur, his luster, his magnificence, his majesty, his effulgence, his resplendence, his glory, his beauty, all in one.

3.6.2 Attribute or Being?

Looking back at what we just studied, I admit that Althaus and Brunner certainly had a point. Yet, I wonder whether the question that they raise is not simply a problem with *all* so-called divine "attributes." God *is* love (1 John 4:8, 16), God *is* light (1:5), God *is* spirit (John

---

62. Brunner (1950, 188-92).
63. Cf. "long-suffering will" in 1 Clement 19:3 (http://www.newadvent.org/fathers/1010.htm).
64. Otto (1958).
65. Brunner (1950, 157-74); Althaus (1952, 289-92).

4:24). Is love or light or spirit only one attribute out of many? God *is* altogether love, he *is* altogether light, he *is* altogether spirit—but in exactly the same way he *is* altogether holiness, altogether goodness, blessedness, glory, majesty, and so on. Yet, his love and his spirituality and his righteousness and his holiness, though never in conflict with each other, are not identical. Here again we have the problem of ancient substantialism, which plays off God's being (Lat. *substantia*) against God's attributes (Lat. *accidentia*).

Because of this substantialist embarrassment in how to express these things as accurately as possible we keep speaking of distinct "attributes," as long as we maintain that each of them could also be called his being (*against* substantialism). To repeat: God's being *is* his attributes in their unity, totality, and fullness, while his attributes *are* his being in its diversity and variability. I think here of the well-known prism metaphor (often used by Reformed philosopher Herman Dooyeweerd): the one beam of white light *is* the many colors in their unity, totality, and fullness, while the many colors *are* the one beam of light in its diversity and variability.

I am encouraged in defending this unifying approach by Scripture itself placing God's holiness alongside other divine attributes: "Holy and awesome" (Ps. 111:9); "holy and beautiful" (Isa. 64:11); "righteous and holy" (Mark. 6:20); "holy . . . righteous Father" (John 17:11, 25); "the Holy and Righteous One" (Acts 3:14); "holy and righteous and good" (Rom. 7:12); "holy and beloved" (Col. 3:12); "holy and true" (Rev. 6:10); "blessed and holy" (20:6). As soon as we abandon the traditional substantialist dualism of being and attributes, the problem identified by Althaus and Brunner disappears: God's attributes *are* his being, and *vice versa*.[66] Choosing whether certain features of God are part of—or consti-

---

66. See Ouweneel (2007b, 293–96).

Salvation and God's Being

tute—his being *or* are instead divine attributes is a false choice.

3.6.3 Terminology

In the Old Testament, the Hebrew root *q-d-sh* refers primarily to the cultic service. It has to do with what differs from the secular, that is, what has been withdrawn from profane use, and set apart for and consecrated to God.[67] The ground around the burning bush (Exod. 3:5), Gilgal (Josh. 5:15), Jerusalem (Neh. 11:1, 18; Isa. 48:2; 52:1; Dan. 9:24; Matt. 4:5; 27:53; Rev. 11:2; cf. 21:2, 10), the temple area (Ps. 48:1; Isa. 11:9; 56:7). and the temple itself (1 Chron. 29:3; Ps. 5:7; 79:1; 138:2; Isa. 64:10 etc.) are all holy because the presence of YHWH is associated with it. We call God holy because he himself is separate from all that is secular or profane (Isa. 5:16; 6:3; Hos. 11:9).

Where God is revealed or presented in his holiness, or praised for his holiness, he is sanctified (hallowed, declared holy; Num. 20:12-13; Isa. 5:16; Ezek. 20:41; 28:22, 25; 36:23; 38:16; 39:27; cf. Matt. 6:9; Luke 11:2; 1 Pet. 3:15).[68] Because God is holy, that which expresses his being—his name—is holy (Lev. 20:3; 22:2; 1 Chron. 16:10, 35; Ps. 33:21; 103:1; Ezek. 36:20-23). His Word (Ps. 105:42, "promise" = Heb. *dabar*, "word"; Jer. 23:9, lit., "the words of his holiness") and his Spirit (Ps. 51:11; Isa. 63:10) are holy because they are opposed to all that is creaturely and secular. Isaiah calls God "the Holy One of Israel" twenty-nine times, in connection with both judgment and redemption.

Herman Bavinck referred to Hermann Cremer,[69]

---

67. Von Rad (1975, 272-74); *TDNT* 1:90. Remarkably enough the root can also be used for what has been consecrated to idols, and thus is very *unholy*; e.g., the *qadēsh* (fem., *qedēshah*) is the temple prostitute (both in Deut. 23:18).
68. The words "holy," "hallow," "saint," and "sanctify" all basically refer to the same matter.
69. Bavinck (*RD* 2:219); Cremer (1917).

who emphasized that holiness is not primarily a relationship from below to above but from above to below. That is, it must be attributed primarily to God, and only then, secondarily, to creatures. Creatures are never holy in themselves, and cannot sanctify themselves (make themselves holy). All holiness and sanctification proceed from God. This point alone suffices to make us very careful to call prelapsarian Adam "holy" if we have no explicit biblical proof for this.[70] God can sanctify things or people, that is, separate them from the profane, but only he is holy in himself. It is this very attribute that, in every manifestation of God, impresses people with his deity. When God swears by his holiness (Amos 4:2), this is the same as swearing by himself (6:8), or people swearing by his name (Deut. 6:13; 10:20). This holiness is manifested in redemption, consolation, faithfulness, but also in punishment and chastisement.[71]

In the New Testament, the use of the Greek term *hagios* largely corresponds to that of Hebrew *q-d-sh* in the Old Testament. God is the "holy Father" (John 17:11), the "holy and true" Sovereign Lord (Rev. 6:10). In 1 Peter 1:15–16, God is called holy in correspondence with Leviticus 19:2. The term *hagios* is also used for Jesus Christ (Mark 1:24; Luke 1:35; 4:34; John 6:69; Acts 3:14; 4:27, 30; 1 John 2:20; Rev. 3:7), and of course many times for the "Holy" Spirit. In addition to this, God is *hosios*, which also means "holy," but then, if we follow the Septuagint, as the equivalent of Hebrew *chasid*, never of *qadosh*. It has connotations of being "pure" and "righteous" (Rev. 15:4; 16:5; cf. Heb. 7:26).

Much more clearly than in the Old Testament, the God who himself is holy becomes the God of sanctification (making holy), the God who sanctifies, that is, the God who consecrates people to himself, brings to expression in them his own image of holiness, and thus

---

70. See Ouweneel (2008a, §§5.1.3, 9.2.3; 2016, 17).
71. See extensively Bavinck (*RD* 2:220–21).

separates them from the domain of sin. The latter is negative, but the former is positive: God's holiness—splendor, brilliance, grandeur, luster, magnificence, majesty, effulgence, resplendence, glory, and beauty—is to be reflected in his people: in their behavior and their actions. In my view, this is the essence of sanctification: God's glory reflected in regenerated and Spirit-filled people.

3.7 God's Faithfulness

3.7.1 New Testament

The salvation of human beings cannot be severed from the faithfulness of God; he is faithful to his eternal counsels as well as to his partner, humanity, also after it had fallen into sin. God is faithful to his promises despite the fact that, also after the Fall, humans depart from him time and again. Departures even occurred, and occur, in the heart of the Christian world (cf., e.g., 1 Tim. 4:1; 2 Tim. 3:1-5; Rev. 2-3). Therefore, God's faithfulness includes his being faithful to himself, to his holy and righteous being. As a consequence, he cannot turn a blind eye to sin, and a sacrifice is needed to bring sinners back to him: "What if some were unfaithful? Does their faithlessness nullify the faithfulness of God? By no means! Let God be true though every one were a liar, as it is written, 'That you may be justified in your words, and prevail when you are judged'" (Rom. 3:3-4; cf. Ps. 51:4). "[I]f we deny him, he also will deny us; if we are faithless, he remains faithful—for he cannot deny himself" (2 Tim. 2:12-13).

Emil Brunner noted that God's faithfulness plays a fundamental role in the Bible but occupies a small place in the traditional doctrine of the divine attributes.[72] He suggested interestingly that the cause of this was the speculative idea of the Absolute with its timeless immutability, which leaves no room for God's faithfulness because, in this view, the latter would merely be a synonym

---
72. Brunner (1950, 271).

for his immutability.[73] What would it mean to speak of the faithfulness of an immutable God in the traditional ontic sense of the term? However, the living, loving God of the Bible is very different from the God of philosophical speculation,[74] who by definition is immutable. The God of the Bible is faithful because he wishes to realize his counsels (cf. Rom. 8:29), because he suffers with his people (Isa. 63:9), and because he loves them (§3.5).

Wherever God or Christ are said to be faithful, we find the same term that is also used for human faithfulness *or* faith (the same Greek word: *pistis*; adjective: *pistos*). In all these cases, the sense is that God, or Christ, is absolutely faithful to himself as well as to others. Because God is faithful he is trustworthy; those who have faith in him, trust him. To someone who is "faithful" (*pistos*) one can "entrust" (*pisteuō*) matters, or even oneself (for this meaning of *pisteuō*, cf. Luke 16:11). In Matthew 23:23, faithfulness is mentioned as one of the essential aspects of the Torah, together with justice and mercy; in Romans 3:3, God's faithfulness is contrasted with human unfaithfulness (Gk. *apistia*).

Of great importance in salvation is that God is faithful to the work of Christ, so to speak. We read in 1 John 1:9, "If we confess our sins, he [i.e., God] is *faithful* and *just* to forgive us our sins and to cleanse us from all unrighteousness." John could also have said that God is gracious and merciful when he forgives those who confess their sins. But instead, he underscores here the faithfulness and righteousness of God in forgiving. God is faithful and just when he applies the atoning work of Christ to a confessing sinner, since because it was for this purpose that he gave his Son in the first place: "He who did not spare his own Son but gave him up for us

---

73. Ouweneel (2008b, §6.2.2); see also Wentsel (1987, 406– 13); Pannenberg (1991, 1:436–38).
74. Think of the famous note by Blaise Pascal, found after his death: "God of Abraham, God of Isaac, God of Jacob, not of the philosophers and the scholars."

all, how will he not also with him graciously give us all things?" (Rom. 8:32). Reverently speaking, God would be unfaithful to both the work of Christ and the penitent sinner were he not to make this work effective for the latter. God shows his righteousness in being just (or righteous) and the justifier of (i.e., the One making righteous) the person who has faith in Jesus (Rom. 3:26).

3.7.2 Old Testament

We read in Lamentations that "The steadfast love [mercies (N)KJV][75] of the LORD never ceases; his mercies [Heb. *rahamayw*, from *rechem*; compassions (N)KJV] never come to an end; they are new every morning; great is your faithfulness [Heb. *emunah*]" (Lam. 3:22–23). Conversely, it is asked with respect to humans: "[A] faithful man [Heb. *ish emunim*] who can find?" (Prov. 20:6). In comparison to God's faithfulness, where can we find a true equivalent among humans? All too often, God's faithfulness collides with human unfaithfulness.

We see here that in the Old Testament, too, God's faithfulness comes to light. It is described by the Hebrew root '-m-n and its cognates (Deut. 7:9; 32:4; Neh. 9:33; Ps. 33:4; Isa. 49:7). These terms can also be rendered as "truth" and related forms, especially "truthfulness"; the word "truth" is etymologically related to Dutch *trouw* and German *Treue*, which mean "faithfulness."[76] Whenever someone says "Amen," they are testifying not only to the truth of what was just said (or prayed; cf. 1 Cor. 14:16), but even more to the general faithfulness or truthfulness of God. God speaks the truth, that is, he tells us things as they really are, and we can rely on this because God is trustworthy. God *is* truth (Ps. 31:5; Jer. 10:10; Rom. 3:4, 7) in the sense that he is absolutely reliable in what he says and what he does, and is thus wor-

---

75. One Heb. word: *chesed*; actually the text has the plural: *chasdē YHWH*.
76. Cf. *TDNT* 1:232-37; 6:182-96; *DOTT* 1:427-33.

thy of our unconditional and devoted trust (confidence). He shows himself truthful to people, which means that he is faithful to them (Gen. 24:27; Ps. 57:3; 61:7; 89:14,; cf. each verse in the KJV ["truth"] and modern translations ["faithfulness"]). All God's words, ways and works are truth, that is, truthful, faithful, and trustworthy (2 Sam. 7:28; Ps. 19:9; 25:10; 33:4; 111:7; 119:86, 142, 151; Dan. 4:37). He *abounds* in faithfulness or truth (Exod. 34:6); it extends to the clouds (Ps. 33:5).

People must be and practice truth/faithfulness, as well (Exod. 18:21; Neh. 7:2; Ps. 45:4). Therefore, the Hebrew word *emet* entails both "truth(fulness)" and "trustworthiness." The Greek word *pistis* entails both "faith" and "faithfulness." All three—truth, faith (confidence), and faithfulness—characterize the relationship between God and human beings on a transcendent-religious level. Through words of the same root '-m-n, we can say that because God is faithful, he confirms his word (1 Kings 8:26; 2 Chron. 6:17), establishes it (1 Chron. 17:23–24), fulfills it (2 Chron. 1:9), makes it "stand firm" or "remain faithful" (cf. Ps. 89:28), or "what is sure" (Hos. 5:9).

Artur Weiser observed that these terms refer to God's being: "[T]he fundamental meaning [of *emet*] is 'that which is essential,' i.e., 'that which makes God God.'"[77] This seems to be the meaning of 2 Timothy 2:13 as well: "[I]f we are unfaithful, he remains faithful—for he cannot deny himself." God cannot become unfaithful to himself; he cannot be in conflict with his own being; in short: he cannot stop being God. Whether this means that the Lord remains faithful to his promises once given,[78] of that he remains faithful to his holiness when he chastises people's unfaithfulness,[79] in both cases he remains faithful to *himself*.

---

77. *TDNT* 6:185.
78. Ridderbos (1967, 207–208).
79. Bouma (1937, 144–45); Vine (1985, 3:316).

3.7.3 Faithfulness, Reason, Will

Astonishingly, Herman Bavinck concluded that because *emet* means both "truth" and "faithfulness," God's veracity or truth(fulness) (Lat. *veracitas*) is a virtue of both the intellect and the will.[80] Let me try to explain this in terms associated with H. Dooyeweerdian.[81] If Bavinck had used these terms, his approach might have been more or less as follows.

There is certainly a logical and a historical-formative (conative) element in God's *emet*—viewed as the meaning nucleus of the pistical modality—just as *all* other modal aspects are encountered within the pistical modality in the form of modal analogies. For instance, we encounter in faithfulness also a kinematic element if we think of the steady constancy of God's promises (*'-m-n* meaning "to be firm/steady/established"); a physical element in the force of his faithfulness; a perceptive element in the self-awareness of his faithfulness; a social element in the relationships with humans that are presupposed in God's faithfulness; an aesthetic element in the inner harmony of God's faithfulness, and in his attitude to erring humans; a juridical element in his faithfulness as it manifests itself in a righteous way both in judgment and in redemption; and an ethical moment in the love that is presupposed in his faithfulness toward humanity.

Is God's faithfulness then the sum of all this? No, these are only analogous elements within something—faithfulness—that itself is irreducible to any other modal idea. God's faithfulness cannot be expressed in purely logical, nor in purely historical-formative (conative) terms, nor in both together; it is essentially irreducible. Bavinck could just as well have said of God's love, or God's righteousness, or God's holiness, that they are virtues of the intellect and of the will. This can be easily explained:

---

80. Bavinck (*RD* 2:207).
81. By way of introduction, see Ouweneel (2014).

what is love, or righteousness, or holiness, if they have not been thought through, or if there is no will to show them toward humans in God's relationship with them? However, if these analogous elements would be emphasized too much, this would be just as mistaken, namely, one-sided, as in the case of God's faithfulness.

3.8 God's Peace[82]

3.8.1 The God of Peace

We have seen that in the being of God are also found the *goals* of salvation. This is true also with respect to God's peace (§3.8), God's bliss (§3.9) and God's glory (§3.10). These are characteristics that, to the extent this is possible for creatures, God shares with redeemed people (§3.5). Let us now considers these characteristics, beginning with peace.

Remarkably, God is never called the God of joy. In Psalm 43:4, God is called "my exceeding joy"; this means not that God *is* joy but that he embodies the psalmist's joy at that moment. By way of contrast, seven times God is called the "God of peace" (Rom. 15:33; 16:20; 1 Cor. 14:33 ["God is not a God of confusion but of peace"]; 2 Cor. 13:11 ["the God of love and peace"]; Phil. 4:9; 1 Thess. 5:23; Heb. 13:20). This phrase means "the peaceful God" or "the God who embodies and works peace." Therefore we read about the "peace of God" (Phil. 4:7), it is said that he has "thoughts of peace" about his people (Jer. 29:11 [N]KJV), "he will speak peace to his people, to his saints" (Ps. 85:8), he "will ordain peace for" his people (Isa. 26:12), he will "reveal to them the abundance of peace and truth" (Jer. 33:6 [N]KJV), and he fills them "with all joy and peace" (Rom. 15:13).

In the address of their various letters, the New Testament writers (Paul, Peter, John, Jude) wish for their readers the peace of God, their Father, and sometimes

---

82. *TDNT* 2:400–17; *DOTT* 4:130–35; *DNTT* 2:776–83; Pop (1999, 547–51).

we find such a wish at the end of a letter (Eph. 6:23; 1 Pet. 5:14; 3 John 1:15). Usually, peace is here connected with grace; in some personal letters, mercy is added (1 Tim. 1:2; 2 Tim. 1:2; 2 John 1:3).

What is true for God is true also for his Son, the Messiah: "[T]his [One] shall be peace," that is, the embodiment of peace for his redeemed people (Micah 5:5 NKJV; cf. Isa. 9:6, "Prince of Peace"). "[H]e himself is our peace," "our" referring again to God's people (Eph. 2:14). The "peace of Christ" must rule believers' hearts (Col. 3:15), and Paul hopes that "the Lord of peace himself [may] give you peace at all times in every way" (2 Thess. 3:16). Jesus is the true Melchizedek, king of Salem, that is, "king of peace" (Heb. 7:2; cf. v. 3b; Gen. 14:18). In John 14:27, Jesus grants this promise to his disciples: "Peace I leave with you; my peace I give to you."

3.8.2 Peace and Salvation

Peace is an important soteriological term; see, for instance, the parallelism in Isaiah 52:7, "How beautiful upon the mountains are the feet of him who brings good news, who publishes *peace*, who brings good news of happiness, who publishes *salvation*." As we saw, in its broadest sense "salvation" (Heb. *yeshuʿah*) overlaps with Hebrew *shalom*, which entails "peace" but also well-being, harmony, wholeness, prosperity, blessing, and bliss (§§1.3.1, 1.7.1). The world is craving this *shalom*, the kingdom of peace and righteousness, rest and safety: "Of the increase of his government and of *peace* there will be no end, on the throne of David and over his kingdom, to establish it and to uphold it with justice and with righteousness from this time forth and forevermore" (Isa. 9:7). "Behold, I will extend *peace* to her [i.e., Jerusalem] like a river, and the glory of the nations like an overflowing stream" (66:12).

In those days that the prophets envisioned, people will follow God's Torah (cf. 2:3-4), and this will be the guarantee for their peace: "Oh that you had paid attention to my commandments! Then your peace would have been like a river, and your righteousness like the waves of the sea" (48:18; cf. Ps. 119:165, "Great peace have those who love your law; nothing can make them stumble"). Notice the contrast with the lawbreakers: "There is no peace . . . for the wicked" (48:22; 57:21).

Christians could easily imagine such a world without war and conflict, while yet leaving God out of consideration. This would be like the paradise of the Islamic tradition, which tells us much about its alleged pleasures but hardly anything about God in paradise. Jesus said, however, "I have said these things to you, that *in me* you may have peace" (John 16:33). As G. C. Berkouwer said, "It is a peace which would depart from us and become unrecognizable just as soon as it is isolated from his person."[83] There is no true peace *in itself*; it is the "peace *with* God" (positional peace, the consequence of the justification by faith), the "peace *of* God" (Phil. 4:7, experiential, everyday peace), the "peace of Christ" (Col. 3:15; cf. John 14:27), which believers enjoy, and which cannot for a moment be separated from its root.

I see three elements in biblical peace. First, peace is *order;* notice this contrast: "God is not a God of confusion but of peace" (1 Cor. 14:33; VOICE: "God is the author of *order*, not confusion"). Second, peace is *harmony*; see, for instance: "It is he who shall build the temple of the LORD and . . . shall sit and rule on his throne. And there [or, he] shall be a priest on his throne, and the counsel of peace shall be between them both" (Zech. 6:13; MSG: ". . . showing that king and priest can coexist in *harmony*"). Third, peace is *rest*; notice the following parallelisms: "Ask ye the peace of Jerusalem, at *rest* are those loving thee" (Ps. 122:6 YTL). "And the work of righteousness shall be peace; and the effect of righteousness *rest* and security for ever. And my people shall dwell in a habita-

---

83. Berkouwer (1965, 19).

tion of peace and in secure dwellings and in the refreshing of *rest*" (Isa. 32:17-18 JUB).

3.8.3 Peace and the Eschaton

Many of the Bible passages mentioned so far show clearly that to a large extent peace is an eschatological notion. Believers already *possess* positional "peace with God" (Rom. 5:1), and *may* possess experiential "peace of God" (Phil. 4:7), but the full meaning of this will be disclosed only in the *eschaton*. "[T]here remains a Sabbath rest [one Gk. word: *sabbatismos*] for the people of God" (Heb. 4:9). In my view, this refers not to heaven but, as everywhere in the book of Hebrews, to the Messianic kingdom ("the world to come," 2:5; "the age to come," 6:5; "the good things to come," 10:1; "the kingdom that cannot be shaken," 12:28; "the city that is to come," 13:14).[84]

Paul says, "[T]he kingdom of God is not a matter of eating and drinking [i.e., of trivialities] but of righteousness and peace and joy in the Holy Spirit" (Rom. 14:17). In the present age, this kingdom is being realized in the midst of a world full of *un*righteousness, of war and conflict, of sadness. Only in the Messianic kingdom will God's peace be fully manifested: "[T]he meek shall inherit the land and delight themselves in abundant peace" (Ps. 37:11). "In His days the righteous shall flourish, and abundance of peace" (72:7 NKJV). "Of the increase of his government and of peace there will be no end, on the throne of David and over his kingdom, to establish it and to uphold it with justice and with righteousness from this time forth and forevermore" (Isa. 9:7). "My people will abide in a peaceful habitation, in secure dwellings, and in quiet resting places" (32:18). "For you shall go out in joy and be led forth in peace; the mountains and the hills before you shall break forth into singing, and all the trees of the field shall clap their hands" (55:12). "'Peace, peace, to the far and to the near,'

---
84. Ouweneel (1982, 1:56-57).

says the L‍ORD, 'and I will heal him [i.e., Israel]'" (57:19). "[H]e shall speak peace to the nations; his rule shall be from sea to sea, and from the River to the ends of the earth" (Zech. 9:10).

In the Messianic kingdom, peace will be realized in heaven as well as on earth, but only "among those with whom he is pleased" (Luke 2:14; cf. 19:38); these are the people who have peace *in Christ* (John 16:33). "You keep him in perfect peace whose mind is stayed on you, because he trusts in you.... O L‍ORD, you will ordain peace for us, for you have indeed done for us all our works" (Isa. 26:3, 12). These are the people who stand in a covenant relationship with the Lord: "'For the mountains may depart and the hills be removed, but my steadfast love shall not depart from you, and my *covenant of peace* shall not be removed,' says the L‍ORD, who has compassion on you" (54:10). "I will make a *covenant of peace* with them. It shall be an everlasting covenant with them. And I will set them in their land and multiply them, and will set my sanctuary in their midst forevermore" (Ezek. 37:26).

3.9 God's Bliss
3.9.1 Terminology

Already the church fathers considered the contemplation of God (Lat. *contemplatio Dei*) to be the highest form of bliss for the saved. We could also say that this highest bliss is sharing in God's own bliss. This bliss is not only an objective reference to a state of perfection in God himself, but also a subjective reference to the awareness of it, the experience of joy that belongs to it.[85] In the Old Testament, the Hebrew root ᶜ-*sh-r* means "to declare happy" or "blissful." The common English rendering is something like "to call blessed," but "blessed" is an unfortunate rendering. The translation "blessed" should be reserved for the Hebrew word *barukh* (see, e.g., Gen.

---
85. Althaus (1952, 296).

9:26; 14:19-20). This is a concept very different from one derived from the Hebrew root ᶜ-sh-r, namely, ᶜashrey, for instance in this: "Happy [or blissful] is the man who walks not," and so on (Ps. 1:1).

Some modern translations do make this important distinction: "The truly happy person . . ." (CEB), "Happy is the man . . ." (HCSB, NLV; cf. ICB), "Happy are those . . ." (EXB, gnt, NCV, NRSV), "Oh, the joys of those . . ." (NLT, TLB), "O the happiness of that one . . ." (YLT). "Happy" may sound colloquial (therefore I give the alternative "blissful"), but it is the exact rendering of ᶜashrey; the rendering of "blessed" is simply wrong, despite its long translational history. A blessed person is not necessarily happy at all; the two concepts are quite different.

The corresponding Greek term in the New Testament is *makarios*, which in English Bibles is often rendered as "blessed" as well. But "blessed" is the proper rendering of the Greek word *eulogētos* (e.g., 2 Cor. 1:3; Eph. 1:3; 1 Pet. 1:3); *makarios* means "happy, blissful" (e.g., Matt. 5:3-11). Here again, it is only a few modern translations that give the proper rendering (CEB, GNT, NLV, OJB, Phillips, YLT; cf. "fortunate," TLB). We speak here of the *Beatitudes*, which is a correct term because the Latin equivalent of *makarios* is not at all *benedictus* ("blessed") but *beatus*, "happy," from the verb *beare*, "to make happy."

The Hebrew term ᶜashrey is never used for God, but the Greek term *makarios* is used twice for God, both in 1 Timothy. The first reference is: ". . . the gospel of the glory of the blissful [Vulgate: *beatus*[86]] God" (1:11). Interestingly, no English translation renders *makarios* correctly here (cf. MSG, "this great God"; NLV, "our honored God"). Other languages do provide the correct rendering: *gelukzalig* (Dutch); *selig* (Luther); *bienheureux* (French);

---

86. Cf. 2 Cor. 1:3; Eph. 1:3; 1 Pet. 1:3, where the Vulgate correctly renders *benedictus*. The English translational tradition has not done justice to a distinction that is clearly made in Hebrew, Greek, and Latin (as well as in Dutch and German).

beato (Italian), and so on. The failure to render *makarios* correctly is inherent to the English language. The matter is important, for how will readers understand 1 Timothy 1:11 if they get the impression that the verse speaks of the *praise* of God instead of the *bliss* of God?

3.9.2 Happiness

I did find the correct rendering in the *Expositions* by Alexander MacLaren: "The gospel of the glory of the happy God." MacLaren wrote of this,

> There are two Greek words which are both translated "blessed" in the New Testament. One of them, the more common [Gk. *eulogētos*], literally means "well spoken of," and points to the action of praise or benediction; describes what a man is when men speak well of him, or what God is when men praise and magnify His name. But the other word, which is used here [Gk. *makarios*], and is only applied to God once more in Scripture [see below], has no reference to the human attribution of blessing and praise to Him, but describes Him altogether apart from what men say of Him, as what He is in Himself, the "blessed," or, as we might almost say, the "happy" God. If the word happy seems too trivial, suggesting ideas of levity, of turbulence, of possible change, then I do not know that we can find any better word than that which is already employed in my text, if only we remember that it means the solemn, calm, restful, perpetual gladness that fills the heart of God.[87]

I could not have said it any better! It is so much better than the argument of the *Expositor's Greek Testament:*

---

87. http://biblehub.com/commentaries/maclaren/1_timo thy/1.htm; cf. Matthew Henry: "the holy happiness of heaven"; Jamieson-Fausset-Brown: "The term, 'blessed,' indicates at once immortality and supreme happiness"; Matthew Poole: "God . . . being infinitely happy in the possession of his own excellencies"; Bengel: "supreme happiness" (http://biblehub.com/ commentaries/1_timothy/1-11.htm).

"We may call God *blessed*, but not *happy*; since happiness is only predicated of those whom it is possible to conceive of as unhappy."[88] If this were so, then neither we could say that God is "blessed"—or righteous, gracious, loving, holy, etc.— because it is not possible to conceive of him as "unblessed" (or unrighteous, ungracious, unloving, unholy, etc.). This is a strange argument.

The other reference is 1 Timothy 6:15, "the blissful and only Sovereign, the King of kings and Lord of lords." The phrase in Titus 2:13 ("the blissful hope") comes close to this because it refers to "the sphere of the incorruptible and blessed [Luther: *selig* = blissful] God."[89] Perhaps the greatest miracle of God's salvation is that human beings—creatures—will ultimately be included in this sphere of bliss, love, and fellowship: "[I]ndeed our fellowship is with the Father and with his Son Jesus Christ" (1 John 1:3; cf. John 17:22-26).

If the word "happy" sounds too trivial or earthly, let us follow the description given by Friedrich Hauck: *makarios* denotes "the transcendent happiness of a life beyond care, labour and death," especially "the happy state of the gods above earthly sufferings and labours," and then of human beings: "the state of godlike blessedness [Ger. *Seligkeit:* bliss] hereafter in the isles of the blessed Ger. [*Seligen:* blissful ones]."[90] In addition to the Bible passages mentioned, *makarios* and related forms refer "overwhelmingly to the distinctive religious joy which accrues to man from his share in the salvation of the kingdom of God,"[91] both in the Septuagint and in the New Testament. In addition, God's bliss is different from that of the pagan gods, because in him it never consists of a certain elevation above, and thus a lack of interest for, human circumstances (Gk. *apatheia*). God's

---

88. http://biblehub.com/commentaries/1_timothy/1-11.htm.
89. *TDNT* 4:370.
90. Ibid., 4:362.
91. Ibid., 4:367.

bliss cannot be severed from his love and grace toward humanity. Regarding this *apatheia* we must now add a few more thoughts.

3.9.3 *Apatheia* and Other Errors

Strangely enough, Albrecht Ritschl believed that it is wrong to speak of Jesus' soul sufferings under human sin because this would not comport with his bliss.[92] This notion is nothing less than the idea of *apatheia*, the ancient pagan view of bliss that entails elevation above human circumstances.[93] One of the true aspects of God's love and bliss is that he *can* suffer with humans (cf. Isa. 63:9a, "In all their affliction he was afflicted"), and yet can fully maintain his intrinsic bliss. There can be no true mercy of God without this element of sympathizing emotionality (cf. Jer. 31:20; Hos. 11:8).

Emil Brunner fell into the opposite misunderstanding by denying God's bliss—he dismissed 1 Timothy 1:11 and 6:15—because this would exclude God's sympathizing care.[94] However, both bliss and compassion are undeniable divine features. They appear incompatible only if one mistakenly deals with them in a logical-conceptual way, so that logical contradictions between them can be construed. Instead, we can use only such terms as "ideas," that is, notions that are logical but not exhaustive; they can only approximate the subject concerned.[95]

Herman Bavinck saw three elements in God's bliss.[96]

(1) Absolute perfection, for bliss is the part of every being that lives perfectly, without any internal or ex-

---

92. Ritschl (1966, 573).
93. Althaus (1952, 298); cf. Ouweneel (2007b, 115; *EDR* 4:§6.6.3).
94. Brunner (1950, 287–88).
95. Regarding this, see Ouweneel (2008a, §§1.2, 1.3; 2014).
96. Bavinck (*RD* 2:250–51); the English translation uses the word "blessed(ness)" for this attribute.

ternal disturbance. In this sense, eternal life is eternal bliss, both for God and for believers (cf. John 17:3).

(2) God knows his absolute perfection and loves it. There is no perfect bliss without perfect knowledge and perfect love.

(3) God enjoys himself, and in himself, he rests in himself, is sufficient in himself, and all of this in an absolute sense. It is eternal peace.

This description is good as it stands, but I have little appreciation for Bavinck's scholastic assertion that God "eternally loves himself with divine love."[97] This is more neo-Platonic than Christian.[98] Where we can speak of God's love only in an approximate way (not in a conceptual way), the highest criterion for love is not "self-love"—Bavinck followed Augustine[99] in using this expression with respect to God[100]—but love for others.

We can easily go beyond Scripture here, unless we take the Trinity into account. Then self-love no longer comes to the fore but love toward the Other, even if the Other is an intra-Trinitarian Other. Thus, God's eternal, perfect bliss, including his eternal, perfect love, is understood as the love *between* divine persons,[101] the bliss of undisturbed, peaceful, harmonious, happy fellowship. Rather than speaking of "self-love," we are thereby helped to see the wonder of God's bliss in the Father's eternal love for the Son from before the foundation of the world (John 17:24), and conversely, there is the eternal love of the Son for the Father, connected with the love of the Spirit (Rom. 15:30).

3.10 God's glory
3.10.1 Displayed Beauty
God's glory is also very important for soteriology be-

---

97. Bavinck (*RD* 2:232).
98. Althaus (1952, 297).
99. De Trinitate IX.2.
100. Bavinck (*RD* 2:232).
101. Cf. Ouweneel (2007b, 80, 278).

cause Scripture promises believers "an eternal weight of glory beyond all comparison" (2 Cor. 4:17). The gospel is about the bliss of God (§3.9) but also about "the light of the knowledge of the glory of God in the face of Jesus Christ" (cf. v. 4, "the light of the gospel of the glory of Christ, who is the image of God"). Regarding the New Jerusalem, which is the bride of the Lamb (Rev. 21:9), we are told that it has "the glory of God" (v. 11). Heav-en, where Jesus is and where he expects his people to be with him as well (John 17:24), is filled with the glory of God (Acts 7:55). Please note, this does not mean that a place itself (a city, heaven) can have glory; only God has glory. The New Jerusalem and heaven have glory be-cause God fills them with his glory.

Human beings by nature *fall short* of the glory of God (Rom. 3:23), whereas redeemed people *inherit* the glory of God: "[W]e rejoice in hope of the glory of God" (5:2); "if children, then heirs—heirs of God and fellow heirs with Christ, provided we suffer with him in order that we may also be glorified with him" (8:17); "those whom he justified he also glorified" (v. 30).

Traditional dogmatics tells us that God's perfection is the intrinsic ground for his bliss (§3.9), and entails his glory.[102] I would describe glory as the displayed excellency of God; as Psalm 145:5 puts it, "the glorious splendor [lit., glory of the splendor] of your majesty" (cf. Isa. 2:10, 19, 21). This element of display is essential for the notion of God's glory; among other things, it implies that, since there are creatures, God's glory is *observed*; his glory "shines" (Luke 2:9; John 1:4–5, 14; 2 Cor. 4:4, 6).[103] In other words, God's glory is related to the fact that he is called "light" (1 John 1:5), which refers to his shining splendor, brilliance, luster, majesty, brightness, and re-

---

102. See Bavinck (*RD* 2:252); a standard work is still Von Gall (1900); cf. Barth (*CD* 2/1=8, §29, 66; =9, §31.3:209–47).
103. Cf. Althaus (1952, 293–94).

splendence.

One way to put it is to speak of God's beauty. In Exodus 33:18-19, the glory of YHWH reveals itself in his "goodness" (Heb. *tub* or *tuv*), which here has the sense of "beauty."[104] Zechariah says, "[H]ow great is his [i.e., God's] goodness [Heb. *tub*], and how great his beauty [Heb. *dagan*]" (9:17).[105] Another Hebrew term with the meaning of "beauty" is *noʿam*, which means "loveliness" and is used for God in Psalm 27:4 and 90:17. A reference to God's beauty is found in Exodus 24:10, in the collateral phenomenon of "a pavement of sapphire stone" under God's feet, "like the very heaven for clearness."

Augustine liked to speak of the "beauty of God" (Lat. *pulchritudo Dei*); he called God the highest beauty because in his being there is absolute oneness, measure, and order;[106] in short: God is harmony. God is "the most beautiful thing/matter/entity there is" (Ger. *das Schönste*), as is sung in the hymn "The Golden Sun" (Ger. *Die güldne Sonne*) of the German Pietist poet Paul Gerhardi: "God is the greatest, the most beautiful, the best there is, the sweetest, the surest, of all riches the most noble treasure."[107] A modern song by Tim Hughes says, "How glorious, how beautiful you are! Beautiful One I love, Beautiful One I adore."

B Wentsel emphasized the beauty of God, and pleaded for a corresponding aesthetics of worship (cf. Phil. 4:8, "whatever is lovely, whatever is commendable, if there is any excellence, if there is anything worthy of praise, think about these things").[108] Christians are

---

104. For Heb. *tob*, "good," in the sense of "beautiful," see Exod.2:2; Judg. 15:2; 1 Sam. 16:12; 1 Kings 1:6; Dan. 1:4.
105. Expositors differ about whether God's beauty or Israel's beauty is meant here.
106. *De ordine* I. 26; II. 51; *De beata vita* 34; *Contra Academia* II.9; cf. Bavinck (*RD* 2:254).
107. Brunner (1950, 287-88) had scarcely any appreciation for this notion.
108. Wentsel (1987, 464-67).

called to be beautiful because God is beautiful. The music and the poetry of their worship must be beautiful because God's beauty deserves it. Although it may not be very common to speak of beauty in regard to salvation, if God is beautiful, the beauty of his being is manifested also in his plan of salvation. Those who are saved are brought into a domain of many blessings—they are also led into the greatest *beauty*.

3.10.2 Glory and Light

The glory of which we are speaking here is the glory of God's being; it is God himself.[109] God *is* light. In Psalm 102:15 and Isaiah 59:16, we find parallelism between the glory of the Lord and his person or his name. In the Old Testament, the Hebrew phrase *kabod* YHWH refers to the glory of God that comes to expression when he reveals himself in an exceptionally impressive way.[110] This may be in a thunderstorm, as suggested by Psalms 29 and 94 (cf. Job 37:2–5; 38:1). In Exodus 24:15–16, the glory of the Lord is like a consuming fire in a cloud on a mountain (cf. 19:16). Although the term "glory" is not mentioned in Judges 5:4–5, we see there how the appearance of the Lord is linked with a trembling earth, dropping clouds, and quaking mountains. In Ezekiel 1, God's glory becomes visible in storm, cloud, fire, lightning, and the sound of raging water (for the cloud see vv. 26–28; 10:4, 18; 11:22–23; 40:34–35; 43:2–5).

Of course, this never implies that the thunderstorm *is* the glory of YHWH. He cannot be compared with a pagan god of thunder (Baal, Bel/Marduk, Zeus/Jupiter, Donar/Thor), whose being more or less coincides with the thunder, or is the embodiment of thunder (or should we say, the thunder is the embodiment of the god?). God *reveals* himself sometimes in thunder and lightning, but on other occasions the glory of God reveals itself

---

109. See extensively, Ouweneel (*EDR* 2:293–96).
110. *TDNT* 2:238–39.

Salvation and God's Being

precisely *not* in storm wind, earthquake and fire but in "the sound of a low whisper" (1 Kings 19:11-12).

Isaiah describes the glory of the LORD as a light that breaks through like dawn, which clearly refers to the sun (58:8; 60:1-2; cf. Mal. 4:2). This image returns in the New Testament with regard to Christ: "[H]is face shone like the sun" (Matt. 17:2); "a light from heaven, brighter than the sun, that shone around me" (Acts 26:13); "his face was like the sun shining in full strength" (Rev. 1:16). The technical term for "glory" here is the Greek word *doxa*, derived from *dokeō*, "to seem," here with the special meaning—found rarely in secular Greek but found often in Flavius Josephus—of "radiance," "luster," "effulgence."[111] With respect to God it is more specifically "divine and heavenly radiance," the "luster" or "splendor" of God.[112] God is the "God of glory" (Acts 7:2; cf. v. 55; 2 Thess. 1:9). The word occurs many times; these are only a few passages that shed light on its special meaning.[113]

Of primary importance are the associations with light, as in the expression "the glory of that light" (of the appearance of the glorified Jesus; Acts 22:11 KJV). It is the glory of God that "gives light" to the New Jerusalem, "and its lamp is the Lamb" (Rev. 21:23). The Son is the "radiance [Gk. *apaugasma*] of the glory of God" (Heb. 1:3). The "Majestic Glory" of 2 Peter 1:17 is that of the "bright cloud" (Matt. 17:5), reminding us of the pillar of cloud in the Old Testament. In Revelation 15:8, the heavenly temple "was filled with smoke from the glory of God and from his power," that is, the smoke of the

---

111. The Dutch verb *schijnen* and the German verb *scheinen*) can mean both "to seem" and to shine."
112. In the discussion found in *TDNT* 2:237 and 247, we find lan guage—more Greek than biblical—about God's "(mode of) being."
113. Cf. Danker (2000, s.v. *dokeō* and *doxa*). It is striking that the original meanings of both Heb. *kabod* ("weight") and Gk. *doxa* ("opinion"; cf. the related word "dogma") are far removed from the notion of "glory."

judgment to be poured out on the earth by God's glory (cf. 9:2; 14:11; Ps. 18:7-9; Isa. 6:3-4). But this smoke also reminds us again of the cloud that filled the tabernacle (Exod. 40:34-35) and the temple (1 Kings 8:10-11).

3.10.3 Glory and Salvation

One of the most significant descriptions of salvation might be this one: salvation involves the paradoxical access to a glory that is actually inaccessible; it consists of dwelling in the light of God himself. As Jesus said, "Father, I desire that they also, whom you have given me, may be with me where I am, to see my glory that you have given me" (John 17:24; cf. Rev. 21:23; 22:5). We find this paradox in several passages: Paul speaks of God "who alone has immortality, who dwells in unapproachable light, whom no one has ever seen or can see" (1 Tim. 6:16), but also: "[N]ow we see in a mirror dimly, but then face to face" (1 Cor. 13:12); and Jesus says, "Blessed are the pure in heart, for they shall see God" (Matt. 5:8); and Isaiah, "They shall see the glory of the LORD, the majesty of our God" (Isa. 35:2).

Paul also paradoxically speaks about knowing "the love of Christ that surpasses knowledge" (Eph. 3:19). In the senses just described, salvation is inaccessible and inexpressible and unknowable—and is yet accessed and expressed and known. This is the redemptive wonder of God. At the Fall, the door to Paradise was closed (Gen. 3:22-24). In the realization of salvation, the door is opened again—to an indescribably more glorious Paradise than Adam lost: ". . . access by faith into this grace in which we stand, and we rejoice in hope of the glory of God" (Rom. 5:2); ". . . access in one Spirit to the Father" (Eph. 2:18; cf. 3:12).

It is understandable that many have speculated about the inaccessible und inexpressible.[114] Rabbinic tradition considered the *kabod* YHWH to be a *created*, visible radi-

---
114. Bavinck (*RD* 2:253-54).

ance, a "body of light," through which God made known his presence within creation. This idea was adopted in theosophy (by Jakob Boehme). In 1493, the Eastern Orthodox Church accepted the doctrine of an uncreated, divine light, distinct from God's being, without explaining how something could be uncreated without being essentially divine. Early Lutheran theology speculated about whether God is light in a factual or in a figurative sense, apparently without realizing that *all* speaking about light in connection with God is necessarily metaphorical. God *is* light (1 John 1:5), although what is said about God here can be approximated only with the aid of creaturely terms, in this case: physical light. These terms are not used here as concepts, in which we logically *enclose* a matter, but as ideas, with which we logically *approximate* a matter.[115]

The proximity of this to the idea of literal physical light can be seen in Psalm 104:1-2:

"You are clothed with splendor and majesty, covering yourself with light as with a garment." This is light that might blind a person (Acts 9:3, 8-9); it might even consume him (cf. 1 Tim. 6:16; Exod. 3:6; 33:20; Judg. 6:22-23; 13:22; Isa. 6:5; 1 John 4:12). The highest salvation entails this wonderful paradox: the contemplation of a glory that cannot be contemplated. This glory is consuming, yet does not consume the believer. It is blinding, yet does not blind him. It is inaccessible, yet he enters it. It is infinite, yet opens itself for finite creatures.

3.11 God's Invisibility
3.11.1 Mediated Vision

Finally, we investigate how God's glory—his *displayed* excellencies—relates to what Scripture teaches about God's invisibility: "No one has ever seen God" (John 1:18; cf. 6:46; 1 John 4:12; cf. v. 20); God's "invisible at-

---

115. See again Ouweneel (*EDR* 3:§1.2, 1.3; 2016); cf. also Brümmer (2005, 18, 30).

tributes, namely, his eternal power and divine nature" (Rom. 1:20); "the invisible God" (Col. 1:15; cf. 1 Tim. 1:17; Heb. 11:27). This invisibility finds its counterpart in the contemplation of God (Lat. *visio Dei*) by believers, to some extent even here on earth, and ultimately in the heavenly state of glory (Lat. *status gloriae*).

An important question, which occupied traditional theology with intensity, is the nature of the earthly *visio Dei*, as occurred with the elders of Israel (Exod. 24:10-11), Moses (33:23), Isaiah (6:1), Ezekiel (1:26-28), Daniel (7:9), Stephen (Acts 7:55), the apostle John (Rev. 4:2-3), and possibly Paul (2 Cor. 12:2). The great majority of theologians believed that this was a mediated *visio*, that is, in a form in which the glory of God was veiled.[116] This is understandable: "revelation" is not only *taking away* a veil (Gk. *apokalypsis*), but in another sense also *assuming* a veil, putting on a physical covering, through which human beings—physical beings—can come to know God.[117] Even as the "revealed God" (Lat. *Deus revelatus*), God remains in a certain sense the "concealed God" (Lat. *Deus absconditus*), as Martin Luther put it.[118] God's revelation always occurs within human experience, and with (physical) means that are suited to the created cosmos.

God's Word always needs a "revelational carrier" (Ger. *Offenbarungsträger*), to use Gerhard Ebeling's phrase.[119] This is what Karl Barth called the "worldliness" (Ger. *Welthaftigkeit*) or creational character of revelation.[120] Even with the most direct (immediate) revelation, like God speaking with Moses "face to face" (Exod. 33:11; Num. 7:89; 12:8; Deut. 34:10), this speaking necessarily covers itself in the form of a human voice in order

---

116. Cf. Bavinck (*RD* 2:188).
117. See Ouweneel (1993, 226).
118. Cf. Ebeling (1979, 256).
119. Ibid., 250.
120. Barth (*CD* 1/1=1, §5.4:178-83).

to be audible to Moses. We see this clearly illustrated in 1 Samuel 3:4-9, where Samuel confuses the voice of the LORD with the voice of Eli.[121]

Please note that we are speaking here of the glory of God's *being*, and of whether believers will see this glory in the *eschaton*. In other senses, seeing God's glory is no issue at all, namely, seeing God's glory as it comes to light in his works: "The heavens declare the glory of God" (Ps. 19:1). God's "invisible attributes, namely, his eternal power and divine nature, have been *clearly perceived*, ever since the creation of the world, in the things that have been made" (Rom. 1:20). Jesus said to Martha at the tomb of Lazarus, "Did I not tell you that if you believed you would *see the glory of God?*" (John 11:40), namely, in the imminent resurrection of Lazarus. We see God's glory in his works, and thus in a *derived* sense; but this is quite different from seeing God's *intrinsic* glory, the glory of his *being*.

3.11.2 Immediate Vision?

Will there be a real, *im*-mediate contemplation of God according to his being (Lat. *visio Dei per essentiam*) in the heavenly bliss. Herman Bavinck discussed the various views of this matter.[122] The Lutherans were inclined to assume such a *visio*, not only with the mind (Lat. *mentalis*) but also with the eyes of the renewed body (Lat. *corporalis*). Most Reformed theologians, however, rejected this idea on the basis of Ephesians 3:19 ("the love of Christ that surpasses knowledge") and Philippians 4:7 ("the peace of God, which surpasses all understanding"). If the love of Christ and the peace of God surpass all comprehension, will not a *visio per essentiam*, which *is* a form of comprehension, lie beyond the reach of believers? God is infinite, and human beings remain finite, even in glory. Therefore, this contemplation, even when

---

121. Cf. Berkhof (1986, 48-49).
122. Bavinck (*RD* 2:187-91).

in eternity humans to some extent behold God's infinite glory, will remain finite.[123]

I would state the matter this way: if a *visio Dei per essentiam* were possible in heavenly glory, then human beings would be able to observe in supernatural categories. This would imply that human beings themselves would surpass creaturely boundaries, and thus would become divine. If human beings will eternally remain creatures—even slaves (Rev. 22:3 HCSB)—then God can never be known in any other way than in creaturely categories, no matter how much more perfectly than today. Paul says that God "dwells in unapproachable light, whom no one has ever seen or can see" (1 Tim. 6:16). What basis do we have for saying that this will no longer be the case with *glorified* human beings? If God reveals himself to believers on earth in a mediated way, how do we know this will be different in eternity?

I wonder if our contemplation of God will ever extend any further than what Jesus himself said, "Whoever has seen me has seen the Father" (John 14:9). In other words, will believers ever see the Father apart from the Son, that is, the Son as the incarnate Man Jesus Christ? Now already, the fullness of deity dwells in him bodily (Col. 2:9), that is, the fullness of the Trinity dwells in the body of the glorified Man Jesus Christ, who is the Son himself. So will we ever see the Godhead *apart from* its full manifestation in the *body* of the incarnate Son? Compare this with John's statement: "[W]e shall see him as he is" (1 John 3:2). This "he" is God—but then the God who will "appear" (same verse), that is, as the incarnate and glorified Son. "[W]e shall be like him"—but this can only be said of the Son as the One who is now the glorified Man in heaven, the "firstborn among many brothers" (Rom. 8:29).

One more point. Compare here John 17:22, where Jesus speaks of glory that the Father had *given* him, and

---

123. Cf. Heyns (1988, 63).

that he gave to (shared with) the believers. But in verse 24, we read of a glory of Jesus that believers will "see" but apparently not share.

By way of summary, the Bible teaches us about three kinds of glory.

(a) *A glory not seen, not shared.* There is the purely divine glory of the eternal Son in the bosom of the Father that, just like the intrinsic glory of the Trinity, cannot be perceived by believers, leave alone be shared. There is no divine glory seen apart from the Son, the glorified Man in heaven.

(b) *A glory seen, but not shared.* There is a *given* glory of the Son as the glorified *Man* in heaven that can be seen by believers, but at the same time surpasses their own glory (as, e.g., they are kings, but he is the King of kings; they are priests, but he is the high priest; they are the members of the body, but he is the head; etc.) (John 17:24).

(c) *A glory seen as well as shared.* There is a *given* glory of the Son as the glorified *Man* in heaven that can be seen by believers, and can be shared by them; this is what John 17:22 and 1 John 3:2 refer to (cf. other important passages: Rom. 8:29; Phil. 3:21; Col. 3:4; 2 Thess. 1:10).

3.11.3 More on the Trinity

Again, my thesis is that there is no divine glory contemplated by human beings apart from the Son, the glorified Man in heaven. Believers have been *saved* by this person, and can now contemplate God, but only through this very same Savior. Let me underscore this with three references to the Old Testament, without entering more deeply into the mysteries of the Trinity.[124]

First, in Isaiah 6 we find a vision of the prophet Isaiah in which he saw the glory of YHWH. Too many Chris-

---

124. See extensively, Ouweneel (2007b, chapter 2).

tians think too easily that YHWH and the Father are more or less identical, instead of realizing that the name YHWH necessarily stands for the Trinity. When the apostle John refers to Isaiah's vision, he tells us that the prophet beheld the glory of *Christ* (John 12:41). Where God reveals himself, already in the Old Testament, the person of the Godhead that comes to the fore is apparently the Son, that is, the pre-incarnate Christ (that is, through the Holy Spirit; cf. Acts 28:25–27).

Second, quite remarkable is what the prophet Ezekiel tells us after he had arrived at the summit of the description of his heavenly vision:

> And above the expanse over their heads there was the likeness of a throne, in appearance like sapphire; and seated above the likeness of a throne was a likeness with a *human* appearance. . . . Like the appearance of the bow that is in the cloud on the day of rain, so was the appearance of the brightness all around. Such was the appearance of the likeness of the glory of the LORD (Ezek. 1:26, 28).

The prophet saw the glory of YHWH in the form of a *man*, which I understand to mean in the form of the pre-incarnate Christ, and, by way of anticipation, in the form of the glorified *Man* Jesus Christ.[125]

Third, Daniel 7 seems to distinguish clearly between the Ancient of Days (God) and the Son of Man (v. 13).[126] However, at that point in the text when we expect to hear further about the coming of the Son of Man on the clouds of heaven we read, "As I looked, this horn made war with the saints and prevailed over them, until *the Ancient of Days came*, and judgment was given for the saints of the Most High, and the time came when the saints possessed the kingdom" (vv. 21–22). And what

---

125. Cf. Grant and Bloore (1931, 22–23); Gaebelein (1972, 21).
126. I am using the uppercase ("Son of *Man*") because of the use of this verse in Matt. 24:30, 26:64, Mark 13:26, 14:62, and Luke 21:27.

is even more striking, in Revelation 1:14–15 the Son of Man is described in terms of features that in Daniel 7:9 are attributed to the Ancient of Days (whiteness like that of snow and wool; fiery flames). Here again, God and the glorified Son of Man seem to merge in a mysterious way.[127]

We get the strong impression that, wherever and whenever God reveals himself, it is in and through either the pre-incarnate or the incarnate Christ, that is, the *Logos* (this term denoting an inner mystery coming to a [verbal] expression): "the Word was *with* God," as the expression (revelation, manifestation) of him, and he could be such in a perfect way because "the Word *was* God" (John 1:1). If this principle is true both before and after the incarnation, why would it not be the case in the *status gloriae*? Christ is the One who, through his redemptive work, brings believers to God (1 Pet. 3:18)—the Triune God. The *Man* Christ Jesus brings us to the Father, the Son and the Holy Spirit, at the same himself being in person the Son.

It pleased *God*—not "the Father" (KJV) but the Triune Godhead—that in the Man Christ the fullness of the Godhead would dwell, and still *bodily* dwells (Col. 1:19; 2:9), this Christ being himself the Son. It is not the Father who, in the eternal state, is "all in all" but the Triune *God* (1 Cor. 15:28). Jesus Christ is the One in and through whom alone the Triune God reveals himself, and who is himself one of the three persons: the Son. It is he who brings us to God—and when, one day, believers will behold this God, it will still be this Christ *in* and *through* whom they will behold God. For not only is it true that whoever has seen him has seen the Father (John 14:9), but there is no *other* way to see the Father.

---

127. See Ouweneel (1988, 155).

Chapter 4
Old Testament Sacrifices

*T]he life of the flesh is in the blood,
and I have given it for you on the altar
to make atonement for your souls,
for it is the blood that makes atonement by the life.*
Leviticus 17:11

*Indeed, under the law almost everything is purified with blood,
and without the shedding of blood
there is no forgiveness of sins.*
Hebrews 9:22

Summary: *The sacrifice of Christ cannot possibly be understood without some knowledge of the Old Testament sacrifices, of which Christ's sacrifice was the divine fulfillment. Of central importance is the notion of atonement, in which we notice the elements of propitiation and reconciliation. Atonement is brought about by a sacrifice, whose blood "covers" (blots out) the sins committed by the offerer(s). The blood is the key element. The blood takes away the wrath of God; at the same time, it is God himself who supplied the sacrificial ministry, and ultimately even his own Son.*

To approximate the significance of Christ's sacrifice, no less than four bloody offerings are prescribed in Leviticus. First, the burnt offering (with the grain offering belonging to it) makes the offerer acceptable in God's eyes. Second, the peace offering (re-)establishes fellowship between God and his people, and between people and people. Third, the sin offering takes away (blots out) specific sins (the role of the priest is very important here). Fourth, the guilt offering repairs certain guilt, both toward the neighbor and toward God.

4.1 The Notion of Atonement
4.1.1 Root Meaning of Atonement

AFTER THREE CHAPTERS of a more introductory nature with respect to the field of soteriology, we are now prepared to discuss the atoning sacrifice of Christ. As happens so often, we must begin by resolving some terminological problems that have often blurred the discussion. We are going to use the term "atonement," but we notice immediately that in the ESV this term occurs only in the Old Testament. In the KJV, it only occurs in Romans 5:11, ". . . our Lord Jesus Christ, by whom we have now received the atonement." Other translations, including the NKJV, use the term "reconciliation" (Gk. *katallagē*) here. Indeed, this latter term is the closest in meaning to "atonement," a word that was derived from "at-one-ment," being "at one," bringing parties to agreement with each other, "reconcile" (people and people, and people and God). However, in the Old Testament, the term "atonement" renders the root *kpr* and its cognates (see §4.1.2), which means something closer to "propitiation" (a term found in the ESV in Rom. 3:25; Heb. 2:17; 1 John 2:2; 4:10). One of the tasks of the present sections is to clearly differentiate between reconciliation (Gk. *katallagē*) and propitiation (Gk. root *hilask*).

The need for this differentiating—and fortunately it has often been done before—is evident from the fact that in the KJV these terms are sometimes confused. A quite disturbing example is Hebrews 2:17, where the KJV speaks about Jesus as the "merciful and faithful high priest in things pertaining to God, to make *reconciliation* for [Gk. *hilaskesthai*] the sins of the people." For this word, the NKJV has rightly substituted the term "propitiation." In the Old Testament as well, the KJV sometimes reads "reconcile" where "propitiate" is meant (e.g., Lev. 6:30; 8:15; 16:20). Thus, although the root meaning of "atonement" reminds us more of reconciliation than of propitiation, we must keep in mind that in the Old Testament "atonement" usually has the sense of "propitiation."[1]

One may regret this confusion about such very different matters: reconciliation and propitiation. Yet, it is also important to emphasize that the two terms are closely related, since both tell us something of the way God solves the problem of sin.[2] Reconciliation pertains to the *sinner*, who must be brought back into harmony with God; propitiation pertains to *sin*, which must be blotted out. Although the two are clearly distinct, the one does not occur without the other. It is futile to blot out the sinner's sin if they are not simultaneously brought back to God. And it is futile to reconcile the sinner with God if the person's sins have not been taken away. This is nicely illustrated by Romans 3:25, Christ being the One "whom God put forward as a propitiation by his blood." The word that Paul uses here for "propitiation" (Gk. *hilastērion*) is the word used in various Septuagint passages for the "mercy seat" (DRA; WYC: "propitiatory"), the cover of the ark that stood in the tabernacle, and lat-

---

1. Dutch has its own terminological problems: the word *verzoening* means both "propitiation" and "reconciliation." German distinguishes between *Sühnung* and *Versöhnung*, but these terms obviously have the same root. Bolkestein (1945, 45) suggested using *zoening* for the former meaning, but this proposal has not found acceptance.
2. Berkouwer (1965, 263).

er in the temple. This propitiatory (Heb. *kapporet*) was the place of propitiation because of the sprinkled blood for blotting out sins. However, since the ark was the center of the "tent of *meeting*," it was also the place of encounter between God and his people (Exod. 29:42-43) (reconciliation). Paul calls Christ the personal *hilastērion* because he blots out the sins of his people *and* facilitates their encounter with God again in peace (cf. Rom. 5:1, 10).

In summary, we must keep the meanings distinct: it is linguistically and theologically incorrect to say that Jesus made propitiation between God and believers, or that Jesus reconciled our sins. Yet, the meanings are closely related. As Karl Barth said about Christ as the propitiatory (the Old Testament point of meeting between God and human beings),

> The life of Jesus is the place in history fitted by God for propitiation and fraught with eternity— .... At this place [i.e., Christ, i.e., the propitiatory] the Kingdom of God has come nigh: ... so near, that here God dwells with men and His communing is unmistakable [cf. Rev. 21:3]; ...., God's speaking with them [cf. Exod. 29:42; Num. 7:89], God's will to appeal to the world to come home, in his peace, cannot possibly be ignored.[3]

It is one act of God in Christ to *reconcile* the world with himself (2 Cor. 5:19) as well as to send Christ as the *propitiation* for our sins (1 John 4:10). In one word, this is what *atonement* is all about, as we will extensively consider in this and following chapters.

4.1.2 Old Testament Atonement

One of the key statements for any Christian soteriology is that it is impossible to understand the New Testament doctrine of atonement without sufficient knowledge of

---

3. Barth (1976, 105).

the Old Testament principles of atonement. As A. van de Beek wrote, "[W]ithout the ceremonial laws we will never understand Christ. Probably the reason why we have so much difficulty with the New Testament Christology and atonement doctrine is that we are not steeped in the Torah and the theological exegesis of it, like the authors of those writings were."[4] The book of Hebrews in particular endeavors to explain the New Testament atonement from the Old Testament, especially from the various aspects of the Day of Atonement (Heb. *Yom hak-Kippurim;* in current vernacular: *Yom Kippur*). We will have difficulty understanding the message of Hebrews if we are not familiar with the details of the Day of Atonement rituals.

In the Hebrew expression *Yom Kippur*, we encounter the Hebrew root that we wish to discuss first.[5] The Hebrew word *kippur* comes from the root *k-p-r*, of which the *qal*[6] has the basic meaning of "to cover, to paint." The *qal* form occurs only in Genesis 6:14, where "to cover with pitch" is the Hebrew *kapharta bakkopher*; the word *kopher*, "pitch, bitumen, tar," probably comes from *k-p-r*, although some think set of consonants belongs to two different roots. In the great majority of cases, the root occurs in the *piel* form (Heb. *kipper*), usually in passages in Exodus, Leviticus, and Numbers that deal with the sacrificial and priestly ministry. In some passages, the basic meaning of "covering" comes through:

---

4. Van de Beek (2002, 276); see also J. Vlaardingerbroek in Elsinga (1998, chapter 2).
5. See *TDNT* 3:302-310, *DOTT* 2:689-712, Pop (1999, 498-505), and the standard lexica. See these sources for the complex question whether a single root or multiple roots have provided the various meanings of *k-p-r*: (a) "to cover," (b) "to ransom," and (c) "to blot out," meanings that are not necessarily mutually exclusive; cf. Wenham (1979, 27-28); Harris (1990, 538).
6. The *qal* is the common form of the Hebrew verb, the *niphal* is the passive form, the *hiphil* is the causative form, the *piel* is the intensive form, and the *pual* is the passive intensive form; the *hithpael* has several meaning aspects.

"I [i.e., Jacob] may *appease* him [i.e., Esau] with the present that goes ahead of me" (Gen. 32:20; lit., cover his face, i.e., pacify him [NIV], make him friendly [CEV], some even: propitiate him [DARBY, EXB]). See Proverbs 16:14 as well: "A king's wrath is a messenger of death, and a wise man will appease [pacify, calm down] it/him [i.e., cover the wrath, blot it out]." However, with regard to God we never find this notion of the *placation*, that is, appeasing the wrath of God (pacifying God, calming, soothing, placating, or mollifying him, mitigating his wrath). See §§9.3–9.4 on this important subject.

4.1.3 "Covering, Blotting Out"

In Isaiah 28:18, the root meaning of *k-p-r* (here the *pual*, Heb. *kippur*), "to cover, to blot out," clearly comes to light: "Then your covenant with death will be annulled [erased, dissolved, abolished, wiped away, canceled]." Here, and at many other places, it is obvious that *k-p-r*, as has been alleged,[7] does *not* mean "to cover" in the sense of "to cover over," as if, when the cover is removed, the sin would come to light again. The mistaken idea here is that the sins were temporarily covered over until the actual and definitive atonement by Christ. Thus, Pentecostal Bible teacher Derek Prince suggested that the Day of Atonement was a day of covering. Through the sacrifices that were offered on that day, the sins of the people were covered—but only for a year. Exactly a year later, on the same day, their sins had to be covered again. Thus, the sacrifices that were brought on that day did not offer a lasting solution to the problem of sin; they provided only a temporary coverage.[8]

Pentecostal theologians Duffield and Van Cleave similarly argued that believers receive in Christ more than a covering of their sins. In him these sins are forgiven, and thus completely blotted out. The blood of the sacri-

---

7. E.g., Harris (1990, 538) refers to this error.
8. Prince (2001, 13–14).

ficial animals was sufficient to cover the sins of the people only as long as Christ had not come in order by his blood not only to cover them but also to blot them out entirely.[9]

Of course, if the authors mean to say that the blood of bulls and goats in itself cannot remove sins, they are right (Heb. 10:4). On the Day of Atonement, "there is a reminder of sins every year" in the sacrifices (v. 3). Animal blood *as such* cannot blot out sins. But this has nothing to do with the root meaning of *k-p-r*, as if this would "only" mean "to cover," and *therefore* not "to atone." In Isaiah 28:18 the word does mean "to cover" in the sense of "to annul, erase, dissolve, abolish, wipe away, cancel." The Greek words (derived from the root *hilask-*), which in the New Testament mean "to propitiate," are used in the Septuagint to render the Hebrew root *k-p-r*. The meaning is "to blot out," "to annul," *so that what is "covered" no longer exists*. The quoted authors confuse two things: the ineffectiveness of animal blood and the root meaning of *k-p-r*, whereby they confuse theological and linguistic categories. Victor Cole saw it more sharply: Christ's atoning blood provides the ultimate covering that is needed to blot out our sins, and give satisfaction to God (Heb. 10:4, 10, 15–16).[10]

In Exodus 32:20, the expression "make atonement for your sin" literally means "cover your sin" (cf. CEV, "keep this sin from being held against you"). Thus, in 2 Samuel 21:3, "make atonement" literally means "cover" in the sense of "make good" (AMP), "make amends" (LEB), "make up for the harm done" (EXB; NCV), or also "take away Israel's sin" (ICB). In all these cases, it might be wise to avoid the word "atone(ment)" because no sin offering is involved (cf. §6.5). This is even clearer in passages such as: "[D]isaster shall fall upon you, for which you will not be able to atone" (Isa. 47:11), where, instead

---

9. Duffield and Van Cleave (1996, 200).
10. V. B. Cole in Adeyemo (2008, 139).

of "atone," we should instead read, "put off" (KJV), "turn aside" (CJB).

In the notion of *k-p-r* in the Old Testament, the basic issue is always one of finding a way to cover sin in the sense of putting it away, warding it off, making up for it, or also: no longer reckoning sin to the sinner. The latter meaning is found, for instance, in Ezekiel 16:63, ". . . when I atone for you for all that you have done." Recall the even clearer case of murder by an unknown killer: "Accept atonement, O LORD, for your people Israel, whom you have redeemed, and do not set the guilt of innocent blood in the midst of your people Israel" (Deut. 21:8). This is atonement without a true sin offering, simply because there is no ascertainable guilt. The meaning is simply: do not impute the shed blood to your innocent people.

If there *is* ascertainable guilt, the situation is totally different; in this case, a "cleansing from sin" is needed. Basically, this can occur only through forgiveness of God's people on the basis of an atoning sacrifice, as we will see at length. At this point, notice the other manner of cleansing, namely, revenge on the enemies of his people: "He will avenge the blood of His servants, and render vengeance to His adversaries; He will provide atonement for His land [and] His people" (Deut. 32:43 NKJV), that is, "cleanse his people's land" (ESV). This aspect, too, comes to light in the atoning work of Christ: not only is the sin "covered" (i.e., blotted out) but vengeance is executed upon the *power* of sin and upon Satan, so that they are destroyed.

4.2   Atonement Through a Sacrifice
4.2.1 The Sacrificial Blood Effects Atonement

In the great majority of cases, *k-p-r* occurs in connection with a *sacrifice* that brings about the atonement (the covering, i.e., blotting out of sin). In Daniel 9:24, "to atone for iniquity" is more literally "to cover [and thus blot out] iniquity." The same occurs in, for instance, Psalm 65:3 ("you atone for our transgressions") and 78:38 ("he ... atoned for their iniquity and did not destroy them"). In all three cases, this must be taken to mean that God covers (i.e., blots out) sins through a sacrifice. The need for such a sacrifice comes to light in this painfully negative sentence: "[T]he iniquity of Eli's house shall not be atoned[11] for by sacrifice [Heb. *zēbach*] or offering [Heb. *minchah*] forever" (1 Sam. 3:14). The Hebrew word *minchah* probably has the broader meaning here of "offering" in general (see note 27 and §4.4.4).

A very extensive description of the principle of sacrificial atonement is found in Leviticus 19:22, "And the priest shall make atonement for him [i.e., the guilty person] with the ram of the guilt offering before the LORD for his sin that he has committed, and he shall be forgiven for the sin that he has committed." Here we find (a) an animal sacrifice, in this case a guilt offering (see §§4.3.1 and 4.7), (b) the "making atonement [one word: *k-p-r*] for" the sins committed, (c) the LORD, against whom the guilty person has sinned and for whom the atonement is necessary, and (d) the forgiveness that is possible on the basis of the atoning sacrifice.

The essential element of the atoning sacrifice is the shedding of blood:[12] "[T]he life of the flesh is in the blood, and I have given it for you on the altar to make atonement for your souls, for it is the blood that makes atonement by the life" (Lev. 17:11). Here the Hebrew word for "life" is *nephesh*, traditionally rendered "soul," the vital power of the animal. It is thought to reside in the blood for the simple reason that, when the blood has flowed out of the animal, the animal is dead. Compare verse 14: "[T]he life [*nephesh*] of every creature [lit., of all flesh] is its blood" (cf. Deut. 12:23). The blood, as the

---

11. Here we find the *hithpael* form: *yitkappēr*.
12. For the meaning of this, see extensively, Morris (1955, chapter 3).

vital power, effects atonement in the following way: sacrificing the life of an innocent sacrificial animal brings about the restoration of the guilty person's life by blotting out (covering) the latter's guilt. The vicarious death of the sacrificial animal saves the sinner from death.[13]

Normally, a person themselves must bear the consequences of their sin, as Numbers 35:33 makes clear: "[B]lood pollutes the land, and no atonement can be made for the land for the blood that is shed in it, except by the blood of the one who shed it." Shedding the blood of the guilty person annuls the desecration of the land. If the slayer has shed blood by accident, they must still stay in the "city of refuge" (vv. 13–15) to save the land from desecration as a consequence of the killing. Timothy Ashley added to this the remarkable thought that it was the death of the high priest that atoned for the shed blood, and blotted out the guilt (cf. vv. 25, 28).[14] He presumed that behind this is the principle of Genesis 9:6: shed human blood can only be atoned for by shed human blood. However, Numbers 35 refers only to the death of the high priest, not to his shed blood. I can find no reference in the text that the high priest's death has any atoning meaning. Moreover, Genesis 9 is not about atonement but about vengeance.

In my view, Jewish expositor Rabbi Shlomo Yitzhaki (Rashi) made it even worse by assigning part of the guilt for the bloodshed to the high priest: the latter should have prevented the manslaughter by his prayers.[15] Much better is the explanation of A. Noordtzij, who denied that the death of the high priest had any atoning effect.[16] In his view, the manslayer had to stay in the city of refuge because the ending of a period in office (i.e.,

13. So Rashi and Ibn Ezra (Cohen (1983, 714).
14. Ashley (1993, 654), with reference to C. F. Keil, J. Sturdy, P. J. Budd, and the Talmud (Makkot 11); cf. Allen (1990, 1004).
15. Cohen (1983, 980).
16. Noordtzij (1983, 301).

the high priest's death) ended an era. Noordtzij compared this with a new king who has just been installed, and who grants mercy to a number of prisoners.

When a person must bear the consequences of their own blood guilt in that the judicial system demands their own life, this is *retribution*, or even *revenge*: "Whoever sheds the blood of man, by man shall his blood be shed" (Gen. 9:6; cf. Lev. 24:17, "Whoever takes a human life shall surely be put to death"). However, when an innocent, vicarious sacrificial animal bears the consequences of the person's blood guilt, this is *atonement*: the guilt is covered (i.e., blotted out), the punishment has been averted, the guilty person goes free, and is viewed as never having committed the sin. If we take the two aspects together, we may say that atonement is God's revenge executed upon an innocent substitute.

4.2.2 Appeasing God?

Sometimes a distinction is made between the person (the priest) who makes atonement through a sacrifice, and God who makes atonement without any means, out of pure grace.[17] Indeed, where God is the subject of atonement, there is never any doubt about what atoning means (e.g., Ps. 79:9, "Help us, O God . . . deliver us, and atone for our sins"; Isa. 27:9, "Therefore by this the guilt of Jacob will be atoned for . . . when he makes all the stones of the altars like chalkstones crushed to pieces"; Ezek. 16:63, "that you . . . never open your mouth again because of your shame, when I atone for you for all that you have done").

Yet we should not create a false contrast here, for it is God himself who has instituted the sacrificial and priestly ministry in order thereby to prepare a way of atonement for his people. It is *never* the opposite, as if—as has been suggested—atonement in the Old Testament would be the means to appease the wrath of a God who

---
17. Koehler and Baumgartner (1953, 452).

is enraged by his people's sins. In fact, this notion may be current in paganism but is entirely foreign to the Old Testament. The sacrifice is not a means to atone an angry God but a means that God himself has prepared so that people may receive propitiation for their sins and be reconciled with him.

The thought of appeasing God is based on only a few passages (Gen. 32:20; Prov. 16:14). but these verses do speak of angry people. Nowhere it is said in the Old Testament that a sacrifice must pacify *God*, calming, soothing, placating, or mollifying him, or mitigating his wrath. Insofar as God's wrath is mentioned, which must be soothed, it is God himself who does so: "So will I satisfy my wrath on you, and my jealousy shall depart from you. I will be calm and will no more be angry" (Ezek. 16:42; cf. Zech. 6:8, they "have set my Spirit at rest," where judgment is spoken of) (see more extensively §§9.3–9.4).

We must keep in mind that God himself instituted the sacrificial and priestly ministry as a way—and apparently the *only* way—to bring sinful human beings back to himself. It is not the priest who intervenes between sinful humans and an angry God to appease the latter, but out of love the holy God offers to his people a way for coming to terms with him again. Sure, when the people have fallen into idolatry, Moses says angrily, "You have sinned a great sin. And now I will go up to the Lord; perhaps I can make atonement for your sin" (Exod. 32:30). And sure, God is wrath (v. 10) so that he sends a plague on the people (v. 35). And sure, it is Moses who must beg God for mercy. However, this mercy is not *wrung* from God; this is so because, first, mercy is rooted in God's very being: "The Lord, the Lord, a God merciful and gracious, slow to anger, and abounding in steadfast love and faithfulness, keeping steadfast love for thousands, forgiving iniquity and transgression and sin" (Exod. 34:6-7). And second, this mercy is founded upon the way God himself had already stipulated, namely, the way of the sin offering: "Aaron shall make atonement on its horns once a year. With the blood of the sin offering of atonement he shall make atonement for it once in the year throughout your generations. It is most holy to the LORD" (Exod. 30:10).

God's wrath against sinners and their sins is real. But this does not mean that he forgives reluctantly as if he were forced to do so by the priest's intervention. On the contrary, "he does not willingly bring affliction or grief to anyone" (Lam. 3:33 NIV). "I have no pleasure in the death of the wicked, but that the wicked turn from his way and live" (Ezek. 33:11). "For you, O LORD, are good and forgiving, abounding in steadfast love to all who call upon you" (Ps. 86:5). Conversely, this does not mean that forgiveness occurs "just like that." Two things are indispensable for it. First, *toward God*, satisfaction must be given in the form of a sin offering. Second, *in people— not in God, for he does not need to be appeased—a ch*ange must occur: they must repent and confess their sins (Lev. 5:5), and come to God on the basis of an innocent, vicarious sacrifice. All of this will be explained further in coming sections and chapters.

4.2.3 Other Aspects

By way of summary, with the addition of some details, let me explain once more the central function of blood in atonement, viewed from the various meanings of the one root (*or* the various roots?[18]) of *k-p-r*:

(a) The righteous and holy God not only *demands* blood—"when I see the blood, I will pass over you" (Exod. 12:13)—but he is also the One who himself *provides* it: "I have given it [i.e., the blood] for you on the altar to make atonement for your souls" (Lev. 17:11). This point is very important in connection with whether God is the subject of atonement (he reconciles himself with humans),

---
18. See §4.1.2 and note 5.

or the object of atonement (he is the One who must be reconciled in the sense of appeased) (§§9.3–9.4, 10.4).

(b) Blood covers the sin, so efficiently that it can no longer be found (cf. §12.4.2). It is gone, it has disappeared never to be found again. Here are related metaphors: sins are "carried to a remote place" (Lev. 16:22 NIV); "you have cast all my sins behind your back" (Isa. 38:17). "I have blotted out your transgressions like a cloud and your sins like mist" (44:22). "You will cast all our sins into the depths of the sea" (Micah 7:19); "as far as the east is from the west, so far does he remove our transgressions from us" (Ps. 103:12). "I will forgive their iniquity, and I will remember their sin no more" (Jer. 31:34).

(c) Blood wipes out or blots out sin (exterminates, extinguishes, obliterates, annuls, abolishes, erases, extirpates, and nullifies it), so that it no longer exists. This notion is closely related to the metaphor of washing: "Wash me thoroughly from my iniquity . . . wash me, and I shall be whiter than snow" (Ps. 51:2, 7); "though your sins are like scarlet, they shall be as white as snow; though they are red like crimson, they shall become like wool" (Isa. 1:18). "[Y]ou were washed, you were sanctified, you were justified in the name of the Lord Jesus Christ and by the Spirit of our God" (1 Cor. 6:11). "To Him who loved us and washed us from our sins in His own blood . . ." (Rev. 1:5 NKJV). "They have washed their robes and made them white in the blood of the Lamb" (Rev. 7:14; cf. Heb. 9:14; 1 John 1:7). All dirty stains have been dissolved in the blood of Christ.

(d) Blood is the ransom for sin, for blood stands for life: with the life of the innocent substitute—the animal sacrifice—the live of the trespasser is ransomed: "[T]he Son of Man came not to be served but to serve, and to give his life as a ransom for many" (Matt. 20:28); "this is my blood of the covenant, which is poured out for many for the forgiveness of sins" (26:28). "[T]here is one God, and there is one mediator between God and men, the man Christ Jesus, who gave himself as a ransom for all" (1 Tim. 2:5-6). Just as in the old covenant (Exod. 24:8), the new covenant is founded upon blood. Regarding the aspect of the ransom, see our more extensive discussion in §§6.1-6.3.

For the sake of completeness, let us briefly look at some other words related to the root *k-p-r*.

The Hebrew noun *kippurim*, a plural with singular meaning, has the sense of "atoning act," in short: "atonement" (Exod. 29:36; 30:10, 16; Num. 5:8; 29:11). We know it especially in the Hebrew expression *Yom hakKippurim*, "Day of Atonement" (Lev. 23:27-28; 25:9; Heb. *Yom Kippurim* in 23:28), currently called *Yom Kippur*, an expression that does not occur in the Old Testament. The sin offering of the Day of Atonement is called "sin offering of atonement" (Heb. *chattat hakkippurim*, Exod. 30:10; Num. 29:11).

The Hebrew word *kapporet* refers to the cover or lid ("mercy seat") that rested on the ark of the covenant (see especially Exod. 25:17-22; 37:6-9). If *k-p-r* means "to propitiate," then "propitiatory" is a good rendering (DRA; WYC). The traditional English rendering "mercy seat" originated through passages such as Psalm 99:1, "The LORD . . . sits enthroned upon the cherubim" (cf. Exod. 25:17-22), and through the Greek term *hilastērion*, "mercy seat" (Heb. 9:5), derived from *hileōs*, "merciful" (Luke 18:13, Gk. *hilasthēti*).

In 1 Chronicles 28:11 we find the special Hebrew expression *bet hakkapporet*, "room for the mercy seat," shorter: "the place of atonement" (NIV). This refers to the Most Holy place, where the ark with its cover stood. Possibly, the Hebrew term *kapporet* is related to the original meaning of *k-p-r*, "to cover," hence: "cover."[19] But I deem

---

19. Wenham (1979, 229). Also *kopher*, plur. *kepharim*, "henna blossoms" (Song 1:14; 4:13; 7:11), comes from *kpr*, here in the original meaning "to cover," namely, with paint, because

it more likely that it is called this because once a year, on the Day of Atonement, the high priest "made atonement" on the *kapporet* by sprinkling on it the blood of the sin offering (Lev. 16:13–15).

4.3 Introduction to the Atoning Sacrifices[20]
4.3.1 The Five Offerings of Leviticus

In Leviticus 1–7 we find the five offerings that play an essential role in the Mosaic ministry: the *burnt offering* (or entirely burned offering, holocaust;[21] 1:1–17; 6:8–13), the *grain offering* (or meal offering, oblation; 2:1–16; 6:14–23), the *peace offering* (or fellowship offering, offering of thanksgiving; 3:1–17; 7:11–21, 26–36), the *sin offering* (or purification offering; 4:1–5:13; 6:24–30), and the *guilt offering* (or trespass offering, restitution offering; 5:14–6:7; 7:1–10). Actually, we find only four atoning offerings here; the grain offering is not a bloody offering—it is entirely vegetative—and occurs only in connection with the burnt offering. The guilt offering is actually a special form of the sin offering, so that among the atoning offerings three main types remain: the burnt, the peace, and the sin offerings.

Often, the burnt and sin offerings are mentioned in one breath. Examples are the purification ritual for the woman who has given birth (Lev. 12:6, 8), the ritual for the leper (14:19, 22, 31), the ritual for the man with

---

with this plant, hair, nails, fingers, and toes were painted orange-yellow (cf. *kopher*, "pitch," in Gen. 6:14).

20. See extensively *DNTT* 3:418–28, 996–1022; and further Darby (n.d.-b, ad loc.); Grant (1890; 1956); Kelly (1896/1897); Stuart (n.d.); Milgrom (1970; 1976; 1991); Mackintosh (1972); Levine (1974; 1989); Jukes (1976); Heijkoop (1977); Coates (2007); Newberry (2014); I have made ample non-referenced use of these works.
21. Gk. *holokautōma* ("wholly burned") in the New Testament (adopted from the Septuagint); the word "holocaust" has been derived from it; see §4.4.1.

an unclean discharge (15:15), the ritual for the woman with an unclean discharge (v. 30), and on the Day of Atonement (16:3, 5; see chapter 5). The reason for this combination will be explained later. Burnt, peace, and sin offerings sometimes occur together, as in the consecration of the priests (Lev. 8-9; see §5.7.1), when a Nazirite vow ends (Num. 6:14, 16-17), and in the consecration of the tabernacle (7:15-17, 21-23). In all these cases, the peace offering has the character of a consecration or ordination offering.

It is necessary to clearly distinguish between (I) obligatory offerings and (II) freewill offerings. The former (I) category contains again two different kinds:

(a) Fixed, *periodic* offerings, namely, the daily morning and evening burnt offering (Exod. 29:38-42; Num. 28:3-10), the burnt and sin offerings on the occasion of every new moon (Num. 28:11-15), and further the offerings at the appointed festivals of the LORD: the Passover (*Pesach*), the Feast of Unleavened Bread (*Matsot*), the Feast of Weeks (or Pentecost, *Shavuʿot*), the Feast of Trumpets (*Yom Teruʿah*[22]), the Day of Atonement (*Yom Kippur*), and the Feast of Booths (*Sukkot*) (Lev. 23:4-43; Num. 28:16-29:39; cf. Deut. 16)

(b) *Occasional* offerings: I just mentioned examples of various purifications and consecrations. Other occasional obligatory offerings include the sin and guilt offerings that had to be brought after certain trespasses (Lev. 4-6).

The latter (II) category contains the *freewill* offerings. Notice the way the book of Leviticus opens: "When any one of you brings an offering to the LORD . . ." (Lev. 1:2; cf. 2:1). The intention is obviously that this would occur at the offerer's own initiative. Especially burnt offerings (22:18) and peace offerings (7:16; 22:21) could have the

---

22. Today Jews call this *Rosh Hashanah*, the Jewish New Year (in the Jewish civil calendar, the seventh month of Lev. 23 is the first month).

character of a freewill offering. The Lord prescribed in detail which conditions such offerings had to satisfy, but that did not change their voluntary character.

4.3.2 Obligatory and Voluntary

In order to understand the spiritual significance of the offerings, we must realize the important distinction between obligatory and voluntary offerings. In the obligatory offerings, the *objective* meaning of the offerings comes to the fore. Apparently, they refer to the atoning work of Christ as the objective ground on which God can have fellowship with his people; we will investigate this point extensively. The offerings ensured that the relationship between God and his Old Testament people could be maintained (the daily burnt offering), or was restored (sin offerings), as well as the relationship between an Israelite and their neighbor (sin offerings). The people had been redeemed from Egypt on the basis of the blood of the Passover Lamb (Exod. 12; see §5.1), and God had made a covenant with them on the basis of burnt and peace offerings (Exod. 24:5-8). The other obligatory offerings served to guarantee the relationship between God and his people, and mutually between Israelites, through continual purification and sanctification.

This continual aspect (Heb. *tamid*) is seen, for instance, in the commandment that the fire on the altar of burnt offering should never stop burning (Lev. 6:9, 12-13).[23] We remember that this fire on the altar came "from the LORD," that is, it was fire that had descended from heaven (9:24; cf. 2 Chron. 7:1 mentions this fire in Solomon's temple). The sin of Nadab and Abihu was that they offered "strange fire" (Lev. 10:1), that is, not fire from the altar, fire "from the LORD." The parallel suggested by Gordon Wenham with the "fire" in a believer that

---

23. Cf. Keil and Delitzsch (2:318); Gispen (1950, 104).

should never stop burning seems to me irrelevant.[24]

In the freewill offerings we are dealing with the *subjective* meaning of offerings, that is, the realization of the meaning of the sacrifice in the offerer's soul, which as a "spiritual sacrifice" of thanksgiving and praise returns to the LORD (cf. the New Testament application in Heb. 13:15; 1 Pet. 2:5). Take, for instance, the burnt offering, first as to its objective meaning: in order for the people to be, and to remain, acceptable (pleasing) to the LORD, he *demanded* the daily morning and evening burnt offering. In themselves, the people were not pleasing to God; but he accepted the people on the basis of the acceptability of the sacrifice (Exod. 29:41). Because of the pleasing aroma of the offering he could dwell in their midst (vv. 42-45). However, the Israelite who presented to the LORD a freewill burnt offering did so out of their own desire to be acceptable to him (Lev. 1:4). The deeper significance of this will be dealt with in §4.4.

4.3.3 The Atoning Sacrifices and the New Testament

The New Testament refers extensively to the Old Testament sacrifices, and consistently applies them to the atoning work of Christ. Sometimes reference is made to specific Old Testament offerings. More generally, John the Baptist called Jesus "the Lamb of God, who takes away the sin of the world" (John 1:29; cf. v. 36), which may refer to the Passover lamb (Exod. 12:3-14; see §5.1), or to the lamb of the morning and evening burnt offering (29:38-42), or the lamb of the sin offering (e.g., 4:32), or the lamb of the guilt offering (6:6; 14:13; Num. 6:12), or very generally to "the" sacrifice, as in Isaiah 53:7, "like a lamb that is led to the slaughter." In an equally general way, Peter says that believers have been "ransomed . . . with the precious blood of Christ, like that of a lamb without blemish or spot" (1 Pet. 1:18-19). And John says, "[Y]ou [i.e., the Lamb] were slain, and by your blood you

---

24. Wenham (1979, 120).

ransomed people for God from every tribe and language and people and nation" (Rev. 5:9; cf. 1:5; 7:14).

Some New Testament passages are more closely related to the various types of Old Testament sacrifices, as will be explained more extensively in §§4.4 to 4.7.[25]

(a) *The burnt offering:* through Christ's God-pleasing atoning death, now believing sinners themselves are pleasing to God: "I appeal to you therefore, brothers, by the mercies of God, to present your bodies as a living sacrifice, holy and acceptable to God, which is your spiritual worship" (Rom. 12:1); "walk in love, as Christ loved us and gave himself up for us, a fragrant offering and sacrifice to God" (Eph. 5:2); believers have been "taken into favor in the Beloved" (1:6 DARBY).

(b) *The peace offering:* through Christ's atoning death, peace and resulting communion have been established between God and his people, and between the members of his people. In 1 Corinthians 10:18–21, Paul draws a parallel between eating the peace offering and eating the Lord's Supper; this suggests that the Christ whom we commemorate in the Lord's Supper is presented in the peace offering. It is the sacrifice that establishes peace between God and people ("since we have been justified by faith, we have peace with God through our Lord Jesus Christ," Rom. 5:1), and between people and people (Christ "is our peace, who has made us both [i.e., Jewish and Gentile believers] one," Eph. 2:14).

(c) *The sin offering:* through Christ's atoning death, the sins of believers have been blotted out, and they themselves have been ransomed: "[T]he blood of Christ, who through the eternal Spirit offered himself without blemish to God, [will] purify our conscience from dead works . . . he has appeared once for all at the end of the ages to put away sin by the sacrifice of himself . . . Christ, having been offered once to bear the sins of many . . ." (Heb. 9:14, 26, 28). "He Himself is the propitiation for

---

25. Cf. Chafer (*ST* 3:75–76).

our sins, and not for ours only but also for the whole world" (1 John 2:2 NKJV). God "loved us and sent his Son to be the propitiation for our sins" (4:10).

(d) *The guilt offering:* through Christ's atoning death, what the sinner has corrupted and robbed has been restored and restituted. This type of sacrifice is not explicitly mentioned in the New Testament, but various verses of Isaiah 53 are applied to Christ (cf. v. 3 in Mark 9:12, v. 4 in Matt. 8:17, v. 5 in Rom. 4:25 and 1 Pet. 2:24, v. 7 in Acts 8:32, v. 9 in 1 Pet. 2:22, v. 12 even by Jesus himself in Luke 22:37). In Isaiah 53 it is said of him: "[W]hen his soul makes an offering for guilt, he shall see his offspring; he shall prolong his days; the will of the LORD shall prosper in his hand" (v. 10).

4.4 The Burnt Offering[26]
4.4.1 The Old Testament Form

Regarding three of the four bloody sacrifices in the Old Testament, we read that they make atonement for the offerer. Of a fourth sacrifice, the peace offering, we can only conclude this in an indirect way (cf. Exod. 29:32-33; Lev. 4:26, 35; Ezek. 45:15, 17). Of the first three, the burnt offering must be dealt with first, not only because it comes first in Leviticus but also because it is the only bloody sacrifice that is mentioned earlier in Genesis (8:20; 22:2-3, 6-8, 13).[27]

The Hebrew term for "burnt offering" is *ʿolah*, derived from the root *ʿ-l-h*, "go up." The sense is that this is

---

26. See *DOTT* 3:405-15; *DNTT* 3:421.

    Cf. the Heb. word *minchah* in Gen. 4:3-5, which has substantially the same meaning (in Lev. *minchah* is the grain offering). Often, the morning and evening burnt offering is also called *minchah* (Exod. 29:40-41; Num. 28:5-8; 1 Kings 18:29, 36; 2 Kings 3:20; 16:15; Ezra 9:4-5; Ps. 141:2; Dan. 9:21). The ninth hour (about 3:00 p.m.), the "hour of prayer" (Acts 3:1; cf. 10:2), which is the time of the evening burnt offering, is still called *minchah* by the Jews.

a sacrifice from which nobody eats but that in its entirety "goes up" in smoke on the "altar of burnt offering" (Heb. *mizbach ha-ᶜolah,* Exod. 30:28) before and for the LORD. Hence the Septuagint rendering is *holokauston* or *holokaustōma* or *holokaustōsis,* "that which is burnt entirely" (holocaust). Sometimes, the verb and substantive are connected: *wayyaᶜal ᶜolot,* "he offered burnt offerings," literally, "he made go up [things] going up" (Gen. 8:20; cf. 22:2; 1 Sam. 7:9). The word "holocaust" as a reference to the destruction of the Jewish nation under the Third Reich indicates its massive and total character (*entirely* burned); it also refers to the cremation ovens, and suggests the offering character of this genocide.

The description of the burnt offering in Leviticus 1 concerns the freewill burnt offering. It is remarkable that W. H. Gispen did not discuss at all its voluntary character.[28] His colleague A. Noordtzij—both were Reformed—rightly spoke of an offering "that comes from the urge of the heart."[29] Rabbi Samuel Lehrman said, "The sacrifice was not acceptable unless the owner spontaneously declared, 'I choose, of my free will, to bring this offering.' . . . His free will was essential for its acceptance *before the* LORD."[30] And Laird Harris said, "The offerer brings the offering because he feels the need to be accepted before God."[31] Gordon Wenham briefly described the offerings of Leviticus 1–3 as "a personal act of devotion or atonement."[32]

In my view, the Hebrew word *lirtsonu* (not *kirtsonu*) in Leviticus 1:3 does not mean "of his own voluntary will" (KJV), nor "for *its* [i.e., the offering's] acceptance" (CEB), but "for *his* [i.e., the offerer's] acceptance" before

---

28. Gispen (1950, 35–36).
29. Noordtzij (1982, ad loc.).
30. In Cohen (1983, 605–606).
31. Harris (1990, 538 note 3).
32. Wenham (1979, 50).

the LORD (LEB).³³ This is directly related to verse 4, "He shall lay his hand on the head of the burnt offering, and it shall be accepted for him to make *atonement* for him [Heb. *lekapper ʿalaw*]." The specific point here is that the burnt offering is *not* brought in view of specific sins. To this end, the sin offering was given; the two offerings, the burnt and sin offerings, should never be confused. Moreover, this is a freewill offering; the occasion for it is not a specific sin. Nevertheless, the purpose of the burnt offering is that the offerer may be acceptable (pleasing) to God due to the atonement that is effected by this sacrifice (this is the subjective aspect; §4.3.2). This point must now be investigated more closely.

4.4.2 The Burnt Offering and Sin

In reference to the burnt offering, commentator A. Noordtzij spoke specifically about "impurity and sin," and of a "sinful soul content,"³⁴ but in my view this goes too far; for specific sins, sin offerings were demanded. Gordon Wenham pointed to the prayers of psalmists, who ask the LORD to be pleased with his people by hearing their prayer and blessing them (Ps. 40:13; 77:7-9; 85:1).³⁵ Wenham's explanation came close to acknowledging the atoning significance of the burnt offering: not only does the burnt offering express "complete surrender to the Lord ... consecration ... to a course of life pleasing to God,"³⁶ and "an act of homage, expressed by a gift,"³⁷ but it *atones*—not by blotting out specific sins but by bringing God's pleasure to rest on someone who by nature is a sinner.³⁸

Indeed, in my view, it is not specific sins but human

---

33. Cf. Cohen (1983, 605-606).
34. Noordtzij (1982, ad loc.).
35. Wenham (1979, 56).
36. So Keil (1887, 317); cf. Harris (1990, 538).
37. So De Vaux (1964, 37).
38. Wenham (1979, 57).

sinfulness in general that comes to the fore here. The offerer brought a voluntary burnt offering, not because they was aware of specific sins but (negatively) because they was aware of their vanity and unworthiness as a sinful human being, and (positively) because they nevertheless wished to be pleasing to God, not on the basis of their own *unworthiness* but of the *worth(iness)* of the vicarious offering, whose fragrance ascended to God as a pleasing aroma (Lev. 1:9, 13, 17). This is basically what was being expressed in the offerings brought by Abel (Gen. 4:4) and Noah (Gen. 8:20).

The atoning value of the burnt offering was seen also in the purification of the leper (Lev. 14:20), in which the leprous disease is not the picture of concrete sins but of someone's general impurity because of their sinfulness (see further §5.6).

Gordon Wenham mentioned other examples of the connection between sinfulness and the burnt offering,[39] but in my view not all of these are equally viable. Thus, the burnt offerings of Job 1:5 and 42:8 presumably belonged to the patriarchal time, when the sin offering had not yet been introduced; this offering appears for the first time in Exodus 29:14. We read in 2 Chronicles 29:7-8 about the failure of bringing the daily burnt offerings, which provoked God's anger. We read in 2 Samuel 24:25 (1 Chron. 21:26) about the restoration of the normal relationship between God and his people, which was guaranteed by the daily burnt offering. I do support Wenham's important conclusion, though:

> [W]e conclude that one function of the burnt offering was to prevent God's displeasure at man's sin [read: sinfulness] from being turned into punishment. Because man's very nature is sinful, there is always friction between him and his maker.[40]

---

39. Ibid., 57-58).
40. Ibid., 58).

4.4.3 The Laying On of Hands

In several passages, the laying on of hands (Heb. *semichah*) was an essential part of the offering ritual (Lev. 1:4; 3:2, 8, 13; 4:4, 15, 24, 29, 33).[41] By placing their hands on the head of the animal, the offerer made themselves one with the offering in the awareness of the fact that the animal would die in their stead. In connection with the burnt offering, Felix Chingota summed up four explanations of that laying on of hands:[42] (a) the transference of sins to the animal, (b) the identification of the offerer with the sacrificial animal, so that this could die as a substitute for him, (c) a symbolic oath, indicating the intention or innocence of the offerer, and (d) an indication that the animal belonged to the offerer, and was brought as a sacrifice. However, explanation (c) cannot be correct because the offering was intended to make atonement for the offerer (Lev. 1:4). This instead suggests explanation (b). Explanation (a) was true for the sin offering but not for the burnt offering.

In my view, the idea is this: in the sin offering, the deeper significance was that the offerer transferred their sins to the sacrificial animal, so to speak, in order that the animal, loaded with the sins of the offerer, would die in their stead. In a similar way, the Israelites laid their hands on the Levites, in order that these would take the place of their firstborn (Num. 8:10; cf. 3:40–51), and Moses laid his hands on Joshua in order that the latter would take his place (27:18, 23; Deut. 34:9). We see this in a very special way on the Day of Atonement: the high priest laid "both his hands on the head of the live goat" (the scapegoat), and confessed "over it all the iniquities of the people of Israel, and all their transgressions, all their sins" (Lev. 16:21). Afterward, the scapegoat was sent into the wilderness to perish there.

Gordon Wenham called this explanation of the lay-

---

41. Cf. Budiman (1971, 58–66).
42. Cf. Budiman (1971, 58–66).

ing on of hands, along with some other explanations, less acceptable.[43] However, it seems to me that this interpretation of the sin offering is perfectly correct—but with the burnt offering it does not seem to work. The similarity between the two offerings is that the offerer identified themselves with the sacrificial animal. But when the offerer brought a sin offering, they wished to *get rid* of something, namely, their sins, whereas in the burnt offering they wished to *obtain* something, namely, the pleasure and favor of God, which they would receive because of the pleasing aroma of the offering. In other words, in the sin offering, through the laying on of hands, the *unworthiness* (sins, iniquities) passed from the sinner to the sacrificial animal, and was vicariously judged in this animal. But in the burnt offering, the *worthiness* (acceptability) of the sacrificial animal, whose fragrance was a pleasant aroma for God, passed from the animal to the offerer, who thus became acceptable to God.[44] In both cases, there is a symbolic identification as well as transference: in the sin offering from the offerer to the animal, in the burnt offering from the animal to the offerer.

4.4.4 The New Testament Application

The New Testament significance of the burnt offering is considerable: the believer knows Christ not only as the sin offering that took away all their sins, but also the burnt offering through which they can now be acceptable (pleasing) to God: "taken into favor in the Beloved" (1:6 DARBY). There is also a collective aspect: just as all Israel was pleasing to God through the daily burnt offering, the church is pleasing to God through Christ's

---

43. Wenham (1979, 62); cf. Shelton (2006, 53–57), who, in my view, makes an unjustified distinction between
laying on of one hand or of two hands.
44. *Contra*, e.g., Wenham (1979, 94), who assumes that in both the sin and the burnt offering the laying on of hands involved the transference of sin.

once accomplished atoning work. The acceptability of Christ, of his person (Matt. 3:17; 17:5) as well as of his work (Eph. 5:2), has passed on to the church.

At the same time, the voluntary character of the burnt offering refers to the believer as well, who, because of his acceptability in Christ, devotes himself to God. Just as the burnt offering was not eaten but was entirely burned on the altar, Christ had consecrated himself entirely to God on the cross. Similarly, believers devote themselves to God: "[W]alk in love, as Christ loved us and gave himself up for us, a fragrant offering and sacrifice to God" (Eph. 5:2). This is perfect consecration, which has the character of a sacrifice.[45] Thus, Paul encourages believers: "I appeal to you therefore, brothers, by the mercies of God, to present your bodies as a living sacrifice, holy and *acceptable* to God, which is your spiritual worship" (Rom. 12:1). "Whoever thus serves Christ is *acceptable* to God and approved by men" (14:18). "[L]et us offer to God *acceptable* worship, with reverence and awe" (Heb. 12:28; cf. 13:21; 2 Cor. 5:9; Eph. 5:10; Col. 1:10; 2 Thess. 1:11; 1 John 3:22). "For we are the aroma of Christ to God" (2 Cor. 2:15). Thus, believers' good work is also called "a fragrant offering, a sacrifice *acceptable* and *pleasing* to God" (Phil. 4:18).

When coming to God, the first thing the sinner needs is the sin offering, that is, the sacrifice that takes away their sins. In the experience of faith, this person may come under the impression of the significance of the burnt offering—the pleasure that God takes in him in Christ—only much later, and some never seem to reach this point. However, with God it is the reverse: when in Leviticus he thinks of the atoning sacrifice of Christ, he begins with the burnt offering, and thus with the pleasure he takes in Christ's atoning death *for himself*. Whereas the sin offering presents to us God's solemn

---

45. Notice the etymological connection between "consecration" and "sacrifice" (Lat. *sacer*, "holy, sacred").

judgment upon sin, the burnt offering speaks of that perfect surrender of Christ to the will of God—tested by, and displayed at, the cross—that brings about the Father's highest pleasure: "For this reason the Father loves me, because I lay down my life that I may take it up again" (John 10:17). This is the criterion for the acceptability to God of believers.[46]

Of the sin offering, it is said only once that its fat, put on the altar, was a "pleasant aroma to the LORD" (Lev. 4:31). For the rest, the emphasis lies much more on the disgusting character of the animal upon which sin is being transferred, which animal therefore had to be burned "outside the camp," that is, far from God's people (4:12, 21; 6:11). Hebrews 13:11-12 says of this, "For the bodies of those animals whose blood is brought into the holy places by the high priest as a sacrifice for sin are burned outside the camp. So Jesus also suffered outside the gate in order to sanctify the people through his own blood." The burnt offering, however, is consumed entirely on the alter, for "a pleasing aroma to the LORD." Viewed from the standpoint of the sinner's needs and experience, the sin offering came first; viewed from the standpoint of *God's* desires, the burnt offering came first. The very first thing about which he spoke, as soon as the tabernacle had been erected and the glory of the LORD had descended, was the burnt offering (Exod. 40:1-38; Lev. 1).

The burnt offering is followed, in Leviticus 2, by the grain offering (Heb. *minchah*; on this, see note 27 above). This offering was inseparably connected with the burnt offering. As far as we can assess, there was never a separate grain offering, and conversely, there was never a burnt offering without the concomitant grain offering. Therefore, the latter is dealt with immediately after the burnt offering, without a separate introduction (such as "And the LORD spoke to Moses, saying . . ."; cf. 4:1). Like

---

46. Grant (1956, 33).

the burnt offering, it too was a pleasing aroma to the Lord: a part of it came on the altar as "a food offering with a pleasing aroma to the Lord" (Lev. 2:2, 9). It was called "most holy" (Lev. 2:3, 10).

With others, I believe that the grain offering—which was not a bloody offering, yet was closely connected with a bloody offering—speaks of Christ's true and pure humanity. There may be a parallel here with the type of the manna, but I also see a distinction. The manna suggests Jesus' perfectly consecrated *life* on earth (cf. John 6:31-33, 49-51, 57-58), whereas the grain offering seems to suggest Christ in the glory of his *person* as the perfect Man of God: flour, which is from the earth (cf. Isa. 53:2), mixed with oil, the well-known type of the Holy Spirit (cf. Luke 1:35). The manna was eaten by all the people, but the grain offering only by the priests (Lev. 6:14-18), that is, by those who were familiar with the holy presence of God.

In the New Testament application, only believers are spiritually capable of realizing and enjoying what Christ as the perfect Man here on earth meant to the heart of God. It was only *this* person, in all the glory of his person and in all the glory of his earthly life, in all his loveliness before God, who was fit to become on the cross the true burnt offering. Thus, burnt and grain offerings are inseparably linked: we cannot behold the burnt offering death of Christ without realizing who was the glorious Man who gave himself into death. First, there was the perfect Man Jesus Christ, then the God-consecrated life of this Man, then the God-consecrated surrender of this life into death as a pleasing aroma to the Lord.

4.5   The Peace Offering[47]
4.5.1 The Old Testament Form
We seldom read that the peace offering has atoning significance: "Aaron and his sons . . . shall eat those things

---
47. See *DOTT* 4:135-43; *DNTT* 3:422-23.

[i.e., the peace offering] with which atonement was made at their ordination and consecration" (Exod. 20:32-33). "[A]ll its [i.e., the sin offering's] fat he shall burn on the altar, like the fat of the sacrifice of peace offerings. So the priest shall make atonement for him for his sin" (Lev. 4:26; cf. v. 35). "And one sheep ... for grain offering, burnt offering, and peace offerings, to make atonement for them" (Ezek. 45:15; cf. v. 17). In the peace offering we do find the same notion of the offerer's acceptability as we found in the burnt offering: "When you offer a sacrifice of peace offerings to the LORD, you shall offer it so that you may be accepted" (Lev. 19:5). "If any of the flesh of the sacrifice of his peace offering is eaten on the third day, he who offers it shall not be accepted, neither shall it be credited to him" (Lev. 7:18; cf. 19:7). This aspect is underscored through the connection with the burnt offering: the peace offering's fat is burnt on the altar of *burnt* offering: "Then Aaron's sons shall burn it on the altar on top of the burnt offering, which is on the wood on the fire; it is a food offering [lit., a fire offering, (H)CSB] with a pleasing aroma to the LORD" (Lev. 3:5).

The Hebrew phrase for "peace offering" is *zebach shelamim*, in which we recognize *zebach*, "sacrifice" (any bloody animal offering), and the root *sh-l-m* (see §4.5.3). Often the word *zebach* alone means "peace offering" (7:16-17), especially when listed together with other offerings: "In sacrifice [*zebach*, read: peace offering] and offering [*minchah*, read: grain offering] you have not delighted, but you have given me an open ear. Burnt offering and sin offering you have not required" (Ps. 40:6; cf. Lev. 23:37, "... presenting to the LORD food offerings, burnt offerings and grain offerings, sacrifices [read: peace offerings] and drink offerings"; Josh. 22:29, "an altar for burnt offering, grain offering, or sacrifice [read: peace offering]"). Often we find the combination "burnt offerings and sacrifices [read: peace offerings]" (e.g., Exod. 10:25; 18:12; Lev. 17:8; Num. 15:3, 5, 8; Deut.

12:6, 11, 27; Josh. 22:26-28[48]), which again underscores their connection.

Whereas the Sinaitic Law contains many obligatory burnt, grain, and sin offerings, Gordon Wenham suggests that only one obligatory peace offering is mentioned: at the Feast of Weeks (Lev. 23:19). This is not entirely correct, for the obligatory consecration offerings (Lev. 8-9; Num. 6-7) also had the character of a peace offering (§5.7.1). Peace offerings were also involved in the consecration of Solomon's temple (1 Kings 8:63-64; 2 Chron. 7:7), as well as in the renewed consecrations under Hezekiah and Josiah (2 Chron. 30:22; 31:2; 33:16). They will be involved again in the consecration of Ezekiel's temple (Ezek. 43:27). However, these were all one-time offerings; indeed, I am not aware of regular obligatory peace offerings.

4.5.2 The Eating Aspect

In Leviticus 3, the emphasis is on the part of the peace offering that is for the LORD, namely, certain parts of the fat and the kidneys, which were burned on the burnt offering altar: "And the priest shall burn it upon the altar: it is the food [Heb. *lechem*, lit. "bread," YLT] of the offering made by fire unto the LORD" (v. 11), "with a pleasing aroma" (v. 16). The idea is that part of the offering is "eaten" by the LORD; it is his "bread." This aspect of eating is very important, as we see in Leviticus 7:32-36. The text speaks of the "wave breast and the heave shoulder" (KJV), that is, the animal's breast that is waved before the Lord and the thigh that is heaved before him (GNT: the breast shaken to and fro, and the shoulder lifted up). These parts were given to the priests to be eaten by them. The rest of the animal's meat was eaten by the offerer and their companions if they were ceremonially "clean" (Lev. 7:15-16, 18-19). Thus we see there were

---

48. In v. 27 (Heb. *bizbachēnu ubishlamēnu*) "sacrifices" and "peace offerings" seem to be distinguished.

three participants in this meal: the LORD (for the fat is his "bread"), the priest who brought the offering (he got the shoulder and the thigh), and the people. This meal aspect is underscored by the fact that the altar is called a "table" (Ezek. 41:22; 44:16;[49] Mal. 1:7, 12; cf. 1 Cor. 10:21).

According to Leviticus 17:3-6, every meat meal of the Israelites had the character of a peace offering, at least during their wilderness journeys: the fat was God's "food," the breast and the thigh were given to the priest, and the rest was for the people. Thus, just like the grain offering, the peace offering was a genuine *meal* offering. Of the burnt offering all the meat was consumed on the altar, whereas of the grain offering (Lev. 6:16, 18), of certain sin offerings (vv. 26, 29-30), and of the guilt offering (7:6-7), only certain parts could be eaten, and only by the priests. But in addition to the fat, the breast, and the thigh, all the meat of the peace offering was eaten by the people. Thus, the ritual of the peace offering ended with a meal, in which the offerer with their relatives and friends ate the meat of the sacrificial animal. A biblical example of this is the sacrificial meal that Samuel organized in Bethlehem (1 Sam. 16:2-5; cf. Gen. 31:54; Deut. 12:7; 27:7; 1 Chron. 29:21-22).

The peace offerings mentioned in Leviticus 3 were freewill offerings as well, just like the burnt and grain offerings of chapters 1 and 2. In Leviticus 7:12, 16 (cf. 22:21), three possible motives for bringing a peace offering are mentioned. It could be (a) a "thanksgiving sacrifice," that is, an utterance of praise or thanksgiving, whether for something special, like answered prayer (cf. Ps. 50:14; 54:6-7; 56:12-13; 100; 107:21-22),[50] or as an expression of general gratitude, (b) a votive offering,

---

49. In Ezekiel, it is not clear, though, whether the altar of incense or the altar of the burnt offering is meant; Alexander (1986, 964, 976).

50. Ibn Ezra, Rashi: deliverance from suffering or trial, return after a dangerous journey, release from prison, recovery after illness; see Cohen (1983, 636).

namely, in connection with a vow that the offerer had made and was now fulfilling (cf. Gen. 28:20-21; 1 Sam. 1:3-4, 9-11; Ps. 116:17-19), or (c) a freewill offering, that is, a spontaneous gift, without any special reason (Ps. 54:6-7; Ezek. 46:12).

Gordon Wenham refers to the thanksgiving offering as a "confession offering" because the meaning of the Hebrew word *todah* is broader than praise or thanksgiving, and can also mean "confession" of a person's faith or of their sins (cf. Josh. 7:19; Ezra 10:11). However, the peace offering as such is never connected with any confession of sin.[51]

4.5.3 Function and Meaning

The things discussed so far can help us understand the function and meaning of the peace offering. Because of its meal character it is obvious why the peace offering was a *fellowship* offering; this is how many translations render the Hebrew phrase *zebach shelamim*. Let us now look a little more closely at the meaning of the Hebrew word *shelamim* in the phrase *zebach shelamim* ("peace offering"), because this meaning is not at all immediately evident.[52] In addition to the traditionally mentioned connection with the Hebrew word *shalom*, "peace" (hence "peace offering,"[53] possibly "offering of well-being," CEB), connections have been sought with possible other *sh-l-m* roots, which would lead to renderings such as "reward offering," "greeting offering," or "closure offering." Yet, the notion of peace seems to fit best the character of the peace offering as a fellowship offering: the peaceable sacrificial meal, of which both God and the people ate, presupposed rest and harmony between God and his people, and between the individual mem-

---

51. Wenham (1979, 78n11).
52. See *DOTT* 4:136-41; *DNTT* 3:422-23, and the lexica.
53. Cf. Septuagint: Gk. *eirēnikē*, an adjective derived from *eirēnē*, "peace."

bers of his people. Elsewhere, I have discussed the connection between the Old Testament peace offering meal and the New Testament Lord's Supper (cf. 1 Cor. 10:18-21).[54]

When it comes to peace between God and his people (cf. §3.8), we think first of Romans 5:1,[55] "[S]ince we have been justified by faith, we have peace with God through our Lord Jesus Christ." In addition to this positional peace *with* God, we must certainly mention the experiential peace *of* God that is granted to the believers: "[T]he peace of God, which surpasses all understanding, will guard your hearts and your minds in Christ Jesus" (Phil. 4:7; cf. Rom. 14:19; 15:13; 2 Cor. 13:11; Gal. 5:22; 6:16; Eph. 6:23; 2 Thess. 3:16; 1 Pet. 5:14; 2 John 1:3; Jude 1:2). Rashi thinks of peace for the world.[56]

In all these cases, we are dealing with a peace that—this is essential—does not come about by itself, and does not remain intact by itself, but is founded upon, and in the Old Testament must be repeatedly founded upon, the *atoning* sacrifice. In the New Testament sense, this means that all true peace and harmony between God and people, and between people and people, is based upon the atoning sacrifice of Christ. As in the burnt offering, the connection between the peace offering and atonement is seldom mentioned because this offering does not involve specific sins that must for atoned for. However, this does not remove the need for the peace and fellowship of God's people to be based only upon an *atoning* sacrifice. Here is a brief summary.

First, in a negative sense, the *sin* offering takes away sins.

Second, in a positive sense, the *burnt* offering makes the offerer acceptable (pleasant) to God; this can all be very individual.

---

54. Ouweneel (1999, 31-54; 2010b, §§8.1.2 and 8.5.1).
55. Harris (1990, 543).
56. Cohen (1983, 612).

Third, the *peace* offering establishes peace between God and his people, and mutually between the members of his people; this is always collective.

Peace and fellowship between God and his people are embedded in the covenant that he made with Israel. It is no wonder that, precisely when the covenant is at stake, peace offerings are often mentioned (e.g., Exod. 24:3-9; Deut. 27:1-8; 1 Kings 8:59-63). It is possible that especially here the aspects of the votive offering and the freewill offering come to the fore.[57] Especially the meaning of votive offerings clearly seems to explain why consecration offerings had the character of a peace offering (see above): through this offering, the consecrated person was obliged to faithful devotion to the LORD. The concomitant burnt and sin offering formed the foundation: the sin offering atoned for the sins of the consecrated person, the burnt offering made such a person acceptable (pleasant) to the Lord. On this foundation one's faithful dedication to the LORD was based.

In almost all offerings we see a difference in the animals that were allowed to be offered. In the burnt offering a bull, a male sheep or goat, a pigeon or a turtledove could be offered. In the peace offering a male *or* a female animal could be offered: cow, sheep or goat; presumably, female animals were allowed because the demands were less strict here than with the burnt offering, which had to be offered in its entirety on the altar. In these offerings, the size, and thus the worth, of the animal depended on the *prosperity* or on the *generosity* of the offerer. However, in the sin offering (§4.6), one's *social status* was decisive: a bull for the priest or the entire nation, a male goat for a tribal head, a female sheep or goat for an ordinary Israelite; a pigeon or turtledove if the latter was poor (cf. Luke 2:22-24).

---

57. Wenham (1979, 79).

4.6 The Sin Offering[58]
4.6.1 The Old Testament Form

The offering that was the Old Testament atoning sacrifice *par excellence*, namely, the offering that took away sins, was the sin offering, Hebrew *chataa* or *chattat*.[59] It is striking that these words mean both "sin" and "sin offering," that is, a means *against* sin. This is because the root *ch-t-'* does mean "to sin," but the *piel* form *chitte'* means "to purify from sin," and hence, "offer as a sin offering."[60] Thus, *chattaa* and *chattat* mean both "sin" and "purification from sin," and hence, "means for purification from sin," that is, "sin offering."

The sin offering was for the purification of people who had sinned unintentionally, or by mistake, that is, without evil intention (Lev. 4:2, 13, 22, 27; 5:15, 18). The assumption here is not that these people would never sin without their conscience protesting; this kind of sin is even explicitly mentioned in the guilt offering (6:2-3). The actual sense becomes clear from the contrast between Numbers 15:27-28, sinning unintentionally, or by mistake, and Numbers 15:30, sinning "with a high hand," that is, in a spirit of rebellion, with a fist clenched toward heaven, as it were.[61] An example of this follows in Numbers 15:32-35, namely, the case of the Sabbath breaker. The preeminent New Testament example of this is blasphemy against the Holy Spirit (Matt. 12:32).[62]

The sins involved were not necessarily direct sins against God; for premeditated murder there was no sin offering, either (Num. 35:16-21). This corresponds with Hebrews 10:26-29,

---

58. See *DOTT* 2:93-103; *DNTT* 3:419-20.
59. See Ouweneel (2008a, §13.1.2).
60. Lev. 8:15; Num. 19:19; Ps. 51:9; Ezek. 43:20, 22-23; 45:18; Lev. 6:26; 9:15; 2 Chron. 29:24.
61. Cf. Harris (1990, 547-48); Allen (1990, 829-30).
62. See Ouweneel (*EDR* 1:150-52).

For if we go on sinning deliberately after receiving the knowledge of the truth, there no longer remains a sacrifice for sins, but a fearful expectation of judgment, and a fury of fire that will consume the adversaries. Anyone who has set aside the law of Moses dies without mercy on the evidence of two or three witnesses. How much worse punishment, do you think, will be deserved by the one who has trampled underfoot the Son of God, and has profaned the blood of the covenant by which he was sanctified, and has outraged the Spirit of grace?

We also think here of the strong emphasis in the New Testament on sins committed in ignorance, which can be forgiven: "Father, forgive them, for they know not what they do" (Luke 23:34). "And now, brothers, I know that you acted in ignorance, as did also your rulers" (Acts 3:17). "[F]ormerly I was a blasphemer, persecutor, and insolent opponent. But I received mercy because I had acted ignorantly in unbelief" (1 Tim. 1:13).

In Leviticus 5:1-4 we find a few examples of unintentional sins of omission: the trespasser failed to testify before a judge about the sins he had observed; or he forgot that he had touched an unclean thing: a dead animal, or human uncleanness; or he forgot that he had uttered a rash oath. As an afterthought, he realized that he had become guilty of one of these sins, so he had to confess his sin and bring a sin offering.

4.6.2 The Role of the Priest

In Leviticus 1-3 scarcely any attention is paid to the role of the priest, without whose help the Israelite could not bring any freewill offerings. In Leviticus 4 this priestly role cannot be omitted, because here a significant, though unstated, distinction is being made between sins in which the priest was involved, and sins in which he was not involved. These are the two distinct situations:

(a) Sin by the anointed priest (vv. 3-12) or by the whole congregation of Israel (vv. 13-21);[63] in both cases the priest is involved in the guilt.

(b) Sin by a leader (tribal head) (vv. 22-26) or by an ordinary Israelite (vv. 27-35); in these cases the priest himself is not guilty.

These instances share two features with respect to the offering: the animal's fat is burned on the altar "for a pleasing aroma to the LORD" (v. 31), and part of the blood is poured out at the foot of the altar. In addition to these two shared features, there are three conspicuous differences between the two described situations:

Type (a): the priest is involved in the committed sin(s):
* Part of the blood is brought into the sanctuary (the first part of the tabernacle) and sprinkled in front of the veil (Lev. 4:6, 17).
* Another part of the blood of the sin offering is put on the horns of the altar *of incense* (vv. 7, 18).
* The priest is not allowed to eat the meat of these sin offerings; it is entirely burned[64] at a "clean place outside the camp" (vv. 12, 21; 6:30).

Type (b): the priest is not involved in the committed sin(s):
* The blood of the sin offering is not brought into the sanctuary.
* Part of the blood of the sin offering is put on the horns of the altar *of burnt offering* (vv. 25, 30).
* The meat of the sacrificial animal was eaten by the priests in the sanctuary (Lev. 6:22-29).

What is the meaning of the differences between the

---

63. The Midrash and Rashi apply the Heb. term ʿedah, "congregation," to the Sanhedrin; Cohen (1983, 616).
64. In v. 10 the word "burned" (Heb. *hiqtir*) means "gone up in smoke" on the altar; this always involved presenting a pleasing aroma to the LORD. In v. 12 the word "burned" (Heb. *s-r-ph*) refers to ordinary burning (here of something disgusting) leading to destruction.

two types of offering? Various answers have been given to this question. For instance, Gordon Wenham said that the sprinkling of the animal's blood within the sanctuary "protected the sinner from the holiness of God expressing itself in righteous anger."[65] However, why then was this needed when a priest had sinned, but not when a tribal head had sinned?

Indeed, in my view the key lies in whether the priest was involved in the sin. He was the mediator between God and the people; as a reward he received the meat from the peace and sin offerings. However, when the priest himself was involved in a serious trespass, either of himself or of the entire nation, this mediatorship itself was at stake, as we see in Leviticus 4:3, "[I]f it is the anointed priest who sins, thus bringing guilt on the people . . . ." The sin of the (high?) priest brought the entire people under its consequences so that he was no longer capable of making atonement for them.[66] When a non-priest sinned, the tabernacle was still holy; but when the priest, or the whole congregation (including the priest) sinned, it was no longer holy.[67] In the latter case, the priest was not allowed to eat the meat of the sin offering; moreover, the way into the sanctuary—the way from the people to the Most Holy place, where God dwells—had again to be cleansed, sanctified, and consecrated (cf. more generally Lev. 15:31, "Thus you shall keep the people of Israel separate from their uncleanness, lest they die in their uncleanness by defiling my tabernacle that is in their midst").

The principle can also be formulated spatially: the blood moves as far as the person or group involved is allowed to move, and purifies the tabernacle to that point.[68] An ordinary Israelite can never enter the sanc-

---

65. Wenham (1979, 93).
66. Cf. Rashi; see Cohen (1983, 615).
67. Cohen (1983, 617).
68. Kiuchi (1987, 124).

tuary; thus, when they have sinned, the sanctuary does not have to be purified, for they were not able to defile it. However, a priest was allowed to enter the sanctuary daily, so when he had sinned it had to be purified. To be sure, the Most Holy place was not entered; nor was the priest allowed to enter it. Only the high priest could do this, and only on the Day of Atonement (Lev. 16:2). However, the blood was brought as near as possible to the ark of the covenant by being sprinkled in front of[69] the veil, and was put on the altar of incense. On the Day of Atonement, the blood was sprinkled both over (on) and in front of (before) the mercy-seat (Lev. 16:14–15). In this way, the way of the people to God were purified.

4.6.3 The New Testament Application

In the New Testament application, our previous considerations may become even clearer. With his own blood, Christ has entered the (heavenly) sanctuary (Heb. 4:14; 9:11–12, 24–26), so that the way into the sanctuary has now been purified, and believers can freely approach God:

> Therefore, brothers, since we have confidence to enter the holy places by the blood of Jesus, by the new and living way that he opened for us through the curtain, that is, through his flesh, and since we have a great priest over the house of God, let us draw near with a true heart in full assurance of faith, with our hearts sprinkled clean from an evil conscience and our bodies washed with pure water (cf. 1 Pet. 1:2) (see further in §§5.3–5.4).

The role of the blood in the sin offering is essential, as the New Testament clearly shows: "[T]his is my blood of the covenant, which is poured out for many for the forgiveness of sins" (Matt. 26:28); "... the church of God, which he obtained with his own blood" (Acts 20:28). ".

---

69. According to some, "against" (wyc) or "toward" (ceb).

. . Christ, whom God put forward as a propitiation by his blood" (Rom. 3:25). "In him we have redemption through his blood, the forgiveness of our trespasses" (Eph. 1:7; cf. Col. 1:20); ". . . how much more will the blood of Christ . . . purify our conscience from dead works to serve the living God. . . . [W]ithout the shedding of blood there is no forgiveness of sins" (Heb. 9:14, 22). "[Y]ou were ransomed . . . with the precious blood of Christ, like that of a lamb without blemish or spot" (1 Pet. 1:18-19); "the blood of Jesus his Son cleanses us from all sin" (1 John 1:7). "To him who loves us and has freed us from our sins by his blood . . ." (Rev. 1:5); "you were slain, and by your blood you ransomed people for God from every tribe and language and people and nation" (5:9). "They have washed their robes and made them white in the blood of the Lamb" (7:14).

Whereas in the burnt and peace offerings the blood was sprinkled "against the sides of the alter" of burnt offering (Lev. 1:5, 11; 3:2, 8, 13), in the sin offering the blood was sometimes sprinkled in front of the veil, but also put on the horns of the altar. As we saw, in the former offerings these were the horns of the altar of incense, in the latter offering the horns of the altar of burnt offering. The difference was due to the seriousness of the trespass, which depended on the status of the trespasser. But at any rate the sin had affected the location of the sacrificial ministry: in each situation the altar of burnt offering, and when the priest was involved in the sin also the altar of incense.

To understand the sin offering it is essential to grasp the basic thought that the defilement of the offerer was transferred to the sacrificial animal, and was taken away by its death (cf. §4.4.3). This defilement could be physical (Lev. 12-15; see §§5.6-5.7) or spiritual: unintentional sin against the Lord (4:2, 13, 22-27; 5:1-4). As soon as the defilement had been transferred to the sin offering, a person was defiled by touching the blood of the sacrificial animal; earthenware vessels that had been used for the sin offering had to be broken 6:27), bronze vessels hand to be scoured and rinsed in water (v. 28; 11:33, 35; 15:12; Num. 31:22-23). The one who had burned the sin offering outside the camp had to be purified (Lev. 16:16, 28; cf. Num. 19:8-9, 21). But if the blood of the sin offering was applied according to the rules, it brought about the very purification of the offerer(s) (Lev. 16:33).[70]

We have seen before that the burnt and sin offerings were the chief, basic offerings in the Mosaic sacrificial ministry. Consecrations and various purification rituals (Lev. 8-9, 12-15; Num. 8:8, 12) were all based upon a burnt offering and a sin offering (see §§5.3-5.7). Together they formed the foundation for God's relationships with his people, as illustrated by the two great obligatory atoning rituals in Israel: the daily morning and evening burnt offerings, and the annual sin offering on the Day of Atonement. In Christ, the meanings of these two foundational offerings merge.

(a) *The sin offering:* as we saw, this takes away the (sinful) *unworthiness* of believers: "He himself bore our sins in his body on the tree, that we might die to sin and live to righteousness. By his wounds you have been healed" (1 Pet. 2:24). "For our sake he [i.e., God] made him [i.e., Christ] to be sin who knew no sin, so that in him we might become the righteousness of God" (2 Cor. 5:21). As the Hebrew word *chattat* means both "sin" and "sin offering," the expression "made him to be sin" (Heb. *hamartian epoiēsin*) could be read as: "made him to be a [or, the] sin offering."[71] Compare here also Romans 8:3, "By sending his own Son in the likeness of sinful flesh

---

70. Incidentally, the blood that, in the case of the priest (Lev. 8:23-24) or the leper (14:14), was put on the lobe of the right ear, on the thumb of his right hand, and on the big toe of his right foot, did not come from a sin offering but from the consecration offering, which had the character of a peace offering (see §§5.6 and 5.7.1).
71. Cf. Ouweneel (2007b, 347).

and for sin [ESV note, as a (or, the) sin offering], he condemned sin in the flesh."[72]

(b) *The burnt offering:* as we saw, this grants to the believer the *worthiness* of Christ himself. Of him God said, "This is my beloved Son, with whom I am well pleased" (Matt. 3:17; cf. 17:5). Thus the apostle Paul could say that believers had been "taken into favor in the Beloved" (Eph. 1:6 DARBY). And in the practical elaboration of believers' spiritual life, this means: "[W]alk in love, as Christ loved us and gave himself up for us, a fragrant offering and sacrifice to God" (5:2).

4.7 The Guilt Offering[73]
4.7.1 The Old Testament Form

In more contemporary translations, the "trespass offering" of the KJV has become a "guilt offering" (ESV), a "compensation offering" (CEB), a "reparation offering" (NABRE), a "restitution offering" (HCSB), or a "penalty offering" (NCV). These translations render the Hebrew term *asham*, from the root *'-sh-m*, "to make guilty, to be guilty" (Lev. 4:13, 22, 27 [cf. 3]; 5:2-5, 17, 19; 6:4, etc.), hence "to be held guilty," hence "to pay for the guilt," or short: "to pay" (Ps. 5:10; 34:21-22; Prov. 30:10; Hos. 10:2; 14:2). Among cognate terms I mention the Hebrew words *ashem*, "guilty" (2 Sam. 14:13), *ashmah*, "guilt" (Lev. 6:7; 22:16), and especially *asham*, which means both "guilt" and "penitence" (that through which guilt is settled; Gen. 26:10; Jer. 51:5; plur.: Ps. 68:21), hence "guilt offering" (Lev. 5:6-6:7, 17; 7:1-7; Num. 5:7-8; 1 Sam. 6:3-4, 8, 17; Isa. 53:10). Just as the Hebrew word *chattat* means both sin and that through which sin is blotted out, so too the Hebrew word *asham* means both guilt and that with which guilt is paid.

The guilt offering could be called a special form of the sin offering as long as we recognize that it differs

---
72. Cf. ibid.
73. See *DOTT* 1:557-66; *DNTT* 3:420-21, and the lexica.

considerably from the ordinary sin offerings. These differences are estimated rather differently. Gordon Wenham claimed, "Closer examination shows that the two sacrifices were quite distinct."[74] But Laird Harris observed,[75] "The sin offering . . . and the guilt offering . . . are very similar." This corresponds with Leviticus 7:7, "The guilt offering is just like the sin offering; there is one law for them."

A striking difference is that only a ram qualified as the guilt offering animal (Lev. 5:15-16, 18; 6:6; 19:21-22; cf. 4:12-13; Num. 6:12). Rams could also be used as burnt or peace offerings, but for the guilt offering rams alone were allowed, whereas, conversely, rams did not qualify as sin offering animals. Another difference is that no blood sprinkling occurred, unlike with the sin offerings. As with all other animal sacrifices, the fat parts and the kidneys went up in smoke on the altar of burnt offering (Lev. 7:3-5). As with some of the ordinary sin offerings, the meat was eaten by the priests near the sanctuary.

Many attempts have been made to formulate the difference between the sin offering and the guilt offering. Jacob Milgrom, an authority in the field of the Mosaic sacrifices, connected the sin offering with defilement, and the guilt offering with desecration. In the former case, the defiled person must be purified, whereas in the latter case, the profane must be consecrated again.[76] Notice here Leviticus 10:10: it may be expected that the priest would be able "to distinguish between the holy and the common, and between the unclean and the clean."

4.7.2 Various Cases

The first reason for bringing a guilt offering is this: "If anyone commits a breach of faith and sins unintention-

---

74. Wenham (1979, 105).
75. Harris (1990, 547).
76. Milgrom (1976, 127; 1991, 49-50, 339-78).

ally in any of the holy things of the Lord..." (Lev. 5:15). This presumably refers to, for instance, "the bread of his God, both of the most holy and of the holy things" (Lev. 21:22), of which someone of the priestly family was allowed to eat but not the ordinary Israelite. Therefore, Leviticus 22:14 says, "And if anyone eats of a holy thing unintentionally, he shall add the fifth of its value to it and give the holy thing to the priest"—which is characteristic of the guilt offering (see below). To the edible "most holy things" belonged the "bread of the Presence" (or "showbread," Lev. 24:9), the grain, sin and guilt offering (Lev. 2:3, 10; 6:10, 18, 22; 7:1, 6; 10:12, 17; 14:13; 18:9). To the edible "holy things" belonged the priestly parts of the peace offerings (Exod. 29:27-28; Lev. 7:31-36; 10:14-15; 23:20; Num. 6:20), and the firstfruits of the harvest and of the clean cattle (Num. 18:12-18). Gordon Wenham assumed that, also in cases when people had failed to fulfill a vow or to bring a tithe, a guilt offering was demanded.[77]

The trespasser had to make restitution for unintentionally robbing from the priest; in addition to restitution, a penalty of twenty percent had to be paid. Moreover, the trespasser had to consider that they had not only robbed from the priest but that such a sin was also sin against *God*.[78] Therefore, a ram had to be offered as a guilt offering. The worth of that ram apparently had to satisfy a certain minimum, to be determined by the priest (Lev. 5:15-16).

A second case of trespassing for which a guilt offering had to be brought was this: "If anyone sins, doing any of the things that by the LORD's commandments ought not to be done, though he did not know it, then realizes his guilt, he shall bear his iniquity" (Lev. 5:17). The expression "bear his iniquity" is crucial here, and means something like "suffer under (the consequenc-

---

77. Wenham (1979, 106).
78. Strack (1894, ad loc.).

es of) the illegitimate act." The person concerned was afraid that they had unintentionally sinned, and had called down upon themselves the wrath of God. They did not know exactly *what* their trespass was, but they did suffer under the matter.[79] In this case no restitution could be made, but a guilt offering had to be brought, so that "he has paid full compensation to the LORD" (v. 19 ESV note; cf. EXB, ICB, NABRE).

In the third case requiring a guilt offering involved sins that were definitely known to the trespasser:

> If anyone sins and commits a breach of faith against the LORD by deceiving his neighbor in a matter of deposit or security, or through robbery, or if he has oppressed his neighbor or has found something lost and lied about it, swearing falsely—in any of all the things that people do and sin thereby . . . (Lev. 6:2-3).

The sin involved here is not only theft, extortion, and the like, but also lying or perhaps committing perjury about it (cf. Exod. 22:7-9).[80] These are definitely not unconscious or unintentional sins. Yet, here, too, an atoning sacrifice was allowed, and even commanded. Of course, atonement could occur only if there was genuine repentance and sincere confession of sin. Not only was restitution required to the person robbed or extorted, or for the lost deposit, plus a penalty of twenty percent, but the LORD, too, had to receive satisfaction: both because of the theft as such—for every sin against one's neighbor is also a sin against God—and because of having taken the LORD's name in vain.

---

79. Gispen (1950, 95-96); Wenham (1979, 108).
80. Wenham (1979, 108) puts too much emphasis on the latter, for v. 4 does emphasize the restitution to the person robbed: he "will restore what he took by robbery or what he got by oppression or the deposit that was committed to him or the lost thing that he found."

4.7.3 Function and Meaning

As always, the sacrificial animal takes the place of the guilty person. Here, Isaiah 53:10 is quite remarkable: "he made himself[81] a guilt offering" (cf. CJB, ERV, NASB, RSV) because this poetic line stands entirely in the context of substitution:

> [H]e was pierced for our transgressions; he was crushed for our iniquities; upon him was the chastisement that brought us peace, and with his wounds we are healed. All we like sheep have gone astray; we have turned—everyone—to his own way; and the LORD has laid on him the iniquity of us all" (vv. 5-6).

The notion of *substitution* could hardly be expressed in a more poignant way (see further §§9.1-9.2).

However, the guilt offering also involved that other aspect, lacking in the sin offering, namely, that of *restitution*, that is, the compensation for, or restoration of, what went wrong. This can be clearly seen in Psalm 69, which no doubt has Messianic features:[82] "I restored that which I took not away" (v. 4 KJV). Arthur Clarke stated that Psalm 69(:4) shows to us the guilt offering aspect of Christ's vicarious suffering, which implies both the ideas of restoration and propitiation.[83] Here, the Messiah is the One who must make restitution vicariously of what others have "taken away" (stolen, ESV), whether from their neighbor or (especially) from God.[84] Christ restored the honor that humanity had stolen from God

---

81. The pronoun "himself" is in the accusative, not the dative.
82. Cf. v. 10 with John 2:17 and Rom. 15:3, and v. 22 with Matt.27:34, 48.
83. Clarke (1949, 175); so also Gaebelein (1965, 272).
84. Cf. Belgic Confession, Art. 21: "Therefore, He [Christ] 're stored that which He took not away' . . ."
(Dennison, 2008, 2:436). A tenor recitative in Bach's *St. Matthew's Passion* sings: "He must pay for the robbery of others" (Ger. *Er soll vor fremden Raub bezahlen*).

by glorifying him in and through his atoning death. As Jesus said (if we take the participle instrumentally, as many translations do), "I have glorified you on earth *by* finishing the work you gave me to do" (John 17:4 CJB).

The burnt offering and the sin offering had to be brought for the people at fixed times; I referred to the fixed morning and evening burnt offering (Exod. 29:38-46) and the fixed annual sin offering on the Day of Atonement (Lev. 16; see §§5.3-5.4). There was only one regular peace offering, namely, that of the Feast of Weeks (Pentecost; Lev. 23:19). However, there was no regular guilt offering. Perhaps we may say that, in the regular sacrifices, the notion of the guilt offering was implied in the fixed sin offerings. This supports our thesis that the primary sacrifices were the burnt and sin offerings. On all days, at all New Moon festivals, and at all seven annual festivals, burnt offerings were brought, and at all New Moon festivals and all annual festivals, sin offerings were brought as well, except on the Day of the Firstfruits (Heb. *Yom habBikkurim*) (Lev. 23; Num. 28-29).

To be sure, there were fixed peace and guilt offerings, but these were connected not with the festivals but with certain rituals. We find the peace offering in consecration rituals (see §4.5), and the guilt offering in purification rituals. Thus, Leviticus 14:12-14 prescribes a guilt offering for the purification of the leper (see §5.6). This probably has to do with leprosy being viewed as an expression of guilt toward God, especially in the holy things (cf. Num. 12:10-15; 2 Kings 5:25-27; 2 Chron. 26:16-21, and Lev. 5:17-19).[85] Some believe that a guilt offering had to be brought because one had failed to give the LORD his due: for the duration of the leper's illness, they were unable to fulfill their religious duties.[86] How-

---

85. Milgrom (1976, 80-82); Wenham (1979, 210); Obadiah ben Jakob Sforno thinks of blasphemous and haughty behavior which led to the judgment of being slain with leprosy; Cohen (1983, 691).
86. Gispen (1950, 223); Allis (1970, 147); Wenham (1979, 210).

ever, this can hardly be correct: why were those who had been ill for a long time not obliged to bring a guilt offering, too (cf. Luke 8:43)?[87]

A guilt offering was also brought after sexual intercourse with a female slave (Lev. 19:20-22), or when the Nazirite vow had been broken or was being renewed (Num. 6:12), or with sending away pagan women (Ezra 10:19). In all these cases, the people involved had brought guilt upon themselves that had to be atoned—guilt not only toward the neighbor but also, and particularly, toward the Lord God.

---

87. Noordtzij (1982, ad loc.).

Chapter 5
Special Atonement Rituals

[W]hen I see the blood,
I will pass over you,
and no plague will befall you
to destroy you,
when I strike the land of Egypt.
Exodus 12:13

Christ, our Passover lamb, has been sacrificed.
Let us therefore celebrate the festival,
not with the old leaven, the leaven of malice and evil,
but with the unleavened bread of sincerity and truth.
1 Corinthians 5:7–8

Christ entered once for all into the holy places,
not by means of the blood of goats and calves
but by means of his own blood,
thus securing an eternal redemption.
Hebrews 9:12

Summary: *Following our discussion of the ordinary Old Testament offerings (chapter 4), in the present chapter we discuss additional Old Testament atoning rituals: the Passover (Pesach) (with special emphasis on the lamb), the Day of Atonement (Yom Kippur) (with special emphasis on the two goats, one representing the principle of satisfaction, the other that of substitution), the law about leprosy (being a picture of outbreaking sin) (with special emphasis on the meaning of the two birds), the consecration of the priests (why did this include a burnt offering and a sin offering, and what is the nature of the consecration offering?), the cleansing of women in childbed and of persons with a discharge (why was purification in such cases necessary?), and finally, the water of purification and its practical use for the wilderness journey. All of these rituals shed light on atonement in the New Testament sense of the term.*

5.1   Pesach[1]

5.1.1 The Institution of Pesach

ALL OF THE ATONING rituals discussed thus far, as well as those treated in this chapter, shed light on atonement in the New Testament sense. This is evident from the frequent references to these Old Testament rituals in the New Testament. Therefore, it is worthwhile to devote attention to them.

The first annual festival on Israel's religious calendar[2] was also the festival that was instituted first (Exod. 12), viz., Passover (Heb. *Pesach*). Both this festival and the Feast of the Unleavened Loaves (Bread) (Heb. *Chag haMatsot*; shortened to *Matsot*) were established for the

---

1. For more details, see Ouweneel (2001b, chapter 3); see also the bibliography in that volume for many publications dealing with the biblical festivals. For the names and spelling of various Hebrew festivals and sacrifices mentioned in this chapter, we are following largely the stylistic standards set forth in *The BL Hanbook of Style (2nd ed.)*.
2. The seventh month of the religious calendar is the first month of the civil calendar.

Israelites during their stay in Egypt (cf. Exod. 12:1). So these festivals are closely linked with the most ancient historical event of Israel as a nation: the exodus from Egypt.[3] Shortly before the people of Israel left the land of Egypt, where they had served as slaves for such a long time, the LORD through his servant Moses gave them the Passover (Heb. *Chag haPesach*, "Feast of the Passover [Lamb]"[4]). The very first Passover festival occurred in connection with the event of the exodus itself; all the subsequent Passover festivals served, and serve, to commemorate the exodus.

What remained the same in all Passover festivals after the exodus from Egypt was that each family—or a somewhat larger group, as many as could eat an entire lamb in one evening—had to pick a lamb from the flock. A lamb is a young sheep, but also a young goat could be taken (v. 5, "You may take it from the sheep or from the goats"). I will continue to speak of a lamb because in later practice this was the only animal that was used. According to Rabbi Nachmanides (d. ca. 1270), a lamb (a young ram) was chosen because it was the sacred animal of the Egyptians; by killing it, the Israelites wanted to show the impotence of the Egyptian god. He also pointed out that the ram was the Zodiac sign for the month of spring (Nisan).[5]

The lamb is often depicted as a very young animal; but in fact it had to be a ram of one year old. It was supposed to exhibit no defects. It was slaughtered, roasted in its entirety, and then the meat of the ram had to be completely eaten during the same night, together with bitter herbs" (Heb. *merorim*, v. 8) and unleavened bread (plural: *matsot*, loaves).

---

3. In Deut. 16 :1, 3, 6, 12 this fact is mentioned no fewer than five times; see also Exod. 12:17, 42; 13:3-4, 8-9, 14, 16; 23:15; 34:18.
4. Only in Exod. 34:25; also called "Festival of the Ears [of Grain]" (Heb. *Chag ha'Abib*) and "Spring Festival."
5. Cohen (1983, 387); cf. on this point extensively, Ouweneel (1998, 303-12).

5.1.2 The Blood on the Doorposts

Only during the very first celebration of the Passover festival was the blood of the slaughtered lamb put "on the two doorposts and the lintel of the houses in which they eat it" with a bunch of hyssop (vv. 7, 22). Hyssop (Heb. *ezob*—the words in both English and Hebrew appear etymologically related) was probably a kind of Majorana (*Origanum syriacum*). The plant was also used in the purification of the leper (Lev. 14:4, 6, 49, 51-52; see §5.6) and of someone who had touched a corpse (Num. 19:6, 18; see §5.7.4). Thus, it was a means of symbolic purification, as confirmed by Psalm 51:7a, "Purge me with hyssop, and I shall be clean" (also see §7.6.5).

This putting the blood on the doorposts and the lintel made that first celebration absolutely unique. The reason for it was that, during the Passover night, the "destroyer" would pass through the land of Egypt. In all houses where the blood had *not* been smeared, he would kill the firstborn son (Exod. 12:23; cf. Ps. 78:51; 135:8; 136:10). This was indeed what happened with the firstborn sons of the Egyptians (cf. v. 29, the crown prince; the daughters are not mentioned; also cf. son[s] in 12:24, 26; 13:8, 12-15). The firstborn of Israel were saved from this, not because they were better, stronger, or more devoted than the firstborn of Egypt but because they had found refuge under the blood of the Passover lamb. However, the LORD did not have in view only the firstborn at that time; in Exodus 13:1-2 and 11-15 we see that, henceforth, *all* the firstborn sons of Israel had to be sanctified to the Lord, that is, consecrated to his service, even though, as far as this task was concerned, they were later replaced by the Levites (Num. 3:13, 44-51; 8:16-18; 18:15-18).

Because the firstborn sons of Israel took refuge under the blood of the Passover lamb during the last night of their sojourn in Egypt, they were safe from the "destroyer" (12:23; cf. 1 Cor. 10:10 and Heb. 11:28). Sometimes

Special Atonement Rituals

God spoke of himself as the One who would kill the firstborn of Egypt (Exod. 11:4; 12:23a, 29), sometimes he distinguished himself from the "destroyer," just as the Angel of YHWH is sometimes identified with him, and sometimes distinguished from him.[6] In Psalm 78:49 it is God himself who brought destruction but for this he used "a company of destroying angels" (lit., "angels of evil," ASV, WEB). Some understand the "destroyer" to be an evil, competing power, which was stopped by the LORD. However, the passages mentioned point instead to an "angel" (messenger, representative) of God himself (see the parallel accounts in 2 Sam. 24:15-17 and 1 Chron. 21:14-18).

5.1.3 Terminology

The Hebrew name *Pesach* was not primarily the name of the festival but of the Passover lamb itself (in the Pentateuch: Exod. 12:11, 21, 43, 48; 34:25; Lev. 23:5; Num. 9:2-14; 28:16; 33:3; Deut. 16:1-2, 5-6). The Hebrew of Exodus 12:27 speaks of *zebach-pesach*, that is, "Passover sacrifice," and in 34:25 of *zebach chag hapesach*, that is, "sacrifice of the Passover festival." For our purpose, these verses are particularly important because they show that the Passover lamb had indeed sacrificial meaning, and thus atoning significance (see below).

In the Septuagint the word *pesach* has been changed into *Pascha*; in the Dutch Bible translations, *Pascha* has become the common word for "Passover," both in the Old and the New Testament. The Septuagint also has *Pasek* or *Pasech* (in 2 Chron. 30 and 35), and the Vulgate has *Phase* or *Pase* (cf. Dutch *Pasen*, French *Pâques*, Spanish *Pascua*, Italian *Pasqua*, Swedish *Påsk*, and Danish *Påske*[7]).

---

6. Ouweneel (2007b, §7.3).
7. Interestingly, the English and the German church adopted the ancient pagan designations: *Easter*, *Ostern*, respectively, referring to the Germanic goddess Ostara.

The Hebrew term *Pesach* is usually derived from the root *p-s-ch*, "be crippled, to limp" (2 Sam. 4:4; 1 Kings 18:21, 26), hence "to pass limping," hence "to skip over, to pass over." Indeed, we find the meaning "pass over" in Exodus 12:13, "[T]he blood shall be a sign for you, on the houses where you are. And when I see the blood, I will pass over [Heb. *pasachti*] you, and no plague will befall you to destroy you, when I strike the land of Egypt" (also see vv. 23 and 27). In addition to this passage, *p-s-ch* only occurs in Isaiah 31:5 (NKJV), "Passing over, He will preserve" Jerusalem (ESV, "he will spare and rescue it"). Again, this concerns Egypt (vv. 1, 3)! Perhaps we can translate, "rescue it by passing over," just as God had done during the Passover night (notice the quotation marks in NIV, "he will 'pass over' it and will rescue it").

The Passover lamb was slaughtered on the fourteenth of the month of Abib (or Aviv; post-exilic name: Nisan), literally "between the two evenings" (Exod. 12:6; Lev. 23:5; Num. 9:3), that is, "at twilight" (ESV, NKJV, NIV), or simply "in the evening" (KJV). Some think of the time between sunset and dusk, others think of the time between the sun's descent (3:00 to 5:00 p.m.) and sunset (cf. Deut. 16:6, "in the evening at sunset"). Still others think of the midpoint between noon and the beginning of the evening, that is, according to Jewish parlance, around the "ninth hour" (3:00 p.m.).[8] In connection with the latter, it is important that the evening burnt offering was also brought "between the two evenings" (Exod. 29:39), and in the later Jewish tradition this was the ninth hour (cf. Acts 3:1). For our purpose, this is highly significant because this was also the hour when Christ, the true Passover lamb, died (Matt. 27:46; Mark 15:34; Luke 23:44; see §5.2.2).[9]

---

8. Cf. Talmud: Pesachim 58a; Yomah 28b; see also Wenham (1979, 302); Cohen (1983, 387); Kaiser (1990, 373).
9. Cf. Ouweneel (2007b, 408).

5.2 The Spiritual Meaning of Pesach
5.2.1 The Lamb in Paul's and John's Writings

The clearest New Testament reference to the spiritual significance of Pesach is found in 1 Corinthians 5:7, "Christ, our Passover lamb [Gk. one word: *pascha*], has been sacrificed." G. Sevenster said of this, "Apparently, the apostle could assume that the church would understand his thought without further explanation. The chief point is that Paul deems it utterly obvious here that Christ's death can be viewed as an offering for others."[10] In this regard, this passage can be linked with several others that speak of Christ as a "Lamb."

The first time Jesus is referred to as "the Lamb" is by John the Baptist: "Behold, the Lamb of God, who takes away the sin of the world" (John 1:29; cf. v. 36, "Behold, the Lamb of God"). It is most likely that John was referring here to the Passover lamb. At any rate, the quotation in John 19:36 ("Not one of his bones will be broken") suggests a clear link between Jesus' death on the cross and the Passover by referring to Exodus 12:46 ("you shall not break any of its bones"). A question that must be raised concerning this interpretation is whether the Passover lamb does indeed "take away sin," as John the Baptist seemed to suggest. Is it indeed an *atoning* sacrifice? Jewish tradition took it this way—just as *every* bloody offering in Israel had an atoning character, though with widely varied nuances (see §§4.3–4.7). The Passover lamb is a sacrifice (Heb. *zebach*), as well (§5.1.3). W. Kaiser thought implicitly of an atoning sacrifice by pointing out that in Exodus 12 all the people functioned as priests (cf. 19:56, "you shall be to me a kingdom of priests").[11] According to Deuteronomy 16:1–8, in the Promised Land Pesach had to be connected with the future temple, which underscored its sacrificial character.[12]

---

10. Sevenster (1946, 172).
11. Kaiser (1990, 372).
12. Craigie (1976, 242).

At a minimum we can say is that the firstborn of Israel found refuge under the blood of the Passover lamb, just as the New Testament believers find refuge under the blood of Christ (see, e.g., Eph. 1:7; Col. 1:14; 1 Pet. 1:18-19; 1 John 1:7; Rev. 1:5). This does not mean that John the Baptist's reference to the "Lamb of God" could not (also) refer to other Old Testament images, such as the daily burnt offering (Exod. 29:38-42; Num. 28:3-8), various special offerings (Lev. 1:10; 3:6; 5:6, 15, 18; 6:6; 12:8; 14:10; 22:19, 21, 28), and the Messiah as the true Lamb of Isaiah 53:7 (cf. the application to Christ in Acts 8:32-35). We might think also of the lamb or ram in Genesis 22:7-13, which in Jewish tradition plays a great role as well; it often speaks of the "binding" (Heb. *ᶜakedah*) of Isaac, especially at Rosh Hashanah, the Jewish New Year.[13]

All these references, including those to the Passover lamb, find their culmination in the person of Jesus Christ and his atoning work on the cross. Also in the book of Revelation, the apostle John many times calls Jesus the Lamb (from Rev. 5:6 to 22:3),[14] in which all the meanings we have mentioned seem to be united, from Exodus 12 to Isaiah 53.

5.2.2 The Ninth Hour

Another important reference to Jesus as the true Lamb of God is found in Peter's letters: believers, you know "that you were ransomed from the futile ways inherited from your forefathers, not with perishable things such as silver or gold, but with the precious blood of Christ, like that of a lamb without blemish or spot" (1 Pet. 1:18-19). Peter, too, seems to refer primarily to the Pass-

---

13. Ouweneel (2001b, 145).
14. In this context, I will not be discussing the possible but irrelevant differences between the usual Gk. word for "lamb" (*amnos*) and the one used in Rev., viz., *arnion*.

over lamb, especially because of the addition "without blemish or spot" (cf. Exod. 12:5, "without blemish," Gk. *amōmos*, also in Heb. 9:14, ". . . Christ, who through the eternal Spirit offered himself without blemish to God"). We notice, though, that other lambs used as sacrifices had to be without blemish, too (Exod. 29:1; Lev. 1:3, 10; 3:1, 6; 4:3, 23, 28, 32; 5:15, 18; 6:6 etc.). Moreover, 1 Peter 2:22-24 refers to Isaiah 53 (especially vv. 7 and 9), where the Messiah is the true sacrifice. Yet, as I see it, in 1 Peter 1 the Passover lamb comes primarily to the fore because the subject here is not so much atonement for sins but rather the redemption from the slavery of sin, just as Israel had been redeemed from the slavery of Egypt.

One of the most remarkable parallels between the Passover lamb and Jesus is that Jesus seems to have died at the place where, and at the moment when, the Passover lambs were slaughtered. The synoptic Gospels tell us emphatically that he died in Jerusalem at the ninth hour (Matt. 27:45-46; Mark 15:33-34; Luke 23:44), and we have already seen that this was the hour of the daily burnt offering in the temple but probably also of the death of the Passover lambs. In an analogous way, Christ arose from the dead precisely on the Day of the Firstfruits (Heb. *Yom HaBikkurim*), and the Holy Spirit was poured out precisely on the day of the Feast of Weeks or Pentecost (Heb. *Shevu'ot*).[15]

The hour of the evening offering, or the ninth hour (i.e., about 3:00 p.m.), the "hour of prayer" (Acts 3:1; cf. 10:2-3), plays a remarkable role in redemptive history. It was the hour when fire descended from heaven upon the sacrifice that the prophet Elijah offered on Mount Carmel in order to lead Israel back to God (1 Kings 18:36). It was the hour when the prophet Daniel was visited by the angel Gabriel, who revealed to him the subsequent history of Jerusalem (Dan. 9:21). It was the hour when Ezra the scribe humbled himself before God on behalf

---

15. Ouweneel (2001b, §§4.1.1, 4.2.3-4).

of the people, and subsequently together with the people (Ezra 9:15). It was the hour when the lame man at the Beautiful Gate was healed through Peter and John—the first miracle after Pentecost (Acts 3:1). It was also the hour when the Roman centurion Cornelius received his vision with the aim of inviting to his home Peter, who would open the door of the gospel to the Gentiles (Acts 10:3). In short, it was at the very hour when the evening sacrificial animal as well as the Passover lambs as well as Jesus himself died that God brought redemptive blessing on people who were to receive it.

5.3 The Day of Atonement: the Ritual
5.3.1 Introduction

No Old Testament passage describes the atoning work of Christ, as God intended it to be, more extensively, and thus anticipates Christ's atoning death more clearly, than the one about the Day of Atonement (Lev. 16; 23:27-32; Num. 29:7-11).[16] The seventh month of Israel's religious calendar, that is, the first month of the civil year, the month of Tishri, features on 1 Tishri the Jewish New Year (Heb. *Rosh Hashanah*, "Head of the Year"), which is also called "Day of the Blast [of Trumpets]" (Heb. *Yom Teruʿah*), then on 10 Tishri the Day of Atonement (Heb. *Yom Hakkippurim* [cf. Lev. 23:27], or *Yom Kippur*), and finally on 15-22 Tishri the Feast of Booths or Tabernacles (Heb. *Sukkot*).

The festival of *Rosh Hashanah* is the first of ten days of penitence, of which *Yom Kippur* is the last and most important. These ten days are called the "Days of Awe" (Heb. *Yamim Noraim*). During the times of the tabernacle, the First Temple and the Second Temple, these ten

---

16. See Ouweneel (2001b, §5.3), plus the bibliography in that volume (206-08). Here in this volume, I am providing a further development of and commentary on that text. See also Noordtzij (1982, ad loc.); Gispen (1950, ad loc.); Grant (1956, chapter 13); Wenham (1979, ad loc.); Hoek (1998, chapter 5).

days of repentance at the beginning of the new calendar year formed the prelude to the great atonement accomplished through the sin offering brought on the Day of Atonement. Israel's redemptive history began in Egypt with the Passover lamb (Exod. 12), of which the poured out blood formed the foundation for the ultimate restoration of Israel. Look at this brief survey:

(a) The Passover (Heb. *Pesach*) was fulfilled in Christ's atoning death on the cross.

(b) The Day of the Firstfruits (Heb. *Yom Habikkurim*) was fulfilled in his resurrection on the third day.

(c) The Feast of Weeks or Pentecost (Heb. *Shavu'oth*) was fulfilled in the outpouring of the Holy Spirit (Acts 2).

(d) The Day of Atonement (Heb. *Yom Kippur*) will be fulfilled completely at the second coming of Christ (see §13.7).

We are struck by the severity of this "Sabbath of Sabbaths," which is not a weekly Sabbath but the great annual Sabbath (see Lev. 16:29–32; 23:28–32). These strict rules involved absolute rest, abstaining from every kind of work, and complete fasting. In the Jewish tradition, this not only means abstaining from food and drink but also refraining from washing the body, refraining from stimulants, and even from the "luxury" of leather shoes.[17] These rules underscore the important fact that humans cannot contribute anything to their own atonement. It is only the LORD God who, through these prescriptions and their fulfillment in Christ, has brought about atonement for his people.

5.3.2 The First Goat

In order to better understand the Day of Atonement, let us summarize the chief elements of the sin offering, as these are extensively described in Leviticus 16 (see this

---

17. Talmud: Mishnah Yomah 73b.

and the next section; in §5.4.2 the burnt offering on the Day of Atonement will be discussed).[18]

(1) The high priest purified himself: he bathed his body and put on special white garments (v. 4). Jesus is the "merciful and faithful high priest in the service of God, to make propitiation for the sins of the people" (Heb. 2:17).

(2) The high priest took the two goats, which together constituted the one sin offering for Israel, that is, they presented two aspects of the work of Christ (see below). He cast lots over them: one goat was for the LORD, and one was "for Azazel" (regarding this, see §5.4.1) (vv. 5-10). Tradition tells us that the lot "for the LORD" always landed in high priest's right hand, which was considered to be a good omen. However, throughout the forty years preceding the destruction of Jerusalem (AD 30-70) it landed in the high priest's left hand. (Note also that the red ribbon put between the horns of the scapegoat, which, if it turned white, proved that the LORD had accepted the Day of Atonement sacrifice, stayed red after AD 30.[19]) This is quite remarkable because the year AD 30 was the presumed year of Jesus' death.[20] After he had brought the true Day of Atonement sacrifice, the usual animal sacrifice of that day could no longer be acceptable to God, particularly if it was not connected with Christ's sacrifice.

(3) The high priest slaughtered a bull for himself and his "house" (i.e., family) (v. 11). The "house" of the high priest Jesus Christ is the New Testament church (Heb. 3:6; 10:21; cf. Eph. 2:19; 1 Tim. 3:15; Titus 1:7; 1 Pet. 2:5; 4:17). This is important because it shows that the prophetic future of this world involves not only Israel. The

18. See also extensively, the Talmud tract Yomah, also called Kip purim.
19. Rosh Hashanah 31b; Yomah 39b (fol. 39a) says, though, that this had been the case from the time of Simon the Just (ca. 300 BC).
20. See Ouweneel (2007b, 374-75).

church will occupy an important position as nothing less than the "house" of the great high priest himself.[21]

(4) *First entrance into the Most Holy Place.* The high priest took a censer filled with coals of fire from the altar, his hands filled with sweet incense beaten small, and brought all of this inside the curtain (veil), and put the incense on the fire of the altar of incense (vv. 12-13). The purpose of this may have been to create a smoke screen, so that the high priest would not see the Shekinah,[22] or perhaps conversely, that God would not see the sinner.[23] On some occasions, incense did turn away God's wrath (Num. 16:46-48; cf. Ps. 141:2).

(5) *Second entrance into the Most Holy Place.* The high priest brought part of the blood of the bull into the Most Holy place, and sprinkled it in front of, and on, the ark of the covenant (v. 14).

(6) *Third entrance into the Most Holy Place.* He slaughtered the "goat for the LORD," brought part of the goat's blood into the Most Holy place, and sprinkled it in front of, and on, the ark of the covenant (v. 14). The book of Hebrews deals extensively with this matter, and refers it to the sacrifice of Christ on the cross (2:17; 7:27; 9:7, 14, 23-28; 10:1-14). Since his ascension, Christ is in the heavenly sanctuary (9:12, 24), where he awaits his second coming (10:13). Therefore, despite the cross, for Israel, the Day of Atonement has not yet been entirely fulfilled, as we will see in point (9) (next section).

(7) The high priest put another part of the blood of the bull and the goat on the horns of the altar of burnt offering "all around," and sprinkled some of the blood on the altar itself (vv. 18-19). It was the blood that blotted out the sins of the people, and reconciled them with God. Similarly, the blood of Christ brought this about, this time genuinely and perfectly, once for all.

---

21. See extensively, Ouweneel (2012a).
22. Hertz (1932, 156).
23. Keil and Delitzsch (2:399).

(8) The high priest symbolically purified the tabernacle with the blood, and thereby consecrated it anew (vv. 16–19).

5.3.3 The Second Goat

(9) Subsequently, the high priest loaded all the sins of the people upon the second goat, the one "for Azazel" (see §5.4.1), and sent it away into the wilderness (vv. 20–23). Apparently, the intention was that it would perish there. To be sure of this, it became the Jewish custom to cast the goat down from a cliff on to jagged rocks.[24] Only then were the sins of the Israelites actually removed. In the sanctuary, the *objective* foundation for their atonement had been laid with the blood of the first goat. However, *subjectively* the people took part in the atonement only when the second goat had been sent away. Similarly, on the cross the foundation for Israel's future restoration has been laid; but as a *nation*, Israel will share in the atonement only when Jesus returns from the heavenly sanctuary, and eternally removes the sins of the people on the basis of his own work on the cross (vv. 17–21). At that time, the Day of Atonement will become a complete spiritual reality for Israel (see §13.7).[25]

During the time of the Second Temple, the people were so glad that the high priest had returned from the sanctuary unhurt that the afternoon of the Day of Atonement was a time of great festival joy.[26] This was a clear anticipation of the joy connected with the coming of the Messiah and of his kingdom of peace and righteousness. Some rabbis believed that the Messiah would appear on the Day of Atonement,[27] one that occurred in a Year of Jubilee (cf. Lev. 25:8–34). Today, Isaiah 58 belongs to the Scripture readings in the synagogue service

---

24. Ibn Ezra mentioned this tradition; Cohen (1983, 706).
25. Coates (2007, 200–03).
26. Talmud: Ta'anit 26b.
27. Cf. Talmud: Yomah 19b.

on the Day of Atonement,[28] and in earlier days the readings went to Isaiah 61. Therefore, some assume that the synagogue service in which Jesus read Isaiah 61, and applied it to himself (Luke 4:16-22), occurred on a Day of Atonement. In any case, some rabbis believed that one day the Messiah will appear to Israel with the words of Isaiah 61.

For those who believe in Jesus Messiah today, the Day of Atonement is already a complete spiritual reality. For Israel it will be so at the second coming of Christ, at the end of the seventy "weeks" (periods of seven years): "Seventy weeks are decreed about your people and your holy city, to finish the transgression, to put an end to sin, and *to atone for iniquity*, to bring in everlasting righteousness" (Dan. 9:24). For Israel, that day will be a day of repentance and confession of sin (cf. Zech. 12:10-11). At the beginning of the month of Tishri (that is, in the autumn), Israel says as it were, "The harvest is past, the summer is ended, and we are not saved" (Jer. 8:20). But then, on the tenth day, the Day of Atonement is celebrated, the day of salvation, just before the great harvest festival, the Feast of Booths. The end of the great harvest from Israel as well as from the Gentiles is at the same time the day of great redemption.

(10) The high priest took off his white garments, bathed his body in water, and put on his regular high priestly garments (vv. 23-24; cf. Exod. 28). The person who led the second goat away also had to wash his clothes and bathe his body (v. 26).

(11) The high priest put the fat of the bull and of the goat on the altar of burnt offering, where it went up in smoke (v. 25) for a pleasing aroma to the LORD (cf. Lev. 4:31; Eph. 5:2).

(12) Another person took the skin, the flesh, and the dung of the bull and of the goat, and burned it all outside the camp (v. 27).

---

28. See Ouweneel (2001b, §5.3.2).

5.4 Various Sacrificial Animals
5.4.1 The Goat for Azazel

The expression "goat for Azazel" (called "the scapegoat" in Lev. 16:8, 10, 26) is quite remarkable. The four chief explanations of this expression are the following:

(a) Azazel means "the goat [Heb. ^{c}ez] that departs" (from the root ^{c}-z-l), a meaning we find in the Septuagint (Gk. *apopompē*) and the Vulgate (Lat. *caper emissarius*; cf. DRA: emissary goat; KJV: the scapegoat [i.e., escaping goat]).[29] The derivation is debatable, especially because Leviticus 16 speaks of a male goat (buck, he-goat, Heb. *sa^{c}ir*), not of a female goat (^{c}ez).

(b) The word is derived from a supposed verbal form *azalzel* (whose basic form does occur in Arabic), which means "to remove" or "to carry away"; that is, the "goat for the removal" (viz., of the sins).[30]

(c) The word is the proper name of a wilderness area (cf. v. 22), or for a part of it: "steep rock" (Rashi).

(d) The word is the name of a desert demon, which perhaps means "strong [from ^{c}azaz] god [el]" (Ibn Ezra, Maimonides). Nachmanides believed that this referred to the angel Samael, and that the second goat was meant to be a sacrifice to him.[31]

Most expositors understand Azazel as a spiritual power hostile to God, which belongs to the wilderness (cf. the ESV, which renders the term as a proper name). They do so especially because of the parallelism in verse 8 (lit., "one lot for YHWH and one lot for Azazel").[32] Reference is often made also to the fallen angel Azazel or Azael in 1 Enoch 6:7 and 8:1. He is supposed to be the angel who gave direction to the *grigori* (from Gk. *egrēgoroi*,

---

29. This is argued by Harris (1990, 590).
30. See the various references in Gispen (1950, 243).
31. Cohen (1983, 706).
32. Noordtzij (1982, ad loc.); Gispen (1950, 243–44); Wenham (1979, 234), who mentions other possible renderings as well.

"watchers";[33] cf. this notion in Dan. 4:13, 17, 23). These were supposedly the fallen angels who had intercourse with earthly women, from whom issued the giants and through whom the Flood was brought about (Gen. 6:1-4). Islam contains a similar tradition: here, Azazel is a *jinn* (demon) who was cast from heaven because he desired earthly women. Azazel has also been viewed as the leader of the *se͑irim* (plural of Heb. *sa͑ir*, "goat [demon]"), the demons looking like he-goats (RSV: satyrs!) in the wilderness (Lev. 17:7; 2 Chron. 11:15; Isa. 34:14). In the so-called Apocalypse of Abraham, Azazel is identified with the serpent that tempted Eve (Gen. 3:1-6).

Of course, in Leviticus 16, the intention of all this is not that the second goat was to be *sacrificed* to someone called Azazel. First, such a sacrifice was strictly forbidden (Lev. 17:7; Deut. 32:17); second, the scapegoat was not a sacrifice in the actual sense of the word. Rather, the meaning is that the goat, loaded with the sins of the people, was sent into the wild where the unclean spirits belong. One might even say: the goat (Heb. *sa͑ir*) was sent to the domain where the goat demons (Heb. *se͑irim*) belong: "[W]ild animals will lie down there, and their houses will be full of howling creatures; there ostriches will dwell, and there wild goats [KJV: satyrs] will dance" (Isa. 13:21). "[W]ild animals shall meet with hyenas; the wild goat [KJV: satyr] shall cry to his fellow" (34:14).[34]

The destruction of Babylon is the subject of Isaiah 13:21 and 34:14, and also of Revelation 18:2: "Fallen, fallen is Babylon the great! She has become a dwelling place for demons, a haunt for every unclean spirit, a haunt for every unclean bird, a haunt for every unclean and detestable beast." Here again, we find a description of

---

33. Cf. Ouweneel (2004, 37-38).
34. A satyr is a being from Greek mythology (Latin counter part: *faun*) often depicted with a goat's tail, goat's ears, and sometimes goat's legs. The Greek forest god Pan is also depicted as a human with goat's legs and horns. Later Christian tradition applied these features to Satan.

a domain filled with demons, unclean spirits, unclean birds and beasts. Consider as well, in connection with the sending of the scapegoat into the wilderness, what Jesus said, "When the unclean spirit has gone out of a person, it passes through waterless places seeking rest, but finds none" (Matt. 12:43; cf. Luke 11:24). A striking episode featuring an unclean place to which demons can be sent is that involving the pigs in Matthew 8:31-32 (and par.), which rushed down the steep bank into the sea nd drowned.

5.4.2 Other Sacrificial Animals

On the Day of Atonement the *sin offering* was the central point of attention—but a *burnt offering* could not be omitted. No wonder: in Christ's atoning work, not only carrying away believers' sins is important but also establishing their new status and acceptability in Christ before God (see §4.4). Therefore, the high priest offered as a burnt offering a ram for himself and for his house as well as a ram for the rest of the people of Israel (Lev. 16:3, 24; Num. 29:8-9).

It is remarkable that whereas the high pries administered the sin offering act in white garments, he administered the burnt offering act in his ordinary high priestly garments (Lev. 16:24): the breastpiece, the ephod, the robe, the coat of checker work, the turban, and the sash (Exod. 28:4). Perhaps this was because these ordinary high priestly garments were connected with the high priest's *daily* ministry: representing God's people in the sanctuary. This came to expression in that he *continually* wore the names of Israel's tribes on his shoulders and on his breast (Exod. 39:2-14). Typologically this pointed to the *heavenly* ministry of our great high priest: Christ (Heb. 2:18; 4:14-16; 6:20; 7:24-25; 8:1-2; 9:11-15; 10:19-22). Only in Hebrews 2:17 do we hear about his *earthly* and *one-time* work as a high priest: his self-sacrifice on the cross. Each year, on the Day of Atonement, the high priest administered the sin offering while wearing the white garments as a one-time annual ministry that was exceptional.

The bull and the two goats of the sin offering and the two rams of the burnt offering numbered five animals in total. According to Numbers 29:8-11, in addition to this, there were the same offerings as for the New Year's festival: as a burnt offering a young bull, a ram, and seven one-year-old sheep; as a sin offering a he-goat. In addition to this were the two sheep for the morning and evening burnt offerings. In total these numbered seventeen animals.[35] In comparison with the number used for the New Year's festival, this was not conspicuously many: on that day, twenty-three animals were offered, but this was also because that day coincided with a New Month festival.

5.5 The Significance of the Day of Atonement
5.5.1 Satisfaction and Substitution

The central sacrifice on the Day of Atonement was the sin offering; for its meaning I refer to §4.6. The most remarkable new element is that on the Day of Atonement the two meanings, normally combined in the sin offering, were separated by sacrificing two animals instead of one: one goat for the Lord and one goat for Azazel. Together these two goats constituted the one sin offering for the people. This helps us understand why the high priest did not lay his hands on the first goat but only on the second goat. (When the sin offering consisted of only one animal this occurred with the animal that was to be slaughtered.[36])

In the light of both the Old and New Testaments, the

---

35. In Jewish tradition, 17 is a sacred number: the numerical sum of the letters in the name YHWH (6+5+10+5) is 26; if we add the numbers (6+5+1+0+5) it is 17. Recall as well the number 153 in John 21:11, which is the sum of the first 17 integers.
36. *Contra* Shelton (2006, 54, 61-62).

meanings of the two goats seem readily apparent. The first goat illustrated what theologians have come to call *satisfaction*, that is, what in the work of atonement is necessary *for God* (i.e., "satisfying" his offended holiness and righteousness). The second goat illustrated what theologians have come to call *substitution*, that is, what in the work of atonement is necessary *for the people* (the scapegoat being sent to its death as their substitute). In the present book, these terms will be dealt with extensively in chapter 9, but it is important to briefly refer to them here.

Before God could show his mercy to a sinful people (second goat) something had to be offered to God himself (first goat). The satisfaction of God's honor and God's justice had to be provided. We have seen that the sins of the people, including those committed against the neighbor, were also sins against God. Therefore, the blood of an innocent sacrifice had to be carried into the Most Holy Place, the figurative dwelling place of God. The blood had to be sprinkled on the mercy seat as a confirmation and coronation of a perfectly borne judgment on sin. The blood was also sprinkled in front of the ark to indicate that, through this atoning blood, the way for humanity to approach God had been purified and sanctified again, and that, henceforth, priestly ministry in the sanctuary was again possible (cf. §4.6.1).

The *second* goat carried the iniquities of the people to a "remote area" (v. 22). As I said, this is prophetically applicable to the coming Day of Atonement for the penitent remnant of Israel (Dan. 9:27; see §13.7). However, the principle that is presented here is also applicable to the members of the Gentile church. The first goat shows how Christ underwent God's fatal judgment on sin, and how in this way God found such perfect satisfaction that, on the basis of this offering, he could provide the "ministry of reconciliation." This is the ministry through which God implores all people: "[B]e reconciled to God" (cf. 2 Cor. 5:18–21).[37] However, for those who are attracted by the gospel of God's love, and come to plead on the basis of this sacrifice, there is a second problem: not only must God's honor be restored through his judgment on sin as an evil power, but the sinners' sins—the acts flowing from their sinful natures—must also be blotted out. Christ has accomplished this, too. On the cross, he "confessed," so to speak, all the believers' sins as the true high priest (Lev. 16:21) as if they were his own sins, and as the true sacrifice he bore all their sins in his body on the cross (1 Pet. 2:24).

This "confessing" of believers' sins by the sinless One as if they were his own sins comes to light in some psalms that are clearly Messianic. In Psalm 40, Jesus prophetically presents himself as the burnt, grain, peace and sin offerings (vv. 6–8; cf. Heb. 10:5–10); but then he continues, "[E]vils have encompassed me beyond number; my iniquities have overtaken me, and I cannot see; they are more than the hairs of my head; my heart fails me" (v. 12). Psalm 69 is another Messianic psalm (cf. v. 9 and John 2:17; Rom. 15:3; v. 21 and Matt. 27:34, 48; John 19:28–29; also ponder v. 4b). Yet, the protagonist says, "O God, you know my folly; the wrongs I have done are not hidden from you" (v. 5). Jesus committed no sin (1 Pet. 2:22), he knew no sin (2 Cor. 5:21), in him was no sin (1 John 3:5)—yet, on the cross he identified himself with the sins of believers.

5.5.2 Cleansing of the Tabernacle

We must mention still one other effect of the blood of the first goat, and of the bull. The sprinkled blood atones for the sanctuary, then Aaron atones for the entire tabernacle with it, and lastly with it he atones for the altar of burnt offering (Lev. 16:15–16, 18–20a). In addition to several other meanings, the tabernacle is an image of the heavens, as the book of Hebrews makes clear:

---

37. See Ouweneel (2008b, §13.2).

Indeed, under the law almost everything is purified with blood, and without the shedding of blood there is no forgiveness of sins. Thus it was necessary for the copies of the heavenly things to be purified with these rites, but the heavenly things themselves with better sacrifices than these. For Christ has entered, not into holy places made with hands, which are copies of the true things, but into heaven itself, now to appear in the presence of God on our behalf (9:22-24; cf. 4:14; 6:19-20; 7:26; 8:1-2; 9:6-12; 10:19-20).

In relation to the tabernacle, an image of heaven, the court of the tabernacle is apparently a picture of the earth. In the altar of burnt offering we may see an anticipation of the cross of Christ. It was here, on earth, that he shed his blood, that is, poured out his human life into death. At the same time, the image shows us Christ as presenting his blood to God in the heavenly sanctuary: "[H]e entered once for all into the holy places, not by means of the blood of goats and calves but by means of his own blood, thus securing an eternal redemption" (Heb. 9:12).

Why did the altar and the tabernacle, and thus also the "heavenly things," need to be purified? Of course, these "things" have not sinned; therefore, there is no link between them and the second goat. However, they have been defiled by sin as an evil power because of the presence of sinful humanity. Therefore, sin must be put away not only from individual people but also from the *cosmos* (John 1:29): "Behold, the Lamb of God, who takes away the sin of the *world!*" Not only humanity, but the entire *creation* was "subjected to futility," and therefore must "be set free from its bondage to corruption" (Rom. 8:20-21). On the basis of the blood of Christ, sin as an evil power will be abolished from the universe.

In the Roman Catholic mass, John 1:29 has always been wrongly quoted: "Lamb of God, who takes away the *sins* (Lat. *peccata*) of the world," instead of "sin" (Lat.

peccatum), as the Vulgate has it. Using the plural "sins" suggests that Jesus takes away the sins of all people instead of only the sins of all believers (unbelievers must bear their own sins; see §12.3). This is why I prefer to render 1 John 2:2 as follows: Christ "is the propitiation for our sins, and not for ours only but also for the whole world" (NKJV), rather than: ". . . but also for the *sins* of the whole world" (KJV). In terms of the Day of Atonement, the first goat represents the whole world (Christ's atoning work of satisfaction is so great that all can come)—but the second goat carries away the sins of God's people (Christ blotted out the sins of those who believe; not the sins of all humans, because then nobody could be condemned for their own sins) (see more extensively in chapter 12).

5.5.3 Special New Testament Aspects

It is remarkable how many references to the Day of Atonement the New Testament contains, especially in Hebrews.[38]

(a) Christ is both the high priest (Heb. 2:17; 4:14; 5:10; 6:20; 8:1; 9:11) and the sacrifice of the Day of Atonement (Heb. 8:26-27; 9:11-14, 26, 28; 10:10, 12, 14).

(b) The tabernacle is an image of the heavens (Heb. 4:14; 6:19-20; 7:27; 8:1-2; 9:6-12, 23-24; 10:19-20).

(c) The ark of the covenant, more concretely, its cover (the "mercy seat," Lev. 16:2, 13-15), is an image of the throne of God (Heb. 4:16; 8:1-2; cf. Ps. 80:1).

(d) The curtain, passed through by the high priest, is an image of the flesh of Christ (Lev. 16:2, 12, 15; Heb. 10:20).

Remarkably enough, the "scapegoat," the goat "for Azazel," does not appear in the book of Hebrews; but of course, this does not imply that it has no connection with the atoning work of Christ. At any rate, since the

---

38. See extensively, Ouweneel (1982); cf. Grant (1956, chapter 20).

so-called Epistle of Barnabas (c. AD 200), and since Justin Martyr and Tertullian, Christians have seen the scapegoat as a type of Christ as well.[39] Another remarkable thing is that Hebrews always speaks of the tabernacle in the wilderness, never of the temple of Solomon or the temple of Herod.

Also notice the following contrasts:

(a) Aaron was a sinful, mortal high priest. Christ is the sinless, eternal high priest (Heb. 5:1-10; 7:23-28; cf. Lev. 16:1-2, 6, 11, 24, 32).

(b) The sacrifices on the Day of Atonement were repeated annually because they could not bring about actual atonement; they merely pointed forward to the true sacrifice of Christ. Christ offered himself once for all, thus securing an eternal redemption (Heb. 8:27; 9:6-12, 25-28; 10:1-13; cf. Lev. 16:29, 34).

(c) During the time of tabernacle and temple, the way through the curtain, into the Most Holy Place, was open to the high priest alone, and this only once a year (Lev. 16:1-2; cf. 10:1-2). At present, the way into the heavenly sanctuary is open to all New Testament priests, and this continually (Heb. 10:19-22; cf. 1 Pet. 2:5; Rev. 1:6; 5:10; 20:6).

Please note that in Hebrews there is *no* torn curtain,[40] just as in the tabernacle, too, there never was a torn curtain (or rent veil). It just creates confusion to bring in here the torn curtain of the temple (Matt. 27:51). In Hebrews 10:20, the curtain is not torn but intact. The great point in Hebrews is that the way into the Most Holy Place is open to the worshipers, not because the curtain has been torn but because it no longer forms a hindrance for them, as it did for the high priest in the tabernacle.

---

39. Epistle of Barnabas 7.6-11; Justin, *Dialogue with Trypho* 40.4; Tertullian, *Against the Jews* 14; cf. Schilder (1940, 381).
40. *Contra* Wenham (1979, 237), and hymns like "The veil is rent! Lo! Jesus stands before the throne of grace."

(d) In the Old Testament, the (high) priest stood in front of the "throne of God" (the mercy seat). – In the heavenly sanctuary, Christ does not *stand* before the throne of God but is *seated* at the right hand of the throne of God, until his second coming (Heb. 1:3; 8:1-2; 9:24, 28; 10:11-13; 12:2). Incidentally, notice the remarkable passage where Stephen sees Jesus *standing* at the right hand of God (Acts 7:55). Could we say that, at that moment, Jesus had not yet sat down as long as the rejection by Israel was not yet complete and definitive (cf. 3:19-21)?[41]

5.6 The Law about Leprosy

5.6.1 The Meaning of Leprosy

In the atoning sacrifice of Christ, there is a very important element that finds minimal expression in the sacrificial ministry of the Old Testament, namely, the atoning significance of Christ's resurrection and glorification (see §§10.1-10.2). Those who attach great value to Old Testament typology, especially in the sacrificial ministry, have for centuries thought they could detect a reference to the resurrection in the purification ritual required for the *leper*.[42]

The text tells us:

> [T]he priest shall command them to take for him who is to be cleansed two live clean birds and cedarwood and scarlet yarn and hyssop. And the priest shall command them to kill one of the birds in an earthenware vessel over fresh water. He shall take the live bird with the cedarwood and the scarlet yarn and the hyssop, and dip them and the live bird in the blood of the bird that was killed over the fresh water. And he shall sprinkle it seven times on him who is to be cleansed of the leprous disease. Then he shall pro-

---

41. Kelly (1952, 102-103).
42. Darby (n.d.-b, ad loc.); Grant (1890, 321-34); Mackintosh (1972, ad loc.); Coates (2007, ad loc.).

nounce him clean and shall let the living bird go into the open field (Lev. 14:4-7; also cf. vv. 49-53).

At this point it does not matter precisely which disease was meant (cf. more generally the EXB: "a harmful skin disease"). For the sake of convenience, we will borrow the terms "leper" and "leprosy" from the traditional translations. In the Bible, leprosy was a well-known symbolic picture of sin as the evil that is present in a person and erupts in wicked actions. These actions consist of self-aggrandizement; compare the cases of Miriam (Num. 12:10), Gehazi (2 Kings 5:26-27), and king Uzziah (2 Chron. 26:19-21).

The significance of this symbolic picture is underscored by the fact that the leprosy was not really treated as a disease, which we can see from two facts. First, with the cleansing of the leper, a guilt offering was required (Lev. 14:12, 21); apparently, the leper was viewed as a guilty person. Second, it is interesting that the Bible seldom speaks of any healing of the leper (Lev. 14:3) but rather of their cleansing (purification). This term referred both to the healing as such (Matt. 8:2; 11:5; Luke 4:27; 17:14, 17) and to the purification ritual associated with the priest (Lev. 14). By the blood of the sacrificial animal, the leper was cleansed, just as the penitent sinner is cleansed (purified) by the blood of Christ (Heb. 9:14; 1 John 1:7).

5.6.2 The Two Birds

The two birds required for sacrifice by the law of leprosy together represented the one offering of Christ, just as the two goats on the Day of Atonement did, though in quite a different way. The first and the second goats represented the principles of satisfaction and substitution, respectively. The two birds pointed to the death and resurrection of Christ, respectively; on the one hand, Christ "was delivered up for our trespasses," and the other hand, was "raised for our justification" (Rom. 4:25).

The bird that was slaughtered pointed to Christ the Substitute, granting satisfaction to God and bearing believers' sins in their stead. The bird that was dipped in the blood of the first bird, then covered with the first bird's blood, and then allowed to fly away free in the open field, pointed to the risen and ascended Christ. He "entered the Most Holy Place once for all by[43] his own blood, having obtained eternal redemption" (Heb. 9:12 NIV). The first bird had died, yet life continues beyond the grave in the second bird; this life has passed through death, taking death captive and making it subservient to God's purposes.[44]

The blood of the first bird was put on the leper in order to cleanse them, namely, on the lobe of their right ear, their right thumb, and their right big toe, the ear, standing for all the five senses, the thumb for the hands, and the big toe for the feet. Thus, the healed leper's entire life of listening (obedience[45]), acting, and walking was brought under the atoning blood. Then came the oil, on the head of the healed leper (Lev. 14:14–18). The oil is the well-known image of the Holy Spirit: Old Testament anointing with oil corresponds with New Testament anointing with the Spirit (cf. Acts 10:38). The Spirit gives to the healed leper the strength to live their new life the way God intends it (also see §5.7.1).

The second bird carried that same blood of the slaugh-

---

43. Gk. *dia*; the ESV renders this as "by means of"; in my view, the shorter form must be preferred: "by" (KJV), in the sense of "[characterized] by"; cf. the NKJV, "with." The rendering of the ASV, "through," has the same disadvantage as "by means of" because it suggests that Christ needed his own blood in order to be able to enter the sanctuary.
44. Grant (1956, 93–94).
45. The word "obedience" comes from Latin *ob*, "to," and *au dire*, "to listen"; cf. Dutch: *horen* ("to hear") and *gehoo rzamen* ("to obey").

tered bird into the air, toward God, as it were. Thus, believers have been cleansed by the blood of the Christ who died, *and* the risen and glorified Christ stands with this same blood before God in the heavenly sanctuary. After the offering of the two birds, a week later, guilt, sin, burnt, and grain offerings followed (Lev. 14:10-20); their significance was discussed earlier (§§4.4-4.7).

5.7 Other Atoning Rituals
5.7.1 The Consecration of the Priests[46]

In my view, Old Testament typology has become richer and more relevant through the growing insight that the types underscore especially the subjective side of the life of faith. Thus, the typological lessons of the Old Testament priesthood are not so much about what all New Testament believers become in Christ, objectively, as a matter of principle. Rather, they deal with the practical, spiritual realization of believers' priestly ministry during their life of faith.

In opposition to the Roman Catholic view of the priesthood, Protestant churches rightly recovered the priesthood of all believers: believers are a holy and royal priesthood (1 Pet. 2:5, 9), and individually priests of God (Rev. 1:6; 5:10; 20:6). In Hebrews 3:6 and 10:21, believers constitute the "house" (family) of which Christ as high priest is the head, and in 13:15 they are the true sacrifice offerers of the present era.[47] However, in what way does this priesthood come to concrete expression in the Protestant church service and in church's life? What sense does it make to the average Protestant that he/she is a priest? I have devoted much more attention to this matter in my work on ecclesiology;[48] here I will

---

46. See Darby (n.d.-b ad loc.); Grant (1890, 233-37, 307-13); Mackintosh (1972, 202-204); Coates (1930, ad loc.; 2007, ad loc.).
47. See extensively, Ouweneel (1982, passim).
48. See especially Ouweneel (2010b, chapter 3).

restrict myself to the consecration sacrifices of the Old Testament priests. This priestly consecration is not an image of conversion (becoming a Christian), for Aaron and his sons had belonged to the people of God for a long time. It is rather an image of the practical, spiritual realization of the priesthood in the Christian walk of faith, specifically, learning to practice genuine praise and worship (cf. Eph. 5:18-20; Heb. 13:15; 1 Pet. 2:5).

Without entering into all the details, I would point to the three sacrifices of priestly consecration: the burnt and sin offerings (Lev. 8:14, 18), which are like all ordinary burnt and sin offerings (§§4.4 and 4.6), and the actual consecration offering: the "ram of ordination" (or "of consecration," v. 22, 28-29, 31, 33; Exod. 29:22, 26-27, 31, 33-34). Literally, the text speaks of the "ram of fillings" (Heb. *eyl millu'im* or *eyl hammillu'im*). This terminology reflects that during the consecration of the priests their hands were filled with the fat from the ram together with "one loaf of bread and one cake of bread made with oil, and one wafer out of the basket of unleavened bread that is before the LORD" (Exod. 29:22-23; Lev. 8:27-28). By and by, the expression "filling the hand(s)" received the figurative meaning of "consecration" (Exod. 28:41; 29:9, 29, 33, 35; 32:29; Lev. 8:33; 9:17; Judg. 17:5, 12; 1 Kings 13:33; 1 Chron. 29:5; 2 Chron. 13:9; Ezek. 43:26).

As always, when they are mentioned together, the burnt and sin offerings present to us the two sides of Christ's atoning work: in the burnt offering we see how the worthiness of Christ passes to the offerer, and in the sin offering we see how the sinful unworthiness of the offerer passes to Christ, and has been blotted out by him. The priesthood of believers, that is, bringing spiritual offerings of praise and worship, is a high office. But in the very performance of the highest office, the office-bearer is reminded time and again of the atoning work of Christ, which forms the basis for his office: all hindrances for this office have been removed by the sin offering, all worthiness for the office is derived from the burnt offering. The more that a person practically realizes the meaning of the burnt offering in one's soul, the more they may enjoy the worthiness with which they are now allowed to approach God: "[B]e imitators of God, *as beloved children*. And walk in love, as Christ loved us and gave himself up for us, a fragrant offering and sacrifice to God" (Eph. 5:1-2), that is, be likewise "a fragrant offering and sacrifice to God."

The actual consecration offering, the "ram of ordination," had the character of a peace offering (see §4.5): the fat came on the altar (Exod. 29:22; Lev. 8:25, 28), and the "wave breast and the heave shoulder" were eaten by the newly consecrated priests (Exod. 29:26-28; Lev. 8:29-31). The exceptional aspect of this peace offering was that part of the blood had to be put on the right ear lobe of Aaron and his sons, on their right thumb, and their right big toe (Exod. 29:20; Lev. 8:23-24). This was the most essential act of consecration: in this way, the entire life (listening, acting, walking) of the priest-to-be was brought under the blood of the sin offering. It is remarkable that this application of the blood on ear, thumb, and toe is mentioned only in the cases of the priestly consecration and the cleansing of the leper (§5.6.2). With regard to what humans are by nature, the person who is consecrated to the priesthood is on the same level as the leper: both must be brought under the blood, and only in this way can they function before God.

5.7.2 Purification After Childbirth[49]

Leviticus 12:6-8 deals with the purification of the woman who has borne a son or a daughter. In the former case, she was unclean for seven days, in the latter case fourteen days. These days were followed by thirty-three

---

49. See Darby (n.d.-b, ad loc.); Grant (1890, 320-21); Mackintosh (1972, ad loc.); Coates (2007, ad loc.).

Special Atonement Rituals

days and sixty-days of purification, a total of forty and eighty days, respectively. This is by far the longest period of uncleanness and purification that is dealt with in the Sinaitic Torah. Expositors have suggested that the background of these stipulations is the problem of original sin: children are unclean because they come from unclean parents. However, the difficulty with such an interpretation is that in these stipulations, the person viewed as unclean is not the newborn baby,[50] but the mother, apparently because of the discharge of blood connected with the birth (vv. 4–5, 7).

Since such a discharge can continue for six weeks, the total time of her purification was set at forty and eighty days, respectively. Yet, this case was not identical to that of menstruation, because an offering was required after childbirth, but not after menstruation. Apparently, childbirth in some way involved sin that had to be atoned for. Even though the child was not unclean, through the sin offering the mother was reminded that she was the unclean source of her child (cf. Gen. 8:21; Job 14:4; 15:14; 25:5–6; Ps. 14:2–3; 51:5; 53:2–3; 58:3; John 3:6; Rom. 2:5; Eph. 2:3).[51]

We cannot enter here into all exegetical issues, such as the difficult—perhaps no longer answerable—such as why the time of purification for a daughter lasted twice as long as that for a son. Rather, two issues are particularly relevant for our present discussion. First, why did a discharge of blood, or a discharge more generally (see Lev. 15), make a person unclean? And second, what was the meaning of the prescribed purification offerings? Regarding the first issue, it appears that everything that flowed from the sexual body parts (semen, blood, pus— but not urine) was viewed as uncleanness; this is discussed further in the next section.

Regarding the second issue, at the end of the time

---

50. Wenham (1979, 187–88).
51. See more extensively, Ouweneel (2008a, chapter 12).

of purification, the woman who had given birth had to "bring to the priest at the entrance of the tent of meeting a lamb a year old for a burnt offering, and a pigeon or a turtledove for a sin offering" (Lev. 12:6). Or, if she could not afford this, she could bring "two turtledoves or two pigeon, one for a burnt offering and the other for a sin offering" (v. 8). This was also what Joseph and Mary offered after Jesus' birth (Luke 2:22-24). The priest offered the animals to "make atonement for her." Here again, the two sides of Christ's atoning work come to light in the burnt offering and the sin offering. The latter had the special meaning, as in all cases of cultic uncleanness, of re-opening for the person the way to the altar: "Thus you shall keep the people of Israel separate from their uncleanness, lest they die in their uncleanness by defiling my tabernacle that is in their midst" (Lev. 15:31).

In various Protestant traditions, the underlying thought of a necessary purification period after childbirth continued until the beginning of the twentieth century. In various parts of the Netherlands, under no condition would a woman who had recovered after giving birth go out socially, or work in her field, until she had first gone to church, and the pastor had publicly thanked God that she, after her "hour of peril," had appeared again in God's house.

5.7.3 The Purification of the Person with a Discharge[52]

In Leviticus 15 we hear about various discharges from the sexual body parts:

(a) an (uncommon) discharge from the male member (vv. 2-12); presumably referring (particularly) to gonorrhea;

(b) ejaculation apart from sexual intercourse (vv.

---

52. See Grant (1890, 335-36); Mackintosh (1972, ad loc.); Coates (2007, ad loc.).

16-17), or during intercourse (v. 18; the latter event made the woman unclean as well);

(c) menstruation (vv. 19-23; cf. Gen. 31:35; 2 Sam. 11:4); and

(d) prolonged vaginal bleedings (vv. 25-27).

In cases (b) and (c), normal, in (a) and (d) abnormal (sickly) discharges were implied. We should note that after ejaculation or menstruation a certain time of cultic uncleanness had to be observed, but no atonement was needed. This means that none of these two normal biological events were viewed as sinful. It *was* true, however, that Israelites were not allowed to have sexual intercourse just before a sacred act (Exod. 19:15; 1 Sam. 21:4-5; cf. 2 Sam. 11:9-13; 1 Cor. 7:5), because this would make them unclean (i.e., unfit to participate in any tabernacle ritual) for the rest of the day. A woman was unclean for seven days after the end of her menstruation. In practice, given what we know today, this meant that, after about five days of menstruation plus the seven additional days of uncleanness, she had reached at the precise beginning of her fertile time. After about twelve days of sexual abstinence, this practice greatly enhanced the expansion of the nation.

Not only did abnormal (sickly) discharges, both in men and in women, make the person involved unclean, but they also required an atoning sacrifice. In Numbers 5:2, "everyone who is leprous or has a discharge and everyone who is unclean through contact with the dead" were put into one category: all three groups had to be sent "outside the camp," "that they may not defile their camp, in the midst of which I dwell" (v. 3). This is the pivotal point: as mentioned earlier (previous section), Leviticus 15:31 explains why the person involved needed atonement: the sickly discharge made him or her unfit to participate in the ministry of the tabernacle for the duration of the sickness. This is no wonder: sexual diseases are almost always the consequence of promiscuity, that is, of sin. A sexual disease was on the same level with leprosy in the sense that in both cases atonement was demanded. This does leave us with the question why atonement was not demanded in *all* cases of prolonged periods of illness, for leprosy was not necessarily a consequence of sin (though it was a symbolic picture of it).

We read of the purified man and woman that, on the eighth day after the discharge had stopped, they had to take two turtledoves or two young pigeons, and had to give them to the priest at the entrance of the tent of meeting. He had to prepare one pigeon as a sin offering, and the other as a burnt offering: "And the priest shall make atonement for him/her before the LORD for his/her unclean discharge" (Lev. 15:14-15, 29-30). As always, we find here the two chief offerings representing the two sides of the work of Christ: the burnt offering, which makes the person acceptable (pleasing) in the eyes of God, and the sin offering, which takes away his/her sinfulness.

5.7.4 The Water of Purification

It may be useful for our purpose to add a few words on "the water for impurity" in Numbers 19 (see vv. 9, 13, 20-21; KJV: "the water of separation"; DRA: "the water of aspersion"; ISV: "the water of purification"; NIV: "the water of cleansing"; OJB: "the water of sprinkling"; Heb. *mey niddah*).[53] Given the thousands who died during the wilderness journey (recall that the many dead are mentioned in Num. 14-16), clearly the Israelites could not avoid coming into contact with death.

Numbers 19 deals with the practical issue of managing to reach the end of this journey in ceremonial purity. To this end, Israel needed a protocol that would purify them from every contact with death. This does not

---

53. Cf. the elaboration of it in the Mishnah tracts Ohalot (= Tents) and Para (= Cow).

Special Atonement Rituals

involve a sacrifice in the actual sense (see below), but only the purification protocol needed repeatedly during the wilderness journey.[54]

The priest Eleazar, Aaron son and successor as high priest (Num. 20:25-28), had to slaughter outside the camp "a red heifer[55] without defect, in which there is no blemish, and on which a yoke has never come" (Num. 19:2). He then took some of its blood and sprinkled it toward the front of the tent of meeting seven times. Then the heifer was burned by an unknown person, but in Eleazar's presence. The latter threw cedarwood, hyssop,[56] and scarlet yarn on the burning heifer. The ashes of the heifer were deposited outside the camp in a clean place. When an Israelite had defiled themselves by touching a corpse, or touching the bones of a corpse, or a grave, a portion of these ashes was put into a vessel, water from a well was poured on them ashes, and this "water of cleansing" was sprinkled on the defiled person with some hyssop. The motivation given is "for purification from sin" (NIV; Heb. *chattat hi*); this is more correct than "sin offering" (ESV), which it was not in the actual sense of the word because no part of the heifer was placed on the altar of burnt offering (see below).

Remarkably, this purification law is not given in Leviticus, along with the common atoning rituals, although it is related to them: the cleansing with water was based on the sacrificial death of the red heifer, whose blood had atoning value as is evident from its sprinkling toward the altar, even though no part of the cow came on the altar. Yet, the law of the water of purification is given only in Numbers 19, near the end of the forty-year wilderness journey.[57] Thus, this law occupied a distinctive

54. Darby (n.d.-b, ad loc.).
55. Other translations: "young cow" or simply "cow"; cf. Ashley (1993, 363-64).
56. Here again the role of hyssop is remarkable; cf. §§5.1.2, 5.6.1, and 7.6.5.
57. Coates (191, 246-47); Grant (1956, 111); Mackintosh

position. The protocol involving the water of purification did not belong to the actual atoning rituals, for the sacrifice was not linked with the altar of burnt offering, and the word "atonement" is not mentioned. Therefore, we will not discuss the many exegetical details; for that, the reader is encouraged to consult the commentaries.

Because of this distinctive position, it is doubtful that we should read the phrase "sin offering" in verses 9 and 17 (see above). Commentators A. Noordtzij and T. Ashley[58] wished to read "sin offering" here, though Noordtzij relativized his own rendering by saying: "[T]he words 'it is for the purification from sin' (v. 9) are a correct render of *hatta'at* (the word for 'sin offering'), because this is not a true sin offering; if it were, the heifer would have to be slaughtered at the altar (Lev. 4), and then of course not by a layperson" (cf. Num. 19:3). Yet, there is a clear link with the sin offering, perhaps a special form of the sin offering.[59] At least this is the view of Hebrews 9:13-14,

> For if the blood of goats and bulls, and the sprinkling of defiled persons *with the ashes of a heifer*, sanctify for the purification of the flesh, how much more will the blood of Christ, who through the eternal Spirit offered himself without blemish to God, purify our conscience from dead works to serve the living God.

The word "sin" (with the associated meaning of "sin offering" and "purification from sin") in Numbers 19 is remarkable because contact with death was viewed as inevitable, and therefore one could hardly speak of guilt. It was a matter of defilement, not guilt.[60] Yet, the

(1972, ad loc.).
58. Noordtzij (1983, 169); Ashley (1993, 365). Gispen (1959, 303) rightly opposed this exegesis.
59. See Vonk (Forthcoming, 131), and especially Milgrom (1983, 85-95).
60. See Darby (*CW* 19, 292).

word "sin" is used, apparently because sin and death are inseparably joined. Coming into contact with death implied defilement with what is a consequence of sin. Thus, cleansing from contact with death also implied cleansing from what has caused death. Apparently for this reason, the water of purification was derived from something that, if it was not distinctive kind of sin offering, at least exhibited strong similarities to it.

It reminds us of what Jesus said to Peter, "If I do not wash you, you have no share [or, communion] with me . . . . The one who has bathed does not need to wash, except for his feet, but is completely clean" (John 13:8, 10).[61] Peter had "bathed," that is, he was born again (cf. 3:5; 1 Cor. 6:11; Titus 3:5); but just like every believer, he needed the regular and repeated cleansing by Christ: purification from the defilements with which believers come into contact up during their earthly walk (cf. the bronze basin, Exod. 30:17–21). Numbers 19 point not only to justification but also to undisturbed fellowship with God despite all the contacts with death that we unintentionally incur in our walk on earth. Not only personal sin, but death, hinders the believer from boldly drawing near in the sanctuary (cf. Heb. 10:19–22). The blood of the unblemished heifer, pointing to Christ who knew no sin and could not be brought under its power, was sprinkled seven times in front of the tabernacle, that is, in front of the place of fellowship ("tent of meeting"), not (in this case) the place of atonement.[62]

Reformed authors A. Noordtzij and W. Gispen repeatedly wrestled with the typological interpretation of this passage, while missing a great number of significant aspects.[63] C. Vonk paid more careful attention to those as-

---

61. Dennett (1888, 165) made this connection because of Zech. 13:1.
62. Darby (*CW* 9, 292).
63. Regarding Num. 19, see Darby (*CW* 9, 206); Gispen (1959, 302–03).

pects.[64] Gispen referred to the Johannes Lundius,[65] who contributed much to the typological understanding of the Israelite sacrificial ministry, leaving us an extensive typological explanation of Numbers 19. Gispen was dissatisfied with this explanation, perhaps because Lundius went too far afield in his typological interpretation. But that should not lead us to discard that kind of interpretation altogether, for it does lend deep insight into the meaning of atonement in the Old Testament, and thereby also into the meaning of atonement in the New Testament atonement.

Let me conclude this chapter with these brief comments about three related Bible passages:

1. The washing with the "water of purification," recorded in Numbers 19, was in view of a pure *journey through the wilderness.*

2. The washing of the hands and feet with water drawn from the bronze basin, recorded in Exodus 30:17-21, was in view of *holy ministry in the sanctuary.*

3. The footwashing, recorded in John 13:1-15, was in view of *holy communion with Christ.*

---

64. Vonk (Forthcoming, 129).
65. Lundius (1726).

Now Available from Paideia Press
www.paideiapress.ca

Chapter 6
Special Aspects of Atonement

> "In overflowing anger for a moment
>   I hid my face from you,
> but with everlasting love
>   I will have compassion on you,"
>   says the LORD, your Redeemer [Heb. Go'el].
>
> Isaiah 54:8

> [T]he Son of Man came not to be served
>   but to serve,
> and to give his life as a ransom for many.
>
> Matthew 20:28

Summary: *Of special interest in the Old Testament is the Go'el, the "Redeemer," who had four tasks: he "redeemed" the lost inheritance of his relatives, he set a relative free who had felt obliged to sell himself as slave, he married a widow tied in with an inheritance, and he performed as the "avenger of blood." All of this pointed elsewhere, namely, to God himself as the Redeemer of his people, performing these very same four tasks with respect to them. In the ultimate fulfillment, Christ is the Redeemer, performing these* *tasks for his followers.*

Another remarkable point is that Christ is both the offerer (even high priest) and the offering in the Aaronic sense. However, he is not priest after the order of Aaron but after that of Melchizedekian; there are important similarities as well as differences between the two orders.

Some attention is given to forms of Old Testament atonement involving no animal sacrifices. They shed light on other aspects of Christ's work.

All the points considered so far are beautifully illustrated in several Genesis types: the offerings of Adam, Abel, Noah, and Abr(ah)am.

Defective offerings were not simply offerings that violated the rules but especially offerings brought in the wrong attitude. Sin offerings had no value to God in the absence of true contrition and confession. Especially the prophets strongly underscored the need for a proper attitude, that of repentance combined with love and mercy.

6.1 The *Go'el*
6.1.1 The Lost Inheritance

IN DIRECT CONNECTION WITH the subject of atonement, one of the most fascinating figures in the Old Testament goes back to Israelite family law. It is that of the "redeemer," Hebrew *go'el*, whose task it is to keep the family and its possessions intact.[1] The Hebrew word *go'el* is the present participle, "redeeming," of the root *g-'-l*, "to redeem," or more extensively: "to lay claim (to a person or thing)" (cf. Job 3:5, "Let gloom and deep darkness claim it," i.e., the day of my birth), and hence: "to claim back," "reclaim," release from another's authority and carry back to one's own authority.[2] The person who performed this was the "claimer, releaser, redeemer." I will pass by two less rele-

---

1. See *TDNT* 4, 330–335; *DOTT* 1, 789–94; for New Testament applications, see North (1954).
2. Koehler and Baumgartner (1953, 162).

vant passages: Leviticus 27, where the original owner of sacrificial animals is at the same time the redeemer, and Numbers 5:8, where the redeemer is receives a ransom to repay a debt. Apart from this, in the Old Testament we find four forms of "redeeming" (Heb. *g'ullah*) for protecting the following matters or persons:

(a) *A lost inheritance.* If, because of impoverishment, an Israelite was obliged to sell a piece of land or a house, the redeemer—a close relative—could redeem this possession for them, that is, buy it back, and hand it over to the original owner (Lev. 25:23-37; cf. Jer. 32:7-8). In any case, the land that had passed into foreign hands would be released in the so-called Year of Jubilee, and returned to its original owner. This meant that the ransom that had to be paid for it was in fact the possession's rental value during the years remaining until the Year of Jubilee.[3] The theological basis for this form of redemption was this: "The land shall not be sold in perpetuity, for the land is mine. For you are strangers and sojourners with me" (Lev. 25:23). The land belongs to YHWH, and he gave it to Israel only as a loan, but in such a way that each family had its own inalienable loan of land (Num. 32; Josh. 13 etc.; cf. 1 Kings 21:3). It was allowed pass into other hands, but only for a limited time. (With houses it was different; they could be sold forever, Lev. 25:30.)

6.1.2 Other Forms of Redemption

(b) *Enslaved persons.* The "brother"—that is every close male relative—could become so poor that he no longer saw any other solution to his poverty than to sell himself as a slave to pay for his debts (Lev. 25:47-54). In this case again, the enslaved Israelite would automatically become free in the Year of Jubilee (Exod. 21:1-6; Deut. 15:12-18). This meant that the ransom to be paid to release the enslaved Israelite equaled the value of the working years that remained until the Year of Jubilee.

---

3. Thus Rashi; Cohen (1983, 768).

Here, the theological basis was the redemption from Egypt: the Israelites had been delivered from slavery, and therefore none of them should ever become a slave again (Lev. 25:42, 55; 26:13; Deut. 15:15)—unless God would have to punish them for persistent apostasy: "And the LORD will bring you back in ships to Egypt, a journey that I promised that you should never make again; and there you shall offer yourselves for sale to your enemies as male and female slaves, but there will be no buyer" (Deut. 28:68).

(c) *Sonless widows.* If a man died without leaving a son who could inherit his land, one of his close relatives had to marry his widow in order to father a son from her on behalf of the deceased man, so that this son could inherit the deceased man's possessions (Deut. 25:5–10). In such a case, people speak of a *levirate marriage* (from Lat. *levir*, "brother-in-law," that is, brother of the husband). To be sure, in the Torah the term "redemption" is not used for this situation. It is especially in the book of Ruth that we see how the redeemer also married the sonless widow who was, so to speak, attached to the deceased man's inheritance (Ruth 2:20; 3:9–13; 4:1–8, 14). Notice the self-evidence for such a marriage for the redeemer-to be: "The day you buy the field from the hand of Naomi, you also acquire Ruth the Moabite, the widow of the dead, in order to perpetuate the name of the dead in his inheritance" (Ruth 4:5). This was why the redeemer who was first in line could not redeem, so that Boaz, who was second in line, took over.

(d) *Killed persons.* If a person had been killed, the redeemer—a close relative of the killed man, if possible his son—took upon himself the task of killing the manslayer, and thus of blotting out the guilt of the manslaughter. He was called in Hebrew the *go'el haddam*, the "avenger [lit., redeemer, here better: reclaimer] of blood" (Num. 35:12, 19–27; Deut. 19:6, 12; Josh. 20:3, 5, 9; 2 Sam. 14:11; 1

Kings 16:11).[4] He was called *go'el* because the avenging restored the balance of justice. However, if the manslaughter had occurred unintentionally, the manslayer could seek a hiding-place in one of the cities of refuge, where the verdict over him would be announced. If it had been unintentional manslaughter, the manslayer could stay in the city of refuge. But if it had been (intentional) murder, the elders of the city handed him over to the "avenger of blood," who thus was allowed to kill him (Num. 35:12, 22-25; Deut. 19:4-7; Josh. 20:2-3, 5, 9).

This is what the redeemer did: he released a land that, or a person who, had fallen into foreign hands, in certain cases he even fathered an heir who could possess the land of his family, and if a close relative had been murdered he executed the death sentence on perpetrator. In short: he helped to preserve the balance of justice in his part of the families of Israel.

6.2 God As *Go'el*

6.2.1 Introduction

Remarkably, in the Old Testament, all four meanings of *go'el* mentioned so far are applied to God himself as well. Especially in lawsuits, the Lord can function as a *go'el* for the disadvantaged person (Ps. 119:154; Prov. 23:10-11; Jer. 50:33-34; cf. Job 19:25). Here, the theological basis is first the familial relationship between God and his people: "[Y]ou are our Father, though Abraham does not know us, and Israel [i.e., Jacob] does not acknowledge us; you, O LORD, are our Father, our Redeemer [Heb. *go'el*] from of old is your name" (Isa. 63:16; cf. 64:8; Deut. 32:6; Ps. 103:13; Mal. 1:6). Israel's fathers in the ordinary sense of the word were Abraham, Isaac, and Jacob, but these were not able to rescue the people in the Babylonian captivity. YHWH was Israel's Father in a deeper sense, on whom they could rely as Redeemer. Here, it is

---

4. Cf. the proper name Igal (*Yig'al*, see CJB; from *g-'-l*), "revenger" (Num. 13:7; 2 Sam. 23:36; 1 Chron. 3:22).

not a brother but a father who takes upon himself the task of redeeming, but it is still a close relative. God is the Redeemer, and his sons (Deut. 14:1; sing.: Exod. 4:22) are the redeemed (Heb. *g'ulim*, Isa. 35:9; 62:12). (In Isa. 54:1-8 he is not the Father but the Husband; see below.)

A second theological basis is the redemption from Egypt: "I am the LORD, and I will bring you out from under the burdens of the Egyptians, and I will deliver you from slavery to them, and I will redeem [Heb. *v'ga'alti*][5] you with an outstretched arm and with great acts of judgment" (Exod. 6:6). At the beginning of Israel's history, God had proven himself as the Redeemer of his people: "You have led in your steadfast love the people whom you have redeemed [Heb. *ga'alta*]; you have guided them by your strength to your holy abode" (15:13). In many ways, the exodus from Babylon resembled the exodus from Egypt (cf. Isa. 35:8-10; 43:16-21; 51:9-11). No wonder, then, that especially throughout Isaiah 40–66, YHWH is often called the Redeemer of his people. Israel could appeal to him as such: "[O]ur Redeemer [Heb. *go'el*] from of old is your name" (Isa. 63:16; cf. Ps. 78:35, "They remembered . . . the Most High God their redeemer").

6.2.2 A Lost Inheritance

Let us look again at the four aspects of redemption. First there was a *lost inheritance* that had to be reclaimed. God redeemed not only Israel but also the Holy Land—holy because God had dwelt there—in which they had lived for so many centuries (Ps. 74:2; Isa. 52:9; 59:20; 62:12). In Isaiah 63:16, God is the Redeemer in connection with the estranged inheritance: "Your holy people held possession for a little while; our adversaries have trampled down your sanctuary" (v. 18; cf. 65:9-10).

---

5. In Jewish tradition, the third verb in this verse is connected with the third cup of the Passover (or *Seder*) meal: the "cup of salvation" (cf. Heb. *kos-yeshuʿot*, Ps. 16:13).

Of special interest is Ezekiel 11:15, "Son of man, your brothers, even your brothers, your kinsmen [lit., the men of your redemption, Heb. *anshey g'ullateka*], the whole house of Israel, all of them, are those of whom the inhabitants of Jerusalem have said, 'Go far from the LORD; to us this land is given for a possession.'" Those who had stayed behind in Jerusalem spoke in such a repulsive way concerning the exiles in Babylon; however, the latter were their relatives, the "men of their redemption," that is, the persons who had the right of redemption: they were fully allowed to return, and to reclaim their own possession. According to Ralph Alexander, the Hebrew term *g'ullateka* describes a close relationship that existed within a family, and that made it necessary that possessions returned to that family in the Year of Jubilee (Lev. 25). Tribal solidarity is emphasized here. In this context, the word referred to land that those who had stayed behind had stolen from absent original owners. Leviticus 25 had not been followed.[6] The return from the Babylonian captivity also implied "redemption" of the land: restoration of the land to the original owners or their offspring.

6.2.3 Enslaved Persons

God "redeemed" Israel from Egypt (Exod. 6:6; 15:13), and after they had becomes slaves in Babylon, he "redeemed" them again from that empire: "Go out from Babylon, flee from Chaldea, declare this with a shout of joy, proclaim it, send it out to the end of the earth; say, 'The LORD has redeemed his servant Jacob!'" (Isa. 48:20). "Was it not you who . . . made the depths of the sea a way for the redeemed [Heb. *g'ullim*] to pass over? And the ransomed of the LORD shall return and come to Zion with singing" (51:10–11; cf. 35:9). "The people of Israel are oppressed, and the people of Judah with them. All who took them captive have held them fast; they refuse

---

6. Alexander (1986, 794).

to let them go. Their Redeemer is strong; the LORD of hosts is his name. He will surely plead their cause, that he may give rest to the earth, but unrest to the inhabitants of Babylon" (Jer. 50:33-34). "There [i.e., in Babylon] you shall be rescued; there the LORD will redeem you from the hand of your enemies" (Micah 4:10).

In such passages, it is often also implied that the exile, the captivity in the foreign land, is also an image of the slavery of sin: "I have blotted out your transgressions like a cloud and your sins like mist; return to me, for I have redeemed you [Heb. *g'altika*] . . . For the LORD has redeemed [Heb. *ga'al*] Jacob, and will be glorified in Israel" (Isa. 44:22-23). "For thus says the LORD: 'You were sold for nothing, and you shall be redeemed [Heb. *tigga'elu*] without money'" (52:3). "For the LORD has ransomed Jacob and has redeemed [Heb. *ug'alu*] him from hands too strong for him" (Jer. 31:11) (regarding the LORD as Redeemer, in addition to the passages mentioned, see also Isa. 41:14; 43:14; 44:6, 24; 47:4; 48:17; 49:7; 60:16; also cf. Gen. 48:16; Ps. 19:14; 69:18; 77:15; 103:4; 106:10; Isa. 43:1; Lam. 3:58; Hos. 13:14.) One of the new names of Israel will be: "The redeemed of the LORD" (Heb. *geule* YHWH, Isa. 62:12; cf. Ps. 107:2).[7]

It is remarkable that Israel was redeemed "without money" (Isa. 52:3); instead, other nations were given as a kind of "ransom" (*kopher*, cf. §4.2.3) in Israel's place: "I give Egypt as your ransom, Cush and Seba in exchange for you" (Isa. 43:3). To King Cyrus God paid no ransom for Israel's release; on the contrary, the wealth of Egypt and Cush will come to Israel: "I have stirred him [i.e., Cyrus] up in righteousness, . . . he shall build my city and set my exiles free, not for price or reward, . . . The wealth of Egypt and the merchandise of Cush, and the Sabeans, men of stature, shall come over to you and be yours; . . . They will plead with you, saying: 'Surely God

---

7. Cf. the related expression "ransomed of the LORD" (Heb. *feduye* YHWH, from *p-d-h*, "to ransom," Isa. 35:10; 51:11).

is in you, and there is no other, no god besides him'" (Isa. 45:13-14).

6.2.4 The Abandoned, Childless Wife

After the Babylonian exile, God as the Redeemer took Israel—more specifically Judah—as his wife again. In Isaiah 50:1 the LORD had said: "Where is your mother's certificate of divorce, with which I sent her away? Or which of my creditors is it to whom I have sold you? Behold, for your iniquities you were sold, and for your transgressions your mother was sent away." After the exile came Israel's restoration.

Here, the redeemed woman is not the widow of the brother but rather the temporarily abandoned wife:

> ". . . For your Maker is your husband, the LORD of hosts is his name; and the Holy One of Israel is your Redeemer, . . . For the LORD has called you like a wife deserted and grieved in spirit, like a wife of youth when she is cast off, says your God. For a brief moment I deserted you, but with great compassion I will gather you. In overflowing anger for a moment I hid my face from you, but with everlasting love I will have compassion on you," says the LORD, your Redeemer (Isa. 54:5-8).

From this childless woman a rich offspring will come forth who will possess the inheritance: "Sing, O barren one, who did not bear; break forth into singing and cry aloud, you who have not been in labor! For the children of the desolate one will be more than the children of her who is married" (54:1). "Then you will say in your heart: 'Who has borne me these? I was bereaved and barren, exiled and put away, but who has brought up these? Behold, I was left alone; from where have these come?'" (49:21). These children will receive the Holy Land as their inheritance: ". . . then you shall take delight in the LORD, and I will make you ride on the heights of the earth; I will feed you with the heritage of Jacob your father, for the mouth of the LORD has spoken" (58:14) "Lift up your eyes all around, and see; they all gather together, they come to you; your sons shall come from afar, and your daughters shall be carried on the hip" (60:4).

6.2.5 The Blood Revenge

The Lord took revenge on the enemies of Israel, who had oppressed it: "Come down and sit in the dust, / O virgin daughter of Babylon; / . . . Your nakedness shall be uncovered, / and your disgrace shall be seen. / I will take vengeance, / and I will spare no one./ Our Redeemer—the LORD of hosts is his name— / is the Holy One of Israel" (Isa. 47:1-4; cf. 59:17). "I will make your oppressors eat their own flesh, / and they shall be drunk with their own blood as with wine. / Then all flesh shall know / that I am the LORD your Savior, / and your Redeemer, the Mighty One of Jacob" (Isa. 49:26). "For the day of vengeance [on Israel's enemies] was in my heart, / and my year of redemption [Heb. *geulay*] had come. / . . . [I]n his love and in his pity he redeemed them; / he lifted them up and carried them all the days of old" (Isa. 63:4, 9; see more generally Deut. 32:43; 2 Kings 9:7; Ps. 9:12).

Quite remarkable in this context is Job 19:25 (CJB), "I know that my Redeemer is alive, that in the end he will rise on the dust."[8] According to one interpretation, which is of special interest to us, *go'el* has here the ancient meaning of the avenger of blood.[9] He "stands" on the victim who had been turned to dust, or "rises" on his behalf. The remarkable point here is here that it is God himself who "slays" Job (see, e.g., 13:15). Therefore, if God rises here in Job's lawsuit as Job's avenger of blood, he rises *against himself*. We find this thought also at other places in Job: God is both the judge and the accused as well as the defender (9:19, 33-35; 10:2, 7,

---

8. Cf. Ouweneel (2000a, 174-75).
9. So O. Procksch (*TDNT* 4:330).

17; 13:3, 8, 18, 23; 16:19-21; 17:3; 23:3-7, 10-12; 24:1-12; 31:37; 33:23-24).[10] When Job, after his death or after his resurrection, "in his flesh" shall "see God" (19:26-27), he will know that the same God who "killed" him, will also be his "avenger of blood." The God in whose hands Job is at the moment of his lamentation is the same God who, one day, will turn everything to his good.

6.3 Christ As *Go'el*
6.3.1 Introduction

Many of the passages mentioned, especially in Isaiah 40-66, have clearly Messianic overtones; in the end, it will be the Messiah who will be the *go'el* of his people. In Isaiah 49:7, the LORD is Israel's Redeemer, who, through the suffering Servant of the Lord (see vv. 1-7), will accomplish the work of redemption. He had said in verse 6: "I will make you [i.e., the Messiah] as a light for the nations, / that my salvation may reach to the end of the earth." Isaiah 59:20 says, "And a Redeemer [Heb. *go'el*] will come to Zion, / to those in Jacob who turn from transgression." Paul implicitly applies these words to Christ: "And in this way all Israel will be saved, as it is written, 'The Deliverer will come from Zion, he will banish ungodliness from Jacob'; 'and this will be my covenant with them when I take away their sins'" (Rom. 11:26-27; the latter part seems to be a quotation from Isa. 27:9 LXX or Jer. 31:34).

The royal psalm, Psalm 72, looks forward prophetically to the Messiah, of whom Solomon was a type; in verses 13-14 we read, "He has pity on the weak and the needy, / and saves [Heb. *yoshia*^{c}, from *y-sh-^{c}*] the lives of the needy. / From oppression and violence he redeems [Heb. *yig'al*, from *g-'-l*] their life,/ and precious is their blood in his sight."

In Luke 4:18-19 Jesus applies another Messianic passage to himself (Isa. 61:1-2), "The Spirit of the Lord

---
10. See Ouweneel (2000a, 170-73).

God is upon me, because the LORD has anointed me . . . he has sent me . . . to proclaim liberty to the captives, and the opening of the prison to those who are bound; to proclaim the year of the LORD's favor, and the day of vengeance of our God." Here we find the Hebrew word *deror*, "liberty (or release)," a word that is used in Leviticus 25:10 in connection with the Year of Jubilee: "[Y]ou shall consecrate the fiftieth year, and proclaim liberty [Heb. *deror*, release] throughout the land to all its inhabitants. It shall be a jubilee for you" (cf. Jer. 34:8-10; also "year of liberty/release" in Ezek. 46:17). The "year of the LORD's favor" (Isa. 61:2) presumably refers to this Year of Jubilee, the year of the "restoration of all things" (Acts 3:21 NKJV). Jewish scholar Philo used the term "restoration" (Gk. *apokatastasis*) as a reference to the Year of Jubilee.[11] Apparently, this year, that is, the "year of release (or, redemption)," refers to the Messianic kingdom.

6.3.2 The Four Tasks of the *Go'el*

Especially in the book of Revelation, Christ is the great *go'el*, even though the verb "to redeem, to free" (Gk. *luō*) occurs only in 1:5 ("To him who loves us and has freed[12] us . . ."), where his own blood is the ransom. The starting point for recognizing Christ as the *go'el* in Revelation is the scroll in chapter 5. I prefer the interpretation that identifies this scroll as the purchase deed or title deed of the entire creation, in analogy with such a document in Jeremiah 32:10-12, which had to do with the redemption of the land.[13] In this sense, one could interpret the question of Revelation 5:2 ("Who is worthy to open the scroll and break its seals?") as follows: Who has both the (legal) right and the (physical) power to act as the *go'el* of creation? In short: who *may* do it, and who

---

11. Decalogue 164.
12. The Byzantine text has "washed"; see the KJV.
13. See Ouweneel (1988) on Rev. 5.

can do it? Compare verse 3: "[N]o one . . . was *able*." The redeemer's *worthiness* refers to his legal right (he *may* do it); his *ability* refers to his physical power (he *can* do it). The world needs a redeemer who fulfills both conditions: he must be worthy, and he must be able.

Indeed, all four aspects of redeemership (the task of the *go'el*) that we discussed early return here.[14]

(a) *The lost inheritance.* Revelation 5 and following chapters are about the question who has the right and the power to regain for God and his people the creation that was lost to Satan. The opening of each seal of the scroll in turn leads to a new judgment, each implying a further purifying God's creation from every foreign element. In the book of Revelation, this entire process is depicted as a conflict between the Lamb and the dragon (i.e., Satan, Rev. 12:9; 20:2)—a war in which, humanly speaking, the most unlikely protagonist by far, the Lamb, will prevail. Just as all facets of the redemption in Isaiah 40-66 find their consummation in the new heavens and the new earth of 65:17-25, the same is seen in Revelation 21:1-8. The Lamb redeems the creation for God, and causes all his followers to dwell in the renewed inheritance.

(b) *Enslaved persons.* Not only are the heavens and the earth that are redeemed, but so are a people: "To him who loves us and has *freed* us from our sins by his blood and made us a kingdom, priests to his God and Father, to him be glory and dominion forever and ever" (Rev. 1:5-6). "Worthy are you to take the scroll and to open its seals, for you were slain, and by your blood you *ransomed* people for God from every tribe and language and people and nation" (5:9). This word "ransomed" (from Gk. *agorazō*; cf. 14:3-4, where "redeemed" is also from *agorazō*) reminds us again of the redeemer, who paid the ransom to redeem the enslaved people.

(c) *The redeemed bride.* Closely connected with the

---

14. See more extensively, Ouweneel (2012a).

inheritance redeemed by Christ is a bride, the church of Christ (cf. 2 Cor. 11:2; Eph. 5:22-32): "Let us rejoice and exult and give him the glory, for the marriage of the Lamb has come, and his Bride has made herself ready" (Rev. 19:7). "And I saw the holy city, new Jerusalem, coming down out of heaven from God, prepared as a bride adorned for her husband. . . . Then came one of the seven angels who had the seven bowls full of the seven last plagues and spoke to me, saying, 'Come, I will show you the Bride, the wife of the Lamb'" (Rev. 21:2, 9). "The Spirit and the Bride say, 'Come'" (Rev. 22:17).

(d) *The blood revenge.* The Redeemer will also execute revenge on all those who have oppressed his people: "O Sovereign Lord, holy and true, how long before you will judge and avenge our blood on those who dwell on the earth?" (Rev. 6:10). Here, the Redeemer is addressed as the One who reclaims the blood of his people (cf. v. 9, "slain"). The greatest enemy on whom the blood revenge must be executed is the dragon, Satan: "[T]he devil who had deceived them was thrown into the lake of fire and sulfur where the beast and the false prophet were, and they will be tormented day and night forever and ever" (Rev. 20:10).

6.4 The Place of the High Priest
6.4.1 Offering As Well As Offerer

In studying the types of the Old Testament sacrificial laws, we encounter the remarkable fact that Christ is presented not only as the atoning offering but also as the high priest who brings it. It goes even further than this: the altar as well, as the point of encounter between God and his people, seems to refer to Christ; Matthew 23:10 even says, "[W]hich is greater, the gift or the altar that makes the gift sacred?" The implication is that the altar it not *less* than the offering. Now what is as great as the offering of Christ other than Christ himself? The tabernacle and the temple also refer to Christ, who, when he lived on this earth, was in his body the dwelling place of God: "[T]he Word became flesh and tabernacled among us" (John 1:14 TLV). "'Destroy this temple, and in three days I will raise it up.' . . . [H]e was speaking about the temple of his body" (John 2:19, 21).

Let us now turn to consider the (high) priest. It is worth noting that Christ is both the offering and the offerer. A large part of the book of Hebrews speaks of the fact that Christ, although he is priest "after the order of Melchizedek" (Heb. 5:6, 10; 6:20; 7:11, 17), at present performs in heaven a typically Aaronic priesthood of intercession and mediation (Heb. 4:14-16; 7:25-28; 8:1-2). Also specifically Aaronic is the fact that he, following the typology of the Day of Atonement, as the high priest has brought his blood into the sanctuary (§§5.3-5.5).

The only reference to Jesus' (high) priesthood on earth is Hebrews 2:17, where Christ is presented as "a merciful and faithful high priest in the service of God, to make propitiation for the sins of the people." At the same time he is the atoning sacrifice:

> For if the blood of goats and bulls . . . sanctify for the purification of the flesh, how much more will the blood of Christ, who through the eternal Spirit offered himself without blemish to God, purify our conscience from dead works to serve the living God . . . [Christ did not come] to offer himself repeatedly, . . . [b]ut as it is, he has appeared once for all at the end of the ages to put away sin by the sacrifice of himself . . . Christ [has] been offered once to bear the sins of many (Heb. 9:13-14, 25-28).

The offering of Christ is elaborated further in Hebrews 10:4-14, again in contrast with the Old Testament sacrificial ministry:

For it is impossible for the blood of bulls and goats to take away sins. Consequently, when Christ came into the world, he said, "Sacrifices and offerings you have not desired, but a body have you prepared for me; in burnt offerings and sin offerings you have taken no pleasure. Then I said, 'Behold, I have come to do your will, O God, as it is written of me in the scroll of the book'" [Ps. 40:6-8]. . . . And by that will we have been sanctified through the offering of the body of Jesus Christ once for all. And every priest stands daily at his service, offering repeatedly the same sacrifices, which can never take away sins. But when Christ had offered for all time a single sacrifice for sins, he sat down at the right hand of God, waiting from that time until his enemies should be made a footstool for his feet. For by a single offering he has perfected for all time those who are being sanctified.

Notice this phrase: "Christ had offered [thus, he is the offerer] for all time a single sacrifice for sins," that is, he is the offering.

6.4.2 The Two Priestly Orders

The argument of Hebrews strongly emphasizes that, although Christ's priestly ministry exhibits so many Aaronic features, he could not be a priest after the *order* of Aaron. This was because he did not belong to Aaron's family, nor to the tribe of Levi, but to the tribe of Judah (Heb. 7:13-14). A different order was needed, not as an emergency provision in order to enable Christ to be priest, but an order that was both new and much older, as well as more elevated, than the order of Aaron. This is the order of Melchizedek. He was king of Salem, priest of the Most High God, and met Abraham after the latter's victory over the four kings (Gen. 14:18-19). David quotes YHWH who spoke of his (i.e., David's) "Lord" (i.e., the Messiah): "The LORD says to my Lord: 'Sit at my right hand, until I make your enemies your footstool'" (Ps. 110:1; cf. Matt. 20:23; 22:44; Acts 2:34; Heb. 1:13), and then says, "The LORD has sworn [to the Messiah] and will not change his mind, 'You are a priest forever after the order of Melchizedek'" (Ps. 110:4).

This order of Melchizedek is more elevated than the order of Aaron for the following seven reasons (notice especially the Gk. key terms *kreitton* or *kreisson*, "better," *pleion*, "greater/better," and *meizon*, "greater").[15]

(a) Although the Melchizedekian priesthood is not yet mentioned in Hebrews 3, we do read there of the "more glory" and the "more honor" of Christ in regard to the entire Mosaic system (v. 3).

(b) The Aaronic priesthood contained many defective, sinful, and mortal priests, who had to bring sin offerings also for themselves. However, the Melchizedekian priesthood contained/contains only one priest, who is perfect, sinless, and immortal, a priest who offered *himself for others* (Heb. 5:1-10).

(c) The Aaronic priesthood was not, but the Melchizedekian priesthood was, based upon a divine oath (Heb. 6:16-17; 7:20-21, 28). Thus, it was/is characterized by "better things—things that belong to salvation" (Heb. 6:9), a "better" covenant, "enacted on better promises" (Heb. 8:6).

(d) In his forefather Abraham, Aaron gave tithes to Melchizedek, who therefore was his superior in this respect. Conversely, in his forefather Abraham, Aaron was blessed by Melchizedek, and thereby the inferior was blessed by the superior. Both points indicate that Melchizedek was more than Aaron, and therefore the Melchizedekian priesthood is more than the Aaronic priesthood (Heb. 7:1-10).

(e) The Aaronic priesthood was temporary "because of its weakness and uselessness (for the law made nothing perfect)" (Heb. 7:18-19). However, the Melchizedekian priesthood is everlasting, and does contain a "better hope" (Heb. 7:19), that is, a hope for "a better possession and an abiding one" (Heb. 10:34).

(f) The Aaronic priesthood led God's people into an earthly sanctuary and an earthly land. However, the

---

15. See Ouweneel (1982, 1:16); see also the diagram there (65).

Melchizedekian priesthood leads God's people into "the greater and more perfect tent (not made with hands, that is, not of this creation)" (Heb. 9:11), and into a "better country, that is, a heavenly one" (Heb. 11:16). During the time of the Aaronic priesthood, occasionally a temporary raising of the dead occurred, that is, a return to the mortal body (Heb. 11:35). However, the Melchizedekian priesthood leads to a superior resurrection, to an immortal, incorruptible resurrection body (cf. v. 40; 1 Cor. 15:51-57; Phil. 3:21).

(g) Above all, the Aaronic priesthood was based upon defective (animal) sacrifices, which in reality cannot remove sins. In contrast with this, the Melchizedekian priesthood was based upon "sprinkled blood that speaks a better word than the blood of Abel" (Heb. 12:24), and better than the blood of animal sacrifices. It is the blood of a "better sacrifice" (cf. 9:23), namely, the sacrifice of the high priest himself, who gave himself up into death (Heb. 9:11-14, 23-28; 10:1-18; cf. 11:4; Gal. 1:4; 2:20; Eph. 5:2, 25; 1 Tim. 2:6; Titus 2:14).

6.4.3 The High Priest's Heavenly Ministry

In the book of Hebrews, the high priestly ministry is linked not only with the atoning work of Calvary, but also, and in particular, with the ministry that the high priest Jesus Christ performs at present in heaven. This is a ministry of intercession (Heb. 7:25; cf. Rom. 8:34; 1 John 2:1), but more than that, a ministry of mercy: "For we do not have a high priest who is unable to sympathize with our weaknesses, but one who in every respect has been tempted as we are, yet without sin. Let us then with confidence draw near to the throne of grace, that we may receive mercy and find grace to help in time of need" (Heb. 4:15-16; cf. 2:18). However, there is still more. Often, Christians view Christ's heavenly ministry only from this perspective: intercession, mercy, help in time of need. But for the author of Hebrews, "the point in what we are saying is this: we have such a high priest, one who is seated at the right hand of the throne of the Majesty in heaven, *minister in the holy places*, in the true tent that the Lord set up, not man" (8:1–2).

It seems to me that the transition from the ministry of intercession and help in need to the latter ministry is found in Hebrews 7:25, Jesus "is able to save to the uttermost those who draw near to God through him, since he always lives to make intercession for them." Here, believers are seen not only as being in trouble down here on earth, needing salvation and intercession, but *as those who draw near*. I link this with the word "minister" in 8:2, Greek *leitourgos*, from which the English word "liturgist" was derived, a word that fits here very well. Christ is the great liturgist in heaven, and those "who draw near" to God, join him in this heavenly ministry of worship. Notice that it is Christ who says, "I will tell your name to my brothers; in the midst of the congregation I will sing your praise" (2:12; cf. Ps. 22:22). The "congregation" mentioned here—in its New Testament application the company of Christian believers—is the church, which answers to the appeal: "Through him [i.e., Christ] then let us continually *offer up a sacrifice of praise to God*, that is, the fruit of lips that acknowledge his name" (Heb. 13:15).

Christ is not only the One through whom we are reconciled to God but also the One through whom we, as a reconciled people, draw near to God as priestly worshippers. This is the way they are described in Hebrews 10:19–22:

> Therefore, brothers, since we have confidence to enter the holy places by the blood of Jesus, by the new and living way that he opened for us through the curtain, that is, through his flesh, and since we have a great priest over the house of God, let us draw near with a true heart in full assurance of faith, with our hearts sprinkled clean from an evil conscience and our bodies washed with pure

water.

The closing lines clearly remind us of the Old Testament priestly consecration (Lev. 8:6, 23–24) (see §5.7.1). We come to God, not only as the poor and needy, but as priests and worshipers.

In the expression "a sacrifice of praise" (Gk. *thysian aineseōs*) in Hebrews 13:15, the word *thysia* is the common word for a literal (animal) sacrifice, as in 5:1; 7:27; 8:3; 9:9, 23, 26; 10:1, 5, 8, 11, 26; 11:4. Thus, the author is again thinking of the Old Testament sacrificial ministry, but this time to describe not the one-time offering of Christ to God but *our* continual offerings of praise through Christ to God. This is also evident from the reference to Hosea 14:2—we offer "the calves of our lips" (KJV)—where the Septuagint reads, "the fruit of our lips" (as do many English translations). If we accept the Masoretic text here, this suggests that already in the Old Testament, sacrificial animals could be spiritualized as offerings of praise, which were brought by the mouth. We find the same in Psalm 50:14 and 23, "Offer to God a sacrifice of thanksgiving.... The one who offers thanksgiving as his sacrifice glorifies me."

The emphatic contrast with verse 13 ("Do I eat the flesh of bulls or drink the blood of goats?") clearly suggests that, although the sacrificial terminology is maintained, the text is referring to spiritual offerings. Thus, we should notice the enormous difference between "offerings of thanksgiving" that are literal animal sacrifices (Lev. 7:12–15; 22:29; 2 Chron. 33:16; Amos 4:5) and "offerings of thanksgiving" in the figurative sense: offerings of the heart and the mouth (Ps. 50:14, 23; in 107:22 and 116:17; both meanings can be involved).

This figurative way of speaking is continued in the New Testament. Thus, Peter says that God's people are "a holy priesthood, to offer spiritual sacrifices acceptable to God through Jesus Christ" (1 Pet. 2:5). These are first and foremost offerings of praise, thanksgiving, and worship, but on a more basic level the believer's entire life ("body") is involved, a life consecrated to God "as a living sacrifice, holy and acceptable to God, which is your spiritual worship [Gk. *latreia*]" (Rom. 12:1).

The fact that the terminology of the bloody sacrificial ministry is being used in these formulations may be taken to indicate that believers' offerings are always rooted in, and refer back to, the bloody atoning sacrifice of Christ himself: "Therefore be imitators of God, as beloved children. And walk in love, *as* Christ loved us and gave himself up for us, a fragrant offering and sacrifice to God" (Eph. 5:1–2). Christ brought himself as a sacrifice to God for *his people—they* bring sacrifices to God as well, namely, the fruit of their lips; and bringing their entire lives as offerings is but a weak analogy to the self-surrender of Christ.

6.5 Atonement Without a Bloody Sacrifice
6.5.1 Covering Over Without Punishment

In §4.1.2 we briefly considered a few meanings of the Hebrew root *k-p-r* and its cognates, especially those having to do with the bloody sacrifices. Sometimes, *k-p-r* means "to atone" in the sense of covering sin so that no punishment is needed, not reckoning a person's sin to them, leaving them free of punishment. When some people in Israel had not purified themselves in preparation for the Passover feast, King Hezekiah interceded for them: "'May the good LORD pardon everyone who sets his heart to seek God, the LORD, the God of his fathers, even though not according to the sanctuary's rules of cleanness.' And the LORD heard Hezekiah and healed the people" (2 Chron. 30:18–20). This was forgiveness without a special bloody sacrifice, but we may be allowed to say that this atonement of *God's people* was conceivable only within the framework of the daily burnt offering as well as the annual sin offering of the Day of Atonement.

In Jeremiah 18:23, the prophet prayed in view of those who sought to kill him: "Forgive not their iniquity, nor blot out their sin from your sight. Let them be overthrown before you; deal with them in the time of your anger." This prayer seems to presuppose the possibility that God could cover the sins of Jeremiah's opponents without a special offering. This case and the previous one are exceptional because they presuppose a form of atonement without an atoning sacrifice. In fact this was also the case in Isaiah 6:7, "Behold, this [burning coal from the altar] has touched your lips; your guilt is taken away, and your sin atoned for [Heb. *kuppar*, pual form of *k-p-r*]." However, this atonement was connected with the altar. This was the altar on which the offerings were sacrificed, so that Isaiah's atonement could not be severed from the atoning sacrifices. This atoning coal was one of the coals that had consumed the sin offering, and thus had brought about a holiness that could be granted to the prophet.[16]

Of special interest is also Proverbs 16:6, "By steadfast love [one Heb. word: *chesed*] and faithfulness [Heb. *emet*] iniquity is atoned for [LEB: covered over]." It is hard to assume that the Bible would suggest here that a person's good works would outweigh their iniquity. In my view, W. H. Gispen did not get this straight; his thesis, "True atonement for sin is attained only through perfectly keeping the law of the ten commandments,"[17] is not valid, for it is a self-contradiction: a person who perfectly keeps the ten commandments does not do any sins for which they would need atonement.

As I see it, H. A. Ironside came closer to the solution by distinguishing between atoning for sins toward God and putting things straight between people. Proverbs 16:6 deals with the latter: atonement for iniquity is made through love and faithfulness. As to God, no

---

16. Grant (1956, 117).
17. Gispen (1954, 12).

loving acts and faithful words can cleanse a person's conscience from guilt and bring about acceptance with God. But if a person sins toward another person, that person will repent and try as much as possible to remedy what went wrong. That person will be much more careful in the future, and thus manage to some extent to purify their mind from the evil committed.[18]

6.5.2 Atonement Through a Ransom

Besides the bloody sacrifices, the Old Testament mentions another special means of atonement: ransom. As we have seen, the Hebrew word is *kopher*, derived from *k-p-r*, and thus has the root meaning of "covering, compensation, amends." As such, it can even mean "bribe" (1 Sam. 12:3; Prov. 6:35 CJB; Amos 5:12). Elsewhere it means a "ransom" that is paid to escape from punishment or to be freed from the hands of evildoers (Prov. 13:8; Isa. 43:3). It can also function within civil jurisprudence as instituted by God (negative: Num. 35:31-32). In the latter case, what is meant is a compensation (Exod. 21:30 CEB, NLT), or a true ransom in the sense of atonement, a vicarious means of atonement, with which a person saves their life. An example is Exodus 30:12 (see next section).

With regard to eternal life or eternal death, no human can pay the ransom for another person: "Truly no man can ransom another, or give to God the price of his life, for the ransom of their life is costly and can never suffice, that he should live on forever and never see the pit" (Ps. 49:7-9). Centuries later, one great exception to this "no man" appeared: "[T]he Son of Man came not to be served but to serve, and to give his life as a ransom for many [Gk. *anti pollōn*]" (Matt. 20:28; cf. Mark 10:45). Christ "gave himself as a ransom for all [Gk. *hyper pantōn*]" (1 Tim. 2:6).[19] "[Y]ou were bought with a price"

---
18. Ironside (1907, 194).
19. I understand the difference between "many" and "all" to

(1 Cor. 6:20; 7:23). In both Old and New Testaments, this ransom is normally the blood of the innocent substitute. This was a costly price: it was "precious blood" (1 Pet. 1:19). However, also other atoning means are mentioned (see below).

In Job 33:23–26, too, we hear about an effective ransom:

> If there be for him an angel, / a mediator, one of the thousand, / to declare to man what is right for him, / and he is merciful to him, and says, / "Deliver him from going down into the pit; / I have found a *ransom*; / let his flesh become fresh with youth; / let him return to the days of his youthful vigor"; / then man prays to God, and he accepts him; / he sees his face with a shout of joy, / and he restores to man his righteousness.

A rabbinic reading of verse 23 explains: "If there be one angel [a *defender*], out of a thousand *prosecutors*, who will intervene for him . . . God will show grace to him."[20] This passage is especially interesting because the one who pays the ransom is called an "angel" (or messenger), "a mediator, one of the thousand." This mediator intervenes to save the guilty person from the hands of the angel of death.[21] This "angel" can be none other than the Angel of YHWH, that is, the pre-incarnate Christ.[22] Only he could pay the demanded ransom on behalf of people.[23]

In Job 36:18, Elihu says, "Beware lest wrath entice you into scoffing, and let not the greatness of the ransom turn you aside." The English translations show the

---

mean that the ransom is offered to all people but becomes effective only for the many who believe.
20. Targum, Rashi, Ibn Ezra; see Reichert (1985, 173).
21. Hartley (1988, 446).
22. Ouweneel (2007b, §7.3); cf. De Wilde (1981, 316).
23. Berechiah and Metsudat David also made the link between the "angel" and the ransom; see Reichert (1985, 173).

many ways this verse can be rendered. Some expositors see here some kind of bribing (e.g., CEB, CJB, NIV; see MSG: "don't think you can bribe your way out of this"),[24] but perhaps it is better to assume here the same meaning as in Job 33:24. The sense would then be that Job might feel aversion against the high ransom that had to be paid for him, and thus might turn away from God.[25]

Quite strange in this context is Proverbs 21:18, "The wicked is a ransom for the righteous, and the traitor for the upright." R. Whybray understood the verse to say that the wicked undergoes the evil that he had prepared for the righteous (cf. 11:8; 28:10).[26] W. H. Gispen thought a bit similarly; he referred to the fact "that the wicked is struck by God's judgment already here on earth, which judgment passes by the righteous. And as far as this judgment is concerned, the faithless one comes in the place of the upright." In this approach, justice was scarcely done to the root meaning of "ransom," but Gispen did bring Jesus into his interpretation: "Jesus as the Righteous One is a ransom for the wicked because he was reckoned as a wicked one by God." This is too far-fetched, though: Jesus was a ransom for the wicked, not for the righteous—but the text is precisely about the latter ones. Therefore I prefer the view of H. Ironside, which turned the matter around.[27] He understood this to be an expression of "intrinsic righteousness," and adduced 2 Samuel 20:14–22 as an example: an entire city was saved through the death penalty for a guilty man. But when grace was proclaimed in Christ Jesus, things were turned around: the Righteous One became a ransom for the wicked, and the Upright One for traitors. Justice demands the punishment of the guilty ones, so that the guiltless ones are set free; but love led the Guilt-

---

24. Cf. Kroeze (1960, 253); (1961, 402).
25. Hartley (1988, 474).
26. Whybray (1972, 121); cf. Ross (1991, 1055).
27. Ironside (1907, 289).

less One to death, so that the guilty ones would be justified.

6.5.3 Forms of Ransom

In the law of Moses, we encounter several times the notion of a ransom consisting not of blood but of silver or gold. Thus, the firstborn of Israel had primarily been destined to perform ministry in the sanctuary, but afterward they were replaced by the Levites. In this transference, the firstborn outnumbered the Levites with 273 persons. These 273 were exempt from ministry in the sanctuary, but to this end a ransom, or redemption price, had to be paid for them, consisting of five silver shekels per person, for a total of 1,365 shekels (Num. 3:40–51).

Even more striking are the cases in which the term "atonement" is explicitly mentioned in connection with the ransom. Thus, in Exodus 30:11–16 a census had to be taken, that is, the entire nation was numbered. Each Israelite had to pay a half (silver) shekel as "a ransom [*kopher*] for his life [lit., soul] to the LORD when you [i.e., Moses] number them, that there be no plague among them when you number them" (v. 12). It was "to make atonement for your [i.e., Israel's] lives. You [i.e., Moses] shall take the atonement money [lit., silver, from Heb. *kesef hakkippurim*] from the people of Israel and shall give it for the ministry of the tent of meeting, that it may bring the people of Israel to remembrance before the LORD, so as to make atonement for your lives."

Apparently, numbering the people was a risky business, as we see in the history of David (2 Sam. 24:1–17). It was Satan who incited David to number the people (1 Chron. 21:1), with was followed by so much misery. Rashi argued that everything that is numbered stands under the influence of the "evil eye" and the dramatic consequences of it.[28] Such counting brings guilt upon

---

28. Cohen (1983, 540).

Special Aspects of Atonement

Israel (v. 3), either because taking a census usually involves mustering troops, that is, potential manslayers (2 Sam. 24:9; 1 Chron. 21:5), or because the census of the people could generate haughty thoughts.[29] Because *k-p-r* can also mean "to pay a ransom," the money mentioned here can be called an "atonement," though atoning sacrifices are not mentioned.[30]

In Numbers 31, the judgment is described that the Israelites had to execute on the Midianites because of the sins into which they had seduced Israel (cf. 25:16–18). After this had been carried out, each fighter paid for himself a ransom: "[W]e have brought the LORD's offering, what each man found, articles of gold, armlets and bracelets, signet rings, earrings, and beads, to make atonement [Heb. *lekapper*] for ourselves [lit., for our souls] before the LORD" (Num. 31:50). The gold and silver was "brought into the tent of meeting, as a memorial for the people of Israel before the LORD" (v. 54). Why had "atonement" to be made? W. H. Gispen and T. R. Ashley saw a parallel with Exodus 30:11–16 about the ransom that had to be paid for numbering the Israelites (see above).[31] A. Noordtzij rejected this view because no census was involved; he thought instead of "an acknowledgement that during the campaign much has happened that was contrary to God's law, and an attempt to receive forgiveness for these actions by increasing the temple treasure."[32] This comes nearer to R. B. Allen's view, who believed that this text is referring to a gesture of pure gratitude.[33]

In the New Testament, the notions of "buying" and "ransom" can refer to blood (Rev. 5:9), but in principle the metaphor can also refer to silver, which was used for

---

29. Gispen (1939, 172).
30. Ashley (1993, 599).
31. Gispen (1964, 236); Ashley (1993, 599–600).
32. Noordtzij (1983, 276).
33. Allen (1990, 973).

centuries as money (cf. Gen. 23:13–14); compare Paul's statement: "[Y]ou were bought with a price" (1 Cor. 6:20; 7:23). In 1 Peter 1:18–19 we find this contrast: "[Y]ou were ransomed from the futile ways inherited from your forefathers, not with perishable things such as silver or gold, but with the precious blood of Christ, like that of a lamb without blemish or spot" (cf. a similar contrast in Acts 3:6). However, this does not contradict using silver and gold typologically to refer to the ransom that Christ has paid for his people. This is because such a contrast makes sense only if there are points of similarity (for a very different, yet similar example, see being intoxicated with wine and being filled with the Spirit in Eph. 5:18).

As to the gold, it is suggestive of the glory of God since, for instance, the purely golden cherubim on the mercy seat are called the "cherubim of glory" (Heb. 9:5). And the silver is suggestive of the price that is paid for the atonement of believers. Thus, the forty silver bases under the gold-covered frames of the tabernacle (Exod. 26:19–21, 25)—which as God's dwelling place is also a type of the church—might refer to the redemption in Christ upon which the church has been built.[34]

6.6 Types in Genesis
6.6.1 Adam

Everything that the Old Testament teaches about atonement shows clearly that people cannot stand before God on the basis of their own achievements but only on the basis of vicarious sacrifice.[35] This truth comes to light, although in a hidden manner, in Genesis 3:21, where YHWH covers Adam and Eve with garments of skins. This presupposes that one or more animals had to die. The first couple had initially covered themselves with loincloths of fig leaves, but that would not do. These cloths

---

34. See, e.g., Chambers (1958, 80–82); Pollock (2009, 49–51).
35. Cf. generally, Verkuyl (1992, chapter 9).

reflected as well as exhausted their possibilities, and had merely demonstrated their helplessness.[36] Now they could begin to discover how this helplessness supplied them with the opportunity to come to know God's tender mercies. These mercies could be bestowed only through the death of *another*, a substitute that itself was innocent of the sin that Adam and Eve had committed. This vicarious death supplied them with a covering that answered to God's thoughts. The first couple could do nothing else than accept God's grace and the covering that he, in his grace, had supplied for them.

Theologian and philosopher Francis A. Schaeffer argued that these were the first animals that ever died. He believed that this shows that people cannot stand before God in their own covering (the fig leaves) but that they need a covering from God, a very special covering demanding the death of a victim, a covering not supplied by people themselves but by God. Schaeffer warned against drawing too many conclusions from Genesis 3:21 alone, yet maintained—and I agree with him—that here we find the roots of the Old Testament sacrificial system. Verse 21 looks forward, as it were, to the fulfillment of verse 15: the coming of him who would bruise the head of Satan (cf. Rev. 12:9; 20:2).[37] Redemption is not only about atonement for sins but also about defeating the tempter (Matt. 4:3; 1 Thess. 3:5), the one who incited, and incites, people to sin.

Henry M. Morris suggested that Adam and Eve perhaps watched with sadness as God picked out two of their animal friends—probably two sheep—and killed them before their eyes, pouring out their innocent blood before their eyes. In typological form they learned that a true atonement or covering can be supplied by God alone.[38] Two additional thoughts are appropriate here.

---

36. Grant (1956, 24).
37. Schaeffer (1982, 75); cf. Ouweneel (2008a, §10.2.1).
38. Morris (1976, 130).

First, sheep are an obvious suggestion because in the Torah these are the most common sacrificial animals (Gen. 4:4; 22:7, 13; Exod. 12:3-6; 29:38-41); moreover, their skins are good for clothing. Second, if Adam and Eve did indeed watch God kill animals, this must have been the first time they observed physical death (the second time could have been when they found their dead son Abel).

6.6.2 Abel

The first two sons of Adam and Eve, Cain and Abel, picked up the message of Genesis 3 in different ways (4:3-5). Abel brought a sacrifice (Heb. *minchah*), which here is not a grain offering (cf. Lev. 2:1) but an offering with the character of a burnt offering.[39] Cain brought the fruits of his own achievements—work that sin had necessitated (3:19-21) as well as stained—but Abel came to God realizing his own sinfulness and unworthiness, and hiding, so to speak, behind a substitute in the form of a stainless sacrifice.[40]

Incidentally, the point is not to what extent Cain and Abel themselves were consciously aware of these things, but how much we, in retrospect, identify these features in the light of God's entire revelation. Even the earliest revelation (Gen. 3:21), though, should have sufficiently instructed Cain and Abel. Thus, Henry Morris rightly remarked that the entire event can be genuinely understood only in the context of God's original revelation concerning the necessity of a vicarious sacrifice as a prerequisite for approaching God. This cannot have been anything other than what God showed to Adam and Eve in killing the animals and clothing them with the animals' skins. No doubt Adam and Eve explained this to their sons. However, Cain came to believe that his own fruits in every respect were just as valuable, and at least

---

39. Cf. chapter 4 note 26 above.
40. Grant (1956, 25).

Special Aspects of Atonement

as attractive and useful for people, as Abel's animals. Therefore, Cain brought the fruits that his own efforts had extorted from the earth that God had cursed.[41]

Francis Schaeffer, too, presumed that Abel knew, through his parents, of the promise (Gen. 3:15) and of the garments of skins.[42] This may be speculation, he added, but one thing is not speculation: since the time of Abel, the activity of sacrifice was known and practiced. Thus, he said of Noah's sacrifice (8:20) that apparently he too possessed knowledge that we would not have expected at such an early stage, and that must be traced to special revelation from God.[43]

Of course, in principle other interpretations of Genesis 4:4–5 are conceivable:[44] (a) What grows spontaneously constitutes a sacrifice that is more appropriate than what was cultivated (Flavius Josephus). (b) Cain's fruits were no firstfruits, unlike Abel's sacrificial animals (Philo, Ibn Ezra). (c) God esteems the roaming shepherd better than the agrarian who is bound to one place (Hermann Gunkel). (d) Cain was frugal.[45] (e) Abel's sacrifice smelled better than Cain's sacrifice (Saul Levin). (f) We cannot know why Abel's offering was better than Cain's (Victor Hamilton).

None of these explanations satisfies me. I strongly prefer Calvin, who did not work out the point, but stated,[46] "[T]he sacrifice of cattle [by Abel] and the effusion of blood contains something further, namely, that the offerer should have death before his eyes; and should, nevertheless, believe in God as propitious to him." He-

---

41. Morris (1976, 136–37); cf. older authors (ad loc.): Darby (n.d.-b, 1); Kelly (1970); Macintosh (1972); Grant (1890; 2013); Coates (1922).
42. Schaeffer (1982, 79).
43. Ibid., 103.
44. Summarized by Hamilton (1990, 224).
45. So R. E. Averbeck (*DOTT* 2:982).
46. http://biblehub.com/commentaries/calvin/genesis/4.htm.

braist F. Böhl said, "The ground had been cursed by God (3:17–18). However, if our interpretation of 3:21 is correct, the animal sacrifice had been instituted by God himself. Thus, we understand that God rejects the offering of the agrarian, and accepts that of the shepherd."[47]

The Annotations of the Dutch States Translation (1637) comment in the same vein: "That is, Abel's person and offering were pleasant to God because of his faith, looking forward to the offering of the promised Messiah," and refers to Hebrews 11:4, "By faith Abel offered to God a more acceptable sacrifice than Cain, through which he was commended as righteous, God commending him by accepting his gifts. And through his faith, though he died, he still speaks."[48] This is remarkable because, at this early point, justification (declaring someone righteous) is seen as rooted in faith, namely, the faith that, in the vicarious sacrifice, looks forward to the work of Christ, and not to one's own works. Earlier in this series, I have explained that the Old Testament religion in no way implied a justification by works of the law;[49] in the Old Testament, justification is by faith alone.

1 John 3:12 says that "Cain . . . was of the evil one and murdered his brother. And why did he murder him? Because his own deeds were evil and his brother's righteous." The evil element in Cain's works can hardly have been in the external nature of these works; rather, they were evil because Cain was "of the evil one," that is, of his spiritual father, the devil (cf. John 8:44). In contrast with him, Abel was righteous, and his works were righteous. Nevertheless, this was not the reason why Abel's offering was accepted, and Cain's offering was not accepted. Abel's offering was inherently a better offering, as we have seen.

---

47. Böhl (1923, 73).
48. Haak (1918, ad loc.).
49. Ouweneel (*RT* I/2).

6.6.3 Noah

Quite special is the burnt offering (Heb. ʿ*olah*) that Noah brought after the Flood: "Then Noah built an altar to the Lord and took some of every clean animal and some of every clean bird and offered burnt offerings on the altar. And . . . the Lord smelled the pleasing aroma" (Gen. 8:20–21). The human heart had not changed on account of the Flood, as is shown by the important parallelism between Genesis 6:5 ("The Lord saw that the wickedness of man was great in the earth, and that *every intention of the thoughts of his heart was only evil continually*") and Genesis 8:21 ("I will never again curse the ground because of man, *for*[50] *the intention of man's heart is evil from his youth*"). The great difference was this: from now on, God would regard the earth and humanity from the viewpoint of the sacrifice and its pleasant aroma: "[W]hen the Lord smelled the pleasing aroma, the Lord said in his heart, 'I will never again curse the ground. . . . Neither will I ever again strike down every living creature as I have done'" (8:21). Henceforth, what primarily determines God's attitude toward humanity is not human sinfulness but the pleasing aroma of the burnt offering. Not a changed humanity but the sacrifice changes everything. We can hardly overlook the New Testament significance of this: God does not regard repenting people (cf. Ps. 51:16–17) on the basis of their sinfulness (or their supposed goodness, for that matter), but only on the basis of Christ's atoning sacrifice.

In a certain sense, God himself provided this burnt offering. If I read Genesis 7:2–3 correctly, the unclean animals came to the ark two by two, that is, as pairs, but at God's command, seven of each clean animal species boarded the ark—not seven *pairs*, but seven *individual animals*, that is, three and a half pairs.[51] Three pairs

---

50. Heb. *ki*; the translation "even though" (NIV) is also possible.
51. Elsewhere (Ouweneel (1976, 88), I refer to Calvin, W. Gesenius, J. C. Sikkel, J. Schoneveld, H. C. Leupold, and J. C.

wereneeded for procreation after the Flood, but apparently the seventh animal had been pre-ordained as a sacrifice. Indirectly, God had thus provided the clean sacrificial animals (cow, sheep, goat, pigeon, turtledove; cf. 15:9) as a burnt offering for himself (cf. 22:8, and see the next section).

In God's nostrils, the fragrance of the burnt offering that Noah offered was a "pleasing aroma" (Gen. 9:21; Heb. *reah hannihoha*, literally "savor of rest" GNV, JUB). The Hebrew word *nihoah* reminds us of what Noah's name means: "the bringer of rest," and of his function as a type of Christ. God finds rest for his heart, not primarily in the purified earth, and even less in unchanged humanity (their heart was still evil, Gen. 8:21), but in the sacrifice brought by Christ. As the hymn of Julius Anton von Poseck says it, *Auf dem Lamm ruht meine Seele ... Da, wo Gott mit Wonne ruhet, bin auch ich in Ruh gesetzt* ("On the Lamb my soul is resting ... There where God rests with pleasure [viz., in the Lamb and his blood], I have been placed in rest as well"[52]).

6.6.4 Abraham

Of the greatest possible significance is the second occurrence in Genesis of the word "burnt offering." This is found in chapter 22:2, "Take your son, your only son Isaac, whom you love, and go to the land of Moriah, and offer him there as a burnt offering on one of the mountains of which I shall tell you." A father must go and bring his own son as a burnt offering! Equally important are verses 7–8, where Isaac says, "Behold, the fire and the wood, but where is the lamb for a burnt offering?" Abraham said, "God will provide for himself the lamb for a burnt offering, my son." The remarkable thing is that,

---

Whitcomb, who supported this interpretation (*contra* the ESV, NIV; the NKJV and the NLV follow the reading as given above).

52. The official translation (by Mrs. Frances Bevan) says, "On the Lamb my soul is resting ... God is satisfied with Jesus, I am satisfied as well."

Special Aspects of Atonement

more clearly than before, the offering is indeed brought *to* God, but it is God who provides *for himself* the lamb for a burnt offering. To put it even more strongly—in New Testament language—God is the Father who provides the Lamb by offering his own Son (cf. John 1:29; 3:16; Rom. 8:3, 32; 1 John 4:9–10, 14).

That this is indeed the deeper significance of Genesis 22 is evident from, among other things, the fact that Matthew 3:17 ("This is my beloved Son, with whom I am well pleased") contains an allusion not only to Isaiah 42:1 ("my chosen,[53] in whom my soul delights") but also to Genesis 22:2 ("your son, your only son Isaac, whom you love"; cf. v. 16). The implicit parallelism between Isaac and Christ in Hebrews 11:17–19 (Isaac, figuratively speaking, raised from the dead) points in the same direction.[54]

With Abr(ah)am we find exactly the same principle of faith as with Abel: "[H]e believed the LORD, and he counted it to him as righteousness" (Gen. 15:6; cf. Rom. 4:3, 9, 18, 22; Gal. 3:6; James 2:23). This means *in concreto* that Abram believed that all blessing for him and his offspring lay in the "son of promise" (cf. Gal. 4:23), who through death would come to life and who, as such, pointed forward to *the* "Son of promise" (cf. 2 Cor. 1:19–20): Abr(ah)am

> did not weaken in faith when he considered his own body, which was as good as dead (since he was about a hundred years old), or when he considered the barrenness [lit., deadness] of Sarah's womb. No unbelief made him waver concerning the promise of God, but he grew strong in his faith as he gave glory to God, fully convinced that God was able to do what he had promised. That is why his faith was "counted to him as righ-

---

53. Cf. what is probably the best alternative reading in Luke 9:35, "This is my Son, my Chosen One" (so most modern translations).
54. See Grant (1956, chapter 5).

teousness." But the words "it was counted to him" were not written for his sake alone, but for ours also. It will be counted to us who believe in him who raised from the dead Jesus our Lord, who was delivered up for our trespasses and raised for our justification" (Rom. 4:19-25).

Two elements of this are explained in other volumes in the present series: justification by faith[55] and the covenant, because the words of Genesis 15 stand in the context of God's covenant with Abram.[56] Here I am emphasizing that, also with Abram, the offering is central: God fulfills his promises only on the basis of the offering, that is, *the* Offering. In Christ (and his atoning work), all the promises of God find their Yes and their Amen (2 Cor. 1:20). When the covenant of Genesis 15 was made, the offering was "a heifer three years old, a female goat three years old, a ram three years old, a turtledove, and a young pigeon" (v. 9). We find these exact five animal species in the atoning sacrifices of Leviticus 1-7. Thus, there was on God's side the vicarious offering that he provided himself *and* that was brought to him: God gave his Son as a sacrifice (John 3:16; Rom. 8:32), the Son gave himself as a sacrifice to God (Gal. 1:4; Eph. 5:2; Heb. 9:14).

On the human side there is only one condition: faith whereby one entrusts oneself to God's promises (Gen. 15:6; Rom. 4:19-25). However, faith is connected here with two important matters:

(a) It is connected with the (literal or figurative) *circumcision* prescribed by God, that is, the acknowledgement of God's judgment upon the flesh (Gen. 17:10-14; cf. Rom. 2:29; Acts 7:51; Col. 2:11; Old Testament: Lev. 26:41; Deut. 10:16; 30:6; Jer. 4:4). Through the very recognition that in a person's own flesh nothing good is dwelling (Rom. 7:18; cf. John 6:63), he/she learns to cast

---

55. Ouweneel (*RT* III/2).
56. Ouweneel (*RT* IV/2).

him/herself entirely on God in faithful confidence.

(b) Faith cannot be severed from Abr(ah)am's own conduct, which was both the result and the proof of his faith: "When Abram was ninety-nine years old the L*ORD* appeared to Abram and said to him, 'I am God Almighty; walk before me, and *be blameless*'" (Gen. 17:1).[57] "I have chosen [lit., known] him, that he may command his children and his household after him to *keep the way of the L*ORD *by doing righteousness and justice*, so that the L*ORD* may bring to Abraham what he has promised him" (18:19).

6.7 Defective Offerings
6.7.1 Offering in the Right Attitude

From Genesis we move through the Mosaic Torah to the books of the prophets, especially the twelve so-called "minor prophets," whose attitude toward the sacrificial ministry at first glance seems rather strange.[58] Actually, this strangeness began already with what the Jews call the "early" prophets (the authors of the books of Joshua, Judges, Samuel, and Kings), Thus, Samuel said, "Has the L*ORD* as great delight in burnt offerings and sacrifices, as in obeying the voice of the L*ORD*? Behold, to obey is better than sacrifice, and to listen than the fat of rams" (1 Sam. 15:22). Of course, this was a condemnation of the sacrificial ministry as such; how could this ever be the case, given that God himself had instituted it? However, Samuel did condemn a ministry that was performed in a wrong spiritual attitude, as was the case with King Saul (13:12).

The sacrificial ministry did not have some automatic, magical effect independent of the offerer's disposition; on the contrary, their moral attitude determined its value. Psalm 66:13 says, "I will come into your house with burnt offerings; I will perform my vows to you" (cf.

---

57. Cf. ibid., §3.9.2.
58. Cf. Verkuyl (1992, 182).

v. 15); but verse 18 adds, "If I had cherished iniquity in my heart, the Lord would not have listened." Solomon said, "To do righteousness and justice is more acceptable to the Lord than sacrifice" (Prov. 21:3). Again, this did not mean that sacrifices as such had no value but that they lacked value only if the offerer acted in unrighteousness and iniquity. Such an offering was an offering in foolishness: "Guard your steps when you go to the house of God. To draw near to listen is better than to offer the sacrifice of fools, for they do not know that they are doing evil" (Eccl. 5:1).

Sometimes the comparison—the attitude is more, or at least as, important than the offering—is absent in statements that seem quite absolute:

> What to me is the multitude of your sacrifices? / ... I have had enough of burnt offerings of rams / and the fat of well-fed beasts; / I do not delight in the blood of bulls, or of lambs, or of goats. / When you come to appear before me, / who has required of you / this trampling of my courts? / Bring no more vain offerings; / incense is an abomination to me. / New moon and Sabbath and the calling of convocations— / I cannot endure iniquity and solemn assembly. / Your new moons and your appointed feasts / my soul hates; / they have become a burden to me; / I am weary of bearing them. / When you spread out your hands, / I will hide my eyes from you; / even though you make many prayers, / I will not listen (Isa. 1:11-15a).[59]

The problem here is not only an insincere attitude but concrete evil that the people being addressed had committed toward their neighbors: "[Y]our hands are full of blood. / Wash yourselves; make yourselves clean; / remove the evil of your deeds from before my eyes; / cease to do evil, / learn to do good; / seek justice, / correct oppression; / bring justice to the fatherless, / plead the widow's cause" (Isa. 1:15b-17; cf. 58:3-10; Prov. 14:9;

---

59. See Berkouwer (1965, 300).

15:8; 21:3, 27). The LORD said, "What use to me is frankincense that comes from Sheba, / or sweet cane from a distant land? / Your burnt offerings are not acceptable, / nor your sacrifices pleasing to me" (Jer. 6:20). "Though they fast, I will not hear their cry, and though they offer burnt offering and grain offering, I will not accept them. But I will consume them by the sword, by famine, and by pestilence" (Jer. 14:12). "As for my sacrificial offerings, / they sacrifice meat and eat it, / but the LORD does not accept them. / Now he will remember their iniquity / and punish their sins; / they shall return to Egypt" (Hos. 8:13; cf. 5:6; Amos 4:4–5).

6.7.2 Love Better Than Offerings

Remember, in *all* these cases mentioned the point is not that there might be something wrong with the sacrificial ministry as such, for that is impossible: God himself is its source. However, a sacrificial ministry performed by people who have deviated from the Lord, who live in sin and yet bring their offerings, out of habit or hypocrisy, is *very* wrong. A simple example: any sin offering is worthless without the attitude of contrition, repentance, confession, and faith in the Lord's provisions.

What is needed is not just the absence of indifference, hypocrisy, and other forms of sinfulness but, first, the positive presence of *love*: "For I desire steadfast love [one word: *chesed*], goodness, lovingkindness, faithfulness] and not sacrifice, the knowledge of God rather than burnt offerings" (Hos. 6:6; cf. Matt. 9:13; 12:7; Mark 12:33). Second, the positive presence of *justice* and *righteousness:*

> I hate, I despise your feasts,
>   and I take no delight in your solemn assemblies.
> Even though you offer me your burnt offerings and grain offerings,
>   I will not accept them;

and the peace offerings of your fattened animals,
    I will not look upon them.
Take away from me the noise of your songs;
    to the melody of your harps I will not listen.
But let *justice* [Heb. *mishpat*] roll down like waters,
    and *righteousness* [Heb. *tsedaqah*] like an ever-flowing
    stream (Amos 5:21–24).

In the following well-known passage both elements appear:

"With what shall I come before the LORD,
    and bow myself before God on high?
Shall I come before him with burnt offerings,
    with calves a year old?\
Will the LORD be pleased with thousands of rams,
    with ten thousands of rivers of oil?
Shall I give my firstborn for my transgression,
    the fruit of my body for the sin of my soul?"
He has told you, O man, what is good;
    and what does the LORD require of you
but to do *justice* [*mishpat*], and to *love kindness* [*chesed*],
    and to walk humbly with your God? (Micah 6:6–8).

Love, justice, and righteousness are to be expressed in a very down-to-earth manner: God demands social justice and love toward the widows and orphans, the poor and needy, the oppressed and defenseless, the foreigners and the sojourners:

They [i.e., the wicked] hate him who reproves in the gate,
    and they abhor him who speaks the truth.
Therefore, because you trample on the poor
    and you exact taxes of grain from him,
you have built houses of hewn stone,
    but you shall not dwell in them;
you have planted pleasant vineyards,
    but you shall not drink their wine.

> For I know how many are your transgressions
>   and how great are your sins—
> you who afflict the righteous, who take a bribe,
>   and turn aside the needy in the gate (Amos 5:10-12; cf. 2:6-8; 4:1; 8:4-6; Micah 2:1-2; Zech. 7:10; Mal. 3:5; New Testament: James 1:27; 2:14-16; 5:1-6).

Sacrifices have no value apart from the right attitude, from which follow the right actions. Of course, this concerns primarily a person's attitude toward God. However, there can be no right attitude toward God without the right attitude toward fellow human beings (cf. 1 John 3:17; 4:20; 5:1).

Quite astonishing is the language of Jeremiah 7:22-23,

> [I]n the day that I brought them out of the land of Egypt, I did not speak to your fathers or command them concerning burnt offerings and sacrifices. But this command I gave them: "Obey my voice, and I will be your God, and you shall be my people. And walk in all the way that I command you, that it may be well with you."

Does the prophet really wish to deny here the Mosaic origin of Israel's sacrificial ministry? J. A. Thompson and others proposed the artificial solution that during the actual exodus from Egypt or when giving the Ten Commandments God had not yet given a sacrificial ministry to his people.[60] This view had been refuted by G. C. Aalders.[61] The ESV and many other translations provide the literal rendering, which does not mean that Jeremiah did not honor the temple ministry, or did not recognize it as God-given (cf. 17:26; 33:18).

The best explanation is probably that we are dealing here with a special aspect of Hebrew idiom: "not A but

---

60. Thompson (1980, 287).
61. Aalders (1923, 66).

B" sometimes means "not so much A but rather B," or "not just A but especially B," that is, B is more important than A. Such an form of expression is found in New Testament Greek as well: Hate your parents and love me (cf. Luke 14:26) means: Love me more than your parents. Or Mark 9:37, "whoever receives me, receives not me but him who sent me," that is, receives not *just* me but rather, or especially, him who sent me. Similarly, Jeremiah seems to be saying that God did not just give the sacrificial ministry as such—as if the offerer's attitude would not matter—but emphasized especially inner obedience, the desire to walk after the Lord.[62] Thus, the NIV renders the text as follows: "[W]hen I brought your ancestors out of Egypt and spoke to them, I did not just give them commands about burnt offerings and sacrifices, but I gave them this command: Obey me . . . ."

6.7.3 The True Attitude

In neither the New nor the Old Testament do the sacrifices do not automatically accomplish their work as if the offerer were required only to follow the procedures scrupulously. What really matters is the offerer's inner, spiritual attitude. As far as God was concerned, he made all necessary provisions in the sacrificial ministry, which anticipated the sacrifice of Christ. Now, everything depended not only on whether the offerer genuinely repented of their sins (cf. Lev. 5:5; 16:21; 26:40) but also on whether they purposed to forsake the path of unrighteousness. As Solomon said, "Whoever conceals his transgressions will not prosper, / but he who confesses *and forsakes* them will obtain mercy" (Prov. 28:13). The sinner brought their sacrifice to receive atonement for their sins—but this "works" only if they sincerely confess their sins, and moreover decide to pursue the path of justice.

David marvelously expressed this in his greatest pen-

---

62. Ibid., 68–69; Frost (1971, ad loc.); Feinberg (1986, 431).

itential psalm, which ends as follows:

> [Y]ou will not delight in sacrifice, or I would give it;
>   you will not be pleased with a burnt offering.
> *The sacrifices of God are a broken spirit;*
>   a broken and contrite heart, O God, you will not
>   despise.
> Do good to Zion in your good pleasure;
>   build up the walls of Jerusalem;
> then will you delight in right sacrifices,
>   in burnt offerings and whole burnt offerings;
>   then bulls will be offered on your altar (Ps. 51:16-19).

Thus, David does not push aside the animal sacrifices, but he argues that they have value to God only if *other* "sacrifices" have been brought to God first: a broken spirit, a broken and contrite heart. "For thus says the One who is high and lifted up, / who inhabits eternity, whose name is Holy: / 'I dwell in the high and holy place, / and also with him who is of a contrite and lowly spirit, / to revive the spirit of the lowly, / and to revive the heart of the contrite'" (Isa. 57:15).

In a somewhat different sense, David says,

> In sacrifice and offering you have not delighted,
>   but you have given me an open ear.
> Burnt offering and sin offering
>   you have not required.
> Then I said, "Behold, I have come;
>   in the scroll of the book it is written of me:
> I delight to do your will, O my God;
>   your law is within my heart" (Ps. 40:6-8).

Here we find a second reason why the Old Testament sacrifices had no value in themselves. The first reason was that God did not take any pleasure in offerings that were brought by evil hands and evil hearts. The second reason is that, even if hearts were contrite and repentant, the Old Testament sacrifices had no atoning power in themselves: "For it is impossible for the blood of bulls and goats to take away sins" (Heb. 10:4). Therefore, all hope was on him who one day would say, "Behold, *I have come*." Thus, the text of Hebrews 10 continues:

> When he [i.e., Christ] said above, "You have neither desired nor taken pleasure in sacrifices and offerings and burnt offerings and sin offerings" (these are offered according to the law), then he added, "Behold, I have come to do your will." He does away with the first in order to establish the second. And by that will we have been sanctified through the offering of the body of Jesus Christ once for all (vv. 8-10).

6.7.4 Forgiveness in the Old Testament

The point is not, as has sometimes been claimed (§4.1.3), that the atoning sacrifices in the Old Testament merely covered but did not really blot out sins because, in this view, this could only be achieved by the offering of Christ. This was the view, for instance, of Duffield and van Cleave as well as of Derek Prince (all three Pentecostals),[63] but a similar view was held in the seventeenth century by Johannes Cocceius.[64] If this view were correct, no single believer could have ever been genuinely atoned for in the Old Testament. No, the point is rather that, on the basis of the Old Testament atoning sacrifices, sins *were* really atoned for, but this was possible only because they pointed forward to the true offering of Christ.

To be sure, Romans 3:25 only speaks of a (Greek) *paresis*, "passing over" (ESV); not "forgiveness" (GNV) or "remission" (KJV), for *paresis* is less strong than *aphesis*, the common word for "forgiveness" ("remission"). Yet, the Old Testament definitely had the awareness of true for-

---

63. Duffield and Van Cleave (1996, 199-200); Prince (2000, 13-14).
64. See Berkouwer (1954b, 149-51; 1965, 302n80).

giveness, as is evident from many passages:

> Blessed is the one whose transgression is forgiven,
>   whose sin is covered.
> Blessed is the man against whom the LORD counts no iniquity
> . . . I acknowledged my sin to you,
>   and I did not cover my iniquity;
> I said, "I will confess my transgressions to the LORD,"
>   and you forgave the iniquity of my sin (Ps. 32:1-2, 5).

"For you, O LORD, are good and forgiving, / abounding in steadfast love to all who call upon you" (Ps. 86:5). "O LORD our God, . . . you were a forgiving God to them, / but an avenger of their wrongdoings" (Ps. 99:8). "If you, O LORD, should mark iniquities, / O Lord, who could stand? / But with you there is forgiveness, / that you may be feared" (130:3-4). "[L]et the wicked forsake his way, / and the unrighteous man his thoughts; / let him return to the LORD, / that he may have compassion on him, / and to our God, for he will abundantly pardon" (Isa. 55:7). "Who is a God like you, pardoning iniquity / and passing over transgression / for the remnant of his inheritance? / He does not retain his anger forever, / because he delights in steadfast love" (Micah 7:18).[65]

On the one hand, there was genuine atonement for Old Testament believers because God looked forward to the atoning work of Christ. On the other hand, the truly serious believers must have felt a deficiency. Would they, too, not have understood to some extent that animal blood *in itself* cannot genuinely remove sins (Heb. 10:4)? Is it not possible that, therefore, they too presumed that there were "hidden things" that they could not yet fully grasp (Deut. 29:29 JUB)? The *true* way of atonement still had to be introduced. Perhaps the most spiritually intelligent among them surmised that this reality would be

---

65. See also Exod. 34:7, 9; Num. 14:19-20; 1 Kings 8:30-39; Neh. 9:17; Ps. 25:11, 18; 103:3; Isa. 33:24; Jer. 31:34; and Dan. 9:9.

connected with the Messiah who one day would arrive:

> Surely he has borne our griefs
> 	and carried our sorrows, . . .
> [H]e was pierced for our transgressions;
> 	he was crushed for our iniquities;
> upon him was the chastisement that brought us peace,
> 	and with his wounds we are healed. . . .
> By oppression and judgment he was taken away;
> 	and as for his generation, who considered
> that he was cut off out of the land of the living,
> 	stricken for the transgression of my people?
> 		(Isa. 53:4–5, 8).

Now Available from Paideia Press
www.paideiapress.ca

Chapter 7
The Cross of Christ

[B]eing found in human form,
he humbled himself
by becoming obedient to the point of death,
even death on a cross.
Philippians 2:8

[F]ar be it from me to boast
except in the cross of our Lord Jesus Christ,
by which the world has been crucified to me,
and I to the world
Galatians 6:14

[T]he word of the cross is folly
to those who are perishing,
but to us who are being saved
it is the power of God.
1 Corinthians 1:18

Summary: *The work of Christ on the cross has been interpreted in many ways. In this chapter, I mention the ran-*

som-to-Satan model, the recapitulation model, the sacrificial or vicarious model, the satisfaction model, the ethical model, the exemplary model, the mystical model, and the theopaschitic model. All of these contain certain elements of biblical truth. The most elementary question is whether the work on the cross was "constitutive" (objectively constituting salvation) or "illustrative" (subjectively indicating the way of salvation). Other basic questions are how the models mentioned relate to the "modern mentality," and whether the significance of the cross was gradually revealed to the apostles, or in essence had already been indicated by Jesus himself.

The thesis is presented that the four gospels each cast light upon another aspect of the work on the cross: the guilt offering in Matthew, the sin offering in Mark, the peace offering in Luke, and the burnt offering in John.

Finally, the seven Sayings of Jesus on the cross are briefly dealt with, especially viewed from the soteriological standpoint: they underscore, respectively, the principle of forgiveness, the kingdom of God, fellowship, the vicarious sacrifice, the significance of Scripture, the glorification of the Father, confidence in God.

7.1   Models

7.1.1 A Brief Enumeration

IN MY VOLUME ON Christology, I entered extensively into the Christological and the redemptive-historical aspects of Christ's sufferings on the cross.[1] Now we must deal with the soteriological, as well as the ethical, ecclesiological, and eschatological aspects of these sufferings. These aspects are highly important; Scottish theologian P. T. Forsyth spoke of the "cruciality of the cross," a word play based on the fact that "crucial" comes from Latin word *crux*, which means "cross."[2]

---

1. Ouweneel (2007b, chapter 12, especially §12.2).
2. Demarest (1997, 147).

This is the gospel, not in its fullness, but certainly in its essence: the "word of the cross" (1 Cor. 1:18); Paul preached to the Corinthians "Jesus Christ and him crucified" (2:2). The gospel is the "word of reconciliation" (2 Cor. 5:19 KJV), that is, reconciliation through the cross of Christ (Eph. 2:16; Col. 1:20). This message creates a separation of spirits: "For the word of the cross is folly to those who are perishing, but to us who are being saved it is the power of God" (1 Cor. 1:18). The cross is *the* stumbling-block for both Jews and Gentiles (Gal. 5:11). Even among those who did confess the name of Christ there were "enemies of the cross of Christ" (Phil. 3:18). It is the "cross of our Lord Jesus Christ, by which the world has been crucified to me, and I to the world" (Gal. 6:14). The main reason for the "offense of the cross" (Gal. 5:11) is that it involves the radical end of the "old self," that is, of the sinful flesh, including the religious flesh (Rom. 6:6; Gal. 2:20, 24). It is the "offensive" idea of another person having to die for *one's own* sins, and doing so in such a horrendous way.

Here we arrive at the pivotal question: What is the exact significance of Christ's work on the cross? Answering this fundamental question has generated many theories throughout the history of theology. Mark Baker mentioned three: the conflict theory (cf. §2.6.2: the ransom-to-Satan model; see also §§8.7–8.8), the satisfaction theory (Anselm; see below and chapter 9), and the moral theory (Abelard; see below).[3] Hendrikus Berkhof mentioned "six important conceptions, with which the possibilities within the Western way of thinking are likely exhausted": (a) that of Anselm of Canterbury, (b) that of Peter Abelard, (c) that of John Calvin (as opposed to the Socinians), (d) that of Socinianism, (e) that of Albrecht Ritschl, and (f) that of Karl Barth and Jürgen Moltmann.[4]

In his older work, L. Berkhof gave an even larger

---

3. Baker (2006, 18–24).
4. Berkhof (1986, 311).

number of theories, without mentioning Karl Barth, and J. van Genderen gave a still different enumeration.[5] L. Shelton identified three classical atonement theories (cf. §2.6), and three forensic theories: the satisfaction theory (Anslem), the vicarious punishment theory (Luther, Melanchthon, Calvin), and the governmental theory (Socinians), and various other, partly contemporaneous, less influential models.[6]

7.1.2 The Term "Model"

I speak here of "models," entirely in line with Dutch theologian B. ter Schegget (with whom I do differ on many points):

> The Bible undoubtedly contains no rigidly formulated doctrine of atonement, like what is presented in some handbooks of dogmatics. Scripture speaks of this matter in distinct, variegated, alternating images. Nowadays, we refer to this with the less-than-elegant word "models." Models that are so different that at certain points they contradict, and even exclude, each other. Models that are never elaborated entirely consistently, either. We should view this not as regrettable but rather as encouraging. The biblical witnesses, each in his own way, testify about God's love toward humanity, and in so doing use all the linguistic means, all kinds of images and stylistic devices at their disposal.[7]

I would note, first, we need this variety. Many modern theologians correctly believe that the wide variety of models and metaphors simply render it impossible to

---

5. Cf. Bavinck (*RD* 3:§§378-80); Chafer (*ST* 3:135-64); L. Berkhof (1949, 424-33); Van Genderen and Velema (2008, 519-23); cf. Erickson (1998, 800-817); Heyns (1988, 288-90); McGrath (2007, 251-55); Demarest (1997, 149-66); Van der Veer in Elsinga (1998, chapter 6).
6. Shelton (2006, chapters 9-11).
7. Ter Schegget (1999, 10); cf. Brümmer (2005, 20).

fix upon a uniform and universally valid model. Thus, pastor R. Lanooy offered no fewer than seven perspectives on Christian soteriology: Pentecostal, Baptist, modern Catholic, Lutheran, Calvinist, Eastern Orthodox, and philosophical views.[8] Indeed, I am convinced that fixing upon one uniform and universal model does not do justice to the variegated expressions of Scripture. Most models contain definite elements of truth, which we must respect and allow to complement one another as much as possible.

Second, we need to consider the cultural and historical background of the proposed models. Many theologians believe that certain models, in particular the sacrificial or satisfaction model, have arisen in a certain cultural environment that is no longer ours, and thus no longer fit our time.[9] Thus, Mark Baker has offered a number of modern metaphors for atonement that attempt to recontextualize the stumbling block of the cross.[10] However, my reply to this, especially to the claim that the satisfaction model is no longer satisfactory, is that neither former nor modern culture ought to decide the durability and relevance of a particular model, but only Scriptural-theological arguments—although we indeed should always be aware of the cultural glasses through which we are viewing the biblical evidence.

7.2 Satisfaction, Ethics, Example
7.2.1 Four Classical Approaches

Three of the principal models have already been discussed in §2.6, namely, those that were current among the church fathers. These were (1) the *ransom-to-Satan model* (Jesus Christ saved believers by paying the ransom for them, that is, to Satan, in order to release them from his power; a pivotal Bible verse: Matt. 20:28), (2)

---

8. Lanooy (1994).
9. Regarding this, see Wentsel (1991, 364–66).
10. Baker (2006, 13).

the *recapitulation model* (this is a collective model, which involves the entire creation: the world as it was ruined through Adam's sin is recapitulated by Jesus Christ; a pivotal Bible verse: Eph. 1:10), and (3) the *sacrificial* or *vicarious model* (Jesus offered himself as the vicarious sacrifice in our stead; he underwent the punishment for our sins; he died so that we would live; a pivotal Bible verse: 1 Pet. 2:24).

In this and the next two sections I will discuss five other soteriological models, which were developed in later times. One of these is a medieval model that by now can definitely be reckoned among the classical models. It is the *satisfaction model* set forth by Anselm of Canterbury, described in his famous work *Cur Deus Homo* ("Why God Became Man," 1198). Building blocks for it can be found in the writings of Origen, Tertullian, Cyprian, and Augustine.[11] This view is quite similar to that of the Reformers, but there are differences. L. Berkhof explained the differences this way: with Anselm, the emphasis is on the satisfaction that is given on behalf of God's wounded honor rather than on satisfaction given on behalf of God's righteousness.

In the New Testament, this element is certainly important: humans have been destined to be a "vessel for (or, to) honor" (Rom. 9:21 NKJV, GNV; cf. 2 Tim. 2:20), and "honor" is due to God (see, e.g., 1 Tim. 1:17; 6:16; Rev. 4:9, 11; 5:12-13; 7:12). Paul asks Israel, "You who boast in the law dishonor God by breaking the law" (Rom. 2:23). Where humanity has violated God's honor by transgressing God's law, Christ has restored it. As Jesus said, "Now is the Son of Man glorified, and *God is glorified in him*" (John 13:31). "I glorified you on earth *by*[12] finishing the work you gave me to do" (17:4 CEB, CJB). (This can be

---

11. Bolkestein (1945, 86); Van de Beek (1998, 189); Van Ve luw (2002, 161-62).
12. The participle "having finished (or, completed)" (Gk. *te leiōsas*) clearly indicates *in what way* Jesus had glorified the Father on earth.

viewed as a pivotal Bible verse for this approach to salvation.)

J. A. Heyns explained the difference between Anselm and the Reformers this way: Anselm taught that satisfaction occurred *instead of* the punishment, whereas the Reformers taught that satisfaction occurred *through* undergoing the punishment (Isa. 53:5).[13] J. van Genderen emphasized especially the rationalist, scholastic character of Anselm's doctrine. Both he and Heyns pointed to the notion, which had supposedly been neglected in Anselm's approach, that Christ in his mediatorial work represented his people, and involved them in it.[14] At a minimum, then, every traditional Protestant approach to Christ's work of atonement includes the notion of satisfaction. On the cross, Christ rendered satisfaction for God's honor and righteousness (in a short, rhyming, and well-known Dutch phrase: *verzoening door voldoening,* "atonement through satisfaction").

7.2.2 Other Older Models

In modern times, the *ethical model* of Peter Abelard has been defended by, for instance, H. Bushnell, A. Ritschl, and G. J. Heering.[15] This model emphasizes not so much on God's *righteousness*, for which satisfaction must rendered, but rather the *love* of God, who took the sufferings and sorrows of sinners upon himself (a pivotal Bible verse: John 3:16). Here again, the notion of satisfaction is clearly being downplayed; but, conversely, it is quite possible that the element of God's love, or Christ's love, which seeks to stimulate the human response of love in order to displace hostility toward God, is neglect-

---

13. Heyns (1988, 289).
14. Van Genderen and Velema (2008, 519).
15. See Abelard's Commentary on Romans; regarding Anselm and Abelard, see Lekkerkerker (1949, 48-55); Van de Beek (1998, 186-97); Van Egmond (2001, 47-59); and Borger-Koetsier (2006, 32-39).

ed in the traditional doctrine of satisfaction.[16] A pivotal Bible verse here is Jesus' saying in Luke 7:47 (about the repentant sinful woman): "Therefore I tell you, her sins, which are many, are forgiven—for she loved much. But he who is forgiven little, loves little."

Views that (over)emphasize certain unbiblical ideas, such as that *God* must be reconciled with humanity, or that God's fury against humanity must be appeased (see §§9.3-9.4), ignore that it was God himself who in love supplied for us the sin offering in the person of his own Son (cf. John 3:16; Rom. 4:25 ["delivered up"]; 8:31-32; especially 1 John 4:8-10, 14, 16). God not only *righteously demands* and *receives*, namely, the satisfaction that Christ rendered to him, but he also *gives in love* (namely, his own beloved Son).[17] No proper view of atonement exists that does not keep the balance between God's *demanding* and God's *giving*. If only a the *love* of God were involved, then why would this love have had to travel the burdensome path leading to the cross? If only the *righteousness* of God were involved, the love dimension of God's "inexpressible gift" (2 Cor. 9:15) would not be manifested.

In summary: there ought to be no Anselmian model without its Abelardian counterpart; but there ought also to be no Abelardian model without its Anselmian counterpart. Each model that we are discussing in these sections has an element of truth. But each model also is one-sided. Amid all these models we must try to find the most appropriate soteriological path.

Consider this very different model: *the exemplarist (example) model* of the Socinians (followers of Fausto Sozzini).[18] This model does not speak of substitution and satisfaction, either; rather, it refers to the moral ex-

---

16. König (2006, 458).
17. Cf. Heyns (1988, 284).
18. See especially Faustus Socinus, *De Jesu Christo servatore* ("On the Preserver/Savior Jesus Christ").

ample that Christ provided in his sufferings and death. Without wishing to surrender the previous two elements—satisfaction to God, love from God—we must indeed leave room for the example aspect of his work on the cross. A pivotal Bible verse here is 1 Peter 2:21-24,

> For to this you have been called, because Christ also suffered for you, *leaving you an example, so that you might follow in his steps.* "He committed no sin, neither was deceit found in his mouth" [Isa. 53:9]. When he was reviled, he did not revile in return; when he suffered, he did not threaten, but continued entrusting himself to him who judges justly. He himself bore our sins in his body on the tree [Isa. 53:4], that we might die to sin and live to righteousness. "By his wounds you have been healed" [Isa. 53:5].

The closing verse 24 emphasizes the vicarious aspect of Jesus' work, but verses 21-23 underscore the example aspects far more. The former shows us what Jesus did *for* us, the latter shows us what *we* must do in following his example.[19] The passage is—if the reader will bear with me—both Anselmian and Socinian. No model can be called fully biblical if it is *only* Anselmian (or Abelardian) or Socinian.

Emphasizing Christ's example, also in his sufferings and death, may never occur at the expense of emphasizing the elements of substitution, satisfaction, and divine love in these same sufferings and death. This was done, for instance, by A. Bartlett,[20] who rejected the ransom-to-Satan model, the sacrificial-vicarious model, and the satisfaction model as being too violent. Another ex-

---

19. Cf. the word play by Velema (2008, 658), who distinguished between "what he did for us and what he demonstrated to us [Dutch: wat Hij voor on heeft gedaan en wat Hij ons heeft voorgedaan]."
20. Bartlett (2001).

ample is S. Finlan,[21] who pleaded especially for the recapitulation (or "theotic") model instead of the sacrificial model. He belongs among those theologians who brush aside as non-authentic those passages in the Gospels that do not fit their own views.

7.2.3 Modern Models

The nineteenth century gave us the *mystical model* of F. Schleiermacher, E. Irving, and others. This model presupposes that Jesus was born with a corrupt nature just like every other human being. The difference was that he never yielded to this evil nature, that is, he never sinned. Moreover, in his work on the cross he triumphed over this evil nature, and united his human nature with God. In this, he took all believers with him, who undergo the same inner transformation he did. The most repugnant element in this view is the notion that, through his descent from Adam, Christ inherited the latter's sinful nature. I have refuted this doctrine extensively elsewhere (cf. 2 Cor. 5:21; 1 Pet. 2:22; 1 John 3:5).[22]

Yet, there is one positive element in this view: Christ descended to the depth of our sin—though *not* as a consequence of his own supposedly corrupt nature—in order to carry us to the highest heights, so that we would be glorified with him. Jesus "descended into the lower regions, the earth.... He who descended is the one who also ascended far above all the heavens, that he might fill all things" (Eph. 4:9–10). "The glory that you [i.e., the Father] have given me [i.e., the Son] I have given to them [i.e., his followers]" (John 17:21).

The twentieth century yielded the *theopaschitic model* of K. Barth and J. Moltmann. According to this view, God gave himself on the cross; it was God who suffered and died on the cross. Notice the title of Moltmann's

---

21. Finlan (2005, 114).
22. Ouweneel (2007b, §§10.4 and 10.5).

book: *The Crucified God*. In this view, there is room for notions such as substitution and satisfaction, but then in such a way that the Judge himself was judged instead of humanity. No satisfaction is rendered *to* God, but through his self-surrender God himself has supplied satisfaction in some general sense.

The element of truth in this view is that the Man Christ Jesus, who suffered and died on the cross, is truly God, more specifically: God the Son. However, this does not entail that Christ died also "according to his divine nature," for God cannot die (1 Tim. 6:16). We are necessarily walking here on the razor's edge. In my view, we cannot say that *God* died on the cross. However, we should not separate the two natures of Christ as if, for instance, only a part of Christ died on the cross. It is *Christ* who died, and this Christ is God and Man in one person.[23] The problem is comparable with that of calling Mary the "mother of God," as do the Roman Catholics and the Eastern Orthodox, as also, for instance, the Lutherans in their Formula of Concord. On the one hand, many Protestants would prefer to say that Mary was the mother of Jesus according to his human nature, for God cannot be conceived and born. On the other hand, we should not separate the two natures as if only a part of Christ was born of Mary. It is *Christ* who was born of her, and this Christ is God and Man in one person.

I would refer the reader to a recent collection of articles by a number of theologians who dealt with the dilemma: "Atonement or kingdom?"[24] The reply of several of them was that this dilemma must, and can, be overcome by placing atonement within the framework of the kingdom, helping us to view it in an eschatological way. For example, consider the thesis of H. J. de Jonge: "Atonement by Christ occurs when God makes followers of Jesus, who, after his death, live in corporative

---

23. Cf. Ouweneel (2007b, 115).
24. Van den Brom et al. (1998).

communion with him, and share in Christ's rehabilitation."[25]

This is a typical example of a view with a kernel of truth (cf. §§1.5.6 and 1.7), but a truth that gets lost when severed from notions such as satisfaction through the sacrifice, as H. Noordegraaf has rightly emphasized: we do

> our contemporaries a disservice if we do not dare to speak anymore of sin and guilt, of forgiveness and atonement. . . . A preaching that one-sidedly emphasizes the ethical imperative ["Thou shalt"], saddles [people] with all kinds of guilt complexes because they fail time and again when it comes to realizing ethical ideals. According to the New Testament, the imperative is rooted in the indicative of salvation. In the very light of the liberating message of atonement and redemption, there will be room to speak of guilt, and for an appeal going forth from the preaching of the kingdom. For it is from the wood [of the cross] that God reigns . . . ."

This last comment is an allusion to the hymn of the cross (*Vexilla Regis*) by Venantius Fortunatus (d. 609), which goes back to Psalm 96:10 in an old Latin manuscript: *regnavit a ligno Deus* ("God reigned from the wood").[26]

In 2014, a similar collection of articles appeared that dealt with the various meanings of the cross (victory, liberation, sacrifice, atonement, redemption, justice), to which I myself was allowed to make a contribution.[27] Here again, the authors endeavor to show that the meaning of the cross definitely includes substitution and satisfaction, but is much wider than that.

---

25. H. J. de Jonge in ibid., 75.
26. Ibid., 44.
27. Burger and Sonneveld (2014).

7.3 Pivotal Questions
7.3.1 Constitutive Versus Illustrative

It is not difficult to see that the most important models in the previous sections fall into two groups: those that emphasize the substitution and/or satisfaction aspects (ransom-to-Satan model, vicarious-sacrificial model, satisfaction model, theopaschitic model), and those that have a more ethical and exemplarist significance (ethical model, exemplarist model, mystical model).[28] Sometimes, these two groups are referred to as the *objective* and the *subjective models*, respectively, of which Anselm (satisfaction model) and Abelard (ethical model) are viewed as the great medieval pioneers.

A. McGrath asked the following central questions, which correspond precisely with the two types of models: Are Christ's sufferings on the cross *constitutive* in the sense that, through this work on the cross, salvation is brought about, Christ being the vicarious sacrifice, giving satisfaction to God? *Or* are these sufferings rather *illustrative* in the sense that they indicate an (ethical, exemplarist) way by which salvation can be attained?[29] Did salvation come to us through the cross, *or* was it only hinted at? In other words, during those few hours of Christ's sufferings, was God's salvation accomplished once for all, so that all the Old Testament saints looked forward to *that* moment, and all New Testament Christians look back to *that* moment? *Or* are Christ's suffering on the cross only *one* (albeit an essential) phase in the work of atonement and redemption, with which God was occupied from the time of creation or the Fall, and which he will continue until the end of time? Did God effectively realize his redemptive will through the work

---

28. Wiersinga (1971; 1972) caused a stir in the Netherlands by emphasizing the second category; see Generale Synode van de Gereformeerde Kerken (1977); cf. De Kruijff (1998, 48–53); Borger-Koetsier (2006, 165–71).
29. McGrath (2007, 248), regarding Kähler (1898).

on the cross,? *Or* does the cross merely reveal God's redemptive will, his longing for the salvation of believer, and does its realization still lie in the future?

Of course, the work on the cross is not yet the consummation of the ages; most theologians agree that the full realization of salvation lies in the future. Those who, in faith, entrust themselves to Christ's work on the cross *have been* washed, sanctified, and justified "in the name of the Lord Jesus Christ and by the Spirit of our God" (1 Cor. 6:11), whereas it is equally true that their cleansing, sanctification, and justification—and salvation—have a future dimension, including a future completion. As the apostle Paul wrote, "He delivered us from such a deadly peril, and he will deliver us. On him we have set our hope that he will deliver us again" (2 Cor. 1:10). Salvation has an inherent eschatological dimension: "Since, therefore, we *have* now *been justified* by his blood, much more *shall we be saved* by him from the wrath of God. For if while we were enemies we *were reconciled* to God by the death of his Son, much more, now that we are reconciled, *shall we be saved* by his life" (Rom. 5:9–10).

But this is not the point of debate. The pivotal question instead is whether Christ's work on the cross is a step toward salvation—no matter how important this step may have been—*or* that the foundation for this salvation was laid once for all through this work on the cross. Again, did this work *point out* the way of salvation, or did it basically *accomplish* this salvation?

The answer to this question has profound practical consequences. In the former case, the crucified Christ is particularly an *example* that must be followed. He indicates a *way* that people must go. This is what McGrath called the *illustrative* aspect of the sufferings on the cross. In the latter case, Christ is especially the *Redeemer* who must be accepted in faith. This is the *constitutive* aspect of the sufferings on the cross. In the former case, a person follows the suffering Christ on a path leading to increasing inner transformation. In the latter case, the person who accepts Christ as their Redeemer is inwardly transformed at that very moment (regeneration).

Again, the two approaches should not be opposed to each other. For instance, look at the way the responsibility of believers is involved in their ultimate salvation: "[T]he one who endures to the end will be saved" (Matt. 10:22). "And if those days had not been cut short, no human being would be saved. But for the sake of the elect those days will be cut short" (24:22). "And you ... he [i.e., Christ] has now reconciled in his body of flesh by his death, in order to present you holy and blameless and above reproach before him, *if indeed* you continue in the faith, stable and steadfast" (Col. 1:21-23). "[W]e are his [i.e., Christ's] house, *if indeed* we hold fast our confidence and our boasting in our hope ... we have come to share in Christ, *if indeed* we hold our original confidence firm to the end" (Heb. 3:6, 14). "[T]he righteous is scarcely saved" (1 Pet. 4:18) (see chapter 13).

7.3.2 *Contra* the Modern Mentality?

It is somewhat understandable why the exemplarist approach has become so popular during recent centuries. The idea that, for our redemption, God gave his own Son unto death as a sacrifice for our sins, has met with increasing resistance. J. Hoek wrote about the "modern mentality [Dutch: *levensgevoel*]": "People wish to be responsible for their own actions, and thus have insurmountable difficulty with the idea that another (the Other!) would pay for their sin."[30] Joseph Ratzinger saw this resistance against the doctrine of the vicarious sacrifice as due to, among other things, "our individualistic view of man": "We can no longer grasp substitution because we think that every man is ensconced [Ger. *eingehaust*] in himself alone. The fact that all individual beings are

---

30. Hoek (1988, 54).

deeply interwoven and that all are encompassed in turn by the being of the One, the Incarnate Son, is something we are no longer capable of seeing."[31] As a consequence, not only is the substitution model usually replaced by an exemplarist model but attempts have been made as well to construe the notion of substitution in an entirely new way.

An example of this was Dorothee Sölle, who, after the "death of God" (Friedrich Nietzsche)[32] described Jesus as the One who represents the God who is absent, here and now, through other people.[33] If Jesus had only died vicariously 2,000 years ago, this would move us to passivity, *and* the particular people for whom Jesus suffered vicariously would be forgotten. However, Jesus represents God precisely toward the lower people, in order that the more highly placed people would come to know through him these lower people, and through them would come to know Jesus.

Others have radically rejected the notion of substitution in the sense of a "transference of guilt." In §2.5.1 I mentioned some clear examples. These may be shocking to the orthodox Christian—but let such a Christian realize that the notion of a "transference of guilt" does indeed contain many riddles. H. Berkhof rightly said,

> [N]o one has the power to transfer his guilt. But as the covenant representative Jesus is apparently able to assume our guilt. Apparently—again we face the question: why? Why is representation possible? and why does this require the total sacrifice of a life? and how is this sacrifice related to the assumption of the guilt? The NT asserts the "that," but has no answer to the "why" and the "how." This is God's secret [cf. also §§11.7-11.8 below].[34]

---

31. Ratzinger (2007, 159-60).
32. See especially Altizer and Hamilton (1966).
33. Sölle (1967).
34. Berkhof (1986, 310).

Even though we do not understand the secret, both the objective-constitutive-substitution model, but also the subjective-illustrative-exemplarist approach contain important elements of truth. Humans *change* through conversion and regeneration in order to undergo *further* changes (renewal, spiritual growth). The reborn person *is* a sanctified and justified person who may now *learn* to *live* in a holy and righteous way by the power of the Holy Spirit. All of this has been discussed in an earlier volume in this series,[35] and will be discussed further in the next volume of this series. In the present volume, we will first consider the cross of Christ as an *arena* or *battlefield* (§§8.7 and 8.8). In chapter 9, we will take a closer look at the *sacrificial* character of Christ's work on the cross, and concomitantly also at the two main aspects of substitution and satisfaction. In this way, we will try to remove from the doctrine of atonement traditional errors as well as newer aberrations, in which atonement is viewed only in an illustrative-ethical-exemplarist way.

7.3.3 Gradual Revelation?

From the book of Acts one might get the expression that the actual redemptive significance of Christ's work on the cross penetrated the disciples' minds only gradually. Thus, A. König pointed out that in Acts Peter accuses the Jews several times of having killed Jesus (2:23–32; 3:15; 4:10; 5:30; cf. Stephen in 7:52), which identifies the cross as an instrument of martyrdom, without Peter entering into the redemptive significance of that same work on the cross.[36] Even when Peter speaks of the forgiveness of sins (2:38; 3:19; 5:31; 10:43), he does not refer to the cross but speaks of it as the Old Testament does: if a person confesses their sins, God will forgive them (2 Sam. 12:13; Ps. 32:5; Prov. 28:13). This might be taken to suggest that the soteriological meaning of Christ's work

---

35. Ouweneel (*RT* III/2).
36. König (2006, 291).

on the cross dawned upon the disciples only gradually. Chronologically, Paul would have been the first to grasp it, as he expressed this in Galatians:[37] "... the Lord Jesus Christ, who gave himself for our sins to deliver us from the present evil age, according to the will of our God and Father" (1:4). "I have been crucified with Christ ... I live by faith in the Son of God, who loved me and gave himself for me" (2:20). "But far be it from me to boast except in the cross of our Lord Jesus Christ, by which the world has been crucified to me, and I to the world" (6:14).

This notion of a gradually growing understanding must be modified somewhat, however. In Acts 5:30–31, Peter says that, to be sure, the Jews had killed Jesus by hanging him on a tree (through the Romans, that is), but also that "God exalted him at his right hand as Leader and Savior, *[in order] to* give repentance to Israel and forgiveness of sins." Here, very shortly after the Day of Pentecost, a connection is made—though not elaborated—between, on the one hand, Jesus's death, resurrection, and glorification, and, on the other hand, repentance and forgiveness of sins. Paul, too, refers to such a connection in Acts 13:27–39, though only implicitly: "through [Gk. *dia*]" the crucified and risen Jesus—in this quality—"forgiveness of sins is proclaimed," and "in" (Gk. *en*) him everyone who believes is "justified" from all things from which they could not be justified in the law of Moses (vv. 38–39).

Paul spoke more clearly to the Ephesian elders about "the church of God, which he obtained with his own blood [or, the blood of his own, or, of his own (Son)]" (Acts 20:28). Here, the blood of Christ is the foundation of salvation, as it took shape in the church, linking with Jesus' own words, "[T]his is my blood of the covenant,

---

37. According to some, this epistle was written in AD 48/49, according to others, in 54 or 56, that is, between 15 and 26 years after the crucifixion (which has occurred in AD 30, or perhaps in AD 33).

which is poured out for many for the forgiveness of sins" (Matt. 26:28). However, presumably the words of Acts 20 date from after Galatians, so that the latter is the first testimony regarding the redemptive significance of the cross of Christ (see in the later New Testament letters, e.g., Rom. 3:25; 5:9-10; 6:3-6; 8:3; 1 Cor. 15:3; 2 Cor. 5:18-21; Eph. 1:7; 2:13-16; 5:2, 25; Col. 1:14, 20, 22; 2:14-15; also cf. Heb. 2:9; 9:12, 14, 26; 13:12; 1 Pet. 1:2, 19; 1 John 1:7; Rev. 1:5; 5:9; 12:11).

7.3.4 Jesus' Own Testimony

In a sense, John the Baptist spoke implicitly of the atoning significance of Jesus' death by comparing him to a sacrificial lamb, well-known from Old Testament sacrificial rituals: "Behold, the Lamb of God, who takes away the sin of the world" (John 1:29; cf. v. 36). It is uncertain how much of this he himself had understood (cf. 1 Pet. 1:10-11). Later, the apostles would need the enlightenment of the Holy Spirit in order to understand the words of John the Baptist, as well as those of Jesus himself.

Indeed, in John's Gospel Jesus is recorded as having spoken several times about the vicarious meaning his death would have, most clearly so in the parable of the good shepherd. In this parable, Jesus is not the Lamb (the young ram) but, with a remarkable shift of metaphor, he is the Shepherd, who lays down his life for the sheep (10:11, 15; cf. 15:13). Apparently, these sheep can receive eternal life because he lays down *his* life (10:28). Similarly, in 3:16 we read that God gave the Son, in order that those who believe in him would not perish but have eternal life. In John 6, he connects this "holy exchange" explicitly with his blood: "Whoever feeds on my flesh and drinks my blood has eternal life" (v. 54; cf. vv. 53-58), that is, eternal life is for those who, in faith, appropriate my surrendered body and my poured out blood in their spiritual meaning.

In the synoptic Gospels, the following statement by Jesus is especially important: "[T]he Son of Man came not to be served but to serve, and to give his life as a ransom for many" (Matt. 20:28; cf. Mark 10:45). We will return to the ransom metaphor in chapter 8. Here we must note that Jesus himself indicated that the "many" (believers from both Israel and the Gentiles) would be saved on the basis of his life delivered up to death. That this statement of Jesus, like many statements in John's Gospel, has often been viewed as non-authentic is based not on internal evidence within the Gospels themselves but on theological prejudices, which claim that a doctrine of salvation based upon Jesus' blood and his work on the cross was developed much later, as an element of church-produced theology, a pious afterthought.[38] In other words, such a doctrine was not preached by Christ at all, but invented by the early church, and then put on Jesus' lips.

In the time of the apostolic fathers, the notion of Christ's atoning sacrifice as a substitute was well established. Thus, Clement of Rome wrote (1 Clemens 49:6), "[F]or the love which He had toward us, Jesus Christ our Lord hath given His blood for us by the will of God, and His flesh for our flesh and His life for our lives."[39] And Ignatius wrote (Letter to the Smyrnaeans 1:2–2:1):

> . . . truly nailed for us unto the cross in the flesh in the time of Pontius Pilate and Herod the tetrarch; from the fruit of which cross are we, even from his divinely blessed passion, that he might raise up a sign unto the ages, by means of the resurrection, even unto the saints and them that believe in him, whether they be among the Jews or the Gentiles, in one body of his church. All these things

---

38. Cf. Ouweneel (2007b, chapter 6).
39. http://www.earlychristianwritings.com/text/1clement-lightfoot.html.

did he suffer for our sake, to the end that we might be saved.[40]

The Epistle of Barnabas (7:3; cf. 8:2, 5) says, "He was in His own person about to offer the vessel of His Spirit [i.e., his body] a sacrifice for our sins, that the type also which was given in Isaac who was offered upon the alter should be fulfilled."[41] It is quite interesting that, at this early stage, the typology of Genesis 22 was perceived.

We may conclude that the doctrine of salvation as based on Christ's work on the cross is found in the earliest New Testament writings, and before the end of the first century had become a settled matter in the early Christian church. Insofar as there has been a certain conceptual development during the time of the apostles, we notice that among the apostolic fathers this development had already come to completion. Yet, it is equally remarkable that the (late second-century?) Apostles' Creed states very little of a soteriological nature. It tells us the facts of Jesus' sufferings, death, burial, and resurrection, but not the redemptive significance of these events. Only near the end do we hear about "forgiveness of sins." The Nicene Creed (AD 325) is rather meager on this point: "Christ . . . who for us humans, and for our salvation, came down . . . ." These creeds reflect a time when Christological and Trinitarian matters were much more disputed than soteriological matters.

7.4   Matthew and Mark
7.4.1 Forsaken by God

When comparing the passion stories in the for Gos-

---

40. http://www.earlychristianwritings.com/text/ignati us-smyrnaeans-hoole.html; cf. Letter to the Trallians, Introd. (http://www.earlychristianwritings.com/ text/ignatius-trallians-lightfoot.html).

41. http://www.earlychristianwritings.com/text/barna bas-lightfoot.html.

pels,[42] we notice that Jesus' saying about his being forsaken by God occurs only in Matthew (27:46) and in Mark (15:34). The wordings are a little bit different, but both times the reference is obviously to Psalm 22:1, "My God, my God, why have you forsaken me?" David himself clearly spoke a Messianic-prophetic word here because it is the rule in the Psalms that the godly are *not* forsaken by God: "[T]hose who know your name put their trust in you, / for you, O LORD, have not forsaken those who seek you" (9:10). "I have been young, and now am old, / yet I have not seen the righteous forsaken / or his chil-dren begging for bread. . . . [God] will not forsake his saints" (37:25, 28). "[T]he LORD will not forsake his people" (94:14). Paul, too, could say, ". . . persecuted, but not forsaken" (2 Cor. 4:9). However, through the prophetic Spirit, David uttered in Psalm 22 the words of the Messiah, forsaken by God (see further §7.6.4).

Other experiences described in Psalm 22 could never have been fully applicable to David; instead, they are applied to Jesus: the mocking ("He trusts in the LORD; let him deliver him; let him rescue him, for he delights in him," v. 8; cf. Matt. 27:43), the disjointed bones (v. 14), the sticking tongue (v. 15; cf. John 19:28), the pierced hands and feet (v. 16), dividing the garments and casting lots for his clothing (v. 18; cf. Luke 23:34; John 19:24)—all these things speak of the great Son of David rather than of David himself.[43]

David's statement in Psalm 22:1 was uttered by Jesus during the three hours when darkness reigned on Calvary. During the first three hours, when darkness had not yet fallen, those passing by and standing at the cross mocked Jesus continually; but we hear nothing of this during the hours of darkness. It is quite conceivable that the darkness scared the bystanders as well. But it

---

42. Ouweneel (2007b, chapter 14, especially 477).
43. Grant (1956, 172).

goes deeper than this (see §§11.1-11.3 below): during the first three hours, Jesus suffered from hostile people (just as he had during the preceding three and a half years). But during the last three hours he was dealing above all with a holy and righteous God. *These* were the hours when not the strikes of mocking humans but the strikes of a judging God descended upon him: "'Awake, O sword, against my shepherd, against the man who stands next to me,' declares the LORD of hosts. 'Strike the shepherd, and the sheep will be scattered'" (Zech. 13:7).

The difference between these time periods goes deeper than many seem to have realized. In the first three hours he could still address God as "Father" (Luke 23:34), and at the end of his sufferings he could do so again (v. 46). But during the hours of darkness, he addressed him as "God," for during these hours the wrath of God rested upon him because the sins of believers that had been laid upon him. To be sure, Jesus called him "*my* God," for Jesus never surrenders his bond with God. But when God had made him to be sin for all those who would believe in him (2 Cor. 5:21), God had to forsake him, that is, turn his holy and righteous face away from him for a limited period of time.

7.4.2 Guilt and Sin Offering

In the light of the previous comments, we would suggest that, of the four bloody sacrifices in Leviticus—the burnt, peace, sin, and guilt offerings (§§4.4-4.7 above)—we find in Matthew 27 and Mark 15 especially the guilt and sin offering. Luke 23, too, tells us about the darkness that descended upon Calvary, but not about Jesus being forsaken by God. In John 19, neither the darkness at Calvary nor the forsakenness is mentioned.

Only in Matthew (20:28) and Mark (10:45) does the notion appear of Jesus giving his life as a ransom for his people. This implies that Matthew and Mark emphasize that Jesus on the cross really *paid* for his people's sins.

Only in Matthew (1:21) do we find this interpretation of name "Jesus": "[Y]ou shall call his name Jesus, for he will save his people from their sins." Jesus himself referred to the sins of his people when he instituted the Lord's Supper: "[T]his is my blood of the covenant, which is poured out for many for the forgiveness of sins" (Matt. 26:28); the latter words are lacking in Mark and Luke. Because of these two occurrences of the term "sins," if one were to further distinguish between Matthew and Mark, one might say that in Matthew the guilt offering—dealing with concrete sins—comes somewhat more to the fore, whereas in the sin offering it is more sin in its general heinous character that comes to the fore.[44]

It is remarkable that the four bloody offerings seem to correspond not only with the four Gospels, but also with four Messianic Psalms. In summary:

* *Matthew: the guilt offering – Psalm 69.*
* *Mark: the sin offering – Psalm 22.*
* *Luke: the peace offering (see §7.4.3) – Psalm 133.*
* *John: the burnt offering (see §7.4.4) – Psalm 40.*

Psalm 22 seems to present especially the aspect of the sin offering because of its starting point: the Messiah forsaken by a holy and righteous God.[45] Similarly, Psalm 69 presents especially the guilt or restitution offering because of the well-known verses 4b–5 (NIV): "I am forced to restore what I did not steal. You, God, know my folly; my *guilt* is not hidden from you." Here, the innocent, suffering Messiah makes himself one with his guilty people.[46]

The other two Messianic Psalms, 133 and 40, will be discussed in the following sections.

---

44. Ibid., 136.
45. Ibid., 125.
46. Ibid., 130.

7.4.3 Luke: the Peace Offering

The peace offering was the only sacrifice from which all the people of Israel were allowed to eat, and that sacrifice expressed the fellowship between God and his people. Its character is seen most clearly in the Gospel of Luke. Peace is a central theme throughout Luke: Zechariah says that the Messiah would guide his people's feet "into the way of peace" (1:79). The angels in the fields of Bethlehem spoke of "peace on earth" (2:14). Simeon spoke of peace (2:29). Jesus sent restored people away in peace (7:50; 8:48). He sent out his disciples with the message: "Whatever house you enter, first say, 'Peace be on this house!' And if a son of peace is there, your peace will rest upon him. But if not, it will return to you" (10:5-6). (By way of contrast see 12:51.) At his entrance into Jerusalem the people shouted, "Blessed is the King who comes in the name of the Lord! Peace in heaven and glory in the highest!" (19:38). But Jesus wept over the city saying, "Would that you, even you, had known on this day the things that make for peace! But now they are hidden from your eyes" (v. 42). After his resurrection he greeted his followers with the words, "Peace to you" (24:36).

The cross is the place where peace between God and his people was established; as the apostle Paul put it (Col. 1:20), ". . . making peace by the blood of his cross." It was at the very cross of Jesus that peace was brought to the heart of the dying criminal (Luke 23:39-43).[47]

The theme of fellowship, which characterizes the meal of the peace offering, is also expressed in Luke in a remarkable way. No other Gospel records so many meals; I found ten: the meal in the house of Levi (5:29), in that of Simon the Pharisee (7:36), the feeding of the five thousand (9:12-17), the meal in the house of another Pharisee (11:37), in that of a ruler of the Pharisees (14:1), the parables of a banquet (14:12-13, 16-17) and

---

47. Ibid., 137.

ETERNAL SALVATION

of the prodigal son (15:23; cf. 17:8), the Passover meal (22:14-23), the meal with the Emmaus disciples (24:29-30), and the meal after the resurrection (24:41-43). In the latter meal—foreshadowing the future fellowship of all God's people—Jesus brings to light the atoning significance of his sufferings and death: "Thus it is written, that the Christ *should* suffer and on the third day rise from the dead, and that [on the basis of this death and resurrection] repentance for [or, and] the forgiveness of sins should be proclaimed in his name to all nations, beginning from Jerusalem" (24:46-47). This atonement is the foundation for all peace and fellowship.

The Psalm that most clearly expresses the idea of peace, fellowship, and harmony is, of course, Psalm 133, "Behold, how good and pleasant it is when brothers dwell in unity! It is like the precious oil on the head, running down on the beard, on the beard of Aaron, running down on the collar of his robes! It is like the dew of Hermon, which falls on the mountains of Zion! For there the LORD has commanded the blessing, life forevermore." Here, the center is not so much the offering; rather, it is no one less than the high priest, that is, the one who brings the offering. After the priests have been mentioned in the preceding Psalm (132:9, 16), now the high priest himself appears on the scene as the great Peacemaker. The quality, the fragrance of the fellowship of God's people is that of the anointing oil that rests upon the high priest's head. This fellowship is founded upon the peace offering that the priest brings, but characterized by the oil, an image of the Holy Spirit (cf. Acts 10:38).[48]

Incidentally, no Gospel is more priestly than Luke's. It begins with a priest in the temple, Zechariah, who was slain with muteness because of his unbelief (1:22). (Another failing priest is found in the parable of the good

---

48. For the notion of peace, see also Psalms 29:11; 37:11; 72:7; 85:8, 10; 122:7-8.

Samaritan, 10:31.) It ends with a crowd or worshipers in the temple, continually blessing God (24:52-53). The child Jesus was presented in the temple, and later, as a boy, spoke with the teachers in the temple (2:22-38, 41-51). None of these events is mentioned in any of the other Gospels.

7.4.4 John: the Burnt Offering

The burnt offering, the only sacrifice that was burned in its entirety on the altar to be a pleasing aroma to the LORD, seems clearly to correspond with the Gospel of John. This Gospel speaks nowhere of forgiveness and atonement except in terms of canon law (20:23). Instead, the total self-surrender of Christ is in the foreground: "I glorified you on earth *by* finishing the work you gave me to do" (17:4 CJB). Please note that, here, this work is not so much the reconciliation of the sinner but rather the glorification of the Father. It is similar earlier in John: "Now is my soul troubled. And what shall I say? 'Father, save me from this hour'? But for this purpose I have come to this hour. Father, glorify your name.' Then a voice came from heaven: 'I have glorified it [i.e., my name], and I will glorify it again'" (12:27-28). The punctuation of a colon after "hour" seems appropriate: for this purpose I have come to this hour, namely, that the Father's name may be glorified. The "for this purpose" is crowned with the "Father, glorify your name."[49]

I think that in John 13:31, Jesus is speaking about the "now" of the cross: "Now is the Son of Man glorified, and God is glorified in him." Even when he speaks of his intercession with the Father for his disciples, the glorification of the Father comes first: "Whatever you ask in my name, this I will do, that the Father may be glorified in the Son" (14:13). Also in his disciples' practical walk of faith the honor of the Father is the highest aim: "By this my Father is glorified, that you bear much fruit and

---

49. Kelly (1966, 247); cf. Vine (1985, 1:302).

so prove to be my disciples" (15:8).

In addition to this, no Gospel shows us more clearly how much the disciples enjoy the favor of the Father. This, too, fits entirely with the character of the burnt offering because this offering is brought in order that the offerers may enjoy the pleasure (acceptance) of God. They stand before God enveloped, as it were, by the pleasing aroma of the burnt offering: "[A]ll who did receive him, who believed in his name, he gave the right to become children of God. . . . For from his fullness we have all received, grace upon grace" (John 1:12, 16), with these words as highlight: "*[T]he Father himself loves you*, because you have loved me and have believed that I came from God" (16:27). Because of this favor, no Gospel accords Jesus' followers a higher place than John's: they are going to be with the Son in the house and glory of the Father (14:1-3; 17:22, 24).

In no Psalm is the truth of the burnt offering expressed in a more beautiful way than in Psalm 40.[50] Here, four of the sacrifices are mentioned in verse 6: sacrifice (read: peace offering), offering (read: grain offering), burnt offering, and sin offering (which includes the guilt offering). But the words voluntarily spoken by the Messiah fully represent the spirit of the burnt offering: "Behold, I have come: in the scroll of the book it is written of me: I delight to do your will, O my God; your law is within my heart" (vv. 7-8; cf. Heb. 10:7, 9). The sound of Jesus' words reverberate throughout John's Gospel: "My food is to do the will of him who sent me and to accomplish his work" (4:34). "I seek not my own will but the will of him who sent me" (5:30). "I have come down from heaven, not to do my own will but the will of him who sent me" (6:38). In this perfect self-surrender we are reminded of the complete consuming of the sacrifice on the altar of burnt offering; it is entirely for the Lord, for his pleasure, a sweet aroma for him.

---

50. Cf. Grant (1956, 129).

7.5 The Seven Sayings On the Cross
7.5.1 The Chiastic Structure

When studying the sufferings of Jesus on the cross and their redemptive meaning, as described in the Gospels, we find that considering the soteriological significance of the seven sayings of Jesus on the cross is quite profitable. There are clearly three groups of sayings: the first three of the seven sayings were pronounced by Jesus before the three hours of darkness (Period 1), the middle one of the seven at the lowest point of his suffering during the three hours of darkness (Period 2), and the last three of the seven sayings just before his death (Period 3). The chiastic structure of these sayings is as follows:

Saying (Number)	Adresse	Period
1– Luke	The Father	1
2– Luke	A person	1
3– John	Two people	1
4– Matthew/Mark	God (from Ps. 2)	2
5– John	All people (from a Ps.)	3
6– John	All people (from a Ps.?)	3
7– Luke	The Father (from a Ps.)	3

The chiasm appears in the addressees of the sayings:

   The Father
      Human(s)
         God
      Humans
   The Father

7.5.2 Three + Four

In addition to the chiastic structure of these sayings, as

happens usually with groups of seven in Scripture, we find a three + four or a four + three structure: three of the Sayings were addressed to God, or the Father, but not (or not specifically) the four others. Three, or four, of the saying go back to quotations from the Old Testament (in the case of the sixth saying this is doubtful), the other four (or three) do not. Luke and John each mention three of the seven last words.

The first four words cover four great soteriological subjects: (1) forgiveness of sins, (2) the kingdom of God, (3) adoption into the family of God, and (4) the forsakenness of the sin offering, leading to atonement.

The last three words cover (5) the fulfillment of the prophetic word, (d) the completion of the glorification of God, and (7) entrusting oneself to God for the entire future that is ahead of the Messiah.[51]

7.6 The Seven Sayings
7.6.1 The First Saying

The first of Jesus' sayings was this: "Father, forgive them, for they know not what they do" (Luke 23:34). We pass by the remarkable absence of these words in several ancient manuscripts. Bruce Metzger believes that these words were inserted early, when Luke's Gospel was copied,[52] others view the words as authentic.[53]

This first saying was uttered while Jesus was nailed on the cross, or immediately after this (v. 33). There was no bitterness, no vindictiveness in his heart toward those who martyred him. The forgiveness that he asked for became the contents of the marvelous message of salvation with which he, after his resurrection, sent his disciples into the world: "Thus it is written, that the Christ should suffer and on the third day rise from the dead, and that repentance for the *forgiveness of sins* should be

---

51. See extensively, Schilder (1940, chapters 7, 8-15, 17-20).
52. Metzger (1975, 180).
53. See, e.g., Liefeld (1984, 1044n34).

proclaimed in his name to all nations, beginning from Jerusalem" (24:46-47). Of course, from the side of humanity, repentance and confession of sins was a prerequisite for such forgiveness. But what Jesus basically prayed here was that *God* would accept his sacrifice so that on this foundation forgiveness could be granted to all repentant sinners.

Both Jews and Gentiles have made themselves guilty of the death of Jesus, and both will hear the message of forgiveness of sins. Of what people was Jesus primarily thinking of when he spoke his first saying? He prayed not only for the Roman soldiers who nailed him on the cross, for these were only carrying out orders and were not guilty of his condemnation. He definitely also prayed for the Jewish people, whom he had addressed just before this (vv. 27-31).[54] The majority of the people was still blind, and did not discern the signs of Jesus' Messiahship. Jesus himself had said of Jerusalem, "Would that you [sing.], even you, had known on this day the things that make for peace! But now they are hidden from your eyes" (19:42). The apostle Paul wrote that, if "the rulers of this age" had understood the "hidden wisdom of God," "they would not have crucified the Lord of glory" (1 Cor.2:7-8).

Therefore, shortly after Jesus' resurrection, the apostle Peter addressed the Jews as follows, "[Y]ou killed the Author of life, whom God raised from the dead. To this we are witnesses. . . . And now, brothers, I know that you acted in ignorance, as did also your rulers. . . . Repent therefore, and turn back, that your sins may be blotted out" (Acts 3:15, 17, 19). Paul said of himself, "[F]ormerly I was a blasphemer, persecutor, and insolent opponent. But I received mercy because I had acted ignorantly in unbelief" (1 Tim. 1:13). Just as the vinedresser asked the owner to give the fig tree one final chance (Luke 13:8-9),

---

54. Greijdanus (1941, 265-66); Schlatter (1961, 393-94); Geldenhuys (1983, 614).

ETERNAL SALVATION

Jesus asked the Father as it were for one final chance for the guilty and unbelieving nation. Similarly, just before *his* death, Stephen prayed, "Lord, do not hold this sin against them" (Acts 7:60). This prayer was answered: God gave the Jewish nation forty more years,[55] until the time when God's judgment descended upon the city (cf. Matt. 22:7, "The king was angry, and he sent his troops and destroyed those murderers and burned their city"). During those forty years, thousands of Jews came to believe in Jesus (Acts 21:20), but unfortunately not the nation as a whole.

Of course, the "for" in this first saying did not indicate the *ground* for the forgiveness as such but rather the motivation why Jesus deemed this prayer to be justified. As the Torah expresses it, this was not a sinning "with a high hand" (Num. 15:30) but "unintentional" sinning (cf. vv. 22–29) (see §4.6.1). For the former, there was no sin offering, and therefore no forgiveness; for the latter there was (cf. the much repeated "unintentional" in Lev. 4 and 5). In fact, Jesus was pleading for the forgiveness of his oppressors, a forgiveness based upon the sacrifice he himself was about to bring to God.

7.6.2 The Second Saying

The second word of Jesus on the cross was of special redemptive significance as well. It was his reply to the request of one of the criminals crucified with him: "Jesus, remember me when you come into your kingdom." Jesus said to him, "Truly, I say to you, today you will be with me in paradise" (Luke 23:42–43). Incidentally, it is quite understandable why some manuscripts replaced the name "Jesus' by the title "Lord": apparently, "Jesus" was viewed as too colloquial. However, this is the very

---

55. From AD 30 (cf. Ouweneel [2007b, 374–75]) until 70 (destruction of Jerusalem); cf. other periods of testing lasting forty years: Moses (Acts 7:23, 30), the wilderness journey (v. 42; 13:18), and the rule of Saul (13:21).

reason why "Jesus" is most likely the correct reading.

Initially, this criminal along with the other criminal had mocked Jesus (Matt. 27:44). But afterward the eyes of the former were opened, apparently because of the impression that Jesus made upon him by his words and behavior. He rebuked the other criminal saying, "Do you not fear God, since you are under the same sentence of condemnation? And we indeed justly, for we are receiving the due reward of our deeds; but this man has done nothing wrong" (vv. 40-41). These were the first signs of a converted heart: fearing God, recognizing his guilt, speaking well of Jesus, and especially the subsequent prayer, "Jesus, remember me when you come into your kingdom." It is quite remarkable that the Holy Spirit had worked this insight in the man's soul. Apparently, he recognized that this miserable crucified Man was the Messiah (Anointed King) of Israel, and that, in his case, death could not have the last word. He believed that one day this very Jesus would appear in glory; say, according to general Jewish hopes, as the Son of Man coming with the clouds of heaven (Dan. 7:13-14).

In some manuscripts, the Greek words *eis tēn basileian sou* are rendered in most translations as "into your kingdom"; in other manuscripts we find *en tēi basileiai*, that is, "in your kingdom (or, kingly glory/power)" (AMPC, RSVCE). In the former case, the criminal said: ". . . when you enter your kingdom," that is, at your second coming, or: ". . . when you accept your kingly dignity," which expression is a Semitism.[56] In the latter case, the presumed meaning is again a Semitism: "in your kingly dignity (power, glory)," or simply, "as King."[57] No matter how one reads the text, the meaning is clear: "Let me be with you when you will return as King," namely (apparently) by raising me from death. The suggestion by Alexander Bruce that the former expression refers to

---

56. Bruce (1979, 641); cf. Greijdanus (1941, 269).
57. See Ouweneel (2007b, 469n127 and references).

an immediate entrance into the "kingdom of heaven," and that the criminal at his death hoped to arrive there as well, misses the point entirely.[58] First, the "kingdom of heaven" in the New Testament *never* means heaven but rather a heavenly kingdom *on earth*.[59] Second, such a hope of entering heaven at death was virtually unknown among the Jews; all their expectation was directed toward resurrection and the Messianic kingdom. Third, Jesus' reply made a precise distinction between the (far) future to which the repentant criminal looked forward *and* that very same day.

Concerning my second mentioned objection: the prayer of the repentant criminal indeed reflected the general expectation of Old Testament believers. Their hopes never involved "going to heaven" after death, for such an idea was completely unknown in the Old Testament. Such a notion was often inferred from Jacob's final words: "I wait for your salvation, O Lord" (Gen. 49:18).[60] However, within the framework of his prophetic blessings it is obvious that he was looking forward to the redemption (Heb. *yeshuʿah*) awaiting the faithful during the Messianic kingdom (cf. v. 10, "to him [i.e., the prince from Judah] shall be the obedience of the peoples"). A similar verse that refers to this is Psalm 73:24, "afterward you will receive me to glory," where some translations even introduce the word "heaven" (TLB, NIRV), or render it as "take me up" (CSB), which is utterly mistaken. The literal rendering would be, "after the glory [of Messiah's appearance?] you will receive me [in your kingdom]" (cf. DARBY).[61]

The enormous significance of Jesus' reply is its clear

---

58. Bruce (1979, 641).
59. Ouweneel (*RT* IV/3, §2.3.1).
60. In Dutch, the misconception arose still more easily because the traditional translation was not something like "salvation" but "bliss" (Dutch: *zaligheid*); there is a similar confusion in English: "... to rescue *me*" (GW, NOG).
61. See extensively, Ouweneel (2012a, §2.5.2).

announcement that the repentant criminal did not have to wait until the "last day" (cf. John 11:24) but that he would be with Jesus in Paradise that very same day. This is an important testimony that those who fall asleep in Christ are with him (cf. Phil. 1:23). At the same time Jesus did not deny or amend the criminal's request, but rather confirmed it: there *will* indeed be a day when Jesus will appear in his kingly glory and establish God's kingdom on earth in glory and majesty. All believing Jews and all believing Christians have looked forward, and continue to look forward, to this glorious day of the Messianic kingdom. If Jesus, in his first word, spoke of forgiveness *now*, in his second word he implicitly confirmed the repentant criminal hope pertaining to the *future* kingdom of peace and righteousness.

7.6.3 The Third Saying

The third Saying of Jesus is again addressed to people, namely, to his mother Mary and his disciple John: "Woman, behold, your son! . . . Behold, your mother!" (John 19:26–27). Remarkably, during his earthly ministry, Jesus did not allow his mother to meddle in his affairs (cf. 2:4 DLNT, "What do I have to do with you, woman?"). However, at the end of his earthly life, Jesus gave her special attention—we might say, because of the "sword" that, at that very moment, was piercing through her soul (Luke 2:35). In both cases, he used the same form of address, Greek *gunai*, which in classic literature is a very unusual way for a son to address his mother, both among Jews and among Greeks.[62] The word indicates that, at the beginning of his ministry, a new relationship had arisen between Jesus and Mary. This does not mean, though, that the address of *gunai* was discourteous or impersonal. It was an expression of respect, and sometimes even clearly of affection (cf. Matt. 15:28; Luke 13:12; John 4:21; 8:10; 20:13, 15; 1 Cor. 7:16).

---

62. Morris (1971, 180).

It has been generally accepted (e.g., by Irenaeus) that "the disciple whom Jesus loved" (19:26 Gk. *ēgapa*; see further John 13:23; 21:7, 20 [Gk. *ēgapa*]; 20:2 [Gk. *ephilei*]) was the writer of this Gospel: John, the son of Zebedee.[63] We can imagine that, as the writer, he was reluctant to mention his own name, but did want to point out what was most precious to him: Jesus' love for him. Tradition tells us that John's mother, Salome (Mark 15:40; 16:1), was a half-sister of Mary.[64] Other connections have been suggested as well, for instance, that Salome was a daughter of a sister of Anna, the mother of Mary, and thus a cousin of Mary. At any rate, tradition viewed John as a close relative of Mary, which would make it understandable that Jesus entrusted his mother to *him*. This would be all the more understandable if Jesus' "brothers" were not children of Mary but, as Eastern Orthodox tradition has it, children of Joseph from an earlier marriage.[65] In this case, these stepbrothers were not, as John was, real blood relatives of Jesus.

According to Roman Catholic tradition, these "brothers" were cousins of Jesus, that is, sons of the Mary who was a sister of Mary the mother of Jesus. If this is correct, they had no priority over John, if we assume that he was a son of another sister of Mary. If Jesus were Mary's only son, he could, shortly before his death, entrust her to the care of a close relative of his own choice. Those who maintain that Jesus' brothers *were* Mary's own sons can adduce as an argument for Jesus choosing John the fact that Jesus' brothers did not believe in him (John 7:5) whereas Mary and John did. Moreover, the brothers were absent at the cross, whereas John was present. Yet, Jesus knew that his brother James would believe in him a few days later (1 Cor. 15:7), *and* how can one brother make decisions regarding the mother without the other

---

63. Ibid., 625, incl. note 49.
64. Ouweneel (2007b, 393n5).
65. Ouweneel (2007b, 326n5; 359n4).

brothers—believing or not—having any say in the matter? Therefore, in my view the Eastern Orthodox or Roman Catholic interpretation is more likely.

It is not necessarily strange that this Galilean fisherman was said to have taken Mary "to his own home [Gk. *eis ta idia*]" (John 19:27), and did so immediately, that is, there in Jerusalem. Earlier we had learned that John "was known to the high priest" (18:16). Possibly, Zebedee was a quite well-to-do fisherman (he has his own "hired servants," Mark 1:20) with a house and commercial contacts in Jerusalem, perhaps within the high priestly family.[66]

The deeper redemptive significance of this saying is that "God settles the solitary in a home" (Ps. 68:6), or in more New Testament language: God makes his people live in a "family" (Gk. *patria*, cf. Eph. 3:15), the family of God (cf. §1.4.2). Believers are children of the same God, and thus each other's brothers and sisters. Within the family of God, however, there are not only brother/sisterly relationships but also "fathers" and "mothers in Christ." The apostles regularly present themselves as spiritual fathers (1 Cor. 4:14–15; Gal. 4:19; 1 Thess. 2:11; 1 Tim. 1:2; 2 Tim. 1:2; Titus 1:4; Philem. 1:10; 1 Pet. 5:13; 1 John 2:1; 3 John 1:4), or even as a "nursing mother" (Gk. *trophos*, 1 Thess. 2:7; cf. Gal. 4:19). In Romans 16:13, Paul speaks of the mother of Rufus, who also was his (spiritual) "mother." Part of the redemptive blessing is receiving spiritual parents: "[T]here is no one who has left house or brothers or sisters or mother or father or children or lands, for my sake and for the gospel, who will not receive a hundredfold now in this time, houses and brothers and sisters and *mothers* and children and lands, with persecutions, and in the age to come eternal life" (Mark 10:29–30). Thus, Jesus entrusting a son to his mother, and a mother to her son, beautifully reflects vital relationships within the family of God.

---

66. Ibid., 397n92.

7.6.4 The Fourth Saying

Jesus' fourth saying—the middle one of the seven—in Matthew 27:46 is this: *Eli, Eli, lema sabachtani?*, and in Mark 15:34, *Eloi, Eloi, lema sabachtani?* That is, "My God, my God, why have you forsaken me?" This is the first of the last four last words, most, if not all, of which involve allusions to, or quotations from, the book of Psalms. In this case, it is Psalm 22:1, "My God, my God, why have you forsaken me?" The manuscripts exhibit some differences in Matthew and Mark: *Ēli* or *Elōi, lema* or *lama* or *lima, sabachthani* or *sabaktani* or *zaphthani*. Psalm 22:1 has Ēli, Ēli, lama *ᶜazavthani?* The version *Elōi, Elōi, lema sabachtani?* is the Aramaic rendering of the Hebrew text.[67]

Psalm 22 is not necessarily primarily Messianic;[68] thus, Calvin thinks first and foremost of David suffering under Saul (although this exegesis faces significant objections[69]). Only secondarily can we accept that David is going beyond himself in his descriptions, and that Psalm 22 has a Messianic referent (see §7.4.1).[70] Hence the many Messianic allusions in the New Testament to this Psalm, not only with regard to verse 1 (Matt. 27:46; Mark 15:34) but also, in particular, verses 7–8 (Matt. 27:39, 43); verse 13 (1 Pet. 5:8); verse 16c (John 19:18; 20:25, 27); verse 18 (John 19:24); verse 22 (John 20:17; Heb. 2:12); verse 24 (Heb. 5:7); and verse 27 (Rev. 15:4). We must ask the basic question here whether any saint has ever really been forsaken by God; such a thought conflicts directly with, for instance, Psalm 9:10; 37:25; and 94:14. David may have *felt* this way when he penned Psalm 22:1, but it became full *reality* only in the case of

---

67. Ibid., 435n28; see also Bruce (1979, 331–32); Carson (1984, 578–79).
68. *Contra* many church fathers; see J. Mudde in Knevel and Paul (1995, 59–60, 67–68). Regarding this passage, see Ouweneel (2007b, 184).
69. Ridderbos (1955, 185–86).
70. Ibid., 182–86; Van Gemeren (1991, 199).

Jesus on the cross, when the wrath of God was upon him because of his people's sins (Matt. 1:21; 20:28; 26:28).

At noon, after Jesus had been hanging on the cross for three hours, the sun was darkened in the entire country, again for three hours, that is, between about noon and three o'clock in the afternoon (Matt. 27:45-54; Mark 15:33-39; Luke 23:44-48).[71] We are not told what caused this darkening. It cannot have been an eclipse of the sun, for such an eclipse was possible only at new moon, whereas the beginning of Pesach occurred at full moon.

The Bible is silent about this most horrible phase in the sufferings of Jesus, in which God's full judgment descended upon him (cf. §11.3). The only thing we hear is the cry of dismay from Jesus' own mouth at the end of these three hours: "My God, my God, why have you forsaken me?" In his first and his seventh saying he was addressing his Father, whereas here he was addressing God. This was not only because he quoted Psalm 22. We see here the Man Jesus Christ being smitten by the hand of a holy and righteous God. We should not say that on the cross Jesus was forsaken by his Father. On his way to the cross he had said, "Yet I am not alone, for the Father is with me" (John 16:32). But neither should we say that Jesus was *not* forsaken by his Father. We must leave intact the secret of his being; as F. W. Grosheide said, "What being forsaken by God fully involves, how it is possible that the Son of God was forsaken by God, we humans cannot understand."[72] The reason why we cannot understand this is because it involves two unfathomable mysteries: the Trinitarian mystery (one God, three divine subsistences) and the Christological mystery (Christ, God and Man in one person).

In the face of this forsakenness, it is remarkable that

---

71. Regarding this passage, see Ouweneel (2007b, 408).
72. Grosheide (1954, 435); cf. Van Leeuwen (1928, 200); Liefeld (1984, 782).

Jesus kept clinging to his God, as is evident from the words "*my* God, *my* God."[73] Also important is the interrogative form, "*why* have you forsaken me?" One could imagine how a reply to this question was given in the word that the Messiah himself spoke prophetically in verse 3: "Yet you are holy." In Jesus himself there was no reason why God should forsake him. On the contrary, as the sinless One he was the only human in history who was entitled to ask the "Why?" question. But he also knew the reply: when he ("who knew no sin") had been "made to be sin" (2 Cor. 5:21), a holy and righteous God had to turn away his face from him. Compare here Isaiah 59:2, "[Y]our iniquities have made a separation between you and your God, and your sins have hidden his face from you, so that he does not hear"; and Habakkuk 1:13, "You who are of purer eyes than to see evil and cannot look at wrong, ..."[74] Jesus underwent the hellish sorrows vicariously for his people; as Grosheide put it, "Jesus dies the eternal death still during his life, before he underwent the natural death."[75]

7.6.5 The Fifth Saying

The fifth saying of Jesus was "I thirst" (John 19:28). John adds to this that Jesus said this "knowing that all was now finished," and "to fulfill the Scripture." It is known that, because of blood loss, intense physiological and psychological pain, and extreme temperature, crucifixion leads to indescribable thirst. Nevertheless, as always, John presents Jesus as someone who, despite his horrible sufferings, is fully in control of his situation, and does not think of himself first.[76] One of the words

---

73. Seven times in the New Testament Jesus says "my God": here (2x), in John 20:17 (1x), and in Rev. 3:12 (4x).
74. Cf. Lane (1974, 573) with references to Deut. 21:23; Gal. 3:13; 2 Cor. 5:21.
75. Grosheide (1954, 436).
76. Vine (1985, 1:351).

by which John indicates this is the verb "to go (or come) out" (Gk. *exerchomai*). In John's Gospel, Jesus is rarely led, brought, or taken, but he usually takes the initiative: "Jesus, knowing all that would happen to him, *came forward* and said to them, 'Whom do you seek?'" (18:4). "Jesus *came out*, wearing the crown of thorns and the purple robe" (19:5). "[H]e *went out*, bearing his own cross, to the place called The Place of a Skull" (v. 17).

John wishes to make clear that, in an analogous way, Jesus did not speak of thirst because he was in danger of collapsing, but "to fulfill the Scripture." These words *can* be applied also to the preceding words (Jesus knew "that all was now finished"), or possibly to both phrases.[77] At any rate, this saying involved the fulfillment of a prophetic statement because this verse is generally identified with Psalm 22:15 ("my strength is dried up like a potsherd, and my tongue sticks to my jaws"), and especially to Psalm 69:21 (NKJV),[78] "They also gave me gall for my food, and for my thirst they gave me vinegar to drink." Regarding the gall and the vinegar (sour wine), we read: "They gave Him sour wine mingled with gall to drink" (Matt. 27:34 NKJV). "Immediately one of them ran and took a sponge, filled [it] with sour wine and put [it] on a reed, and offered it to Him to drink" (v. 48 NKJV; cf. Mark 15:36; Luke 23:36). Thus also John 19:29 says, "Now a vessel full of sour wine was sitting there; and they filled a sponge with sour wine, put it on hyssop, and put it to His mouth" (NKJV).

The "hyssop" (Gk. *hyssōpos*) must refer here to a plant stem that was strong enough to bring a sponge to someone's mouth; it was probably a kind of Majorana (*Origanum syriacum*) (see §5.1.2). The use of the word "hyssop" is noteworthy because it seems to contain a ref-

---

77. Morris (1971, 813).
78. This is the third time that John alludes to this psalm (John 2:17 refers to Ps. 69:9; John 15:25 to Ps. 69:4); see Bouma (1927, 233).

erence either to Pesach (Passover, Exod. 12:22)—because Jesus died at Pesach—or to the cleansing ritual for the leper (Lev. 14:4, 6; cf. §5.6), or to the preparation of the purification water (Num. 19:6; see §5.7.4). David speaks of it in Psalm 51:7, "Purge me with hyssop, and I shall be clean."[79]

James Spurrell suggested that we must explain Jesus' thirst spiritually.[80] It was a thirst for the living water, about which Jesus himself had spoken to the Samaritan woman (4:10, 13-14), and which must be linked with the Holy Spirit (cf. 7:38-39).[81] This would provide a link between this saying and the preceding saying: Jesus would have felt cut off from the knowledge and the Spirit of God. In my view, such an interpretation does not fit the character of Jesus as that is depicted in John's Gospel. For instance, the being forsaken by God is not at all described in this Gospel; nor are the hours of darkness. Here, the emphasis is much more on what Jesus was actively accomplishing. Therefore, I would rather link this saying with the next one, which is also mentioned in John: "It is finished" (v. 30). This is exactly what verse 28 says: "Jesus, *knowing that all was now finished*, said (to fulfill the Scripture), 'I thirst.'"

At the beginning of the crucifixion Jesus refused the sour wine (Matt. 27:34; Mark 15:23), presumably because the wine was meant to alleviate the pain somewhat.[82] At the end of his work on the cross, he himself asked for the sour wine and accepted it, possibly to wet his throat and gather all his strength one more time in order to utter the sixth and seventh last words. Yet, John apparently does not wish to suggest that Jesus needed the sour wine. Jesus instead was longing to fulfill the

79. Morris (1971, 813-14n71).
80. Spurrell (1966).
81. Cf. Ouweneel (2007a, 153-54).
82. Cf. Sanhedrin 43a, in reference to Prov. 31:6: "Give strong drink to the one who is perishing, and wine to those in bitter distress."

prophecies in their smallest details. He said so himself (cf. 13:18; 15:25; 17:12; also cf. 12:38; 18:9, 32; 19:24, 36).

The fifth saying linked him with Scripture, and thus with the entirety of God's revelation. He stood in a centuries-long tradition, which began in Genesis 1.

7.6.6 The Sixth Saying

The second to the last saying of Jesus was: "It is finished [completed, accomplished, ended, all done]" (John 19:30), which in Greek is one word: *Tetelestai*, from *teleō*, "to finish, complete, accomplish, bring to fulfillment, to its goal" (from *telos*, "end, goal") (cf. Latin *Consummatum est*). The perfect tense points to a past action whose effects continue in the present and the future. We are dealing with an accomplished work, whose redemptive significance is preserved in all eternity.

It is quite possible that here again we have an allusion to the Psalms, for instance: the coming generation will "come and proclaim his righteousness to a people yet unborn, that he has done [accomplished] it" (22:31) (even though the Septuagint reads *epoiēsen* here).[83] Also compare 71:19, "Your righteousness, O God, reaches the high heavens. You who have done great things, O God, who is like you?"

In my view, we must not think here primarily of Jesus suffering as "guarantor" (cf. Heb. 7:22) and as the "redemption of his church" (C. Bouma), or as the salvation of the world and the mighty work of redemption (L. Morris; see §9.6.1).[84] These do not belong to the theological subject matter of John's Gospel; the word "redemption" does not even occur, nor the word "forgive(ness)" (except in the sense of canon law, 20:23). Instead, we should consider the parallel with 17:4, "I glorified you on earth, having accomplished [Gk. *teleiōsas*] the work that you gave me to do." Earlier, Jesus said, "My food is

---

83. Fromm (1967, 231–36).
84. Bouma (1927, 233); Morris (1971, 815).

to do the will of him who sent me and to accomplish [Gk. *teleiōsō*] his work" (4:34), and: "For the works that the Father has given me to accomplish [Gk. *teleiōsō*], the very works that I am doing, bear witness about me that the Father has sent me" (5:36). In John's Gospel, the supreme emphasis is not on what Jesus accomplished for people but what he was to the Father. In the accomplished work of the Son, the emphasis *here* is not on the redemption of sinners but first and foremost the glorification of the Father through his death, which was a pleasing aroma to the Father. *It is not the sin offering that comes to the fore here, but the burnt offering* (see §7.4.4).

We do have to distinguish here; it has been suggested, though, that we should not ignore the forensic aspect of "It is finished." In the first and second century, the Greek verb *teleō* was used in the sense of paying a debt, and was often written on receipts.[85] Jesus' saying can also be read this way: The debt has been paid (cf. *teleō* in Matt. 17:24; Rom. 13:6, "paying taxes"). Yet, I wonder again whether this interpretation fits John's Gospel. As we saw, in 4:34; 5:36; 17:4 it is the *work* of Jesus that was "finished (accomplished)," which in 17:4 was specifically the work of glorifying the Father, and in view of people: "This is the work of God, that you believe in him whom he has sent" (6:29); ". . . if I do them [i.e., the works of my Father], even though you do not believe me, believe the works, that you may know and understand that the Father is in me and I am in the Father" (10:38). Faith is coming to know the glory of the Son, and the glory of the Father as revealed in him: "[T]his is eternal life, that they know you, the only true God, and Jesus Christ whom you have sent" (17:3)—words that immediately precede those of verse 4, quoted above.

Of course, when he said, "It is finished," Jesus was speaking in an anticipatory way because he still had to die, and still had to rise from death. Without his death

---

85. Tenney (1981, 185).

and resurrection, neither the work of glorifying the Father nor the work of redemption would have been completed (cf., e.g., Rom. 4:25; 1 Cor. 15:12-19). Earlier in John 13:31-32, Jesus had spoken in an anticipatory way of "now," but actually describing himself as the source of his work on the cross: "Now is the Son of Man glorified, and God is glorified in him. If God is glorified in him, God will also glorify him in himself [by placing him at his right hand], and glorify him at once [by raising him from the dead]." Also in 17:4-5 Jesus spoke in an anticipatory way (CEB): "I *have* glorified you on earth by finishing the work you gave me to do. *Now*, Father, glorify me in your presence with the glory I shared with you before the world was created." Similarly, Jesus could say just before dying: "It *is* finished."

7.6.7 The Seventh Saying

The last of Jesus' sayings was: "Father, into your hands I commit my spirit!" (Luke 23:46). Jesus spoke "with a loud voice," which normally would have been impossible for a crucified person at the end of his strength. Thus, we read elsewhere: "Jesus cried out again with a loud voice and yielded up his spirit" (Matt. 27:50; cf. Mark 15:37). Recall what Jesus said about this strength in the fifth of his sayings (§7.6.5).

This last saying alludes to a statement in the Psalms: "Into your hand I commit my spirit; you have redeemed me, O LORD, faithful God" (Ps. 31:5). Jesus adds here, as a form of address, "Father," as he did in the first saying (regarding the chiastic structure of the sayings, see §7.5.1). For the rest, Jesus is here placing himself on one line with the faithful of former days, who during the last moments of their lives committed their spirit (or soul) to the hands of God (compare Stephen's last word, "Lord Jesus, receive my Spirit," Acts 7:59). This, too, has redemptive significance: salvation comprises both present and future; therefore, believers place both their present and their future in the hands of his God and Father. This redemptive meaning is underscored by the rest of Psalm 31:5, "... you have redeemed me, O Lord, faithful God."

In a beautiful way this is expressed in Psalm 16, which, as we see from verse 10 (see Acts 2:31), has a Messianic character.[86] In his profound dependence as Man on his God and Father, he says in verse 1, "Preserve me, O God, for in you I take refuge" (in Heb. 2:13a this statement is placed on Jesus' lips).[87] And then he says, in view of his death (vv. 8–11),

> I have set the Lord always before me; because he is at my right hand, I shall not be shaken. Therefore my heart is glad, and my whole being rejoices; my flesh also dwells secure. For you will not abandon my soul to Sheol, or let your holy one see corruption. You make known to me the path of life; in your presence there is fullness of joy; at your right hand are pleasures forevermore.

These verses indicate that the deepest significance of Jesus' seventh saying involves the expectation of his resurrection, ascension, and glorification. He does not explicitly ask for it, but expresses only in general terms his confidence that, also after this death, the Father will take care of him. Indeed, Jesus was "raised from the dead by the glory of the Father" (Rom. 6:4), was "taken up in glory" (1 Tim. 3:16), and was exalted by God at his right hand (Acts 2:33; Eph. 1:20).

In summary, the seven sayings of Jesus emphasize:
(1.) The principle of forgiveness.
(2.) The kingdom of God.
(3.) Fellowship within the Christian community.
(4.) The substitutionary-sacrificial aspect of the cross.

---

86. Ouweneel (2007b, 183–84).
87. See ibid., 312.

(5.) The significance of Scripture.
(6.) The glorification of the Father.
(7.) Confidence in God with regard to one's further destiny.

Chapter 8
Theological Metaphors for Redemption

Let all the house of Israel therefore know for certain that God has made him both Lord and Christ, this Jesus whom you crucified.
Acts 2:36

*[I]n him all the fullness of God was pleased to dwell,
and through him to reconcile to himself all things, whether on earth or in heaven, making peace by the blood of his cross.*
Colossians 1:19–20

. . . Jesus, the founder and perfecter of our faith, who for the joy that was set before him endured the cross, despising the shame,and is seated at the right hand of the throne of God.
Hebrews 12:2

Summary: *Regarding spiritual, divine matters, we can speak only with metaphors, whether biological-medical, so-*

cial-economic, or other metaphors (cleansing, pottery, refinery). They refer to individuals, to families, to entire nations, or to the whole world. Christ's death on the cross was an act of love and self-surrender, of solidarity with the sufferings of humanity, a form of martyrdom, a battle against the powers, the payment of a ransom, a satisfactory sacrifice. The first three metaphors on this list identify his death was exemplary, the last three identify it as vicarious, and the middle of the seven identify it as both. In some of his sufferings Jesus was alone and unique as the Vicarious One. In other sufferings, he is joined by his followers, who must bear their own crosses, must suffer for righteousness' sake, and must wage war against Satan and his powers as Jesus did.

8.1 Introduction
8.1.1 Biological-Medical Metaphors

THE REDEMPTION THAT CHRIST accomplished on the cross is essentially a mystery that can be neither adequately fathomed nor adequately described by any single model (cf. §§2.5 and 7.1). Regarding the redemptive necessity of Jesus' suffering and death, H. Berkhof observed that

> [f]resh attempts are always made to verbalize it [this redemptive necessity], yet [these have] never led to a theological consensus. There remains an impenetrable haze, making it impossible for us to express in words the decisive connection between death and salvation; and one who thinks that he is able often makes the connection superficial, rational, and all too human.[1]

As with all mysteries in Scripture, the mystery of redemption is approximated through various metaphors. Here and in the following sections I mention fourteen such metaphors (the first of them being that of the sacri-

---

1. Berkhof (1986, 309).

ficial ministry, dealt with earlier in chapters 4-6).[2]

(a) *Rural life*. From this comes the image of the shepherd, who risks his life for his sheep in order to defend them against the lion and the bear, against thieves and robbers. Jesus adopted this image in John 10:8, 10-17, and said he would *lay down* his life for his sheep (cf. David in 1 Sam. 17:34-37, who exhibited the same attitude). It is the image of the strong shepherd, who takes care of the "weak, sick, injured, straying" sheep by expending his own life for them (cf. the contrast in Ezek. 34:3-4). Through his vicarious death, Jesus saved the flock, and even acquired new sheep (John 10:16, 27-29).

(b) *Botany*. The sinner is like a bad tree that, because it is bad, produces bad fruit (cf. Matt. 3:10; 7:16-20; 12:33). Sometimes botanical or agricultural metaphors are used to describe redemption: "For if we have been planted together in the likeness of his death, we shall be also in the likeness of his resurrection" (Rom. 6:5 KJV); "some of the branches were broken off, and you, although a wild olive shoot, were grafted in among the others and now share in the nourishing root of the olive tree" (11:17; also cf. John 15:1-8). "I planted, Apollos watered, but God gave the growth" (1 Cor. 3:6); ". . . you, being rooted and grounded in love . . ." (Eph. 3:17; cf. Col. 2:7).

(c) *Medical care*. Sin is often compared to illness, involving wounds, fractures, tumors, and cancer (Isa. 1:5-6; Jer. 8:22; 30:12-15; 46:11; Ezek. 34:4, 16; 2 Tim. 2:17). We have seen that leprosy is a well-known metaphor for sin (§5.6). Forgiveness and atonement are sometimes compared to healing: "By his wounds you have been healed" (Gk. *iaomai*, 1 Pet. 2:24b; quotation from Isa. 53:5b). Mention must also be made of the Greek verb *sōzō*, the common word for "to save" in a soteriological

---

2. Cf. ibid., 310; Heyns (1988, 282-83); see also Ouweneel (2008a, chapter 7), for the various aspects of sin, each of which implies its own metaphor.

sense, but a verb that also means "to heal" in the medical sense (Matt. 9:22; Mark 10:52; Luke 17:19): salvation is a form of healing (see chapter 14).[3]

8.1.2 Social-Economic Metaphors

(d) *Social-societal life.* With an appeal to 1 Corinthians 7:11, H. Ridderbos described "reconciliation" as speaking "in general of the restoration of the right relationship between two parties, a notion that stems from "the social-societal sphere."[4] It refers to "the restoration of the right relationship between two parties," a restoration—I add—that must not necessarily be viewed from a forensic standpoint. B. Demarest therefore thinks of a metaphor adopted from the sphere of the family.[5] Just as relatives who behave in a hostile and estranged way toward each other (cf. Isa. 59:2) must be reconciled in order to live together in harmony (cf. the parable of the prodigal son, Luke 15:11–32), so people must be reconciled to God.

(e) *The legal order.* Christ's work on the cross clearly exhibits judicial aspects. The human condition involves guilt or debts, in the form of transgressions of God's law, and these debts must be paid (cf. Matt. 6:12; Rom. 2:23; 4:25; 5:15–18; 8:3; 2 Cor. 5:19; Gal. 3:13; Eph. 1:7; 2:1, 5; Col. 2:13; James 2:10). These so-called forensic aspects play a significant role especially in the New Testament doctrine of justification.[6]

(f) *Marriage.* Christ has obtained his church as a bride by surrendering himself for her all the way to death:

---

3. In Eddy (2006), Bruce R. Reichenbach presents a "healing view" on atonement besides the *Christus victor* view of Greg Boyd, the substitution view of Thomas S. Schreiner, and the "kaleidoscopic" view of Joel B. Green.
4. Ridderbos (1975, 182).
5. Demarest (1997, 180).
6. See §9.5 below, and especially my separate volume on this subject (Ouweneel [*RT* III/2]).

"Husbands, love your wives, as Christ loved the church and gave himself up for her, that he might sanctify her, having cleansed her by the washing of water with the word, so that he might present the church to himself in splendor, without spot or wrinkle or any such thing, that she might be holy and without blemish" (Eph. 5:26-27). In Hosea 1-3, Israel is the "wife" of God, like Gomer is the wife of the prophet. If Gomer is the same as the woman in chapter 3, she is "bought" for a high price, that is, "bought back," redeemed, ransomed (v. 2; cf. MSG, "I paid good money to get her back. It cost me the price of a slave"). In the spiritual restoration of Israel as bride or wife of God, God calls himself her "Redeemer": "'[Y]our Maker is your husband, / the LORD of hosts is his name; / and the Holy One of Israel is your, *Redeemer*, / .... For the LORD has called you / like a wife deserted and grieved in spirit, / like a wife of youth when she is cast off,' / says your God. / 'For a brief moment I deserted you, / but with great compassion I will gather you. / In overflowing anger for a moment / I hid my face from you, / but with everlasting love I will have compassion on you,' / says the LORD, your *Redeemer*" (Isa. 54:5-8; italics added).

(g) *Commerce*. Here we find the image of the slave that is ransomed from the hands of their owner (Matt. 20:28; 1 Cor. 6:20; 1 Tim. 2:6; Titus 2:14; 1 Pet. 1:18; see more extensively §§4.2.3 and 8.2.1). The price that Christ paid to ransom his own was his own blood, that is, his own life (Matt. 26:28; Rev. 5:9; cf. Mark 10:45; 1 Cor. 6:20; Gal. 3:13; Col. 2:14; 1 Pet. 1:18-19). By nature, humans are slaves of sin (John 8:34; Rom. 6:16-17, 20). Released from sin, they become slaves of God (Acts 4:29; 16:17; Rom. 6:22; Titus 1:1; James 1:1; 1 Pet. 2:16; Rev. 7:3; 10:7; 11:18; 19:2, 5; 22:3, 6), or slaves of Christ (Matt. 10:24-25; John 13:16; 15:20; Rom. 1:1; 1 Cor. 7:22; Gal. 1:10; Eph. 6:6; Phil. 1:1; Col. 4:12; 2 Tim. 2:24; 2 Pet. 1:1; Jude 1:1; Rev. 1:1; 2:20), or slaves of righteousness (Rom. 6:18-19).

The metaphor of ransoming from slavery reverberates in expressions like "set free from sin" (Rom. 6:18, 22), or "from the law" (7:2-3, 6 [cf. Gal. 5:1]), or "from the law of sin and death" (8:2), or "from the bondage to corruption" (v. 21).[7]

(h) *Military service.* Christ's work on the cross was not only an atoning sacrifice to God, but also a battle, a war, in which Christ as a warrior gained the victory over sin and death, and in particular over Satan and his powers (Mark 3:27; John 16:33; Acts 26:18; Eph. 2:2; Col. 1:13; 2:15; Heb. 2:14-15; 1 John 3:8). In this war, the final victory is not gained before the end of ages (Rev. 17:14; 20:7-10). We will return to this more extensively in §§8.7-8.8.

(i) *Prison.* Augustine described sin as a debt (see point [e]), as a disease (see point [b]), and as a power that holds humans captive (§8.7).[8] Sinful humans must be released, set free, ransomed, from the prison of sin, death, and Satan. Isaiah 61:1 speaks metaphorically of "liberty to the captives, and the opening of the prison to those who are bound" (cf. Luke 4:18; here, Gk. *aphesis,* which normally means "forgiveness," has the sense of "release"). Also compare: ". . . saved from our enemies and from the hand of all who hate us . . . delivered from the hand of our enemies" (Luke 1:71, 74); ". . . they may turn from darkness to light and from the power of Satan to God, that they may receive forgiveness of sins and a place among those who are sanctified by faith in me" (Acts 26:18); "delivered us from the domain of darkness" (Col. 1:13); "set free from sin" (Rom. 6:18, 22); "released from the law" (7:6; cf. 8:2); "to redeem us from all lawlessness" (Titus 2:14; cf. 1 Pet. 1:18); he destroyed "the one who has the power of death, that is, the devil, and

---

7. See Grau (2004) for a postmodern use of the metaphor of commerce (Gk. *oikonomia*), both to explore new paths in theology and to offer a fresh Christian look at economics.
8. McGrath (2007, 271).

deliver all those who through fear of death were subject to lifelong slavery" (Heb. 2:14-15).

8.1.3 Other Metaphors for Redemption

(j) *Washing or cleansing.* Sin is like a stain that adheres to a person, and must be washed away (cf. Isa. 1:16-18). Jesus alluded to this metaphor when he washed his disciples' feet: "The one who has bathed does not need to wash, except for his feet, but is completely clean" (John 13:10; cf. 3:5, "born of water and the Spirit"). Paul says, "[Y]ou were washed, you were sanctified, you were justified in the name of the Lord Jesus Christ and by the Spirit of our God" (1 Cor. 6:11), and: "Christ loved the church and gave himself up for her, that he might sanctify her, having cleansed her by the washing of water with the word" (Eph. 5:25-26), and: God "saved us, . . . by the washing of regeneration and renewal of the Holy Spirit" (Titus 3:5). This metaphor becomes quite unusual when blood is called the means by which this washing takes place: "[T]he blood of Jesus his Son cleanses us from all sin" (1 John 1:7; cf. Rev. 1:5 KJV). The (red) blood can wash "white": "They have washed their robes and made them white in the blood of the Lamb" (Rev. 7:14).

(k) *Self-sacrifice,* in the sense of one person through his death sacrificing himself for others in order that they stay alive: "You do not realize that it is better for you that one man die for the people than that the whole nation perish" (John 11:50 NIV). We find an illustration of this in the case of Jonah: "Pick me up and hurl me into the sea; then the sea will quiet down for you" (Jonah 1:12), with this difference: Jonah knew he was guilty (". . . for I know it is because of me that this great tempest has come upon you"), whereas Jesus was innocent: Christ "suffered once for sins, the righteous for the unrighteous, that he might bring us to God" (1 Pet. 3:18; cf. 2 Cor. 5:21). The good person can sacrifice himself for bad people, but also the shepherd for his sheep (John 10:11,

15), the friend for his friends (15:13-14), or the husband for his wife (Eph. 5:25).

(l) *Pottery.* Several times in the Bible, people are compared to pots of the potter, particularly to express their relationship to God as their Maker, or their fragility (Job 10:9; 33:6; Ps. 2:9; Isa. 29:16; 41:25; 45:9; 64:8; Jer. 18:3-6; 19:1,11; Lam. 4:2; Rom. 9:21-23; 2 Cor. 4:7; 2 Tim. 2:20-21). In Jeremiah 18-19 the question is brought up what God will do with pots or jars that are defective. The answer is that he, just like the potter, can only break and throw away the defective pot. But when the unbaked pot is still on the wheel, it can be kneaded to plain clay again, and something new can be made of it. Although the imagery is applied more to judgment than to restoration, the principle of Jeremiah 18:4 can also be applied positively: on his wheel God can turn failed vessels into vessels of honor (cf. Rom. 9:21-23; 2 Tim. 2:20-21).

(m) *The gold- and silversmith.* Often the renewal of people is also compared to refining gold or silver. See, for instance, this parallel: "Take away the dross from the silver, and the smith has material for a vessel; take away the wicked from the presence of the king, and his throne will be established in righteousness" (Prov. 25:4-5). This image can refer to believers who are refined in the sense of tried and purified, as this verse indicates: "Behold, I have refined you, but not as silver; I have tried you in the furnace of affliction" (Isa. 48:10; cf. Ps. 66:10; Dan. 11:35; 12:10; 1 Pet. 1:7). It can also be used for people who departed from God, and are restored in their service, for instance: "He will sit as a refiner and purifier of silver, and he will purify the sons of Levi and refine them like gold and silver, and they will bring offerings in righteousness to the LORD" (Mal. 3:3; cf. Zech. 13:9s).

8.2 Aspects and Circles
8.2.1 Seven Aspects
What do all these things imply for our understanding of

the many-sided meanings of Christ's work on the cross? I distinguish seven main aspects.[9] The first three Christ shares with the believers, who must endure similar forms of suffering. In the last three aspects, the absolutely unique aspects of Christ's work on the cross come to the fore. In the middle one of the seven aspects we distinguish both an objective-constitutive and an illustrative-exemplarist element.

(1) *Christ's act of love and self-surrender.* This point, which involves the deepest motivation behind Christ's work on the cross and is of an illustrative-exemplarist nature, is elaborated in §8.3.

(2) *Christ's solidarity,* namely, his solidarity with the sufferings of humanity in general, and of Israel in particular, will be discussed in §8.4.

(3) *Christ's martyrdom.* This aspect, which is also of an illustrative-exemplarist nature, will be extensively elaborated in §§8.5 and 8.6. It entails the crucifixion as a "shameful act" (cf. Heb. 12:2), just as the sacrificial meaning of the cross (see points 5 and 6) entails that it was also a "saving act."[10]

(4) *Christ's warfare.* In a sense, Christ's battle against, and triumph over, sin, death, and Satan was unique. But at the same time in a certain sense believers imitate his warfare against the evil powers (Eph. 6:12). Regarding this, see §8.7.

(5) *Christ's payment of the ransom.* In this and the subsequent aspect, Jesus' sufferings were unique (see Matt. 20:28; Mark 10:45; 1 Tim. 2:6). Regarding this see §7.1.1.

(6) *Christ' vicarious sacrifice.* §§9.1–9.3 deal with this very important and unique aspect of the cross of Christ.

(7) *Christ's satisfactory sacrifice.* Regarding this see §9.5; see also extensively, chapters 12–14 on the scope

---

9. Cf. the distinctions by Bavinck (*RD* 3:382–86); Berkouwer (1965, 8).
10. König (2006, 291).

and the consequences of Christ's atoning sacrifice.

8.2.2 Four Circles

I just used the word "scope" with reference to Christ's atonement, something we will consider more extensively in chapters 12–14. At this point, we can describe it in terms of four concentric circles:

(1) *The individual person.* Salvation is first and foremost an absolutely individual matter of everlasting life versus everlasting death, of everlasting light versus everlasting darkness, for each person separately. No person is saved merely because he was born into a Christian family or a Christian church. The terms "conversion" is often reserved for people who convert from one ideology or religion to another one ("Ahmed converted from Islam to Christianity"). This is *never* the way the Bible speaks of conversion. In the book of Acts Jews were not converted from Judaism to Christianity, but converted from godly Messiah-expecters (or legalistic Jews, or indifferent Jews, etc.) to godly Messiah-believing Jews. Similarly, Gentiles converted from idols to God through faith in Jesus, to serve the living and true God (1 Thess. 1:9 JUB). Even within the most godly family or church, the individual must convert from their *personal* state of darkness, death, and evil to the light, life, and love that are in Christ. Only through one's personal regeneration, can one become an *intrinsic* member of the family or church into which they were born.

The biblical illustration of this is Nicodemus. He was no doubt raised in a godly family, and in addition belonged to the Pharisees, was a ruler of the Jews, and one of *the* teachers of Israel—and yet he could not enter, or even "see" (perceive, grasp, discern), the kingdom of God without personal regeneration (John 3:1–10). There is no salvation without a *personal* confession of sins, a *personal* surrender in faith to the person and atoning work of Christ, a *personal* acceptance of him as one's

Savior as well as Lord. This salvation involves (a) forgiveness of sins, justification by faith, (b) redemption from the power of sin, death, and the devil, (c) cleansing, renewal, rebirth, new life, (d) devotion, dedication, sanctification, and conformity to the image of Christ.

(2) *The family.* God envisions saving entire families, in both Old and New Testaments. This divine principle comes to light in the earliest part of the Bible: in the families of Noah, of Abraham, and of Rahab (Gen. 7:1; 18:19; Josh. 6:17; cf. Heb. 11:7). In the book of Acts and in 1 Corinthians, several times a person is referred to *along with* his "house" as experiencing salvation, which is often expressed in baptism (Acts 11:14; 16:31, 34; 18:8; 1 Cor. 1:16; 7:14; 16:15). Of course, there is never any formal guarantee that, if the head of the family comes to faith, all his family members will be saved as well. Salvation within the family can never be severed from personal conversion and faith. Yet, there are special promises for families: "[T]he promise is for you and for your children" (Acts 2:39). "[T]he unbelieving husband is made holy because of his wife, and the unbelieving wife is made holy because of her husband. Otherwise your children would be unclean, but as it is, they are holy" (1 Cor. 7:14).

The Reformed and Presbyterians may link this with infant baptism and the meaning of the covenant.[11] Many Evangelicals may link this significance of the family with the truth of the kingdom of God:[12] "Let the children come to me; do not hinder them, for to such belongs the kingdom of God" (Mark. 10:14). For our present purpose, it is of secondary importance how the principle of the family in God's plan of salvation is supported theologically.

(3) *Israel and the church.* God has promised that one day, at the second coming of Christ, "all Israel will be

---

11. Cf. Ouweneel (*RT* IV/2).
12. Cf. Ouweneel (*RT* IV/3).

saved" (Rom. 11:26); this is the salvation of an entire nation: "In the LORD all the offspring of Israel shall be justified and shall glory" (Isa. 45:25). "[O]ur people shall all be righteous; they shall possess the land forever, the branch of my planting, the work of my hands, that I might be glorified" (Isa. 60:21). The same is true with respect to the New Testament church comprised of both Jews as well as Gentiles: "God first visited the Gentiles, to take from them a people for his name" (Acts 15:11). Jesus Christ "gave himself for us to redeem us from all lawlessness and to purify for himself a people for his own possession who are zealous for good works" (Titus 2:14).

In the church of God, salvation has acquired a collective form (Eph. 2:14-22; 5:23b, 25-27). "Apart from the church there is no salvation" (Lat. *extra ecclesia non salus est*; cf. §1.4.2 with note 33)—referring not to the denominational identity that the Roman Catholic Church as well as many Protestant sects and cults attach to it ("Apart from *our* church there is no salvation") but the church in the sense of the "holy congregation of true Christian believers" (Belgic Confession, Art. 27). As such it is the embodiment of salvation: the circle of those who share in salvation coincides with the circle of "true Christian believers."

Incidentally, a similar ecclesiological confusion exists in the Belgic Confession, Articles 27–29, which on the one hand speak of the church in an existential-transcendent sense ("the holy congregation of true Christian believers"), and on the other hand in a denominational sense (". . . all men are in duty bound to join and unite themselves with it; maintaining the unity of the church; . . ."—how can one "join" a church to which one already belongs by faith?).[13] Elsewhere I examined this

---

13. Dennison (2008, 2:440–41); Art. 29 speaks about the "true" and the "false church" on the basis of a contrast between *denominations* (Roman Catholic versus Reformed).

confusion and other ecclesiological aspects far more extensively.[14]

(4) *The entire world.* In the end, salvation will encompass the entire world—not in the sense that all individual people will be saved (cf. Rev. 21:5-8), but that one day sin will be removed from the world (*cosmos,* John 1:29), and a new creation will arrive (2 Cor. 5:17; Gal. 6:15; 2 Pet. 3:13; Rev. 21:1).

In one meaning of the Greek word *cosmos,* the *cosmos* is a Satanic system of sin and death (John 12:31; 14:30; 16:11), which Christ has "overcome" (John 16:33), and which one day will "pass away" (1 John 2:15-17). In another sense, the *cosmos* is identical with God's creation (Heb. 1:2; 11:3), which will one day be renewed. Therefore, on the one hand, people are redeemed *from* this world (in the former sense), while on the other hand, the *cosmos* itself (in the latter sense) is set free from the power of sin, death, and the devil, renewed to everlasting glory, "set free from its bondage to corruption and obtain the freedom of the glory of the children of God" (Rom. 8:21). "God did not send his Son into the world to condemn the world, but in order that the *world might be saved* through him" (John 3:17). Christ is "the Savior of the *world*" (John 4:42); "the bread that I will give for the life of the *world* is my flesh" (John 6:51). Here I am simply stating the general principle, which I explain and elaborate far more extensively in the volume in this series dealing with eschatology.[15] That general principle is this: God's plan of salvation is never about individuals *only*—it is about all of his creation.

8.3 Christ's Work As an Act of Love
8.3.1 Active Surrender

Few passages depict more profoundly Christ's surrender of love, as this came to expression already in his in-

---
14. Ouweneel (2010a; 2010b; 2016, ad loc.).
15. Ouweneel (2012a).

carnation, than this verse (even if it does not mention the word "love"): "[Y]ou know the grace of our Lord Jesus Christ, that though he was rich, yet for your sake he became poor, so that you by his poverty might become rich" (2 Cor. 8:9). This is the self-surrender of One who, out of love for others, gives everything away, in order that the others will receive everything. This is not the great act of Saint Martin, bishop of Tours, who gave half of his garment to a beggar,[16] but the much greater act of him who kept nothing for himself in order that his people would possess everything. He even "emptied Himself [without renouncing or diminishing His deity, but only temporarily giving up the outward expression of divine equality and His rightful dignity]" (Phil. 2:7 AMP). Of course, we must add here that, in the end, Christ too receives everything, and much more: "Therefore God has highly exalted him and bestowed on him the name that is above every name" (Phil. 2:9). "Jesus, . . . who *for the joy that was set before him* endured the cross, despising the shame, and is seated at the right hand of the throne of God" (Heb. 12:2).

The notions of "giving him/himself" and "giving him/himself up" are well-known in the New Testament as acts of the love of God, who gives (up) his Son (cf. John 3:16; Rom. 8:32), and the love of Christ, who gives (up) himself: ". . . who gave himself for our sins to deliver us from the present evil age, according to the will of our God and Father" (Gal. 1:4); "who gave himself as a ransom for all" (1 Tim. 2:6); "who gave himself for us to redeem us from all lawlessness and to purify for himself a people for his own possession" (Titus 2:14). More specifically in connection with his love: ". . . the Son of God, who loved *me* and gave himself for *me*" (Gal. 2:20). "Christ loved *us* and gave himself up for *us*, a fragrant

---

16. Perhaps he did give everything, as some say: half of his garment belonged to the Roman Empire (and thus could not be given away), the other half he himself had financed.

offering and sacrifice to God ... Christ loved the *church* and gave himself up for *her*" (Eph. 5:2, 25). Jesus is the good shepherd, who lays down his life for his sheep because he *cares for* them (cf. John 10:11, 13–15).

Self-surrender is an active term. It implies that Christ did not undergo his sufferings passively but took them upon himself and very actively endured them. He was not simply led to Calvary but, "he *went out*, bearing his own cross, to the place called The Place of a Skull" (John 19:17); "he *makes himself* an offering for sin" (Isa. 53:10 RSV), "he *poured out* his soul to death" (v. 12). He not only "breathed his last" (Gk. *aphēken to pneuma*, Matt. 27:50 GNT, NRSV) but actively "gave up his spirit" (Gk. *paredōken to pneuma*, John 19:30) in the sense that he himself had explained earlier, "For this reason the Father loves me, because I *lay down* [Gk. *tithēmi*] my life that I may *take it up* [Gk. *labō*] again. No one takes it from me, but I *lay it down* of my own accord. I have authority to *lay it down*, and I have authority to *take it up* again" (John 10:17–18).[17]

8.3.2 Love and Returned Love

Salvation on God's part is not simply a formal, judicial, or administrative act. It cannot be understood if we do not understand it—in addition to many other aspects—as the expression of the love of Christ. Therefore, the apostle Paul prays with regard to the Ephesian believers "that you, being rooted and grounded in love, may have strength to comprehend with all the saints what is the breadth and length and height and depth, and to know the love of Christ that surpasses knowledge, that you may be filled with all the fullness of God" (Eph. 3:17–19). There is no salvation apart from the love of Christ. He gave up *himself*, salvation is embodied in him as it were. As G. Berkouwer put it, "Every gift would lose its richness and vivifying power when isolated and consid-

---

17. Berkouwer (1965, 183, 320).

ered apart from his person."[18]

Peter Abelard saw this love aspect in particular as the actual basis and significance of the work on the cross (§7.2.2), and this view could still be found in the twentieth century as well.[19] In this view, people's love in return (Dutch *wederliefde;* Ger. *Wiederliebe*) plays a great role. In Jesus we see how great is God's (and Christ's) love for us, and this should move people to abandon their hostility, and start loving *him.* The idea is that because of this returned love God forgives people their sins. The prodigal son returned to his father, and therefore the father forgave him (Luke 15:17-24). It is said of the sinful woman in the house of Simon the Pharisee, "[H]er sins, which are many, are forgiven—for she loved much" (Luke 7:47). (However, the rest of the verse—"But he who is forgiven little, loves little"—instead suggests the opposite causal relationship: people are not forgiven because they love, but they begin to love because they have been forgiven.)

Of course, such an emphasis can become one-sided and neglect elements such as satisfaction and substitution[20]—aspects that had been underscored by the somewhat older Anselm of Canterbury. However, Anselm's presentation can be one-sided as well. People must not only believe in the satisfaction that was secured almost two thousand years ago, they must *personally change.* This involves not only conversion and regeneration but also the reconciliation with God (see extensively §§10.4-10.7). To be sure, salvation is *sola fide,* by faith alone, but this faith is not merely the formal intellectual acceptance of a truth but an event that radically *renews* the person. There is no genuine faith without the effect of loving God and the neighbor *on the basis* of the love that God in Christ first bestowed upon the person. Jesus not only preached love but accomplished the ultimate act

---

18. Ibid., 20).
19. See, e.g., Heering (1937, 175-76).
20. Berkouwer (1965, 272-75).

of love, total self-surrendering: "By this we know love, that he laid down his life for us"; but this is followed by this immediate and unavoidable consequence: ". . . and we ought to lay down our lives for the brothers" (1 John 3:16).

In several of the Bible passages mentioned, Christ's self-surrender was especially motivated as being done "for our sins" or to "redeem us from all lawlessness." In this respect Jesus was unique. But the self-surrender as such, as an act of love toward others, is definitely an example for the believers. Consider, in addition to 1 John 3:16, this statement of Jesus: "If I then, your Lord and Teacher, have washed your feet, you also ought to wash one another's feet. For I have given you an example, that you also should do just as I have done to you" (John 13:14–15).

Of the very generous churches in Macedonia it is said, "[T]hey gave themselves first to the Lord and then by the will of God to us" (2 Cor. 8:5). Paul wrote to the Corinthians, "For the love of Christ controls us, because we have concluded this: that one has died for all, therefore all have died; and he died for all, that those who live might no longer live for themselves but for him who for their sake died and was raised" (5:14–15), and: "I will most gladly spend and be spent for your souls. If I love you more, am I to be loved less?" (12:15). To the Ephesians: "[W]alk in love, as Christ loved us and gave himself up for us, a fragrant offering and sacrifice to God" (Eph. 5:2). To the Philippians: "So if there is any encouragement in Christ, any comfort from love . . . [h]ave this mind among yourselves, which was also in Christ Jesus, who . . . emptied himself . . . humbled himself by becoming obedient to the point of death, even death on a cross" (Phil. 2:1, 5–8). And to the Thessalonians: "So, being affectionately desirous of you, we were ready to share with you not only the gospel of God but also our own selves, because you had become very dear to us" (1

Thess. 2:8).

In all these passages, the Master's loving surrender is reflected in his followers. People are saved by faith alone; but since *genuine* faith is inconceivable without being joined to love returned to God and to Christ we can definitely claim that *no one is saved who did not love God and Christ as well as his brothers and sisters:* "We know that we have passed out of death into life, because we love the brothers. Whoever does not love abides in death. Everyone who hates his brother is a murderer, and you know that no murderer has eternal life abiding in him" (1 John 3:14-15). "Anyone who does not love does not know God, because God is love" (4:8). "If anyone says, 'I love God,' and hates his brother, he is a liar; for he who does not love his brother whom he has seen cannot love God whom he has not seen" (v. 20; also see 2:11; 3:10-12, 16-18, 23; 4:7, 11-12, 21; 5:1-2; cf. James 1:27; 2:14-16; 5:1-6).

Remarkably, several times in the New Testament, believers are described not only as "believers," or "Christians," or "disciples (followers) of Jesus," and so on, but as people who love God: "And we know that for those who love God all things work together for good" (Rom. 8:28); "if anyone loves God, he is known by God" (1 Cor. 8:3). "Blessed is the man who remains steadfast under trial, for when he has stood the test he will receive the crown of life, which God has promised to those who love him" (James 1:12). "Listen, my beloved brothers, has not God chosen those who are poor in the world to be rich in faith and heirs of the kingdom, which he has promised to those who love him?" (2:5). A true believer is characterized, so to speak, as a *theophilus* (cf. Luke 1:3; Acts 1:1), a "lover of God."

8.4 Christ's Work As an Act of Solidarity
8.4.1 The Sufferings of All Humanity

There is an element in the sufferings of Christ that unfortunately has drawn little attention, namely, his solidarity with the sufferings of humanity. *He was one of us,* as R. Poortvliet expressed it, meaning that Christ was a human like all of us.²¹ The Son of God took the form of a servant, being born "in the likeness of men," that is, like every other human (Phil. 2:7). "Since therefore the children share in flesh and blood, he himself likewise partook of the same things, that through death he might destroy the one who has the power of death, that is, the devil" (Heb. 2:14). The point was not only that a human could become the substitute for other humans, and therefore the Word had to become flesh (John 1:14). No, the cross was also the highlight of solidarity, the preeminent identification of the very human Jesus' with a suffering humanity.

On the cross, Jesus not only brought the atoning sacrifice for people's sins, but also underwent the sufferings of all humanity since the Fall (as, in fact, he had undergone them since his birth). For humanity, these sufferings were the consequences of their own sins, whereas Jesus was sinless.²² Nevertheless, in his innocence he demonstrated his solidarity with people's sufferings. There was a clear prophetic undertone in what Pontius Pilate said about Jesus after he had him severely flogged: "Behold the man" (John 19:5).²³ Here, Jesus was the human being *par excellence*, representing suffering humanity as a whole. This is how we may understand Pilate's words: Behold, here is humanity, concentrated in one suffering person, in the only One who could thus represent humanity as a whole.

One reason why Jesus suffered with humanity was to be able to help others in their afflictions: "[B]ecause

---

21. Poortvliet (1974).
22. See Ouweneel (2007b, §§10.4, 10.5).
23. This translation suggests that the Gk. word for "man" is in the accusative case. However, more correct is the nominative rendering of the AMPC: "See, [here is] the Man!" (Lat. *Ecce Homo*, not *Hominem*).

he himself has suffered when tempted, he is able to help those who are being tempted" (Heb. 2:18). "[W]e do not have a high priest who is unable to sympathize with our weaknesses, but one who in every respect has been tempted as we are, yet without sin" (4:15). "[H]e is able to save to the uttermost those who draw near to God through him, since he always lives to make intercession for them. For it was indeed fitting that we should have such a high priest, holy, innocent, unstained, separated from sinners, and exalted above the heavens" (7:25–26).

The reality of Christ's solidarity is shown especially in the case of his people of Israel.[24] Jesus enters into, and shares, the sufferings that his people must undergo at the hands of their enemies, i.e., those who persecute and oppress them. This is an aspect that we see especially in the Psalms (see next section) but also, for instance, in Isaiah 53. In this chapter, the Spirit of Christ identifies himself with the faithful of Israel in their sufferings and tribulations. If we begin to see this aspect of solidarity, we will more easily understand that in the suffering Servant of YHWH being described in the four relevant passages (Isa. 42:1-7; 49:1-7; 50:4-11; 52:13-53:11) we are seeing both Israel and the Messiah of Israel, who in the spirit identifies himself with his people.[25] The Servant is explicitly called "Israel" (49:3) but he is also the One who was rejected by his own people (53:3). This remarkable tension is noteworthy. The Servant is Israel suffering on the part of the nations, but he is also the One suffering at the hands of Israel.

Here we encounter is a profound mystery, if not an outright paradox, which we may begin to understand when we grasp the idea of Jesus' identification with his people. As theologian and cultural philosopher F. de Graaff (d. 1993) put it, Jesus is the true "self" of Isra-

---

24. See Darby (*CW* 7:139-237); cf. extensively, Ouweneel (2000a).
25. See Ouweneel (2007b, §5.5.2).

el.²⁶ When he suffers, Israel suffers; when Israel suffers, he suffers. Jesus was "like a lamb that is led to the slaughter" (Isa. 53:7) but Israel was that, too, numerous times, with Auschwitz as the nadir.²⁷ Too often, we one-sidedly consider only that Jesus has suffered *for* his own, and we have overlooked that he also suffered *with* his own.

8.4.2 Christ in the Psalms

If we understand what was claimed in the previous section, we will also grasp how Psalm 69, for instance, can speak of the faithful, albeit guilt-conscious Israelite, whereas at the same time several verses of this Psalm are applied in the New Testament to Christ (v. 4: John 15:25; v. 9a: John 2:17; v. 9b: Rom. 15:3; v. 21: John 19:28-30). Jesus made the sufferings of his fellow-Israelites to be his own sufferings. He proved his solidarity with them, all the way to the cross. People have often wondered how passages in the Psalms can be applied to Christ in the New Testament when they seem to speak of Israel or of the individual Israelite. When we understand the principle of solidarity, we will regularly observe the solidarity of Israel's Messiah in and behind the sufferings of God's people. This extends to the point that what is said about the people is often applicable to him as well, and *vice versa*.

Precious in the sight of the Lord was the death of his "saint" or "godly man" (Heb. *chasid*), that is, the Messiah. However, Psalm 116:15 says, "Precious in the sight of the LORD is the death of his *saints*" (Heb. *chasidim*) (cf. 72:14, "precious is their blood in his sight"). It is the godly Israelite who, in Psalm 22, experiences being forsaken by God and fellow human beings—but in him we unmistakably recognize the Messiah who lives in solidarity with his people (cf. v. 1: Matt. 27:4; Mark 15:34; v. 7-8: Matt. 27:39, 43; v. 18: John 19:24; v. 22: Heb. 2:12). We find

---

26. De Graaff (1987, 91, 96); Ouweneel (2000a, 49-52).
27. De Graaff (1987, 93-95).

this in Psalm 16 (cf. v. 10-11 with Acts 2:25-28; 13:35), Psalm 40 (cf. vv. 7-9 with Heb. 10:5-7), Psalm 44, Psalm 69, Psalm 88, Psalm 102,[28] and others. Such Psalms are not primarily Messianic; see, for instance, Psalm 40:12 ("my iniquities have overtaken me, and I cannot see; they are more than the hairs of my head") and 69:5 ("O God, you know my folly; the wrongs I have done are not hidden from you"). Nevertheless, the Holy Spirit, particularly through the New Testament quotations, points to Christ, whom we observe behind and in the suffering—and often guilt-conscious—nation of Israel.

Incidentally, we also find examples of the opposite. Psalms 44 and 74 are (partially implicit) testimonies about the innocence of the suffering people of Israel, whereas genuine innocence is to be expected more with the Messiah than with Israel. Yet, the Messiah identifies himself here with the faithful in the nation, the Daniels and the Ezekiels, who were carried into exile together with the others, although they were personally innocent. This is the faithful remnant mentioned in Isaiah (10:20-21; 11:11, 16; 28:5; 37:4, 31-32; 46:3).

8.4.3 The Spirit of Christ

What we have been considering here also sheds some light on certain important types in the Old Testament. During the wilderness journey of Israel, Moses was a type of Christ, who, together with his people, travels through the wilderness of church history (cf. 1 Cor. 10:1-5; Heb. 3:7-4:13), whereas Christ is not literally with his people on earth. Thus, Moses was a type of the *Spirit* of Christ (see Acts 16:7; Rom. 8:9; Gal. 4:6; Phil. 1:19; 1 Pet. 1:11), who travels with his people. Similarly, Joshua brought the people into the Promised Land, being a type of the *Spirit* of Christ bringing God's people into

---

28. Vv. 24b-27 are applied to Christ in Heb. 1:10-12, where as in Ps. 102 they refer to YHWH; however, the "distressed" one of vv. 1-11, 23-24a can refer to Christ as well.

the blessings of the "heavenly places" (Eph. 1:3; for the battle involved see 6:12). Similarly, David traveled with his men through the wilderness, continually persecuted by King Saul. Again, David was a type of the *Spirit* of Christ, who identifies himself with his people who are still persecuted and oppressed here on earth.

The Messiah who is glorified at God's right hand in heaven is at the same time with his people in the wilderness of distress, oppression, and persecution, namely, *in the Spirit*, who is the Spirit of Christ. This we see in Moses as well as in David before his enthronement. Similarly, the Messiah shares his glorification with his glorified people, as we see in the types of Joshua and of the enthroned David, followed by Solomon. Jesus himself already attained the end goal: heavenly glory (cf. Heb. 12:1-2), but in the Spirit he is with his people to show his solidarity with them in their afflictions. Consider the following beautiful passage, even though it is not typically Messianic: "When they suffered, he suffered also, and the angel of his presence [i.e., the Angel of YHWH, i.e., the pre-incarnate Christ] saved them. He redeemed them because of his love and compassion; he lifted them up and carried them all the days of the past" (Isa. 63:9 CSB; cf. Moses in vv. 11-14).

In the New Testament we find the same principle, in which Jesus identifies himself with the poor and afflicted:

> Then the King will say to those on his right, "Come, you who are blessed by my Father, inherit the kingdom prepared for you from the foundation of the world. For I was hungry and you gave me food, I was thirsty and you gave me drink, I was a stranger and you welcomed me, I was naked and you clothed me, I was sick and you visited me, I was in prison and you came to me." Then the righteous will answer him, saying, "Lord, when did we see you hungry and feed you, or thirsty and give you drink? And when did we see you a stranger and welcome you, or naked and

clothe you? And when did we see you sick or in prison and visit you?" And the King will answer them, "Truly, I say to you, as you did it to one of the least of these my brothers, you did it to me" (Matt. 25:34–40).

Because of this identification, Jesus could say to Saul of Tarsus, "Saul, Saul, why are you persecuting *me*?" (Acts 9:4; 22:7; 26:14). Whoever persecutes the Messiah's people, persecutes the Messiah himself.

8.5 Jesus' Martyrdom
8.5.1 Torturers and Tortured Ones

We may easily regard the cross one-sidedly as the place of atonement through the vicarious sacrifice, and the place of spiritual warfare against sin, death, and the devil, both of which emphasize the soteriological significance of the cross for penitent sinners. However, the cross of Christ was also a place of *martyrdom*, where hostile people tortured and killed the innocent One. Jesus became the "victim" of human hate and envy—and that is something very different from being the innocent "victim" who was sacrificed in the sinners' stead (cf. Eph. 5:2; Heb. 7:27; 9:14, 26, 28; 10:12).

Yet, we must maintain the deeper link between the two aspects: "[T]his Jesus, [*on the one hand*] delivered up according to the definite plan and foreknowledge of God, [*on the other hand*] you crucified and killed by the hands of lawless men" (Acts 2:23). In other words, *you* made him an innocent martyr, and you bear the guilt for this, whereas *God* made him a vicarious sacrifice precisely for such guilty sinners. The remarkable thing is that this happened at the very same time. Sinners made him a victim by killing him—God made him a victim to die for sinners. The moment when humanity's sinfulness came to light in the most horrible way was the very moment when God made him the vicarious sacrifice to solve the problem of sin.

Let me delve into this a little further. The crime of Jews and Romans as such did not contribute to the salvation of humanity; on the contrary, it only increased the guilt of humanity (see extensively §11.5). Yet, the two belong together. Jewish and Roman guilt helps us to grasp the size of *humanity's* guilt toward God, thereby affording a better view of both the necessity and the scope of Christ's atoning work. In this respect, not only was Jesus' atoning death unique but also his martyr's death.[29] On the one hand, Jesus' *atoning* death was for the benefit of millions of penitent sinners. On the other hand, Jesus' *martyr's* death identified him with the millions of believers who, like him, gave their lives to God "for the cause of truth and meekness and righteousness" (Ps. 45:4; cf. 1 Pet. 3:14).[30]

K. Berger put these words to all humanity on Jesus' lips: "Either you belong to those who brought the Son of Man to death, or you belong with him to the victims."[31] Berger added: "A third possibility is excluded" (except, I would say, that a former torturer can be converted into a tortured victim). You are "offerers" of Jesus, or you are "offerings" yourselves; you are a torturer or a tortured one. If Jesus "had to" suffer (cf. Matt. 16:21; 26:54; Luke 24:26; John 3:14-15; Acts 17:3), then his followers do too; as Jesus said himself, "A servant is not greater than his master. If they persecuted me, they will also persecute you" (John 15:20). In Berger's words: "He who belongs to God must suffer. Often others must suffer too, but he

---

29. *Contra* Den Heyer (1997, 8). In his view, because of the multiplicity of New Testament atonement metaphors, the traditional model can no longer satisfy him; for the arguments of his opponents, see, e.g., Baarlink (1998); Hoek (1998, chapter 2); Boukes in Elsinga (1998, chapter 3); De Kruijff (1998); Borger-Koetsier (2006, 240-45).
30. The question is interesting as to whether we can say, as did Verkuyl (1992, 232), that Jesus' death also identifies him with all *non*-Christians who died as martyrs.
31. Berger (2004, 115).

who belongs to God suffers almost inevitably."[32]

8.5.2 Biblical Examples

In the Messianic Psalms, the Messiah is often the One who suffers especially on behalf of the people. For instance, Psalm 22 does begin with the touching words, "My God, my God, why have you forsaken me? Why are you so far from saving me, from the words of my groaning?" (v. 1, cf. Matt. 27:46; Mark 15:34). But for the rest, the Psalm deals with what *people* (compared to bulls, lions, dogs, and wild oxen) did to him (vv. 7–21; also see, e.g., Ps. 40:13–15; 69; 88 and 102).

Yet, even in this respect there is a clear difference:[33] the Messiah points out that the "fathers" could trust in God, and that he delivered them (v. 4). But then, as a contrast, he says, "To you *they* cried and were rescued; in you *they* trusted and were not put to shame. But *I* am a worm and not a man, scorned by mankind and despised by the people" (vv. 5–6; italics added). At the very moment the bulls, lions, dogs, and wild oxen were arrayed against Jesus, a holy and righteous *God* forsook him. The essential difference with believers is that, when the bulls, lions, dogs, and wild oxen are arrayed against them, *God* is with them—more than ever, so to speak.

Also in the Gospels and in the book of Acts, what *people* did to Jesus on the cross is emphasized several times. He himself said, "[T]he Son of Man will be delivered over to the chief priests and scribes, and *they* will condemn him to death and deliver him over to the Gentiles to be mocked and flogged and crucified" (Matt. 20:18–19). The apostle Peter said, "The God of our fathers raised Jesus, whom *you* killed by hanging him on a tree" (Acts 5:30). At various other places, it is said that Israel (Acts 2:36; 3:15; 4:10; 7:52; 1 Thess. 2:14–15), or "they" (Acts 10:39),

---

32. Ibid., 309–10.
33. Grant (1956, 125).

killed Jesus. Romans executed this judicial verdict, but they acted at Jewish initiative, as we are told time and again. Our point is not whether Jews or Romans were more guilty, but that it was *humans* who did these heinous things to him. This is captured by the statement of H. Berkhof: "In the earliest proclamation of the Palestinian church, . . . the cross is especially the sign of human wickedness that is obliterated by God in the resurrection."[34]

Each of the Old Testament types shows us a certain aspect of New Testament truth. Thus, we might be tempted to look at the cross only from the viewpoint of Genesis 22: the Father and the Son, going together to Calvary, with God providing for himself the Lamb for the burnt offering. There are no enemies in Genesis 22. We might be tempted to look at Jesus' enemies only as two-bit players in the redemptive drama. This would be a mistake. The enemies are key players. They are not just the executors of God's judgment against Jesus. In fact, they were not this at all; they were only executors of the wicked *human* judgment against Jesus. God alone was the executor of *his own* judgment against Jesus. And these two events had to coincide: humanity's most heinous crime was the occasion of God's vicarious sacrifice for human crime. Believers experience both: they may suffer *with* Jesus, and they are the happy beneficiaries of Jesus' sufferings *for* them.

8.5.3 Jesus' Exemplary Death

The significance of the cross for believers is that they follow Jesus, if necessary even to the point of martyrdom. If the bulls, lions, dogs, and wild oxen were against Jesus, they will also be against them. Especially in Peter's first letter, which speaks so much of the sufferings and persecutions of Christians, this point is very important:

---

34. Berkhof (1986, 309).

> For to this you have been called, because Christ also suffered for you, leaving you an *example*, so that you might follow in his steps. He committed no sin, neither was deceit found in his mouth. When he was reviled, he did not revile in return; when he suffered, he did not threaten, but continued entrusting himself to him who judges justly. He himself bore our sins in his body on the tree, that we might die to sin and live to righteousness. By his wounds you have been healed" (1 Pet. 2:21-24).

In this passage, the exemplarist function and the atoning significance of the cross are mentioned in one breath. Believers follow Jesus in the moving way in which he endured his sufferings, *and* they *can* follow him in this because he himself, through his sufferings on the cross, blotted out their sins, and enabled them, through regeneration and the gift of the Holy Spirit, to live for righteousness. Paul wrote, "[L]et no one cause me trouble, for I bear on my body the marks of Jesus" (Gal. 6:17). He therefore had this desire: ". . . that I may know him and the power of his resurrection, and may share his sufferings, becoming like him in his death, that by any means possible I may attain the resurrection from the dead" (Phil. 3:10-11).

Elsewhere, Paul said, ". . . provided we *suffer with him* in order that we may also be glorified with him" (Rom. 8:17); "if we *endure* [with him], we will also reign with him" (2 Tim. 2:12). Peter said, "[R]ejoice insofar as you *share Christ's sufferings*, that you may also rejoice and be glad when his glory is revealed" (1 Pet. 4:13). And in Hebrews 12:2-4 we read,

> . . . looking to Jesus, the founder and perfecter of our faith, who for the joy that was set before him endured the cross, despising the shame, and is seated at the right hand of the throne of God. Consider him who endured from sinners such hostility against himself, so that you may not grow

weary or fainthearted. In your struggle against sin you have not yet resisted to the point of shedding your blood.

This aspect of shame is quite important for deepening our understanding of the cross. For later generations of Christians, the cross became a token of honor, and this obscures the shame that death on a cross involved in antiquity. Only the worst criminals, such as slaves who had killed their masters, were crucified. It was quite audacious for Paul to emphasize in Corinth the crucifixion of Jesus (1 Cor. 2:2). For many Gentiles, that Jesus died in a disgraceful way was enough to scornfully decline the gospel. Thus, the ancient Gentile writer Celsus said (as quoted by Origen), "How should we deem him to be a God, who . . . performed none of his promises, but who also, after we had convicted him, and condemned him as deserving of punishment, was found attempting to conceal himself, and endeavoring to escape in a most disgraceful manner, and who was betrayed by those whom he called disciples?"[35]

Trypho (a Jewish rabbi, or possibly a fictional character) wrote (as quoted by Justin Martyr), "But this is what we are most at a loss about: that you . . . [are] resting your hopes on a man that was crucified."[36] And, "prove to us whether He [i.e., the Messiah] must be crucified and die so disgracefully and so dishonorably by the death cursed in the law. For we cannot bring ourselves even to think of this." The early Christians faced the challenge of having to make clear to the Gentile world how salvation could be based upon someone who had died the death of a martyr on a cross.

---

35. Origenes, *Contra Celsum* 2.9 (http://www.newadvent.org/fathers/04162.htm); cf. 2.35, 68; 6.10, 34, 36.
36. Justinus Martyr, *Dialogue with Trypho* 10.3 and 90.1, respectively (http://www.earlychristianwritings.com/text/ justin-martyr-dialoguetrypho.html).

8.6 Suffering for Righteousness' Sake
8.6.1 Bearing One's Cross

In the Bible passages just mentioned, the emphasis lies not lie on the atoning but on the exemplarist significance of Jesus' sufferings on the cross. It is incorrect to reduce the meaning of these sufferings on the cross to this exemplarist aspect, but this does not render the exemplarist significance unimportant. Scripture gives us ample illustrations of this importance.

In line with this, we must also consider the following encouragements by Jesus: "If anyone would come after me, let him deny himself and take up his cross daily and follow me" (Luke 9:23). "Whoever does not bear his own cross and come after me cannot be my disciple" (14:27). These passages (also cf. Matt. 10:38; 16:24; Mark 8:34) have often been misunderstood (see more extensively, §12.5.2). First, Jesus does not speak here of his own cross but of the disciple's cross. Simon of Cyrene had to carry Jesus' cross (Luke 23:26), but Jesus' disciples must bear their own crosses.

Second, this also shows that Jesus' admonition is not about what believers must do with their sinful desires. Therefore, application of verses like these is incorrect: "We know that our old self was crucified with him" (Rom. 6:6); "I have been crucified with Christ" (Gal. 2:20); "those who belong to Christ Jesus have crucified the flesh with its passions and desires" (Gal. 5:24). Crucifying the flesh—nailing it to the cross of *Christ*—is necessary for each Christian, but this has little to do with bearing *one's own* cross.

Third, bearing one's cross refers not to a person's coming to faith, as if a believer takes up their cross once and for all at the moment of conversion. Luke 9:23 speaks of a taking up one's cross *daily* as a constantly repeated act of renewed commitment.

Fourth, bearing this cross has nothing to do with what people call the "bearing one's cross" of daily bur-

Theological Metaphors for Redemption

dens and personal vicissitudes: financial, relational, medical, and so on. There are two big differences: (a) such burdens are borne by *all* people, not just by disciples of Christ, and (b) these burdens are endured passively; but "taking up one's cross" is a disciple's active, daily decision: one can take it up, but one can also leave it lie.

Fifth, it is the cross of the self-denial: "If anyone would come after me, let him *deny himself* and take up his cross and follow me" (Matt. 16:24; Mark 8:34; Luke 9:23). Such self-denial refers not to acts of altruism, sacrificing oneself for others, but rather to accepting the consequences of consistently following Christ: persecution, oppression, imprisonment, and martyrdom. By totally dedicating oneself to Christ, the disciple sacrifices their own interests. The person who in faith comes to the cross of *Christ* receives eternal salvation, and has heavenly bliss and the kingdom of God as their prospect. However, as long as one is yet in this life, they must learn to daily take up *their own* cross and follow after the humble Lord here on earth, even to the point of martyrdom. One is saved by (the Spirit of) the *glorified* Christ in heaven, but it does not make sense to speak of *following* the glorified Christ. The One whom the believer follows is the Christ who lived here on earth in simplicity and humility, glorifying God and being a blessing for his fellow-humans. It is a following to the point of the cross.

On the one hand, the cross is the place where devil-dominated people tortured and killed Jesus; in one sense, he lost against them. On the other hand, the cross is the place where Jesus waged war against sin, death, and the devil—and he *won* this battle (see §8.7). This is one of the greatest paradoxes of the cross: it is the place where Jesus, in his warfare against Satan and his powers, *perished*, but it is also the place where he *triumphed* over them. He won *by* losing, as became evident in his resurrection. As a prisoner he entered the dungeon of death, and destroyed it from the inside (see §8.8.3 on Samson).

8.6.2 Various Kinds of Suffering

Viewing the cross as the place where Jesus suffered his martyrdom will be clarified when we explicitly distinguish the various *kinds* of suffering that Jesus endured. Thus, we must sharply distinguish between the sufferings that he endured at the hand of *other people*, and those that he underwent from the hand of *God*. Sometimes these are mentioned in one breath, as we saw in 1 Peter 2:22–24, but this does not mean that they are one and the same. We will discuss this matter more deeply in chapter 11, but the point is relevant here.

In his *atoning* sufferings, which Jesus endured from the hand of God, he was absolutely alone. No human could have ever shared in this work. However, there are also sufferings that Jesus does share with us. The apostle Peter speaks of "sharing" Christ's sufferings (1 Pet. 4:13), and Paul, too, speaks of "sharing" his sufferings, "becoming like him in his death" (Phil. 3:10). He can even say, "I am filling up what is lacking in Christ's afflictions for the sake of his body, that is, the church" (Col. 1:24). There is a suffering "for righteousness' sake" (1 Pet. 3:14; cf. v. 17; 2:19–20), which Jesus underwent here on earth, but which believers undergo as well when they stand firm for righteousness in an evil world. Peter calls them "blessed" for such suffering (cf. James 1:2–3), as Jesus himself said, "Blessed are those who are persecuted for righteousness' sake, for theirs is the kingdom of heaven" (Matt. 5:10). Thus, B. van de Beek rightly said that Jesus' death was not only an atoning sacrifice but also the "death of a righteous one,"[37] or, as we might say, the death of a *chasid* ("godly one," cf. Ps. 116:15 NASB).

Everything *people* did to Jesus, people would do to believers as well: "If they persecuted me, they will also

---
37. Van de Beek (1998, 151, 169).

persecute you" (John 15:20). This could almost be called a spiritual law: "[T]hrough many tribulations we *must* enter the kingdom of God" (Acts 14:22). "[N]o one be moved by these afflictions. For you yourselves know that we are *destined* for this. For when we were with you, we kept telling you beforehand that we *were to* suffer affliction" (1 Thess. 3:3-4). This is a fixed rule: "[A]ll who desire to live a godly life in Christ Jesus *will* be persecuted" (2 Tim. 3:12).

God *allowed*, and *allows*, all these things to happen to Jesus as well as to believers. But this is essentially different from what God *actively did* to Jesus, things that he *never* does to believers, or to any other people: "'Awake, O sword, against my shepherd, against the man who stands next to me,' declares the LORD of hosts. 'Strike the shepherd, and the sheep will be scattered; I will turn my hand against [others, to] the little ones'" (Zech. 13:7). "[I]t was the will of the LORD to crush him; he has put him to grief" (Isa. 53:10). Everything God did to Jesus on the cross was done in order that those who would believe would never have to endure *these* sufferings: "For our sake he [i.e., God] made him [i.e., Christ] to be sin who knew no sin, so that in him we might become the righteousness of God" (2 Cor. 5:21).

Let us carefully note what this means. Hostile people persecuted the Righteous One, just as they persecute the righteous ones even today.[38] But all the righteous ones by nature were at one time unrighteous, and were *made* righteous by faith in Christ, through his atoning work: "Christ suffered once for sins, the righteous for the unrighteous, that he might bring us to God" (1 Pet. 3:18). Christ died *for* the unrighteous, and the righteous may die *with* him. The unrighteous may suffer *because of* their own iniquities, but they cannot suffer *for* iniqui-

---

38. Notice the ambiguity in James 5:6, "You have condemned and murdered the righteous person. He does not resist you," which may refer to *any* righteous martyr, but also to the Righteous One, Jesus Christ (cf. DRA, NTE).

ties (i.e., to blot them out). Conversely, the justified ones can suffer for the sake of righteousness.

8.7 The Cross As Arena
8.7.1 Warfare Against Satan[39]

In chapter 9 we will discuss more extensively the contrast between models that view atonement in terms of substitution and satisfaction, and those that view it in an ethical-exemplarist way. At this point we will consider quite a different approach, namely, one that views atonement in terms of a dramatic metaphor,[40] that of warfare between Jesus and the evil powers and Jesus' victory over them. These powers are Satan and sin (§8.7) as well as death (§8.8). This approach is highlighted not so much by the Western (Catholic and Protestant) tradition of "Christ the Atoning Sacrifice" (Lat. *Christus Propitiatio)*, as it is by the Eastern Orthodox tradition of "Christ the Overcomer" (Lat. *Christus Victor*).

Incidentally, Robert Sherman associated the three main atonement models—the warfare, the vicarious and the exemplarist model—with the Father, the Son and the Spirit (and with the three Messianic offices: king, priest, and prophet), respectively.[41] In my view, his arguments for this are hardly convincing. Often, such views suffer from the problem of insufficiently distinguishing between the Trinitarian aspects and the Christological aspects (Christ, God and Man in one person).[42]

In the Heidelberg Catechism, Answer 1, both aspects—*Christus Propitiatio* and *Christus Victor*—are mentioned implicitly: "... Jesus Christ ... with His precious blood (1 Peter 1:18-19) has [a] fully satisfied for all my sins (1 John 1:7; 1 John 2:2), and [b] redeemed me from

---

39. Cf. Chafer (*ST* 3:109-111).
40. Van Genderen and Velema (2008, 532).
41. Sherman (2004).
42. See extensively, Ouweneel (2007b).

all the power of the devil (1 John 3:8); . . . ."⁴³ A. Moerkerken has pointed out that "satisfying" is objective (what was done *for* the believers), and "setting free" is subjective (what was done *to* the believers).⁴⁴ G. Aulén called the dramatic approach to Christ's atonement the classical doctrine of atonement, that is, the approach adopted and taught by the earliest church fathers.⁴⁵ Martin Luther paid attention to this approach as well, which is beautifully shown in one of his best known hymns, *A Mighty Fortress Is Our God* (Ger. *Ein' feste Burg ist unser Gott*): "The Prince of Darkness grim, / we tremble not for him; / his rage we can endure, / for lo! his doom is sure, / one little word shall fell him."

There is no doubt that the New Testament views Christ's work on the cross also in terms of warfare and victory. This comes to expression prophetically in the book of Genesis: the woman's seed will bruise the heel of the serpent's seed (Gen. 3:15; cf. Rev. 12:9; 20:2),⁴⁶ and Shiloh is the (fighting) lion from the tribe of Judah (Gen. 49:9 KJV; cf. Rev. 5:5). The Messiah is the "mighty One," who girds his sword on his thigh, and who rides out "victoriously for the cause of truth and meekness and righteousness" (Ps. 45:3-4). He is not only the defenseless Lamb (Isa. 53:7), but also the mighty One who will "divide the spoil with the strong" (v. 12).

In the New Testament this comes to light even more strongly. There are adversaries enough: angels, rulers, powers, authorities, thrones, dominions, and spiritual forces of evil in the heavenly places (Rom. 8:38-39; Eph. 1:21; 2:2; 3:10; 6:12; Col. 1:16; 2:15; 1 Pet. 3:22; cf. Matt.

---

43. Dennison (2008, 2:771); cf. Ouweneel (2016, ad loc.).
44. Moerkerken (2004, 17).
45. Aulén (1951); regarding the classical atonement motif of Christianity, see Aulén (1931, 513); regarding this, see Berkouwer (1965, 327-42), who also pointed out the dangers of one-sidedness and secularization in this approach.
46. See Ouweneel (2007b, 162); cf. Grant (1956, chapter 3).

24:29; Luke 22:53; Col. 1:13) (§2.3), not to mention sin and death, and the devil himself: "The reason the Son of God appeared was to destroy the works of the devil" (1 John 3:8). Jesus partook of "flesh and blood, . . . that through death he might destroy the one who has the power of death, that is, the devil, and deliver all those who through fear of death were subject to lifelong slavery" (Heb. 2:14–15). J. Hoek put it like this: "By his very bearing the curse of God, Jesus severed the nerve of Satan, the fearsome adversary of God."[47] This is all the more striking because Jesus was "crucified in weakness" (2 Cor. 13:4); precisely in this weakest condition (cf. Matt. 27:42), he triumphed over his enemies.

The Greek verb used in Hebrews 2:14 that is rendered "to destroy" (*katargeō*) means "to put out of action," "to render invalid," "to suspend," and hence "to destroy, to extirpate, to switch off." The same verb is used not only of the devil (Heb. 2:14) but also of sin ("our old self was crucified with him in order that the body of sin might be *brought to nothing*, so that we would no longer be enslaved to sin," Rom. 6:6) and of death ("our Savior Christ Jesus, who *abolished* death and brought life and immortality to light through the gospel," 2 Tim. 1:10). The New Testament often refers to the spiritual warfare that believers must wage; however, the fight that Jesus had to fight on the cross was absolutely unique and solitary. It reminds us of Isaiah 63:3, "I have trodden the winepress alone, and from the peoples no one was with me; I trod them in my anger and trampled them in my wrath; their lifeblood spattered on my garments, and stained all my apparel."

8.7.2 Destroyed and Conquered

On the cross, in the power of his divinity, but also as Man in the power of the Holy Spirit, Jesus destroyed these enemies, put them out of action, rendered them

---

47. Hoek (1998, 106).

impotent, extirpated them, and dismantled them. Jesus never experienced the warfare against his own sinful flesh, for his flesh was not sinful (2 Cor. 5:21; 1 Pet. 2:24; 1 John 3:5). However, when the cup of sufferings was presented to him, he was "in agony" (Gk. *agōnia*, lit. "struggle, wrestling"; Luke 22:44). And even more clearly, the work on the cross led to a real victory, for sin is presented as an evil power that must be "destroyed," done away with," brought to nothing," "rendered powerless," "defeated" (Rom. 6:6, Gk. *katargeō*).

Such victories always have an eschatological dimension: as a matter of principle, sin *was* defeated on the cross—yet people, even believers, still sin. Only at the consummation of the ages will sin be definitively abolished from the cosmos (cf. John 1:29). As a matter of principle, death *was* defeated on the cross— yet people still die. Only at the consummation of the ages will death be definitively thrown into the lake of fire (Rev. 20:14; cf. 1 Cor. 15:26). As a matter of principle, the devil *was* defeated on the cross— yet the devil still prowls around like a roaring lion (1 Pet. 5:8). Only at the consummation of the ages will he too be definitively thrown into the lake of fire (Rev. 20:10; cf. John 12:31). As a matter of principle, the world *was* defeated on the cross— yet it still lies in the power of the evil one (1 John 5:19). Only at the consummation of the ages will it be definitively brought to an end (2:17).

To use Oscar Cullmann's well-known analogy from the Second World War,[48] this is the difference between D-day (Decision Day, June 6, 1944, the Invasion of Normandy), where the war took a decisive turn, and V-day (Victory Day, May 8, 1945, capitulation of Germany). Jesus' death on the cross was on D-day: the day of decision; his final victory at the consummation of the ages will be V-day.

Especially in the book of Revelation, Jesus conquer-

---

48. Cullmann (1962, 84).

ing and overcoming the evil powers is mentioned several times: "The one who conquers, I will grant him to sit with me on my throne, as I also conquered and sat down with my Father on his throne" (Rev. 3:21). "[B]ehold, the Lion of the tribe of Judah, the Root of David, has conquered" (5:5). In the final victory over Satan, as founded upon Christ's work on the cross, the believers will be involved as well: "The God of peace will soon crush Satan under your feet" (Rom. 16:20). The metaphor of the conqueror (overcomer, victor) is so remarkable because in Revelation 5 the Lamb is presented in its weakest condition: its throat has just been slit. This weak, vulnerable Lamb opposes the seemingly supreme dragon ("that ancient serpent, who is called the devil and Satan, the deceiver of the whole world," 12:9; cf. 20:2). In response to this question: "[T]hey worshiped the dragon, for he had given his authority to the beast, and they worshiped the beast, saying, 'Who is like the beast, and who can fight against it?'" (13:4), we find this reply: Jesus' enemies "will make war on the Lamb, and the Lamb will conquer them, for he is Lord of lords and King of kings, and those with him are called and chosen and faithful" (17:14).

8.7.3 Disarmed

Jesus' work on the cross featured warfare against, and victory over, the evil powers: "He disarmed [Gk. *apekdusamenos*] the rulers and authorities and put them to open shame, by triumphing [Gk. *thriambeusas*] over them in him [or, it, i.e., the cross]" (Col. 2:15), and thus, Jesus' ascension to heaven was also a triumph over the defeated powers. Interestingly, the commentaries that I have consulted usually conclude that Christ is the subject of this sentence,[49] whereas it seems more obvious to take God as the subject (see vv. 13–14, "And you . . . *God* made alive together with *him* [i.e., Christ] . . . having for-

---

49. So, e.g., Berkouwer (1965, 340).

given us ... by canceling the record of debt ... This *he* set aside, nailing it to the cross. *He* disarmed ... ," etc.). This was the view of A. Schlatter, who, however, like others, thought of positive powers.[50] B. Demarest saw as the subject both God and Christ.[51]

The earlier Greek verb in verse 15, *apekduomai*, reminds us of the statue of a dethroned monarch divested of his official garment.[52] The latter verb, *thriambeuō*, reminds us of the picture, well-known in the Roman world, of a triumphing general leading his troops through the streets of the city with a miserable group in his wake consisting of conquered kings, officers, and soldiers, exposed to the mockery of the citizens.[53] Here the cross is not an instrument of death, that is, of the defeat of Christ by death, but it is here, as it were, the triumphal chariot of Christ.[54] We have a similar metaphor in 2 Corinthians 2:14–16,

> ... God, who in Christ always leads us in triumphal procession, and through us spreads the fragrance of the knowledge of him everywhere. For we are the aroma of Christ to God among those who are being saved [i.e., the conquering army] and among those who are perishing [i.e., the conquered army], to one [i.e., the latter] a fragrance from death to death, to the other [i.e., the former] a fragrance from life to life.

The one aroma of Christ and his work means both

---

50. Schlatter (1963, 283); cf., in opposition to this, Peake (1979, 529).
51. Demarest (1997, 150 resp. 181).
52. *DNTT* 1:315.
53. Originally, *thriambos* was a processional hymn sung to Dionysus, among the Romans to Jupiter, and secondarily to any triumphing army commander; later, *thriambos/triumphus* became a reference to the procession as such: a celebration of victory.
54. Vaughan (1978, 202).

life to the conquering ones and death to the conquered ones.

Similarly, Paul speaks of God's

> great might that he worked in Christ when he raised him from the dead and seated him at his right hand in the heavenly places, far above all rule and authority and power and dominion, and above every name that is named, not only in this age but also in the one to come. And he put all things under his feet (Eph. 1:19–22).

"God has highly exalted him and bestowed on him the name that is above every name" (Phil. 2:9). The glorified Christ "is the head of all rule and authority" (Col. 2:10). Jesus Christ "has gone into heaven and is at the right hand of God, with angels, authorities, and powers having been subjected to him" (1 Pet. 3:22).

Paul describes Jesus' ascension as follows:

> "When he ascended on high he led a host of captives, and he gave gifts to men." (In saying, "He ascended," what does it mean but that he had also descended into the lower regions, the earth? He who descended is the one who also ascended far above all the heavens, that he might fill all things.) (Eph. 4:8–10).

Paul was here quoting Psalm 68:18, "You ascended on high, leading a host of captives in your train and receiving gifts among men, even among the rebellious, that the Lord God may dwell there." Words that historically referred to bringing the ark of the covenant up to Mount Zion (2 Sam. 6; 1 Chron. 13) are prophetically applied to the ascension as Jesus' triumphal procession, with the prisoners of war in his wake whom he defeated (see further §14.5).

8.8 Warfare Against Death
8.8.1 The Last Enemy

It is easier to imagine a battle against Satan and his consorts than a battle against death. Yet, death, too, is an enemy that must be destroyed:

> When the perishable puts on the imperishable, and the mortal puts on immortality, then shall come to pass the saying that is written: "Death is swallowed up in victory." "O death, where is your victory? O death, where is your sting?" The sting of death is sin, and the power of sin is the law. But thanks be to God, who gives us the victory through our Lord Jesus Christ" (1 Cor. 15:54-57; quotations from Isa. 25:8; Hos. 13:14).

> "The last enemy to be destroyed is death" (1 Cor. 15:26).

Eastern Orthodox theologian John of Damascus described the battle against death in quite a graphic way:

> [D]eath approaches, and swallowing up the body [of Christ] as a bait is transfixed on the hook of divinity [i.e., the divine nature of Christ], and after tasting of a sinless and life-giving body, perishes, and brings up again all whom of old he swallowed up [see next section]. For just as darkness disappears on the introduction of light, so is death repulsed before the assault of life, and brings life to all, but death to the destroyer.[55]

The metaphor of bait, which originated with Origen and appealed to Augustine, is thought provoking.[56] Death is the wages of sin (Rom. 6:23; cf. 1 Cor. 15:56). So what happens when a *sinless* person enters death voluntarily? Not only does such a person not belong there, but

---

55. *An Exact Exposition of the Orthodox Faith* 3.27 (http://www.documentacatholicaomnia.eu/03d/0675-0749,_Ioannes_Damascenus,_De_Fide_Orthodoxa,_EN.pdf).
56. Cf. Van Veluw (2002, 160-61).

by his entrance he will "blow up" the domain of death from the inside: "God raised him up, loosing the pangs of death, because it was not possible for him to be held by it" (Acts 2:24). At the price of his own life, Jesus destroyed death (2 Tim. 1:10); by entering this very death, Jesus robbed it of its power.

Death is the power domain of Satan (Heb. 2:14-15). Satan is the prince of death, who through death wields power over sinners (same passage), but Jesus is the "Author (Prince, Lord, Source) of life" (3:15). Through his very death Christ destroyed the adversary. The devil still prowls around (1 Pet. 5:8), but with regard to "the children" (Heb. 2:14a) he has become powerless; though he still attacks them, he does so less by his power and more by his schemes (Eph. 6:11); we should "not be outwitted by Satan; for we are not ignorant of his designs" (2 Cor. 2:11).[57] The powerlessness of Satan is also illustrated by the fact that believers may still "die" (John 11:14; Acts 9:37), but the more common description is that they "fall asleep" (Matt. 27:52; John 11:11; Acts 7:60; 13:36; 1 Cor. 15:6, 18, 20; 1 Thess. 4:13-15; 5:10). Jesus himself said, "Everyone who lives and believes in me shall never die" (John 11:26). Death has lost its power; for the believer death is only the passage to being "with Christ" (Phil. 1:23) and to resurrection.

8.8.2 The Rulers Overcome

Let me add a few comments at this point. First, note in the quotation of John of Damascus the line: "and brings up again all whom of old he swallowed up." This refers to the so-called "Harrowing of Hell" (Lat. *Descensus Christi ad Inferos*, "Christ's Descent into Hell"), a doctrine that was very popular in early Christianity. It teaches that between his death and resurrection, Christ descended into hell (or Hades) to bring redemption to all the righteous who had died during Old Testament times. I will

---

57. Ouweneel (1982, 1:44).

discuss this subject in §14.5 below.

Second, the description by John of Damascus of death swallowing the body of Christ as a bait implies that death was an enemy who did not really recognize what was at stake when he assaulted Jesus. A parallel to this is the notion that the satanic powers were unaware of what they could expect when waging war against Jesus. As Paul says,

> Yet among the mature we do impart wisdom, although it is not a wisdom of this age or of the rulers of this age, who are doomed to pass away. But we impart a secret and hidden wisdom of God, which God decreed before the ages for our glory. None of the rulers of this age understood this, for if they had, they would not have crucified the Lord of glory" (1 Cor. 2:5-8).

These "rulers" (Gk. *archontes*) remind us of "Beelzebul, the prince [Gk. *archōn*] of demons" (Matt. 12:24; Luke 11:15), or Satan, the condemned "ruler [Gk. *archōn*] of the/this world" (John 12:31; 14:30; 16:11; cf. Eph. 2:2).[58] The rulers (1 Cor. 2:6-8) were made powerless by the Lord of glory, whom they had made their prey, ignorant as they were of God's plan of salvation.[59]

Third, the battle metaphor is implicitly present in those passages that tell us how believers were set free from certain powers: the Father "has delivered us from the domain of darkness and transferred us to the kingdom of his beloved Son" (Col. 1:13); ". . . him who called you out of darkness into his marvelous light" (1 Pet. 2:9); ". . . turn from darkness to light and from the power of Satan to God" (Acts 26:18). A foreshadowing of this is

---

58. Cf. "the prince of the world" (Heb. *sar haʿolam*) in Exod.R. 17.4 on Exod. 12:23. For the view that 1 Cor. 2:8 is about demonic powers, see Fee (1987, 103n21 and n22 with many references), although Fee himself thought of earthly "rulers" (1987, 104n24).
59. G. Delling (*TDNT* 1:489).

found in Jesus' casting out demons: "[H]ow can someone enter a strong man's house and plunder his goods, unless he first binds the strong man? Then indeed he may plunder his house" (Matt. 12:29; Mark 3:27). The "strong one" here is Satan; the demons are his helpers. Through his moral victory during his temptations in the wilderness, and through his casting out demons, Jesus showed that he was stronger than the "strong one"; he robbed him of his "goods." Luke's version is even more powerful: "When a strong man, fully armed, guards his own palace, his goods are safe; but when one stronger than he attacks him and overcomes him, he takes away his armor in which he trusted and divides his spoil" (11:21-22). This is what Jesus did during his ministry, and what he completed at the cross.

8.8.3 Old Testament Illustrations

In §8.8.1, I argued that by entering the domain of death, Jesus "blew it up" from the inside, as it were. What comes to mind here is the story of the judge Samson, who was led as a derided prisoner into the temple of the god Dagon. A "god" like Dagon is in fact an angelic prince who is subservient to Satan. By his enormous strength, Samson made the temple collapse from the inside, and thus humiliated Dagon (Judg. 16:30). Dagon was humiliated once again when the Philistines brought the ark of the covenant into his temple:

> [W]hen the people of Ashdod rose early the next day, behold, Dagon had fallen face downward on the ground before the ark of the Lord. So they took Dagon and put him back in his place. But when they rose early on the next morning, behold, Dagon had fallen face downward on the ground before the ark of the Lord, and the head of Dagon and both his hands were lying cut off on the threshold. Only the trunk of Dagon was left to him (1 Sam. 5:3-4).

The thought that the vicarious sacrificial meaning of Christ's atoning work on the cross is foreshadowed in detail in the Old Testament sacrificial ministry is supported extensively in the book of Hebrews (see §§4.3–4.7). However, we should not overlook so many other Old Testament types, which relate much more to the warfare model of Christ's work on the cross. Even before the sacrificial ministry was instituted at Mount Sinai, the exodus from Egypt and the passage through the Red Sea show us a very different side of Christ's work. God said, "[O]n all the gods of Egypt I will execute judgments: I am the LORD" (Exod. 12:12b; cf. Num. 33:4b). This points to warfare between God and these "gods," as God himself declared, "The LORD will fight for you, and you have only to be silent" (Exod. 14:14). At the exodus, God "cut Rahab [i.e., the angelic prince of Egypt] in pieces," and "pierced the dragon" (Isa. 51:9). At the next confrontation, with another enemy, Moses said, "The LORD will have war with Amalek [type of the adversary powers] from generation to generation" (Exod. 17:16).

Goliath was another enemy, who represented the Philistines as well as their gods. When he met David, he cursed him "by his gods" (1 Sam. 17:43). David's reply was very telling:

> You come to me with a sword and with a spear and with a javelin, but I come to you in the name of the LORD of hosts, the God of the armies of Israel,[60] whom you have defied. This day the LORD will deliver you into my hand, and I will strike you down and cut off your head. And I will give the dead bodies of the host of the Philistines this day to the birds of the air and to the wild beasts of the earth, that all the earth may know that there is a God in Israel, and that all this assembly may know that the LORD saves not with sword and spear. For *the battle is the LORD's*, and he will

---

60. The terms "hosts" and "armies" may refer to the army of Israel, but more likely they refer to God's heavenly armies (cf. 2 Kings 6:15–17; see also Isa. 13:13; Hag. 2:6).

give you into our hand (1 Sam. 17:45-47).

There are many Old Testament examples of Israel's warriors engaged in battles, battles that were types of the warfare that New Testament believers experience. However, when God—or his man, such as David—does the fighting alone, we are always reminded of Christ's work on the cross: "I have trodden the winepress alone, and from the peoples no one was with me; I trod them in my anger and trampled them in my wrath; their lifeblood spattered on my garments, and stained all my apparel. For the day of vengeance was in my heart, and my year of redemption [or, my redeemed] had come" (Isa. 63:3-4). "There has been no day like it before or since, when the LORD heeded the voice of a man, for the LORD fought for Israel.... And Joshua captured all these kings and their land at one time, because the LORD God of Israel fought for Israel" (Josh. 10:14, 42). "[T]he LORD has driven out before you great and strong nations. And as for you, no man has been able to stand before you to this day. One man of you puts to flight a thousand, since it is the LORD your God who fights for you, just as he promised you" (Josh. 23:9-10).

We encounter the warfare model especially in some Old Testament types of Christ.[61] Think of Abel, the first of the woman's seed in his battle against the serpent's seed, represented by Cain (Gen. 4 Think of Moses, who led the people of Israel out of Egypt, and through a series of battles brought them to the Promised Land. Some of those who were called judges, who freed the Israelites of their enemies, demonstrate clear Messianic traits: Gideon (versus the Midianites), Jephthah (versus the Ammonites), Samson (versus the Philistines). Of David (see above) many examples of warfare and victory could be given; he triumphed over both Saul and the neighboring nations, all of whom threatened the people

---

61. See Ouweneel (2007b, §7.6.2).

of God. Finally, we think of Mordecai, who redeemed the people of God from the power of Haman, and became "second in rank to King Ahasuerus, and he was great among the Jews and popular with the multitude of his brothers, for he sought the welfare of his people and spoke peace to all his people" (Est. 10:3).

Chapter 9
Substitution and Satisfaction

> *Surely he has borne our griefs*
> *and carried our sorrows; . . .*
> *[H]e was pierced for our*
> *transgressions;*
> *he was crushed for our iniquities;*
> *upon him was the chastisement that*
> *brought us peace,*
> *and with his wounds we are*
> *healed. . . .*
> *By oppression and judgment he was*
> *taken away;*
> *and as for his generation, who*
> *considered*
> *that he was cut off out of the land of the*
> *living,*
> *stricken for the transgression of my*
> *people?*
>
> Isaiah 53:4–5, 8

Summary: *This chapter discusses some key terms in the doctrine of atonement. The first is substitution: the innocent victim dies for, and instead of, the guilty person. The second is expiation: the blotting out of human guilt. The* *third is propitiation: the satisfaction given to the divine Judge in view of the sins committed. Through this satisfaction, God's honor has been restored as far as his relationship to humanity is concerned. God's justice is satisfied in view of human guilt.*

On the one hand, propitiation must not be debased into a pagan form of placation: appeasing a furious God. On the other hand, it must not be distorted into some form of theopaschitism: the notion that God himself suffered on the cross, or even that God made himself to be sin. One of the underlying problems here is failing to distinguish adequately between the God-Man and the Father-Son relationship. Basic to all understanding of biblical atonement is seeing that God himself, in his endless love, took the initiative for atonement by giving his own Son to death. However, neither love nor righteousness has the priority in atonement: they are in perfect balance from beginning to end.

9.1   Substitution
9.1.1 Introduction

In §5.3 we discussed the two goats of the sin offering on the Day of Atonement, and distinguished between the principle of *satisfaction* represented by the first goat, and the principle of *substitution* represented by the second goat. Both aspects, which are quite different, must now be explained with regard to the sacrifice of Jesus. Let us first look at the principle of *substitution*: the vicarious aspect of the cross (an innocent victim dying instead of, and for the benefit of, a guilty person).

The essence of substitution is this: through the Fall, humanity had forfeited every title to blessing, or even more strongly, had become worthy of eternal condemnation (John 5:24, 29; Acts 24:25; Rom. 2:2-5; Heb. 6:2; 9:27; 10:27; James 2:13; 3:1; 1 Pet. 4:17; 2 Pet. 2:9; 3:7; Jude 1:15). The only way people's sins could be blotted out is through this eternal judgment, that is, an everlasting punishment.[1] No mere person can pay for another person's sins (Ps. 49:7-9), nor could any person do this for themselves. Sins can be wiped out *without* the person having to undergo eternal condemnation only through a substitute that is acceptable to God, one that undergoes God's judgment instead of the guilty person, and thus acquires an eternal redemption for each person who in faith receives this work of atonement.

Two comments are relevant here. First, in practice, being "acceptable to God" amounts to saying that it must be God himself who, in his love and mercy, makes this substitute available (cf. §6.6.4). Second, substitution goes much further than sympathy and empathy. A friend may help carrying the sorrows of another person but they cannot carry these sorrows *instead* of that other person; one cannot "take them over" from another person. Thus, the atoning sufferings of Christ were not just sympathizing with the sinners, but a vicarious suffering, one that was accomplished *instead of* or *in place of* sinners: he "stood in their shoes."[2] Jesus "bore" the sins of believers on the cross (1 Pet. 2:24) *because* believers themselves *could* not "bear" their own sins, and *in order that* they themselves would not *have to* "bear" them.

A terminological comment: the terms "vicarious" and "substitution" refer to the same thing. The term "vicarious" comes from Latin *vicarius*, "substituted, delegated," from *vicis*, "change, exchange, interchange, substitution." The term "substitution" comes from Latin *substitutio*, "a putting instead of (another)," from *sub*, "under," and *statuere*, "to set (up)."

---

1. Cf. Matt. 18:34, "And in anger his master delivered him to the jailers, until he should pay all his debt"—which would take forever: how can a poor, imprisoned man pay his debt?
2. Van de Beek (2000, 107).

9.1.2 Old Testament Evidence

What is the Old Testament evidence for this substitution? We have seen (chapter 4) that the Old Testament sacrificial ministry very clearly entailed this substitution, and we do not have to repeat these arguments here. Moreover, we have seen that in explaining Christ's sacrifice on the cross, the New Testament is in full harmony with the terminology and essential elements of the Old Testament sacrificial ministry. We have seen that the laying on of hands implies that the offerer makes themselves one with the sacrificial animal: the innocent animal dies vicariously for the sins of the offerer (see especially Lev. 16:20–22). Hebrews 2:17 ties in with this: Christ was "a merciful and faithful high priest in the service of God, to make propitiation for the sins of the people." Here as elsewhere in the letter, Hebrews draws a clear parallel between the Day of Atonement and the atoning sacrifice of Christ: the sacrifice atones vicariously for the sins of the people.

This parallel also comes to light in Isaiah 53, where the Servant of YHWH is the true vicarious Lamb:

> Surely he has *borne* [Heb. *n-s-'*] our griefs / and *carried* [*s-b-l*] our sorrows . . . he was pierced *for* our transgressions; / he was crushed *for* our iniquities; / upon *him* was the chastisement that brought *us* peace, / and with *his* wounds *we* are healed . . . / the LORD has laid on *him* / the iniquity of *us* all . . . / like a *lamb* that is led to the slaughter . . . / [he was] stricken *for* the transgression of my people. . . . / Yet it was the will of the LORD to crush him; / he has put him to grief; / when his soul makes an *offering for guilt*, / he shall see his offspring: . . . . [B]y his knowledge shall the righteous one, my servant, / make many *to be accounted righteous*, / and he shall *bear* [*s-b-l*] their iniquities. . . . / he poured out his soul to death / and was numbered with the transgressors; / yet he *bore* [*n-s-'*] the sin of many, . . . (Isa. 53:4–12; italics added).

In no other Old Testament passage is the notion of the Messiah's vicarious sacrifice expressed more clearly than here, and this entirely in terms of the Sinaitic sacrificial ministry. Especially the Hebrew verbs *n-s-'* and *s-b-l*, both in the sense of "bearing/carrying vicariously," are important here. We know the Hebrew verb *n-s-'* from Exodus 28:38 ("Aaron shall bear any guilt from the holy things that the people of Israel consecrate as their holy gifts"); Numbers 14:33 ("your children ... shall suffer for your faithlessness"); Ezekiel 4:5–6 ("So long shall you bear the punishment of the house of Israel," etc.).[3] We know the Hebrew verb *s-b-l* from Lamentations 5:7, "Our fathers sinned, and are no more; and we bear their iniquities," that is, we bear the consequences of *their* sin: *they* sinned, *we* undergo the punishment for those sins. To be sure, this is not a description of atonement, but it does illustrate the principle of substitution: one party sins, and the other party undergoes the punishment for those sins.

9.2 New Testament Evidence

9.2.1 Terminology

The Greek word for "to atone" is *hilaskomai*,[4] which, according to the Septuagint, is the equivalent of the Hebrew root *k-p-r* (see §4.1). The first meaning of this word is "to be merciful (conciliatory)" (Luke 18:13). The tax collector prays, "God, be merciful to me, a sinner!" One could also translate: "God, reconcile me, a sinner" (JUB), that is, "God, atone for my sins." This is remarkable because Jesus adds, "[T]his man went down to his house justified" (v. 14)—a first, very important link between

---

3. Cf. *n-ç-'* in the sense of "loading up oneself," "bearing," with regard to one's *own* guilt ("being responsible for") in Exod. 28:43; Lev. 5:1; 7:18; 17:16; 19:8; 20:20; 22:9; Num. 5:31; 9:13; 14:34; 18:1; Ezek. 44:10.

4. See *TDNT* 3, 300–23; *DNTT* 3:148–66; Morris (1955, chapters 4–5); the Septuagint usually has the intensive form *exhilaskomai*, which does not appear in the New Testament.

atonement and justification, anticipating Paul's expositions on this matter. Because of the atonement brought about by Jesus, the believing sinner can be justified before God.

For the meaning of *hilaskomai* compare the adjective *hileōs*, "merciful" (Matt. 16:22; Heb. 8:12). The Greek words *hileōs* and *hilaskomai* are related to *hilaros*, "merry" (cf. Latin *hilaris*, from which English "hilarity" and "hilarious" were derived). God's atoning mercy makes people merry (see, e.g., Isa. 12 and many Psalms)![5] However, merriness (happiness) does not imply superficiality; on the contrary, the price for God's mercy, and thus for atonement, was simply too high for that. This price is nothing less than the blood of the atoning sacrifice. The blood of Jesus, appointed by God as the true and only atoning sacrifice, is the foundation of the believer's justification (Rom. 5:8), redemption (Eph. 1:7 [cf. 2:13]; 1 Pet. 1:18–19; Rev. 1:5), cleansing (Heb. 9:14; 1 John 1:7; Rev. 7:14), and sanctification (Heb. 10:29).

The related word *hilasmos* means "atonement" (or "atoning sacrifice") or "propitiation": Christ "is the propitiation for our sins" (1 John 2:2; 4:10). This expression ties in entirely with what John said earlier about cleansing—the sin offering is an offering of cleansing (§4.6)!—through the blood of Christ: "[T]he blood of Jesus his Son cleanses us from all sin. . . . If we confess our sins, he is faithful and just to forgive us our sins and to cleanse us from all unrighteousness" (1 John 1:7, 9; cf. Rev. 1:5; 5:9; 7:14; 12:11).

Worth noticing here is the Greek preposition *peri*, "for," in 1 John 2:2 and 4:10, that is, "in view of," namely, to take them away. We encounter the same preposition in the expression *peri (tēs) hamartias*, "for sin." This is the common Septuagint rendering of *chattat*, which means both "sin" and "what is *for* sin," the "sin offering" (Lev.

---

5. Cf. a similar development with the Heb. word *cheyn*, "grace," from which the Yiddish word *gein* ("fun") was derived.

6:30; 7:37; 14:19; 16:5). Also in Hebrews 10:6 and 8, *peri hamartias* means "sin offering." When Paul writes that God sent his Son "for sin" (*peri hamartias*), this probably also means "as [or, to be] a sin offering" (thus NIV; cf. Heb. 10:12, 26; 1 Pet. 3:18). Peter says that Christ suffered "for sins" (Gk. *peri hamartiōn*; 1 Pet. 3:18). Sometimes, the Greek preposition *huper* is used (cf. §9.2.2); thus, the book of Hebrews says, "Christ had offered for all time a single sacrifice for sins [Gk. *mian huper hamartiōn thusian*]" (10:12); but see verse 26, "there no longer remains a sacrifice for sins [Gk. *peri hamartiōn thusia*]" (v. 26; cf. 1:3; 2:17; 5:1, 3; 7:27; 9:7). The difference between *huper* and *peri* here is negligible.

We also find *peri* in Matthew 26:28, but now in a different way: "[T]his is my blood of the covenant, which is poured out for many [Gk. *peri pollōn*] for the forgiveness of sins."[6] Here, *peri* means "for the benefit of," even with the undertones of "instead of" (although this is more *anti*, as in Matt. 20:28). Christ's sacrifice is "for" (in view of) sins, and it is "for" (the benefit of) people; that is, this sacrifice is to take the sins away, and to set believers free from them.

Finally, I mention *hilastērion* in Hebrews 9:5 ("mercy seat"), and especially Romans 3:24–25, ". . . the redemption that is in Christ Jesus, whom God put forward as a propitiation [AMPC: mercy seat] by his blood, to be received by faith." The English word "mercy" is related to the Greek word *hileōs*, and the words "merciful," and

---

6. Note the parallel in Luke 22:20, "This cup that is poured out for you is the new covenant in my blood," where the demonstrative pronoun "that" refers back to "cup," not to "blood" (this fact is ignored in many English translations [e.g., (N)KJV, ASV, NIV], but is rendered properly in the RSV and the ESV). J. Vos (2005, 109–10, 120–21) used this fact to cast doubt on the idea of Jesus' atoning death in Luke. He concluded, in my view incorrectly, "that the traditional doctrine of the vicarious atoning death of Jesus is not found with any clarity in any of the four canonical gospels" (2005, 132). This depends on one's definition of "clarity."

"mercy seat" with the Hebrew word *kappōret*, the cover of the ark that was for atonement (cf. its role on the Day of Atonement, Lev. 16:13-15). The passage tells us that by shedding his blood, Christ has effectuated atonement for sins (the objective aspect), and people will share in this by their faith (the subjective aspect). The original meaning "mercy seat" is clearly involved here: just as the mercy seat in the Old Testament was the place where God and people—in the person of their representative, the high priest—met each other on the Day of Atonement, today Christ is the true "meeting point" between God and people.[7] This idea of a meeting point may be referred to the cross, but also to the preaching of Christ in the gospel.

9.2.2 Application of the Old Testament in the New Testament

Karl Barth said about the blood in Romans 3:25,

> Consequently, in Jesus also atonement occurs only through the faithfulness of God, *by his blood*: only, that is to say, in the inferno of His complete solidarity with all the sin and weakness and misery of the flesh; .... By His blood, then, Jesus is proved to be the Christ, the first and last word to men of the faithfulness of God. By His death He declares the impossible possibility of our redemption, ...[8]

Romans 3:25, along with Hebrews 2:17, 1 John 2:2, and 4:10, make clear that the New Testament applies the terminology of the Sinaitic sacrificial ministry directly to the offering of Christ. Moreover, Christ is called the true Passover lamb (one Gk. word: *pascha*, 1 Cor. 5:7). Here the New Testament does the same as the Old Testa-

---

7. *TDNT* 3:321; see the quotation from Karl Barth in §4.1.1 (note 3),as well as the discussion in *DNTT* 3:163-64, and Den Heyer (1997, 68-72).
8. Barth (1976, 105).

ment did in Isaiah 53, where the Sinaitic sacrificial terminology was applied to the Servant of YHWH.[9]

We have seen that the New Testament extensively applies Isaiah 53 to Christ.[10] The notion of Christ having vicariously borne (Gk. *anapherō*) the sins of his people is therefore quite common in the New Testament: "Christ, having been offered once to *bear* the sins of many . . ." (Heb. 9:28). "He himself *bore* our sins in his body on the tree, that we might die to sin and live to righteousness" (1 Pet. 2:24; cf. John 1:29, "Behold, the Lamb of God, who takes away [Gk. *airō*] the sin of the world!"). Even stronger is the description in 2 Corinthians 5:21, "For our sake he [i.e., God] *made him* [i.e., Christ] *to be sin* who knew no sin, so that in him we might become the righteousness of God." Opinions differ about whether the phrase "to be sin" means "to be our sin offering" (cf. §9.2.1);[11] but regardless of the opinion chosen, this verse clearly implies substitution. In other words, note the "sweet exchange" (§9.6.3): the Righteous One was made to be sin "for us," in order that "we," sinners, could be made righteous.

The expression "for our sake" (Gk. *huper hēmōn*) means "on our behalf" (cf. Phlm.13), or "for our benefit," sometimes with the connotation "instead of us," "in our place" (cf. Rom. 5:6-8; 8:32; 2 Cor. 5:15; Gal. 2:20; Heb. 2:9; 1 Pet. 3:18).[12] In the prophetic word of Caiaphas

---

9. Let me add here this note on Isa. 53: it is remarkable that the Heb. word *talia* means both "lamb" and "youth," and hence "servant": the Servant of God is the Lamb of God. The cognate form *talēh* appears in 1 Sam. 7:9; Isa. 40:11; 65:25 ("lamb"); and the feminine form *talyeta* (altered into *talitha*) in Mark 5:41 ("little girl"); see *TDNT* 1:339; cf. Ratzinger (2007, 21).
10. Ouweneel (2007b, §5.5.2); cf. Verkuyl (1992, 235-36).
11. See Hughes (1962, 213-15); Sabourin and Lyonnet (1970, 250-53); Harris (1976, 354-56); Bernard (1979, 73); *DNTT* 3: 170-71.
12. In 1 Cor. 15:3 we find the Gk. preposition *huper* "for (the purpose of) [our sins]"; see Berkouwer (1965, 308-11); cf. Trench (1953, 310-13) and *DNTT* 3:1179-80, on the

(John 11:50, "it is better for you that one man should die *for* the people, not that the whole nation should perish"; cf. v. 51), *huper* clearly means "instead of." We find this preposition in Galatians 3:13, "Christ redeemed us from the curse of the law by becoming a curse *for* us," and in 1 Timothy 2:6, Christ "gave himself as a ransom *for* all." Here the word "ransom" renders the Greek word *antilutron*, in which the preposition *anti* emphasizes the notion of substitution even more clearly (cf. Matt. 2:22; 5:38; Luke 11:11).[13]

In Matthew 20:28 and Mark 10:45, "[T]he Son of Man came not to be served but to serve, and to give his life as a ransom for many," the last phrase is the Greek *lutron anti pollōn*.[14] H. Ridderbos spoke here of "a substitute [payment] for the life that the person really had a right to."[15] And H. Baarlink wrote: "Summing up everything, it is clear that the words of Jesus at the institution of the Lord's Supper speak of the disciples' sharing in his atoning death."[16] He did not intend to say that the disciples contributed to the actual work of atonement, but rather that they were the beneficiaries of Christ's atoning death.

9.2.3 Conclusion

When we consider the totality of the biblical testimony concerning Christ's work of atonement, we cannot doubt that Christ bore the sins and died "instead of" his people, "in their place." With this basic commitment,

---

relationships between the Gk. prepositions *anti* and *huper*.
13. Baarlink (1998, 54–61); Vos (2005, 105–108) tried to eliminate the traditional meaning of "ransom."
14. Cf. *lutrōtēs*, "redeemer" (Acts 7:35), *lutrōsis*, "redemption" (Luke 1:68; Heb. 9:12), and *lutroō*, "to redeem" (Luke 24:21; Titus 2:14; 1 Pet. 1:18–19), in which the notion of a ransom to be paid is often clearly implied; see extensively, Morris (1955, chapter 1).
15. Ridderbos (1987, 373).
16. Baarlink (1998, 75; cf. 62–74).

we must vigorously reject any standpoint that views Christ's work on the cross exclusively in an illustrative-ethical-exemplarist way. Jesus did not simply die "for" believers in the sense of showing them the way they themselves must walk, but he died especially "for" them in the sense of dying instead of them, in their place, on their behalf.

The argument that God was unfair in making the innocent One suffer for guilty ones. For instance, according to J. Weaver, the substitution model implies an unbiblical notion of violence, which supposedly contradicts God's nature.[17] He therefore prefers the *Christus Victor* model. This is a helpful model, but it represents only one aspect of Christ's work on the cross; the substitution model is just as important, and represents another important aspect of Christ's work. Those who wish to eliminate violence from their model of redemption must also surrender the idea of divine judgment altogether, which contains just as much violence; consider this, for instance:

> God considers it just to repay with affliction those who afflict you, . . . when the Lord Jesus is revealed from heaven with his mighty angels in flaming fire, inflicting vengeance on those who do not know God and on those who do not obey the gospel of our Lord Jesus. They will suffer the punishment of eternal destruction, away from the presence of the Lord and from the glory of his might (2 Thess. 1:6–9).

With regard to an innocent One suffering for others, let us not forget that God did not arbitrarily select a will-less victim. Jesus ho voluntarily presented *himself* to God as the required offering (John 10:17–18; 15:13; Gal. 1:4; 2:20; Eph. 5:2, 25; Titus 2:14):

---

17. Weaver (2001).

When he said above [v. 5-6], "You have neither desired nor taken pleasure in sacrifices and offerings and burnt offerings and sin offerings" (these are offered according to the law), then he added [v. 7], "Behold, I have come to do your will." He does away with the first [i.e., the Sinaitic sacrifices] in order to establish the second [i.e., Christ's own sacrifice]. And by that *will* [of Christ] we have been sanctified through the offering of the body of Jesus Christ once for all (Heb. 10:4-10 [Ps. 40:6-8]).

We must keep in mind yet another point. On the cross, Jesus was in fact no longer the innocent One because—in a mysterious way, which we cannot fathom—God had made him *to be* sin (2 Cor. 5:21), and had laid the sins of believers upon him (1 Pet. 2:24). He died as if he were the very cause or essence of sin. *In this sense*, he was so disgusting to God that the latter had to turn his face away from him; he forsook him.

Some people have difficulty with the traditional model because, to them, it implies that God is a cruel monster who wants to see blood (cf. §§2.5.4 and 11.6.1). For instance, V. Brümmer believed that the traditional atonement model might suggest that "it seems as if God wants to see blood before he can accept us again."[18] In my view, such an idea overlooks the fact that Christ's vicarious offering cost *him*—God—everything: his own beloved Son (Rom. 8:32). God is not a bloodthirsty dragon looking around for a victim. He is not just the demanding God but first and foremost the *giving* God: to be sure, he demanded a sacrifice—but he himself provided that. This is the grand and glorious message of Genesis 22: "God will provide for himself the lamb for a burnt offering" (v. 8).

There is also this aspect: if it is unfair that the innocent die for the guilty, God amazingly expects the very same attitude and willingness from his children; or, to put it more gently: he want his children to be ready to

---

18. Brümmer (2005, 13).

give their lives for their fellow believers: "By this we know love, that he laid down his life for [Gk. *huper*, for the benefit of] us, and we ought to lay down our lives for [*huper*, for the benefit of] the brothers" (1 John 3:16).

In Malachi 3:17 we find a rule that every sensible human can understand and accept. God says, "I will spare them [i.e., the faithful of Israel] as a man spares his son who serves him" (cf. Exod. 4:22–23). A man may chastise a son who misbehaves—but everyone understands that a man cherishes the son who behaves according to his wishes. However, God himself did the reverse: he said, "This is my beloved Son, with whom I am well pleased" (Matt. 3:17; 17:5). Yet, he "did *not* spare his own Son but gave him up for us all" (Rom. 8:32).

9.3 Expiation and Propitiation
9.3.1 God's Fury Appeased?

The aspect of *satisfaction* is much more complex than that of substitution, and therefore involves many more questions and misunderstandings. In this and the next sections, I will try to shed some light on these matters. We must begin by explaining the important difference between the theological terms *expiation* and *propitiation*,[19] before we discuss the subject of satisfaction (§9.5). The Latin term *expiatio* comes from the verb *expio*, "to cleanse from sin (through an atoning sacrifice), set free from guilt, do penance, patch up, mend, turn off the bad effects (of something)." These meanings connect very well with those of the Hebrew root *k-p-r* and the Greek verb *hilaskomai*. Yet, the word "expiation" and its cognates rarely occur in English Bible translations; I found one reference in the NASB (Num. 35:33), and three in the AMPC (Dan. 9:24; Hos. 12:8; Heb. 10:9), and a few others (none in the KJV, ESV, and NIV).

The enumerated meanings of *expiation* indicate what the focus of an atoning (expiating) sacrifice is the guilty

---
19. Cf. *DNTT* 3:151; Demarest (1997, 180).

person, whereas *propitiation* focuses more on God. The atoning sacrifice provides satisfaction to God (this is more the *propitiation* aspect), and involves blotting out human guilt (this is more the *expiation* aspect): "I, I am he who blots out your transgressions for my own sake, and I will not remember your sins" (Isa. 43:25; cf. Jer. 31:34).

The meanings of expiation and propitiation overlap. For instance, sometimes the verb *expio* has the meaning of "conciliatorily appeasing (the fury of) God (or the gods)." This meaning is closely related to the Latin term *propitiatio*, derived from *pro*, "for," and *peto*, "to reach (for something), seize, aspire, strive." The Latin noun *propitiatio* is related to the English adjective *propitious*, which is used of God, or the gods, and means "merciful, benevolent, favorably minded." Thus, the Latin verb *propitio* means, "to render merciful, benevolent, favorably minded," in short: "to propitiate." Thus, propitiation is the action through which God, or the gods, is/are propitiated, rendered merciful, benevolent, conciliatory. A parallel term is the Latin term *placatio*, "soothing (appeasing, mitigating, pacifying, mollifying, alleviating)" the fury of God, or the gods. We know this idea in everyday life through expressions such as making a conciliatory gesture, speaking in a conciliatory (soothing, appeasing) way, in order to propitiate the other person, calm down their fury, render them in a favorable, gentle mood.

Applied to God, this seems to mean that the sacrifice of Jesus brought about a certain change of mind or mood in God: his fury (wrath, anger) has been replaced with mildness, affability, gentleness.[20] In coming sections we must investigate whether such an idea of placating the God of the Bible is indeed biblical. In other words: what may be common in the case of the pagan gods (appeasing their fury, rendering them benevolent), might not

---

20. Berkouwer (1965, 267); Hodges (1955, 45).

be the case at all with the God of the Bible.

The Vulgate clearly shows a preference for *propitiatio* and its cognate forms. Thus, *propitius* appears in Luke 18:13, *propitiatio* in 1 John 2:2, 4:10, *repropitio* in Hebrews 2:17, and *propitiatorium*, "mercy seat," in Hebrews 9:5; *propitiatio* or *propitiatorium* in Romans 3:25. In the English translations, however, "propitiation" and related words are almost as rare as expiation; the KJV uses it only in Romans 3:25, 1 John 2:2, and 4:10. The usual terms are "atonement" and" reconciliation" and their cognate forms.

9.3.2 The Placation

The notion of propitiation in the sense of placation (soothing, appeasing) has deeply penetrated traditional theology. The Latin *placatio* comes from the verb *placo*, "to bring to rest, to calm," and hence: "to propitiate." In connection with atonement this means propitiating God, bringing about his change to a favorable mood with regard to the sinner, namely, through a sacrifice.

Let me mention here a few examples of the theological application of this idea. John Calvin wrote,

> The Spirit usually speaks in this way in the Scriptures: "God was men's enemy until they were reconciled to grace by the death of Christ" [Rom. 5:10 p.]. "They were under a curse until their iniquity was atoned for by his sacrifice." [Gal. 3:10, 13 p.] . . . [Scripture teaches that Christ] purged with his blood those evils which had rendered sinners hateful to God; that by this expiation he made satisfaction and sacrifice duly to God the Father; that as intercessor he has appeased God's wrath [Lat. *Iram eius fuisse placatum*]; *that on this foundation rests the* peace of God with men; that by this bond his benevolence is maintained toward them.[21]

---

21. Calvin (1960, 2.16.2).

I cannot agree that this is a proper presentation of the matter. God is *never* called the "enemy" of humanity (see below), and similarly, the Bible *never* says that God had to be "reconciled" to humanity. Nevertheless, the Canons of Dordt (5.7) also speak of believers experiencing "the favor of a reconciled God."[22] The Annotation to 1 John 2:2 in the Dutch States Translation stated that Christ "satisfying the righteousness of God, pacifies the wrath of God, and so reconciles God to men,"[23] referring to 2 Corinthians 5:21, whereas verse 20 says exactly the opposite: people must be reconciled to *God*. The Belgic Confession begins Article 21 by stating,

> We believe that Jesus Christ is ordained with an oath to be an everlasting High Priest, after the order of Melchizedek; and that He has presented Himself in our behalf before the Father, to appease His wrath [Lat. *ad iram ipsius . . . placandum*] by His full satisfaction, by offering Himself on the tree of the cross, ...[24]

Another example is L. Berkhof, who wrote that "the atonement was intended to propitiate God and to reconcile Him to the sinner."[25] Notice the distinction between atonement and propitiation: atonement has the aim of propitiating (appeasing) God. For the rest, we find here once again the unbiblical statement that it is God who must be reconciled to the sinner, instead of the reverse (or at least the reverse is not mentioned). Please note that it would be entirely incorrect to argue that, if A is reconciled to B, then B is reconciled to A. If A behaves consistently as a hostile enemy, whereas B remains friendly toward A, then A must be reconciled to B, but not B to A.

In my view, this entire view starts from various im-

---

22. Dennison (2008, 4:145).
23. Haak (1918, ad loc.).
24. Dennison (2008, 2:436); cf. Van Genderen and Velema (2008, 523).
25. L. Berkhof (1981, 411); see also Lekkerkerker (1949, 67–72).

balanced or exaggerated notions.[26] In the New Testament God is *never* described as an enemy of people, but by nature people are definitely enemies of God (Rom. 5:10; 8:7; Col. 1:21; James 4:4). Therefore, the New Testament never says that God must be reconciled to sinners, but it definitely says that sinners must be reconciled to God (Rom. 5:10; 2 Cor. 5:18-20; Eph. 2:16; Col. 1:20-21). The Bible does not contain the thought that the atoning sacrifice would be needed to appease a furious God. The idea that Jesus, the Mediator, intervened between God and humanity to prevent him from destroying all people—like an anxious mother intervening between a furious father and his naughty children—is totally foreign to Scripture. On the contrary, I cannot emphasize enough that it was the *loving* God himself who took the initiative in providing the atoning sacrifice, and who was prepared to sacrifice even his only beloved Son. It is not a furious God who must be appeased, but people raging against the Most High in their sins (Ps. 2:1 KJV).

Thus, J. Verkuyl correctly observed that "God was not moved to love through the drama of Golgotha, but the drama of Golgotha is the deepest expression of God's love."[27] He and others have properly contradicted, implicitly or explicitly, contrary utterances of Calvin or of ancient confessional writings. It is therefore strange that C. van der Wal wrote, "The Reformed confession has never said that the Judge of heaven and earth had to be moved to another, milder attitude toward guilty, sinful humans through the bitter sufferings and death of the Lord Jesus Christ on the cross."[28] The quotations from confessional documents given above prove the opposite.

---

26. Cf. Brunner (1934, 470-71); Korff (1942, 2:180, 193-94); Bolkestein (1945, 95-98); Shelton (2006, 63-74), and references there.
27. Verkuyl (1992, 242).
28. Van der Wal (1973, 69).

9.3.3 More Comments

Of course, rejection of such notions as placation has all too easily led theologians to opposite extremes. This was certainly the case, for instance, with theologians like G. H. ter Schegget and H. Wiersinga. Yet their criticism of the placation idea was perfectly correct.[29] For instance, Ter Schegget wrote, "Reconciliation is not that people. . . . propitiate God through religious acts [such as sacrifices]. It is God himself who comes to us, and reconciles the world. The world must be renewed, not he."[30] And later,

> God (subject!) is reconciling the world to himself. The fact that God remains subject of his reconciliation, that from eternity he is the One loving humans, is the unrelinquishable freedom of his subjectivity. It is not the other way round: we are not "reconciling" God, changing his mood, pleasing God, getting God on our side, making God different.[31]

The New Testament does not teach that Jesus appeased the wrath of God, let alone the wrath of "the Father" (see the quote from the Belgic Confession in the previous section). It does speak of the wrath of God, but this concerns the irreconcilable wicked people who continue to manifest themselves as enemies of God (Matt. 3:7; Luke 3:7; John 3:36; Rom. 1:18; 2:5, 8; 3:5; 4:15; 5:9; 9:22; 10:19; Eph. 2:3; 5:6; Col. 3:6; 1 Thess. 1:10; 2:16; 5:9; Rev. 6:16–17; 11:18; 14:10; 16:19; 19:15). Jesus vicariously underwent the consequences of this wrath, namely, the punishment for sins. But nowhere in the New Testament do we encounter the idea that Jesus' sacrifice was needed to bring God in a favorable mood with respect to sinners. God *already* was in a favorable mood toward

---

29. Wiersinga (1971; 1972); Ter Schegget (1999); see also Brümmer (2005, 131–39).
30. Ter Schegget (1999, 7).
31. Ibid., 63.

Substitution and Satisfaction

sinners, for it was he himself who, in perfect love, gave his own beloved Son as an atoning sacrifice for them.

Some have tried to read the notion of placation into 1 John 2:1-2:

> My little children, I am writing these things to you so that you may not sin. But if anyone does sin, we have an advocate with the Father, Jesus Christ the righteous. He is the propitiation for our sins, and not for ours only but also for the sins of the [better: also for the] whole world.

Jesus being the advocate with the Father would then suggest that Jesus function is to bring the Father in a favorable mood.[32] However, this example is quite inappropriate because verse 1 does not at all refer to the One bringing about reconciliation by appeasing God's wrath with regard to sinners. On the contrary, he is the intercessor with the *Father* for the benefit of those who are already God's own *children*, and thus already beloved by him (cf. Heb. 2:18; 4:14-16; 7:25; John 16:27; 1 John 3:1).[33] In fact, the idea that God the Father can still be angry with his children is unknown in the New Testament.

The entire issue is related to the distinction between propitiation and reconciliation, which is sometimes blurred by the word "atonement." As we have seen, the latter word, "at-one-ment," was derived from the idea of reconciliation—making two formerly hostile parties into "one"—but in practice the term is often used in the sense of propitiation. The two are both sides of the one work of Christ on the cross, but the distinction must be carefully maintained. Propitiation is that aspect of Christ's work that is *directed toward God*, in order to remove sin by enduring in his own person the divine judgment upon sin. Reconciliation, however, is *directed*

---

32. Morris (1965, chapters 5 and 6); Hill (1967, chapter 2).
33. *Contra* Marshall (1978, 118-19), although he expresses himself carefully.

toward people, in order to bring repentant sinners back to God.³⁴ Both aspects are perfectly true and appropriate; confusing them means losing much and attenuating everything. Far more serious is that this confusion leads to presenting God's character mistakenly, as if through Christ he changed from a furious Judge into a loving Father. Even in judgment, God was and is always the loving God. He himself lovingly prepared the sacrifice, which would accomplish both what was needed for God (satisfaction), and what was need for humanity (reconciliation, redemption, forgiveness).

9.4 Placationism *versus* Theopaschitism
9.4.1 Propitiation and the Wrath of God

Although the idea of the placation goes much too far, propitiation cannot be entirely severed from the notion of the wrath of God.³⁵ But the opinions differ widely as to the extent of such a connection. Some have argued that it is not God who is propitiated but sin; it is not God who must be appeased—on the contrary, God himself is the giver of the sacrifice—but sin must be removed from before him.³⁶ C. Brown has dealt extensively with the objections to the notion of propitiation, and prefers the notion of expiation.³⁷ Brown concluded that the authors of the Old Testament as well as the translators of the Septuagint were unsympathetic to the gross pagan idea of propitiating a capricious and malevolent deity.³⁸

In my view, this is correct with respect to placation. Yet, we may distinguish between the notion of appeasing a furious deity, and rendering a holy God favorable

---

34. Kelly (1927, 24).
35. Cf. Berkouwer (1965, 258-61).
36. Westcott (1883, 85-87); Dodd (1935, 82-95); Verkuyl (1992, 241).
37. *DNTT* 3:151-60; he referred to G. F. Oehler, G. von Rad, and J. Herrmann for the Old Testament teaching, and to C. H. Dodd and L. Morris for the New Testament teaching.
38. *DNTT* 3:157.

toward the sinner. The Greek verb *(ex)hilaskomai* can indeed involve the notion of propitiation, even though in the Septuagint this appears only three times: "Now the people of Bethel had sent Sharezer and Regem-melech and their men to entreat the favor of [lit., appease the face of; YLT] the LORD" (Zech. 7:2). "Many peoples and strong nations shall come to seek the LORD of hosts in Jerusalem and to entreat the favor of [lit., appease the face of; YLT] the LORD" (8:22). "And now entreat the favor of [lit., appease the face of; YLT] God, that he may be gracious to us. With such a gift from your hand, will he show favor to any of you? says the LORD of hosts" (Mal. 1:9). These are *only* three times; C. H. Dodd therefore treats them as exceptions.[39] Moreover, there is no parallel for this in the New Testament, though it is true that both Philo and Flavius Josephus, as well as the apostolic fathers, always use the Greek verb *hilaskomai* in the sense of propitiation (appeasing God).

Perhaps C. K. Barrett offered the proper balance here.[40] He argued that it would be wrong to ignore that expiation has, as it were, the effect of propitiation. That is, the sin that could have aroused God's anger is expiated, according to God's own will, and thus is no longer able to arouse God's anger. M. Erickson referred to Romans 3:24–26:

> . . . Christ Jesus, whom God put forward as a propitiation [Gk. *hilastērion*] by his blood, to be received by faith. This was to show God's righteousness, because in his divine forbearance he had passed over former sins. It was to show his righteousness at the present time, so that he might be just and the justifier of the one who has faith in Jesus.

Here, Erickson argued, the notion of propitiation cer-

---

39. Dodd (1935, 86–87).
40. Barrett (1957, 78).

tainly seems to be in the background: in the past, God had left sins unpunished.[41] It was conceivable that God could be accused of having condoned sin since he had not demanded any punishment for it. However, now he has put forward Jesus as a *hilastērion*. This proves both that God is righteous (his *wrath* required the sacrifice), and that he is the justifier of those who have faith in Jesus (his *love* provided the sacrifice for them).

No expositor has expressed the matter as sharply as J. Murray. He argued that it is one thing to say that Jesus' atoning sacrifice has led the angry God to an attitude of love toward sinners. That would be totally incorrect. It is another thing to say that the angry God loves. That is to say (I would add), the angry God finds a way of love to appease, so to speak, his own anger. This seems to me perfectly correct.

In summary, the propitiation that Jesus brought about did not bring a furious God into a favorable mood. In other words, it was not a *placation*, so that we could better avoid this word altogether. What propitiation did accomplish was that God prepared a way whereby both his wrath toward human sins and his love for sinners found perfect satisfaction. Or even more sharply—for we cannot deny that God's wrath also involved the *sinner* (John 3:36; Rom. 2:8; 9:22; Eph. 5:6; Col. 3:6; 1 Thess. 1:10; 5:9; Rev. 6:16; 14:10)—the *same* propitiation that gave satisfaction to God's wrath toward the sinner also furnished a way for God to show his love for the sinner.

9.4.2 Theopaschitism

One who vigorously rejects the notion of the placation (appeasing God's wrath), and vigorously insists that the initiative for reconciliation began with God himself, and that he gave his own Son for this purpose, can easily land in the other extreme. Over against placationism, we find *theopaschitism*, the doctrine that God himself

---

41. Erickson (1998, 829).

suffered on the cross.[42] Sometimes this doctrine took the form of *patripassianism*, which argues that, because the Son is only a "mode (of being)" of the Father, it was the Father himself who suffered on the cross.[43] Father and Son coincide here to such an extent that it is one and the same to say that the Son suffered on the cross and that the Father suffered there.

The whole idea is the very opposite of the early Christian (but in fact pagan) doctrine of God's *impassibility*: God cannot suffer. This idea even seems to reverberate in the Westminster Confession of Faith (II.1), which claims that God is "without body, parts (Deut. 4:15–16; John 4:24; Luke 24:39), or *passions* (Acts 14:11, 15); . . . ."[44] Such a statement clearly conflicts with the many biblical passages about God's emotions, such as his anger (e.g., Rev. 14:10; 16:19), joy (e.g., Zeph. 3:17), grief (e.g., Gen. 6:6; Ps. 78:40), love (e.g., John 3:16) hatred (e.g., Ps. 5:5; Isa. 1:14; Amos 6:8), and even disappointment (e.g., Isa. 5:2) and fear (e.g., Deut. 32:27).

Especially in Lutheran tradition, the notion of the "crucified God" is well-known, beginning with Martin Luther himself,[45] and culminating in the twentieth-century work of J. Moltmann.[46] Whether one begins with the thought that Christ is God, or with the thought that God is "in Christ" to such an extent that he experiences everything that Christ experiences, one is led to the notion of the suffering God. Not in the sense that God, or the Father, "suffers with" the Son (in sympathy or empathy with him), for that idea would be fully acceptable. No, the idea is that God suffers in his person.[47] "In Christ" it is God himself who bears our sins, or, as P.

---

42. Cf. Ouweneel (2007b, 115).
43. See ibid., 81–82, 84, 91.
44. Dennison (2008, 4:236–37; italics added).
45. See Olivier (1984).
46. Moltmann (1972).
47. See the discussion in Berkouwer (1965, 264–87).

Roscam Abbing put it, "He [God, not Christ!] made the affliction, the distress, the guilt, the sin of humanity to be his affliction, his distress, guilt, sin."[48] And, "[U]ltimately it is the case that also in heaven, in God's heart, judgment prevails because God denies himself and thus directs judgment at himself, and grants it validity; . . ."[49]

This is entirely in line with Karl Barth, who, when speaking of Christ's work on the cross, repeatedly adds in the same breath words like "that is, God himself": it is God who suffers, who bears the curse, who sacrifices himself for us.[50] Similarly, M. H. Bolkestein said, "God himself has brought the conflict between himself and us to a solution by bearing it in himself."[51] A. van de went to the point of saying that God pronounced the curse upon himself, and that God has borne the curse;[52] and elsewhere: "God has himself crucified . . . God himself accomplishes the work of atonement."[53] The last step in this thought development is that God made *himself* to be sin (cf. 2 Cor. 5:21).

This entire line of argument is incredibly inconsistent. This is immediately evident from the facts that Christ vicariously suffered under the wrath of God, and had to endure being forsaken by God. These matters cannot be reconciled with the notion of a "suffering God," unless one accepts the utter consequence, as Karl Barth indeed seemed to do, that *God* underwent the wrath of *God*, and that *God* was forsaken by *God*. In my view, we are just as far removed from biblical parlance here as in those views that interpret reconciliation as appeasing

---

48. Roscam Abbing (1950, 36).
49. Ibid., 129.
50. Barth (*CD* 2/1=8, §30.2:145).
51. Bolkestein (1945, 115) with reference to this same passage in Barth.
52. Van de Beek (1998, 155–56).
53. Van de Beek (2000, 106–107).

God's wrath in the primitive-pagan sense. Neither placationism nor theopaschitism satisfies in explaining the significance of propitiation.

9.4.3 The Middle Way

Between strict placationism and theopaschitism lay John Calvin's theological struggle, as he endeavored to give due honor both to the wrath of God and to the love of God.[54] The wrath of God, not only toward sin but also toward the sinner (e.g., Rom. 1:18), as well as the love God toward the sinner (e.g., John 3:16), are both biblical realities. In theopaschitism, the former threatens to be obliterated, in placationism, the latter. God himself is the subject of atonement: he took the initiative of stretching out his hand of reconciliation toward humanity, namely, by giving his own Son: "[I]n Christ God was reconciling the world to himself, not counting their trespasses against them, and entrusting to us the message of reconciliation. Therefore, we are ambassadors for Christ, God making his appeal through us. We implore you on behalf of Christ, be reconciled to God" (2 Cor. 5:19-20).

God made Christ, not himself, to be sin (2 Cor. 5:21). He made Christ, not himself, a curse (Gal. 3:13). Scripture supplies no basis for the speculation that God made *himself* to be sin and a curse. On the contrary, the face of a holy and righteous God had to turn away from him who, on the cross, had been made to be sin and a curse. It is no use arguing that Christ is God. That is true, but God is not Christ—God is Father, Son, and Holy Spirit, the Son being the person who became incarnate in the person of Jesus Christ.

It is perfectly true that God made our case—our lostness and guilt—to be his cause, in order to bring it to a solution in his endless love, without this love ever coming into conflict with his wrath toward sin as well as the

---

54. Berkouwer (1965, 284-87); cf. also Bavinck (*RD* 3:447-50).

sinner. It is perfectly true that God brought our case to a good outcome by paying a high price: his own beloved Son. It is perfectly true that, in and through Christ's work on the cross, both God's righteousness and his love have found perfect satisfaction. It is also perfectly true that the Christ who gave himself for his people is God: God the Son, the second person in the Godhead. But it is *not* biblical to say that God *himself* was made to be sin, or that (the immortal!) God *himself* gave himself unto death. God cannot die (1 Tim. 6:16)—but God the Son can "partake in blood and flesh"[55] (Heb. 2:14), and as such become able to die. This does not mean that God does die after all, but that God-the-Son-become-flesh died, which is not the same.

Placationism leaves insufficient room for the fact that God himself provided for himself a Lamb for the burnt offering (Gen. 22:7–8, 14), and that this was an act of his supreme love: "God is love. In this the love of God was made manifest among us, that God sent his only Son into the world, so that we might live through him. In this is love, not that we have loved God but that he loved us and sent his Son to be the propitiation for our sins" (1 John 4:8–10).

Theopaschitism lands in the other extreme: it emphasizes this aspect of God's love so strongly and one-sidedly that God is said to have given himself to be the Lamb for the burnt offering. What we emphasize over against placationists is that God himself gave his Son unto death. But what we emphasize over against theopaschitists is that this does *not* mean that God gave *himself* unto death. The Father and the Son go together, even to the cross (cf. Gen. 22:6, 8); they go together, even during the three hours of darkness. But the Father *is not* the Son. The Father gives the Son—not himself. To say otherwise would, as G. Berkouwer called it, be a "viola-

---

55. I have no idea why so many English translations transpose the order into "flesh and blood."

tion of the Trinitarian mystery."[56]

9.5 Satisfaction

9.5.1 Violated Justice

It is important to realize that criticizing the doctrine of propitiation, especially in its traditional placation form, does not necessarily affect the doctrine of satisfaction.[57] In the placationist version, we are dealing with a more psychological approach, as if atonement aimed at appeasing a furious God, and bring him to a more favorable mood. In the satisfaction doctrine, we are dealing with a more forensic approach; that is, not the wrath of God, but his honor and rights come to the fore. God's honor was violated by humanity: "You who boast in the law dishonor [Gk. *atimazeis*, from *timē*, "honor"] God by breaking the law" (Rom. 2:23). Compare Jesus' statement, "I do not have a demon, but I honor my Father, and you dishonor me" (John 8:49).

This is what satisfaction means in everyday parlance, as well. The injured party tells the injuring party, "I demand satisfaction," that is, the restoration of my violated honor and remuneration for the injustice done to me. Sometimes, in earlier centuries this was said in order to challenge another party to a duel (which could have left the dishonored person dead). Doing injustice to a person is to violate their rights, that is, to withhold from them what they are entitled to have, or to hurt, injure, or offend them.[58]

Of course, this does not mean that God's *intrinsic* honor could ever be violated by humans. Anselm of Canterbury wrote that "it is impossible for God to lose his honor,"[59] and that "as far as God is concerned, to his

---

56. Berkouwer (1954b, 352; 1965, 279-80).
57. Cf. Berkouwer (1965, 281-82).
58. Against this very doctrine of satisfaction Wiersinga (1971; 1972) aimed his arrows.
59. Cur Deus homo 1.14.

honor nothing can be added, and nothing can be taken from it."[60] What is at stake is his honor in relation to humanity: God honor that he should receive from humans is shortchanged.[61] In other words, his *rights* as Creator with regard to his creatures, which they must respect, have been violated. God is dishonored when he does not receive from his creatures what he is entitled to.

As far as the latter point is concerned, the Greek term *dikaiōma* is important, especially in the sense of "righteous decree" (or "just requirement," ISV):[62] of the wicked ones it is said, "Though they know God's righteous decree that those who practice such things deserve to die, they not only do them but give approval to those who practice them" (Rom. 1:32). "Righteous decree" is here this one word *dikaiōma* ("just requirement," the demands of God's justice), which also occurs in 8:4, "... in order that the righteous requirement of the law might be fulfilled in us, who walk not according to the flesh but according to the Spirit." As Creator and Lawgiver, God is the righteously requiring and demanding God. Where his requirements are not honored, and thus, where he himself is dishonored, it is consistent with his righteous being not to leave such behavior unpunished.

9.5.2 Satisfied Justice

No matter how loving God may be, no redemption can be valid in his eyes that does not involve satisfying his *justice*: "Zion shall be redeemed by *justice*, and those in her who repent, by *righteousness*" (Isa. 1:27). This implies that God does justice not only to *Zion* by judging Zion's enemies, but also to *himself* by bringing Zion

---

60. Ibid., 1.15.
61. Regarding the teaching of Anselm, cf. Ter Schegget (1999, 137-38); Van Veluw (2002, 163, 165-66), and Borger-Koetsier (2006, 32-34, 37-39).
62. See *TDNT* 2:219-23; *DNTT* 3:360-65.

to repentance and conversion through chastisement. Therefore, the gospel reveals not only God's love, but especially his *righteousness* (Rom. 1:17). Remarkably, in the sermons and speeches in the book of Acts, God's love is not mentioned once, but the term "right(eous)(ness)" and "justification" are emphasized so much more (3:14; 7:52; 10:35; 13:10, 39; 17:31; 22:14; 24:15, 25).

This righteousness that is presented in the gospel is not a threatening righteousness, as young Luther believed, but a redeeming righteousness: ". . . Christ Jesus, whom God put forward as a propitiation by his blood, to be received by faith. . . . It was to show his *righteousness* at the present time, so that he might be *just* [righteous] and the justifier [righteous-maker] of the one who has faith in Jesus" (Rom. 3:24–26). "If we confess our sins, he [i.e., God] is faithful and *just* [righteous] to forgive us our sins and to cleanse us from all unrighteousness" (1 John 1:9).[63]

No matter how loving God may be, he cannot deny his own being (2 Tim. 2:13): "For it was *fitting* [Gk. *eprepen*] that he, for whom and by whom all things exist, in bringing many sons to glory, should make the founder of their salvation perfect through suffering" (Heb. 2:10). The Greek verb *prepō* indicates what was "fitting" for God (KJV), what was appropriate in terms of his being (CSB). This is what he cannot escape or avoid, simply because he is *God*. There is a holy "must" here, which is entailed by his very being, and which we find several times in Jesus' own words: "From that time Jesus began to show his disciples that he *must* go to Jerusalem and suffer many things from the elders and chief priests and scribes, and be killed, and on the third day be raised" (Matt. 16:21, italics added; cf. Luke 9:22; 17:25). "[A]s Moses lifted up the serpent in the wilderness, so *must* the Son of Man be lifted up, that whoever believes in

---

63. For more discussion regarding justification, see Ouweneel (*RT* III/2).

him may have eternal life" (John 3:14-15). "The prophets said the Messiah *must* suffer these things before he begins his time of glory" (Luke 24:26 ERV; cf. vv. 44, 46; 22:37; Mark 8:31). "[H]ow then should the Scriptures be fulfilled, that it *must* be so?" (Matt. 26:54; cf. John 20:9). Paul "explained and proved that the Christ *must* die and then rise from death" (Acts 17:3 ICB, italics added).

All of this mean that the criterion for the nature and the extent of Christ's atoning sacrifice lay, on the one hand, in the love, grace, and mercy of God, but on the other hand, in God's righteousness and holiness. The two sides must never be played off against each other. The sacrifice *could* not be other than it actually was without falling short of God's love. But neither *could* it be other than it was without falling short of his righteousness.

Therefore I have difficulty accepting what K. Berger wrote:

> Of course one could wonder for what purpose Jesus' death on the cross was at all "necessary." *No, necessary it was not.* It [i.e., the crucifixion] was free wickedness of people. . . . [Their] wickedness and opportunism are in no way necessary for God's forgiveness. With respect to the murder of Jesus, God rather *repeats*, out of free grace, his willingness to forgive, as Jesus himself had already announced.[64]

If Berger puts the question in this form: Was this wickedness of people, that is, the crucifixion of Jesus, necessary for the salvation of believers?, then the answer is, strictly speaking: No. For their salvation, believers do not depend on the wicked acts of people (see §11.5). And yet, as to whether the *sacrificial death* of Jesus was necessary for the salvation of believers, the answer is a hearty Yes.

People killed Jesus; nobody is saved by this act as

---

64. Berger (2004, 315, italics added).

such; on the contrary, it simply increased human guilt. Jesus was "sacrificed"—but, strictly speaking, he was murdered but not "sacrificed" by people; their act did not have the character of a sacrifice to God. It was *God* who sacrificed Jesus, and it was Jesus who sacrificed himself. *God* gave his Son into death—*this* is what saves everyone who believes in him. The tension between these various statements will be explored more fully in chapter 11.

9.5.3 Satisfaction and Punishment

As far as the sinner is concerned, God requires satisfaction, namely, in the form of punishment; note the italics words in what follows: the wicked "will go away into eternal *punishment*" (Matt. 25:46; cf. Jude 1:7); they "will suffer the *punishment* of eternal destruction, away from the presence of the Lord and from the glory of his might" (2 Thess. 1:9; cf. Heb. 10:29); "the Lord knows . . . to keep the unrighteous under *punishment* until the day of judgment" (2 Pet. 2:9; cf. Jude 1:15). It belongs to the essence of the gospel of atonement that Christ vicariously endured this punishment: "[H]e was pierced for our transgressions, he was crushed for our iniquities; the *punishment* that brought us peace was on him, and by his wounds we are healed" (Isa. 53:5 NIV; cf. 1 Pet. 2:24b).

On the face of it, H. Berkhof was right in pointing out that, in the New Testament, the notion of punishment is not explicitly used with regard to Jesus' sacrificial death.[65] However, first, at least two passages come very close to this: "By sending his own Son in the likeness of sinful flesh and for sin, he condemned sin in the flesh" (Rom. 8:3); and, "Christ redeemed us from the curse of the law by becoming a curse for us" (Gal. 3:13). Second, from the absence of certain *terms* it cannot be concluded that the *content* of these terms is absent as well (think

---

65. Berkhof (1986, 310).

of terms like "substitution" and "Trinity," which are not in the Bible, but their content definitely is).

Berkhof pleaded for approximating Jesus' sacrificial death not in a one-sided judicial or cultic way, as has become common since Anselm, but also from the viewpoint of "the Johannine concepts of love, obedience, and glorification" (see 1 John 4:8–10; John 4:34; 8:29; 13:31; 17:4; cf. §7.2.2).[66] Indeed, I find this so important that I wish to maintain, on the one hand, with the synoptics Gospels and Paul, that a holy and righteous *God* made Jesus to be sin (2 Cor. 5:21), condemned sin in him (Rom. 8:3), and therefore had to forsake him during the three hours of darkness (Matt. 27:46; Mark 15:34). But on the other hand, I wish to maintain with John that the *Father*, together with the Son, went through the valley of the shadow of death:[67] "And he who sent me is with me. He has not left me alone, for I always do the things that are pleasing to him" (John 8:29). And just before going to his cross: "Behold, the hour is coming, indeed it has come, when you will be scattered, each to his own home, and will leave me alone. Yet I am not alone, for the Father is with me" (16:32).

What reader is not reminded here, again, of Isaac's "being bound" (Heb. *aqedah*, Gen 22:9), to ask it in the rabbinic way?

> And Abraham took the wood of the burnt offering and laid it on Isaac his son. And he took in his hand the fire and the knife. *So they went both of them together*. And Isaac said to his father Abraham, "My father!" And he said, "Here I am, my son." He said, "Behold, the fire and the wood, but where is the lamb for a burnt offering?" Abraham said, "God will provide for himself the lamb for a burnt offering, my son."

---

66. Ibid., 311.
67. Regarding the contrast between, on the one hand, God and the Man Jesus and, on the other hand, the Father and the Son, see Ouweneel (2007b, 115).

So they went both of them together—father and son (Gen. 22:6–8) (cf. §7.3.4). I think this is one of the most touching passages in the book of Genesis.

These two aspects (the God–Man relationship and the Father–Son relationship) can be confused is two ways. In my view, H. Berkhof confuses them by concluding from the latter that one should preferably not speak of the former (including the being forsaken by God).[68] J. Verkuyl confuses them by associating the fourth word on the cross with the "salvation bringing drama between Father and Son" instead of "between a holy God and the Man Jesus." We should not separate here, but we should certainly distinguish.[69] The *Father* gave his Son and, together with the Son, the *Father* went the Son's hard way of suffering. However, this way of the Father with the Son does not exclude the notion of a holy and righteous *God,* who had to forsake the *Man* Jesus Christ on the cross. Theologically, the two aspects should be carefully discerned. They touch not only upon the Trinitarian mystery but also upon the Christological mystery of the two natures of Christ; perhaps these two mysteries can be called the two greatest stumbling blocks in systematic theology.

9.6 Satisfaction, Love, Righteousness
9.6.1 Love

Traditional theology had little room for this aspect of the Son glorifying the Father out of love (cf. §§7.4.4 and 7.6.6). H. Berkhof emphasized this very aspect and sacrificed the traditional one for this one, whereas traditional theology has done the opposite. Time and again, the work that Jesus accomplished in John's Gospel was understood in a forensic sense. Take, for instance, the Annotation to the Dutch States Translation at John 17:4: "namely, [the work] of the reconciliation and redemp-

---
68. Berkhof (1986, 292).
69. Verkuyl (1992, 233); cf. Ouweneel (2007b, 115).

tion of mankind"; and regarding the saying, "It is finished," in John 19:30, "Namely, all that I was to suffer to reconcile men unto God, and that was foretold thereof by the prophets." But John's Gospel never speaks of reconciliation (atonement, propitiation, expiation) (and of forgiveness only once [20:23] in the sense of canon law). That is, in the Annotation, John's Gospel is treated in a synoptic and Pauline way, not in a Johannine way.

L. Morris came closer to the truth in saying, "*[E]rgon* here [John 17:4] stands for His complete life work. . . . Jesus' whole life was consistently spent in doing the will of God and in accomplishing His purpose."[70] In §7.6.6 we saw, though, that the forensic aspect is not entirely lacking here: the Greek word *tetelestai* ("It is finished") may contain the element of "paying off" a debt. Jesus really paid a debt on the cross; compare: "Does your teacher not pay [Gk. *telei*] the tax?" (Matt. 17:24); "because of this you also pay [Gk. *teleite*] taxes" (Rom. 13:6). Thus, *tetelestai* can mean "the price has been paid."

Indeed, the forensic aspect is not lacking in the Gospel of John; see especially: "Behold, the Lamb of God, who takes away the sin of the world! (1:29). And of course: "He Himself is the propitiation for our sins, and not for ours only but also for the whole world" (1 John 2:2 NKJV). "God . . . sent his Son to be the propitiation for our sins" (4:10). Conversely, the elements of the love of God (Rom. 8:32), the obedience of Christ (5:19; Phil. 2:8), and the glorification of God in and through Christ (2 Cor. 1:20; 4:6), are not at all lacking in Paul's letters. Thus, we emphasize the Johannine aspects without neglecting the Pauline aspects, in which the forensic element has its clearest place. The Belgic Confession (Articles 20 and 21) says,

> We believe that God, who is perfectly merciful and just, sent His Son to assume that nature in which the disobe-

---

70. Morris (1971, 689-91).

dience was committed, to make satisfaction in the same, and to bear the punishment of sin by His most bitter passion and death.... For it is written: "... the chastisement of our peace was upon Him; and with His stripes we are healed."[71]

The demanding righteousness of God is given primacy of place also in the Heidelberg Catechism (Q/A 40):

Why was it necessary for Christ to suffer "death"?
Because the justice and truth (Gen. 2:17) of God required that satisfaction for our sins could be mad in no other way than by the death of the Son of God (Heb. 2:9)."[72]

And the Canons of Dordt (2.1-3):

Article 1
God is not only supremely merciful, but also supremely just. And His justice requires (as He has revealed Himself in His Word) that our sins committed against His infinite majesty should be punished, not only with temporal but with eternal punishments, both in body and soul; which we cannot escape, unless satisfaction be made to the justice of God.

Article 2
Since, therefore, we are unable to make that satisfaction in our own persons, or to deliver ourselves from the wrath of God, He has been pleased of His infinite mercy to give His only begotten Son for our Surety, who was made sin, and became a curse for us and in our stead, that He might make satisfaction to divine justice on our behalf.

Article 3
The death of the Son of God is the only and most perfect sacrifice and satisfaction for sin, and is of infinite worth

---

71. Dennison (2008, 2:435-46).
72. Ibid., 2:779; see Ouweneel (2016, 124-25).

and value, abundantly sufficient to expiate the sins of the whole world.[73]

The word "Surety" (Gk. *engyos*), used in Article 2, appears in the New Testament only in Hebrews 7:22, but in the traditional doctrine of atonement appears much more often. This word, too, has a forensic meaning (see more extensively §10.6.2).[74] Jesus serves as the surety or guarantee of the new covenant. Particularly in Hebrews 7:22, this has an eschatological significance: he is the guarantee that all God's promises will be fulfilled. In the traditional doctrine of the atonement this word has especially a forensic meaning: Jesus is the guarantee that whoever comes to God in faith and pleads on the basis of the atoning work of Christ, will indeed receive salvation.

9.6.2 Righteousness

It is of essential importance to recognize that the cross is more than a proof of God's love, and that the gospel is about more than a God who in love accepts the penitent sinner. Regrettably, however, most people, including Christians, prefer hearing about God's love rather than about God's righteousness. Every Christian can quote John 3:16 ("For God so loved the world . . ."), but few Christians can quote Romans 1:17, which says that in the gospel "the *righteousness* of God is revealed from faith for faith, as it is written, 'the righteous shall live by faith.'"

As mentioned earlier, the sermons and speeches recorded in the book Acts remarkably speak of "righteous(ness)" but do not contain the term "love." If salvation were only a matter of the love of God, who graciously overlooks the sins of the penitent person, it would be incomprehensible why Christ's horrible work on the cross

---

73. Dennison (2008, 4:130).
74. See *TDNT* 2:329; *DNTT* 1:372.

was at all necessary. However, the gospel *is not* about the love of God only but about the *righteousness* of God: "[N]ow the righteousness of God has been manifested apart from the law, although the Law and the Prophets bear witness to it—the righteousness of God through faith in Jesus Christ for all who believe" (Rom. 3:21-22).[75] In other words, God grants salvation to a person not only because God is full of love but also because he is righteous: ". . . Christ Jesus, whom God put forward as a propitiation by his blood, to be received by faith. This was to show God's *righteousness* . . . at the present time, so that he might be *just* [righteous] and the justifier [righteous-maker] of the one who has faith in Jesus" (Rom. 3:24-26).

John expresses the same thought: "If we confess our sins, he is faithful and *just* [righteous; not only gracious and merciful] to forgive us our sins and to cleanse us from all unrighteousness" (1 John 1:9). This righteousness of God has to do with his holy demands. However, for the very reason that full satisfaction has been given on the cross to the *justice* of God, he does not have to demand anymore, but he can give. He is as magnanimous in his giving as he is strict in his demanding. Now that God's *justice* (righteousness) has been satisfied, it is also *just* (righteous) of God to forgive every person who penitently comes to plead on the basis of the atoning blood of Christ.

This point is of eminent importance. *Satisfaction* (if you wish, payment) has been given for every penitent sinner who comes to God, so that—reverently speaking—God would be unrighteous if he were to reject the sinner who comes to him with the confession of and sorrow for their sins. The sinner has not merited anything; but comes pleading on the basis of a Guarantor

---

75. Regarding this important expression "righteousness of God" in Rom. 1:17 and 3:21-22, see Ouweneel (*RT* III/2, especially §1.7).

who has merited it *for* him. Through the price that Christ has paid, God's honor and God's justice have been restored; satisfaction has been given to these divine requirements. Jesus Christ took upon himself the guilt of believers, so that through faith they now stand before God guiltless and sinless (cf. Matt. 18:27). He took upon himself their guilt (sins), so that they have been set free from the curse (Gal. 3:13). Even though, in a sense, it was Caiaphas and Pilate who pronounced this curse upon him, yet it was actually God himself who pronounced the curse upon his Son.[76] Jesus took upon himself the sin of believers, so that they could receive perfect forgiveness for these sins (1 Pet. 2:24).

9.6.3 The Sweet Exchange

This is the point where substitution and satisfaction come together; as the Latin phrase expresses the matter, *satisfactio vicaria*, "vicarious satisfaction." In the believers' stead, Jesus gave God satisfaction. The *Letter of Mathetes to Diognetus* IX (middle second century?) speaks here of a "sweet exchange":

> But when our wickedness had reached its height, and it had been clearly shown that its reward, punishment and death, was impending over us; and when the time had come which God had before appointed for manifesting His own kindness and power, how the one love of God, through exceeding regard for men, did not regard us with hatred, nor thrust us away, nor remember our iniquity against us, but showed great long-suffering, and bore with us, He Himself took on Him the burden of our iniquities, He gave His own Son as a ransom for us, the holy One for transgressors, the blameless One for the wicked, the righteous One for the unrighteous, the incorruptible One for the corruptible, the immortal One for them that are mortal. For what other thing was capable of covering

---

76. Van de Beek (1998, 155).

our sins than His righteousness? By what other one was it possible that we, the wicked and ungodly, could be justified, than by the only Son of God? *O sweet exchange!* O unsearchable operation! O benefits surpassing all expectation! that the wickedness of many should be hid in a single righteous One, and that the righteousness of One should justify many transgressors! (italics added).[77]

Martin Luther used the expression "wonderful exchange" in his work *The Freedom of the Christian*, as we hear in these words:

That is the mystery which is rich in divine grace to sinners: wherein by a *wonderful exchange* our sins are no longer ours but Christ's and the righteousness of Christ not Christ's but ours. He has emptied Himself of His righteousness that He might clothe us with it, and fill us with it. And He has taken our evils upon Himself that He might deliver us from them . . . in the same manner as He grieved and suffered in our sins, and was confounded, in the same manner we rejoice and glory in His righteousness (italics added).[78]

John Calvin, too, used the phrase:

This is the *wonderful exchange* [Lat. *mirifica commutatio*] which, out of his measureless benevolence, he has made with us; that, becoming Son of man with us, he has made us sons of God with him; that, by his descent to earth, he has prepared an ascent to heaven for us; that, by taking on our mortality, he has conferred his immortality upon us; that, accepting our weakness, he has strengthened us by his power; that, receiving our poverty unto himself, he has transferred his wealth to us; that, taking the weight of

---

77. http://www.earlychristianwritings.com/text/diognetus-roberts.html; cf. Eveson (1966, title: *The Great Exchange*).
78. Luther, WA 5, 608 (https://tollelege.wordpress.com/2009/11/19/a-wonderful-exchange-by-martin-luther/).

our iniquity upon himself (which oppressed us), he has clothed us with his righteousness (italics added).[79]

The latter phrase refers to 2 Corinthians 5:21, where this exchange is expressed as follows: the sins of believers descend upon him, the sinless One, and his righteousness descends upon them, the unrighteous ones.[80] A disparaging phrase like "the receipt theory of the atonement" does not do justice to this view of the atonement. We should not forget that phrases like "making satisfaction to God" and "making payment in the believer's stead" express only a forensic and a commercial metaphor, respectively, and taken together with other metaphors (§8.1), cannot fathom the depths of the divine atonement.

Regarding, on the one hand, propitiation and placation, and on the other hand, satisfaction, we should never overlook that the initiative for making atonement proceeded from God himself. God's love did not begin to function, in any sense whatsoever, only after his righteousness had received satisfaction (or after his fury had been appeased). His love and his righteousness existed and operated from the very beginning: God's love prepared a righteous path to atonement, and his righteousness prepared a path along which his love could become effective. His love for humanity was so great that he himself gave his own Son unto death. And his righteousness was so great that he did not diminish his holy and righteous judgment because this person was his Son. But his love was so great that this judgment descended not on guilty sinners but on his Son (cf. again John 3:16; Rom. 8:32; 2 Cor. 5:18-21; Col. 1:21; 1 John 4:10). This is what J. Heyns meant when speaking of both the *giving* and the *receiving* God in making atonement:[81] God received

---

79. Calvin (1960, 4.17.2).
80. Van Genderen and Velema (2008, 617).
81. Heyns (1988, 284-85).

full satisfaction, and he gave everything imaginable as a result of Christ's atoning work.

These two sides have received proper and timely emphasis lately—in part due to criticism of the traditional doctrine of satisfaction. Whatever modern people may think of it, we must maintain the notion of satisfaction because it is covered by the testimony of Scripture. But we should do this without any hint or taint of some kind of placation (appeasing the wrath of God), emphasizing instead the *giving* God. This is indeed "atonement through satisfaction" (Dutch: *verzoening door voldoening*)—but in this, God is not primarily the *Object* but the *Subject* of atonement.

Chapter 10
Resurrection and Reconciliation

[I]f while we were enemies we were reconciled to God by the death of his Son, much more, now that we are reconciled, shall we be saved by his life.
More than that, we also rejoice in God through our Lord Jesus Christ, through whom we have now received reconciliation.
Romans 5:10–11

For the love of Christ controls us, because we have concluded this:
that one has died for all, therefore all have died;
and he died for all, that those who live might no longer live for themselves
but for him who for their sake died and was raised. . . .
All this is from God, who through Christ reconciled us to himself
and gave us the ministry of reconcilia-

> *tion;*
> *that is, in Christ God was reconciling the world to himself,*
> *not counting their trespasses against them,*
> *and entrusting to us the message of reconciliation.*
> *Therefore, we are ambassadors for Christ,*
> *God making his appeal through us.*
> *We implore you on behalf of Christ, be reconciled to God.*
> *For our sake he made him to be sin who knew no sin,*
> *so that in him we might become the righteousness of God."*
>
> 2 Corinthians 5:14–15, 18–21

Summary: *Christ's resurrection is of essential importance: without it, believers would still be lost. Christ's glorification was the goal and crown of his work of redemption; we could not imagine redemption without the glorious Man at God's right hand. In both cases, the view of the Heidelberg Catechism is considered. Special attention is given to Hebrews 9:12 as to its correct translation and the redemptive significance: when and how did Jesus enter the heavenly sanctuary?*

Another important subject is reconciliation. The traditional view (God had to be reconciled to people) is incorrect: Scripture never calls God an "enemy" of humanity, and similarly never says that God had to be reconciled to people. It is rather the other way round: people must be reconciled to God, and—not to be forgotten—to each other.

Attention is paid to the crucial terms "mediator" (Christ is the intermediary between God and humanity) and "guarantor" (through his work, Christ has supplied the guarantee of salvation for all those who believe). Another subject is the threefold ministry in 2 Corinthians 5 and 3: the ministry of reconciliation, of righteousness, and of the Spirit.

Finally, attention is given to the theological distinctions between the blood, the cross, and the death of Christ.

10.1 The Resurrection of Christ
10.1.1 Saved by Christ's Death *and* Resurrection

CHRIST'S ATONING SACRIFICE contains a very important element that finds minimal expression in the Old Testament sacrificial ministry. This is the atoning significance of Christ's resurrection (§10.1) and glorification (§10.2).[1] In §5.6.2 we noted a reference to the resurrection in the living bird that, covered with the blood of the sacrificed bird, rises to the sky (in the law on leprosy). Generally speaking, though, it is difficult to imagine how the burnt, peace, sin, and guilt offerings could contain a metaphorical hint at the resurrection of Christ.

However, in the New Testament, the resurrection and glorification of Christ are of essential importance in his atoning sacrifice. To be sure, Jesus said at the end of his sufferings on the cross: "It is finished" (John 19:30)—but if, for some reason, he had *not* died a few moments later, the work certainly would *not* have been finished. Before his work on the cross, the Son had said to his Father, "I glorified you on earth, having accomplished the work that you gave me to do" (17:4). In both cases, Jesus spoke anticipatorily (§7.6.6): literally speaking, Jesus had not yet fully accomplished his work, but in his mind he saw himself beyond the cross (cf. Heb. 12:2, ". . . for the joy that was set before him . . ."). Moreover, even his dying was not enough: Jesus' work would not have been finished if he had not risen from the dead: "[I]f Christ has not been raised, your faith is futile[2] and you are still in your sins" (1 Cor. 15:17). An accomplished redemption

---

1. Cf. Ouweneel (2007b, 425–31); cf. extensively, Prince (2004).
2. Gk. *mataia*; "vain" KJV; "worthless" CSB; "useless" CJB; "a delusion" GNT.

is inconceivable without the glorified Man in heaven: "After making purification for sins, he sat down at the right hand of the Majesty on high" (Heb. 1:3); "when Christ had offered for all time a single sacrifice for sins, he sat down at the right hand of God" (10:12)

Regarding the resurrection, the testimony of Scripture is clear and manifest: Jesus "was delivered up for our trespasses and raised for our justification" (Rom. 4:25). "[I]f while we were enemies we were reconciled to God by [Gk. *dia*, through] the death of his Son, much more, now that we are reconciled, shall we be saved by [*Gk. en*, in (the power of)] his life" (Rom. 5:10). People are baptized into the death of Christ Jesus:

> We were buried therefore with him by baptism into death, in order that, just as Christ was raised from the dead by the glory of the Father, we too might walk in newness of life.... We know that Christ, being raised from the dead, will never die again; death no longer has dominion over him. For the death he died he died to sin, once for all, but the life he lives he lives to God. So you also must consider yourselves dead to sin and alive to God in Christ Jesus (Rom. 6:3-4, 9-11; cf. Col. 2:12).

"[I]f you confess with your mouth that Jesus is Lord and believe in your heart that God raised him from the dead, you will be saved" (Rom. 10:9). "[A]s by a man came death, by a man has come also the resurrection of the dead. For as in Adam all die, so also in Christ shall all be made alive" (1 Cor. 15:21-22). "[H]e died for all, that those who live might no longer live for themselves but for him who for their sake died and was raised" (2 Cor. 5:15). "According to his [i.e., God's] great mercy, he has caused us to be born again to a living hope through the resurrection of Jesus Christ from the dead" (1 Pet. 1:3; see further Rom. 7:4; 8:11; Eph. 2:6; Phil. 3:10; Col. 3:1; 1 Pet. 1:21; 3:18).

10.1.2 The View of the Heidelberg Catechism

The matter of which we are speaking has been summarized by the Heidelberg Catechism as follows (Q/A 45):

> *What benefit do we receive from the "resurrection" of Christ?*
> First, by His resurrection He has overcome death, that He might make us partakers of the righteousness which He has obtained for us by His death (1 Cor. 15:15, 17, 54-55; Rom. 4:25; 1 Peter 1:3-4, 21). Second, by His power we are also now raised up to a new life (Rom. 6:4; Col. 3:1-4; Eph. 2:5). Third, the resurrection of Christ is to us a sure pledge of our blessed resurrection (1 Cor. 15:12; Rom. 8:11).[3]

Here we find—not three but in fact—four important aspects of the resurrection of Christ summarized in one sentence:

(1) In the first point we see the *objective* aspect of the resurrection of Christ: together with his glorification, it formed the closure of his redemptive work. By overcoming death he was able to save those who had been held in the bondage of death.

(2) At the end of the first point we find the *subjective* aspect of Christ's resurrection, namely, regarding our *position in Christ*: believers have become God's righteousness in him (2 Cor. 5:21).

(3) In the second point mentioned in the Catechism we again see the *subjective* aspect of the resurrection of Christ, but now in its practical application regarding the believer's Christian walk in faith: they have been baptized into the death of Christ, in order that, just as Christ was raised from the dead, they too might walk in newness of life (Rom. 6:4).

(4) In the third point we find the *eschatological* dimension in Christ's resurrection: as Christ was raised, one day believers will be raised as well: "If the Spirit of

---

3. Dennison (2008, 2:779); see also Ouweneel (2016, 138-41).

him who raised Jesus from the dead dwells in you, he who raised Christ Jesus from the dead will also give life to your mortal bodies through his Spirit who dwells in you" (Rom. 8:11). Jesus said, "As the living Father sent me, and I live because of the Father, so whoever feeds on me, he also will live because of me" (John 6:57; cf. vv. 39-40, 44, 54). "Because I live, you also will live" (14:19). Paul wished to "know him and the power of his resurrection, and may share his sufferings, becoming like him in his death, that by any means possible I may attain the resurrection from the dead" (Phil. 3:10-11). I take this to mean that Paul wished to attain the resurrection either through the transformation of his body at Christ's second coming (vv. 20-21; cf. 1 Cor. 15:50-55), or, if necessary, through dying (even dying a martyr's death) first.

10.1.3 Theological Meaning of the Resurrection

Let me provide a brief seven-point summary of what the theological significance of the resurrection of Christ for the salvation of the believers.[4]

(1) *Forgiveness and justification:* Their sins have been forgiven, they have been justified by faith, and nothing or nobody can ever destroy them: "[H]e whom God raised up did not see corruption. Let it be known to you therefore, brothers, that through this man forgiveness of sins is proclaimed to you, and by him everyone who believes is freed from everything from which you could not be freed by the law of Moses" (Acts 13:37-39). The apostle Paul wrote:

> It will be counted [as righteousness] to us who believe in him who raised from the dead Jesus our Lord, who was delivered up for our trespasses and raised for our justification. Therefore, since we have been justified by faith, we have peace with God through our Lord Jesus Christ.

---

4. Ouweneel (2007b, 426).

> Through him we have also obtained access by faith into this grace in which we stand, and we rejoice in hope of the glory of God (Rom. 4:24–5:2);

Paul also wrote about "... his Son ..., whom he raised from the dead, Jesus who delivers us from the wrath to come" (1 Thess. 1:10).

(2) *A new creation:* Believers have been set free from a meaningless and empty sinful life, and transformed into new creatures in Jesus Christ, with a magnificent new significance and destination: you, believers, "have died to the law through the body of Christ, so that you may belong to another, to him who has been raised from the dead, in order that we may bear fruit for God" (Rom. 7:4). Christ "died for all, that those who live might no longer live for themselves but for him who for their sake died and was raised. ... Therefore, if anyone is in Christ, he is a new creation. The old has passed away; behold, the new has come" (2 Cor. 5:15–17).

(3) *Baptism:* Through baptism God's people have been made one with Christ, "in order that, just as Christ was raised from the dead by the glory of the Father, we too might walk in newness of life" (Rom. 6:4). Believers have "been buried with him [i.e., Christ] in baptism, in which you were also raised with him through faith in the powerful working of God, who raised him from the dead" (Col. 2:12). "Baptism, which corresponds to this [the salvation of Noah and his family through water], now saves you, not as a removal of dirt from the body but as an appeal to God for a good conscience, through the resurrection of Jesus Christ" (1 Pet. 3:21).

(4) *Seated in heaven:* Believers have received the life of the risen Christ, so that God now views them as having already been (spiritually) raised with Christ, and in him they have even been seated in the heavenly places: God raised Christ

from the dead and seated him at his right hand in the heavenly places.... And you were dead in the trespasses and sins in which you once walked.... But God, being rich in mercy, because of the great love with which he loved us, even when we were dead in our trespasses, made us alive together with Christ—by grace you have been saved—and raised us up with him and seated us with him in the heavenly places in Christ Jesus (Eph. 1:20; 2:1–6).

(5) *Intercession:* During their walk of faith, they may know that the risen Jesus, sitting at God's right hand, intercedes there for them: "Christ Jesus is the one who died—more than that, who was raised—who is at the right hand of God, who indeed is interceding for us" (Rom. 8:34). "[H]e is able to save to the uttermost those who draw near to God through him, since he always lives to make intercession for them" (Heb. 7:25; cf. 4:14–16).

(6) *Spiritual life:* Their actual spiritual life is there where the risen Lord is: "If then you have been raised with Christ, seek the things that are above, where Christ is, seated at the right hand of God. Set your minds on things that are above, not on things that are on earth. For you have died, and your life is hidden with Christ in God" (Col. 3:1–3).

(7) *Resurrection of the body:* If believers pass away before the second coming of Christ, they will be raised from the grave at his return: "If the Spirit of him who raised Jesus from the dead dwells in you, he who raised Christ Jesus from the dead will also give life to your mortal bodies through his Spirit who dwells in you" (Rom. 8:11). "God raised the Lord and will also raise us up by his power" (1 Cor. 6:14; cf. 15:12–23). "[H]e who raised the Lord Jesus will raise us also with Jesus and bring us with you into his presence" (2 Cor. 4:14). "[S]ince we believe that Jesus died and rose again, even so, through Jesus, God will bring with him those who have fallen asleep" (1 Thess. 4:14).

10.2 Glorification
10.2.1 Redemptive Significance

In a way similar to what we saw in §10.1, the ascension and glorification of Christ are of essentially important for the salvation of believers: "Christ Jesus is the one who died—more than that, who was raised—who is at the right hand of God, who indeed is interceding for us" (Rom. 8:34). God

> worked in Christ when he raised him from the dead and seated him at his right hand in the heavenly places, far above all rule and authority and power and dominion, and above every name that is named, not only in this age but also in the one to come . . . God . . . made us alive together with Christ—by grace you have been saved— and raised us up with him and seated us with him in the heavenly places in Christ Jesus (Eph. 1:20; 2:4-6).

Baptism is "an appeal to God for a good conscience, through the resurrection of Jesus Christ, who has gone into heaven and is at the right hand of God, with angels, authorities, and powers having been subjected to him" (1 Pet. 3:21-22). Christ entered heaven as our "great high priest" (Heb. 4:14), our "forerunner" (Heb. 6:20), our intercessor, "exalted above the heavens" (Heb. 7:26; cf. 9:24), and the One "securing an eternal redemption" (Heb. 9:12).

Notice especially the five times that the book of Hebrews speaks of the fact of Jesus being seated at God's right hand:

(1) *Accomplished work:* "After making purification for sins, he sat down at the right hand of the Majesty on high" (1:3). Here, Jesus' sitting at God's right hand is viewed as the result of—one could say, reward for—having accomplished the work of atonement.

(2) *Ruler of all:* "[T]o which of the angels has he ever said, 'Sit at my right hand until I make your enemies

a footstool for your feet'?" (1:13). Here, the sitting is viewed as placing the glorified *Man* Jesus higher than all the angels of heaven. A *Man* now rules the universe, including all spiritual powers.

(3) *Heavenly ministry:* "[W]e have such a high priest, one who is seated at the right hand of the throne of the Majesty in heaven, a minister in the holy places, in the true tent [or, tabernacle] that the Lord set up, not man" (8:1-2). Here, Jesus being seated is connected with his holy ministry, compared to that of the high priest in the Old Testament tabernacle.

(4) *Accomplished work:* "[W]hen Christ had offered for all time a single sacrifice for sins, he sat down at the right hand of God" (10:12). Compare (1).

(5) *Accomplished martyrdom:* "[L]ooking to Jesus, the founder and perfecter of our faith, who for the joy that was set before him endured the cross, despising the shame, and is seated at the right hand of the throne of God" (12:2). Here, Jesus sitting at God's right hand is viewed as the result of his martyrdom, and set as an example to believers.

The believers' "sitting in heaven" is viewed from two angles:

(1) *Present meaning:* In and with Christ, believers are sitting in the heavenly places (Eph. 2:5-6). That is, their place in heaven is so secure, as a result of Christ's work, that they are viewed as sitting there already now.

(2) *Future meaning:* Believers' sitting in heaven is viewed as a future prospect, to be reached at the end of their Christian walk of hardship and sufferings, just like Jesus' own walk on earth (Heb. 12:1-2). His *work* puts them there already now; his *example* places heaven before them as the end goal of their life of faith.

10.2.2 The View of the Heidelberg Catechism

The Heidelberg Catechism is clearly conscious of the redemptive significance of Jesus' ascension and glorification, as we see in Q/A 49:

> *What benefit do we receive from Christ's ascension into heaven?*
> First, that He is our Advocate in the presence of His Father in heaven (1 John 2:1; Rom. 8:34). Second, that we have our flesh in heaven as a sure pledge, that He as the Head, will also take us, His members, up to Himself (John 14:2; 20:17; Eph. 2:6). Third, that He sends us His Spirit as an earnest (John 14:16; Acts 2:33; 2 Cor. 5:5), by whose power we seek those things which are above, where Christ sits at the right hand of God, and not things on earth (Col. 3:1).[5]

This summary is certainly not complete (cf. the next section). But what strikes us is especially the reference to the Holy Spirit; as Jesus himself said, followed by John's comment: "'Whoever believes in me, as the Scripture has said, "Out of his heart will flow rivers of living water."' Now this he said about the Spirit, whom those who believed in him were to receive, for as yet the Spirit had not been given, because Jesus was not yet glorified" (John 7:38-39). Afterward, Jesus said, "[I]t is to your advantage that I go away, for if I do not go away, the Helper will not come to you. But if I go, I will send him to you" (16:7). The Holy Spirit had *worked* on earth from the very beginning (Gen. 1:2), but he could not *dwell* in God's people before Jesus had been glorified, that is, had accomplished his work, had returned to heaven, and had taken his seat at the right hand of God. Without the glorified *Man* in heaven, there could be no dwelling of *God the Spirit* on earth.[6]

Indeed, Jesus' finished work was the prerequisite for the outpouring of the Holy Spirit, and the glorified Jesus himself was the One who brought about this outpour-

---

5. Dennison (2008, 2:780); see Ouweneel (2016, 151-54).
6. See extensively, Ouweneel (2007a, 133-36, 155-56, 162, 164).

ing: "... the Helper comes, whom I will send to you from the Father, the Spirit of truth, who proceeds from the Father" (John 15:26; cf. 14:26). "Being therefore exalted at the right hand of God, and having received from the Father the promise of the Holy Spirit, he has poured out this that you yourselves are seeing and hearing" (Acts 2:33). One of the important aspects of this duality—a glorified Man in heaven, God the Spirit on earth—is that the task of the Holy Spirit on earth would be to bring to light the glory of the glorified Man in heaven. As Jesus said, "He [i.e., the Spirit] will glorify me, for he will take what is mine [i.e., my glory] and declare it to you" (John 16:14).

Characteristic of Judaism is that God is in heaven, and humanity is on earth: "The heavens are the LORD's heavens, but the earth he has given to the children of man" (Ps. 115:16). But characteristic of Christianity is that, since the Day of Pentecost, a glorified *Man* is seated at God's right hand in heaven while *God* the Holy Spirit dwells on earth: a Man in heaven, God on earth.

10.2.3 Theological Meaning of the Glorification

Let me once again provide a brief seven-point summary of the theological significance of the glorification of Christ for the salvation of believers.[7]

(1) *Accomplished work:* This glorification is the closure and crowning of the work of redemption accomplished by Christ: "I glorified you on earth, having accomplished the work that you gave me to do. And now, Father, glorify me in your own presence with the glory that I had with you before the world existed" (John 17:4-5). "[B]eing found in human form, he humbled himself by becoming obedient to the point of death, even death on a cross. Therefore God has highly exalted him and bestowed on him the name that is above every name" (Phil. 2:8-9). "He was manifested in the flesh, vindicated

---

7. Cf. Ouweneel (2007b, 431).

by the Spirit, seen by angels, proclaimed among the nations, believed on in the world, taken up in glory" (1 Tim. 3:16). "After making purification for sins, he sat down at the right hand of the Majesty on high" (Heb. 1:3). "[W]hen Christ had offered for all time a single sacrifice for sins, he sat down at the right hand of God" (10:12).

(2) *Triumph over the powers:* Christ's glorification involved his triumph over all the spiritual powers: "Let all the house of Israel therefore know for certain that God has made him both Lord and Christ, this Jesus whom you crucified" (Acts 2:36). God raised Christ "from the dead and seated him at his right hand in the heavenly places, far above all rule and authority and power and dominion, and above every name that is named, not only in this age but also in the one to come. And he put all things under his feet and gave him as head over all things to the church" (Eph. 1:20-22). "He [i.e., God] disarmed the rulers and authorities and put them to open shame, by triumphing over them in him [i.e., Christ]" (Col. 2:15).

(3) *Ruler over all:* Christ's glorification implies his kingship over all things: "All authority in heaven and on earth has been given to me" (Matt. 28:18). "[Y]ou have been filled in him, who is the head of all rule and authority" (Col. 1:20). ". . . Jesus Christ, who has gone into heaven and is at the right hand of God, with angels, authorities, and powers having been subjected to him" (1 Pet. 3:21-22).

(4) *Heavenly position:* Christ's glorification marks not only Jesus' present position but also that of believers in him: God raised Christ "from the dead and seated him at his right hand in the heavenly places. . . . But God . . . made us alive together with Christ . . . and raised us up with him and seated us with him in the heavenly places in Christ Jesus" (Eph. 1:20; 2:4-6).

(5) *Spiritual life:* The glorified Christ is the active "sphere" in which the believer walks and breathes: "If

then you have been raised with Christ, seek the things that are above, where Christ is, seated at the right hand of God. Set your minds on things that are above, not on things that are on earth. For you have died, and your life is hidden with Christ in God" (Col. 3:1–3).

(6) *Heavenly intercession:* Christ's priestly ministry in heaven is especially characterized by intercession and caring for the interests of believers: "Christ Jesus is the one who died—more than that, who was raised—who is at the right hand of God, who indeed is interceding for us" (Rom. 8:34).

> Since then we have a great high priest who has passed through the heavens, Jesus, the Son of God, let us hold fast our confession. For we do not have a high priest who is unable to sympathize with our weaknesses, but one who in every respect has been tempted as we are, yet without sin. Let us then with confidence draw near to the throne of grace, that we may receive mercy and find grace to help in time of need (Heb. 4:14–16; cf. 7:25; 8:1–2).

"My little children, I am writing these things to you so that you may not sin. But if anyone does sin, we have an advocate with the Father, Jesus Christ the righteous" (1 John 2:1).

(7) *Heavenly liturgy:* The glorified Christ is also the "minister" (Gk. *leitourgos*) in the heavenly sanctuary, the leader of the heavenly priestly worship of God's people: "[W]e have such a high priest, one who is seated at the right hand of the throne of the Majesty in heaven, a minister in the holy places, in the true tent [or, tabernacle] that the Lord set up, not man" (Heb. 8:1–2; cf. 2:12, Christ leading the congregational worship; 13:15, believers continually offering up a sacrifice of praise to God *through Christ*).

10.3 Entering (By? With?) the Blood of Christ
10.3.1 Hebrews 9:12

The previous sections do not necessarily imply that the glorification of Christ as such was part of the actual work of redemption. Hebrews 9:12 does seem to suggest this, at least in the NABRE: "[H]e [i.e., Christ] entered once for all into the sanctuary, not with [Gk. *di'*] the blood of goats and calves but with [Gk. *dia*] his own blood, thus obtaining eternal redemption." Notice two points here: first, the double rendering "with" for the Greek preposition *dia* (also in the NKJV); second, the word "thus" that is inserted (also in the ESV). To begin with the latter: I prefer the rendering "*having* obtained eternal redemption" (KJV).

The central question to be discussed is *when* Jesus' "entering into the [heavenly] sanctuary" actually occurred. If Jesus entered *with* his blood, are we not led to believe that this entering happened when Jesus was on the cross, during, or at the end of, the three hours of darkness? The moment Jesus shed his blood (his physical life) unto death was the moment when all the value of this blood appeared before the face of a holy and righteous God in heaven, and "thus" redemption was obtained. However, when we do not render the Greek preposition *dia* as "with" but "by (means of)" (KJV, ESV) or "through" (ASV),[8] and we translate "*having* obtained . . . ," then Christ's entering is naturally understood as referring to his ascension. After Jesus had obtained redemption when he was on the cross, six weeks later[9] he ascended to heaven "by means of" (which is equivalent to "by virtue of") his blood, which he had shed on the cross. Thus, the best rendering is still that of the KJV (followed by others: DARBY, BRG, CSB): "[B]y his own blood

---

8. Both renderings, "with" and "by," are possible; the choice must be made on contextual grounds; see Ouweneel (1982, 2:15).

9. There are 41 days between Good Friday and the Thursday of Jesus' Ascension; Jewish counting: 42 days.

he entered in once into the holy place, having obtained eternal redemption for us."

As surely as Hebrews 9:12 appears to refer to Christ's ascension, just as surely was eternal redemption obtained forty days earlier: through Jesus' death and resurrection. This work was not in some way completed when Jesus was glorified in heaven. It *was* already a finished work, and on the basis of it ("by, by virtue of, his blood") he ascended to heaven.

Several commentators underscore the important difference between "with" and "by," such as F. F. Bruce: "[O]ur author deliberately avoids saying that Christ carried His own blood into the heavenly sanctuary."[10] Jesus ascended to heaven, not *with* his blood but *by virtue of* his blood, shed six weeks earlier.

Those who still prefer the rendering "with," they have two options. They either may wish to just affirm the unbiblical idea that only at his ascension was Christ's work of redemption completed. Or they identify the "entering" with some other moment: whether the three hours of darkness on the cross, or the three days of Christ's death, or immediately after his resurrection. Such escapes are not needed if we follow the KJV, and the versions that followed it: "Neither by the blood of goats and calves, but by his own blood he entered in once into the holy place, having obtained eternal redemption for us." Redemption was obtained through death and resurrection, whereas the entering into the heavenly tabernacle occurred on the Day of Ascension.[11] The Greek phrase *di' haimatos* (or *dia tou idiou haimatos*) lays the connection between Jesus' death and his ascension. Through shedding his blood on Good Friday, he was able to enter heaven six weeks later.

---

10. Bruce (1964, 200–01); similarly Grosheide (1955, 207); Morris (1981, 85–86).
11. Cf. Berkouwer (1965, 207–209).

10.3.2 Typology

Because of the typological significance of the Day of Atonement, it is very attractive to think that Christ brought his own blood into the heavenly sanctuary at the time of his sacrifice. If so, this could only have been accomplished during his work on the cross. When Jesus surrendered his life in death, his blood, that is, his life as surrendered in death, appeared before God in all its magnificent value. But we must be careful here. It is impossible to extend the typology into the extreme. In the first place, Christ was not literally "slaughtered." His throat was not cut. When a sacrificial animal "gives its blood," so to speak, this means that the blood flows from the slit throat. But when Jesus gave his blood, there was no slit throat. Giving his blood meant precisely the same as giving his physical life into death. "Laying down his life" (John 10:17-18) is identical with "giving his blood."

Notice that in Greek the word "life" is here *psychē*, elsewhere rendered "soul," the equivalent of Hebrew *nephesh*. And notice the link between *nephesh* and *dam* ("blood"): "[T]he life [*nephesh*, soul] of the flesh is in the blood, and I have given it for you on the altar to make atonement for your souls, for it is the blood that makes atonement by the life. . . . For the life [*nephesh*] of every creature is its blood: its blood is its life [Heb. *nephesh*]" (Lev. 17:11, 14). "Only be sure that you do not eat the blood, for the blood is the life [Heb. *nephesh*], and you shall not eat the life [Heb. *nephesh*] with the flesh" (Deut. 12:23). Blood makes atonement through the sacrificial animal giving its life.

We must therefore be careful in linking the atonement with the literal blood that dripped from Jesus' wounds. The Bible teacher W. van de Kamp mentioned seven times that Jesus bled "for us," from Gethsemane to the cross, namely, in view of the believers' forgiveness, redemption, cleansing, healing, deliverance, atonement, and regeneration, respectively.[12] We cannot say, of course, that redemption has *nothing* to do with the blood from his wounds. Yet, I believe that it is not *this* blood that comes to fore when we speak of Jesus giving his blood. It is not true that, if Jesus' wounds had not dripped blood, there would be no redemption. The redemption lies in his giving up his *life*.

Moreover, notice that the wounds were inflicted on Jesus by Roman soldiers. They scourged him (Matt. 27:26), pressed the crown of thorns on his head (vv. 29-30), shed his blood by nailing him to the cross (v. 35), and a Roman soldier pierced Jesus' side so that blood and water came out (John 19:34-35). Scripture never emphasizes any redemptive value that these bleedings might have had. Believers are saved by Jesus' blood—not so much the blood dripping from his various wounds, but rather by the life that he surrendered in death. Take the piercing of Jesus' side after he had died: this was a testimony to Jesus having really died, but it had no atoning value in itself. It was not so much the wounds that people inflicted upon Jesus but the wound that *God* inflicted upon him: "[H]e [i.e., the Messiah] was pierced for our transgressions; he was crushed for our iniquities; upon him was the chastisement that brought us peace, and with his wounds we are healed. . . . [I]t was the will *of the Lord* to crush him [not: to have him crushed by others]; *he* has put him to grief" (Isa. 53:10; cf. 1 Pet. 2:24). "Awake, O sword, against my shepherd, against the man who stands next to me. . . . Strike the shepherd" (Zech. 13:7). I do not wish to *sever* this from the wounds that people inflicted upon him, but let us not say that wicked people contributed, by what they did, to the redemption of believers (see extensively §11.5).

Christ has "freed us from our sins by his blood" (Rev. 1:5; cf. Eph. 1:7), and forgiveness is through his blood "poured out." This is not so much by the blood that oth-

---

12. Van de Kamp (2005, summary: 44-45).

ers made flow from him, but rather the blood that he figuratively shed himself by laying down his life (see again §11.5). "Justified by his blood" (Rom. 5:9) means: justified by his self-surrender in death. Saying that Christ "gave his blood" is the same as saying that Christ "gave his life": "[T]he Son of Man came ... to give his life [Gk. *psychēn*] as a ransom for many" (Matt. 20:28).

In summary:

(a) When Christ laid down his life, his "blood" appeared before God in heaven in all its atoning value, just as the high priest entered the sanctuary with the atoning blood.

(b) Six weeks later, when Christ ascended to heaven, and personally entered the heavenly sanctuary, this was not "with" his blood but "by" (by virtue of) his blood, which had been shed six weeks before.

10.4 Is God an Enemy of Humanity?
10.4.1 The Sense of Reconciliation

In §4.1.1, I pointed to the difference between atonement in the sense of *propitiation* (Gk. *hilasmos*; Ger. *Sühnung*) and atonement in the sense of *reconciliation* (Gk. *katallagē* with the cognate verbs *katallassō, apokatallassō, diallassō*, and *sunallassō*; Ger. *Versöhnung*).[13] In the former case, sins are atoned for, that is, blotted out; in the latter case, people are reconciled to God, that is, brought (again) into harmony with God. Sins are removed *from* God, repentant sinners are brought back *to* God. The Greek verbs *(apo)kat-* and *diallassō* have been derived from *allassō*, "to change" (cf. *allos*, "other"; it is "change from one into the other"), "to alter" (from Lat. *alter*, "other"). The derivations mentioned point to a change in attitude (mentality, orientation); specifically: a person changing from a foe into a friend, either toward God or toward one's neighbor.

---

13. Regarding the latter terms, see *TDNT* 1:254–59; *DNTT* 3:151–66; Morris (1955, chapter 6); Ridderbos (1975, chapter 5, §33).

Often, this distinction has not been very well appreciated. For instance, as we saw, the word "atonement" (from "at-one-ment") originally had more to do with reconciliation (between parties), but in its common usage it is linked more with blotting out ("atoning for") sins. In Dutch, propitiation and reconciliation are both rendered as *verzoening*, apparently because, when Dutch theological terminology developed, the distinction was hardly perceived. German distinguishes between *Sühnung* and *Versöhnung*, but etymologically these words are closely related. Or take the KJV, which renders the Greek verb *hilaskesthai* as "to make reconciliation" (for the sins of the people) in Hebrews 2:17. The KJ21 maintained this mistake, but the NKJV corrected it: "to make propitiation for the sins of the people."

In my view, one reason for this lack of distinction is that propitiation has often been linked with placation, that is, the idea, that God's fury had to be appeased (§§4.2.2, 9.3–9.4). Thus, in *propitiation* the emphasis is not on atoning for sins—which is the root idea of *hilaskomai*—but rather on a change that must be brought about in God himself (cf. "propitiating the deity"). This change is then easily linked with the Greek verb *katalassō*, "to reconcile," in such a way that the emphasis is not on humanity reconciled to God but on God reconciled to humanity. Earlier we quoted L. Berkhof: "[T]he atonement was intended to propitiate God and to reconcile Him to the sinner."[14] Here, propitiation and reconciliation are mentioned in the same breath, as if they amount to the same thing. Here, propitiation is not propitiation for sins but *propitiating God*, and thus reconciling him to humanity. In my view, this error, going back at the earliest to Anselm of Canterbury, is foreign to Scripture; it originated in paganism.

In §9.3.2 I gave a few quotations from the Reformed

---

14. L. Berkhof (1981, 411); similarly Althaus (1949, 42); Murray (1968, 172).

world in which it was claimed that God was (or had been) an enemy of humanity, and that God had to be propitiated, whether in the sense that God must receive satisfaction for sin—which is correct—or in the sense that God must be reconciled to humanity, which is incorrect. The problem is that, in the pagan world, the Greek verb *katallassō* indeed had this latter sense. Here, atonement is always the initiative of humans toward the deity, who must be brought into a favorable mood. However, in the New Testament it is the very reverse. Here, God had not changed, but people had. God did not show hostility toward humanity, but humanity behaved in a hostile way toward God. Thus, God did not have to be reconciled, but *people* did.[15] At the same time, it was not people but God himself who took the initiative for this reconciliation.

Let me mention a few causes for the mistaken idea that God had to be reconciled. For instance, people confuse the fact that God is angry with sinners (e.g., Rom. 1:18) with the idea that therefore he is the enemy of sinners. This is a mistake. People can be very angry with their children precisely because they love them so much, and thus want to see them behave better. Compare this proverb: "[T]he LORD reproves him whom he loves, as a father the son in whom he delights" (Prov. 3:12; cf. Heb. 12:6).

Another confused idea is that, if party A must be reconciled to party B, then B must be reconciled to A. Indeed, this is often the case—but not always. The Latin verb *reconciliare* means "to make friendly again"; if B had remained friendly, and A was hostile, then A must be "made friendly again," not B. Humans had to be reconciled to God, not God to humanity. God may be angry because of people's sins, but he remains benevolent toward them, as he shows in the proclamation of the gospel. Thus, people need not try to render him favorable,

---

15. Grant (1956, 152).

for he *is* already benevolent toward them. Therefore, people do not take the initiative in reconciliation—God does (§10.5).

10.4.2 Biblical References

There are only a few Bible passages where we find the statement that God would have been an enemy to certain people, and they are all in the Old Testament: "But they [i.e., the Israelites] rebelled and grieved his Holy Spirit; therefore he turned to be their enemy, and himself fought against them" (Isa. 63:10). "All your [i.e., the Israelites'] lovers have forgotten you; they care nothing for you; for I have dealt you the blow of an enemy, the punishment of a merciless foe, because your guilt is great, because your sins are flagrant" (Jer. 30:14). "He [i.e., the LORD] has bent his bow like an enemy, with his right hand set like a foe; and he has killed all who were delightful in our eyes in the tent of the daughter of Zion; he has poured out his fury like fire. The LORD has become like an enemy; he has swallowed up Israel; he has swallowed up all its palaces; he has laid in ruins its strongholds, and he has multiplied in the daughter of Judah mourning and lamentation" (Lam. 2:4-5).

These few passages never deal with God's attitude toward the sinner in general, but with his temporary judgment upon Israel, in his ways with his rebellious people. God's "enmity" refers to what *in the end* he must do with people if they stick to their evil ways. His "hatred" refers to the same thing: "My heritage has become to me like a lion in the forest; she has lifted up her voice against me; therefore I hate her" (Jer. 12:8). It means that this enmity and hatred of God is linked with his anger regarding the sins of his people. The thought that God would basically be an enemy to, or would hate, the sinner in general, simply because one is a sinner by nature, appears in neither the Old Testament or the New Testament.

Nor does the New Testament explicitly contain the notion that God would be an enemy to, or would hate, people, or certain people. Therefore, F. Büchsel wrote,

> He [i.e., God] is not reconciled. Nor does He reconcile Himself to us or to the world. On the other hand, we are reconciled to God in R[omans] 5:9-10, or reconcile ourselves to Him in 2 C[orinthians] 5:20. Thus God and man are not on equal terms in relation to reconciliation. Reconciliation is not reciprocal in the sense that both equally become friends where they were enemies. The supremacy of God over man is maintained in every respect.[16]

I would add that this is not just a matter of God's supremacy but of his benevolent love toward humanity despite his anger concerning human sins.

It is true that, in Romans 5:9-10, human enmity is mentioned in the same breath with the wrath of God. But I repeat, wrath does not necessarily imply enmity. Wrath does not exclude benevolence at all. We have a striking example of this in Mark 3:5, "[H]e [i.e., Jesus] looked around at them [i.e., his opponents] with *anger, grieved* at their hardness of heart." Jesus was angry about the evil attitude of his opponents, but he did not hate them. On the contrary, his being grieved about the hardness of their hearts points to benevolence, and even love. As Jesus says elsewhere, "How often would I have gathered your children together as a hen gathers her brood under her wings, and you were not willing!" (Luke 13:34). *He* wanted, but *they* did not want. Notice as well that the book of Revelation can speak of the "wrath of the Lamb" (Rev. 6:16), where the Lamb the expression of self-sacrificing love (cf. 1:5; 3:9, 19).[17]

The very commandment, "Love your enemies" (Matt. 5:44), presupposes that a person does not behave

---

16. *TDNT* 1:255.
17. Hoek (1988, 80).

toward another person who is behaving like an enemy, in a hostile but in a friendly, benevolent way. If the other is an enemy toward you, you yourself are not necessarily an enemy. Thus, if people are called enemies of God, it does not mean that God is naturally an enemy of humanity. Sometimes, God says, "Ah, I will get relief from my enemies and avenge myself on my foes" (Isa. 1:24; cf. Ps. 68:1, 21; 89:10, 51; 92:9; Isa. 42:13; 59:18; 66:6, 14; Nah. 1:2, 8). But at other times, "I spread out my hands all the day to a rebellious people" (65:2; cf. Rom. 10:21). And in the New Testament, the emphasis on the latter is even stronger than in the Old Testament.

10.5 Human Enmity
10.5.1 Enemies of God and Each Other

It is not God who is an enemy of humanity, but it is humans who, because of their sinfulness, are enemies of God: "[W]hile we were enemies we were reconciled to God by the death of his Son" (Rom. 5:10). "[T]he mind that is set on the flesh is hostile to God, for it does not submit to God's law; indeed, it cannot" (8:7; cf. 11:28; 12:20). "And you, who once were alienated and hostile in mind, doing evil deeds . . ." (Col. 1:21). "You adulterous people! Do you not know that friendship with the world is enmity with God? Therefore whoever wishes to be a friend of the world makes himself an enemy of God" (James 4:4).

In general, this common enmity toward God usually does not join people together—with the rare exception of Herod and Pilate (Luke 23:12)—because the same corrupt heart also creates enmity between people; enmity it is a work of the flesh (Gal. 5:20; cf. 4:16). God reconciled Jews and Gentiles through their common faith in Christ, "thereby killing the hostility" that formerly had existed between them (Eph. 2:16). "[W]e ourselves were once foolish, . . . hated by others and hating one another" (Titus 3:3). This is a remarkable fact. We can imagine that, after the Fall, people began to hate God. But in their misery they also began to hate each other. The first recorded sin after the Fall was Cain's hatred toward Abel, which led to murder (Gen. 4:1-17; 1 John 3:12). The Fall was a "vertical sin" of humans toward God; this murder was a "horizontal sin" of one human toward another.

The Holy Spirit is the power by which converted hearts begin to turn hatred into love: "You have heard that it was said, 'You shall love your neighbor and hate your enemy.' But I say to you, Love your enemies and pray for those who persecute you, so that you may be sons of your Father who is in heaven" (Matt. 5:43-45; cf. Luke 6:27, 35). Please note that God never said "hate your enemy"; this was a sinful human addition to God's command. Therefore, Jesus' reply was intended as a correction not of the Mosaic Law but of the Pharisaic distortions of it.

There is another side to this truth as well (as there always is). It is true that the gospel reconciles people to God and to each other. At the same time, it creates a division between those who turn to Christ and those who reject the gospel. Jesus said, "Do not think that I have come to bring peace to the earth. I have not come to bring peace, but a sword. For I have come to set a man against his father, and a daughter against her mother, and a daughter-in-law against her mother-in-law. And a person's enemies will be those of his own household" (Matt. 10:34-36; cf. Micah 7:6; also see Ps. 41:9 [John 13:18]; 55:12-14). This enmity is not intended, but one that it an inevitable result of the gospel.

10.5.2 Active or Passive?
Interestingly, a theological problem is present here over which theologians have fought for centuries. In this human enmity toward God, are we dealing with what has been called the *active* or the *passive* enmity of humans?

The former refers to people's hostile attitude (feelings, utterances) toward God. The latter refers to a hostile relationship that supposedly originated through God's wrath toward humanity; it therefore exists quite apart from people necessarily *feeling* hostile, or *showing* any hostility toward God.

Both standpoints have found their adherents. Thus, Sandlay and Headlam[18] tried to refute J. B. Lightfoot, who believed that in the entire New Testament, the Greek word *echthros,* "enemy," refers to active enmity.[19] James Denney believed that the entire context of Romans 5 requires that we take "enemies" in the passive sense, especially because of Romans 11:28, "As regards the gospel, they [i.e., the Jews] are enemies for your [i.e., the Gentiles'] sake." Denney argued that, in a real sense, by nature all people are objects of divine enmity. As sinners, they lie under God's judgment, and his wrath hangs over them.[20] H. Ridderbos believed that the connection with Romans 5:9b (we shall be saved by Christ from God's wrath) clearly shows that the text is about passive enmity.[21] He and E. Harrison[22] appealed to both Romans 11:28 and Romans 5:9b. J. Murray believed that the kernel of reconciliation is not people's active enmity toward God and its removal, but God's alienation from us, and the means that God has provided for removing this alienation.[23]

Nevertheless, I prefer the view that Romans 5:10 refers to active enmity because I think this standpoint has better arguments. J. B. Lightfoot pleaded for this view. H. Bietenhard argued that, since the natural person rebels against God in their thinking and acting, they are a

---

18. Sanday and Headlam (1901, 129-30).
19. Lightfoot (1895, ad loc.).
20. Denney (1979, 625).
21. Ridderbos (1959, 111; cf. 1975, 184-85).
22. Harrison (1976, 60).
23. Murray (1955, 39-41; 1968, 172).

real enemy toward God.[24] In addition to Romans 5:10, he referred to Colossians 1:21, ". . . you, who once were alienated and hostile in mind, doing evil deeds, . . ." Bietenhard also mentioned Romans 11:28, arguing that, here, the as yet unbelieving Jews are enemies not in the passive but in the active sense, that is, because of their stubbornness. Therefore, R. Tasker argued that the enmity and alienation to be removed lie in humans, not in God.[25] That is, it is not simply the wrath of God that makes them enemies but their own evil attitude: "[W]e ourselves were once foolish, disobedient, led astray, slaves to various passions and pleasures, passing our days in malice and envy, hated by others and hating one another" (Titus 3:3).

Dale Moody called it incomprehensible how someone reading Romans 5:6-11 could entertain the thought that God is the enemy of humanity, even of powerless and wicked sinners. If the phrase, "while we were [still] enemies" (v. 10), is taken to include God—*God* and humanity were enemies—then we must be consistent and also say, "while God and humanity were still weak" (v. 6), and even that both God and humanity were sinners (v. 8). But no, it is humanity, not God, that is in a hostile state. The gradually descending hopeless human condition, in which people are described first as powerless, then as sinners, and finally as enemies, stands in opposition to God's love, which in the death of Christ is oriented toward humanity.[26]

W. Foerster took a middle position. He understood "enemy" in Romans 11:28 as passive because of the passive "beloved" as well as the expression "for your sake." But, he argued, this passage does not decide the proper understanding of Romans 5:10 because in that verse, the enemy is active. This is because Paul intends to show

---

24. *DNTT* 1:554.
25. Tasker (1963, 124).
26. Moody (1970, 194).

the greatness of the divine grace of forgiveness, which is granted to people who in their behavior are enemies of God.[27] Consider also Romans 8:7; Colossians 1:21; James 4:4, each of which verses imply active enmity. Together with Foerster I maintain that, no matter how one reads Romans 11:28 (opinions differ again), this verse must not dominate the exegesis of Romans 5:10. On the contrary, the parallels with the passages just mentioned seem to plead strongly for the notion of active enmity.

10.6 Mediator and Guarantor
10.6.1 Mediator

The New Testament places heavy emphasis on the person through whose mediation the reconciliation is brought about. He is the "mediator" (Gk. *mesitēs*, from *mesos*, "middle"): "[T]here is one God, and there is one mediator between God and men, the man Christ Jesus, who gave himself as a ransom for all" (1 Tim. 2:5-6); "he is the mediator of a better covenant, which was established upon better promises" (Heb. 8:6 KJV); he is "the mediator of a new covenant" (9:15; 12:24). The word *mesitēs* also occurs in Galatians 3:19-20, but here it refers to Moses, so that some translations, including the ESV, prefer the rendering "intermediary" (most translations: "mediator"). The verb that goes with *mesitēs* is *mesiteuō*, "to mediate," "to act as a mediator or guarantee": "So when God desired to show more convincingly to the heirs of the promise the unchangeable character of his purpose, he guaranteed [Gk. *emesiteusen*, AMPC: "intervened (mediated)"; KJV: "confirmed"] it with an oath" (Heb. 6:17).[28]

The New Testament never explicitly and directly links the mediator with the notion of reconciliation. Rather, in a wider sense he is the person who mediates between God and humanity, and through his atoning

---

27. *TDNT* 2:814.
28. See *TDNT* 4:598-624; *DNTT* 1:372-76.

Resurrection and Reconciliation

sacrifice brings people back to God: "Christ also suffered once for sins, the righteous for the unrighteous, that he might bring us to God" (1 Pet. 3:18). Yet, certainly implied in this bringing people back into harmony with God lies the idea of reconciliation.

A mediator is the person who mediates between the two parties involved in a covenant, an agreement, or a will.[29] When a covenant was made, the mediator looked after the interests of *both* parties. Thus, Jesus Christ took care of the interests of humanity by taking upon himself its obligations, and by undergoing for humans the sacrificial death that blotted out the human failures with regard to these obligations. Similarly, he took care of God's interests by furnishing him with a holy and perfect foundation upon which God can bless people, and commune with them.

Hebrews 9:15 makes clear that Christ could not be a mediator within the framework of the old covenant, whether or not on the basis of the death of a sacrificial animal. Instead, he became the mediator on the basis of his own death; for it is by his death that he dealt with God's people's breaking the covenant, and thus opened up the way for God's blessings. In verse 16-17, the Greek word *diathēkē*, "covenant," has the special sense of "testament" ("last will").[30] In such a case, the mediator is the executor, the person carrying out the last will of the testator. Here this is the will of God regarding humanity. At the same time, as the passage shows, Christ himself was the testator, who through his death opened the way for effectuating this will: because he died, the eternal inheritance could be placed at the disposal of the favored party, that is, the heirs, the people of God.

Moses was the mediator of the old covenant, but he

---

29. Ouweneel (1982, 1:109; 2:19); cf. also the "arbiter" and the "mediator" in the book of Job (9:33; 33:23). In Ouweneel (*RT* IV/2, §1.5), we discussed the figure of the mediator more extensively.
30. Ibid., §1.4.2.

did not die for the people. As a sinful man, he would not have been able to do this (cf. Exod. 32:31–34; Ps. 49:7–8). Moses could only employ the death and the blood of sacrificial animals in order to confirm the first covenant (see Heb. 9:18–22). However, Christ is the mediator of a new covenant, which is founded upon nothing less than his own sacrificial death.

10.6.2 Guarantor

In Hebrews 7:22 we find another key term: "This makes Jesus the guarantor [Gk. *engyos*; CSB: guarantee; KJV: surety] of a better covenant."[31] The guarantor is a person who makes himself legally liable for the maintenance of an agreement between two parties. He presents himself as guarantor for one of the parties, or for both of them. When one party fails to fulfill its (e.g., financial) obligations, the guarantor accepts these as his own and fulfills them. A person can be a guarantor only if he can prove that if necessary, he is able to fulfill the obligations of the agreement. The term occurs frequently in the papyri.[32] In some cases, the guarantor had to guarantee with his own life; hence the apocryphal admonition: "Do not forget the kindness of your guarantor, for he has given [i.e., here, put at risk] his life for you" (Sirach 29:15 NRSV).

Thus, Jesus became the guarantor of a covenant (Gk. *diathēkē*), that is, a disposition of God for the benefit of humans. If these humans fulfill certain obligations, that is, if they keep God's commandments, they can have fellowship with God and receive his blessings. If they fail to fulfill these obligations, the guarantor takes them upon himself, with all the consequences of this act. In the old covenant of Sinai, God laid these obligations upon the people in the form of the Torah. But the people failed miserably, and thus forfeited the blessings connected with obedience to the Torah. The new covenant is better

---

31. Ouweneel (1982, 1:95–96).
32. Dods (1979, 315).

because, here, Jesus as the guarantor took all the obligations upon himself. That is, he not only kept the Torah but also took care of the miserable plight of the people by giving his own life for them. As a consequence, we now live in a covenant that has been entirely renewed and is everlasting (Heb. 8:8; 9:15; 12:24; 13:20). It is founded upon the blood of Christ, that is, "the blood of the covenant" (9:20; 10:29; 13:20; Matt. 26:28; Luke 22:20; 1 Cor. 11:25). As such, Jesus has become the guarantor and mediator of this covenant. As the guarantor, he takes the obligations of the covenant upon himself; as the mediator, he established or restores the relationship between the two parties.

In the soteriological context, the word "guarantor" occurs only once in Scripture (Heb. 7:22). However, in the unique language of Dutch hyper-Calvinism, the Dutch word *borg* ("guarantor") occurs numerous times; it is rarely absent from any sermon. We find it especially in mysterious Dutch neologisms such as the *borgwerk* (the "guarantor's work [on the cross]"), the *borgtochtelijk lijden* (the "guarantor's sufferings"), the *schuldovernemende borg* (the "guarantor taking upon himself the guilt"), the *borgmantel* (the "guarantor's garment," under which God's people find refuge)—code words that are completely unknown in ordinary Dutch.

Lutheran and Calvinist expositors believe that Jesus is the guarantor for people before God,[33] and in my view they are right: as the high priest on earth, he atoned for the sins of the people, and thus fulfilled all God's requirements pertaining to sinful humanity (Heb. 2:17). Other expositors believe that Jesus is the guarantor for God before humanity,[34] and in my view they are right, too: as the high priest in heaven, he is the guarantee that now all the blessings of the new covenant that God

---

33. Thus ibid.
34. Hugo Grotius, John Peirce; see ibid.; guarantor for *both* parties: Bleek (1840, ad loc., with references).

has promised will indeed flow to the people of God. All the guarantees of the new covenant are embodied in the heavenly high priest, glorified at God's right hand.[35]

One more point. In Galatians 3:19 we read that God entrusted the Torah to a "mediator," Moses (cf. Deut. 5:5), who passed it on to the people (Exod. 32:15; 34:29; Deut. 9:15; 10:1-5). Then we find these cumbersome words: "Now a mediator does not [mediate] for one [only], but God is one."[36] The simplest and most fitting explanation of this cryptic expression seems to be that the occurrence of a mediator always implies two parties (cf. the ESV), namely, the parties between which he mediates. God is one of these two parties, so that Moses' mediatorship implies a second party, that is, the people of Israel. However, it is remarkable that various expositors have placed heavy emphasis on the Greek article: "*the* mediator," and therefore refer this expression to Christ. This was done by church fathers like Chrysostom and Jerome.[37] These exegetes read the text to imply that Christianity contains a mediator too, namely, Christ, but that, since Christ is both God and Man, this mediatorship does not create any distance between God and humanity—as was the case when the Torah was given—because God in Christ deals directly with humanity.

10.7 Who Is Reconciled to Whom?
10.7.1 Humans Reconciled to Humans

We have extensively discussed the fact that God does not have to be reconciled to humans; the New Testament states only that humans must be reconciled to God as well as to their fellow-humans. Regarding the latter point, these passages come to mind: "[I]f you are offering your gift at the altar and there remember that your brother has something against you, leave your gift

---

35. Cf. Bruce (1964, 151n70).
36. See Ouweneel (1997, 210-12).
37. See Cole (1965, ad loc.).

there before the altar and go. First be reconciled [Gk. *diallagēthi*] to your brother, and then come and offer your gift" (Matt. 5:23-24). Stephen tells the people, "And on the following day he [i.e., Moses] appeared to them [i.e., some Israelite men] as they were quarreling and tried to reconcile [Gk. *synēllassen*] them, saying, 'Men, you are brothers. Why do you wrong each other?'" (Acts 5:26).

Paul argues, "But even if she [i.e., a divorced woman] does depart, let her remain unmarried or be reconciled [Gk. *katallagētō*] to [her] husband" (1 Cor. 7:11 NKJV). And with regard to believing Jews and Gentiles, now united in the one body of Christ, Paul says, "For he himself is our peace . . . that he . . . might reconcile us both to God in one body through the cross, thereby killing the hostility" (Eph. 2:14-16) (see §13.1). This is not only "to God" but also "in one body," thus being reconciled to each other: Jews, Greeks, barbarians, Scythians, circumcised and uncircumcised, slaves and free people, males and females (Gal. 3:28; Col. 3:11).

In recent times, various works have emphasized the importance of reconciliation between various people on the basis of the atonement that Christ has brought about. S. Hines and C. DeYoung see reconciliation as a way of life, and as God's "One Item" agenda: bringing people to God as well as to each other, despite their mutual diversity.[38] In line with the South African Truth and Reconciliation Commission, J. de Cruchy saw reconciliation particularly as a path toward the restoration of justice, not only in the theological but also in the political and social sense.[39] Nigerian theologian Yusufu Turaki argued that the cross of Christ creates not only vertical but also horizontal reconciliation, reconciling groups that before were enemies by making them one in Christ (Eph. 2:11-22). This unity eliminates all barriers brought about by human selfishness, greed, ethnici-

---

38. Hines and DeYoung (2000).
39. De Cruchy (2002).

ty, tribalism, racism, and nationalism. This unity leaves no room for hostility, hatred, prejudice, stereotyping, discrimination, bias, or anything else that tries to exclude others.[40]

10.7.2 Humans Reconciled to God

For our subject—reconciliation to God—the following passage is of primary importance: "[I]f while we were enemies we were reconciled to God by the death of his Son, much more, now that we are reconciled, shall we be saved by his life. More than that, we also rejoice in God through our Lord Jesus Christ, through whom we have now received reconciliation" (Rom. 5:10-11). As we saw, verse 10 presumably deals with a hostile *attitude*, just as in Colossians 1:21. By nature, humans not only are enemies of God in a strictly judicial sense, but they also *exhibit* active hostility. As those fallen in sin, and thus rebellious, humans are by definition enemies of God, even if they speak quite respectfully of him. Usually, however, there is also active enmity, if not directly toward God, then at least toward Christ, or toward Scripture, or toward God's children. The apostle Paul argues that the *guilty* person needs forgiveness and justification, and the *hostile* person needs reconciliation to God (just as the morally impure person needs God's cleansing, the spiritually dead person needs being made alive ["quickening"], and so on).

In Romans 11:15 Paul says, "For if their [i.e., Israel's] rejection means the reconciliation of the world, what will their acceptance mean but life from the dead?" Here, the apostle speaks of the providential ways of God: if at present, because of Israel's apostasy, the mass of the people falls outside God's saving grace, the way is opened for the Gentiles, to whom now the reconciliation can be offered universally.[41] *Propitiation* means: thanks

---

40. Y. Turaki in Adeyemo (2008, 875).
41. See extensively, Ouweneel (*RT* IV/2, §1.3 and chapter 5).

Resurrection and Reconciliation

to Christ's atoning sacrifice, all the sins of those who believe will be blotted out. *Reconciliation* means: thanks to Christ's atoning sacrifice, a person can be turned from an enemy into a friend (i.e., lover) of God (cf. Rom. 8:28; 1 Cor. 8:3; 1 John 4:20-21; 5:2). The one who was an enemy in Romans 5:10, and has now been reconciled to God, becomes one in whose heart the "love of God has been poured out through the Holy Spirit who has been given to us" (v. 5).

Paul deals with reconciliation most extensively in 2 Corinthians 5:18-20,

> All this is from God, who through Christ reconciled us to himself and gave us the ministry of reconciliation; that is, in Christ God was reconciling the world to himself, not counting their trespasses against them, and entrusting to us the message of reconciliation. Therefore, we are ambassadors for Christ, God making his appeal through us. We implore you on behalf of Christ, be reconciled to God.

As we have explained far more extensively elsewhere,[42] according to this passage the way to reconciling humans to God is so magnificent that God, through his ambassadors, implores all people to be reconciled to him. This shows, on the one hand, that it is God who is active in this reconciliation because the imploring goes out from him; it is not people imploring God to be reconciled to him.[43] On the other hand, people are not reconciled to God in a passive way: this imploring aims to bring people into this reconciliation in an active way, by faith. Compare here the same verbal form in 1 Corinthians 7:11, where such activity is expected of the divorced wife.[44]

---

42. Ibid., §13.3.2.
43. People suggesting that the sinner must implore God have sometimes referred to Deut. 28:23, "the heavens over your head shall be bronze," so that God does not listen.
44. *TDNT* 1:256.

If there is any passage where it is evident that God is no enemy of humanity, a God who must be reconciled to humans, it is here. The "wrath of God," mentioned in Romans 1:18, does not conflict with this,[45] for this wrath is not directed against people as such but against "all ungodliness and unrighteousness of men." And if it is at all directed against people, then it is as a final judgment of hardening (cf. vv. 24, 26, 28). I think we can maintain this general rule: the *love* of God reaches out to the *sinner*, the *wrath* of God is directed against *sins* (we may add: as well as against the sinner who rebelliously hardens himself).

10.7.3 Light from the Parables

Because of the work of Christ, God has every reason to implore people out of pure love and the gentle benevolence of his heart: Stop being my enemy, come back to me, let us be friends (again). It is like the father in the parable of the prodigal son. Who would dare to assert that this father was the young man's enemy? On the contrary, he was waiting for him with his arms stretched out, so to speak. As soon as the son made the first move, the father *ran* to him (Luke 15:20). The next moment the son was in his father's arms. The father did not have to be reconciled to the son, but the son to the father. As surely as enmity does not have to be mutual, reconciliation does not have to be mutual either.

The parable of the prodigal son (vv. 11–32) also sheds light on another aspect. Sometimes, reconciliation among humans involves nothing more than untangling some misunderstandings, and removing the resulting alienation. At other times, however, the alienation involves genuine guilt toward the other person; in this case, repentance and confession are needed from the guilty person, and forgiveness from the injured person,

---

45. Contra TDNT 1:257.

as in the parable mentioned.[46] Sometimes the mere fact that the brother "has something against you" may be enough to make the first move (Matt. 5:23-24).

What the parable does *not* clarify is the fact that God can grant forgiveness only on the basis of an atoning sacrifice. People's enmity and alienation toward God cannot be lifted by simply clearing away the possible misunderstandings that might have arisen between the two parties. *Reconciliation* of people to God is possible, just as *atonement* for sins, only through a sacrifice. God reconciles people to himself "in Christ," that is, through the latter's mediatorship and atoning sacrifice.

In another parable in Luke (18:9-14), the one about the Pharisee and the tax collector, some other important aspects are prominent. On the one hand, the Pharisee is an enemy of God because he is an unrepentant sinner. However, he behaves and speaks as if he is a friend of God, imagining that he stands in the latter's favor because of his own good deeds: "God, I thank you that I am not like other men, extortioners, unjust, adulterers, or even like this tax collector. I fast twice a week; I give tithes of all that I get" (vv. 11-12). He does not understand his true condition, he does not see the *need* for reconciliation, and therefore he *is* not reconciled to God. Incidentally, he looks very much like the older son in the parable of the prodigal son.

On the other hand, there is the tax collector, who reminds us of the prodigal son. This man *is* aware of his lost condition, he repents, and he confesses that he is a sinner: "God, be merciful to me, a sinner!" (v. 13). Or, as the JUB says, "God, reconcile me, a sinner"; or the YLT, "God, be propitious to me—the sinner!" (the Greek verb is *hilastheti*, from *hilaskomai*, "to atone" [see §9.2.1]). Jesus adds that the Pharisee was not, and the tax collector was, justified in the eyes of God. This is what the apostle Paul has explained more fully in his letters: justifica-

---

46. König (2006, 455).

tion is based not upon a person's good deeds, but upon his confessing his bad deeds, and for the rest entrusting himself to God's mercy in faith.

10.8   Reconciliation of the World
10.8.1   No Universalism

The reconciliation of "the world" mentioned in Romans 11:15 and 2 Corinthians 5:19 does not imply that ultimately all people will be reconciled to God (universalism; see §12.4.1), nor does it mean that here the term "world" refers to the totality of the elect (predestination doctrine).[47] As we have seen, *propitiation* means that the reconciliation that Christ accomplished is *sufficient* for the entire world, and therefore can be offered to all people. However, it becomes *effective* only to those who accept in faith both Christ and his atonement. The "message of reconciliation"—"be reconciled to God" (2 Cor. 6:19-20)—contains the invitation to surrender in faith. On the one hand, we see Christ's sufficiency here: the gospel can be presented to *all* people (cf., e.g., Rom. 5:18; 1 Tim. 2:4-6; Titus 2:11; Heb. 2:9). On the other hand, we see here the condition consisting of faith: God's invitation must be accepted with a believing heart.

I like the wording of Romans 3:22 in the KJV (cf. BRG, DARBY, DRA), based upon certain important manuscripts: ". . . Even the righteousness of God which is by faith of Jesus Christ unto all and upon all [Gk. *eis pantas kai epi pantas*] them that believe." I take this to mean: the righteousness of God, as presented in the gospel, comes *eis pantas* ("*unto* all [people]"), but it comes only "*over* [Gk. *epi*] all who believe." Most expositors prefer the wording we find in more modern translations, but I quote the KJV's wording to illustrate my point.

Concerning this point, Colossians 1:19-22 is remarkable because here the entire creation is involved in the reconciliation:

---

47. Cf. Ouweneel (*RT* III/1, §§12.3.3, 13.1-13.2).

For in him [i.e., Christ] all the fullness of God was pleased to dwell, and through him to reconcile to himself all things, whether on earth or in heaven, making peace by the blood of his cross. And you, who once were alienated and hostile in mind, doing evil deeds, he has now reconciled in his body of flesh by his death, in order to present you holy and blameless and above reproach before him.

This has been called "cosmic reconciliation," that is, the reconciliation of fallen creation (§12.2.1).[48] It never means, however, that ultimately all *people* will be reconciled to God. On the one hand, the text speaks of "all *things*," that is, the entire cosmos, but it speaks separately of "*you*, who once were alienated and hostile in mind, doing evil deeds," and who are thus contrasted with those are *still* "alienated and hostile in mind, doing evil deeds." "All things" are reconciled in the consummation of the ages (that is, restored to God; cf. Acts 3:21), but believers are being reconciled already now. The reconciliation of "all things" is a reference to a new heaven and a new earth, which will come one day. The reconciliation of those who believe involves the existence of the body of Christ, the whole of all those reconciled, already now and forever.

Notice a similar contrast in Revelation 21. On the one hand, we hear: "Behold, I am making *all things* new" (v. 5), which implies "a new heaven and a new earth" (v. 1). On the other hand, we read: "*But* as for the cowardly, the faithless, the detestable, as for murderers, the sexually immoral, sorcerers, idolaters, and all liars, their portion will be in the lake that burns with fire and sulfur, which is the second death" (v. 8). Thus, the wicked are *not* included in the "all things" that will be made new. This is a strong argument against universalism.

10.8.2 A Threefold Ministry

In 2 Corinthians 5:18 we hear about a "ministry" (Gk.

---

48. See, e.g., Y. Turaki in Adeyemo (2008, 875).

diakonia) of reconciliation, related to the "ministers" (Gk. *diakonoi*) of the new covenant in 3:6. Apparently, there are two parts to this ministry of the new covenant: there is the "ministry of the Spirit" in 3:8, and the "ministry of righteousness" in 3:9. Thus, we find mentioned in 2 Corinthians 3 and 5 a threefold ministry, which constitutes one entity. In the order of application ("redemptive order"):

1. Through the ministry of *reconciliation*, a repentant person is brought into fellowship with God; their enmity is abolished. Where there was once hostility, there is now peace and harmony between this person and God.

2. The ministry of the *new covenant*, consisting of two parts (cf. Jer. 31:31–34):

2.1 Through the ministry of *righteousness* (cf. "I will forgive their iniquity, and I will remember their sin no more," Jer. 31:34), the sins of this person are atoned for (propitiation).

2.2 Through the ministry of the *Spirit* (cf. "I will put my law within them, and I will write it on their hearts," Jer. 31:33), *Christ* is written in the heart of these new believers: "[Y]ou show that you are a letter from Christ delivered [Gk. *diakonētheisa*, administered] by us, written not with ink but with the Spirit of the living God, not on tablets of stone but on tablets of human hearts" (2 Cor. 3:3).[49]

10.9 The Blood, the Cross, and the Death of Christ
10.9.1 The Blood of Christ

G. V. Wigram, the man who, among other things, enabled the publication of the *Englishman's Hebrew and Chaldee Concordance of the Old Testament* and the *Englishman's Greek Concordance of the New Testament,* wrote a remarkable work entitled *The Blood, the Cross and the*

---

49. See more extensively, Ouweneel (*RT* IV/2, chapter 6).

Death of Jesus Christ.[50] As we near the end of our discussion of the principles of atonement (chapters 8–10), it may be good to consider separately these three aspects. What function did the blood, the cross, and the death of Christ, each by itself, have in the work of atonement? I am following Wigram,[51] but the arrangement of the various Bible passages is my own. As far as the blood is concerned:

(a) *Objective aspects.* By virtue of his own blood, Christ entered the heavenly sanctuary once for all, after having obtained an eternal redemption (Heb. 9:12; cf. vv. 25–26). The blood of Christ testifies of blessings to the believers, but of judgment to the world (12:24–25). It is the blood of Christ that, together with the water and the Spirit, constitutes the divine testimony in regard to the significance of Christ's coming into this world (1 John 5:6–8).

(b) *Subjective aspects: conversion.* Christ's shed blood offers to his followers a place within the new covenant (Matt. 26:28; cf. Heb. 12:24). It grants them eternal life (John 6:32–69). It is also the foundation for their justification by faith (Rom. 5:9). Through the blood of Christ, believers have redemption in Christ, the forgiveness of their trespasses (Eph. 1:7; cf. Col. 1:14). Through the blood of Christ, believers, including those from the Gentiles, have been brought near to God (Eph. 2:17). The blood of Christ has purified their consciences from dead works, to serve the living God (Heb. 9:14). The blood of Christ is the ransom by which believers have been bought and released (1 Pet. 1:18–19; cf. Rev. 5:9), and by which they have been washed white (Rev. 7:14; cf. 1:5 KJV; cf. 1 Pet. 1:2, "sprinkling with his blood").

(c) *Subjective: the walk of faith.* Knowing the blood of Christ is evidence of eternal election (1 Pet. 1:2). Through the blood of Christ believers have full liberty

---

50. Wigram (1970); see also Nee (1977, ad loc.).
51. Ibid., 4–49.

and boldness to spiritually enter the heavenly sanctuary (Heb. 10:19). The blood of Christ is the foundation for the daily cleansing of the believers (1 John 1:9). It is through the blood of Christ that believers gain spiritual victories over the devil and his powers (Rev. 12:11).

(d) *Collective.* By the blood of his Son, God has obtained his church for himself (Acts 20:28). Jesus has sanctified his people through his own blood (Heb. 13:12). The blood of Christ is the basis for the unity and fellowship of believers, as this is expressed at the Lord's table (1 Cor. 10:16).

(e) *Eschatological.* Through the "*blood* of his cross" (i.e., the blood that he shed on the cross), Christ has made peace as the foundation for the reconciliation of all things to God (Col. 1:20) (cf. [e] in the next section).

10.9.2 The Cross of Christ[52]

(a) *Objective aspects.* God has canceled "the record of debt that stood against us with its legal demands. This he set aside, nailing it to the cross. He disarmed the rulers and authorities and put them to open shame, by triumphing over them in him [i.e., Christ; or, in it, i.e., the cross]" (Col. 2:14–15). The cross of Christ implies God's judgment on the "old self" (or "old person," Rom. 6:6). The cross is an "offense" (stumbling block) to the world (Gal. 5:11), precisely because it does not leave the "old self" intact. As a consequence, even some so-called Christians do actually walk as "enemies of the cross of Christ" (Phil. 3:18; cf. Gal. 6:12).

(b) *Subjective aspects: conversion.* When people come to God in Christ, they acknowledge that they have been "crucified" with Christ (Gal. 2:20; cf. 3:1), that is, they accept God's judgment on the "old self" as God executed this sentence in Christ on the cross (Rom. 6:6; cf. 1 Pet. 4:1–2).

---

52. Ibid., 50–84; see also Nee (1977, ad loc.).

(c) *Subjective: the walk of faith.* Believers are supposed to take up their own cross daily, and deny themselves (see §12.5.2). The fact that Christ was crucified "in weakness, but lives by the power of God" (2 Cor. 13:4), is a practical example to them. The same is true for Jesus' self-emptying, his humiliation, and his obedience to the point of death (Phil. 2:5-8). "[T]hose who belong to Christ Jesus have crucified the flesh with its passions and desires" (Gal. 5:24), and from now on they boast in nothing "except in the cross of our Lord Jesus Christ, by which [or, through whom] the world has been crucified to me, and I to the world" (6:14). The way Jesus endured the cross is the example for the race set before them (Heb. 12:1-2).

(d) *Collective.* Through the cross of Christ, believing Jews and believing Gentiles have been reconciled to God in one body (Eph. 2:16). The cross of Christ implies God's judgment on all that is sinful, also within the church (1 Cor. 1:17-18; cf. 2:2).

(e) *Eschatological.* Through the "blood of his *cross*," Christ has made peace as the foundation for the reconciliation of all things to God (Col. 1:20) (cf. [e] in the previous section).

By way of summary, we can say that the blood of Christ preeminently effects cleansing and forgiveness, and thus also justification and reconciliation. The entire New Testament use of the phrase "blood of Christ" is linked to the Old Testament sacrificial ministry, directly or indirectly. With the cross of Christ this is not the case; this term sheds light on other aspects of the work of Christ: the shame of the crucifixion as such—and thus also the believer's shame, who is supposed to be a cross-bearer—as well as the humbling of Christ, and his subsequent exaltation, and in particular the judgment of the "old self." God nailed it to the cross, and thus cast it from his presence. A person will share in this practically and internally: *God* has crucified the "old self"

(Rom. 6:6), but the *believer* does the same in their heart (Gal. 5:24), that is, they acknowledge and accept internally and practically what God on the cross did to the "old self."

In the blood, the emphasis is more on the positive side: it restores a person's fellowship with God by blotting out what stood between God and that person. But the cross emphasizes more the negative side: it implies the moral end of the "old self," and of all that is involved in the latter's existence. Thus, the cross of Christ is not just another way of speaking of the death of Christ. That phrase "the death of Christ" is a rather neutral expression; but the phrase "the cross of Christ" expresses much more clearly the infinite love of God for a person as exhibited in the heinous death of his Son. It was *this kind* of death that Jesus died. The cross lays bare the enmity of the human heart toward God, reveals the true nature of sin as it is in the eyes of God, and reveals the impossibility of bridging, though any human effort, the cleft that separates humanity from God.[53] Only the cross itself can supply this bridge.

10.9.3 The Death of Christ[54]

This point relates to what was said in §§10.1 and 10.2 about the redemptive significance of the resurrection and glorification of Christ.

(a) *Objective aspects.* Through his death, Christ dealt once and for all with the problem of sin (Rom. 6:10). His death was the end of his own life of self-emptying, humiliation, and obedience (Phil. 2:6-8). Christ abolished death, and brought life and immortality to light through the gospel (2 Tim. 1:10). He underwent the "suffering of death," "tasted" death "for everyone," in order that whoever believes through him would find life (Heb. 2:9). Through his death, he destroyed him who had the "pow-

---

53. Vine (1985, 1:97).
54. Wigram (1970, 87-232).

er of death," the devil (v. 14). Christ's death redeemed believers from transgressions committed (9:15).

(b) *Subjective aspects: conversion.* Believers may know that they been reconciled to God by the death of his Son, and that therefore they shall also be saved by his life (Rom. 5:10; cf. Col. 1:22). They "have been united with him in a death like his," and they shall also "be united with him in a resurrection like his" (Rom. 6:5). They are "dead to sin and alive to God in Christ Jesus" (v. 11). This Christian position of being "dead" to sin will be worked out in the next volume of this series.

(c) *Subjective: the walk of faith.* The baptism of Christians is "into his death" (6:3-4), the death of Christ; that is, their old life ends in baptism, and in baptism there is "newness of life" beginning, behind the risen Christ. "[A]s those who have been brought from death to life," they must not present their members to sin as instruments for unrighteousness, but present themselves to God, and their members to God as instruments for righteousness (v. 13).

(d) *Collective.* The celebration of the Lord's Supper is a continual proclamation of the death of the Lord (1 Cor. 11:26), as the foundation for their practical unity and fellowship (10:16-17).

(e) *Eschatological.* The proclamation of the Lord's death at the Lord's Supper will be continued "until he comes" (1 Cor. 11:26). It is the calling of at least some believers to come to know "the power of his resurrection," and to "share his sufferings, becoming like him in his death," that is, by losing their lives through martyrdom, in order to receive life again in the "resurrection from the dead" (Phil. 3:10-11).

10.9.4 Review

The *blood* of Christ demonstrates preeminently forgiveness and justification, the *cross* of Christ shows preeminently the abolition of the "old self," and the *death* of Christ points especially to ending the old life and beginning a new life with the risen Christ. The blood of Christ involves the end of the sins of all those who believe, while Christ's death on the cross involves the end of the *person* who committed, and commits, those sins. Christ's blood leads to the restoration of fellowship, Christ's death to renewal and a new life in him.

The natural person needs not only a solution to the problem of their sins—*they themselves* are the problem. The death of Christ implies the person's end, just as the life of the risen Christ implies their new beginning. As we saw, the New Testament speaks of the blood of Christ in a way that relates very closely to the Old Testament sacrificial ministry. However, never does the Mosaic Law clearly state that not only his sins but the person himself is the problem in the sight of God. Putting aside the "old self" is a typical New Testament extension of Old Testament truth. Not only does the sacrifice die *for* the person, but the person *themselves* died in and with the sacrifice. Thus, their former existence has been put aside to make room for a new person. In the Old Testament, the emphasis did not lie on the nature of the sacrificial animal but on the sins that had to be blotted out. But now that we know that no one less than Christ, the Son of God, is the true sacrificial Lamb, the full emphasis is on his person, and not primarily on the needs of humanity. The redeemed person not only rejoices in the solution of the problem of their sins, but *their* full attention, too, is toward the *person* who solved this problem on the cross.

The redeemed person is "in Christ"—such a statement would have been inconceivable and incomprehensible with regard to the Old Testament sacrificial animal. The redeemed person knows not only that Christ gave his blood *for* them, poured out his life into death *for* them, but also that they themselves have died and risen *with* Christ. Atonement is no longer only deliverance *from* evil powers, but especially deliverance *unto* the service of God in the imitation of Christ (cf. 1 Cor. 11:1; Eph. 5:1; 1 Thess. 1:6).

To illustrate this, let us consider the remarkable contrast between Pesach and the Lord's Supper, even though the latter is a continuation of the former (see §5.2). In Pesach the emphasis lies especially on the remembrance of an *event*: the deliverance from Egypt (and of course on the God of redemption). But in the Lord's Supper, the emphasis is on the remembrance of a *person*. Of course, it is important what the Lamb did for God's people (the redemption from a spiritual "Egypt"). But more important than this is the Lamb himself: "Do this in remembrance of *me*," as Jesus explicitly asked (Luke 22:19; 1 Cor. 11:24-25).

Moreover, it would have made no sense to an Israelite to be obliged to "follow" the Paschal Lamb in the wilderness, whereas for the Christian this is essential: the true Paschal Lamb redeems people *for himself*, in order to bind them forever to himself in his resurrection and glorification, and to turn them into followers of himself. The Old Testament does not even *know* such a thing as the resurrection, and even less the glorification, *of the Lamb* (or of any sacrificial animal), whereas the resurrection and glorification of the true Paschal Lamb in the New Testament is essential. The book of Revelation centers on the victorious Lamb (e.g., 5:1-13; 7:10; 17:14). The Israelite knew nothing more than the identification with the sacrificial animal in its death, as was expressed in the laying on of hands. But the New Testament believer identifies with the Paschal Lamb in his resurrection and glorification as a criterion for their Christian walk.

Chapter 11
Some Theological Difficulties

> *[A]s by the one man's disobedience the many were made sinners,*
> *so by the one man's obedience the many will be made righteous.*
> *Now the law came in to increase the trespass,*
> *but where sin increased,*
> *grace abounded all the more,*
> *so that, as sin reigned in death,*
> *grace also might reign through righteousness*
> *leading to eternal life*
> *through Jesus Christ our Lord.*
> Romans 5:19–21

Summary: *Several complicated theological questions are answered in this chapter. First, was the wrath of God upon Jesus throughout all his life, or only during the three hours of darkness on the cross? In my view, it is the latter.*

Second, did Jesus' law-keeping increase human guilt, or did it contribute to vicariously removing this guilt? In my view, it is the former.

Third, did the wounds that people inflicted on Jesus contribute to the salvation of believers? Or did only the wounds that God inflicted on Jesus do this? In my view, it is the latter (and these "wounds" were definitely not the same). Behind this lies the basic question what it means that Jesus "gave his blood," or the relationship between what people did to Jesus, and what God did to him.

Fourth, why was a sacrifice necessary at all, or why can God not forgive the repentant and confessing without anything further? Are the nearly fifty answers to this question sufficient, or must we say that at the deepest level we do not understand why? In my view, it is the latter.

11.1 Expiation Throughout Jesus' Entire Life?
11.1.1 Did Jesus Undergo the Wrath of God?

IN CHAPTER 9, SEVERAL complicated questions arose surrounding the biblical doctrine of atonement, such as: How do the wrath of God and the love of God relate to each other in atonement? Is God the subject of the atonement (propitiation comes from God), or the object (he *is* propitiated), or both? How does satisfaction relate to God's love? There are more such questions that may be asked, which indeed have been asked throughout the centuries, and have sometimes led to fierce controversies.

Let us begin by introducing the following problem. It has often been claimed that Jesus has borne the wrath of God. Is this a biblical way of speaking, and if so, *when* did Jesus bear this wrath? (a) During his entire life on earth? (b) During his entire sufferings at the end of his earthly life? (c) During the entire time that he was on the cross? (d) During the three hours of darkness on the cross?

The first order question is this: Did the wrath of God ever come upon Jesus, and if so, when? We can derive the answer only indirectly from some passages: "[I]f our unrighteousness serves to show the righteousness of God, what shall we say? That God is unrighteous to inflict wrath on us?" (Rom. 3:5). "Let no one deceive you with empty words, for because of these things the wrath of God comes upon the sons of disobedience" (Eph. 5:6). "Put to death therefore what is earthly in you: sexual immorality, impurity, passion, evil desire, and covetousness, which is idolatry. On account of these the wrath of God is coming" (Col. 3:5-6). "But wrath has come upon them [i.e., unconverted Jews in Judea] at last" (1 Thess. 2:16). All these passages involve the wrath of God upon the wicked; one could argue that Christ vicariously underwent this wrath for believers. If God's wrath came upon sinners because of their sins, it is obvious that God's wrath came upon Jesus when he was made to be sin (2 Cor. 5:21).

By the same token, we may argue that God's judgment came upon Jesus, although this is not said explicitly anywhere, either. Romans 8:3 comes close, though: "By sending his own Son in the likeness of sinful flesh and for sin [or, as a sin offering], he [i.e., God] condemned sin in the flesh." Jesus came in human flesh, that is, the flesh that in us, ordinary humans, is defiled by sin. God executed judgment upon this sinful nature, not by condemning these sinful humans themselves, but by condemning him who died in the place of his people, on their behalf, although he himself was sinless.

The fact that God's wrath, or judgment, came upon Jesus may also be concluded from Christ being forsaken on the cross (Matt. 27:46; Mark 15:34; cf. Ps. 22:1): when Jesus had been made to be sin (2 Cor. 5:21), and had borne the sins of believers in his body on the cross (1 Pet. 2:24), God, who is "of purer eyes than to see evil and cannot look at wrong" (Hab. 1:13), turned his face away from him. I will enter into this more deeply later; but first we must deal more extensively with the question *when* Jesus bore the wrath of God.

11.1.2 Was God's Wrath On Jesus Throughout All His Life?

I think A. Moerkerken went far too far when he wrote, "As an innocent Child, he [i.e., Jesus] bore the full burden of God's wrath. When he, as a boy, walked in the streets of Nazareth, and worked in the workshop of his stepfather Joseph, he bore every day and every night the wrath of God against sin."[1] Does this formulation do justice to what bearing God's wrath actually entails, namely, undergoing God's judgment upon sin? I do suppose we can say that Jesus suffered all his life under the presence of sin in this world (we will come back to this), and that, in his own pure soul, he was deeply aware of God's wrath upon sin. But would anyone maintain that, already as a child, Jesus bore the *punishment* for sin? What did this look like or consist of? And where is the evidence for this statement?

We must acknowledge that Moerkerken's view ties in with the Heidelberg Catechism (Q/A 37),[2] where we read:

> *What do you understand by the word "suffered"?*
> That all the time He lived on earth, but especially at the end of His life, He bore, in body and soul, the wrath of God against the sin of the whole human race . . . .[3]

Various versions of the Catechism include reference to four Bible passages as evidence. The first of them, Isaiah 53:4, is indeed applied to Jesus' ministry in Matthew 8:17, and not to his work on the cross. However, the latter text is dealing only with Jesus' healing ministry, *not* with his atoning sacrifice for sins, and even less with the wrath of God.

The other passages mentioned, 1 Peter 2:24; 3:18; 1

---

1. Moerkerken (2004, 210).
2. See Ouweneel (2016, 116–19).
3. Dennison (2008, 2:778).

Timothy 2:6, do speak of Christ's work of atonement, but unmistakably in connection with the cross: Jesus bore the sins of believers *on the tree* (1 Pet. 2:24; see §11.2.3), suffered for the unrighteous in his hour of death (3:18), gave himself as a ransom (1 Tim. 2:6), and did this in his self-surrender *unto death* (Gal. 2:20). I suppose that we may say that as Jesus was accomplishing this work, he "bore the wrath of God," but, notice first that none of these passages explicitly says this, and notice second, none of them says he did this throughout his entire life; they refer to the cross.

11.1.3 Other Reformed Confessions

Of course, the Heidelberg Catechism is not alone in this matter. The classic Reformed Form for the Celebration of the Lord's Supper says, "First, we have full confidence in our hearts that our Lord Jesus . . . was sent by the Father into this world, that he took upon himself our flesh and blood, and that, from the beginning of his incarnation until the end of his life, he bore for us the wrath of God, under which we should have perished eternally."[4] The relevant question is whether this is indeed the doctrine of Scripture. I think not, as we will see.

Interestingly, the Form for the Celebration of the Lord's Supper (1964) of the Christian Reformed Church renders this passage as follows: "[W]e bear witness that our Lord Jesus was sent by the Father into the world, that he took upon himself our flesh and blood, and that he bore the wrath of God on the cross for us."[5] Notice how the phrase "from the beginning of his incarnation until the end of his life" has been replaced with the phrase "on the cross"! I judge this to be a return to bib-

---

4. Dutch version: http://www.hervormdonderdendam.nl/ere diensten/formulier_avondmaal.html.
5. https://www.crcna.org/resources/church-resources/liturgi cal-forms-resources/lords-supper/form-celebration-lords-supper.

lical truth. Thus, the question arises as to how many Reformed theologians would continue to defend the view that Christ bore the wrath of God throughout all his life—other than those who swear by every word of the ancient Reformed confessions.

The Westminster Larger Catechism (Q/A 49) seems to be in line with this more biblical view:

> *How did Christ humble himself in his death?*
> Christ humbled himself in his death, in that having been betrayed by Judas (Matt. 27:4), forsaken by his disciples (Matt. 26:56), scorned and rejected by the world (Isa. 53:2-3), condemned by Pilate, and tormented by his persecutors (Matt. 27:26-50; John 19:34); having also conflicted with the terrors of death, and the powers of darkness, *felt and borne the weight of God's wrath* (Luke 22:44; Matt. 27:46), he laid down his life an offering for sin (Isa. 53:10), enduring the painful, shameful, and cursed death of the cross (Phil. 2:8; Heb. 12:2; Gal. 3:13).[6]

Here, bearing God's wrath appears to be limited to Jesus' sufferings at the end of his life. One of the Bible verses mentioned, Luke 22:44, does refer to Gethsemane, not to the cross; but notice the question asked: **"How did Christ humble himself** *in his death?"*

The Westminster Shorter Catechism (Q/A 27) is much more concise:

> *Wherein did Christ's humiliation consist?*
> Christ's humiliation consisted in his being born, and that in a low condition (Luke 2:7), made under the law (Gal. 4:4), undergoing the miseries of this life (Heb. 12:2-3; Isa. 53:2-3), *the wrath of God* (Luke 22:44; Matt. 27:46), and the cursed death of the cross (Phil. 2:8); in being buried (1 Cor. 15:3-4), and continuing under the power of death for a time (Acts 2:24-27, 31).[7]

---

6. Dennison (2008, 4:308; italics added).
7. Ibid., 4:3, 56-57; italics added.

It is not clear in this concise wording whether the phrase "wrath of God" applies to all of Jesus' life, or only to the cross. But, in my view, the Bible verses mentioned by the Catechism refer only to the cross (Ps. 22:1; Matt. 27:46; Isa. 53:10; 1 John 2:2).

11.2 Christ's Keeping the Law

11.2.1 Active and Passive Obedience

The problem just mentioned is related to the well-known Reformational distinction between the *active* and the *passive obedience* (or *righteousness*) of Christ.[8] His active obedience supposedly refers to his ministry during his walk on earth, his passive obedience to his sufferings and death. My first point of criticism is that I find the terms "active" and "passive" rather unfortunate: is John 10:18 ("No one takes it [i.e., my life] from me, but I lay it down of my own accord") a form of passive obedience? And is Galatians 4:4 ("born under the law"), or John 20:21 ("the Father has sent me"), a form of active obedience?

This distinction between Christ's active and passive obedience has been dealt with in another volume concerning the doctrine of the imputation of the righteousness of Christ.[9] According to H. Bavinck, the righteousness of Christ thought to be imputed to believers is Christ's active obedience (i.e., his keeping the law), though he rightly warns against "too sharp a distinction between Christ's passive and his active obedience."[10] Here again, consider the teaching of the classic Reformed Form for the Celebration of the Lord's Supper, which tells us that Jesus Christ "fulfilled for us all obedience to God's law and the righteousness."[11] *For us*, that

---

8. See extensively, L. Berkhof (1981, 418–20); Berkouwer (1965, 319–27); Grudem (1994, 570–77); Erickson (1998, 835–36, 971).
9. Ouweneel (*RT* III/2, chapter 4).
10. Bavinck (*RD* 4:224).
11. See note 2 above.

is apparently, vicariously, as the believers' substitute. John Piper wrote that Christ suffered and died in order to fulfill for us the righteous requirements of the Law.[12] Many more Reformed witnesses could be quoted.

However, first and foremost, if the righteousness that believers receive is a *legal* righteousness—what has been called the "active righteousness of Christ," that is, his perfect law-keeping—then after all, this righteousness is no more than a righteousness "that comes from the law," or "from *a* law," or that is of a law-like nature (Gk. *tēn ek nomou*), as Paul says in Philippians 3:9. This is *not* what he calls in the same verse the righteousness "from God" (Gk. *tēn ek theou*). What Paul argues here is that he is no longer *interested* in any righteousness that is *ek nomou* (according to the norm of any law) but only in "the righteousness from God that depends on faith." In other words, his concern is not with any *law-keeping* that even Christ might have accomplished for him, in his stead; he is simply uninterested in *that kind* of righteousness.

Second, a righteousness *ek nomou*, now taken especially in the sense of the Sinaitic law, consists only of what we ought to have done ("Do this and you will live," Luke 10:28[13]), *and nothing further*. Such a righteousness would not entitle any person to a relationship with the risen Christ (Rom. 6:7–8), or to the glory of God (3:23–24; 5:1–2), or to eternal life (5:21; cf. John 17:3; 1 John 1:1–4; 5:20), just as Adam was not entitled to these things before the Fall. Not even Israel would have received these New Testament blessings if she had perfectly observed the Torah. Therefore, basing salvation on Jesus' law-keeping, rather than only and exclusively on his work on the cross, during the time he was forsaken by God, is to no avail.

---

12. Piper (2004, 37).

13. This claim is valid apart from whether Gentiles were ever formally under the Sinaitic Law (cf. the problem of Acts 15).

In other words, salvation is based not upon the "entire obedience of Christ" (Lat. *tota oboedientia Christi*) but only and exclusively on the "obedience of Christ's sufferings and death" (Lat. *oboedientia passionis et mortis*). During the first period after the Reformation, this latter view was taught, for instance, by Johann Piscator, following Anselm of Canterbury. Johannes Bogerman (chairman of the Synod of Dordt) and Sibrandus Lubbertus were inclined to this view as well.[14] However, David Pareus urgently warned against this standpoint: "To what purpose, then, is his [i.e., Christ's] preceding humiliation, his assumed form of a servant, his servitude to the law?"[15] This is a fair question—although Pareus should have been aware of the correct answer, which is very different from what he himself suggested (see next section).

11.2.2 No Vicarious Law-Keeping

American theologian Jonathan Edwards believed that the blood of Christ's circumcision (Luke 2:21) was just as atoning as the blood flowing from his side, and that all the sufferings from his early youth, and all those troubles, contempt, and temptations that he underwent during his entire life, brought atonement and satisfaction.[16] Reformed theologians in the Netherlands, H. Bavinck and G. C. Berkouwer, defended this argument by referring to Galatians 4:4-5, "God sent forth his Son, born of woman, born under the law, to redeem those who were under the law."[17] But what is the relevance of this passage? It does not say that Jesus' life under the law, and his keeping it, as such contributed anything to the redemption of those who were under the law (see

---

14. Reformed theologian De Groot (1952, 68) seemed to hold this view as well.
15. See Bos (1932, 10).
16. Edwards (2003, 213).
17. Bavinck (*RD* 3:378-380); Berkouwer (1965, 314-15).

below).

Of course there is a connection between Jesus' law-keeping and his atoning work (and this is the answer to Pareus' argument mentioned in the previous section). It is not that this law-keeping was *part* of the atoning work, but was a necessary *condition*, which is something essentially different. Only this person, Jesus Christ, who had perfectly kept the law, could release those who were held captive by the law (Rom. 7:6; Gal. 4:4–5). But this is very different from the idea that Christ's law-keeping as such was part of the atoning work. This law-keeping was a prerequisite to be able to become the substitute of lawbreakers, but it was not vicarious as such.

Remarkably, those who insist that Christ vicariously kept the law for his people never produce any biblical evidence for their claim. The reason is simple: there is none. The idea is nothing more than a logical inference: humans have broken the law, so that they are condemnable and need someone who kept the law *for* them. But this is not at all logically required. Those who break the law deserve punishment. They need not someone who vicariously keeps the law for them, but someone who takes the punishment for this law-breaking upon himself. Of course, the latter is accepted by all orthodox Christians—but why do some also insist on the former? On what basis?

Jesus' law-keeping was an *example* to humanity. It showed humans how they should have lived; it accused guilty humans; in a sense it even aggravated their guilt because it showed humans that it was possible after all to perfectly keep God's law—this one Man did it. This is the exact opposite of the idea that his law-keeping atoned for human sins, or at least contributed to this atonement. Rather, it increased human culpability; it did not decrease it. How could Jesus' law-keeping as such take away any guilt? It merely showed in a painful and shameful way how sinful humanity was. Before the judgment seat of God, Jesus' law-keeping functions as a proof that God's law was *not* too burdensome for humanity to keep it. It points an accusing finger at the sinner, but it can do nothing positive for the sinner.

The phrase may sound quite familiar: "Christ fulfilled the law for us"—but it is totally foreign to the New Testament, both according to the letter and according to the spirit of the New Testament. If you break the law, you do not need someone who keeps this law in your stead, but you need someone who takes upon himself the punishment for your trespassing the law. It is the same in normal life. If I ignore a red traffic light, I need to pay a fine, or I need someone to pay the fine for me—I do not need someone who vicariously keeps the law for traffic lights on my behalf. Or to use a more drastic example: if I murder another person, I must go to prison, and in some countries I might even receive the death penalty. It would be an enormous peculiarity if another person were to undergo this death penalty in my stead (presuming the law of the state would allow such a thing). But it would not help me one bit if that other person would keep the Sixth Commandment "for" me (whatever such a statement could possibly mean).

11.2.3 Condition or Part?

To be clear, of course it is definitely true that Jesus fulfilled the law in a perfect way in the sense of having kept or observed the law without ever transgressing it.[18] However, Scripture nowhere teaches that he did so "for us," in our stead, vicariously, as our substitute. Jesus' keeping the law was a necessary *condition* for his work of atonement. If he himself had not fulfilled the law, how could he have undergone the punishment for those who had broken it? How could he have taken their trespasses upon himself if he himself had ever transgressed the law? However, this fact is radically differ-

---

18. See extensively, Ouweneel (2001a, 103–06; 2018a, §§4.5-4.8).

ent from the notion that his law-keeping as such would have been *part* of his work of atonement.

Therefore, we must reject this sentence in the Belgic Confession (Art. 22): "But Jesus Christ, imputing to us all His merits, and so many holy works which He has done *for us and in our stead*, is our righteousness" (italics added).[19] The basic mistake that so many Reformational theologians have made here is that they understood the obvious *relationship* between Christ's law-keeping and his work of atonement in such a way that they made of the former a part of the latter.

In fact, the distinction is quite simple. What qualifies a person for a job is not part of the job itself. For many professions, a certain education is obligatory; this education is the *condition* for performing that job. But it is not part of the job as such. Similarly, for great sport events, vigorous physical training is an indispensable condition. But the training is not part of the sport event as such.

The conclusion must be obvious: Jesus' law-keeping was one of the things that made him capable of accomplishing the work of atonement; but this does not make this law-keeping *part* of the work of atonement. I venture to say that those who believe that the righteousness of Christ's life administered to *our* righteousness as received by faith, and who believe that the sufferings of his active ministry were punitive and vicarious, do not possess a clear picture of the biblical gospel.[20]

11.3 Only On the Cross
11.3.1 Grain and Burnt Offering

The error that I described in the previous section is not at all a typically Reformational mistake. I also encountered it in the great work on *Jesus* by Joseph Ratzinger,

---

19. Dennison (2008, 2:437).
20. Darby (*CW* 7, 293); for further extensive discussion of this important matter, see Ouweneel (*RT* III/2).

who drew far-reaching conclusions from Jesus' words at his baptism: "Let it be so now, for thus it is fitting for us to fulfill all righteousness" (Matt. 3:15). Ratzinger stated:

> In a world marked by sin, then, this Yes to the entire will of God also expresses solidarity with men, who have incurred guilt but yearn for righteousness. . . . Jesus loaded the burden of all mankind's guilt upon his shoulders. He bore it down into the depths of the Jordan. He inaugurated his public activity by stepping into the place of sinners.[21]

But what evidence does Ratzinger have that Jesus, during his walk on earth, has borne the sins—not of all humanity but—of his people? Jesus bore them *on the tree*, that is, on the cross (1 Pet. 2:24). The sin offering "bearing" the sins of the people enters into death: when God made the Messiah a guilt offering, the latter was cut off from the land of the living (Isa. 53:8–10, NKJV, NIV). Believers are reconciled to God by the *death* of his Son, not by his life on earth preceding this death; insofar as his life contributes to their salvation, this is not his life on earth but his resurrection life (Rom. 5:10). I am not aware of the slightest New Testament evidence that Jesus, during his entire life, or since his baptism by John, would have borne the sins of believers.

We find the opposite peril in the Catechism of Geneva, prepared by John Calvin (Q/A 55): "*Why do you go immediately from His birth to His death, passing over the whole history of His life?* Because nothing is said here about what belongs properly to the substance of our redemption."[22] So there is *nothing* in the whole history of Jesus' life pertaining to the salvation of believers? This is going to the other extreme.

---

21. Ratzinger (2007, 17–18).
22. Dennison (2008, 1:476); this is also known as Calvin's Catechism (1545) and The Catechism of the Church of Geneva.

Minimally, the life of Jesus was typologically the "grain offering" brought to God, as we find that offering described in the Sinaitic Law (§4.4.4). Of course, typology cannot prove any New Testament doctrine, but it can certainly illustrate them. The grain offering was not a bloody sacrifice; in itself it had no atoning significance, just as the life of Jesus *per se* had no atoning value. The grain offering had meaning only in its combination with a burnt offering, which *was* a blood offering, and *had* atoning significance. However, without the grain offering no burnt offering was conceivable. In its typological meaning, this tells us that we cannot regard Jesus' sacrifice on the cross without viewing his entire preceding life, which was the condition for it.

Reformed theologian J. Verkuyl stated that

> It is a fact of experience that, among all nations and within all cultural circles, the story of Jesus' life and activitry makes a deep impression, and that this story of Jesus' life, also before his great sufferings, must not be withheld from any child or adult. Yet, it is also a fact that all paths and lines in the Gospels culminate in the cross.[23]

How true this is—and what a good (implicit) response to the Geneva Catechism!

11.3.2 Bearing On or Carrying To?

There is one passage that we must examine here, namely, 1 Peter 2:24, "He himself bore our sins in his body on the tree, that we might die to sin and live to righteousness." This "bearing" must be properly understood, although opinions vary widely. Some translations have the rendering, "Christ himself carried our sins in his body *to* the cross" (GNT); or, "He used his servant body to carry our sins to the Cross" (MSG). Reformed theologian S. Greijdanus rendered it as follows: "*Who carried*

---

23. Verkuyl (1992, 230).

our sins in his body to the tree of the cross."²⁴ Bible scholar W. Kelly said that such a rendering, "carrying to the tree," is surely erroneous because for the latter notion the Greek uses the word *prospherō* or *prosagō*, whereas 1 Peter 2:24 has *anapherō*.²⁵ In his view, the latter verb means "to bear" in the specific sacrificial sense of "blotting out," as we find it in the Hebrew of Isaiah 53:4 and 11–12, "Surely he has borne our griefs and carried our sorrows . . . the righteous one, my servant, . . . shall bear their iniquities . . . he bore the sin of many." From the parlance of both Old and New Testaments, this seems to be the meaning of *anapherō*. Christ "bore" the sins of believers on the cross (blotted them out, underwent God's judgment for them), but he did not "carry them to cross."

Bible scholar W. Grant concluded the same, saying that the doctrine of Scripture does not allow for any other construction.²⁶ Bible scholar J. N. Darby also extensively investigated the matter, and concluded that offering (presenting) the sacrificial animal to God—bringing it to him—was expressed with *prospherō*. Its being consumed on the altar was the offering it up as a sacrifice to God; this was expressed with *anapherō*. In the Old Testament sacrificial ministry, there is no ritual significance attributed to bringing a living sacrificial animal to the altar.²⁷ Thus, in Darby's view, there is no doubt that the rendering, "He himself bore our sins in his body on the tree," which we find already in the KJV, is the correct one.

Several nuances should be added to temper the forceful language of Kelly, Grant, and Darby.²⁸ The rendering "bore our sins" is indeed a good one: *anapherō* sometimes means the same as *pherō* (cf. Isa. 53:4 LXX *pherei*,

---

24. Greijdanus (1931, 117–18).
25. Kelly (1923, 166).
26. Grant (1956, 173).
27. Darby (*CW* 7, 300–01).
28. *DNTT* 3:1195–96.

v. 12 *enēnenken*, both as the rendering of Hebrew *n-s-'*), and Greek *epi* ("on") with the noun in the accusative *can* refer to a location ("on the tree"). However, such a location is normally indicated by *epi* plus a genitive, as we find in Deuteronomy 21:23 (LXX; cf. Gal. 3:13, "Cursed is everyone who hangs on a tree [Gk. *epi xulou*]"). Thus, *epi xulon* (accusative) can certainly mean "up to a tree." If we combine this with *ana-* ("upward") in *anapherō*, the rendering, "He carried our sins up to the tree," cannot be excluded.

However, even if we prefer the latter rendering, this does not change the fact that the actual location of the atoning sacrifice was "in his body on the tree."[29] The claim of older Bible scholars such as Kelly, Grant, and Darby, namely, that Christ did *not* bear the wrath of God all his life, but only on the cross, remains fully intact. Whereas Reformed theologian K. Schilder stated, "The preparation is finished; now follows the essence of the sacrifice itself; now He must enter upon the darkness of night."[30] I would say instead that it is not the "essence" of the sacrifice that has now arrived, but the actual sacrifice as such.

11.4 God's Pleasure Rested On Jesus
11.4.1 Pleasure or Wrath?

What is the biblical evidence for the claim that Jesus bore the wrath of God during his entire earthly life? The *counter*-proofs are clear enough: throughout his entire life, Jesus enjoyed fellowship with the Father; in other words, the Father's pleasure rested on him continually: "This is my beloved Son, with whom I am well pleased" (Matt. 3:17; cf. 12:18; 17:5). It was always Jesus' "food" to do the will of him who sent him and to accomplish his work (John 4:34); "I seek not my own will but the will of him who sent me" (5:30; cf. 6:38; 7:18). He therefore

---
29. Blum (1981, 235).
30. Schilder (1940, 372).

could say, "[H]e who sent me is with me. He has not left me alone, for I always do the things that are pleasing to him" (8:29). Even when he was on his way to the cross, he could still say, "I am not alone, for the Father is with me" (16:32). He could also say, "[Y]ou always hear me" (11:42). Now look at the great contrast with the cross; there, he said, "[Y]ou do *not* answer" (Ps. 22:2).[31] It was only in the resurrection that he could say, "You have answered Me" (v. 21 NKJV).

How, then, could anyone claim that throughout all his life (before his sufferings on the cross), the wrath of God rested on him? If one asserts this, one must also assert that Jesus had been made to be sin all his life (cf. 2 Cor. 5:21), and that he had been forsaken by a holy and righteous God all his life (see Ps. 22:1). On the one hand, who would dare to claim that Jesus had been made to be sin throughout all his life, and thus was forsaken by God? On the other hand, who would say that God's wrath rested on Jesus, or that he bore this wrath, during the time when he had *not* yet been made to be sin, and had not yet been forsaken by God? How could we separate these three things? Or who would wish to say that the Father's pleasure rested on Jesus throughout all his life and that, at the same time, God's wrath rested on him?

A. Moerkerken did not see this tension: "Yet, you may never say that the Father was angry with the Son.... God always loved his Son, also when the latter, as our guarantor and substitute, bore God's wrath against the sin of the entire human race."[32] But does he not see the tremendous difference between the Jesus living here on earth in constant fellowship with the Father, the constant object of the Father's pleasure, *and* the Jesus who, during the three hours of darkness on the cross, had to cry out, "My God, my God, why have you forsaken

---

31. Grant (1902, 155).
32. Moerkerken (2004, 212).

me?" The truth is that, as far as we know, Jesus never addressed God as *God* during his life on earth, except on the cross (and later: John 20:17, "my Father and your Father, my God and your God").[33] Can we imagine Jesus saying during his life on earth (conscious of God's wrath supposedly resting upon him), "My God, my God, why have you forsaken me?" And can we imagine Jesus joyfully saying during the hours of darkness, "I am not alone, for the Father is with me"? I would rather say, during his life the *pleasure of the Father* rested on him, whereas during the three hours of darkness the *wrath of God* rested on him.

Do we not appreciate here the great fact that, on the cross, for the first (recorded) time of his life, Jesus no longer said, "My Father," but "my God" (cf. §7.4.1)? Here he said something that he could not possibly have said during his life on earth: "My God, my God, why have you forsaken me?" If Jesus indeed had borne the sins of believers during his entire life, he ought to have been forsaken by God throughout his entire life, for God cannot look upon sin with even the slightest tolerance.[34] God is "of purer eyes than to see evil and cannot look at wrong" (Hab. 1:13). If Jesus had been made to be sin all his life (or at least since his baptism), God could not have had any fellowship with him, and Jesus could not have had a moment of joy. In Luke 10:21 we read, "In that same hour he rejoiced in the Holy Spirit and said, 'I thank you, Father, Lord of heaven and earth.'" Is this the language of someone who had been made to be sin, who had been forsaken by a holy and righteous God, and who was bearing the wrath of God? How then can anyone claim that Jesus bore the wrath of God throughout his entire life?

---

33. Together with Rev. 3:2 and 12, we hear Jesus say "my God" eight times in the New Testament.
34. Kelly (1923, 170).

11.4.2 The Sufferings of the Cross

Lewis Sperry Chafer correctly summarized:

> [T]he Word of God does not assign saving value to any obedience of the sufferings of Christ other than that connected with His death.... Salvation is based on the blood of the cross and not on the blood of circumcision or even the blood which He sweat in the garden.... He provided no redemption, reconciliation, or propitiation when circumcised or when baptized.[35]

Later, Chafer wrote,

> It is thus claimed by not a few that all His sacrifice, even His leaving heaven, and every privation and rejection, was vicarious in character, that is, it was wrought in behalf of others. No doubt others were benefited; but such sacrifice was not in any sense a substitution, since no other was ever appointed to the path which He pursued. All His life was a sacrifice, but by universal Biblical usage only that sacrifice by which He gave His life on the cross is vicarious and substitutionary.[36]

Apparently, Chafer understood the word "sacrifice" broadly, similar to its meaning in reference to ordinary people sacrificing their time, money, and energy for the benefit of others, without such sacrifices contribution to taking away sins. In other words, Jesus' life was a sacrifice in the sense of the grain offering, not in the sense of the burnt offering (cf. §11.3.1).

At a minimum, one must acknowledge the New Testament's clearly distinction between the life of Jesus and his final sufferings. It is certainly true that, in a sense, Jesus suffered all his life "for righteousness' sake" (see §8.6). He suffered as God's faithful witness on earth.

---

35. Chafer (*ST* 3:42–43).
36. Chafer (*ST* 3:65).

He suffered as a perfect, spotless, blameless Man in the midst of wicked sinners. Even in the midst of his closest followers he had to say, "O faithless generation, how long am I to be with you? How long am I to bear with you?" (Mark 9:19). Indeed, he suffered all his life, the Righteous One in the midst of the unrighteous. However, this is all essentially different from vicariously bearing the sins of these unrighteous people, enduring God's wrath upon them, in their stead, as their substitute.

Interestingly, Jesus himself made this distinction when he said, just before the last Passover: "My time is at hand" (Matt. 26:18), and during the Passover meal: "I have earnestly desired to eat this Passover with you *before I suffer*" (Luke 22:15). He had suffered all his life—but now he was going to suffer in a special and unique way: as the true Passover Lamb, the true sin offering. Thus, Jesus himself distinguished between the last night and day of his life and the preceding part of his life. It was only in these final sufferings, yes, in this *having to* suffer during this last day and night, that God's redemptive plan was accomplished (Matt. 16:21; 26:54, 56; Luke 9:22; 17:25; 24:26; John 3:14-15; Acts 17:3).

We could express the difference this way: Jesus had glorified the Father all his life, but when he went to the cross it became a matter of glorifying *God*—the very God who is the Judge of sin—in and through his death. This was not a question of the Son dealing with his loving Father, but of the perfect Man Jesus dealing with a holy and righteous God in view of the problem of sin. As the Son of the Father, he could not say, "My God, my God, why have you forsaken me?" He said this as the Son of Man. At that moment, and only then, God forsook his faithful Servant, the Man Christ Jesus.[37] And yet, although we must distinguish, we cannot separate for a moment the divine and the human natures of Christ. We must *distinguish* what we cannot *separate*.

---

37. Kelly (1927, 21-22).

Just one additional note. F. Grant made the following interesting comparison. The life of Jesus consisted of three parts: the first thirty years were almost entirely hidden, then followed the three and a half years of his public ministry, and then his sufferings on the cross. Grant saw a parallel with the Passover lamb. The first ten days of the first month of Israel's religious year were silent; Grant viewed them as parallel with the first thirty years of Christ's life on earth. Then followed the four days that the Israelites had taken a lamb into their homes, and could become acquainted with the lamb (Exod. 12:3); these days correspond, says Grant, with the three and a half years of Christ's public ministry. Finally, on the fourteenth of the month, the Passover lamb was slaughtered (v. 6), which corresponds with Jesus' death as the true Passover lamb on the cross.[38]

11.5 The Stripes of Pilate?
11.5.1 God's Stripes

We must now enter a little more deeply into whether the sufferings that Caiaphas and Pilate, as well as the raging crowd, inflicted upon Jesus were part of his atoning sufferings. In §8.5 we saw that we must sharply distinguish between the sufferings that Jesus underwent with respect to *people*, and those he underwent with respect to *God*. Sometimes they are mentioned in the same breath, as we saw in 1 Peter 2:22-24, but this does not mean that they are one and the same thing. Thus, when the text says that believers have received healing through the wounds or stripes of Jesus (1 Pet. 2:24), people have often all too quickly applied this to the stripes that Pilate's scourging inflicted upon him.[39] However, Peter was not at all referring here to Pilate but to Isaiah 53:5b, "[W]ith his wounds we are healed," which is explained by verse 10: "[I]t was the will of the Lord to

---

38. Grant (1956, 174-75).
39. So, e.g., Wuest (1977b, 68-69); McCrossan (1982, 26-28).

crush him; *he* has put him to grief." It was *God* who inflicted these wounds upon him.

The reason Pilate is mentioned in the Apostles' Creed and in the Nicene Creed ("suffered under Pontius Pilate") is not because Pilate supposedly contributed something to our salvation. Rather, the reason is explained in the Heidelberg Catechism (Q/A 38):

> *Why did He suffer "under Pontius Pilate" as judge?*
> That He, being innocent, might be condemned by the temporal judge (Acts 4:27-28; Luke 23:13-15; John 19:4), and thereby deliver us from the severe judgment of God, to which we were exposed (Ps. 69:4; 2 Cor. 5:21).[40]

We may read the "thereby" here in a wrong way, as if his condemnation by Pilate as such contributed to believers' eternal salvation; but we might also read it as nothing more than a comparison. The mentioning of Pilate is important because it places Jesus' sufferings and death in a historically verifiable context.[41]

Let us return to an important point made in §10.3.2: the blood of Jesus that brings atonement is not directly related to the blood that *people* caused to flow from Jesus. Rather, the atoning "blood" has to do with his *life*, which he surrendered unto death on behalf of his people. Neither the blood that flowed at his circumcision, nor the blood that he sweated out in Gethsemane (see previous section),[42] nor the blood that flowed because of the crown of thorns or the scourging, not even the blood that ran from the wounds in his hands and feet at the crucifixion, and later from his side, has *as such* atoned for people's sins.

Underlying the opposite conviction is the appalling thought that Jesus would have been literally "slain"

---

40. Dennison (2008, 2:778); cf. Ouweneel (2016, 120-21).
41. See Ouweneel (2007b, 43).
42. So, e.g., Schilder (1950, 369-71).

("slaughtered, immolated"), like the Old Testament sacrificial animals. This is not the case at all. Such would have been impossible because neither the Jews, nor the Romans, were thinking of a sacrificial act when they killed Jesus. Jesus was executed by cruel judges, not slaughtered by a pious priest. Neither the Jews nor the Romans were rendering the sacrifice of Jesus—*God* did that, or Jesus himself did it. He is an "offering and sacrifice" (Eph. 5:2), but not one presented by humans. Jesus was God's sacrifice, or, as we can also say, he was his own sacrifice to God. Therefore, his blood did not literally have to "flow" in order to have atoning value. What has atoning value is not that people killed Jesus, but that he surrendered his own life unto death. Were this not the case, then he should not have been crucified but people should have slit his throat so that all his blood would have flowed out, as in the case of the sacrificial animal.

11.5.2 "Slaughtered"

Just as the word "Lamb" is metaphorical, so too is the word "slaughtered":

> Christ, our Passover lamb, has been sacrificed [Gk. *etuthē*, from *tuō*, to sacrifice, immolate, slay, slaughter]" (1 Cor. 5:7); "... a Lamb standing, as though it had been slain [Gk. *esphagmenon*, from *sphazō*, to slay, slaughter, butcher] ... you were slain [Gk. *esphagēs*], and by your blood you ransomed people for God. ... Worthy is the Lamb who was slain [Gk. *esphagmenon*]" (Rev. 5:6, 9, 12; cf. 13:8).

Jesus was neither literally a Lamb, nor literally slain; but in the imagery of Scripture he is the Lamb that was slain—not by people but by God.

This is the way many painters have depicted Christ, such as Hubert and Jan van Eyck on the famous altar piece in Ghent (Belgium). They painted a Lamb whose throat has just been slit, and the blood is running out. This is the way an *animal* is slaughtered; but it is definitely not the way Jesus was killed. In nailing his hands and feet to the cross, and even piercing his side, the Roman soldiers did not "slaughter" him. In the words K. Schilder: "Without *faith*, no one sees the sacrifice here. For all sacrificial knives so far had been handled by priestly hands. But *here* the nails are driven by the stable hand of Cain's accomplices. And yet here is the *sacrifice*, because *behind* the act of the soldiers there is the entire work of Christ himself."[43]

This is an essential distinction. What biblical evidence shows that even the slightest thing that *people* did to Jesus would have contributed anything to the salvation of believers? Must we not rather say that all rejection of Jesus by people, and all wounds inflicted upon Jesus by people, merely brought to light all the more clearly the wickedness of humanity? The fact that people rejected Jesus, and even crucified him, was given by the Holy Spirit as evidence of their sinfulness: when the Spirit comes, Jesus said, "he will convict the world concerning sin and righteousness and judgment: concerning sin, because they do not believe in me" (John 16:9; cf. 8:24; 9:41; 15:22).

All that people did to Jesus, including the actual crucifixion, only rendered humanity more guilty before God, and contributed nothing toward blotting out this guilt. How could it have been otherwise? How could human *sins* contribute to atoning for these same sins? Even repentance and confession of sins do not as such contribute to atonement—even less so do those sins themselves. *Nothing* that people ever did or do contributes to their salvation—only Jesus' sacrifice saves. And I repeat, people did not sacrifice him—God did, or, Jesus offered himself up to God.

To be sure, God made providential use of Caiaphas and Pilate, Jewish leaders and Roman soldiers, who crucified Jesus. Peter told the gathered Jews, "[T]his Jesus,

---

43. Schilder (1940, 109).

delivered up according to the definite plan and foreknowledge of God, *you crucified and killed by the hands of lawless men.* . . . Let all the house of Israel therefore know for certain that God has made him both Lord and Christ, this Jesus *whom you crucified*" (Acts 2:23, 36; italics added). Jews and Romans acted in ignorance, yet they were fully responsible for what they did. However, it does not mean that they *sacrificed* Jesus. This Jesus did himself: "*Christ* loved us and gave himself up for us, a fragrant offering and sacrifice to God" (Eph. 5:2; italics added). Christ "has appeared once for all at the end of the ages to put away sin by the *sacrifice of himself*" (Heb. 9:26; italics added). "Christ had offered for all time a single sacrifice for sins" (10:12).

Here is the paradox: the moment when wicked hands *killed* Jesus (Acts 2:23; 3:15; 5:30) was the very moment when Christ sacrificed *himself*. The moment when wicked people *took* Jesus' life was the very moment when Jesus actively *laid down* his own life (John 10:11, 15, 17–18). What wicked people did served only to aggravate the human condition. What Jesus did served the salvation of all those who believe.

11.5.3 God and Humans Working Together

Our salvation owes nothing to the wounds that *people* inflicted on Jesus, but it owes everything to those wounds that *God* inflicted on him.[44] He was indeed "despised and rejected by *men*, a man of sorrows and acquainted with grief; and as one from whom men hide their faces he was despised, and we esteemed him not" (Isa. 53:3). However, this rejection could not save anyone. But then we read: "[I]t was the LORD's will to crush him and cause him to suffer, and though the LORD makes his life an offering for sin, he will see his offspring and prolong his days, and the will of the Lord will prosper in his hand"

---

44. See the sharp distinction rightly made by, e.g., Mabie (1906, 21–30); Chafer (*ST* 3:44–51).

(v. 10 NIV). It was *God* who said, "Awake, O sword, against my shepherd, against the man who stands next to me... Strike the shepherd, and the sheep will be scattered; I will turn my hand against [KJV: upon] the little ones" (Zech. 13:7; cf. Matt. 26:31, where Jesus applies these words to himself).

The sword mentioned by Zechariah was not the sword of Pilate, but the sword of God's wrath. The "sword" of human authorities has been *given* to them by God (cf. Rom. 13:4), but they are not *God's own* sword—a sword that can also be used *against* authorities: one day, there will be a "sword" in Christ's mouth "to strike down the nations, and he . . . will tread the winepress of the fury of the wrath of God the Almighty" (Rev. 19:15). But on the cross the sword of the fury of the wrath of God the Almighty was turned against *him*. God had used Pilate's sword to *take* Jesus there, so to speak; but then it was God's own sword that was wielded against Jesus.

What a comfort for the believer to be assured that their salvation does not owe anything to what wicked Pilate ignorantly undertook with his "sword" against the Lord of glory (cf. 1 Cor. 2:8). Believers owe their salvation only to what God's "sword" wrought for wicked people through the opprobrious but glorious death of his Son.[45]

Again we face a paradox here. People crucified Jesus, it was not God who did so—but it occurred "according to the definite plan and foreknowledge of God" (Acts 2:23). God "gave up" (Gk. *paredōken*) his Son (Rom. 8:32), but his hand did not kill him. Rather, it is as Jesus said, "The Son of Man is going to be delivered [Gk. *paradidotai*] into the hands of men, and *they* will kill him" (Mark 9:31). Yet, the Messiah said prophetically, "*[Y]ou* [i.e., God] lay me in the dust of death" (Ps. 22:15b). The two things cannot be separated. As G. C. Berkouwer put it, "God's action [on the cross] does not run like a second

---

45. Kelly (1923, 172).

line beside the line of man's action but like an invisible, mysterious *hand* which rules and guides all human action from beginning to end."[46] That humans rejected the living Stone, and that God made him the corner stone, comprised one action: "The stone that the builders rejected has become the cornerstone. This is the LORD's doing; it is marvelous in our eyes" (Ps. 118:22-23; cf. 1 Pet. 2:4, 7).

According to his own responsibility and the decision of his own will, Pilate delivered Jesus to be crucified (Matt. 27:26)—but at the same time he could not do anything "unless [as Jesus personally told him] it had been given you from above" (John 19:11). In Gethsemane, Jesus saw before him all that people would do to him. But within all these sufferings he was aware of the cup that *the Father* had given him (18:11). In the Garden, he surrendered to people's arbitrary power and injustice, but explains: "[T]his is *your* hour, and the power of darkness" (Luke 22:53) because *God* had ordained it this way (cf. Jesus' statement at a much earlier occasion, "My hour has not yet come," John 2:4).

Thus, we must not separate here—but we certainly must distinguish. The "sword" of Pilate is not identical with the "sword" of God—on the contrary, it is opposed to it; they serve contrary purposes. People struck Jesus because they hated him, and wished to kill him. In fact, they hated God himself. This is the opposite of what God intended: God struck Jesus because he loved humanity such that he was prepared to sacrifice his Son in order to save people. People struck Jesus because they hated him—God struck Jesus because he loved us. Or, people struck Jesus because they hated him—God struck Jesus despite the fact that he loved him. People got rid of the Savior by murdering him—God *made* him the Savior by letting him enter death. People brought judgment upon Jesus because of his alleged sins. God brought judgment

---

46. Berkouwer (1965, 142).

upon Jesus for *other people's* sins, and even for sin as such, sin viewed as a wicked power. We could also put it this way: people killed Jesus *because* they were sinners, God led Jesus to death *for* sinners.

The two matters—what people did and what God did—are each other's very opposites in every respect. They cannot be separated, the two events coincide as it were, but that does not make them one and the same. Look at the Roman centurion; he had overseen Jesus' crucifixion. Did this in any way contribute to anyone's salvation? No, the man himself needed salvation (and this he got, if we understand his words correctly; Matt. 27:54). Jesus died for wicked people, including the men who crucified him, and for whom he had prayed: "Father, forgive them, for they know not what they do" (Luke 23:34). Saul of Tarsus was such a man; if he had stood nearby, he certainly would have helped the soldiers (as he did at Stephen's stoning; Acts 7:58; 8:1). But he would have done so in ignorance: "[F]ormerly I was a blasphemer, persecutor, and insolent opponent. But I received mercy because I had acted ignorantly in unbelief, and the grace of our Lord overflowed for me with the faith and love that are in Christ Jesus" (1 Tim. 1:13). The centurion and Saul were saved not because they had persecuted Jesus (Acts 9:4), but because Jesus died for them.

11.6 The Three Hours of Darkness
11.6.1 Types of Sufferings
When considering the sufferings of Christ, I believe we should properly distinguish various stages:

(a) *Perfect Manhood.* His sufferings as a perfect Man among wicked people. These sufferings lasted from his birth to his death. Even as a child he must have been keenly aware of the enormous differences between himself, the spotless One, and the sinful people around him (including his own brothers; John 7:5). These sufferings were *not* vicarious.

(b) *Divine ministry.* The sufferings that Jesus endured during his ministry as God's faithful witness, sufferings caused by people's resistance to his message and the rejection of his person and works. These sufferings were *not* vicarious, either.

(c) *Gethsemane.* The sufferings that he endured in the Garden when the cup of God's wrath was placed before him, and he realized the sufferings he would have to endure on the cross; he was "in agony," "and his sweat became like great drops of blood falling down to the ground" (Luke 22:44). But it was not yet the moment to *drink* the cup; that is, these sufferings were not vicarious, either. They were preparatory for the actual work of atonement that he would fulfill on the cross.

(d) *Captivity and condemnation.* The physical (and also mental) sufferings that Jesus endured from the moment he was taken captive, led before Annas, Caiaphas, Herod, and Pilate, was scourged, was crowned with thorns, and was nailed to the cross. These sufferings were very grievous, but they were *not* vicarious.

(e) *The three hours of darkness* (cf. §§7.4.1 and 7.6.4). During these hours, the horrific scene at Calvary was withheld from the eyes of the curious and the hostile. It had now become a matter between Jesus and a holy and righteous God only. This was the time when he was forsaken by God. These sufferings were not only very grievous, but *they were also vicarious.* Jesus suffered and died instead of, and for the benefit of, all those who would believe in him.

Jacobus Alting made a similar distinction between the first and the last three hours on the cross.[47] During the first three hours, it was still a matter of *people* inflicting sufferings upon Jesus. They derided him, wagging their heads and scolded him (Matt. 27:39-44). In this sense, there was not yet any essential—only a gradual—

---

47. *Opera Omnia* V.393-395.

difference between the sufferings of Jesus in his preceding life and his sufferings on the cross. However, during the three hours of darkness people were apparently afraid. They were silent; we do not hear their voices anymore. People had to step back as it were—a holy and righteous Judge came to the fore, out of sight of wicked bystanders. Jesus was made to be sin; the wrath of God descended upon him; God had to forsake him. No longer was it human fists, or swords, or whips, or hammers driving nails. Now it was only the sword of the divine Judge. No longer was it a matter of wounds that people inflicted upon him, but the spiritual wounds that God inflicted upon him.

Thus, the Heidelberg Catechism (Q/A 39) confesses,

> *Is there anything more in His having been "crucified" than if He had suffered some other death?*
> Yes, for thereby I am assured that He took upon Himself the curse which lay upon me (Gal. 3:13-14), because the death of the cross was accursed of God (Deut. 21:22-23).[48]

Jesus bore the wrath of God *not* during his life on earth, but on the cross: "Christ redeemed us from the curse of the law by becoming a curse for us—for it is written, 'Cursed is everyone who is hanged on a *tree*'" (Gal. 3:13, with a reference to Deut. 21:23).

11.6.2 "My God, Why..."

Throughout his life, Jesus addressed the Father when he prayed. He did so even in Gethsemane (Mark 14:36, "Abba Father"), as well as during the first hours on the cross (Luke 23:34, "Father, forgive them..."), and immediately before he died (v. 46, "Father, into your hands I commit my spirit"). However, during the three hours of darkness, "the Father's name departs from his lips,"[49]

---

48. Dennison (2008, 2:778); see Ouweneel (2016, 122-23).
49. Berkouwer (1965, 145), who, incidentally, did *not* wish to limit

and he spoke those horrible words of Psalm 22:1, "My God, my God, why have you forsaken me?" (Matt. 27:46; Mark 15:34). Apart from the primary sense that these words have in Psalm 22 (see §7.6.4), they meant to Jesus *literally* that in this darkness (which enveloped Calvary, so that curious looks were no longer allowed, not even our own very sanctified looks) the holy Judge had turned away his face from him. Eyes that were "purer than to see evil" (Hab. 1:13) could no longer regard him who had been made to be sin (2 Cor. 5:21), that is, who had been made the very (source of) evil itself. It is as if all evil of the world was concentrated in him, and then judged in his person.

This was the moment when God's wrath was upon Jesus, and when Jesus bore the sins of his people (1 Pet. 2:24). This was the moment that we can say that Jesus entered into the sorrows of hell, as has often been said, especially as an attempt to give some sense to the dark words in the Apostles' Creed: Greek *katelthonta eis ta katōtata*, Latin *descendit ad infer[n]os*, English "descended into hell," or, as others prefer, "descended to the dead"[50] (cf. §14.5).

The Belgic Confession (Art. 21), too, rightly connects the judgment on the believers' sins with Jesus' words in Psalm 22:1, Jesus

> and "suffered, the righteous for the unrighteous" [1 Pet. 3:18] as well in His body as in His soul, feeling the terrible punishment which our sins had merited; insomuch that "his sweat became as it were great drops of blood falling down upon the ground" [Luke 22:44]. He called out: "My God, My God, why hast Thou forsaken me?" and has suffered all this for the remission of our sins.[51]

Christ's atoning sufferings to the cross, nor to the three hours of darkness.

50. Cf. Ouweneel (2007b, 410).
51. Dennison (2008, 2:436).

Notice the precise wording: in Gethsemane Jesus was only "feeling" the appalling punishment required by our sins, but the Confession does not suggest that at that moment—in Gethsemane—Jesus was already *bearing* the punishment of sins. Jesus felt what horrendous judgment the people's sins had deserved; but it was when he said, "My God, my God, why have you forsaken me?," that he actually bore the sins of his people so that these could be forgiven.

If I am being fair to the Belgic Confession here, and not reading too much into it, a correct distinction is being made here. In Gethsemane, the moment came when the cup in all its horror was placed before Jesus' eyes. (I leave aside the senseless, and unanswerable, question whether it was God or Satan who placed the cup before him.) Jesus *saw* the cup, and was sorrowful and troubled by it. But during the three hours of darkness, he *drank* the cup, and drained it "down to the dregs," so to speak (cf. Ps. 75:8b). Jesus did not drink this cup throughout his entire life (as is suggested by the mistaken idea that he bore the wrath of God throughout his entire life). No, he drank this cup of God's wrath *on the cross*. That, in Gethsemane, this cup was only presented and shown to him, explains that he did not yet *drink* it; he even feared to drink it. Otherwise he could not have prayed, "My Father, if it be possible, let this cup pass from me" (Matt. 26:39).

Notice here this brief dialogue that Jesus had with his disciples John and James: "Jesus answered, 'You do not know what you are asking. Are you able to drink the cup that I am to drink?' They said to him, 'We are able.' He said to them, 'You will drink my cup, but to sit at my right hand and at my left is not mine to grant, but it is for those for whom it has been prepared by my Father'" (Matt. 20:22-23). The best interpretation of this passage is that Jesus first spoke of the cup that he alone would be able to drink, and which at that moment was still future for him! But the second time, he spoke of a cup of sufferings that he would share with his disciples. (See chapter 8 for this important distinction between sufferings that Jesus shares with his own, and sufferings that he could endure only alone.)

11.6.3 The Jewish Remnant

One day the remnant of Israel will say of its Messiah: "[W]e esteemed him stricken, smitten by God, and afflicted" (Isa. 53:4). In this statement, Israel confesses to having made a miserable mistake. However, the remarkable thing is that Jesus was indeed a Man "stricken, smitten by God, and afflicted," but very different from what Israel had thought. We read of Pharaoh in Abram's time, "[T]he LORD afflicted Pharaoh and his house with great plagues" (Gen. 12:17), but this involved God's judgment upon Pharaoh's own sins. This was the mistake of Israel; they thought that Jesus had been "stricken, smitten by God, and afflicted" for his own sins. But it was the reverse, as the faithful in Israel confess in the first part of the same verse and in the next verses:

> Surely he has borne *our* griefs and carried *our* sorrows; yet we esteemed him stricken, smitten by God, and afflicted. But he was pierced for *our* transgressions; he was crushed for *our* iniquities; upon *him* was the chastisement that brought *us* peace, and with *his* wounds *we* are healed. All we like sheep have gone astray; we have turned—every one—to his own way; and the LORD has laid on him the iniquity of *us all* (Isa. 53:4-6).

The apostle Peter explicitly accused the Jerusalem Jews of his days of having killed Jesus through the hands of the Romans (Acts 2:23, 36; 3:15; 4:10; 5:30). Stephen said that they had murdered him (7:52). Paul accused the Jews in Israel: "[T]hough they found in him no guilt worthy of death, they asked Pilate to have him executed" (Acts 13:28). However, both Peter and Paul showed these Jews that there was a way out: "Repent and be baptized every one of you in the name of Jesus Christ for the forgiveness of your sins" (Acts 2:38).

> Repent therefore, and turn back, that your sins may be blotted out, that times of refreshing may come from the presence of the Lord, and that he may send the Christ appointed for you, Jesus, whom heaven must receive until the time for restoring all the things about which God spoke by the mouth of his holy prophets long ago (Acts 3:19-21).

"This Jesus is the stone that was rejected by you, the builders, which has become the cornerstone. And there is salvation in no one else, for there is no other name under heaven given among men by which we must be saved" (Acts 4:11-12). "Let it be known to you therefore, brothers, that through this man forgiveness of sins is proclaimed to you, and by him everyone who believes is freed from everything from which you could not be freed by the law of Moses" (Acts 13:38-39).

In the end, the point is not what hands scourged Jesus, or nailed him to the cross—hands of the Jews, the Romans, or the soldiers—because for these people there is forgiveness. In the end, it was not these people but our sins that nailed Jesus to the cross, so to speak. This truth has been expressed in several literary forms. As Jacob Revius put it: it was not the Jews or the Roman soldiers who crucified you, but *I* did this to you; all those terrible things happened to you because of my sins.

Well-known German hymn writer Johann Heermann wrote in a hymn that was included in the text of Johann Sebastian Bach's *Saint Matthew's Passion*: "What is the reason for all these great torments? Alas, my sins, they have thee sorely stricken; I, ah Lord Jesus, have this debt encumbered which thou art bearing." In summary, Jesus was smitten by three parties: first, by the Romans (which only increased human guilt); second, by confessing believers (it was their sins that struck Jesus); third, by God, who smote him with his wrath, so that all those who believe would go free.

11.7 The Mystery of the Sacrifice
11.7.1 Why the Sacrifice?

Now we have to face what is perhaps the most difficult question: *Why* does God demand an atoning sacrifice for sins? Or, as Anselm of Canterbury formulated the question in his *Cur Deus Homo* ("Why God Became Man"): ". . . for what cause or necessity, in sooth, God became man, and by his own death, as we believe and affirm, restored life to the world; when he might have done this, by means of some other being, angelic or human, or merely by his will."[52]

We have seen that, through the sacrifice, satisfaction had to be given to God, and that his injured honor and justice had to be restored. However, we must now ask why this was possible only in this dreadful way: through offering his own Son. We have also seen that sinners can be saved only by a spotless, innocent sacrifice, which takes their place and sheds its own blood for the guilty one; "without the shedding of blood there is no forgiveness of sins" (Heb. 9:22; cf. Lev. 17:11). But *why* is this so? Here again, we must now ask whether, and why, there was no easier way conceivable. Why does God *require* a sacrifice? Why does this God, who needs nothing from his creatures, need a sacrifice? Why could the sovereign, almighty God not choose a way that was less cumbersome—less cumbersome also for himself!

In the Old Testament, God appears to forgive several times on the basis of a confession of sins, without a special sacrifice that was demanded (see, e.g., Lev. 26:40–46; Num. 14:20; 2 Sam. 12:13; Ps. 32:5; Prov. 28:13; Jer. 50:20; Dan. 9:9; Jonah 2). But we must be careful here. It can

---

52. *Cur Deus homo* I.1 (https://en.wikisource.org/wiki/Cur_Deus_Homo/Book_First/Chapter_1).

be argued that this forgiveness always occurred within the framework of the annual atoning sacrifice rendered on the Day of Atonement (Lev. 16), and thus always presupposed this sacrifice. But even then, the question remains why God cannot grant forgiveness purely and merely on the basis of his gracious, merciful, tolerant, forgiving nature. Apparently, God cannot turn a blind eye to any sin. He needs a *foundation* for being able to forgive and to redeem. But again, *why* is this so? If God desires to forgive, and if he is dealing with a repentant and confessing sinner, why can he not simply *grant* this pardon out of his forgiving mercy? And if he did need a foundation, why did it have to be *this* foundation—a sacrifice that cost God himself so much? Why did God first have to "see blood," as some theologians have expressed it (cf. §§2.5.4 and 9.2.3)?

11.7.2 The Atonement Message of the Gospels

Astonishingly enough, in the Gospels we see at best only dimly the necessity of a sacrifice in order for God to forgive sinners. John the Baptist preached the message that forgiveness of sins and entering the kingdom of God depended only on repentance and conversion. The idea that, in addition to this subjective condition (on the part of humanity), an objective foundation (on the part of God) for this forgiveness and entrance is also needed, hardly comes to expression. It is the same in the parables of Jesus, in which, for God, restoration depends only on conversion; the parable of the prodigal son is the quintessential example here. In the parable of the Pharisee and the tax collector (Luke 18:13; see §9.2.1), we hear at most in the appeal "be merciful to me" (Gk. *hilasthēti moi*) the undertone of God being in an atoning or conciliatory mood (the Gk. verb *hilaskomai* means "to atone for").

The clearest evidence for the necessity of a sacrifice is found in two statements by Jesus (which, of course, because of their exceptional nature have been discarded by some critics as "not authentic"): "[T]he Son of Man came not to be served but to serve, and to give his life as a ransom for many" (Matt. 20:28; Mark 10:45), and concerning the Passover cup: "Drink of it, all of you, for this is my blood of the covenant, which is poured out for many for the forgiveness of sins"(Matt. 26:27-28). In addition to these, we have various statements of Jesus recorded in John's Gospel: the Son of Man who "must" be lifted up, and God "giving" his Son (John 3:14-16), the Good Shepherd "laying down" his life for the benefit of the sheep (10:11, 15-18). And notice especially this remarkable passage:

> [O]ne of them, Caiaphas, who was high priest that year, said to them, "You know nothing at all. Nor do you understand that it is better for you that one man should die for the people, not that the whole nation should perish." He did not say this of his own accord, but being high priest that year he prophesied that Jesus would die for the nation. and not for the nation only, but also to gather into one the children of God who are scattered abroad (John 11:49-52).

K. Berger wrote: "Neither the baptism of John the Baptist 'for the forgiveness of sins,' nor Jesus' acquittal according to Mark 2 [v. 5, 'your sins are forgiven'], nor the parable of the prodigal son are so dogmatic that they would say, Only through the cross sins could be forgiven."[53] This does not imply that the cross was actually unnecessary—although Berger seems to claim this (cf. §9.5.2)—but it does suggest that God, or Jesus, apparently could easily forgive without any reference to a sin offering (cf. Matt. 6:14-15; 12:31-32; Luke 7:47-48).

Why, then, was an atoning sacrifice absolutely required? Or should we rather say that Jesus *could* forgive precisely because he was aware of the sacrificial work

---

53. Berger (2004, 315).

he was going to accomplish? If, in Old Testament times, God showed his "divine forbearance" in passing over the sins of those times *in view of* Jesus' coming work of atonement (cf. Rom. 3:24-25), Jesus could have done the very same during the time of the Gospels. In other words, it is hard to find a biblical case of divine forgiveness that could possibly, in some way or another, *not*, be linked to the sacrifice, either the Day of Atonement, or the cross of Jesus, which was the fulfillment of this Day.

11.7.3 Traditional Answers

From the very beginning of Christian theology, well-known answers have explained the why of Jesus' sacrifice. The tremendous offering that a holy God requires underscores his holy hatred of and aversion toward sin. Scripture speaks of "every abominable thing that the LORD hates" (Deut. 12:21); "his soul hates the wicked and the one who loves violence" (Ps. 11:5b; cf. 45:7). Proverbs 6:16-19 speaks of seven things that the Lord hates (also see Isa. 1:14; 61:8; Jer. 44:4; Amos 5:21; 6:8; Zech. 8:17). Perhaps if we understood much more profoundly how God abhors evil, we would better understand why he requires either retribution, or the highest sacrifice conceivable. By nature we are sinners, and therefore, by nature we are easily inclined not only to do evil to each other, but also to forgive each other. This is sinners dealing with sinners. However, it is so very different with a pure, holy, transparent, spotless, righteous God. If we better understood how, in his relationship with humanity, God's honor was and is injured through the wickedness of sinners, we might better understand the necessity of the sacrifice—even the highest sacrifice possible.

We can turn a blind eye to sin, and behave as if it had never happened. But if we drive our car once it has a fundamental defect, we cannot behave as if nothing has happened. We need a repair, or even a new car. If we have stolen, we must pay back. This is the principle of retribution: "... fracture for fracture, eye for eye, tooth for tooth; whatever injury he [i.e., the evildoer] has given a person shall be given to him" (Lev. 24:20; Exod. 21:24; Deut. 19:21; cf. Matt. 5:38). Sin is guilt that must be compensated, paid back, repaired, *or* a payment must be made: a ransom, a price must be paid (cf. Ps. 49:7–8). In the parable, this is said concerning the wicked servant: "[I]n anger his master delivered him to the jailers, until he should pay all his debt" (Matt. 18:34). And if the person longs to be saved, he will have to find another person to pay this debt for him, or to undergo his punishment for him. *Payment must be made.*

Notice this repeated "must," which is rooted in God's holy being (cf. §9.5.2): it is something he cannot escape, simply because he is *God*. We find this holy "must" in Jesus' own words: "From that time Jesus began to show his disciples that he *must* go to Jerusalem and suffer many things from the elders and chief priests and scribes, and be killed, and on the third day be raised" (Matt. 16:21; cf. Luke 9:22; 17:25). "[A]s Moses lifted up the serpent in the wilderness, so *must* the Son of Man be lifted up, that whoever believes in him may have eternal life" (John 3:14–15). "The prophets said the Messiah *must* suffer these things before he begins his time of glory" (Luke 24:26 ERV; cf. vv. 44, 46; 22:37; Mark 8:31). "[H]ow then should the Scriptures be fulfilled, that it *must* be so?" (Matt. 26:54; cf. John 20:9). Paul "explained and proved that the Christ *must* die and then rise from death" (Acts 17:3 ICB). Or compare Hebrews 9:23, "Thus it was *necessary* for the copies of the heavenly things [i.e., the tabernacle and its contents] to be purified with these rites [i.e., with animal blood], but the heavenly things themselves with better sacrifices than these," namely, the one burnt and sin offering of Christ.

11.8 The "Why" Remains
11.8.1 The Deepest Answers

A. van de Beek, wrote, "Against the background [of substitution], it also becomes clear why atonement is always linked with blood."[54] Well, in my view this is *not* so clear at all. But Van de Beek is right when he says that those asking, "Why could God not forgive just like that? Why did any blood have to be shed for this?" are ignoring the seriousness of sin. It cost *everything* in order to undo *everything* that sin had wrought. Through sin, everything came under the power of death. It cost a *life*—the best, the highest life—in order to blot out this death. But again, we must face the question why it *had to* be like this, why there was definitely no other way.

J. Piper, has summarized this matter with no fewer than fifty reasons why Jesus had to die;[55] to mention just a few: to take the wrath of God upon himself (Gal. 3:13); to please his heavenly Father (Eph. 5:2); to learn obedience and to be sanctified (Heb. 2:10; 5:8); to obtain resurrection from death (Heb. 13:20-21); and to show the riches of God's love and grace to sinners (John 3:16; Rom. 5:7-8; Eph. 1:7). In each of these fifty explanations—and more could be given—there is no doubt a kernel of truth; in previous parts of this volume, we found indeed clear biblical evidence for them.

However, this is about all that can be said, based on what Scripture teaches us. But all of this together does not yet answer the question *why* this had to be so. H. Berkhof observed,

> Apparently—again we face the question: why? Why is representation possible? and why does this require the total sacrifice of a life? and how is this sacrifice related to the assumption of the guilt? The NT asserts the "that," but

---

54. Van de Beek (2000, 108).
55. Piper (2004).

has no answer to the "why" and the "how." That is God's secret.[56]

To this set of questions, the fifty reasons listed by J. Piper do not begin to provide an answer. That's not a criticism. But it is important to acknowledge the legitimacy of questions like those raised by Berkhof.

A. König wrote in a similar vein:

> [N]ot one of these reasons is [explicitly] given in Scripture. Moreover, I do not obtain any clear reason or clarification in the Bible why sacrifices for sin were at all necessary, not even Christ's sacrifice. But the factuality of the sacrifices is clear: offerings are required, and had to be brought in the Old Testament, and Christ's sacrifice was in the end necessary. This is simply part of the biblical message without this being clarified. But does this make God a cruel person, who must see blood in order to forgive? *Yes*, if one undertakes a campaign against the Bible, and wishes to ridicule it at every point. *No*, if one takes the Bible seriously, and tries to understand it.[57]

Perhaps, König's language is a little too sharp: in my view, there *are* clear biblical reasons why Christ's atoning sacrifice was needed. Satisfaction, substitution, ransom, and the like constitute such reasons. However, we must try to understand König at a deeper level: ultimately, the Bible does not reveal to us why satisfaction could be given to God *only* through Christ's sufferings on the cross and his death, and why God can forgive us only on the basis of a vicarious sacrifice, or, why his own loving readiness to forgive was insufficient for this goal.

Scripture is perfectly clear on this: there is no atonement without satisfaction (Dutch: *geen verzoening zonder voldoening*). But the Bible is less clear about the <u>why it could</u> be done *only this* way. Almost from its very

56. Berkhof (1986, 310).
57. König (2006, 292).

beginning, the Bible emphasizes the significance of vicarious sacrifice. However, the Bible in the end provides no fundamental answer as to the why the blotting out of sins and the reconciliation of the sinner with God is possible only in this way. "Without the shedding of blood there is no forgiveness of sins" (Heb. 9:22). But we are not told why this is so. We will simply have to accept this mystery as a divine given.

11.8.2 God's "Own Blood"

One important point must be added. The claim that God is cruel because he allegedly "wants to see blood" must be utterly rejected. This is because the mystery is in fact much greater than those who launch such claims apparently are aware of: God not only *requires* a sacrifice, he himself *supplies* it, as we have seen: "God so loved the world, that he gave his only Son" (John 3:16). He "did not spare his own Son but gave him up for us all" (Rom. 8:32). It was in his Son Jesus Christ that God stretched out to the world the hand of reconciliation (2 Cor. 5:19). "In him all the fullness of God was pleased to dwell, and through him to reconcile to himself all things" (Col. 1:19–20; cf. v. 13). "I will send my beloved son," says the father in the parable of the wicked tenants (Luke 20:13). "God sent his only Son into the world, so that we might live through him. In this is love, not that we have loved God but that he loved us and sent his Son to be the propitiation for our sins" (1 John 4:9–10).

It is true that a holy God required a sin offering for the sins of his people. It is equally true that *God himself supplied* this sin offering, namely, in the person and work of his only, beloved Son. To put it more strongly still, in a sense God gave *himself*. The Word, who was and is God, became flesh (John 1:1, 14). He who was in the form of God came in human likeness (Phil. 2:6–7). We have seen that it goes too far to say that *God* was crucified (§9.4.2)—but it is certainly true that the *Man* Jesus died, and this Man was and is God the Son.

In this mystery lies the explanation, as far as I can see, for the obscure statement in Acts 20:28, ". . . the church, which he obtained with his own blood [Gk. *dia tou haimatos tou idiou*]." The KJV and many others render the Greek phrase by "with his own blood," whereas many others render it by "with the blood of his Own," or "of his own [Son]." It is noteworthy that, apart from theological objections, under normal circumstances every translator would have preferred the former translation as being the most natural:[58] God bought the church with his own blood, that is, God *the Son* did so. Nevertheless, many translations choose the latter option. This is no wonder: there is a healthy fear of theopaschitism (§9.4.2). *God* did not die, but he sent his Son, who became the suffering and dying Man Jesus Christ. *God* did not bear the wrath of God, but the suffering Son of Man bore the wrath of God. God did not forsake *God*, but God forsook the Man Jesus Christ burdened with the sins of believers.

However, it is equally true that this Man was and is God, more specifically, God the Son. In §9.4.3 I quoted the statement by G. C. Berkouwer, who warned that we can easily violate the "Trinitarian mystery" here. It is true that the Man Jesus Christ suffered under the smiting hand of God. But it is equally true that this Man is God, namely, the Second Person in the Godhead, that is, God the Son. We cannot fathom this paradox; we will believe it only if we believe Scripture as the revealed, divinely authoritative Word of God.

11.8.3 The Two Together

Stating that something is a paradox or mystery does not diminish the duty of theologians to draw as near to this mystery as possible, without falling over the edge: God *gave* a sacrifice, namely, his own Son, and God *be-*

---

58. See Ouweneel (2007b, 26–68).

came a sacrifice, namely, in the person of God the Son. Each of these statements demolishes the image of a cruel God who wants to see blood. If God wanted to "see blood," then he did so by giving *his own* blood, namely, the blood of the Man Christ Jesus, who is God the Son. At the deepest level, we do not understand exactly why God could not choose an easier, less troublesome and grievous way. But he did not require from *humans* that they go this most difficult pathway: he went this way alone. In Christ, God gave *himself*.

If we cannot fit these things into a theological paradigm, we can nonetheless admire the biblical *illustration* of the Father and the Son going together (§6.6.4):

> And Abraham took the wood of the burnt offering and laid it on Isaac his son. And he took in his hand the fire and the knife. *So they went both of them together.* And Isaac said to his father Abraham, "My father!" And he said, "Here I am, my son." He said, "Behold, the fire and the wood, but where is the lamb for a burnt offering?" Abraham said, "God will provide for himself the lamb for a burnt offering, my son." *So they went both of them together.* . . . So Abraham called the name of that place, "The LORD will provide"; as it is said to this day, "On the mount of the LORD it shall be provided" (Gen. 22:6–8, 14).

To me this is one of the most magnificent passages in the book of Genesis. Notice what is presented here. God provides the burnt offering—but at the same time he is typologically described as the father, who ascends the mountain to offer his own son, and who, in doing so, in a sense lays himself on the altar. For without the son, the father is nothing—not even a father. Without the son, he is a man without a future. If the son must die on the altar, (something of) the father will die together with him. And yet, it is not the father who is sacrificed but the son.

Jesus himself told his disciples, "Behold, the hour is coming, indeed it has come, when you will be scattered, each to his own home, and will leave me alone. Yet I am not alone, for the Father is with me" (John 16:32). When Jesus went to the cross, it was not to appease an angry God. On the contrary, both the Father and the Son traveled that road together, to the very top of Calvary. On the cross, during the hours of darkness, the *Man* Christ Jesus was forsaken by a holy and righteous *God* (Matt. 27:46)—but both the (divine) *Father* and the (divine) *Son* traveled this entire road together, until the bitter end (cf. §11.3). Again, we cannot fathom this mystery; we must leave it, and believe.

The full picture is not that of a cruel God *demanding* an offering, but rather that of a loving, gracious, merciful God *supplying* the offering, and in a certain sense—in the person of the Man Jesus Christ, who was and is God the Son—himself *becoming* the offering. Many biblical reasons can be adduced as to why it "had" to be like this, and why it "could" not be done any other way. But basically we are at a loss for words. What we can understand, we can worship. And what we *cannot* understand, we can still worship.

Chapter 12
The Extent of Atonement

*This is good, and it is pleasing in
the sight of God our Savior,
who desires all people to be saved
and to come to the knowledge
of the truth.
For there is one God,
and there is one mediator between
God and men,
the man Christ Jesus,
who gave himself as a ransom for all,
which is the testimony given
at the proper time.*
1 Timothy 2:3-6

Summary: *This chapter discusses the issues regarding for whom Christ died (answer: for all people, and for the whole cosmos) and for whose sins he atoned (answer: for those of believers). Because these issues are not identical, the phrase "(un)limited atonement" is ambiguous. The matter is investigated by examining many biblical passages. Christ not only died for all people, but his death has definite consequences for all people (although universalism is rejected).*

In addition to this, three important soteriological is-

sues are discussed. First, the meaning of the cross in the believer's daily walk (in which Christ's cross must be distinguished from the believer's own cross). Second, the meaning and consequences of forgiveness (its cost, its basis, its effects, and its significance in the Christian's practical walk). Third, Eastern Orthodox soteriology with its greater emphasis on Christ as the One who triumphed over death and Satan (more than on Christ as the One who atoned for sins), as well as theosis, in short: God's work in the believer to develop his own image in the latter.

12.1 Four Different Views
12.1.1 Summary

WHAT IS THE SCOPE or extent of Christ's atoning death, or for whom did he accomplish atonement on the cross? Traditionally, four answers have been given to this important question:

(1) Christ died only for the elect, and blotted out only their sins (doctrine of predestination; see the rest of this section).

(2) Christ died for all people, but he actually blotted out the sins only of those who believe in him (sublapsarianism) (§§12.1–12.2).

(3) Christ blotted out the sins of all people, but only those who believe in him will be saved (doctrine of "unlimited atonement," but we will see that this is an ambiguous description) (§12.3).

(4) Christ blotted out the sins of all people, so that all people will ultimately be saved (universalism; in Dutch and German more clearly called *alverzoening* and *Allversöhnung*, respectively: reconciliation of all) (§12.4).

The first two views can be classified under the heading of "partial" (or "limited") atonement, and the last two under the heading "general" (or "unlimited") atonement (but again, these are confusing terms as we will see). The first three views maintain that only those who believe will be saved—the rest are lost—whereas the fourth view maintains that all people will ultimately be saved. The first view maintains that Christ died for the elect alone, whereas the last three views maintain that Christ died for all people (which does not necessarily mean that all people will be saved).

We will see that each of the four views can adduce an entire series of Bible passages as evidence. We are facing here one of those difficult theological situations where scholars must try to enter so deeply into the spirit of Scripture that they manage to get the total picture, and this is always a rather subjective matter. I will defend the claim that sublapsarianism (§12.2) comes closest to the message of the Bible.

12.1.2 "All People," the "Whole World"

Let us now look at the first view mentioned: Christ died for the elect only, and blotted out only their sins. If we omit the word "only" here, it is not difficult, of course, to adduce Bible passages that tell us that Christ died for his people, for believers, for the elect, and has blotted out their sins (e.g., Matt. 1:21; John 10:11, 15, 26-27; 15:13; 17:9; Acts 20:28; Rom. 8:28-33; Eph. 5:25). The truth of this is undisputed among orthodox Christians. This is not the issue, however. The point of discussion is rather whether we can say that Christ died *for all people*, and if so, what is the precise theological significance of this.

Elsewhere I have argued extensively that Christ came into this world for *all* people, and that he can promise salvation to *all* people on the condition that they surrender to him in faith.[1] Note the italicized words in the following citations from Scripture: "Come to me, *all* who labor and are heavy laden, and I will give you rest" (Matt. 11:28; cf. Isa. 55:1); "*all* have sinned and fall short of the glory of God, and are justified by his grace as a gift" (Rom. 3:23-24); "as one trespass led to condemna-

---

1. See Ouweneel (*RT* III/2, chapter 13).

tion for all men, so one act of righteousness leads to justification and life for *all* men" (5:18). "... God our Savior, who desires *all* people to be saved and to come to the knowledge of the truth ... Christ Jesus, who gave himself as a ransom for *all*" (1 Tim. 2:3–6); "the grace of God has appeared, bringing salvation for *all* people" (Titus 2:11); "... not wishing that any should perish, but that *all* should reach repentance" (2 Pet. 3:9; cf. Ezek. 33:11). "Jesus, crowned with glory and honor because of the suffering of death, so that by the grace of God he might taste death for *everyone*" (Heb. 2:9).

Sometimes, Isaiah 53:6 is referred to as well ("the LORD has laid on him the iniquity of us *all*"),[2] but this is hardly appropriate because it is not all people but the faithful remnant of Israel that is in view here.

Notice as well those passages that speak of "the [entire] world" (italicized in what follows) as the object of God's saving love: "Behold, the Lamb of God, who takes away the sin of the *world*" (John 1:29). "God so loved the *world*, that he gave his only Son, that whoever believes in him should not perish but have eternal life" (3:16); "we know that this is indeed the Savior of the *world*" (4:42). Israel's "rejection means the reconciliation of the *world*" (Rom. 11:15); "in Christ God was reconciling the *world* to himself" (2 Cor. 5:19). "He Himself is the propitiation for our sins, and not for ours only but also for the *whole world*" (1 John 2:2 NKJV); "the Father has sent his Son to be the Savior of the *world*" (4:14).

There are three ways to deal with the verses just quoted.[3] First, one may argue that these verses prove that all people will ultimately be saved. This is the (erroneous) view that will be dealt with in §12.4.1. Second, these verses may be taken to show that salvation is *offered* to all people, but is effectively granted only to those who

---

2. E.g., Erickson (1998, 847).
3. See more extensively, Ouweneel (*RT* III/2, chapter 13) and references there.

believe; for this (in my view the biblical) standpoint see §§12.2 and 12.3. Third, it has been argued that the expression "all" in the verses mentioned means "all the elect," and that "the world" means "the world of the elect." This is the (erroneous) view of consistent adherents of the Calvinist doctrine of the double predestination. As I see it, at this point dogmatism is dominating exegesis, and where this happens human reason dominates Scripture—a fundamental theological sin. Only in the Calvinist doctrine of double predestination do people seriously believe that "all" (even "all men," "all people") and "world" (even "the whole world") refer to the elect only. The result is not to proclaim the truth, but to attempt to save one's dogmas. One can imagine people in the sixteenth century, in the infancy of the Reformation, making such suggestions. But it is hard to imagine people in the twenty-first century (except zealous confessionalists) still presenting this as biblical truth.

12.1.3 Between Predestination and Unlimited Atonement

The many Bible passages telling us that salvation is offered to all people on earth indicate that we may indeed say that "Christ died for them." I think here of the Scottish theologian J. McLeod Campbell, who wrote a treatise on Calvinism about the extent of atonement,[4] and was denounced for it by the Presbyterians who alleged that he taught "unlimited atonement" (see §12.3). They could not comprehend that someone can reject "unlimited atonement" (Christ atoned for all the sins of the world), and yet maintain that "Christ died for all." He tasted death *for everyone*, is what we found in Hebrews 2:9. But this is not the same as saying that he blotted out the sins of everyone. We will come back to this, but here I would state the matter this way (as an illustration): such a view results from confusing the two goats on the

---

4. Campbell (1996, especially chapter 3).

Day of Atonement, that is, confusing satisfaction and substitution (see §12.2.1). Campbell's view may have been a threat to consistent Calvinism, but I think it was perfectly correct.

In addition to the passages mentioned earlier, which underscore God's universal offer of salvation, there are four passages that are significant for this discussion, and entail special difficulties for the classic doctrine of predestination. Here are three of the four passages (all italics added): "[I]f your brother is grieved by what you eat, you are no longer walking in love. By what you eat, do not destroy the one *for whom Christ died*" (Rom. 14:15). "And so by your knowledge this weak person is destroyed, the *brother for whom Christ died*" (1 Cor. 8:11). "How much worse punishment, do you think, will be deserved by the one who has trampled underfoot the Son of God, and has profaned the *blood* of the covenant by which he was *sanctified*, and has outraged the Spirit of grace?" (Heb. 10:29). Here it is declared unequivocally that people for whom Christ died, and who had been sanctified by his blood, can still perish. (This is related to the more general question whether the truly regenerate can still be lost; see the next volume in this series.)

The fourth passage is this one: "[T]here will be false teachers among you, who will secretly bring in destructive heresies, even denying the Master who *bought* them, bringing upon themselves swift destruction" (2 Pet. 1:1). What does it mean that the Master "bought" these false teachers? The Annotation to the Dutch States Translation reduces this to the assertion that "they pretend to be such." Now the text is indeed challenging,[5] unless we assume that through his atoning sacrifice, Christ not only redeems all true believers, but through this sacrifice, has acquired title to *every* human being. The Father gave the Son "authority over *all* flesh" (John

---

5. See the discussion in Blum (1981, 276–77) of the various interpretations.

17:2), and the Son uses this power to grant eternal life to all those whom the Father "gave" him (vv. 2b, 6, 9, 22, 24), but eternal destruction to the wicked (see §12.4.2).

In my view, the Remonstrants (Arminians) were wrong in several points, but in this point (Art. II) they were closer to the truth. That is, they rightly argued: "Accordingly Jesus Christ, Savior of the world, has died for each and every man, and through His death on the cross has merited reconciliation and forgiveness of sins for all; nevertheless so that no one in fact becomes a partaker of this forgiveness except believers, . . ." referring to John 3:16 and 1 John 2:2.[6] I would rather say that Christ obtained for each and every man the *possibility* of redemption and forgiveness, but the rest of the statement is fully adequate: Christ died for all, but only the believers profit from it.

12.2 The (Un)limitedness of Atonement
12.2.1 Cosmic Reconciliation

We must look a little more closely at the view that can be summarized by the phrases "the universal offer of salvation" (Christ died for all) and "limited atonement" (only believers profit from his death). It is what has been called sublapsarianism[7]—not a very lucid term.

The phrase "limited atonement" is in some sense ambiguous.[8] This led Millard Erickson to describe sublapsarianism as *unlimited* atonement (God has prepared salvation for all people), and *limited* application (God has chosen some to receive this salvation).[9] I would rather say that the atonement is *unlimited* in that Christ died for all, so that salvation can be fairly and honestly

---

6. Dennison (2008, 4:43).
7. See Ouweneel (*RT* III/1, §14.6.1).
8. Geisler (2011, 923–42) dealt extensively with the problem of (un)limited atonement but is unclear about the ambiguity in the terminology.
9. Erickson (1998, 931).

presented to all people. All people may come and accept the gospel. But atonement is *limited* in the sense that only those who do come—those who truly believe—are allowed to say that Christ blotted out *their* sins. This is why the practice of many gospel preachers is mistaken of saying to an audience that "Christ bore your sins on the cross"; we can say this only to true believers. But gospel preachers *can* say to everyone that "Christ died for you."

This is what I have tried to illustrate by means of the two goats on the Day of Atonement (§5.5.1). The first goat illustrated the principle of *satisfaction*, that is, what in the work of atonement is necessary *for God* (Jesus "satisfied" God's violated holiness and righteousness). The second goat illustrated the principle of *substitution*, that is, what in the work of atonement is necessary *for the people* (the scapegoat being sent to its death as their substitute, carrying their sins). The first goat tells us that the work of Christ is so vast that salvation can be truly offered to all people; all may come and share in God's salvation. The second goat tells us that Christ has blotted out the sins of those who are "his people," that is, who have surrendered to him in faith.

In short: Christ died for all people (in this sense his work is unlimited in scope), but he atoned for the sins of all believers only (in this sense his work is limited in scope). The former point is sufficiently illustrated by the passages quoted in §§12.1.2 and 12.1.3. However, these verses do *not* say that by his death Christ effectually blotted out the sins of *all* people. Further discussion of this matter requires that we examine the exegesis of two passages: 2 Corinthians 5:19 and 1 John 2:2.

12.2.2 Second Corinthians 5:19

The apostle Paul tells us that "in Christ God was reconciling the world to himself, not counting their trespasses against them." This verse is about reconciliation, not about expiation, but for our present purpose this does not make much difference. The GNV has "God reconciled the world to himself." Some have objected to this rendering, arguing that although in Christ God did stretch out his hand of reconciliation to the world, this does not mean that the whole world *has* been reconciled. The point is, however, that translations have often rendered similar constructions in the latter way. An example is the second gerund in this verse: "counting." No translator would object to treating this as an imperfect, like: "In Christ, God did not hold people guilty for their sins" (ERV; cf. EXB, GW). Similarly, there can be no linguistic objection to the rendering: "God reconciled the world to himself."

No matter how one renders the expression, it does not necessarily mean that each separate member of the world population *has been* reconciled to God, perhaps even without such persons being aware of it. The Greek phrase ēn katallassōn does have more emphasis than a simple imperfect (cf. Luke 4:44, ēn kērussōn, "he was preaching"; KJV: "he preached").[10] At any rate we do not find here an aorist, as in verse 18 (Gk. *katallaxantos*; cf. Rom. 5:10-11), where the object is "us" (believers *have been* reconciled), but rather we find the Greek imperfect ēn, "was," which does not indicate any moment of termination; the offer of reconciliation is still going on.[11]

About this P. Hughes stated:

> The implication is, rather, that reconciliation is *cosmic* in its effects: it is applied in the first place to mankind; but since man, as the crown of God's creation, in his fall brought a curse upon the subordinate realm also, so in man's restoration the whole created order (*cosmos*) will also be restored. What the first Adam dragged down the second Adam raises up [with reference to Col. 1:20]."[12]

---

10. Bernard (1979, 72).
11. *TDNT* 1:257.
12. Hughes (1962, 209).

Similarly, F. Grosheide argued,

> What God reconciles to himself are not simply separate individuals, but is a cosmos, an ordered whole. . . . Paul speaks of a cosmos, an entirety, and includes this a little later in *autois* ["them"], in which comes to light that this cosmos is the entirety of those whose sins have been forgiven [in which he interprets the phrase "not counting their trespasses against them" as "forgiving to them their trespasses]."[13]

There is a close parallel here with verse 15: the "all" for whom Christ died are those who "live," that is, who "no longer live for themselves but for him who for their sake died and was raised." Thus, in verse 19, of those to whom God stretches out his hand of reconciliation (i.e., all people), it is only those who *accept* this hand in faith who are indeed saved. For them, the offered reconciliation becomes effectual.

12.2.3 First John 2:2

As we saw earlier, the question arises in 1 John 2:2 as to how we must translate: "He is the propitiation for our sins, and not for ours only but also for the sins of the whole world" (KJV; more correctly: ". . . for [the sins of] the whole world"), or, ". . . not for ours only but also for the whole world" (NKJV). It is debatable whether the context demands that we insert the words "the sins of" here; the Greek phrase *peri holou tou kosmou* allows both possibilities. The Vulgate has *pro totius mundi*, "for [those of] the whole world," which suggests the second rendering. D. Smith argued that the first rendering is indeed possible (cf. for a similar construction Matt. 5:20, "unless your righteousness exceeds [that] of the scribes"),[14] but he is missing the point: there are specific *sins* in the

---

13. Grosheide (1959, 170).
14. Smith (1979, 174).

believer from time to time, and there is *sin* in the world; it is thoroughly sinful. B. Westcott, too, preferred the rendering "for the whole world."[15] The text speaks of the sins of believers, and of the sinfulness of the world, *not* the sins of all people.

G. Barker defended the translation "also for the sins of the whole world," and interpreted this as follows: Christ's offering is sufficient for all, and it is necessary for all.[16] That is, all can indeed come, and none can come without it. It does *not* mean that Christ's sacrifice is efficient, effective, or effectual (Lat. *efficax*) for all, as though Christ's offering had blotted out the sins of all people (cf. §12.3). Therefore, no matter how one translates the verse, it cannot be taken as evidence for the doctrine of unlimited atonement (Christ bore the sins of all people). That is, the formulation "sufficient and necessary to blot out sins" is not identical with the formulating "effectively blotting out all sins."

To put it another way: there is enough soap for everyone; yet, some people remain very dirty. There is enough drinking water for everybody; yet, there are people who die of thirst. There is sufficient water for everyone (there is enough) as well as necessary water for everyone (without water one dies). But water is only effective if one drinks it.

In the light of these arguments, W. Kelly is too fearful when he argues that the inserted words "the sins of" corrupt the sense of the verse, and in fact suggest wrong doctrine. If Christ had indeed atoned for all the sins in the world, the whole world would be saved.[17] Kelly is correct: such a statement nowhere occurs in the Bible. But this is not what the first mentioned translation of the verse necessarily implies. It all depends on the force of the word "for" here: Christ being the propiti-

---

15. Westcott (1883, 44–45).
16. Barker (1981, 314); cf. Marshall (1978, 119).
17. Kelly (1870, 301–302).

ation "for" the sins of all people means that there is a just ground in the sacrifice of Christ on which God can meet the whole world (as Kelly put it himself). Because of Christ's work on the cross, propitiation can be offered to all people.

F. Grant had exactly the same view on atonement as Kelly, yet had no problem accepting the inserted words "the sins of"; in fact, he considered them to be implied.[18] He argued that, if John says, "not for *ours* only," he necessarily derives from this that it is also for the sins of others. But, as Romans 3:25 makes clear, propitiation is made effective only through faith. Grant also emphasized that Christ's perfect sacrifice was sufficient and available for every soul in the world, so that one can say "for the sins of the whole world" without any problem. The appeal and the provision are for all. The sin of rejecting this offer is blamed on the one who rejects it, and they will never be able to say that there was no means of salvation, or that it was not available.

Of course, such an interpretation—and I know no better one—does imply that the two words "for" (Gk. *peri*) in 1 John 2:2 do not mean exactly the same thing. Christ is the propitiation for our sins, and not for ours only but also for the sins of the whole world. In the first case, "for" means not only available but also effective: the believers' sins *have* been atoned for. In the second case, "for" means no more than sufficient and available, but not necessarily effective.

There is one other aspect is worth mentioning: not only is Christ's atoning sacrifice available for the whole world, so that no one has an excuse, but the text also implies that there is *no other* means of atonement.[19] If we take it this way, John's statement would also be directed against the pre-Gnostic heretics whom he was opposing. Nowhere in the world can there be found any

---

18. Grant (1902, 227-28).
19. See, e.g., Medema (1993, 60).

ground on which humans can stand before God except the atoning sacrifice of Christ (cf. Acts 4:12).

12.2.4 Summary

No matter how precisely we render 1 John 2:2, with or without the words "the sins of," the only conclusion that does justice to general biblical teaching is that the atoning sacrifice of Christ is *sufficient* for all people (they do not have to look anywhere else for additional measures), it is *necessary* for all people (there is no salvation without it), but it is *efficient* (having effect) only for those who in faith surrender to Christ and his work. Christ died for all, all people can come and may come, no one excepted—but only those who figuratively lay their hands on this sacrifice, will effectively receive a share in it. Atonement is offered to all people, but only the sins of those who believe *have been* effectively atoned.

I can fully agree here with the Canons of Dordt (2.3): "The death of the Son of God is the only and most perfect sacrifice and satisfaction for sin, and is of infinite worth and value, abundantly sufficient to expiate the sins of the whole world," and a bit later (2.6): "And, whereas many who are called by the gospel do not repent nor believe in Christ, but perish in unbelief, this is not owing to any defect or insufficiency in the sacrifice offered by Christ upon the cross, but is wholly to be imputed to themselves."[20]

One point mentioned earlier deserves more emphasis. It may be useful to point out that the L in TULIP,[21] *limited atonement* (that is, atonement for some, not for all) is in fact not sufficiently precise. We need a clearer definition here. T. Nettles called the view presented above a variation of the "limited atonement" view,[22] whereas Millard Erickson called it a variation of the "unlimit-

---
20. Dennison (2008, 4:130 and 4:131, respectively).
21. See Ouweneel (*RT* III/1, §12.3).
22. Nettles (1986, 302).

ed" or "universal atonement" view.²³ This neatly describes the terminological confusion that easily occurs at this point. Early in the twentieth century, A. Strong expressed the matter more accurately by arguing that what is limited is not the *atonement* but the *application* of the atonement through the work of the Holy Spirit.²⁴ B. Demarest argued that this view is not Arminian at all, but in fact is close to that of Calvin himself, and it was later, scholastic Calvinism that narrowed it down to the first view mentioned in §12.1.²⁵

In summary:

* Atonement is *unlimited* in that Christ's work is sufficient for all people.

* Atonement is *unlimited* in that Christ's work can be, and is, offered to all people (no one is excluded from the possibility of receiving it).

* Atonement is *limited* in that Christ has blotted out the sins only of those who believe.

* Atonement is *limited* in that Christ's work becomes efficient only for those who believe.

Especially these last two points must be investigated more closely, as we will do in the next sections.

12.3 Which Sins Atoned?
12.3.1 The Ambiguous Term "Unlimited"

We now come to the third view mentioned in §12.1.1, which claims that Christ blotted out the sins of all people, but only those who believe in him will be saved. This could be called the doctrine of unlimited atonement in three senses of the word "unlimited": atonement is viewed as unlimited, first, in that Christ's work is sufficient for all people; second, it can be, and is, offered to all people (no one is excluded from the possibility of

---
23. Erickson (1998, 843).
24. Strong (1907, 771).
25. Demarest (1997, 193).

receiving it); and third, it is unlimited in that Christ has blotted out the sins of all people.

This view is often equated with the previous one, but incorrectly so.[26] This and the previous view both state that Christ died for all people, and that all may come to accept salvation in faith. Both also maintain that those who do not accept his salvation will perish. The difference between the two is this: the previous view says that Christ effectively blotted out the sins of *only believers*, whereas the present view says that Christ blotted out the sins of *all people*. The cause of the confusion between the two views is easy to spot. Many people find it hard to imagine how one could distinguish between, on the hand, the statement that Christ died for all, that is, he is the propitiation for all, and on the other hand, the statement that Christ blotted out the sins of all people. It is not understood how Christ can be the propitiation "for" all without the sins of all being effectively atoned (blotted out).

Yet, in my view this is what we learn from John 3:16. God loved the whole world, and gave his Son for the whole world. However, what the Son obtained on the cross—eternal life—is for the benefit only of those who believe. All are in view, but few receive it. And if 2 Corinthians 5:15 says that "he died for all," this is clarified as follows: ". . . that those who live might no longer live for themselves but for him who for their sake died and was raised." Died for *all*—yet, those who effectively "live" are only those who believe in Christ, and are thus identified with him in his death and resurrection. The same Bible that emphasized that all may come because Christ died for all, *never* says that Christ has effectively blotted out the sins of all people. Salvation is *for* everyone—but only if one comes will one *receive* this salvation.

Of course, this view presupposes God's foreknowl-

---

26. See, e.g., the confusion in Van Genderen and Velema (2008, 526–31).

edge as to who would believe and who would not. How this fore*knowledge* (prescience) relates to fore*ordaining* (predestination) has been extensively investigated in an earlier volume.²⁷

12.3.2 "All" and "Many"

We find something similar in a remarkable passage (Rom. 5:18–19): "Therefore, as one trespass led to condemnation for all men, so one act of righteousness leads to justification and life for all men. For as by the one man's disobedience the many were made sinners, so by the one man's obedience the many will be made righteous." Notice here the distinction between "all" in verse 18, and "the many" in verse 19. As I see it, verse 18 deals with the universal offer of God's saving grace—and how could this offer be universal if Christ's atoning sacrifice did not have universal value and significance? Salvation is offered to all people. However, verse 19 deals with the two human families: "the many" who are the family of the first Adam, and "the many" who are the family of the last Adam (cf. 1 Cor. 15:45). Only those who, by faith, have come to belong to the latter human family have effectively become righteous ones.²⁸

Christ's sacrifice is so far-reaching that all people may approach to plead on its basis. This explains the "all" in verse 18. However, this sacrifice becomes effective only for those who believe; this explains the "many" in verse 19. This word "many" is entirely in line with what we find in Matthew 20:28 and Mark 10:45 ("the Son of Man came . . . to serve, and to give his life as a ransom for many [Gk. *anti pollōn*]"), and in Matthew 26:28 ("my blood . . . poured out for [Gk. *peri*] many"). The thought arose from Isaiah 53:11–12 (LXX): ". . . to justify the righteous one who serves *many*, and their sins he will bear.

---

27. Ouweneel (*RT* III/1, §§2.8.1, 4.7, and 11.3.1).
28. William Kelly, http://biblehub.com/commentaries/kelly/romans/5.htm.

Therefore he will inherit *many* . . ." As to the "ransom," compare 1 Timothy 2:6, God gave Christ "as a ransom for *all* [Gk. *huper pantōn*]." Jesus speaks of the "ransom for [*anti*] many," Paul of the "ransom for [Gk. *huper*] all." Perhaps we may go as far as to say that *anti* in Matthew 20:28 implies that Christ vicariously paid the ransom for the many as their substitute, whereas the *huper* in 1 Timothy 2:6 implies that Christ's ransom is offered for the benefit of all people.

A striking example of the difference between "all" and "many" is found in 1 Timothy 4:10, ". . . the living God, who is the Savior [Gk. *sōtēr*] of all people, especially of those who believe." In what sense is God the *sōtēr* of all people? Perhaps *sōtēr* does here means nothing more than "Preserver, Maintainer" (AMPC, DARBY). This is also the way the Annotation to the Dutch States Translation understands it. No matter how this word *sōtēr* is interpreted, the text makes clear that God did, or does, something for all people, but he did, or does, more for believers. What is universal is not effectual salvation, but the *offer* of salvation. We distinguish here between a redemptive universalism in the actual sense (cf. §12.4) and what we could call a kerygmatic universalism (cf. §§12.1–12.3).[29] In the latter case, a further distinction can be made between the *satisfaction* accomplished toward God, and the *substitution* accomplished with regard to people (see chapter 9). The former implies that Christ's sacrifice is sufficient for the salvation of all people. The latter implies that Christ has effectually blotted out the sins only of those who believe. He died "for" all people in the sense of "for the benefit of" all people. He died "for" the believers in the sense of a substitute: he died in their stead.

12.3.3 Alternatives

Many people live uneasily with the idea of an atonement

---
29. Van Genderen and Velema (2008, 529).

that is both unlimited (sufficient for all people, offered to all people) and limited (only the sins of believers have been blotted out). So we repeatedly encounter the tendency either to emphasize the unlimited aspect, which ultimately leads to universalism, or to emphasize the limited aspect, which led to the classic doctrine of predestination. Together with the latter view, I maintain that Christ has not blotted out the sins of all people. We do not find the opposite view in Scripture; moreover, it is difficult to see how any person could still receive eternal condemnation if Christ had blotted out all his sins. Together with the former view, however, I maintain that Christ did not die for the elect only. We do not find the opposite view in Scripture; moreover, it is otherwise difficult to see how we could still seriously and fairly offer the gospel of salvation to all people.[30] But I admit that we are walking a very narrow path here, and we can easily fall into the ditch on either side.

As we have seen, not all those who teach that Christ bore the sins of all people are universalists (i.e., those who believe that all people will ultimately be saved). They argue that, although Christ bore the sins of a certain person, this person can still perish because of their unbelief. For two reasons this must be wrong. First, unbelief is also a sin, which thus, according to this view, must have been blotted out by Christ as well, so that no one can perish because of their unbelief.

Second, Scripture clearly teaches that some people are eternally condemned—not just because of their unbelief but—because of their *works*, as the italicized words in the following verses demonstrate: the Son Man "will repay each person according to what he has *done*" (Matt. 16:27). "For we must all appear before the judgment seat

---

30. The division within the Dutch denomination known as Ge reformeerde Gemeenten (North America: Netherlands Reformed Congregations) that occurred in 1953 was precisely about this point: if God has elected only *some* people, how can he fairly and honestly offer salvation to *all* people?

of Christ, so that each one may receive what is due for what he has *done* in the body, whether good or evil" (2 Cor. 5:10). "He will render to each one according to his *works*" (Rom. 2:6). The dead "were judged, each one of them, according to what they had *done*" (Rev. 20:13). "Behold, I am coming soon, bringing my recompense with me, to repay each one for what he has *done*" (22:12). We read of the "Father who judges impartially according to each one's *deeds*" (1 Pet. 1:17). It is inconceivable to assume that, on the cross, Christ would have blotted out the sins of all people, and that these same people, if they die in unbelief, would have to undergo divine judgment for these very same sins. God cannot possibly punish the same sin twice; if he did, he would be less just than any earthly tribunal. The action of "blotting out sins" entails that they simply no longer exist.

I repeat, sublapsarianism (universal substitution, partial atonement for sins) teaches that Christ's atonement is *available* to all people. On the one hand, those adhering to the doctrine of the double predestination (partial substitution, partial atonement) should have difficulty with this. In their view, atonement cannot possibly be available for all, because Jesus supposedly died only for the elect. On the other hand, those who believe that Jesus bore the sins of all people (universal substitution, universal atonement) should have difficulty with the word "available" as well because it would be too weak: Christ *did* effectually blot out the sins of all people. The latter group consists of two parts, which differ on the question whether this means that all people will ultimately be saved. This question will be discussed in the next sections.

12.4 Consequences For All People?
12.4.1 Universalism
In the views we have considered so far, two questions arose: Is substitution partial or universal (i.e., did Christ

die for some or for all), and is the atonement (the blotting out of sins) partial or universal? Those who say that both substitution and atonement are universal can be further distinguished into two groups: those who say that unbelievers will still perish, and those who say that all people will ultimately be saved. The latter group is described by the (not so explicit and unambiguous) term "universalists." In a sense, the latter group seems more consistent than the former group: if Christ indeed blotted out the sins of all people, how could it be true that some people will ultimately perish?

Elsewhere, I have dealt more extensively with universalism.[31] Here I will simply point out that universalists consistently commit at least seven fundamental errors.

(a) Bible passages that deal with the *offer* of atonement to all people are mistakenly interpreted to mean that all people will effectually be saved. This is a logical mistake. The appeal "Come!" on the part of God or of Christ or of the apostle (e.g., Isa. 55:1; Matt. 11:28; Rev. 22:17b) cannot be interpreted to mean that all will come.[32] "Be reconciled to God" (2 Cor. 5:20) cannot be interpreted to mean that all will be reconciled. If atonement is "*for* all," this does not necessarily mean that all will receive it. And so on. As soon as this rather simple point is grasped, much of the so-called universalist "evidence" disappears.

(b) Similarly, passages like 1 Timothy 2:4 (God desires all people to be saved) and 2 Peter 3:9 (God does not wish that any should perish) do not imply that all people will be saved. God's desire encounters human unwillingness, which he respects but ultimately condemns, as we see clearly in Luke 13:34, where Jesus says,

---

31. Ouweneel (1995; 2012a, chapter 14); cf. also, e.g., Müller and Schirrmacher (1998); Parry and Partridge (2003); Van de Beek (2008).

32. In other words this is unlike the master's command mentioned in Matt. 8:9: "I say to one, 'Go,' and he goes, and to another, 'Come,' and he comes."

"O Jerusalem, Jerusalem, the city that kills the prophets and stones those who are sent to it! How often would I have gathered your children together as a hen gathers her brood under her wings, and you were not willing!"[33] The Lord wanted to save them, but the people themselves were unwilling. Traditionally, theology makes the useful distinction at this point between the resistible and the irresistible will of God. God's will to save *all* people is his resistible will; his will to save at least *some* is his irresistible will.[34]

(c) Sometimes, universalists cling to the word "all" without understanding the word in its broader context. For instance, they emphasize the "all things" in Revelation 21:5, "Behold, I am making all things new." However, first, "all things" is not the same as "all people" (see the distinction, e.g., also in Col. 1:20 ["all things"] and v. 21 [believers]). Second, they argue Revelation 21:8 away: "*BUT* as for the cowardly, the faithless, the detestable, as for murderers, the sexually immoral, sorcerers, idolaters, and all liars, their portion will be in the lake that burns with fire and sulfur, which is the second death."[35]

(d) Notice Philippians 2:10-11, ". . . so that at the name of Jesus *every* knee should bow, in heaven and on earth and under the earth, and *every* tongue confess that Jesus Christ is Lord, to the glory of God the Father." Universalists believe that this passage necessarily means that all people will be saved. They overlook the fact that, one day, even the greatest sinners will have to bow down before Jesus, but their bowing does not at all entail their eternal salvation. They will bow in a fawning (flattering, hypocritical) or cringing manner; compare: "Your enemies shall come fawning to you, and you shall tread upon their backs" (Deut. 33:29). "Those who

---

33. See extensively, Ouweneel (*RT* III/1, passim; see index).
34. See ibid., especially chapters 10-14.
35. This example comes from personal conversations with uni versalists.

hate the Lord would cringe toward him, and their fate would last forever" (Ps. 81:15; cf. Ps. 18:43–45; 66:3).

12.4.2 Eternal Destruction

(e) Universalists ignore the eternal distinction between those who are saved and those who will perish: "[A]n hour is coming when all who are in the tombs will hear his [i.e., the Son of Man's] voice and come out, those who have done good to the resurrection of life, and those who have done evil to the resurrection of judgment" (John 5:28–29). "[T]here will be a resurrection of both the just and the unjust" (Acts 24:15). One day, God

> will render to each one according to his works: to those who by patience in well-doing seek for glory and honor and immortality, he will give *eternal* life; but for those who are self-seeking and do not obey the truth, but obey unrighteousness, there will be wrath and fury. There will be tribulation and distress for every human being who does evil, . . . but glory and honor and peace for everyone who does good (Rom. 2:6–10).

"For the word of the cross is folly to those who are perishing, but to us who are being saved it is the power of God" (1 Cor. 1:18). "For we are the aroma of Christ to God among those who are being saved and among those who are perishing" (2 Cor. 2:15). Moreover,

> [T]he Lord Jesus is revealed from heaven . . . , inflicting vengeance on those who do not know God and on those who do not obey the gospel of our Lord Jesus. *They will suffer the punishment of eternal destruction*, away from the presence of the Lord and from the glory of his might, when he comes on that day to be glorified in his saints, and to be marveled at among all who have believed, because our testimony to you was believed (2 Thess. 1:7–10).

Notice the difference: there are those for whom Christ bore the punishment (Isa. 53:5), and those who will have to undergo the *eternal* punishment for their sins (2 Thess. 1:9).

(f) There is *eternal* (everlasting) life, but also an *eternal* (everlasting) fire and an *eternal* (everlasting) punishment (Matt. 25:41, 46). These expressions are used here as parallels; that is, the fire and the punishment are just as everlasting as eternal life. Arguments (often based upon a fragmentary knowledge of Greek) claiming that the word "eternal" (Gk. *aiōnios*) sometimes means "for a certain age [Gk. *aiōn*]," that is, temporary, are inconsistent. That is to say: why apply such time-limiting interpretations to the eternal fire and the eternal punishment, but not to the eternal life of believers? Is eternal salvation also brought to an end at a certain moment?

(g) Second Corinthians 4:18 makes a clear distinction between what is "transient" (or "temporal, temporary") and what is "eternal" ("everlasting"). This shows that in some cases, *aiōnios* is not limited to a certain time span. Of the wicked it is said, "[T]he smoke of their torment goes up"—not just "eternally" but—*forever and ever* [Gk. *eis aiōnas aiōnōn*]" (Rev. 14:11; cf. 19:3; 20:10), literally: "until the age of ages," or even, "the eternity of eternities."

It is quite remarkable that recently two defenders of universalism wrote that if a person believes that the Bible is the infallible Word of God, they will never believe that God will save all people because there are too many verses about judgment, hell, and eternal punishment to justify such optimism.[36] This is quite true. Therefore, the two authors demonstrate that they themselves can maintain their universalist doctrine only by contradicting or distorting the biblical testimony. They fail to realize that, in this way, *any* heresy can be defended. For more detailed discussion, the reader is encouraged to

---

36. Gulley and Mulholland (2003, 49).

consult my treatment of the subject elsewhere.[37]

12.4.3 Yet Consequences For All People

Earlier in this chapter, we asked whether Christ died for some people or for all people. This issue is linked with another one, namely, whether God's fair and honest offer of salvation comes to all people or only to the elect.[38] Apart from this, however, we may ask whether Christ's atoning sacrifice has certain consequences for *all* people, even if not all people accept the gospel. Earlier in this series, I dealt with the issue of common grace, which is a blessing for *all* people, and which, according to hyper-Calvinists *is not*, and according to others *is*, based on Christ's death on the cross.[39]

The first and foremost observation is that we are speaking here of God's grace as expressed in making the sun rise on the evil and on the good, sending rain on the just and the unjust (Matt. 5:45), and doing good by giving rains from heaven and fruitful seasons, satisfying people's hearts with food and gladness (Acts 14:17). Some would add here 1 Timothy 4:10, ". . . the living God, who is the Savior [Gk. *sōtēr*] of all people, especially of those who believe" (see §12.3.2). The Annotation to this verse in the Dutch States Translation understands *sōtēr* to mean here Preserver, Maintainer, according to the general sense of *sōzō*, "to keep, preserve." The Annotation refers to Psalm 36:5-6, where God "saves" (keeps, preserves) humans and animals. However, since Paul uses the word *sōtēr* consistently in its soteriological sense, it may be better to understand the verse to mean that God is a Savior *for* all people (cf. 2:3-4, God the *Savior* wishes all people to be saved), even if not all people wish to accept this salvation.[40] The work of the Savior is

---

37. Ouweneel (1995; 2012a, chapter 14).
38. See Ouweneel (*RT* III/1, chapter 13), and note 28.
39. Ibid., §2.4.2.
40. Demarest (1997, 191).

sufficient for all people, but *effectual* only for those who believe (§§12.1–12.3).

However, the consequences of Christ's work on the cross with regard to all people extend much further than this (cf. §12.1.3): "Father, the hour has come; glorify your Son that the Son may glorify you, since you have given him authority [Gk. *exousia*] over *all* flesh, to give eternal life to all whom you have given him" (John 17:1–2). Through the cross, the Son has acquired authority (power) over (or, a title to) *all* people, and he uses this power by granting eternal life to believers, and by sentencing unbelievers to eternal death (cf. 5:26–29; Matt. 25:34, 41, 46). Herein we also find the explanation for the remarkable fact that even the "false teachers" among God's people have been "bought" by the Master, even though they will perish (2 Pet. 2:1; see §12.1.3). Through his death, Christ obtained a title to them, which he uses to execute judgment on them unless they repent.

In a more positive sense, we may say that the entire world is affected by Christ's sacrifice, which is universal in extent and intention. D. Bloesch maintained that even unbelievers will share in the resurrection of the dead because of Christ's sacrifice. And they, too, profit from the cross and the resurrection of Christ since the devil and his hosts have been objectively cast down and slain, independently of the human response to the cross.[41] Even though they are not aware of it, unbelievers, too, are allowed to live in a world where Satan does not have the last word, and where sin will not lead to the final collapse of this world. They, too, profit from common grace, which operates in this world due to the cross of Christ. Today, it is still true for kings, as well as for other heads of state and for prime ministers, that "[t]he king's heart is a stream of water in the hand of the LORD; he turns it wherever he will" (Prov. 21:1).

---

41. Bloesch (1978, 167).

12.5 The Cross In the Walk of Faith
12.5.1 The Cross of Christ

In various ways, the believer interacts with the idea of the cross. On the one hand, there is the cross of Christ (this section), while on the other hand, there is the believer's own cross (§12.5.2). For the believer, the cross of Christ has two meanings, which are closely related: Christ was crucified *for* him/her, and he/she was crucified *with* Christ. Let us have a closer look at this matter, adding to these two related meanings, which refer to the cross of Christ in the believer's daily life.

(a) Christ died *for* (in favor of, instead of, on behalf of) the believer at the cross. He reconciled "both [i.e., believers from the Jews and from the Gentiles] to God in one body through the cross, thereby killing the hostility [between the two groups]" (Eph. 2:16). He made "peace by the blood of his cross" (Col. 1:20). God canceled "the record of debt [one Gk. word: *cheirographon*, a handwritten debenture[42]] that stood against us with its legal demands. This he set aside, nailing it to the cross. He disarmed the rulers and authorities and put them to open shame, by triumphing over them in him [or, by it, i.e., by the cross]" (Col. 2:14–15).

Here, various aspects of Christ's work on the cross merge: reconciliation between Jews and Gentiles, blotting out guilt, triumphing over (spiritual) rulers and authorities (in the heavenly places; cf. Eph. 6:12).

(b) Believers themselves died with Christ on the cross, objectively in AD 30 (approximately),[43] and subjectively when they, at their conversion, applied this to themselves, and realized it in their heart: "[O]ur old self was crucified with him [i.e., Christ] in order that the

---

42. *TDNT* 9:435–36; Ridderbos (1960, 184–86); Peake (1979, 527–28); Bruce (1984, 109n91).

43. A Reformed friend of mine was asked by an Evangelical, "When were you saved?" His reply, "In AD 30."

body of sin[44] might be brought to nothing, so that we would no longer be enslaved to sin" (Rom. 6:6). "I have been crucified with Christ. It is no longer I who live, but Christ who lives in me. And the life I now live in the flesh I live by faith in the Son of God, who loved me and gave himself for me" (Gal. 2:20).

Whereas point (a) deals more with atonement for *sins*, the present point deals more with the end of human sinful existence, that is, a person's old life under the power of *sin* (the "old self" or "old person"; cf. Eph. 4:22; Col. 3:9).

(c) Believers must personally and actively nail their sins to the cross: "[T]hose who belong to Christ Jesus have crucified the flesh with its passions and desires" (Gal. 5:24). Believers not only know that they have been crucified with Christ, but have acknowledged this judgment inwardly, and have accepted it. They agree with God's judgment upon their sinful nature, as though they themselves have nailed this sinful nature to the cross.

This subjective aspect must be an ongoing reality in the Christian's life: "For if you live according to the flesh you will die, but if by the Spirit you put to death the deeds of the body, you will live." The body is viewed here as the instrument of the flesh, the evil principle that is constantly inclined to rule it.[45] "Put to death therefore what is earthly in you [lit., your members that are on the earth]: sexual immorality, impurity, passion, evil desire, and covetousness, which is idolatry" (Col. 3:5). "Putting to death" means here radically doing away with these things by acknowledging God's judgment that he executed on them at the cross, and making this a concrete reality in Christian experience: "So you also

---

44. Regarding this expression, see Ridderbos (1959, 130); Murray (1968, 220-21).
45. Vine (1985, 1:456); cf. Ridderbos (1959, 179-80); Murray (1968, 294).

must consider yourselves dead to sin and alive to God in Christ Jesus" (Rom. 6:11).[46]

(d) The believer must bear witness to (the "shame" of) the cross: "For the word of the cross is folly to those who are perishing, but to us who are being saved it is the power of God" (1 Cor. 1:18). "But if I, brothers, still preach circumcision, why am I still being persecuted? In that case the offense of the cross has been removed" (Gal. 5:11). "It is those who want to make a good showing in the flesh who would force you to be circumcised, and only in order that they may not be persecuted for the cross of Christ. . . . But far be it from me to boast except in the cross of our Lord Jesus Christ, by which the world has been crucified to me, and I to the world" (6:12, 14). "For many, of whom I have often told you and now tell you even with tears, walk as enemies of the cross of Christ" (Phil. 3:18).

This is why bearing such witness is so difficult: because the cross involves the absolute end of the "old self," the natural, sinful human existence. Thus, this "old self" enjoys no other prospect than this cross, which in ancient times was so shameful: the cross of Christ (cf. §10.9.2). Those who preach circumcision (see the verses quoted above) wish to maintain a religion of the flesh. However, even when the flesh becomes religious, it remains just as corrupt as ever, and deserves no other termination than the cross. Many want to be known as "friends" (admirers, disciples) of Christ (of his life, of his teachings), while at the same time remaining enemies of his cross because this does not leave intact anything of the "old self," including the religious "old self."

12.5.2 The Believer's Cross

As surely as a believer must learn to figuratively nail his flesh on the cross of *Christ*, just as surely must they

---

46. Cf. Ridderbos (1960, 207-208); Peake (1979, 537-38); Bruce (1984, 140-42); Vine (1985, 2:563).

learn to bear *their own* cross, as Jesus explained several times (Matt. 10:38; 16:24; Mark 8:34; Luke 9:23; 14:27).[47] However, opinions on this matter differ markedly; we must identify and assess three major errors (see what was said earlier in §8.6.1).

First, this bearing one's cross is confused with bearing the cross of Christ, as if believers are comparable to Simon of Cyrene, who was pressed to carry the cross of Jesus (Matt. 27:32). Jesus challenges believers to bear not *his* cross but *their own* cross. And he does not force them to do this—they must voluntarily take up their cross, every day anew.[48]

This leads us immediately to a second point: the text does not speak of a cross that is *placed* upon people, as in the proverbial saying: "Everyone has to bear their own cross," in the sense of common human vicissitudes. This mistake was made by John Calvin:

> Thus, lest in the unmeasured abundance of our riches we go wild; lest, puffed up with honors, we become proud; lest, swollen with other good things—either of the soul or of the body, or of fortune—we grow haughty, the Lord himself, according as he sees it expedient, confronts us and subjects and restrains our unrestrained flesh with the remedy of the cross. And this he does in various ways in accordance with what is healthful for each man. For not all of us suffer in equal degree from the same diseases or, on that account, need the same harsh cure. From this it is to be seen that some are tried by one kind of cross, others by another. But since the heavenly physician treats some more gently but cleanses others by harsher remedies, while he wills to provide for the health of all, he yet leaves no one free and untouched, because he knows that all, to a man, are diseased.[49]

---

47. Regarding this, see the clear explanations of Greijdanus (1941, 146; 1955, 234–35); Lane (1974, 306–307); Bruce (1979, 531); and Geldenhuys (1983, 398).
48. See extensively, Küng (1976, 534–44).
49. Calvin (1960, 3.8.5).

If this approach were correct, there would not be any basic difference between a believer and an unbeliever since both deal with pain and sorrow, sickness and mourning throughout their lives. Job argues that the life of *every* human is hard: "Isn't a mortal's stay on earth difficult like a hired hand's daily work?" (Job 7:1 GW). However, Jesus was not referring in a general sense to a cross of hardship and sorrow that is placed upon us (passive), but to a cross that believers must consciously *take up* (active), and do so every day again: "If anyone would come after me, let him deny himself and *take up his cross daily* and follow me" (Luke 9:23). Notice the last three words: bearing one's cross is about following Jesus, about consecration and dedication, in brief, about discipleship: "Whoever does not bear his own cross and come after me cannot be my disciple" (Luke 14:27).

Third, taking up one's cross is not the same as crucifying one's "passions and desires" (cf. Gal. 5:24). The reason is that believers nail the latter to the cross of *Christ*—which is very different from taking up *one's own* cross. Therefore, in my view, J. Piper is mistaken in explaining Matthew 10:38 to mean that following Jesus as Savior and Lord implies that one's own sinful self must be crucified.[50] Is it so hard to grasp the distinction between nailing sins to *Christ's* cross and bearing *one's own* cross?

A. König rightly distinguishes between, on the one hand, diseases, pain and sufferings that believers must patiently endure throughout their lives and, on the other hand, sufferings that their enemies inflict upon them because they consistently follow Jesus.[51] Yet, even this appropriate distinction still accounts too little for the fact that the cross must be *taken up* daily. Jesus links this to denying oneself (Matt. 16:24), that is, submitting one's own needs and desires to those of Jesus. Every day

---

50. Piper (2004, 109).
51. König (2006, 296).

anew, believers must *choose*, so to speak, whether they wish to serve the honor and interests of Jesus, or their own honor and interests. In the former case they will indeed be persecuted (John 15:20; 2 Tim. 3:12), in the latter case they can avoid persecutions. Notice here the important words that follow in the text: "For whoever would save his life will lose it, but whoever loses his life for my sake will find it" (Matt. 16:25).

12.5.3 A Double Death Sentence

We must take into account here also the negative emotions that "bearing" a cross will have evoked among Jesus' listeners. As we see in the case of Jesus himself (John 19:17), it was the person sentenced to the death on the cross who had to carry his own cross to the place of execution. Jesus challenges his followers to take up their crosses, and thus, so to speak, voluntarily sign their own death sentence. Their Christian life is viewed, so to speak, as a road from the courtroom to the place of execution.

This is *not* the death sentence that was dealt with in the previous section: the acknowledgment that one's old self has died with Christ on the cross. The latter is the judicial death sentence executed by *God* upon the *old self*, which the believer must accept and internally appropriate. However, the passages about bearing one's cross deal instead with the death sentence by *Satan* upon the *new self*. It is a death sentence in the sense of the consistent following of Christ, which could lead to martyrdom at the hands of God's enemies.

Here again we find the two main aspects of the work on the cross that were mentioned earlier: the crucifixion as an act of divine salvation, and the crucifixion as an event of human shame (§§8.4 and 8.5). The first aspect refers to Christ's work on the cross as an atoning sacrifice. In this believers cannot follow him; in this he is unique and alone. The second aspect, however, refers to the cross as a place of martyrdom. In this, believers can—and especially must—follow their Lord by taking up their own cross. In the first case, Christians sign their own *spiritual* death sentence: they believe and acknowledge that in Christ's work on the cross they themselves, that is, their "old self," has died with Christ. In the second case, they sign their own *physical* death sentence: their consistently following their Lord may, as in the Lord's case, lead to they death as martyrs.

In the first case, the believer believes and accepts that they *have been* spiritually crucified, namely, in and with Christ at the moment the latter was crucified for them (AD 30). In the second case, they *might* be physically crucified, as sometimes happened during the Roman Empire, or die as a martyr in another way, as has happened to thousands of Jesus' followers, even after the Roman Empire.

In the first case, the spiritual death on the cross means for the believer the end of the "old self" and the birth of a "new self" on earth. In the second case, the literal death on the cross, or another form of martyrdom, means for the believer a passage from temporary, earthly life to the eternal, heavenly life.

12.6 Forgiveness[52]
12.6.1 God's Heart

The traditional doctrine of atonement puts great emphasis on "satisfaction," on a "ransom" that must be paid, a "debt" that must be met. Those who are familiar with this presentation might get a wrong picture by an emphasis that is too strong or one-sided, viz., forensic and commercial metaphors. It is true, the Bible does speak of "guilt" that humanity has toward God (cf. §4.7); and one might get the impression that this guilt or debt, thanks to Christ's sacrifice, is written off in God's books as though this were merely a bookkeeping transaction:

---

52. See *TDNT* 1:509-512; *DNTT* 1:697-703.

God "canceled the unfavorable record of our debts with its binding rules and did away with it completely by nailing it to the cross" (Col. 2:14 GNT).

However, if we look at God's removing people's debts only from this viewpoint, we will easily overlook the aspect of love and mercy, as it is illustrated in the parable: "So the servant fell on his knees, imploring him [i.e., the master], 'Have patience with me, and I will pay you everything.' And *out of pity for him* [Gk. *splanchnistheis*], the master of that servant released him and forgave him the debt" (Matt. 18:26–27). The prodigal son "arose and came to his father. But while he was still a long way off, his father saw him and *felt compassion* [Gk. *esplanchnistē*], and ran and embraced him and kissed him" (Luke 15:20). Guilt (debt) is not just written off, it is *forgiven*, and genuine forgiveness is inconceivable without the components of grace, mercy, pity, compassion, in short: love.

C. A. Coates described forgiveness as the unconditional declaration on God's part of his inclination toward humanity. God wants people to know that he and his grace are greater than their sins, and to this end he sends forth a gracious proclamation. Forgiveness is entirely *of* and *from* God; here, we are not in the presence of human need and ruin, but in the presence of God's infinite mercy.[53]

It is remarkable that Paul speaks of God's forgiveness in some of his loftiest passages: God

> predestined us for adoption to himself as sons through Jesus Christ, according to the purpose of his will, to the praise of his glorious grace, with which he has blessed us in the Beloved. In him we have redemption through his blood, the *forgiveness* of our trespasses, according to the riches of his grace (Eph. 1:5–7; cf. 4:32).

---

53. Coates (n.d., 6–7).

Elsewhere he speaks of believers "giving thanks to the Father, who has qualified you to share in the inheritance of the saints in light. He has delivered us from the domain of darkness and transferred us to the kingdom of his beloved Son, in whom we have redemption, the *forgiveness* of sins" (Col. 1:12–14). With Christ "you were also raised . . . through faith in the powerful working of God, who raised him from the dead. And you, who were dead in your trespasses and the uncircumcision of your flesh, God made alive together with him, having *forgiven* us all our trespasses" (2:12–13).

No act of God allows us to look more deeply into God's *heart*, and to receive a more glorious impression of his mercy and grace, his patience and goodness, than forgiveness. The first time that God himself spoke of this wonderful forgiveness was on Mount Sinai, at the very moment when the people had sinned terribly against him (the idolatry with the golden calf): "The Lord passed before him [i.e., Moses] and proclaimed, 'The Lord, the Lord, a God merciful and gracious, slow to anger, and abounding in steadfast love and faithfulness, keeping steadfast love for thousands, forgiving iniquity and transgression and sin'" (Exod. 34:6–7). David said, "[Y]ou, O Lord, are good and forgiving, / abounding in steadfast love to all who call upon you" (Ps. 86:5). And another poet of Israel: "If you, O Lord, should mark iniquities, / O Lord, who could stand? / But with you there is forgiveness, / that you may be feared" (130:3–4). And the apostle John: "If we confess our sins, he is faithful and just to forgive us our sins and to cleanse us from all unrighteousness" (1 John 1:9).

D. Pawson described a meeting in India of representatives of all world religions, where each had to describe in a few words the unique contribution of his own religion.[54] The Christian simply said, "Forgiveness." This was greeted with silence. No one else could have said

---

54. Pawson (2005, 45).

this. Forgiveness is one of the greatest wonders that Christians can speak of. The Jewish representative might have answered, "The Torah"—and what a magnificent gift of God it is. But what the Christian was referring to was what, for heaven's sake, must happen when human beings have totally broken God's Torah.

12.6.2 Forgiveness Is Expensive

Forgiveness may seem to be an easy job. You merely have to say solemnly and sincerely, "I forgive you," and everything is fine again. In reality, God purchased forgiveness at an unspeakably high *cost*, and did so in two different senses. First, God cannot forgive by simply turning a blind eye to people's sins. This would be inappropriate for the perfectly holy and righteous being of God, and for the entire system of morals and justice on which he has built the universe.[55] It may sometimes *seem* as though he forgives without an atoning sacrifice, but in reality such a sacrifice is always present in the background: "Indeed, under the law almost everything is purified with blood, and without the shedding of blood there is no forgiveness of sins" (Heb. 9:22). God needs a foundation or basis for his forgiveness, and finds it in the atoning sacrifice, as Jesus himself said, "... my blood ..., which is poured out for many for the forgiveness of sins" (Matt. 26:28). God overcomes sin not by denying it but by taking it utterly seriously. This is why there is no forgiveness of sins without a basis for this forgiveness, which God has provided in Christ Jesus and his crucifixion.

There is no *forgiveness* for guilt if there is no *payment* for that guilt, but then not by the guilty person themselves—that would require an eternity (cf. Matt. 18:34)—but by a vicarious sacrifice, a perfect substitute, which provides satisfaction to God. No forgiveness without retribution, and no retribution without the shedding

---

55. Erickson (1998, 833).

of blood. As A. König put it, "God's forgiveness is expensive, non-affordably expensive. At least it is non-affordable for us. This is the very reason why he provided someone who was able to 'pay': Jesus."[56]

Second, forgiveness cost the Most Holy God also something of his own heart, so to speak.[57] He is the God who cannot tolerate any form of evil (cf. Hab. 1:13), and therefore we should never speak of God's forgiveness in a cheap, superficial manner. This was what D. Bonhoeffer (murdered by the Nazis in 1945) meant when he spoke about "cheap grace" (Ger. *billige Gnade*).[58] God's grace is never cheap because God had to pay a high price to be able to show grace. He was willing to pay this price because he *loves* to show grace. There is no one who hates evil as strongly as he does—but at the same time there is no one who loves the penitent sinner as strongly as he does, and who forgives them as soon as the first traces of contrition and repentance become visible in the sinner.

A remarkable example of this is seen in King Ahab:

> [W]hen Ahab heard those words [by Eiljah], he tore his clothes and put sackcloth on his flesh and fasted and lay in sackcloth and went about dejectedly. And the word of the LORD came to Elijah the Tishbite, saying, "Have you seen how Ahab has humbled himself before me? Because he has humbled himself before me, I will not bring the disaster in his days; but in his son's days I will bring the disaster upon his house" (1 Kings 21:27–29).

This example shows that, if a person possesses and shows a droplet of repentance, God grants an ocean of grace. Sadly, with some people (not the least in hyper-Calvinist circles) the reverse is often true: they de-

---

56. König (2006, 447).
57. Cf. Ratzinger (2007, 207).
58. Bonhoeffer (2001).

mand an ocean of repentance before they are prepared to allow the other a droplet of divine forgiveness. Such people may think they are properly emphasizing God's holiness and righteousness, but they seem to have little understanding of the glory and greatness of Christ's atoning sacrifice. God is so liberal with his forgiveness, not because he takes his own holiness lightly, but because of the wonderful breadth and scope of Christ's work. The greatest guilt—that of humanity—requires the greatest punishment—everlasting damnation—*or* the greatest atoning sacrifice: that of God's own Son. Now that this sacrifice has been offered, God reveals the greatest forgiveness.

12.6.3 Four Aspects of Forgiveness

A terminological note: to forgive sins means "to send" sins "away" (the Gk. verb is *aphiēmi*). Compare the parallel in Leviticus 16:21,

> Aaron shall lay both his hands on the head of the live goat, and confess over it all the iniquities of the people of Israel, and all their transgressions, all their sins. And he shall put them on the head of the goat and *send it away* into the wilderness by the hand of a man who is in readiness.

Sins that have been "sent away" by God no longer exist in his mind or before his eyes. See §4.2 for a number of Bible passages that clearly illustrate this. In Matthew 18:27 and 32, the verb *aphiēmi* is sometimes rendered as "to cancel" (a loan or a debt), and the related noun *aphesis* in Luke 4:19 is rendered as "liberty" ("release, deliverance") for prisoners (captives). Otherwise, *aphesis* always means "forgiveness" of sins: release (deliver, set free) the sinner from them, "sending" their evil acts "away" so that the sins are no longer present.

When we consider this and related aspects, we may distinguish at least four aspects of forgiveness.

(a) *Canceling the debt owed (or the guilt incurred).* The most beautiful illustration of this is found in the parables. First that of the prodigal son (Luke 15:11-24): he confesses his sins (v. 21), which is the condition of all forgiveness (Ps. 32:3-5; Prov. 28:13; 1 John 1:9; James 5:16), and the father forgives him his sins. This is more clear in the parable of Matthew 18:23-35, where, out of pity, a king absolves the enormous debt of one of his slaves (roughly 225 *billion* American dollars). The debt is so great that the slave would not be able to pay even a trifle of his debt. Jesus mentions this gigantic sum to give his listeners an impression of their immeasurable guilt toward God, as well as of God's tremendous mercy.

(b) *Accepting the guilty one.* In the parable of the prodigal son, the father not only grants forgiveness, but he has the best robe put on the young man, and a ring put on his finger, and shoes on his feet, and the fattened calf killed, "... and let us eat and celebrate. For this my son was dead, and is alive again; he was lost, and is found" (vv. 22-24). In Pauline language: forgiveness involves being "*accepted* [KJV; HCSB: *favored*; Gk. *echaritōsen*]" in the Beloved," that is, the beloved Son of God, and becoming oneself an adopted son[59] of God (Eph. 1:5-6).

(c) When Paul deals with the subject of forgiveness, he links it with being *redeemed* through Christ's blood (Eph. 1:7), or being *delivered* from the domain of darkness and being *transferred* to the kingdom of God's beloved Son (Col. 1:13-14).

(d) The person who has received forgiveness possesses the promise of *eternal bliss*: the criminal on the cross confessed his guilt, and asked Jesus to remember him when Jesus entered his kingdom. There was a double blessing for the criminal: that very same day, he would be with Jesus in Paradise, and in the coming age, he

---

59. Gk. *huios*; here, better than the term "child" (Gk. *pais* or *teknon*); the difference between "children" and "sons" of God will be dealt with in the next volume of this series.

would be with Jesus in the Messianic kingdom (Luke 23:40-43). For the rest, forgiveness culminates in justification, a subject I have dealt with in an earlier volume.[60]

Let me add an important point here. Forgiveness is granted out of God's free grace, not because of the sinner's merits. For those who know Paul's testimony, this is self-evident. However, it may be helpful to emphasize that repentance and confession of sins should not be elevated to the status of a "good work": "For by grace you have been saved through faith. And this is not your own doing; it is the gift of God, not a result of works, so that no one may boast" (Eph. 2:8-9). Thus, even the believing surrender *to* God's saving grace is nothing but a work of God's grace.[61] Therefore, Augustine spoke of *gratia praeveniens*, "prevenient grace," that is, the grace that is working in the life of a person already before they repent, a grace working toward this repentance and conversion.[62]

12.7 Conditions of Forgiveness

12.7.1 Repentance, Confession, Faith

Forgiveness is not only a sovereign act of God toward people. In several ways, people's own responsibility is required for forgiveness to be received. To be sure, forgiveness is unmerited and free, but this is not the same as unconditional. There are at least five conditions that the person who wishes to receive this forgiveness must fulfill (see this and the next section).[63]

---

60. Ouweneel (*RT* III/2).
61. The construction of Eph. 2:8 is not entirely clear: the Gk. pronoun *touto* ("this") may refer back to either the Gk. noun *pisteōs* ("faith")—thus Bruce (1984, 289), but *touto* is neuter, and *pistis* is feminine—or to the Gk. participle *sesōimenoi* ("being saved"—thus Salmond (1979, 289)—or to the entire preceding sentence—thus Grosheide (1960, 40) and Wood (1978, 37).
62. McGrath (2007, 334); Ouweneel (*RT* IV/3, §13.8.2).
63. Cf. Pawson (2005, 48-50), who mentions the first and the fifth

(a) There is no divine forgiveness without *contrition and repentance*. David says with confidence: "[A] broken and contrite heart, O God, you will not despise" (Ps. 51:17). God promised his people: "I dwell . . . with him who is of a contrite and lowly spirit, to revive the spirit of the lowly, and to revive the heart of the contrite" (Isa. 57:15); "this is the one to whom I will look: he who is humble and contrite in spirit and trembles at my word" (66:2); "godly grief produces a repentance that leads to salvation" (2 Cor. 7:10). Some formal confession of sins without some measure of contrition and repentance has no value before God. The Lord said to some who confessed to be Christians, "Therefore repent. If not, I will come to you soon and war against them with the sword of my mouth" (Rev. 2:16).

(b) With regard to the confession of sins, the Bible does not call upon people to ask for forgiveness but to *confess their sins*. Of course, we do not take this too strictly; thus, Jesus teaches us in the Lord's Prayer: "Forgive us our debts [or sins]" (Matt. 6:12; Luke 11:4). However, we must not forget that this is a collective prayer ("*Our* Father . . . Give *us* . . . forgive *us* . . . lead *us* not . . . deliver *us*"). In their personal prayers, it would be spiritual laziness if people were simply to ask for forgiveness in a general and noncommittal way; it would only enhance a superficial attitude toward sin. The only exception is Psalm 19:12, "Who can discern his errors? Declare me innocent from hidden faults." That is, forgive me the sins that I have committed but that I was—or am no longer—aware of.

Even where, in the Bible, we hear the prayer. "Forgive!." this generally occurs within the framework of contrition, repentance, and confession: "I have sinned greatly in what I have done. But now, O Lord, please take away the iniquity of your servant, for I have done very foolishly" (2 Sam. 24:10). The context makes clear what

---

conditions.

The Extent of Atonement

David's sin was, and it was evident that his confession of it was implied in his begging for forgiveness.

Solomon prays, "[I]f they [i.e., the Israelites] pray toward this place and acknowledge your name and turn from their sin, when you afflict them, then hear in heaven and forgive the sin of your servants, your people Israel" (1 Kings 8:35–36).

> [I]f they turn their heart . . . and repent . . . saying, "We have sinned and have acted perversely and wickedly," if they repent with all their heart and with all their soul . . . then hear in heaven your dwelling place their prayer and their plea, and maintain their cause and forgive your people who have sinned against you, and all their transgressions that they have committed against you (vv. 46–50).

You can find more general terms in Numbers 14:19; Psalm 25:11, 18; Daniel 9:17–19; Hosea 14:2; and Amos 7:2.

Such passages clearly show the right order of things: contrition, repentance, confession of sins: "I acknowledged my sin to you, and I did not cover my iniquity; I said, 'I will confess my transgressions to the LORD,' and you forgave the iniquity of my sin" (Ps. 32:5). "If we confess our sins, he is faithful and just to forgive us our sins and to cleanse us from all unrighteousness" (1 John 1:9).

(c) It is hard to imagine a person repenting and confessing his sins to God without *some amount of faith* (cf. §13.6.2). "[W]ithout faith it is impossible to please him, for whoever would draw near to God must believe that he exists and that he rewards those who seek him" (Heb. 11:6). What is the benefit of confessing one's sins without some expecting that God is listening and might be willing to forgive? It is the conviction expressed under point (a) (Ps. 51:17; Isa. 57:15; 66:2): if I am really contrite and repentant, and confess my sins, God will not reject me. Afterward, the person discovers that it was

God himself who, in his mercy and through his Spirit, led them to confession: "God's kindness is meant to lead you to repentance" (Rom. 2:4). "The Lord is not slow to fulfill his promise as some count slowness, but is patient toward you, not wishing that any should perish, but that all should reach repentance" (2 Pet. 3:9).

12.7.2 Gratitude and Perseverance

(d) True *gratitude* concerning the received forgiveness, as it comes to expression surrender and dedication. If the cleansing of leprosy is a type pointing to the forgiveness of sins (see §5.6), the healed Samaritan offers us a beautiful example of this gratitude:

> Then one of them, when he saw that he was healed, turned back, praising God with a loud voice; and he fell on his face at Jesus' feet, giving him thanks. Now he was a Samaritan. Then Jesus answered, "Were not ten cleansed? Where are the nine? Was no one found to return and give praise to God except this foreigner?" And he said to him, "Rise and go your way; your faith has made you well" (Luke 17:15–19).

The latter point is quite serious; what may have happened to the other nine, who did *not* come back to give thanks to Jesus? Did they remain healed? What was their relationship to the *God* of this healing?

Paul says, "Rejoice always, pray without ceasing, *give thanks* in all circumstances; for this is the will of God in Christ Jesus for you. Do not quench the Spirit" (1 Thess. 5:16–19). "*[B]e thankful* . . . whatever you do, in word or deed, do everything in the name of the Lord Jesus, *giving thanks* to God the Father through him" (Col. 3:15, 17). "[I]n everything by prayer and supplication *with thanksgiving* let your requests be made known to God" (Phil. 2:6).

(e) True confession of sins is connected with *the inten-*

tion not to fall back again into the sins one has confessed: "Whoever conceals his transgressions will not prosper, but he who confesses and *forsakes them* will obtain mercy" (Prov. 28:13). John the Baptist said, "Bear fruit in keeping with repentance" (Matt. 3:8; cf. Acts 26:20). Jesus not only healed the paralyzed man at Bethesda but also told him, "See, you are well! Sin no more, that nothing worse may happen to you" (John 5:14). Thus, he not only granted forgiveness to the adulteress woman, but also said to her, "[G]o, and from now on sin no more" (8:11). Of course, this does not mean that believers indeed *will* never sin again. James says, "[W]e all stumble in many ways" (3:2). The point is not achieved perfection but the sincere intention of the heart to lead a life—in the power of the Holy Spirit—to the honor and glory of the Lord.

12.7.3 Forgiving Oneself and Others

(f) A person must also learn to forgive *themselves*, which means *accepting* God's forgiveness.[64] Being unable to forgive oneself, that is, to accept God's forgiveness, no matter how psychologically understandable this may perhaps be, is a form of false humility, of an unconscious desire to be wiser than God. It is unbelief, often simply based upon ignorance. Any single sin that we commit is more grave in *God's* eyes than we imagine—more grave than the totality of the world's sins is in *our* eyes—and yet he forgives all sins if they are sincerely confessed. Why then would the confessors themselves not accept this forgiveness?

God is the One "who forgives *all* your iniquity" (Ps. 103:3; cf. v. 12); "you [the LORD] have cast *all* my sins behind your back" (Isa. 38:17). "I have blotted out your transgressions like a cloud and your sins like mist" (44:22; also cf. 1:18; 43:25). "You will cast *all* our sins into

---

64. See Ouweneel (2004, 257-58); cf. Van der Voet (1996); W. Smouter and A. Hegger in Smouter and Blom (2001).

the depths of the sea" (Micah 7:19; also cf. Jer. 31:34; Luke 7:48–50; 1 John 1:7–9; 2:2). Why would sinners wish to be more holy and more righteous than God with respect to their own sins? Paul calls himself the "foremost" of sinners, yet testifies that he received God's mercy and experienced his patience (1 Tim. 1:15–16).

(g) The person who has received forgiveness must also learn to *grant forgiveness to others*. This point is of fundamental importance because Jesus makes God's forgiveness toward the believers explicitly dependent on it. He teaches believers to pray: "[F]orgive us our debts, *as* we also have forgiven our debtors" (Matt. 6:12). He says it even more strongly in the parable on forgiveness: "So also my heavenly Father will do to every one of you [viz., condemn you], if you do not forgive your brother *from your heart*" (18:35).[65] Elsewhere Jesus says, "[W]henever you stand praying, forgive, if you have anything against anyone, so that your Father also who is in heaven may forgive you your trespasses" (Mark 11:25). And Paul says, "Be kind to one another, tenderhearted, forgiving one another, *as* God in Christ forgave you" (Eph. 4:32; cf. Col. 3:13). Literally, the order is turned around here: God has forgiven you, so now you must forgive, too. This is not essentially different from: Forgive each other, else God will not forgive you. The forgiveness that believers have received from God in Christ, and the forgiveness they grant others, are inseparably connected. No one can be saved who is not prepared to forgive others, no matter how badly these others have sinned.

God's grace has the terrific feature that it is inexhaustible: the more a believer gives it away, the more it is multiplied in them, as J. Wimber said. If people refuse to give away what God gave them so freely—by holding sins against certain other people—God's grace dries up, and they will develop a sickness of the mind. Our fail-

---

65. See Brümmer (2005, chapter 4) on the how divine and human forgiveness are correlative.

ure to forgive is bad for people.⁶⁶ And A. König asked his reader, "Whom do you have to grant forgiveness to? Remember: his or her debt [toward you] is totally insignificant in comparison with your guilt toward God."⁶⁷

12.8 The Consequences of Christ's Victory
12.8.1 Eastern Orthodox Soteriology

In chapter 8, we pointed out the great difference between two standpoints—one that views Christ's work on the cross in terms of atoning sacrifice, substitution. and satisfaction, and one that views Christ's work in the light of warfare against the powers, triumph, and victory. Notions like forgiveness, propitiation, and reconciliation clearly belong to the former viewpoint. Notions like redemption and deliverance (from the power of sin, death, and Satan) clearly belong to the latter viewpoint. We are dealing here with two very different ways of considering Christ's sufferings on the cross, but which are not mutually exclusive (so we need to choose between them) but which describe aspects of the same event.

The former standpoint received more emphasis in Western Christianity, while the latter received more emphasis in early Christianity and in Eastern Orthodox Christianity, which was rooted in the thought of the Greek church fathers (Athanasius, John Chrystostom). As J. Verkuyl wrote, "The remarkable thing is that in the Western world those images and metaphors [of warfare and victory] have been greatly neglected in modern time, and that in the Eastern and Southern world they are often central. . . . Eastern Orthodoxy has never neglected this aspect."⁶⁸ This difference is due to Augustine, and especially to Anselm, who, through their doctrine of satisfaction, steered Western soteriology forcefully in the former direction. Despite differences with

---

66. Wimber and Springer (1986, 91).
67. König (2006, 448).
68. Verkuyl (1992, 238).

Anselm, the soteriology of Luther and Calvin can still be called largely Anselmian. In the Eastern Orthodox Church, there is much more emphasis on redemption and deliverance from the powers that held humanity captive since the Fall, viz., death and Satan.

The great metaphor of Western soteriology is—no wonder, given the great influence of Roman jurisprudence in the West—the *courtroom*: people are acquitted because their mediator, Jesus Christ, has paid the ransom for them (cf. chapter 9). *The* great metaphor of Eastern soteriology is the *battlefield*: people are delivered because their victor, Jesus Christ, has defeated their oppressors, viz., death and the devil (cf. §8.7). Greek church father Athanasius (d. 373) called Jesus' resurrection body his "victory trophy."[69] When you enter any ancient church, you will soon see the difference: in a Roman Catholic church building, the crucifix draws one's attention; in an Eastern Orthodox church building, the icon (fresco, mosaic) of the risen Christ is prominent. The crucifix points to Christ the sacrifice; the icon of the risen Christ points to Christ the Victor (Lat. *Christus Victor*). In other words, the crucifix points to Christ as the Lamb of God (Lat. *Agnus Dei*"); the image of the risen Christ points to the conquering Lion (cf. Rev. 5).

In Western soteriology, the central point is sin and atonement, as well as a new way of life, in which sin is increasingly overcome. In Eastern soteriology, the central point is the devil and victory, as well as a new way of life in which the devil is increasingly overcome. As John of Damascus (d. 749) put it,

> [Christ] was put to the test and gained the victory, in order that he would gain the triumph for us, and would give to our nature the strength to overcome the adversary, in order that this nature, which once had been overcome, would overcome its earlier triumpher with the same

---

69. On the Incarnation of the Word, 189, 195, 199-207, 251.

weapons with which it had been overcome itself.[70]

Thank God both are true: on the cross, the "body of sin" has been "destroyed [Gk. *katargēthē*], that henceforth we should not serve sin" (Rom. 6:6 KJV), *and* Christ went "through death" that "he might destroy [Gk. *katargēsē*] him that had the power of death, that is, the devil" (Heb. 2:14 KJV; cf. 2 Tim. 1:10, "abolished [Gk. *katargēsantos*] death"). Believers have been delivered from sin as well as from the devil and death—a great fact, the former part of which is emphasized more heavily in Western Christianity, and the latter more heavily in Eastern Christianity.

12.8.2 Theosis

At the center of Eastern soteriology we find the notion of *theosis*, the process of ever more closely approximating God and ever more closely resembling him.[71] This is indeed not a moment but a development. The Eastern church emphasizes less the statement, "You [plur.] must be born again" (John 3:7), and more the statement, "[Y]ou may become partakers of the divine nature" (cf. 2 Pet. 1:4). The great teacher here is not the Latin father Augustine of Hippo or Anselm of Canterbury, but the Greek father Athanasius of Alexandria. A great man of God indeed, known and appreciated also among Western Christians because of his positive role at the Council of Nicea (325) and because of the Athanasian Creed, which was not written by him, but named after him. Athanasius wrote, "God became Man in order that men would become gods" (cf. John 10:34–35, "Is it not written in your Law, 'I said, you are gods'?"). This must not be understood to mean that the creaturely distance between Creator and creatures would have been elimninated, or that humans would merge into the being of

---
70. An Exact Exposition of the Orthodox Faith, 3.20.
71. See Ouweneel (*RT* II/3, §9.5).

God, or would become equal to God. Rather it means that they have been brought into intimate fellowship with God, and that the image of God is becoming more and more visible in them.

Before the Fall, Adam and Eve, who had been created in the image of God, were called to grow ever more in their fellowship with God. However, through the Fall, the image of God within them had been heavily affected, and their spiritual growth stagnated. They and their offspring had become captives of death and Satan. When Christ became flesh, and descended to earth, not only was the image God in human nature restored, but Christ also waged war against the two powers that held humanity captive: death and Satan,[72] and conquered them. Now that these enemies have been defeated, and human nature has been renewed, humans can again ascend toward God and commune with him in intimate fellowship. This is *theosis*, the fullness of which is attained only in the eternal glory. Notice the emphases here: the actual enemies of humanity are death and Satan, and Christ has defeated them. Less reference is made to human guilt (though this is not denied or ignored, of course), and therefore also to forgiveness and justification. Rather, this approach emphasizes redemption and deliverance.

For a change of pace, let us state the matter this way: in Western Christianity, the emphasis is more on Colossians 2:14—God canceled "the record of debt that stood against us with its legal demands. This he set aside, nailing it to the cross." In Eastern Christianity, the emphasis is more on what comes next in the passage (v. 15)— "He disarmed the rulers and authorities and put them to open shame, by triumphing over them in him [or, it, i.e., the cross]." The jubilation of the West is: All our sins are gone! We have been justified! The East acclaims:

---

72. A more complete list would be: "the *three* powers that held humanity captive, sin, death, and Satan."

The Extent of Atonement

We have been delivered! We are free! Both are great and true shouts of joy.

A problem such as *"Once Saved, Always Saved?"*[73] would not arise that easily in the Eastern church because here the emphasis is rather on "salvation" ("redemption") as a process, which is finished only in eternity. The way of *theosis* is the way of continuous deliverance. This is first deliverance from one's own flesh: "Wretched man that I am! Who will deliver [Gk. *rhusetai*] me from this body of death? Thanks be to God through Jesus Christ our Lord!" (Rom. 7:24-25). This is positively a redemption *unto* good works (Titus 2:14, Gk. *lutrōsētai*), a deliverance from the power of devil and death (Heb. 2:14-15, Gk. *apallaxē*). Western soteriology points especially to the one-time punctiliar event: you *have been* saved (see, e.g., Eph. 2:5, 8). Eastern soteriology emphasizes especially to the succession of moments in a process: you *are being* saved (e.g., Rom. 5:9-10). Western soteriology stresses the positional: what believers *have* become in Christ (justified, sanctified). Eastern soteriology stresses the practical realization of this in a spiritual process of growth: practical justification and sanctification, learning to live as a righteous and holy person.[74]

In the Bible—and in sound theological thought—we clearly find the balance between these two aspects: God's Word is not oriented neither Westward nor Eastward, so to speak. At a certain point in time, believers *were* born again (1 Pet. 1:3), but that new life must be gradually developed within them (Col. 3:1-3). They *were* delivered from the evil one, but they still pray: "[D]eliver us from evil [or, the evil one]" (Matt. 6:13; cf. 2 Cor. 1:10). They *were* saved (Eph. 2:5, 8; 2 Tim. 1:9; Titus 3:5), but they are also still *being* saved (Phil. 1:19). They must work out their own salvation (Phil. 2:12 (cf. 1 Tim. 4:16), and they *will* be saved (Rom. 5:9-10; 13:11; 1 Thess.

---

73. Cf. the title of Pawson and Forster (1996).
74. See more extensively, Ouweneel (*RT* III/2, chapters 7 and 9).

5:8-9; 2 Tim. 4:18; Heb. 7:25; 9:28; 1 Pet. 2:2; 4:18). They *were* sanctified (1 Cor. 6:11), yet must still "strive for . . . the holiness without which no one will see the Lord" (Heb. 12:14). They *were* justified (Rom. 5:1), yet must still "pursue righteousness" (2 Tim. 2:22). They *did* receive the Holy Spirit when they came to faith (Eph. 1:13), yet are called upon to be continually (or, time and again) *filled* with the Spirit (5:18). Only in the consummation of the ages will they also receive the redemption of their mortal bodies (Rom. 8:23), as well as the inheritance that was promised to them (Eph. 1:14; cf. 4:30; Heb. 1:14).

12.8.3 Redemption

This last paragraph is an appendix of a purely technical nature; it deals with the various terms for "redemption."

The notion of redemption, deliverance, salvation, liberation, release, rescuing, setting free—already we have seven English terms—is expressed by several words in Greek as well. First I mention the verb *rhuomai*.[75] It has especially the sense of "deliver (from the hand of)"; thus, it is often used in the Septuagint for both God and human deliverers. In the Gospels, it appears only in Matthew 6:13 ("deliver us from evil"), Matthew 27:43 ("let God deliver him now, if he desires him"), and Luke 1:74 ("being delivered from the hand of our enemies"). In each case, reference is made, implicitly or explicitly, to the power from which one is delivered: "Who will deliver me from this body of *death*?" (Rom. 7:24); "that I may be delivered from the *unbelievers* in Judea" (15:31). "He delivered us from such a *deadly peril*, and he will deliver us" (2 Cor. 1:10). "He has delivered us from the domain of *darkness*" (Col. 1:13). "I was rescued from the *lion's mouth*. The Lord will rescue me from every

---

75. See *TDNT* 6:998-1003; *DNTT* 3:200-205. In Old English, the Indo-European root *w(e)ry* is found in *bewarian*, "to defend" (cf. modern "beware") and *weard*, "guardian, watchman."

The Extent of Atonement

evil deed," namely, which others could do to me (2 Tim. 4:17-18); "the Lord knows how to rescue the godly from *trials*" (2 Pet. 2:9). Often the word has an eschatological dimension: "The Deliverer will come from Zion" (Rom. 11:26); "Jesus who delivers us from the *wrath* to come" (1 Thess. 1:10).

The second Greek verb is *luō* with the related form *lutroō*.[76] The Greek verb *luō*, "to loosen," has many meanings, and only a few times does it have the sense of deliverance, namely in Acts 2:24 ("God raised him up, loosing the pangs of death") and Revelation 1:5 ("To him who loves us and has freed us from our sins by his blood . . ."). The cognates *lutron* and *antilutron* have been discussed in §9.2.2. Other cognates are *lutrōsis*, "redemption" (Luke 1:68 ASV; 2:38; Heb. 9:12) and *apolutrōsis* (Luke 21:28; Rom. 3:24; 8:23; Eph. 1:14; 4:30; Heb. 9:15). Waiting for redemption is looking forward to the Redeemer, *lutrōtēs*, a word that occurs only in Acts 7:35 as a title of Moses, but in a verbal form also in Luke 24:21, "But we had hoped that he was the one to redeem [Gk. *lutrousthai*] Israel." Similarly, Paul speaks of him "who gave himself for us to redeem us from all lawlessness" (Titus 2:14). And Peter: ". . . knowing that you were ransomed from the futile ways inherited from your forefathers, not with perishable things such as silver or gold, but with the precious blood of Christ, like that of a lamb without blemish or spot" (1 Pet. 1:18-19).

In the latter passage, the notion of a paid ransom is clearly present (as the ESV indicates), but this is not always the case. However, *luō* does always have the basic sense of "to loosen": the redeemed or ransomed person has been loosened from the bonds that held him captive. Moses is the type of the Redeemer (Acts 7:35): he who delivers God's people from the bonds of slavery,

---

76. See *TDNT* 4:328-56; *DNTT* 3:180-81, 189-200; the word is found in English words of Greek origin: analysis, hydrolytic, lysosome, etc.

and leads them out of Egypt into freedom.

The third and most important verb is *sōzō*, "to save," with the cognates *sōtēr*, "savior" (cf. §§12.32 and 12.4.3), *sōtēria*, "salvation," and *sōtērios*, "bringing salvation" (only in Titus 2:11).[77] The verb may refer to deliverance from physical death (Matt. 14:30 etc.)—or even *out of* physical death (Luke 8:50)—or to deliverance from sickness (Matt. 9:22 etc.) and from demonic possession (Luke 8:36 etc.). In its soteriological sense, God is the Savior (1 Cor. 1:21), or Christ (1 Tim. 1:15). Others are also mentioned as persons through whom divine salvation comes to people, such as Paul (Rom. 11:14), the believing spouse (1 Cor. 7:16), or the fellow believer (James 5:20).

Both God (Luke 1:47) and Christ (Luke 2:11) are called *sōtēr*, "Savior," the One bringing salvation. In a combined form we find: "our great God and Savior Jesus Christ" (Titus 2:13; cf. 2 Pet. 1:1; also see Isa. 43:3, 11; 45:14–15, 21; 49:26; 60:16; 63:8). Sometimes, Christ is called *sōtēria* ("salvation") in the sense of *sōtēr* (Acts 13:47). The name *Iēsous Sōtēr*,[78] refers to Jesus who "will save his people from their sins" (Matt. 1:21), but also "Jesus the One who saves from the grip of the powers."[79]

The Greek noun *sōtēria*, "salvation," may refer to deliverance from physical perils (Acts 27:34), but the most important meaning involves the entire subject of this and the next volume in this series: "salvation" in its spiritual significance (see § 1.3), both in its present sense (Phil. 1:28) and in its eschatological sense (Rom. 13:11; Heb. 9:28; 1 Pet. 1:5). It appears frequently in composite phrases like "a horn of salvation . . . knowledge of salvation" (Luke 1:69, 77), "the message of this salvation"

---

77. See *TDNT* 7:965–1024; *DNTT* 3:205–221; in English, the root is found in the term "soteriology."

78. Early Christians identified themselves by means of the Gk. word *IChThYS* ("fish"), whose letters stand for *Iēsous Christos Theou Huios Sōtēr*, "Jesus Christ, Son of God, Savior."

79. See Verkuyl (1992, 238).

(Acts 13:26), "the way of salvation" (16:17), the "day of salvation" (2 Cor. 6:2), "the gospel of your salvation" (Eph. 1:13), "the helmet of salvation" (6:17; cf. "for a helmet the hope of salvation," 1 Thess. 5:8), "the founder of their salvation" (Heb. 2:10).

Chapter 13
Atonement for the Church, the World, and Israel

*[Jesus created] in himself one new man
in place of the two [Jews and Gentiles],
so making peace
and [reconciled] us both to God in one
body through the cross,
thereby killing the hostility.*
                    Ephesians 2:15-16

*For when Gentiles, who do not have
the law,
by nature do what the law requires,
they are a law to themselves,
even though they do not have the law
they show that the work of the law is
written on their hearts,
while their conscience also bears
witness.*
                    Romans 2:14-15

*Now if their [i.e., Israel's] trespass
means riches for the world,*

> *and if their failure means riches for the Gentiles,*
> *how much more will their full inclusion mean! . . .*
> *For if their rejection means the reconciliation of the world,*
> *what will their acceptance mean but life from the dead?*
>
> Romans 11:12, 15

Summary: *There is one atonement (through the blood of Christ), but there are various beneficiaries. First, there is the church, which through collective atonement has become a commonwealth showing many different glorious features.*

Second, there is the Gentile world, which involves here especially those who have never heard the gospel. At least five different viewpoints can be discerned regarding the eternal destiny of such people, the most important ones being the exclusivist and the inclusivist viewpoints. In the present chapter, a moderate inclusivism is defended by means of various biblical examples; it is moderate because it is maintained that the possible salvation of the ignorant can be only through the cross of Christ, through the working of the Holy Spirit, and through repentance.

Third, the atonement for Israel is dealt with as it will be realized at Christ's second coming. The most important references are certain prophetic passages (Isa. 53, Zech. 12), the penitential psalms (especially Ps. 51), and institutions in the Mosaic Law with apparent eschatological meaning, especially the Day of Atonement and the water of purification.

13.1 The Church
13.1.1 Collective Atonement

In §10.7.2 we spoke of the "reconciliation of the world" (2 Cor. 5:19), and we saw that this does not mean what

Atonement for the Church, the World, and Israel

it might seem to mean: it does not imply the ultimate reconciliation of all humanity (cf. §12.4.1). In fact, Paul's words deal with the personal salvation of individual people. True, there *is* such a thing as the ultimate reconciliation of "all creation," or of "all things" (Col. 1:20); some speak here of "cosmic reconciliation" (§10.8.1). However, this does not imply the actual reconciliation of "all people."

This distinction may suggest that reconciliation is entirely a personal, individual matter. This is not at all the case, as we see in the important verse of Ephesians 2:16: Christ accomplished his work on the cross such that "both," that is, the believers from the Jews and the believers from the Gentile nations, would be reconciled "to God in one body through the cross, thereby [i.e., by the cross] killing the hostility" that had existed between the two groups. Here, reconciliation is not individual, but collective, namely, first, reconciliation of both groups (Jews and Gentiles) separately with God, and second, reconciliation between Jews and Gentiles within the one church (Gk. *ekklēsia*), the body of Christ.

This second point is the core of the entire passage (Eph. 2:11–22): believing Jews and Gentiles are no longer enemies of God, nor are they any longer enemies of each other, but together they have been included within an entirely new framework, one that is neither Jewish nor Gentile. It is something entirely new: the body of Christ. Formerly, those who are now Gentile Christians were "separated from Christ"; now, those who were "far off" have been "brought near by the blood of Christ." Formerly, they were "alienated from the commonwealth of Israel and strangers to the covenants of promise"; now, they "are no longer strangers and aliens, but . . . fellow citizens with the saints" (v. 19), "fellow heirs, members of the same body, and partakers of the promise in Christ Jesus through the gospel" (3:6). Formerly, they were "having no hope and without God in the world"; now, they are "members of the household of God" (2:19).[1]

It is quite superficial to read in verse 12 that the Gentiles, who were far from the "commonwealth [Gk. *politeia*] of Israel," and are now "in Christ" by faith (v. 13), today *would* share in the commonwealth of Israel. S. Salmond tended to this view: he described the expression "of Israel" as a "theocratic term," and went on to explain the phrase "brought near" in verse 13 as having become members of the theocracy.[2] Discussing verse 19, he stated that the expression "fellow citizens [Gk. *sumpolitai*, cf. *politeia*] with the saints" means that Gentile believers are now part of the greater "Israel of God" (Gal. 6:16). In my view, this is a twofold mistake. First, the "Israel of God" in Galatians 6:16 is not at all the church because it is clearly distinguished from the church, that is, the sum of all who walk by the rule of the new creation. This "Israel of God" points instead to the godly among Israel, especially (or exclusively) those who had come to faith in Jesus as their Messiah, Savior, and Lord.[3] Second, the believing Jews and Gentiles in Ephesians 2 are not "fellow citizens" of the *politeia* of Israel but of that entirely new *politeia*: the church. This is underscored by the addition "members of the household [one Gk. word: *oikeioi*] of God": here the *oikos* (house[hold]) of God is not Israel, but the church (cf. vv. 20-22).

An important term in the passage is Greek word *sussōma* (cf. Gk. *sōma*, "body") in Ephesians 3:6, which is difficult to translate: "members of the same body" (ESV), "members together of one body" (NIV), "fellow members of the body" (NASB), or "of the same body" (KJV). The brief rendering "fellow members" (MEV) might suggest that Gentile believers have become members of Israel.[4] How-

---

1. See Ouweneel (1991, 47-50; 2010a, chapter 3).
2. Salmond (1979, 292-93).
3. See extensively, Ouweneel (1997, 400-402).
4. The rhymed Psalms in Dutch (both 1773 and 1968 editions) say

ever, Scripture nowhere says that post-Pentecost Gentile believers have become members of, or have been incorporated into, Israel. For instance, the olive tree in Romans 11:16–24 is not Israel, for the text makes clear that the "natural branches" (vv. 21, 24) are Israel—and the branches are not the tree. The olive tree lives from the root (v. 16), and this refers to the totality of patriarchal covenant promises and blessings, upon which both Israel and the church are founded (cf. Gal. 3:7, 29).[5] I have explained this far more extensively elsewhere.[6]

The pivotal point in Ephesians 2, and also in 3:6, is that Gentile believers have become *syssōma*, fellow members in one body—not together with *Israel* but with all *Jesus-believers* from Israel. The text makes clear that these two categories of believers, Jewish and Gentile, do not constitute the "true Israel" or the "new Israel," or something similar, but something totally new, which in previous generations had been totally unknown (Eph. 3:3, 5, 9; Col. 1:26): the body of Christ. This is not some "Greater Israel," but is clearly distinct from both Israel and the Gentile nations: "Give no offense to Jews or to Greeks or to the church of God" (1 Cor. 10:32). Here, the church is a distinct entity alongside Israel.

13.1.2 A New Commonwealth

In my view, the course of Paul's argument is this: formerly, the Gentiles had no part in the blessings of *Israel*, but now Jewish and Gentile believers together share in something *entirely new*. In Ephesians 2, this new thing is described in seven different ways:

(1) the one *"new man"* (who is like a new human race, v. 15; cf. the same expression in 4:24);

---

in Psalm 87: "incorporated into Israel," which Reformed singers then apply to themselves.

5. Cf., e.g., Shelton (2006, 42).
6. Ouweneel (2010a, chapter 3).

(2) the one *body* of Christ (he is the head, with Jewish and Gentile believers as members, v. 16);
(3) the one *family* of God (the sum of all those who are children of the Father, v. 18);
(4) the one *politeia* ("commonwealth"), which is no longer Israel but the totality of all the "saints" (v. 19; 3:18);
(5) the one *house* or *household* of God (believers, as it were, living in the same house as God, 2:19);
(6) the one *temple* in the Lord (a place of ministry and worship, v. 20);
(7) the one *dwelling place* of God in the Holy Spirit (which amounts to saying that the church is the dwelling place of the Holy Spirit, v. 22; cf. 1 Cor. 3:16).

Formerly, believing Gentiles could join Israel as proselytes, and become part of the holy nation (cf., e.g., Isa. 56:6-7). However, today the situation is very different: a believing Jew becomes part of the *church*, and a believing Gentile becomes part of the *church*. They have been brought together on equal footing into an entirely new commonwealth: the church. As F. W. Grosheide put it, commenting upon the term *sumpolitai* ("fellow citizens") in verse 19: in the church, "the Gentile Christians differ in nothing from the Jewish Christians."[7] Gentiles have not become spiritual Jews, and Jews have not become spiritual Gentiles; together they are what neither was before: *Christians*. As A. S. Wood put it, being *sumpolitai* and *oikeioi* involves enjoying together all the privileges of God's new people.[8]

The new *politeia* ("commonwealth") and the new *oikos* ("household") are not Israel, but the totality of all those who belong to the Lord, the members of God's household, that is, those who, as his children, constitute

---

7. Grosheide (1960, 47).
8. Wood (1978, 41).

his house and are linked with him, said S. Greijdanus.⁹ It is not the "body of Israel" (whatever that may possibly mean), but the body of Christ, which consists of believers *from* Israel and believers *from* the nations. Nowhere does the text say or suggest that Gentile believers have become citizens of ethnic Israel, as if the distinction between Jews and Gentiles had been abolished. According to the prophetic word, even in the Messianic kingdom, the distinction between Israel and (believing) Gentiles will be maintained (e.g., Isa. 2:1–5; 60:10–12; Zech. 6:15; 8:23; 14:16–21). I have explained this far more extensively in my volumes in this series that deal with ecclesiology and eschatology.¹⁰

Reconciliation between Jews and Gentiles entails that, for the believers, the "dividing wall of hostility" has been "broken down" (Eph. 2:14). This does *not* mean, as many translations suggest, that Jesus has abolished (ESV) or set aside (NIV) the Torah as such. What was abolished was not the Torah but the hostility; see the KJV: "Having abolished in his flesh the enmity, even the law of commandments contained in ordinances," in which the word "even" can best be taken to mean "caused by" or "based upon'; as the CJB has it: ". . . by destroying in his own body the enmity occasioned by the *Torah*, with its commands set forth in the form of ordinances." Because of the sinful flesh of Jews and Gentiles, the Torah, haughtily observed by the Jews and despised by the Gentiles, had generated hostility between the two parties. Through his sacrifice for sin, Christ abolished this hostility in the hearts of those Jews and Gentiles who believe in him.¹¹

Removing that enmity implies reconciliation. Jesus-believing Jews and Jesus-believing Gentiles no longer find any reason in the Torah for animosity. They

---

9. Greijdanus (1925, 63); cf. Schlatter (1963, 188).
10. Ouweneel (2010a; 2010b; 2012a).
11. Stern (1992, 585–88); Ouweneel (2001a, 101).

have become members of one new man, one body in Christ, one commonwealth, one household, one family, one temple, one dwelling place of the Spirit. One in everything. The reconciliation took place "through the cross" (Gk. *dia tou staurou*), and the hostility has been removed "in (the power of) the cross" (Gk. *en autōi*), that is, on the basis of Christ's atoning sacrifice. This reconciliation entails not only a "peace treaty" between (believing) Jews and (believing) Gentiles but even their joining into an entirely new commonwealth.

13.2 The Gentile World
13.2.1 Stating the Problem

We now come to a subject about which I have written elsewhere, though from a different viewpoint.[12] This involves the recurring issue of whether the consequences of Christ's atoning sacrifice extend also to those who have never heard of him: the so-called "ignorant pagans." This discussion applies also (a) to "ignorant pagans" who lived and died before the coming of Christ, (b) to children who die at an early age (see the next volume in this series), and (c) to the mentally handicapped, who may "hear" the gospel but cannot "understand" it. We thus could formulate the question this way: What is the eternal destiny of all those who have never been *able* to accept the gospel of Christ, no matter the reason?

Okholm and Phillips, and also Fackre et al., have presented us with the various viewpoints concerning this question. Apart from the view that the Bible does not speak, or speaks too little, about those who have not heard the gospel, so that therefore we cannot make any definite statements about this matter (J. I. Packer, A. McGrath), the following five views are advocated.[13]

---

12. Ouweneel (*RT* II/3, §10.11).
13. Okholm and Phillips (1995); Fackre et al. (1995, see 20 for a summary); in these works, references can be found to the authors mentioned in the text above. A. Race (1983) gave

(1) *Exclusivism* or *restrictivism:* salvation is only for those who have consciously and explicitly accepted Christ; thus, those who have never heard the gospel are lost forever. This view has often been linked with strict predestinarianism:[14] just as God has *predestined* those who would believe in Christ, so too he can ensure that these people will hear the gospel (Augustine, John Calvin, Jonathan Edwards, C. F. H. Henry, R. C. Sproul, R. Nash, D. Geivett and G. Phillips, D. Strange[15]). Some Bible passages adduced (whose kernel is the notion that outside Christ there is no salvation) are John 14:6; Acts 4:12; 1 John 5:11-12. If I were an adherent of the doctrine of double predestination (which teaches that some people have been predestined for eternal life, and others for eternal destruction), I would be an exclusivist (or restrictivist) without hesitation. But I am not. Yet, I oppose exclusivism not on the basis of rejecting double predestination, but by means of arguments provided under (3) below.

(2) *Universal-chance-before-death* view: all people receive the opportunity to be saved, since God offers them the gospel before, or at the moment of, their death, if necessary by means of angels or dreams. According to some, this gospel comes only to those who have responded positively to what is called "general revelation" (the divine testimony of the creation): God sends more light to those who respond positively to the light that they already have. According to others, God saves those whom he knows *would* have accepted the gospel if they had known it ("middle knowledge"[16]) (without any specification, I mention here Thomas Aquinas, Jacob Arminius, J. H. Newman, J. Oliver Buswell Jr., N. Geisler, R.

---

the first classification: exclusivism, inclusivism, and pluralism.

14. Ouweneel (*RT* III/1, chapters 10-14).
15. Strange (2002) sharply criticized C. Pinnock's inclusivism on the basis of his (Strange's) Reformed covenant theology.
16. Ouweneel (*RT* III/1, §4.6.4).

Lightner). Bible passages that are adduced include Genesis 41:1-7 (the dreams of the Pharaoh); Daniel 2:31-35; 4:10-18 (the dreams of Nebuchadnezzar); Acts 10:1-6 (the angel appearing to Cornelius).

(3) *Inclusivism:* salvation is universally available, therefore also for those who never get to hear the gospel, if they only respond in faith to that (limited) part of God's revelation that they are aware of. The central point is here that this salvation is anchored in all cases in Christ; apart from him, there can be no salvation (Justin Martyr, John Wesley, Augustus H. Strong, C. S. Lewis, W. G. T. Shedd, B. Ramm, C. Pinnock, W. Pannenberg, J. Sanders; cf. K. Rahner's "anonymous Christianity"[17]). Bible passages whose kernel is the notion that salvation is divinely intended for, and offered to, all include Matthew 11:28; John 1:29; 4:42; 12:32; Romans 3:23-24; 5:18; 11:15; 2 Corinthians 5:19; 1 Timothy 2:3-4; Titus 2:11; Hebrews 2:9; 2 Peter 3:9; 1 John 2:2; 4:14.

(4) *Second-chance view:* those who, during their earthly life, have never heard the gospel will receive another opportunity after their death to believe in Jesus. According to this view, God condemns no people apart from an opportunity for them to respond to the gospel. Behind this view lies the conviction that God will ultimately show himself to be the gracious God to *all* people, sometimes with the implication that in effect all people will ultimately share in this grace of God (Clement of Alexandria, G. MacDonald, D. Bloesch, G. Lindbeck, S. Davis, G. Fackre). Bible passages for this view include Romans 3:23-24; 11:32 (salvation comes to be shared by everyone); 1 Peter 3:18-4:6 (there is also a divine testimony to the dead).

(5) *Universalism:* all ethical religions lead to God. Therefore, it does not matter whether the people involved have heard the biblical gospel or not; all sincere people will ultimately find God, or will be saved by Je-

---

17. Rahner (1965).

sus. Among universalists, we distinguish between those who believe that all people will ultimately be saved through the work of Christ, and those who believe that some people will be saved apart from this, on the basis of their own religion (without specifying their particular view, I mention here F. Schleiermacher, W. Barclay, J. Ellul, J. Hick, P. Knitter). The Bible passages adduced include basically those mentioned under (c), but now taken to mean that indeed all people will ultimately be saved.

13.2.2 Analysis of Viewpoints

Does the atoning death of Christ have consequences also for the pagan world, as well as for children who die young, and for the mentally handicapped, that is, for those who never heard the Jewish Torah, and afterward the New Testament gospel? Apparently, this question leads to very different viewpoints. For an explanation and discussion of the fifth viewpoint, a kind of post-modern variety of classical universalism[18] (see §12.4.1), you may consult my volume on eschatology.[19] The fourth view, which is based in particular on a misunderstanding of 1 Peter 3:18-4:6 (cf. §14.5.2), has often been linked with universalism.

The viewpoints mentioned can be distinguished in terms of the following criteria:

(a) Do the adherents believe that all salvation is through Jesus alone, or do they believe that there are other ways of salvation? It is the always the former, according to (1) and (3), it is usually the former, say (2) and (4), and it is sometimes the former, says (5). Verses like John 14:6 ("No one comes to the Father except through me") and Acts 4:12 ("there is salvation in no one else [than Christ]") clearly seem to plead for this option.

---

18. For a presentation of this view, see Gulley and Mulholland (2003).
19. Ouweneel (2012a, §14.4).

(b) Is people's eternal destiny established at the moment of their death, or is there a second chance after death? It is always the former, say (1), (2), and (3). Hebrews 9:27 ("it is appointed for man to die once, and after that comes judgment") clearly seems to plead for this option (cf. also Luke 16:19-31).

(c) Must people, in order to be saved, have heard and accepted the gospel of Christ before they die, or is this not an absolute condition? It is always the former, say (1) and sometimes (2). Some verses clearly seem to plead for the latter option, though: "[I]f anyone is a worshiper of God and does his will, God listens to him" (John 9:31). "I understand that God shows no partiality, but in every nation anyone who fears him and does what is right is acceptable to him" (Acts 10:34-35). God "will render to each one according to his works: to those who by patience in well-doing seek for glory and honor and immortality, he will give eternal life (Rom. 2:6-7; cf. vv. 8-16). All these positions will be explained in the following sections.

13.2.3 All People Enlightened?

Viewpoint (2), the universal-chance-before-death view, has much that is attractive to the reasonable mind: it would solve many of the problems that will be mentioned in the following sections. But this view has one great disadvantage: it lacks any basis in Scripture. For instance, God does reveal himself by way of exception through dreams or angels to people who do not (yet) know him. But from this fact, we cannot derive the claim that God ultimately reveals himself to *all* people who do not (yet) know him. Nor can we derive from it the claim that such a revelation leads the people involved to eternal salvation. King Nebuchadnezzar was not converted by his dreams as such, and Cornelius was not converted by his encounter with the angel as such. If these people came to genuine faith at all (in the case of the king this is doubtful), it was through the preaching of God's human servants: the prophet Daniel and the apostle Peter, respectively.

A unique variant of this view is defended by F. de Graaff, who rendered John 1:9 as follows: "He was the Light, the true one, which gives light to every person, when he (this person) comes into the world," and commented:

> It is said [here] in an irrefutable way that there is no human who did not have to do with the Light of the eternal Torah... The journey *to* the world begins outside the cosmos and ends in birth. Apparently, during this journey, every human is enlightened by the true Light, which is the heavenly Torah.[20]

De Graaff called his view irrefutable, yet few have accepted it. The KJV and others read: "That was the true Light, which lighteth every man that cometh into the world, "while modern translations often link "coming" not to "everyone" but to "light."[21] However, even if we link "coming" to "every man," hardly any expositor explains this to mean that the Logos enlightens a person *before his birth*.

De Graaff was connecting here with a rabbinic tradition: "You give light... to all who come into the world,"[22] but even here it is not being claimed that the Torah enlightens a person before birth. In the Talmud, Job 29:4 ("as I was in my prime, when the friendship of God was upon my tent...") is applied to the time that Job was still in his mother's womb: during this time, God supposedly teaches the entire Torah to the fetus.[23] At birth, an angel hits the child on the mouth, so that it forgets

---

20. De Graaff (1987, 134).
21. Cf. Morris (1971, 93–94).
22. Lev.R. 31.6.
23. Niddah 30b.

the Torah altogether, but afterwards during the person's spiritual development, the remembrance of the Torah is supposedly reawakened. Such speculation has no biblical basis at all.

Apart from this kind of interpretation, the statement in John 1:9 *is* quite remarkable: whether before or—as I prefer—after birth, the Logos who came into the world "gives light to every person." M. Dods pointed out that this is the verse on which the Quakers based their doctrine that God gives enough saving light to every human.[24] Thus, the early Quaker Robert Barclay wrote that some people have called John 1:9 the "Quaker text" because it supposedly proves their claim.[25] The text was adduced by the Greek church fathers as an argument for their thesis that the Logos had led the heathen philosophers in their philosophical investigations.[26]

In my view, it is more in line with the teaching of the entire New Testament to assume that, according to John 1:9, every human receives a certain amount of light from God, even if this consists of no more than God's testimony in nature (Ps. 19:1; Rom. 1:20), or the testimony of people's own conscience (Rom. 2:14-16). John 1:9 does not say that every human is indeed in effect brought to the light; many people prefer darkness (John 3:19-20). In the narrower sense, the verse could mean that "every human who receives light," that is, "comes to knowledge," receives this light "only through Christ."[27] Personally, I prefer to take the verse literally: *every* human is given light, which I take in the wider meaning: every human receives so much light that he/she has no excuse before God. We will return to this in connection with Romans 1:20 (next sections).

John 1:9 does not necessarily mean that a pagan who

---

24. Dods (1979, 686).
25. Barclay (1827, Fifth/Sixth Proposition, § xxi).
26. E.g., Justin Martyr, *Dialogue* 2; Clement of Alexandria, passim.
27. Thus Bouma (1927, 32).

does not know the gospel but does live after the first coming of Christ receives more light than the pagan who lived before this coming. To both, the same light of creation is available (Rom. 1:19-21), as well as the light of conscience (Rom. 2:14-16) (next sections). We may add to this the Noahic oral tradition of judgment and grace, which after the Flood, perhaps in a very mutilated form, passed through Noah and his offspring to all the pagan nations.[28]

13.3 Inclusivism versus Exclusivism
13.3.1 God's Heart For All People

Perhaps an entire volume is needed in order to compare the inclusivist and the exclusivist viewpoint fairly and extensively. Let me refer to the two publications mentioned in note 13. I exclude *a priori* three exclusivist arguments that are usually adduced against inclusivism. At least the variety of inclusivism that I defend, inclusivism does *not* claim that there is any salvation outside Christ (see §13.6.1), it does *not* believe that people who do not know the gospel can come to God apart from the work of the Holy Spirit (§13.6.2), and it does *not* believe that such people can receive salvation without repentance and confession of sin (§13.6.3).

In opposition to exclusivism, inclusivism emphasizes first that salvation is in principle intended for *all* people: "'I, when I am lifted up from the earth, will draw all people to myself.' He said this to show by what kind of death he was going to die" (John 12:32-33). "[A]ll have sinned and fall short of the glory of God, and are justified by his grace as a gift, through the redemption that is in Christ Jesus" (Rom. 3:23-24). "[A]s one trespass led to condemnation for all men, so one act of righteousness leads to justification and life for all men" (Rom. 5:18). ". . . God our Savior, who desires all people to be saved and to come to the knowledge of the truth" (1

---
28. See Ouweneel (2000b, 37-53).

Tim. 2:3-4). "[T]he grace of God has appeared, bringing salvation for all people" (Titus 2:11). "... Jesus, crowned with glory and honor because of the suffering of death, so that by the grace of God he might taste death for everyone" (Heb. 2:9). "The Lord is ... patient toward you, not wishing that any should perish, but that all should reach repentance" (2 Pet. 3:9). Christ "is the propitiation for our sins, and not for ours only but also for the sins of the whole world" (1 John 2:2).

Second, Scripture teaches that God was always interested in and acting on behalf of all people: "Are you not like the Cushites to me, O people of Israel? ... Did I not bring up Israel from the land of Egypt, and the Philistines from Caphtor and the Syrians from Kir?" (Amos 9:7). Paul told the Gentiles that God "did not leave himself without witness, for he did good by giving you [i.e., the Gentiles] rains from heaven and fruitful seasons, satisfying your hearts with food and gladness" (Acts 14:17). They lived, and to some extent still live, in the "times of ignorance" (17:30). There is an element of judgment in this, though, for these are the nations that, after Babel's confusion of languages (Gen. 11:1-9), were dispersed across the earth. Yet, people have wondered repeatedly whether it is not unjust if these Gentiles, who do not know the gospel and thus were unable to accept it, would for this reason be eternally condemned by God.

The Lord commanded that the gospel be preached to all nations: "Go therefore and make disciples of all nations" (Matt. 28:19). "[T]he gospel must first be proclaimed to all nations" (Mark 13:10; cf. 16:15). "Thus it is written, ... and that repentance for the forgiveness of sins should be proclaimed in his [i.e., Christ's] name to all nations" (Luke 24:26-27). "[Y]ou will receive power when the Holy Spirit has come upon you, and you will be my witnesses in Jerusalem and in all Judea and Samaria, and to the end of the earth" (Acts 1:8; cf. 20:25;

Col. 1:23). "I ask, have they [i.e., the Gentiles] not heard [viz., the gospel]? Indeed they have, for 'Their voice has gone out to all the earth, and their words to the ends of the world'" (Rom. 10:18; cf. Ps. 19:4). Jesus even stated as a prophetic fact: "[T]his gospel of the kingdom will be proclaimed throughout the whole world as a testimony to all nations, and then the end will come" (Matt. 24:14). At present, we are living in the time when this prophecy is almost fulfilled.

13.3.2 Ignorance versus Rejection

Are the Gentiles who never heard the gospel, and thus were unable to accept it, lost forever? It may seem that this question can be easily solved with the following (exclusivist) argument. Whoever believes in Jesus Christ, will not perish but have eternal life (John 3:15-16, 36; 5:24; 6:35, 40, 47; 11:25-26; 12:46). Over against this, it is said: "[W]hoever does not believe will be condemned" (Mark 16:16). "Whoever believes in him is not condemned, but whoever does not believe is condemned already, because he has not believed in the name of the only Son of God" (John 3:18). However, such a one-sided appeal to Scripture cannot solve the matter. The last verse of John 3 says: "Whoever believes in the Son has eternal life; whoever does not obey the Son shall not see life, but the wrath of God remains on him" (v. 36). Notice the term "not obey"; this implies that some people *heard* the gospel but did not *obey* it. They are condemned. However, the verse does not tell us anything about those who have *not* heard the gospel, and therefore have *not* disobeyed it. They could not obey it because they did not know it; but neither have they disobeyed the gospel.

In this context, we should notice the remarkable distinction made in 2 Thessalonians 1:8 between "those who do not know God" and "those who do not obey the gospel of our Lord Jesus." Incidentally, both groups fall under God's judgment, and this might seem an argument for exclusivism. The first group apparently includes those who have never heard the gospel: "Pour out your anger on the nations that do not know you" (Ps. 79:6; cf. Jer. 10:25). "Formerly, when you did not know God, you were enslaved to those that by nature are not gods" (Gal. 4:8; cf. 1 Thess. 4:5). The Gentiles "are darkened in their understanding, alienated from the life of God because of the ignorance that is in them, due to their hardness of heart" (Eph. 4:18). Second Thessalonians 1:8 indicates that at least *some* of those who do not know the gospel definitely come under the vengeance of God. This is not simply because they are pagans but because they are immoral pagans in the sense of Romans 1:28-29. Some pagans themselves have *chosen* not to "retain God in [their] knowledge" (v. 28 KJV). As H. Ridderbos put it: "The chosen words express the snooty attitude of people toward God. They have excluded God as a negligible quantity."[29]

This can be understood properly only if we assume that pagans can have *some* knowledge of God. This is exactly what is argued in Romans 1:18, "[T]he wrath of God is revealed from heaven against all ungodliness and unrighteousness of men, who by their unrighteousness suppress [Gk. *katechontōn*] the truth [KJV: hold the truth in unrighteousness[30]]." In other words, they are definitely familiar with (a certain amount of) "the truth," but ignore it. What truth is this? The text continues,

> For *what can be known about God* is plain to them, because God has shown it to them. For his invisible attributes, namely, his eternal power and divine nature, have been clearly perceived, ever since the creation of the world, in the things that have been made. So they are without excuse. For *although they knew God*, they did not honor him as God or give thanks to him, but they became futile in

---

29. Ridderbos (1959, 48).
30. Cf. ibid., 41; Murray (1968, 37); the more common translation of the Gk. verb *katechō* is "to possess, to hold."

their thinking, and their foolish hearts were darkened (Rom. 1:19-21).

In summary, the Gentiles "know" God not in the sense of knowing the gospel, but they know him—at least they are viewed as those who ought to know him—insofar as "his invisible attributes, namely, his eternal power and divine nature" may be perceived in the works of his creation. Despite this knowledge, they have generally followed the way of unrighteousness, in particular that of idolatry in the widest sense of the term (cf. Eph. 5:5; 1 John 5:21).

13.4 Living in the Spirit of the Torah
13.4.1 Romans 2

Many Gentiles have an awareness of God, but this has not led them to serving God; instead, they serve idols. However, according to Romans 2, this is not true of *all* Gentiles: God

> will render to each one according to his works: to those who by patience in well-doing seek for glory and honor and immortality, he will give eternal life; but for those who are self-seeking and do not obey the truth, but obey unrighteousness, there will be wrath and fury. There will be tribulation and distress for every human being who does evil, the Jew first and also the Greek, but glory and honor and peace for everyone who does good, the Jew first and also the Greek. For God shows no partiality" (Rom. 2:6-11).

This is a remarkable statement.[31] Without any reference to the gospel, Paul says here explicitly that to those who "by patience in well-doing seek for glory and honor and immortality," and to "everyone who does good,"

---
31. Cf. Van Leeuwen and Jacobs (1952, 49-53); Ridderbos (1959, 55-61); Murray (1968, 62-76); Harrison (1976, 29-32); Denney (1979, 596-98); Vine (1985, 1:386-89).

God will give eternal life, glory, honor, and peace.

Paul continues,

> For all who have sinned without the law [i.e., the Mosaic Torah] will also perish without the law, and all who have sinned under the law [i.e., the Jews] will be judged by the law. For it is not the hearers of the law who are righteous before God, but *the doers of the law who will be justified*. For when Gentiles, who do not have the law,[32] by nature do what the law requires, they are a law to themselves, even though they do not have the law. They show that the work of the law is written on their hearts, while their conscience also bears witness, and their conflicting thoughts accuse or even excuse them on that day when, according to my gospel, God judges the secrets of men by Christ Jesus" (Rom. 2:12-16).

In other words, the doers of the Torah are justified, whether they have known the Torah, as the Jews do, or not. Those who do not know the Torah but have lived according to their conscience in the spirit of the Torah are saved. In Romans 1:20 people are without excuse because they have the testimony of the creation. In Romans 2:1 they are without excuse because they know how to pass judgment on others who do evil, and this shows that they have a certain awareness of good and evil. But this also shows that they should condemn *themselves* before God.[33] Moreover, they are aware of God's "kindness and forbearance and patience" (Rom. 2:4) in the sense that, apparently, God does not immediately punishes evil but allows time for repentance. This gives them all the more reason to humble themselves before God and throw themselves upon his mercy.

H. Ridderbos was correct when he wrote that Paul's

---

32. Notice that the Gk. noun *nomos* ("law") has no article in these verses; perhaps the meaning is "a law," in the sense of any explicit moral law.
33. Coates (1926, 32).

"description of those who, persevering in good works, will receive eternal life" is "certainly not intended as an unreal hypothesis,"[34] referring to many Bible passages that speak of God judging people "according to their works" (1 Cor. 1:8; 3:12-15; 4:4-5; 2 Cor. 5:10; 1 Thess. 3:13; 5:23; Murray also refers to Matt. 16:27; 25:31-46; John 5:29; Gal. 6:7-10; Eph. 6:8; Col. 3:23-24;[35] cf. Eccl. 12:14). I myself think of Zechariah and Elizabeth, who "were both righteous before God, walking blamelessly in all the commandments and statutes of the Lord" (Luke 1:6). In principle, such godly people might just as well appear among the Gentiles; the description would then be: they are righteous before God, walking blamelessly in the spirit of the Torah.

13.4.2 Cornelius

An interesting example is the Roman centurion Cornelius, who was "a devout man who feared God with all his household, gave alms generously to the people, and prayed continually to God" (Acts 10:2). Peter said of him and his friends, "Truly I understand that God shows no partiality, but in every nation anyone who fears him and does what is right is acceptable to him" (vv. 34-35). Together with earlier theologians such as Johann Bengel and Johannes Weiss, R. Knowling correctly believed that all the terms used here are applicable to the piety that could be reached by any pagan, without the latter necessarily being a Jewish proselyte, or even having any knowledge of the Jewish Scriptures (as Cornelius must have had).[36]

Indeed, Peter's statement is general and universal. God "shows no partiality," that is, a Jew is not *a priori* more pleasing to him than a Gentile. What interests God

---

34. Ridderbos (1959, 55); so too Philippi (1878, ad loc.); Sanday and Headlam (1950, ad loc.); Murray (1968, 63).
35. Murray (1968, 63).
36. Knowling (1979, 259).

is, first, whether a person—Jew or Gentile—is God-fearing (godly, pious), in accordance with as little or as much as the person may know about God. And second, there must be not only the proper attitude but also the proper works: a person must "do what is right." That is, if the person is a Jew they must keep the Torah; if he/she is a Gentile, they must live in the spirit of the Torah. Whether Jew or Gentile (think of Melchizedek, Job, Asenath,[37] Jethro, Rahab,[38] Heber and Jael, Ruth, Naaman, Rechab, Ebed-Melech, and these are only a few), such a person is acceptable to God.

F. F. Bruce wrote, "If, as Micah said, the Lord's primary requirements were that a man should do justly and love mercy and walk humbly with his God (Micah 6:8), then a Gentile might fulfil these requirements as well as an Israelite."[39] Of course, this is a simply a statement of principle; whether such Gentiles have ever existed, and whether their numbers were considerable, is another matter.

13.4.3 Areopagus

Paul seemed to say a similar thing on the Areopagus: all truly godly people are acceptable (pleasant) to God:

> [H]e made from one man every nation of mankind to live on all the face of the earth, . . . that they should seek God, and perhaps feel their way toward him and find him. Yet he is actually not far from each one of us, for "In him we live and move and have our being"; as even some of your own poets have said, "For we are indeed his offspring" (Acts 17:26-28).

---

37. According to the Midrash Tadshe, this pagan woman was a Jewish convert, like Hagar, Zipporah, Shiphrah, Puah, the daughter of Pharaoh, Rahab, Ruth, and Jael.
38. In Heb. 11, apart from the heroes who lived before the patriarchs, Rahab is the only non-Jewish person mentioned (v. 31).
39. Bruce (1988, 225).

Here we learn that (a) all humanity is interconnected through blood relationships; (b) all people were created with the intention that they should seek God, and in some way or another find their way to him; (c) this is not all too difficult because God is very near to humans, and they have "descended" from him.

Paul discerned a deep inner connection between the religion of the Greeks and the worship of the true God by proclaiming that with all their idols, the Greeks also served the God of the Bible—as well or as badly as they could, of course. This was true, even though they could not refer to this One in no other way than as the "unknown God" (Gk. *Agnōstos Theos*). The Athenians had some awareness of the one true God. This corresponds to what Paul wrote in Romans 1 and 2.

Paul was able to see the connection between the Athenian religion and the true God because every pagan religion is nothing but a response, no matter how mutilated, incomplete, and partially deceitful, to the general revelation of God as Creator (i.e., contained in creation), and also partially to the special revelation of God as Judge, passed on through oral tradition from Noah and his sons.

In summary, in my view there can be no doubt that Gentiles "who by patience in well-doing seek for glory and honor and immortality," or, "do good," or, "fear God and do what is right," or, are "doers of the Torah" (though they do not explicitly know it), are certainly and effectively *accepted by God*.[40] In the remarkably insightful words of the blind man who was healed: "We know that God does not listen to sinners, but if anyone is a worshiper of God and does his will, God listens to him" (John 9:31).

---

40. The Gk. term *dektos*, "acceptable" (Acts 10:35) comes from *dechomai*, "to accept"; see, e.g., Acts 8:14; 11:1; 17:11; 1 Cor. 2:14; 2 Cor. 7:15; Gal. 4:14; 1 Thess. 1:6; 2:13; 2 Thess. 2:10).

13.5 The Encounter With Jesus
13.5.1 Saul and Paul

Exclusivists have raised an important objection with regard to inclusivism, to which we must now pay careful attention. If people live faithfully according to the Torah, why then, when they hear the gospel, do they still need to be converted? Saul of Tarsus was (supposedly) an example of such a person. Regarding his life before his conversion, he could claim that he was "as to righteousness under the law, blameless" (Phil. 3:6). He could say to the Jewish Council, "Brothers, I have lived my life before God in all good conscience *up to this day*" (Acts 23:1). Paul seemed to belong entirely to the category of Zechariah and Elizabeth, "righteous before God, walking blamelessly in all the commandments and statutes of the Lord" (Luke 1:6).

Exclusivist R. Nash argued that Saul of Tarsus passed every test of inclusivist salvation. In Nash's view, Saul completely satisfied C. Pinnock's principle of faith. Saul not only believed that God existed, but he also sought him diligently. In fact, he sought Yahweh with such diligence that he cooperated in the persecution and execution of Yahweh's enemies (Acts 22:20). It is appropriate to read Paul's own description of his zeal for God before his conversion (Nash refers to Acts 26:4–5; Phil. 3:4–6, "as to righteousness under the law, blameless"; I would add Gal. 1:14, "I was advancing in Judaism beyond many of my own age among my people, so extremely zealous was I for the traditions of my fathers"). If inclusivism were true, Nash argues, Saul the Pharisee was saved. However, this view was not shared by the divinely inspired author Paul the apostle (Phil. 3:7–11). Even though Paul satisfied every demand of inclusivist salvation, he still was a lost sinner (1 Tim. 1:15).[41]

In answer to this argument by Nash, G. Fackre correctly distinguished between Saul's life of self-righ-

---
41. Quoted in Fackre et al. (1995, 138–39).

teousness by works and Paul's saving faith.[42] He argued that there is an enormous difference between "implicit faith" (which saves the person involved) and religious (often self-conceited, arrogant) moralism (which does not save the person). Zeal, accepting certain truths, and good works are not the same as the saving confidence of faith deeply embedded in a humble, penitent person, whether that person is a Christian or someone who has never heard the gospel. In other words, among both non-Christians and confessing Christians there are those for whom religion is an internal matter, and those for whom it is a purely external matter.[43] When it comes to such pseudo-Christians, it is better to be a pagan who has never heard the gospel than to be a baptized person who neglects such a great salvation.[44]

In summary: Saul of Tarsus did not at all satisfy the "demands of inclusivist salvation" because he was a moralist and a legalist, as well as a religious fanatic. The true condition of his heart became manifest when he began harshly persecuting Christians, followers of Jesus. What Paul said of Israel had been equally true of himself: "I bear them witness that they have a zeal for God, but not according to knowledge" (Rom. 10:2). Saul of Tarsus was zealous enough, but had he ever penitently humbled himself before God? It was only *after* he encountered Jesus that he could truly say, "Wretched man that I am! Who will deliver me from this body of death? Thanks be to God through Jesus Christ our Lord!" (Rom. 7:24–25).

13.5.2 "Anonymous Christians"[45]

The case of Saul and similar cases make clear that

---

42. Ibid., 155.
43. Cf. the psychological distinction of Allport and Ross (1967) between "intrinsic" and "extrinsic religiosity."
44. Kelly (1927, 23).
45. The expression comes from Karl Rahner (see §13.2.1).

among those who have never heard the gospel, we must distinguish between two different groups: those who are moralists, legalists, and self-conceited like Saul, and those who are truly God-fearing like Zechariah and Elizabeth (Luke 1:6). Saul's case shows how difficult it can be to assess to what category a person belongs. This is because we cannot judge a person's *heart*—only God can (cf. 1 Chron. 28:9; Ps. 139:23; Jer. 17:10; Acts 1:24; Rom. 8:27; Rev. 1:23). No doubt there were in Israel many pious people such as rabbi Gamaliel (Acts 5:34-39; 22:3), but, as far as we can tell, this man knew Jesus but never accepted him as Messiah, Savior, and Lord. This showed what was in his heart. (An obscure legend, though, claims that Gamaliel later became a Jesus-follower.[46])

Thank God, other Pharisees, like Nicodemus (John 3:1) and others (cf. Acts 15:5), were "not far from the kingdom of God" (cf. Mark 12:34). And when they encountered Jesus, they indeed entered the kingdom with joy. Thus it was with Lydia, the seller of purple goods, who was a worshipper of God before she heard the gospel. She listened to Paul's preaching, and the "Lord opened her heart to pay attention to what was said by Paul," and she believed (Acts 16:14).

According to E. Sanders, the greatest objection that the apostle Paul had against the Jews of his day was not that they were all hypocrites or legalists, for many of them were not so at all. Paul's objection was that they, in contrast with what he had done, had not accepted Jesus when they had learned about him. The fundamental problem with Judaism was not so much that it preached righteousness by works of the law, but rather that it could not bring about salvation, for this was possible through Christ alone.[47] This is what Paul had against Judaism: it is not Christianity. In other words, there is nothing wrong with the commonwealth of the

---

46. See the Clementine *Recognitiones* I, 65.
47. Sanders (1977, 552); cf. Ouweneel (*RT* III/2, chapter 3).

Torah as such; how could it be otherwise, given the fact that God himself had instituted it. Only, when Christ came, who is the fulfillment of the Torah, did the Jewish commonwealth become meaningless for those who rejected Christ. Therefore, the encounter with Christ was the great test for every Jew: Would such a Jew become a moralist, a legalist, who kept clinging to the obsolete commonwealth? Or would Jesus fill the gap that had existed in his heart for such a long time?

13.5.3 Modern Jews

Incidentally, please note that we cannot speak of modern Jews in the same way that we speak of first-century Jews. The latter group had immediate contact with Jesus, or almost immediate contact, namely, through Jesus' apostles and their collaborators. Modern Jews, however, see Jesus mainly or exclusively through the lens of seventeen centuries of "Christian" persecution. Since at least the Council of Nicaea (AD 325), the Christian church has, at many times and at many places, persecuted Jews "in the name of Jesus." For the latter, unfortunately the name of Jesus stands for the greatest class of enemies Jews have ever had throughout all of world history.

In the Paul's day, the Jews in Rome knew only rumors about the gospel; they told him, "[W]e desire to hear from you what your views are, for with regard to this sect we know that everywhere it is spoken against" (Acts 28:22). In our own day, however, such ignorant Jews no longer exist. To them, there is a chasm between Judaism and Christianity, Jesus did not fulfill the Messianic prophecies, Jesus and his disciples transgressed the Mosaic Torah in various ways. Christianity contains many un-Jewish, even anti-Jewish, doctrines, especially that of the Trinity, which makes Christianity a tri-theistic instead of a monotheistic religion. Jesus cannot be the Messiah because (a) he was not a biological descendant of David in the male line, (b) he was never anointed by any authorized rabbi (Messiah = Anointed!), and (c) his coming did not usher in a world of peace and righteousness, as the prophets had promised. And last but not least, orthodox Jews believe that, if they were to join Christians, they would lose their Jewish identity.

This is not the place to refute all these unfortunate misunderstandings; I have done so elsewhere.[48] Here I would merely observe that a deep chasm now exists between Judaism and Christianity. Of course, in part, Jews themselves are responsible for this (Blaise Pascal already said, "There is light enough for those who wish to see"). But to a great extent, Christians throughout the centuries have presented Jews with a very wrong picture of Jesus and the Christian gospel. How can we bring them to accept "Jesus" if the name "Jesus" means to them injustice and persecution? This is one reason why "Messianic Jews," that is, those who do believe in Jesus as their Messiah and Savior, prefer the Hebrew name Yeshuah to Jesus because of the bad connotations that the latter name historically has for them.[49] If it was hard for Jews to recognize Jesus in the first century, it is hundred times harder for them to recognize him in the twenty-first century. However, in God's time, by his grace, and through his Spirit, they will turn to the Lord (Matt. 24:15-31; Rom. 11:25-27; 2 Cor. 3:16 KJV; Rev. 7:1-8) (see §13.7).

13.6 Conditions
13.6.1 Through Christ Alone
In §13.4 we saw that Gentiles who "by patience in well-doing seek for glory and honor and immortality," or who "do good," or who "fear God and do what is right," or who are "doers of the Torah" (though they are not explicitly aware of it) are accepted by God. Of course, we cannot limit ourselves to this conclusion. This is be-

---

48. See extensively, Ouweneel (2015, especially Excursus 48).
49. Ouweneel (2015, Excursus 50).

Atonement for the Church, the World, and Israel

cause immediately more questions arise: Is this mere theory, or do such people indeed exists among Gentiles who have never heard the gospel? If so, how can this be reconciled with the biblical statement that "no one seeks for God" (Rom. 3:11; cf. Ps. 14:2–3; 53:2–3)? Humans are sinners who are not at all able in themselves to do good or to please God (cf. Titus 3:3, "we ourselves were once foolish, disobedient, led astray, slaves to various passions and pleasures, passing our days in malice and envy, hated by others and hating one another"). Is there for Gentiles who do not know the gospel a possible side-entrance for salvation? Could they in this way be saved apart from Christ?

These are legitimate questions. Without a biblical reply to them, the claim that ignorant pagans can be justified as the "doers of the law" remains mere speculation and has no reality. Appealing to figures like Melchizedek, Job, and Naaman is unhelpful because the first of them knew the name *El ʿEljōn* ("God the Most High,"[50] Gen. 14:19), and Job knew the name Yahweh (Job 1:21). This implies they must have had a certain revelation concerning the God of the Bible. Hagar (Gen. 16) and Asenath (Gen. 41) got to know the true God through the patriarchs, while Reuel/Jethro[51] and Zipporah (Exod. 2:18), Rahab (Josh. 2), Heber and Jael (Judg. 4), Ruth (Ruth 1), Naaman (2 Kings 5), and Ebed-Melech (Jer. 38) came to know the true God through Israelites. Moreover, we want to know whether, especially *after* the birth of Christ, there is a way of salvation apart from him.

John 14:6 is of eminent importance because Jesus claims here to be "*the* way, and *the* truth, and *the* life," with the evident implication that he is the *only* way, the *only* truth, the *only* life. Apart from him, there is no way

---

50. See *TDNT* 8:614–20.
51. Reuel/Jethro, who was already "priest" in Midian before Mo ses met him (Exod. 2:16), is interesting because critics have made the unfounded claim that Jethro did not learn about YHWH from Moses, but rather Moses learned from him.

to the Father, there is no truth in its proper, transcendent sense concerning any matter (there are at most dispersed truth fragments), and there is no genuine life, that is, divine life (life from God). Jesus' claim was either the greatest presumption, or it was self-deceit, or it was the truth: Jesus is the only way to God.

Equally important is Acts 4:12, where the apostle Peter says, "[T]here is salvation in no one else [than in Christ], for there is no other name under heaven given among men by which we must be saved." This means that no humans, from the beginning of creation until the last day of history, are ever, or will ever be, saved apart from Christ and his atoning sacrifice. The Animist, the Hindu, Buddhist or Muslim, who does not know the gospel, and yet—in the sense described above—is truly pious, can come to the Father only through Jesus. The fact that they do not know either Jesus, or the Father—as the eternal Father of the eternal Son—does not change this at all: there is no other way to the Father than through Jesus.

This also means that there is no other way than through the *redemptive work* of Jesus: "For there is one God, and there is one mediator between God and men, the man Christ Jesus, who gave himself as a ransom for all" (1 Tim. 2:5-6). Note the reference here to "men" (humans) and "all," thus not just to Israel. The Gentile who does not know Jesus, yet is truly godly, can come to God only through this mediator. God applies to such a person, who does not know the mediator, the ransom that this mediator has paid also for them. Even though the Gentile is not aware of it, it is only through this ransom that they can be, and are, saved.

13.6.2 Through the Holy Spirit Alone

Redemption for anyone is not only on the basis of Christ's atoning sacrifice alone (the objective aspect), but also through the Holy Spirit alone (the subjective aspect). True, God placed humans on this earth, "that they should seek God, and perhaps feel their way toward him and find him" (Acts 17:27). However, after the Fall, no single human has sought God *by themselves*. If nevertheless there are Gentiles who "do good" and "fear God," this can happen only *through the Holy Spirit*; that is, it is God's own doing in them. The good works in Romans 2:6-13 are not an end in themselves, but a sign of an inner hope for the one, true *God*, for whose glory and honor people are seeking (v. 7), and this can occur only through the Holy Spirit.

Under no condition may the operation of the Holy Spirit be limited to the domain of the church or to the preaching of the gospel. The Spirit "blows where he wishes," "but you do not know where he comes from or where he goes" (cf. John 3:8). Clark Pinnock found this so important that, in his book on the Holy Spirit, he devoted an entire chapter to the work of the Holy Spirit outside ordinary Christian boundaries.[52] God sends forth his Spirit throughout the earth (Ps. 104:30; cf. Gen. 1:2). Church father Irenaeus expressed the conviction that the Holy Spirit was sent "to the entire earth," (Lat. *in omnem terram*), and that he was active among *all* humanity.[53] And to church father Ambrose these Latin words are attributed: *Omne verum, a quocumque dicitur, a Spiritu Sancto est* ("All that is true, said by whomsoever it may be, is of the Holy Spirit").[54] In other words, all truth is God's truth.[55]

Revelation 5:6 says that the "seven eyes" of the Lamb are the "seven spirits [KJV: Spirits]," that is, the Holy Spirit in all his fullness, "sent out into all the earth." This is a reminder of Zechariah 4:10, "These seven are the eyes of the LORD, which range through the whole earth,"

---

52. Pinnock (1996, chapter 6); cf. Ouweneel (*EDR* 1:274-76).
53. *Adversus Haereses* III.11.8-9; cf. 17.1-3.
54. Migne (1879, 17:245).
55. Cf. Holmes (1977, title).

where the Spirit is referred to as well: "Not by might, nor by power, but by my Spirit" (v. 6). If we therefore read, "[T]he eyes of the Lord run to and fro *throughout the whole earth*, to give strong support to those whose heart is blameless toward [NIV: fully committed to] him" (2 Chron. 16:19), this is the same as saying that the Holy Spirit runs to and fro in all the earth to support those whose heart is committed to God. No one can come to God except the person who is personally led by the Spirit to this destination: "No one can come to me unless the Father who sent me draws him" (John 6:44). In other words, there is no salvation without justification, there is no justification without regeneration, and there is no regeneration other than through the Holy Spirit (John 3:5; 1 Cor. 6:11; Titus 3:5).

Others have added the element of *faith* in light of Hebrews 11:6, "[W]ithout faith it is impossible to please him [i.e., God], for whoever would draw near to God must believe that he exists and that he rewards those who seek him." William Kelly argued that godliness and works of righteousness are the fruit of God's grace because there is nothing good in humans themselves unless faith enables them to do what is pleasing to God.[56] Therefore, the principle that Paul describes can become reality only in the Christian. But do we really have to go that far? Does not Hebrews 11:6 support a much wider meaning of "faith"? This verse indicates that the believer need do nothing more than believe that God exists and that he rewards those who seek him.

Apparently, for the Gentile who does not know the gospel this is sufficient. Indeed, true repentance cannot occur without faith (cf. §12.7.1): the person who humbles themselves does so in the (perhaps vague) awareness of a Creator God before whom they humbles themselves, and of the interest that this God takes in humans, of God's approval of true repentance, and of God's mer-

---

56. Kelly (*BT* 6:334).

ciful readiness to forgive sins. But there is nothing more that can be, and must be, expected of Gentiles ignorant about Jesus Christ. Here, the following wise words by the J. Gresham Machen may be relevant: no one knows how little a person can believe, and yet be saved—except God.[57]

13.6.3 Through Repentance Alone

No ignorant Gentile will ever be saved except (a) on the basis of Christ's atoning sacrifice alone (the objective aspect), (b) through the Holy Spirit alone (the subjective aspect, in which the person is passive), and (c) through humble penitence before God (the subjective aspect, in which the person is active). Notice here the unconditional force of 1 John 1:9, "If we confess our sins, he is faithful and just to forgive us our sins and to cleanse us from all unrighteousness." In verses 6–10 the "we" refers alternately to unbelievers (nominal Christians) and true believers; so we would not be amiss in understanding the "we" in verse 9 in a very general sense.

Nothing is said here of the gospel, although of course, in a normal context, no true confession of sins is conceivable without accepting the gospel. But why, in cases where the gospel is not known, could there be no true contrition, repentance, and confession of sins through the power of the Holy Spirit? The person who, according to Romans 1, has some awareness of the Creator, and according to Romans 2, has a conscience (awareness of good and evil), can, on this basis, humble themselves before God if the Spirit directs them to do this. In such a case, without further ado, the powerful principle of 1 John 1:9 is applicable: God is so faithful and just that he grants to such a person forgiveness of sins.

We must add several observations at this point. First, the persons involved cannot really know that their sins are forgiven, because they does not know God's prom-

---
57. Cited in Fackre et al. (1995, 37).

ises in this regard. Second, they do not know that God can forgive only on the basis of Christ's atoning sacrifice. Third, they probably do not realize that only "God's kindness" has led to their repentance (Rom. 2:4). Fourth, they are not, and cannot be, aware of the Holy Spirit, and the latter's guidance in their life. However, none of these five considerations changes in any way the authenticity of God's forgiveness: "[A] broken and contrite heart, O God, you will not despise" (Ps. 51:17). "I dwell in the high and holy place, and also with him who is of a contrite and lowly spirit, to revive the spirit of the lowly, and to revive the heart of the contrite" (Isa. 57:15)—whatever person this may concern. Ulrich Zwingli wrote that there never lived any good person, there never was a single godly heart or believing soul from the beginning of the world until its end, that we will not see in the presence of God.[58]

In his book *The Last Battle* (one of the *Narnia* stories), C. S. Lewis had the Lion Aslan (representing Christ) say to the pagan soldier Emeth (which is the Heb. word for "Truthfulness, Faithfulness"):

> Child, all the service thou hast done to [the idol] Tash, I account as service done to me ... I take to me the services which thou hast done to him. For I and he are of such different kinds that not service which is vile can be done to me, and none which is not vile can be done to him. Therefore, if any man swear by Tash and keep his oath for the oath's sake, it is by me that he has truly sworn, though he know it not, and it is I who reward him. And if any man do a cruelty in my name, then, though he says the name Aslan, it is Tash whom he serves and by Tash his deed is accepted.[59]

This wonderful statement reminds us of the statement by Jesus, who said of every good work done to his

---

58. Quoted in Bromiley (1953, 275–76).
59. Lewis (1956, 149).

"brothers": "Truly, I say to you, as you did it to one of the least of these my brothers, you did it to me" (Matt. 25:40). These good works honor God, and are done to Christ, even if the workers are not aware of it; compare Christ's word about Mary of Bethany: "[S]he has done a beautiful thing to me" (26:10). This is possible only through the Holy Spirit. It is never just a question of any neutral moral or universal human virtue but of that which expresses the very being of Christ, even if the person concerned is ignorant of it.

Incidentally, it is important to note that this principle is valid also where there *is* some knowledge of Christ, and where there is *no* behavior corresponding to the spirit of the Torah. As Jesus himself explained, "On that day many will say to me, 'Lord, Lord, did we not prophesy in your name, and cast out demons in your name, and do many mighty works in your name?' And then will I declare to them, 'I never knew you; depart from me, you workers of lawlessness'" (Matt. 7:22-23). "Afterward the other virgins [who had waited for the bridegroom but had no oil] came also, saying, 'Lord, lord, open to us.' But he answered, 'Truly, I say to you, I do not know you'" (25:11-12). And elsewhere:

> Strive to enter through the narrow door. For many, I tell you, will seek to enter and will not be able. When once the master of the house has risen and shut the door, and you begin to stand outside and to knock at the door, saying, "Lord, open to us," then he will answer you, "I do not know where you come from." Then you will begin to say, "We ate and drank in your presence, and you taught in our streets." But he will say, "I tell you, I do not know where you come from. Depart from me, all you workers of evil!" (Luke 13:24-27).

The most limited knowledge of God combined with a truly godly attitude may lead to salvation. But the most extensive knowledge of God (or Christ) without a truly godly attitude does not lead to salvation. As G. C. Berkouwer put it, "The most impressive works, such as prophesying and casting out of devils in the name of Christ, are no guarantee against the judgment and no security that the prophets and miracle workers are not actually workers of unrighteousness (cf. Matt. 7:22; Luke 13:25, 26),"[60] namely, if the character of Christ was not included in it.

13.6.4 Other Religions

The Holy Spirit works not only among Christians but also among Muslims, (neo-)pagans, Hindus, Buddhists, and atheists. I have met Muslims (such as Rimon Armaly, a Palestinian now working as a pastor in the USA) and Jews (such as Ofer Amitai, currently a Messianic rabbi in Jerusalem) to whom the Holy Spirit gave visions of Jesus Christ, through which they came to faith in Christ. We are told about regions where missionaries found people who had never heard the gospel before but who apparently had been fully prepared for the gospel by the Holy Spirit, and sometimes also by visions.[61] The Spirit is truly omnipresent, also in this respect. John Taylor called the Holy Spirit that incessant, dynamic communicator and intermediary who works upon each element and every process of the material universe, the immanent and anonymous presence of God.[62]

The wisdom of God displayed in his creational works cannot be ignored: "The LORD by wisdom founded the earth; by understanding he established the heavens" (Prov. 3:19). In an earlier volume of this series, we examined the close connection between God's wisdom and his Holy Spirit;[63] see, for instance, the deuterocanonical

---

60. Berkouwer (1954a, 111).
61. See extensively, the missionary anthropologist Richardson (1981).
62. Taylor (1972, 64).
63. See Ouweneel (*RT* II/3, §3.8).

book Wisdom of Solomon:

> Wisdom is a spirit that is friendly to people, but she will not forgive anyone who speaks against God, for God knows our feelings and thoughts, and hears our every word. Since the Lord's spirit fills the entire world, and holds everything in it together, she knows every word that people say (1:6-7 GNT).

It is as if we hear the Holy Spirit himself speaking in Proverbs 8: "Listen! Wisdom is calling out. Reason is making herself heard. On the hilltops near the road and at the crossroads she stands. At the entrance to the city, beside the gates, she calls: 'I appeal to all of you; I call to everyone on earth'" (vv. 1-4). This voice of God's wisdom, which is the voice of his Spirit, is still heard everywhere in this world, not only in the preaching of the gospel but in all forms of true (and therefore divine) wisdom which is known within the human experiential horizon.[64]

Lady Wisdom (cf. "lady Folly" in Prov. 9:13 VOICE) appeals to the wise understanding of humans but also to their consciences. She does so because she "delights" "in the children of men" (8:31): "And now, O sons, listen to me: blessed are those who keep my ways. Hear instruction and be wise, and do not neglect it. Blessed is the one who listens to me, watching daily at my gates, waiting beside my doors. For whoever finds me finds life and obtains favor from the LORD, but he who fails to find me injures himself; all who hate me love death" (Prov. 8:32-36; cf. 9:1-6, 10-11).

13.7 Israel
13.7.1 The Eschatological Yom Kippur
In Romans 11, the great chapter on the future restoration of Israel, Paul says about this nation, "[I]f their

---
64. Pinnock (1996, 193); Ouweneel (2008a, §§4.1-4.2).

rejection means the reconciliation of the world, what will their acceptance mean but life from the dead?" (v. 15). Because Israel rejected its Messiah, the people of Israel have been put aside for a time, thereby creating room in the ways of God to bring about the "reconciliation of the world." However, if Israel's rejection is having such glorious results—a mass of believers from the Gentiles—what glory will result when Israel will be accepted again? This acceptance will have the character of "life from the dead." This is the message of 2 Corinthians 3:16: "But when[65] it [i.e., Israel; sometimes rendered "they"] shall turn to the Lord, the veil [that still lies on their face] shall be taken away" (KJV, BRG, DARBY, DRA, JUB).

The spiritual (as well as literal-physical?) resurrection of Israel is a well-known theme in Old Testament prophecies: "Your dead shall live; their bodies shall rise. You who dwell in the dust, awake and sing for joy! For your dew is a dew of light, and the earth will give birth to the dead" (Isa. 26:19). As God declared through Ezekiel,

> Behold, I will open your graves and raise you from your graves, O my people. And I will bring you into the land of Israel. And you shall know that I am the LORD, when I open your graves, and raise you from your graves, O my people. And I will put my Spirit within you, and you shall live, and I will place you in your own land. Then you shall know that I am the LORD; I have spoken, and I will do it (Ezek. 37:12–14).

"And many of those who sleep in the dust of the earth shall awake, some to everlasting life, and some to shame and everlasting contempt" (Dan. 12:2). "After two days he will revive us; on the third day he will raise us up, that we may live before him" (Hos. 6:2).

---

65. The translation "whenever" cannot be excluded; in this case, the verse is a reference to the conversion of individual Jews at the present time.

In §§5.3–5.5 I briefly indicated that, prophetically speaking, Yom Kippur will become full reality for Israel only at the second coming of their Messiah. In the Old Testament, on that day, once a year, the high priest loaded the sins of Israel on the second goat, the goat "for Azazel" (Lev. 16:8, 10), and sent it into the wilderness, where the animal perished (vv. 20–23). Only then were the sins of the Israelites effectually removed; they received atonement only after the second goat had been sent into the wilderness. Thus, on the cross of Calvary, the foundation for Israel's restoration was laid, as presented in the first goat, and thousands of individual, Jesus-believing Jews have already received a share in it. However, *as a nation* Israel will share in the atonement only when Jesus returns from the heavenly sanctuary, and removes the sins of the nation forever on the basis of his own work on the cross (vv. 17–21). Then, the "Day of Atonement" (Heb. *Yom hakKippurim*) will be fully realized for Israel.

In connection with this, consider once again Daniel 9:24, "Seventy weeks [lit. sevens, i.e., sevens of years] are decreed about your people and your holy city, to finish the transgression, to put an end to sin, and *to atone for iniquity*, to bring in everlasting righteousness, to seal both vision and prophet, and to anoint a most holy place." These seventy "weeks of years" (490 years) encompass the period from the command to restore the city of Jerusalem (probably 457 BC) until the coming of the Messiah (probably AD 27), that is, 483 years. Elsewhere, I have explained, in line with many other authors, why the last "year week" (seven years) is reserved until the end time, just before the second coming of the Messiah.[66] The arrival of the Messianic kingdom will involve for Israel immeasurable blessings; as the text says, it encompasses "finishing" Israel's transgression of rejection and apostasy, putting an end to Israel's sinning, atoning for its

---

66. See extensively, Ouweneel (2012a, §6.5).

iniquities, bringing about their everlasting justification, "sealing" (i.e., probably closing, bringing to fulfillment) the prophecies concerning Israel, and anointing Israel's restored temple.

13.7.2 Israel's Penance

As happened on Yom Kippur throughout the Old Testament, Israel's future day of restoration will be a day of penitence and confession of sin, as prescribed the Lord: "[O]n the tenth day of this seventh month is the Day of Atonement. It shall be for you a time of holy convocation, and you shall afflict [GNT: humble; NIV: deny; AMPC explains: by fasting with penitence and humiliation] yourselves [lit., your souls] and present a food offering to the LORD" (Lev. 23:27; cf. 16:29, 31).

The day of Israel's eschatological restoration will be a day as described in the prophecy of Joel:

> "Yet even now," declares the LORD,
>   "return to me with all your heart,
> with fasting, with weeping, and with mourning;
>   and rend your hearts and not your garments."
> Return to the LORD your God,
>   for he is gracious and merciful,
> slow to anger, and abounding in steadfast love;
>   and he relents over disaster. . . .
> Blow the trumpet in Zion;
>   consecrate a fast;
> call a solemn assembly;
>   gather the people.
> Consecrate the congregation;
>   assemble the elders;
> gather the children,
>   even nursing infants.
> Let the bridegroom leave his room,
>   and the bride her chamber.
> Between the vestibule and the altar
>   let the priests, the ministers of the LORD, weep

and say, "Spare your people, O Lord,
    and make not your heritage a reproach,
    a byword among the nations.
Why should they say among the peoples,
    "Where is their God?' (Joel 2:12-17).

The prophetic character of some of the so-called penitential psalms, like Psalm 51, finds its fulfillment in the great penance of Israel on the day of Christ's return. This is evident from the connection here between the personal penance of the faithful remnant of the nation and the restoration of Zion:

Have mercy on me, O God,
    according to your steadfast love;
according to your abundant mercy
    blot out my transgressions.
Wash me thoroughly from my iniquity,
    and cleanse me from my sin!
For I know my transgressions,
    and my sin is ever before me.
Against you, you only, have I sinned
    and done what is evil in your sight,
so that you may be justified in your words
    and blameless in your judgment. . . .
Purge me with hyssop, and I shall be clean;
    wash me, and I shall be whiter than snow. . . .
Hide your face from my sins,
    and blot out all my iniquities. . . .
Deliver me from bloodguiltiness, O God,
    O God of my salvation. . . .
The sacrifices of God are a broken spirit;
    a broken and contrite heart, O God, you will not despise.
Do good to Zion in your good pleasure;
    build up the walls of Jerusalem;
then will you delight in right sacrifices,
    in burnt offerings and whole burnt offerings;
    then bulls will be offered on your altar.

These last verses have led expositors to wonder whether the psalm is Davidic, because they seem more suited for the time of the exiles from Babylon. I see no basis for this notion, however; David may have wondered what effect the king's sin might have on the city as a whole. At the deepest level these verses must be understood in Messianic terms.

Psalm 102 is another one of the seven penitential psalms, and it is equally prophetic-Messianic (cf. vv. 24–27 with Heb. 1:10–12). In this psalm we find these words, addressed to the Lord God:

> You will arise and have pity on Zion;
>   it is the time to favor her;
>   the appointed time has come.
> For your servants hold her stones dear
>   and have pity on her dust.
> Nations will fear the name of the LORD,
>   and all the kings of the earth will fear your glory.
> For the LORD builds up Zion;
>   he appears in his glory;
> he regards the prayer of the destitute
>   and does not despise their prayer (vv. 13–17).

Note as well the prophetic significance for Israel of Isaiah 53. Strictly speaking, it will not be all believers of all times, but it will be the faithful remnant[67] of Israel that will say of the Lord's Servant (the Messiah):

> [H]e was pierced for *our* transgressions;
>   he was crushed for *our* iniquities;
>   upon him was the chastisement that brought *us* peace,
>   and with his wounds *we* are healed.
> All *we* like sheep have gone astray;
>   *we* have turned—every one—to his own way;
> and the LORD has laid on him
>   the iniquity of *us* all (vv. 5–6).

---

67. For this term, see Isa. 1:9; 10:20–22; 11:11, 16; 37:4, 32; 46:3.

Notice here the eschatological context: "Therefore I will divide him a portion with the many, and he shall divide the spoil with the strong" (v. 12), referring to the power of the Messianic kingdom, which the Messiah will share with the faithful of Israel. It is said of restored Israel in both a soteriological and an eschatological way: "In the Lord all the offspring of Israel shall be justified and shall glory" (Isa. 45:20). "Your people shall all be righteous; they shall possess the land [!] forever, the branch of my planting, the work of my hands, that I might be glorified. The least one shall become a clan, and the smallest one a mighty nation" (Isa. 60:21-22).

Notice also that in the prophetic passage of Deuteronomy 30:1-11, the Hebrew verb *shub* (or *shuv*) means both "to return" to the promised land and "to return" (i.e., to convert in repentance) to the Lord (and it is also used to express the term "again"):[68]

> And when all these things come upon you, the blessing and the curse, which I have set before you, and you call them to mind among all the nations where the Lord your God has driven you, and return [Heb. *weshabta*] to the Lord your God, you and your children, and obey his voice in all that I command you today, with all your heart and with all your soul, then the Lord your God will restore [Heb. *yeshab*, lit. make turn] your fortunes and have mercy on you, and he will gather you again [Heb. *yeshab*] from all the peoples where the Lord your God has scattered you. . . . And the Lord your God will bring you into the land that your fathers possessed, that you may possess it. And he will make you more prosperous and numerous than your fathers. And the Lord your God will circumcise your heart and the heart of your offspring, so that you

---

68. In rabbinic literature, the Heb. word *teshubah* (or *teshuvah*) has received the meaning "repentance" (return to the Lord), and refers to the eschatological restoration of Israel. The Talmud (Nedarim 39b, Pesahim 54a) concludes from Ps. 90:2-3 that God created *teshuvah* before he created the material universe.

> will love the LORD your God with all your heart and with all your soul, that you may live. . . . And you shall again [Heb. *tashub*] obey the voice of the LORD and keep all his commandments that I command you today. The LORD . . . will again [Heb. *yashub*] take delight in prospering you, as he took delight in your fathers, when you obey the voice of the LORD your God, to keep his commandments and his statutes that are written in this Book of the Law, when you turn [Heb. *tashub*] to the LORD your God with all your heart and with all your soul.

The eschatological return to the God of Israel will coincide with the return to the Land of Israel. Therefore, the modern state of Israel is at most a preliminary fulfillment of the Messianic prophecies concerning Israel's restoration.

13.7.3 The Fountain for Cleansing

The prophet Zechariah says of the future propitiation and reconciliation of Israel,

> And I will pour out on the house of David and the inhabitants of Jerusalem a spirit [or, the Spirit] of grace and pleas for mercy, so that, when they look on me, on him whom they have pierced, they shall mourn for him, as one mourns for an only child, and weep bitterly over him, as one weeps over a firstborn. On that day the mourning in Jerusalem will be as great as the mourning for Hadad-rimmon in the plain of Megiddo. The land shall mourn, each family by itself. . . . On that day there shall be a *fountain* opened for the house of David and the inhabitants of Jerusalem, to cleanse them from sin and uncleanness (12:10–13:1).

According to Revelation 1:7, where some of these words are quoted, this statement will be fulfilled at the second coming of Christ: "Behold, he is coming with the clouds, and every eye will see him, even *those who pierced him*, and all tribes of the earth [CJB: the land!] will wail on account of him." Here the reference is not to the "tribes of the earth"—which phrase is linked to the expression "every tribe and language and people and nation" (Rev. 5:9; 13:7; cf. 7:9; 14:6). In the light of Zechariah, here the term "tribes" necessarily refers instead to the tribes of Israel (Rev. 7:4; 21:12), namely, those who will *then* be living in the "land" (!) (cf. Rev. 11:2, 8; 20:9; Matt. 24:30). According to Zechariah 12:11 (cf. vv. 4-9), the lamentation intended in Revelation 1:7 is uttered in Jerusalem, which is indeed the place where Christ will return (Zech. 14:3-4; cf. Acts 1:10-11).

Zechariah 13:1 (KJV) speaks of a "fountain" that is intended for "[the purification from] sin [Heb. *lechattat*[69]] and for uncleanness [Heb. *leniddah*]." The verse refers to a water well; it is referring to purification by blood. From ancient times, Israel was familiar with two purifications by water to which this verse may be alluding, both of which are important for the salvation that is intended for Israel.

The one is the primary and one-time total cleansing of the priests with water during their consecration (Exod. 29:4; Lev. 8:6), followed by the daily washing of their hands and feet in the bronze basin before beginning their ministry. Exodus tells us twice that the priests would be put to death if they did not wash themselves before entering the sanctuary:[70]

> You shall also make a basin of bronze, with its stand of bronze, for washing. You shall put it between the tent of meeting and the altar, and you shall put water in it, with which Aaron and his sons shall wash their hands and their feet. When they go into the tent of meeting, or when they come near the altar to minister, to burn a food offering to the LORD, they shall wash with water, so that they

---

69. The Heb. word *chattat* can mean both "sin" and "purification from sin"; see §4.6.1.
70. Cf. Denham Smith (n.d., 283).

may not die. They shall wash their hands and their feet, so that they may not die" (Exod. 30:18-21).

We read later: "Moses and Aaron and his sons washed their hands and their feet [with the water in the bronze basin]. When they went into the tent of meeting, and when they approached the altar, they washed, as the LORD commanded Moses" (Exod. 40:31-32).

It is conceivable that Zechariah 13:1 refers to the bronze basin, even though we might hardly call this a "fountain" (but neither would we be inclined to call it a "bronze sea," as does 1 Chron. 18:8). If this interpretation is correct, it is referring to Israel's ministry in the sanctuary during the Messianic kingdom, which is explicitly mentioned in the book:

> And on that day there shall be inscribed on the bells of the horses, "Holy to the LORD." And the pots in the house of the LORD shall be as the bowls before the altar. And every pot in Jerusalem and Judah shall be holy to the LORD of hosts, so that all who sacrifice may come and take of them and boil the meat of the sacrifice in them (Zech. 14:20-21; cf. more extensively, Ezek. 43-44).

13.7.4 The Water of Purification

The second purification by water to which Zechariah 13:1 might be referring is the special institution of the "water for impurity" or "water of purification" (Heb. *mey niddah*) in Numbers 19, which we have discussed earlier in §5.7.4. This water was sprinkled on the person who had defiled themselves by coming into contact with death. This contact could have involved a dead body, but contact with human bones, or with a human tomb, was sufficient for defiling an Israelite. The motivation behind the ritual involving the water of purification was clear: "it is for purification from sin" (Heb. *chattat hi*, v. 9 NIV). It is to be noted that we find both Hebrew words *niddah* and *chattat* in Zechariah 13:1 (KJV), "a fountain for "[the purification from] sin [Heb. *lechattat*] and for uncleanness [Heb. *leniddah*]."

I mentioned earlier (§5.7.4) that the law of the water of purification was not given in Leviticus but only in Numbers 19, near the end of Israel's wilderness journey. It is an institution that will be of special significance when Israel ultimately arrives at the end of its twenty centuries of "wilderness journey." We can imagine why, at the beginning of the Messianic kingdom, Israel will need this "purification" and "cleansing." Throughout its history, Israel has come into contact with death in many different ways. It was even "given over to death" (cf. Ezek. 31:14; Ps. 18:4–5; 55:4; 88:15). But the most important point is what we found a little earlier in Zechariah:

> And I will pour out on the house of David and the inhabitants of Jerusalem a spirit [or, the Spirit] of grace and pleas for mercy, so that, when they look on me, on him whom they have pierced, they shall mourn for him, as one mourns for an only child, and weep bitterly over him, as one weeps over a firstborn (Zech. 12:10–11).

The One whom they pierced at the cross—that it was a Roman soldier who literally did this removes nothing from Israel's own responsibility—is the same person as the One represented by the red heifer: he was without blemish, and on him the yoke of sin had never before been placed (cf. Num. 19:2). The *blood* of Christ implies for Israel its sacrificial atonement; and the *water* of purification, based on the same sacrifice of Christ, implies for Israel its cleansing. This very piercing of Christ made clear that both the blood and the water are necessary: "[O]ne of the soldiers pierced his side with a spear, and at once there came out *blood* and *water*. . . . For these things took place that the Scripture might be fulfilled:

'... They will look on him whom they have pierced'" (John 19:34-37).[71] The latter passage suggests a clear connection between Zechariah 12:10 and John 19:34. John comments, "This is he who came by water and blood—Jesus Christ; not by the water only but by the water and the blood" (1 John 5:6).[72] As a variant of this we might say: not only by blood, but by blood as well as by water: blood that reconciles believers with God, water that washes away their sins: "[Y]ou were washed, you were sanctified, you were justified in the name of the Lord Jesus Christ and by the Spirit of our God" (1 Cor. 6:11). Elsewhere, Paul speaks of cleansing "by the washing of water with the word" (Eph. 5:26).[73]

It is remarkable to see that the Day of Atonement occupies the central place in Leviticus (chapter 16), and the water of purification in Numbers (chapter 19).[74] Both find their definitive fulfillment in Israel at the second coming of Christ. The blood was shed on the Day of Atonement in connection with the sin offering, which will one day be seen as the One and the same who brought the true sin offering: the great high priest (Heb. 2:17; 4:14; 10:21). He will return from the heavenly sanctuary (Heb. 9:28), and will send Israel's sins away forever. At the same time, a fountain of water for purification will be opened for Israel, based again upon Christ's atoning sacrifice (represented in the red heifer), in order to wash away all the people's sins.

In this way, they are not only (negatively) delivered from the power of evil, but also (positively) enabled to enter again into temple worship:

> Thus says the LORD of hosts, "Behold, the man whose name is the Branch: for he shall branch out from his place, and

---

71. Cf. Dennett (1888, 165).
72. Cf. Ouweneel (*RT* II/3, §6.8.2).
73. Cf. ibid., §§5.3.1 and 8.2.1.
74. Kelly (*BT* N9:97).

he shall build the temple of the Lord. It is he who shall build the temple of the Lord and shall bear royal honor, and shall sit and rule on his throne. And there [or, he] shall be a priest on his throne, and the counsel of peace shall be between them both." ... And those who are far off shall come and help to build the temple of the Lord. And you shall know that the Lord of hosts has sent me to you. And this shall come to pass, if you will diligently obey the voice of the Lord your God (Zech. 6:12-15).

Chapter 14
Christ's Sacrifice: Healing and Deliverance

Behold Zion, the city of our appointed feasts!
   Your eyes will see Jerusalem,
   an untroubled habitation, an immovable tent,
whose stakes will never be plucked up,
   nor will any of its cords be
   broken....
For the L*ORD* *is our judge; the* L*ORD* *is our lawgiver;*
   the L*ORD* *is our king; he will save*
   us....
And no inhabitant will say, "I am sick";
   the people who dwell there will be
   forgiven their iniquity.
                              Isaiah 33:20, 22, 24

That evening they brought to him [i.e., Jesus]
many who were oppressed by demons,
and he cast out the spirits with a word

> *and healed all who were sick.*
> *This was to fulfill what was spoken by the prophet Isaiah:*
> *"He took our illnesses and bore our diseases."*
> Matthew 8:16–17 (cf. Isa. 53:4)

> *The Spirit of the Lord is upon me, because he has anointed me to proclaim good news to the poor. He has sent me to proclaim liberty to the captives and recovering of sight to the blind, to set at liberty those who are oppressed.*
> Luke 4:18 (cf. Isa. 61:1)

Summary: *In this final chapter, attention is paid to the ministries of healing and deliverance as important results of Christ's work on the cross. The relationship between illness and sin is investigated with a view to asking: Is healing part of Christ's work of atonement? If all sins are forgiven those who confess them, can we similarly guarantee healing to all believers? How is healing included in salvation? What is the place of faith, both before and after a healing?*

Special attention is given to the ancient Christian doctrine that Christ in his resurrection carried Old Testament believers from darkness to light. This idea is analyzed and rejected.

In the ministry of deliverance, the question is essential regarding the extent to which believers can still be under demonic influences. The distinction is made between circumsession, obsession, and possession. Some Christians deny the possibility of such influences, others go to the other extreme and see demonic influences in every ailment and sorrow. A careful balance must be maintained here. A theological analysis is made of the symptoms and the causes of demonic bondage.

14.1 Disease and Atonement[1]
14.1.1 Disease and Sin

PARTICULARLY BECAUSE OF THE rising Pentecostal and Charismatic movements and their theological claims, the question is hotly debated whether the healing of the sick was included in Christ's work of atonement or not. Generally speaking, it is clear that the Bible often refers to a connection between sickness and sin.[2] Thus, Psalm 32:4b says that, as a consequence of sin *and* the refusal to confess it, "[M]y strength was dried up as by the heat of summer." Psalm 103:3 mentions forgiveness and healing in one breath: the LORD is the One "who forgives all your iniquity, / who heals all your diseases." Disease is sometimes a direct consequence of serious sin, as in some cases of leprosy: Miriam (Num. 12:10), Gehazi (2 Kings 5:27), and Uzziah (2 Chron. 26:19). If Israel would remain faithful to the Lord, they would not be plagued with the diseases of the Egyptians (Exod. 15:26). But if they would become *un*faithful, the Lord would punish them with all kinds of diseases (Lev. 26:16, 25; Deut. 28:21-22, 27-28, 35, 60).

The New Testament relates, "And behold, some people brought to him a paralytic, lying on a bed. And when Jesus saw their faith, he said to the paralytic, 'Take heart, my son; your sins are forgiven'" (Matt. 9:2). "Afterward Jesus found him [i.e., the man who had been healed] in the temple and said to him, 'See, you are well! Sin no more, that nothing worse may happen to you'" (John 5:14). "Is anyone among you sick? Let him call for the elders of the church, and let them pray over him, anointing him with oil in the name of the Lord. And the prayer of faith will save the one who is sick, and the Lord will raise him up. And if he has committed sins, he will be forgiven" (James 5:14-15). The conditional word "if"

---

1. §§14.1.1-14.1.4 are an extension and elaboration of Ouweneel (2004, §§7.4.2-7.4.3); see also Ouweneel (2007c).
2. See Ouweneel (2004, chapter 7).

shows that there is no automatic connection between sickness and sin—but the elders do have the duty to investigate whether sin is involved in the disease regarding which they have been called upon.

In Isaiah 53, this connection is expressed in a remarkable manner. In verse 10, the fact that, on the cross, Christ was made to be *sin* for his people (2 Cor. 5:21) is put this way: "Yet it was the will of the LORD to crush him; he has put him to grief [LEB, YLT: He made Him sick; WYC: the Lord would defoul him in sickness]." This is related to the Messiah's atoning sacrifice, for the text continues, ". . . when his soul makes an offering for guilt, he shall see his offspring," and so on.

Isaiah 53:4 says, "Surely he has borne our griefs [CJB: diseases; DRA: infirmities] and carried our sorrows (EXB: sorrows/diseases; ERV: pain(s); NRSV: diseases]." The AMPC says, "Surely He has borne our griefs (sicknesses, weaknesses, and distresses) and carried our sorrows *and* pains [of punishment]." Here again, the connection with the problem of sin is so evident that the Septuagint even translates it this way: "He bears our *sins*, and suffers pain for us." However, when Matthew quotes the verse, he refers to the Hebrew text and applies it to literal diseases: "That evening they brought to him [i.e., Jesus] many who were oppressed by demons, and he cast out the spirits with a word and healed all who were sick. This was to fulfill what was spoken by the prophet Isaiah: 'He took our illnesses and bore our diseases'" (Matt. 8:16–17). Very significantly, this term "bearing" is taken from sacrificial terminology, and means something like "bearing vicariously," or "atoning, blotting out" (cf., e.g., Lev. 16:22, and see §9.1.2 above). It is all the more remarkable that this verb is applied here to Jesus "bearing" diseases.

14.1.2 Jesus "Bearing" Diseases

We see the meaning of the word "bearing" in 1 Peter

Christ's Sacrifice: Healing and Deliverance

2:24, in combination with another quotation from Isaiah 53 (v. 5b): "He himself bore our sins in his body on the tree, that we might die to sin and live to righteousness. By his wounds you have been healed." The latter words are not about the stripes that *Pilate* had inflicted upon Jesus (Matt. 27:26), for these could only aggravate human guilt, not blot it out (see §11.5 above). No, it was *God* who inflicted these "stripes" upon his Son on the cross (cf. Zech. 13:7, "'Awake, O sword, against my shepherd, / against the man who stands next to me,' . . . 'Strike the shepherd'"). Through these "stripes" God's people are *healed* of their sins. It is no wonder that the Septuagint translators thought of a figurative meaning also in verse 4. However, from Matthew 8 we know that Jesus also took upon himself people's literal diseases.

I say this, conscious of the fact that rather different interpretations have been given of Matthew 8:17,[3] and concomitantly also of the references in Isaiah 53 to diseases. D. Kidner believed that the quotation in Matthew 8:17 indicates that also in Isaiah 53:3-5 we must think of literal diseases.[4] D. Prince wrote that he had considered every possible argument to help him escape the literal meaning of Isaiah 53:3-5, but they had failed.[5] Other authors prefer to think of a figurative meaning of "sickness/disease/pain" in Isaiah 53:3-5.[6] J. Ridderbos chose a middle path: "These 'infirmities' and 'sorrows' [in v. 4] include real illnesses and physical defects (cf. Matt. 8:16-17) but are not restricted to them; these categories (as especially the word 'sorrows' clearly indicates) embrace all human suffering. The following verse explains this as punishment for sin."[7]

According to E. J. Young, the image of disease in Isa-

---

3. Cf. Erickson (1998, 853-54), and references there.
4. Kidner (1970, ad loc.).
5. Prince (2001, 30-31; cf. 43-44, 54-57).
6. E.g., Alexander (1953, 294-95); Grogan (1986, 302-303).
7. Ridderbos (1985, 475).

iah 53 refers to sin itself, yet the reference in Matthew 8:17 is appropriate because the verse also includes the notion of removing the consequences of sin, disease being the inseparable companion of sin.[8] Young referred to E. Hengstenberg, who maintained that the Servant of the LORD bore sin in its consequences, and among these, sicknesses and diseases occupy a prominent place.[9] H. Bultema denied that it can be concluded from Isaiah 53:3–5 that believers no longer need to suffer from diseases, yet was convinced that the healing of believers is definitely the fruit of Jesus' work of atonement.[10] J. Piper said concerning Isaiah 53:4 and Matthew 8:16–17 that Christ suffered and died in order to heal us from spiritual and physical diseases. He overcame death and sickness by taking them upon himself and carrying them with him into the grave.[11]

As we saw earlier in §9.1.2, two Hebrew verbs, *n-s-'* and *s-b-l* are both translated as "to bear" or "to carry." With very little difference in nuance, both verbs can have the sense of "to vicariously carry (away)." It is remarkable that Isaiah 53 uses both *n-s-'* and *s-b-l* for both sins and diseases:[12] "Surely he has borne [Heb. *n-s-'*] our griefs [or diseases] and carried [Heb. *s-b-l*] our sorrows [or sicknesses] . . . he shall bear [Heb. *s-b-l*] their iniquities . . . he bore [Heb. *n-s-'*] the sin of many" (vv. 4, 11–12). In my view, in the light of Matthew 8, this combination of these Hebrew verbs removes any doubt that Isaiah 53 is making no distinction between taking away sins and taking away diseases.

We see the same thing in other Bible passages. Thus, in Deuteronomy 28:21–22, 27–28, 35, 60, sicknesses and diseases are included in the curse of the Law, while Ga-

---

8. Young (1972, 345).
9. Hengstenberg (1829–1835, ad loc.).
10. Bultema (1981, 512–14).
11. Piper (2004, 62–63).
12. This point is strangely ignored by Erickson (1998, 855–57).

latians 3:13 says, "Christ redeemed us from the curse of the law by becoming a curse for us—for it is written, 'Cursed is everyone who is hanged on a tree'" (cf. Deut. 21:23). If we take these passages together, this means that Christ redeemed us from the curse of sicknesses and diseases by taking this curse upon himself.

14.2 Is Healing a Part of Atonement?
14.2.1 Not All Are Healed

Is it correct to conclude from the previous section that healing was included in Christ's work of atonement, as Pentecostals and Charismatics claim?[13] R. Nathan and K. Wilson rightly pointed to the perils of this claim.[14] It is God's will to forgive *all* people their sins (cf. 1 Tim. 2:3-4; 2 Pet. 3:9); the only reason why this is not effectuated in certain people is that this is not *their* will (Luke 13:34; Rom. 2:4-8; cf. John 7:17; Rev. 22:17). It is highly questionable whether it is the same with sickness. Is it God's will to heal *all* diseases; so is the only reason why this is not effectuated in certain people—even believers—is that this is not *their* will, or that they do not satisfy one or more conditions for healing (e.g., sufficient faith, no hidden sins, persistent prayer)?

The answer is simple: there is no biblical evidence that God wishes to heal all diseases of all believers if they would only meet the conditions. On the contrary, there is a whole series of believers who were ill without any sins involved, or more strongly, some were at a point of deep faith. Examples include Elisha ("Elisha had fallen sick with the illness of which he was to die," 2 Kings 13:14), Epaphroditus ("was ill, near to death," but was healed; Phil. 2:25-27), Timothy ("use a little

---

13. See Simpson (1880, 30-31); McCrossan (1982, 1-35); Duffield and Van Cleave (1996, 411-15); Bosworth (2000, 11-40).
14. Nathan and Wilson (1995, 71-74). See the nuanced discussion of Wimber and Springer (1986, 164-169); Mayhue (1999, 122-133).

wine for the sake of your stomach and your frequent ailments," 1 Tim. 5:23), and Trophimus ("who was ill," 2 Tim. 4:20).[15] New Testament believers who fell ill but were healed include Lazarus (John 11), Aeneas and Dorcas (Acts 19:32-41), and Eutychus (20:9-10).

Of course, we do know that in certain cases a lack of faith certainly played a role: Jesus "did not do many mighty works there [i.e., in Nazareth], because of their unbelief" (Matt. 13:58; cf. Mark 6:5-6). Also overt or hidden sins may play a role: "[A]nyone who eats and drinks without discerning the body eats and drinks judgment on himself. That is why many of you are weak and ill, and some have died" (1 Cor. 11:29-30; see the passages mentioned above in §14.1.1, such as Psalm 32:4; Matt. 9:2; John 5:14; James 5:14-16). Another reason why believers are not healed might be that they acquiesce to their illness, and do not implore God: "You do not have, because you do not ask. You ask and do not receive, because you ask wrongly" (James 4:2-3). Or perhaps they pray but do not "steadfastly continue" in prayer (Col. 4:2; "at all times," Eph. 6:18); think of Elijah, whom God had promised that he would grant rain when the people would repentantly return to him, yet Elijah had to ask seven times for it (1 Kings 18:42-44).

However, we must not generalize here. In other words, we cannot possibly, in all instances of sick believers, find some reason *why* they are sick. One reason might be that God sends a believer an illness through which he wishes to take him/her to himself; think again of Elisha, who "had fallen sick with the illness of which he was to die" (2 Kings 13:14). More generally we must say that at least one reason why believers often remain ill, even after ardent prayer, is that the fullness of God's kingdom has not yet arrived; recall what the apostle Paul wrote:

---

15. See Ouweneel (2004, §§3.5.1 and 7.2.2).

> For the creation was subjected to futility, not willingly, but because of him who subjected it, in hope that the creation itself will be set free from its bondage to corruption and obtain the freedom of the glory of the children of God. For we know that the whole creation has been groaning together in the pains of childbirth until now. And not only the creation, but we ourselves, who have the firstfruits of the Spirit, groan inwardly as we wait eagerly for adoption as sons, the redemption of our bodies (Rom. 8:20-23).

We do not yet live in the Messianic kingdom of peace and righteousness, in which no inhabitant will say, "I am sick" (Isa. 33:24).

14.2.2 A Balanced View

We have to maintain a careful balance here. On the one hand, the Messianic kingdom has not yet arrived in all its fullness. On the other hand, Jesus *has* "borne" (and thus taken away) the diseases of his people, and Matthew 8:16-17 applies this to literal diseases. This means explicitly that each miraculous healing—but also every "natural" healing, and every healing through medical intervention!—is a consequence of Christ's work on the cross. This is entirely in line with the truth that all blessings that are assigned to God's providence, or his common grace,[16] are direct effects of Christ's work of atonement. For the latter reason, we should not claim that Matthew 8:16-17 is the complete and definitive fulfillment of Isaiah 53, that is, entirely within Jesus' life on earth, and apart from his work on the cross. Notice, for instance, the parallel with Matthew 12:17-21, which is a quotation from Isaiah 42:1-4, or Luke 4:17-21, which is a quotation from Isaiah 61:1-2. In none of these passages we have to do with a complete and definitive fulfillment of the Isaiah passages mentioned.

Moreover, after his death, resurrection, and ascen-

---

16. See extensively, Ouweneel (2004, §3.3-4; 2017, §4.4.1; 2018e, §2.4.2).

sion, Jesus continued his healings: he "worked with them [i.e., the apostles] and confirmed the message by accompanying signs" (Mark 16:20; cf. v. 17). "[H]is [i.e., Jesus'] name—by faith in his name—has made this man strong whom you see and know, and the faith that is through Jesus has given the man this perfect health in the presence of you all" (Acts 3:16). By Jesus, through his servants, "many who were paralyzed or lame were healed" (8:7; cf. 5:16; 6:8; 9:34; 28:8). The believers prayed, "[G]rant to your servants to continue to speak your word with all boldness, while you stretch out your hand to heal, and signs and wonders are performed through the name of your holy servant Jesus" (4:29–30). Paul wrote, "I will not venture to speak of anything except what Christ has accomplished through me to bring the Gentiles to obedience—by word and deed, by the power of signs and wonders, by the power of the Spirit of God" (Rom. 15:18–19). "Does he who supplies the Spirit to you and works miracles among you do so by works of the law, or by hearing with faith . . . ? (Gal. 3:5).

Our conclusion is that it is still Jesus Christ himself who, especially through his servants, continues his work of healing and deliverance, namely, on the basis of this work of atonement, accomplished on the cross. Of course, this in no way excludes the responsibility of his servants: it was, and is, *they* who lay their hands on the sick (Mark 16:18; Acts 9:12, 17; 28:8), anoint them with oil (Mark 6:13; James 5:14), and/or speak the word of power over them (Acts 3:6; 9:34; 14:8–10). It is Jesus who heals the sick; yet, he commanded first his apostles (Matt. 10:8; cf. Mark 6:13), and then the seventy(-two) (Luke 10:9), "Heal the sick." Thus, Jesus' servants are not passive instruments, but they are actively involved in the work of healing; he promised to believers in general, "[W]hoever believes in me will also do the works that I do; and greater works than these will he do" (John 14:12); "these signs will accompany those who believe:

in my name they will cast out demons; they will speak in new tongues; they will pick up serpents with their hands; and if they drink any deadly poison, it will not hurt them; they will lay their hands on the sick, and they will recover" (Mark 16:17-18).

14.3 Forgiveness, But No Immortality
14.3.1 Old Age Ailments

Not all the results of Christ's work become entirely manifest already in the present era, between his ascension and his return.[17] To those who come to him in faith, we are allowed to guarantee the forgiveness of all their sins, whether they have much or little faith. However, we are not allowed to guarantee to them in the same way the healing of all their diseases, even if they have the greatest faith possible.[18] The best proof for this state of affairs is that, ultimately, even the greatest believer in the end dies of a failing body. Some Charismatic theologians believe that a believer need never be sick, and that the Lord, when the time has come, takes his child home, without any sickbed. However, even without a specific disease, almost always a physical cause of death can be identified, even if only the general weakness of advanced age. In the Bible this is perfectly normal as well:[19] several believers had certain ailments due to advanced age.

A good example of such an aged, ailing man was Barzillai, a close companion of David: he

> said to the king, "How many years have I still to live, that I should go up with the king to Jerusalem? I am this day eighty years old. Can I discern what is pleasant and what is not? Can your servant taste what he eats or what he drinks? Can I still listen to the voice of singing men and

---

17. See more extensively, Morphew (1998, 143-47).
18. See, e.g., Nee (2002, 740).
19. See Ouweneel (2004, §3.5.1).

singing women? Why then should your servant be an added burden to my lord the king?" (2 Sam. 19:34-35).

Of David himself we read, "King David was old and advanced in years. And although they covered him with clothes, he could not get warm" (1 Kings 1:1).[20] Of the patriarch Isaac we read that at an advanced age—he had long passed one hundred years—he could no longer see (Gen. 27:1). Of the patriarch Jacob we read that at the end of his life he became ill, and apparently he died from this illness (Gen. 48:1). Of the prophet Ahijah we read, "Ahijah could not see, for his eyes were dim because of his age" (14:4). These were all men of God! The Bible gives us a long list—in metaphorical language—of all the ailments of old age (Eccl. 12:1-7). (Moses and Caleb seem to have represented exceptions rather than the rule; Deut. 34:7; Josh. 14:11.)

In our modern time, it is important to note that great ministers of healing suffered from diseases, and/or eventually died from them.[21] Some of them were richly blessed in their own healing ministry, yet were never healed of some of the diseases from which they themselves suffered. Dozens of solutions have been offered to explain Paul's "thorn in the flesh" (2 Cor. 12:7), about half them explaining it as some kind of sickness or physical handicap (perhaps an eye disease? cf. Acts 23:4-5; Gal. 4:15). Whatever it was, it was severe, but the Lord did not take it away from him:

> Three times I pleaded with the Lord about this, that it should leave me. But he said to me, "My grace is sufficient for you, for my power is made perfect in weakness." Therefore I will boast all the more gladly of my weaknesses, so that the power of Christ may rest upon me. For the sake of

---

20. In fact, he could not have been older than 70: he was 30 when he became king, and he reigned forty years (2 Sam. 5:4; 1 Kings 2:11).
21. For a number of examples, see Ouweneel (2004, §7.3.3).

Christ, then, I am content with weaknesses, insults, hardships, persecutions, and calamities. For when I am weak, then I am strong (2 Cor. 12:8–10).

14.3.2 Salvation and Disease

Although all sins of believers are forgiven, but not all their diseases are necessarily taken from them, we must maintain the link between disease and sin, and thus between healing and salvation. One more linguistic feature illustrates this connection: on the one hand, *atonement* terms are used when a text speaks of the healing of *diseases*, and on the other hand, *healing* terms are used when a text speaks of the forgiveness of *sins*. Thus, the Greek word *sōzō* ("to save"), which is used for forgiveness and eternal salvation, is used more often for healing sickness. This clearly illustrates the close link between the wholeness of the body and the wholeness of the soul. Salvation involves the entire person, and some of this truth comes to light in the healing of believers, or believers-to-be, today.

A few examples may suffice. To a *sinful* woman who asked for Jesus' help he said the same thing that he said to a *sick* woman who asked for his help: "Your faith has saved [Gk. *sesōken*] you; go in peace" (Luke 7:50), respectively, "Daughter, your faith has made you well ["made well" is one Gk. word: *sesōken*]" (Luke 8:48; also see Matt. 9:21–22; 14:36; Mark 5:23, 28, 34; 6:56; Luke 7:3; 8:36, 50; 17:19; Acts 14:9). A sinful person must be "saved" from their sins, a sick person must be saved from their sicknesses; in many cases the same Greek verb *sōzō* is used. One could say that salvation is not unless the entire body is included. This is one reason why Paul says that believers will fully receive or enjoy their "adoption as sons" only when also their bodies will be "redeemed" (Rom. 8:23).

The Hebrew word *r-ph-'*, "to heal," is sometimes used to describe a person's healing after wicked sin: "Because of the iniquity of his unjust gain I was angry, / I struck him; I hid my face and was angry, / but he went on backsliding in the way of his own heart. / I have seen his ways, but I will heal him; . . ." (Isa. 57:17-18). "Return, O faithless sons; / I will heal your faithlessness" (Jer. 3:22). "For the wound of the daughter of my people is my heart wounded; / I mourn, and dismay has taken hold on me. / Is there no balm in Gilead? / Is there no physician there? / Why then has the health of the daughter of my people not been restored?" (Jer. 8:21-22). "Come, let us return to the Lord; / for he has torn us, that he may heal us; / he has struck us down, and he will bind us up" (Hos. 6:1). "I will heal their apostasy; / I will love them freely, / for my anger has turned from them" (Hos. 14:4). Here we could make the opposite claim: there is no real healing if he restoration of the soul is not included, as well.

The indirect testimony of Scripture is that, generally speaking, diseases are a consequence of the Fall. Sickness can often also be closely related to sins that the sick person has committed (see above). Through these sins, an entrance gate is opened for demonic influence, which may cause the disease (see, e.g., Luke 13:11, 16). This implies that, in such cases, the sick person can be healed only through the confession of the sins committed, and subsequently through the casting out of the demons in the name of the Lord Jesus (see §§14.6-14.8). But in other cases, where specific sins are not identified as the cause of the sickness, the Lord often grants healing in response to prayer. Just as sickness has entered the world through the Fall, thus, *due to Christ's atoning work*, all sickness will ultimately be removed (Isa. 33:24; cf. 29:18; 35:5-6; 42:7[22]). Some sick persons receive their healing during this life, but these too will eventually die, if the Lord does not return. Others receive this heal-

---

22. Some of these passages may refer to, or include, spiritual sickness; cf. Isa. 42:18-19; 43:8; 56:10.

ing at the resurrection of their bodies.

Full healing, based on the atonement, will occur only at the consummation of the ages. However, this should not stop us from praying for healing today, since God grants many healings today in response to prayer. The "power of the age to come" (i.e., the power of the coming Messianic kingdom; Heb. 6:5) can be tasted already in the present age. J. Wimber stated that his body wore down as a consequence of the Fall, and that he had no control over the time when God would take him away. But at least, he stated, he did not have to die as a consequence of his personal sins before his appointed time.[23] In other words, God had determined his days; but he himself, had he begun to live in wicked sin, would be responsible for dying before the appointed end of his days (for this possibility, see, e.g., Ps. 102:24; Isa. 38:10).

14.4 The Place of Faith
14.4.1 Faith Before the Healing

In my book on the ministry of healing, I mentioned a number of biblical examples where healing occurred without the persons involved displaying any faith. These included the Syrian commander Naaman (2 Kings 5), the blind man of John 9, and the lame beggar of Acts 3.[24] Although these people did not exhibit any personal faith, yet in all these and other cases, the element of faith was definitely present. For instance, Naaman protested against the prophet Elisha's suggestion to submerge himself seven times in the river Jordan. Yet he was healed because apparently his servants did have some faith, evident when they urged the commander to follow the prophet's recommendation (2 Kings 5:10–14). So faith played a role after all, though not on the part of the sick person himself but in his benevolent companions.

---

23. Wimber and Springer (1986, 174).
24. Ouweneel (2004, 266).

The lame man at the Beautiful Gate, too, had no faith, though neither did he possess unbelief. He simply did not consider the possibility of being healed; he only hoped for alms. Yet, he was healed by faith, though not his own faith but that of Peter (and John): "And his [i.e., Jesus'] name—by faith in his name—has made this man strong whom you see and know, and the faith that is through Jesus has given the man this perfect health in the presence of you all" (Acts 3:16). Although Peter does not explicitly say so, he cannot refer to anything other than his own faith (and that of John).

In the third case mentioned, that of the blind man in John 9, it was Jesus himself who did the healing, so that the question of faith was solved *a priori*. Notice that the healing of the blind man *led to* faith:

> Jesus heard that they had cast him out, and having found him he said, "Do you believe in the Son of Man?" He answered, "And who is he, sir, that I may believe in him?" Jesus said to him, "You have seen him, and it is he who is speaking to you." He said, "Lord, I believe," and he worshiped him (vv. 35-38).

When it comes to healing by faith, there is both a similarity and a difference with regard to the forgiveness of sins. For the forgiveness, too, faith (in God and his mercy) is an indispensable condition; this is because no one would confess their sins to God without some faith in God, both in his existence and in his mercy. The difference, however, is that faith always must be present in the person who is to be forgiven. Other people cannot believe for them, in their stead. The faith of a friend or relative may contribute to bringing them to the confession of their sins, but in the end, *their* confession and *their* faith is required to receive forgiveness. Apparently, in the ministry of healing this requirement is different. The existence of faith in the sick person themselves is

Christ's Sacrifice: Healing and Deliverance

good (cf. Matt. 9:22, 28-29; Mark 10:52; Luke 17:19; Acts 14:9-10), but apparently this is not a necessary condition. Here, the faith of parents or friends can be sufficient basis for healing the sick person. With regard to his sick servant, the centurion believed in Jesus and his power to such an extent that Jesus said of him, "Truly, I tell you, with no one in Israel have I found such faith" (Matt. 8:10; see vv. 5-13). Jesus said something similar about the Canaanite woman who came to him on behalf of her possessed daughter (Matt. 15:28).

Speaking of parents, we also read, "And behold, some people brought to him a paralytic, lying on a bed. And when Jesus saw *their* faith, he said to the paralytic, 'Take heart, my son; your sins are forgiven'" (Matt. 9:2), and then healed the man (vv. 6-7). When Jairus came to Jesus on behalf of his sick daughter, Jesus told him, "Do not fear; only believe, and she will be well" (Luke 8:50). To the father of the boy with the unclean spirit, Jesus said, "All things are possible for one who believes" (Mark 9:23). These three people, the Canaanite woman, Jairus, and the father of the possessed boy, had this in common: they were parents of needy youngsters. Apparently, the faith of parents in view of the needs of their children is of special significance.

In some cases it seemed as if the *unbelief* of the bystanders disturbed Jesus or his servants in their ministry of healing. This might be the reason why in certain situations Jesus drove the bystanders away, or took the sick person away from the crowd:

> [W]hen he had entered [the house of Jairus], he said to them [i.e., the wailing people], "Why are you making a commotion and weeping? The child is not dead but sleeping." And they laughed at him. But *he put them all outside* and took the child's father and mother and those who were with him and went in where the child was. Taking her by the hand he said to her, "Talitha cumi," which

means, "Little girl, I say to you, arise." And immediately the girl got up and began walking" (Mark 5:39-42).

On another occasion:

> [T]hey brought to him a man who was deaf and had a speech impediment, and they begged him to lay his hand on him. And *taking him aside from the crowd privately*, he put his fingers into his ears, and after spitting touched his tongue. And looking up to heaven, he sighed and said to him, "Ephphatha," that is, "Be opened" (Mark 7:32-34).

In summary, unbelief may disturb the healing situation; in Jesus' case we read that on a certain occasion, "he could do no mighty work there, except that he laid his hands on a few sick people and healed them. And he marveled because of their unbelief" (Mark 6:5-6). Conversely, faith is very important. Faith is, as it were, the antenna through which God's power descends in a given situation, or to use another metaphor, the channel through which healing flows to the sick person. But interestingly, whether this is the persons' own faith, or that of the loved ones accompanying them, is less relevant.

14.4.2 Faith After the Healing

Faith is important, not only before but also after the healing. Again, there is a parallel here with the forgiveness of sins: faith is needed to be able to accept forgiveness but it is equally necessary that the forgiven person learns to live out that forgiveness by faith (cf. §12.7).[25] Similarly, the person who has received healing must not allow an unbelieving or semi-believing environment to rob them of that healing. This happens when unbelieving people begin to sow the seed of unbelief in their

---

25. Regarding the significance of faith, see Ouweneel (*RT* III/2, chapters 6 and 7).

heart ("are you really healed?" "did you not just imagine it?" "how do you know that minister of healing was okay?" "do you not feel the pain already coming back?"). If faith plays an essential role *in* the healing—in the sick person or in their companions—faith as well as unbelief may play just as great a role *after* the healing.

Let me give an example. Proverbs 28:13b says, "[H]e who confesses and *forsakes* them [i.e., his transgressions] will obtain mercy." If sin was involved in the causes of the disease that has been healed, it is very important that the healed person develop a new lifestyle. One cannot confess one's sin—and be healed—and simply continue with one's former life. Therefore, Jesus said to the man who had been sick for thirty-eight years: "See, you are well! Sin no more, that nothing worse may happen to you" (John 5:14). On the positive side, the healed person must learn to praise God for their healing (cf. Luke 17:15-18), even if some symptoms temporarily (seem to) return. They must lead a life of devotion and dedication, especially in learning to know and follow Jesus more and more (see John 5:13 and 9:35-38).[26]

This is important particularly when the ministry of healing is a form of, or a part of, the ministry of deliverance (see §§14.6-14.8 below). The latter will avail nothing if believers do not break radically with the sins through which they allowed demons entrance into their lives, and if they do not break with all the objects and literature that were part of these lives. In Acts 19:19 we see how the converts in Asia Minor broke with their former idolatrous life: "And a number of those who had practiced magic arts brought their books together and burned them in the sight of all" (cf. Deut. 7:25-26). Jude wrote (v. 23), "[S]ave others by snatching them out of the fire; to others show mercy with fear, hating even the garment stained by the flesh." It is essential that, after the ministry of healing and/or deliverance the "hole" that

---

26. Cf. Ouweneel (2004, 260).

exists, so to speak, is filled with the Holy Spirit through the believer placing himself entirely under the lordship of Christ. Otherwise the cast out demon may return:

> When the unclean spirit has gone out of a person, it passes through waterless places seeking rest, but finds none. Then it says, "I will return to my house from which I came." And when it comes, it finds the house empty, swept, and put in order. Then it goes and brings with it seven other spirits more evil than itself, and they enter and dwell there, and the last state of that person is worse than the first. So also will it be with this evil generation (Matt. 12:43-45; cf. Eph. 5:18; 2 Pet. 2:20-22).

14.5 Liberated Prisoners?
14.5.1 The View

In §§14.6-14.8 we will discuss the ministry of deliverance, as a further elaboration of the salvation that Christ has wrought. Before we begin that discussion, I must mention an extraordinary aspect of "deliverance," namely, the doctrine concerning Jesus' supposed descent into hell, or into the realm of death, and the supposed release of the believers who supposedly lived in that realm. If this doctrine were correct, this would imply a very special form of the ministry of deliverance, namely, one that supposedly was performed by Jesus himself, in the very domain of death.[27]

This doctrine is found among Roman Catholic and Reformational Christians, and nowadays also among Evangelical theologians. The roots of it lie in the writings of the church fathers. We encounter it in the notion of the *limbus patrum*, which Latin expression literally means "the fathers' limbo."[28] This was the supposed abode of Old Testament believers, a place that since

---

27. Grudem (1994, 582-94); Van de Kamp (2005, 202-03)
28. Not to be confused with the *limbus infantium* or *puerorum*, the supposed limbo for children who die very early without having been baptized.

Christ's death is supposed to be empty. J. MacCullough wrote that, from the time of the second century, no doctrine was better known and more popular, including Jesus' descent into Hades, his triumph over death and Hades, his preaching to the dead, and his release of the souls, and its popularity kept increasing.[29] J. Sanders claimed that the doctrine of Christ's descent into hell (read: Hades[30]) and belief in the release of the souls from this place was established already by the end of the first century. The only remaining point of debate involved *who* exactly had been released.[31]

In its elaborated form, the view we are discussing consists of the following elements:[32]

(a) Jesus descended in person into hell, or Hades, or the realm of the dead, as indicated in the Apostles' Creed in the Latin version as we know it today: *descendit ad infernos*. The Greek version says, *katelthonta eis ta katōtata*, that is literally, "descended into the lower [regions]" (cf. Eph. 4:9). In fact, Latin *infer(n)us* means nothing but "lower" (cf. the word "inferior"), but in antiquity it was used in the sense of the netherworld, the realm of the dead. In Christian thinking, *inferno* by and by received the meaning "hell," without the users making a proper distinction between *hell* (Gk. *gehenna*) and *Hades*, the Greek term for the abode of the dead.

(b) Jesus descended *ad infernos* to "take prisoners with him"; this idea is derived from Ephesians 4:8 (ESV: "he led a host of captives"), which is an allusion to Psalm 68:18 ("You descended on high, leading a host of captives in your train and receiving gifts among men,

---

29. MacCullough (1930, 45).
30. In the New Testament, the word *gehenna* means "hell," the word *hades* means Hades, or the netherworld, or the abode of the disembodied dead. After death, the wicked go to Hades (Luke 16:22–23); the wicked go to hell only after their resurrection (Matt. 10:28; cf. 25:41; Rev. 19:20).
31. Sanders (1992, 183–84).
32. Duffield and Van Cleave (1996, 552).

even among the rebellious, that the LORD God may dwell there [i.e., on Mount Zion]"). While Paul himself in Ephesians 4:8 does draw any significant conclusions for these words, many interpreters have: "When he ascended on high he led a host of captives" (see §14.5.3).

(c) Jesus spent three days and three nights "in the heart of the earth," as he himself put it (Matt. 12:40). Jesus did not stay in the abode of the dead evildoers in Hades (the domain of the dead) but in the part that he himself referred to as "Abraham's bosom," a metaphor for the honorary place at the heavenly supper, that is, for paradisiacal bliss (Luke 16:22 [N]KJV; cf. 23:43).

(d) Jesus took all the righteous from Hades, and brought them with himself into Paradise. Psalm 16:10 ("you will not abandon my soul to Sheol") and its quotation in Acts 2:27 ("you will not abandon [Gk. *enkataleipō*[33]] my soul to Hades," or "leave my soul in Hades" or "in the grave" or "in the realm of death") are adduced as evidence that Jesus was indeed in Hades between his death and resurrection, but was not to stay there.

(e) These righteous whom Jesus brought out of Hades into Paradise are supposedly the "saints" who, after Jesus' resurrection came out of their tombs, and appeared to many in Jerusalem (Matt. 27:52-53).

In a somewhat different sense, we find a reminder of this view with Joseph Ratzinger, who connects Matthew 12:29 with what is said of Jesus in the Latin version of the Apostles' Creed: *descendit ad infernos*.[34] He called the entering into the sin of other people a descent into the "inferno"—not only, as in Dante's description,[35] observing, but suffering with and for these people, and thus transforming them, forcing and opening those doors of the "depth" (his rendering of *inferno*). It was a descent into the house of the evil one, and a struggle with the strong

---

33. Danker (2000, s.v. *enkataleipō*).
34. Ratzinger (2007, 19-20, 26).
35. Dante Alighieri, *Divina Commedia*, Part I: *Inferno*.

one who had kept humanity captive. This strong one, seemingly invincible in world history, was overcome and bound by the stronger one—with Ratzinger's apparent implication that Jesus, at this occasion, plundered the goods of the strong one (Matt. 12:29; Mark 3:27).

14.5.2 Refutation

To begin with, Acts 2:27 indeed seems to suggest that between his death and resurrection, Jesus was in Hades. Yet, to me this is not entirely clear. In Psalm 16, the literal sense is rather, "you will not abandon my soul to Hades," that is, you will make sure—says the godly person—that I do not go to Hades at all. In Luke 16, Jesus tells us that Lazarus was carried to Abraham's side (v. 22), but the rich man lifted up his eyes in Hades (v. 23). This suggests that Abraham, and thus Lazarus, were *not* in Hades. Apparently, they were in the place that Jesus called Paradise (23:43; cf. 2 Cor. 12:3; Rev. 2:7). In other words, there is no clear-cut biblical proof that Jesus ever was in Hades, that is, among the dead who had died in their wickedness.

Of course, we think here immediately of 1 Peter 3:19, where the apostle says that, "in the spirit" (or "in [the] Spirit"), Christ "went and proclaimed to the spirits in prison." People say that there, in Hades, Jesus supposedly put an end to the power of the devil: through death, Jesus destroyed the one who had the power of death, that is, the devil (Heb. 2:14). If before this, the devil had the "power of death," after his triumph Jesus could say, "*I have the keys of Death and Hades*" (Rev. 1:18). We must add here, though, that the meaning of 1 Peter 3:19 is not at all unambiguous.[36] Most expositors identify the "spirits in prison," who had been disobedient in the days of Noah, as the wicked who perished in the Flood, or the fallen angels of Genesis 6:1-4 or their offspring, who

---

36. See more extensively, Ouweneel (2012a, §§3.3.2 and 3.4.1); cf. Blum (1981, 241); Davids (1990, 138-42).

supposedly also died in the Flood. In the former case, the "prison" is Hades, in the latter case it is the Tartarus, the abode of fallen angels (cf. 2 Pet. 2:4 HCSB; the Gk. is *tartarōsas*).

Equally unclear is *when* the Spirit of Christ preached to these "spirits": either in the days of Noah (cf. Gen. 6:3),[37] or between Christ's death and resurrection, or after his resurrection. The context most clearly refers to the risen Christ. Even if we, in line with the Apostles' Creed, think here of the time between Christ's death and resurrection, it would be a "preaching" only to those who perished in the Flood. H. Bavinck pointed out that the text does not speak at all of some gospel preaching to the dead in Hades.[38]

Another difficulty in the ancient view of the Christ's descent into hell is that, until the death of Christ, Old Testament believers would have lived in darkness. An appeal is made to passages such as ". . . I go—and shall not return—to the land of darkness and deep shadow, the land of gloom lick thick darkness" (Job 10:21-22); ". . . if I hope for Sheol as my house, if I make my bed in darkness" (17:13; cf. Eccl. 11:8, "the days of darkness" after death). From this place of darkness, Jesus supposedly redeemed the righteous by leading them out into Paradise at his resurrection or his ascension. However, Job had never been in Hades, and he was speaking as a desperate man. *Scripture* was inspired (2 Tim. 3:16), but Job was not; not everything that a believer says, even if it is recorded in Scripture, is of the Spirit. Moreover, the Hebrew word *Sheol* rarely means Hades (except perhaps in Isa. 14:9-11, but even there the meaning implies the grave; v. 11b). Its common meaning is the grave (cf. the parallel between Job 17:13 and 14; cf. 24:19-20), and in-

---

37. Augustine; Grant (1902, 161-63); Kelly (1923, 200-205); "many Reformed," says Greijdanus (1931, 141); see extensively, Grudem (1988, 157-61, 203-39).
38. Bavinck (*RD* 4:630-31).

deed, there it is always dark.

After his death, Lazarus was carried to "Abraham's side" (Luke 16:22), and no matter how rich the metaphors Jesus' story may be, the response of the rich man certainly does not give us the impression that Abraham's and Lazarus' abode was a gloomy, dark place. Moreover, the converted criminal at the cross received Jesus' assurance that he would be with Jesus "in Paradise" that very same day (Luke 23:43), that is, before Jesus' resurrection. In other words, Scripture does not support the suggestion that the dead and not-yet-resurrected saints before Jesus' death were in a dark place, and only after Jesus' resurrection were brought to a glorious place.

14.5.3 Ephesians 4:8-10

Another difficulty is the phrase in Ephesians 4:8-10,

> When he [i.e., Jesus] ascended on high he led a host of captives [lit, "he led captivity captive," KJV]. (In saying, "He ascended," what does it mean but that he had also descended into the lower regions, the earth? He who descended is the one who also ascended far above all the heavens, that he might fill all things.)"

Theodore of Mopsuestia suggested that the captives (or prisoners) in Psalm 68:18 and Ephesians 4:8-10 are the redeemed. Gottlieb von Harless claimed that these texts speak of people who here on earth had been bound in sins.[39] F. Delitzsch, F. E. König, and others believed that the passages speak of the souls who had been kept in Hades.[40] However, first, the idea of a carrying out and carrying up of Old Testament believers does not fit at all into the context of Psalm 68 and Ephesians 4. These passages speak of very different things, and it is unwarranted speculation to read such things into these texts.

---

39. Harless (1834, ad loc.).
40. König (1927, ad loc.); Keil and Delitzsch (6:261-62).

Second, it is hardly conceivable to identify the "prisoners" as God's own people. The context, especially in Psalm 68, clearly refers to enemies who have been made prisoners of war (cf. Judg. 5:12). This is properly indicated in several translations: "he captured prisoners" (CSB, CEB) and "he led captives into captivity" (ISV). We cannot reverse the argument in Ephesians 4:8-10 by turning God's prisoners into prisoners who had been taken captive by God's *enemies*, and have been set free by Christ.[41] On the contrary, in the application that Paul makes, the point is that Christ "has gained the victory over hell and world, has borne all curse and guilt of his people, has brought about a full atonement for them," as S. Greijdanus put it.[42] Somewhat similarly, K. Wuest identifies the "prisoners" as demons that tried to stop Jesus from his ascension.[43] F. F. Bruce also rejected Ephesians 4:8-10 as evidence for the ancient idea of the plundering of hell. He did so especially because this notion does not do justice to Psalm 68:18, which points to *God's* prisoners of war.[44]

In summary, bundling together a number of speculative exegeses of passages that in themselves are already difficult enough can never yield a reliable theological hypothesis. Ephesians 4:8-10 does point to the idea of a triumphal procession, held by Christ after his victory over Satan and his powers, comparable to 1:20-22, Colossians 2:15, and 1 Peter 3:22. However, this is something very different from a kind of release of Old Testament believers, lifting them from the dark and gloomy realm of death to a illuminated and happy Paradise. Not the slightest unequivocal biblical evidence supports this idea.

---

41. Salmond (1979, 324).
42. Greijdanus (1925, 87).
43. Wuest (1977a, 98-99).
44. Bruce (1984, 344).

14.6 The Ministry of Deliverance[45]
14.6.1 "Pagan" Facets

Let us now pay attention to the ministry of deliverance as Jesus has entrusted it to the believers: "[T]hese signs will accompany those who believe: in my name they will cast out demons," and so on (Mark 16:17).[46] We begin by noticing a particular aspect of the deliverance that Christ has brought about. This aspect is far more obvious for a Third World believer than for a Western Christian. Tokunboh Adeyemo was the general editor of the *Africa Bible Commentary: A One-Volume Commentary*,[47] a complete Bible commentary in one volume. Naturally, a one-volume Bible commentary cannot be very detailed. But one of the most attractive aspects of this work is its many references to the circumstances of African Christians.

In reference to this, in connection with the ministry of deliverance, notice just this one statement of Zechariah the priest: ". . . saved from our enemies and from the hand of all who hate us" (Luke 1:71). I did mention this passage briefly in §§2.4.2-2.4.3, but did not elaborate on it there. The salvation that Christ brought about also involves being saved from "all who hate us," not only from the hate manifested in direct faith persecution, but also from the hate manifested in the "evil eye," in "black magic," and other occult practices whereby people can harm believers.[48] Think of the curses that can be pronounced on people and that can harm Christians too, if they are not spiritually armed against them, or are not released from them. One example is a physical or mental ailment or infertility that, as practice teaches, can be

---

45. See more extensively, Ouweneel (2004, chapter 6).
46. With others, I view Mark 16:9-20 as a later addition to Mark's Gospel (possibly by a collaborator), yet inspired; see, e.g., Metzger (1975, ad loc.).
47. Adeyemo (2006).
48. See extensively, Ouweneel (1978), although several points in this work need to be updated.

consequences of such curses.

It is a serious error if Christians believe that they are no longer susceptible to this kind of curses. American theologian M. F. Unger wrote that at first he believed that demons could no longer affect true believers, but after many reports from missionaries in Africa and Asia he had to revise his opinion.[49] Genuine believers might not be demon-*possessed*—because then their hearts would be occupied by demons—but they can certainly be demon-*circumsessed* (the Christian is "beleaguered" by demons), or even demon-*obsessed* (the Christian is "bound"), to use an ancient Christian distinction (see §14.7.1). In fact, this is also a Western problem because of Satanism, Spiritism, and other forms of occultism, but many Christians seem to be hardly aware of these evil practices. Especially in Africa, it is a very important part of gospel preaching to explain to people that, in Christ, protection is offered also against the evil forces and powers that other people might direct toward them.

Christian preachers must explicitly mention this aspect in their preaching, and offer concrete protection through the application of the gospel, that is, through the ministry of deliverance. If they fail to do so, their listeners will not become free from all kinds of occult influences to which they have been exposed, and are still being exposed. To put it even more strongly, the danger is concretely present that they might consult magicians, shamans, native or traditional or alternative healers (or whatever they might be called) in order to find healing, and thus jump from the frying pan into the fire. What we need here is a full gospel, a gospel for the salvation not only of the soul but also of the mind and the body, concrete release from the grip of the powers of darkness and of those instruments that allow themselves to be used by these powers.

---

49. Unger (1971, 117); cf. Ouweneel (1978, 273-74).

14.6.2 Converts and Bondage

The Western model of redemption, with its great emphasis on sin and atonement but less attention for Satan and his defeat, traditionally had little room for the ministry of deliverance. In the Protestant churches, attention to this was less than traditionally in the Roman Catholic Church with its ancient practices of exorcism. In the early church, it was still very common that persons who came from paganism received the ministry of deliverance together with their baptism. Christians were deeply conscious of the fact that serving pagan idols in fact meant serving demons, and that these converts therefore were probably still in bondage in many respects. They were like the resurrected Lazarus: Jesus had brought him back to life, but Jesus' servants had to free him from the linen strips with which he was still bound; Jesus tells his servants also today, as it were: "Unbind them, and let them go" (cf. John 11:44).

The idea that idolatry consists in service to demons is found in Deuteronomy 32:17 ("They sacrificed to demons that were no gods, to gods they had never known"), 1 Corinthians 10:20 (". . . what pagans sacrifice they offer to demons and not to God"), and Revelation 9:20 (". . . worshiping demons and idols of gold and silver and bronze and stone and wood"). Paul told the Thessalonian believers that one day they "turned to God from idols to serve the living and true God" (1 Thess. 1:9), that is, from the demons to God, from the kingdom of Satan to the kingdom of God (Matt. 12:25–28), from the "power of Satan to God" (Acts 26:18), from "darkness" to the "kingdom of his beloved Son" (Col. 1:13).

From the eighth century, we know the so-called Utrecht or Old Saxon baptismal promise, in which we find the following:

> I forsake all devilish works and words, [the gods] Donar [or Thor] and Wodan and Saxnot, and all demons who are

their companions. I believe in God, the almighty Father. I believe in Christ, God's Son. I believe in the Holy Ghost (Old Saxon: *Ec forsacho allum dioboles wercum end wordum Thunaer ende Woden ende Saxnote ende allum them unholdum the hira genotas sind. Ec gelobo in got alamehtigan fadaer. Ec gelobo in crist godes suno. Ec gelobo in halogan gast*).[50]

It would be a great blessing if modern Christians would recognize that the ministry of deliverance belongs to the normal tasks of the church, exercised toward both believers and unbelievers: "[P]roclaim as you go, saying, 'The kingdom of heaven is at hand.' Heal the sick, raise the dead, cleanse lepers, cast out demons" (Matt. 10:7-8; cf. again Mark 16:17). "The people also gathered from the towns around Jerusalem, bringing the sick and those afflicted with unclean spirits, and they were all healed" (Acts 5:16). "And the crowds with one accord paid attention to what was being said by Philip, when they heard him and saw the signs that he did. For unclean spirits, crying out with a loud voice, came out of many who had them" (8:6-7). "God was doing extraordinary miracles by the hands of Paul, so that even handkerchiefs or aprons that had touched his skin were carried away to the sick, and their diseases left them and the evil spirits came out of them" (Acts 19:11-12).

14.6.3 Ignorance

Unfortunately, many Christians are ignorant about the ministry of deliverance. Paul hoped "that we would not be outwitted by Satan; for we are not ignorant of his designs" (2 Cor. 10:11)—but how many Christians can say Amen to the latter phrase? Therefore, we urgently need information about the consequences of occult contacts, sins, and addictions, about curses, bonds, occult symptoms, Satanic blood pacts, forms of superstition (e.g., amulets), demonic teachings, occult or "alterna-

---

50. See Gysseling (1980, 26).

tive" healing practices,⁵¹ occult books and objects, and so forth.⁵²

Not every Christian is a *minister* of deliverance (see Acts 19:13-16), just as not every believer is a prophet, an evangelist, or a minister of healing. However, this does not deny that, at a given moment, *every* believer can speak a prophetic word (cf. 1 Cor. 12:10; 14:24), can give a testimony about Jesus (cf. Acts 8:4-5), or can lay hands on people (cf. the simple disciple Ananias in Acts 9:10, 17). In the same way, there is a special ministry of deliverance granted to specific believers, but for *all* believers the Lord's promise is true: "[I]n my name they will cast out demons" (Mark 16:17). When necessary, to each believer can be given the charisma of the "working of works of power" (Gk. *energēmata dunameōn*, 1 Cor. 12:10 WYC; Phillips: "the power to do great deeds"; NLV: "doing powerful works").

Three errors need to be avoided in connection with this discussion. The first is that true believers cannot be "possessed."⁵³ As I said, this assertion and debate is rather irrelevant, since believers can certainly be demon-bound to a lesser degree (I will return to this in the next section). Here are some biblical examples: "[Y]ou are to deliver this man [i.e., a confessing Christian] to Satan for the destruction of the flesh, so that his spirit may be saved in the day of the Lord" (1 Cor. 5:5; cf. 2 Cor. 2:10, where the believer involved is seen as restored); ". . . a thorn was given me in the flesh, a messenger of Satan to harass me, to keep me from becoming conceited" (2 Cor. 12:7). "Put on the whole armor of God, that you may be able to stand against the schemes of the devil" (2 Cor. 6:11); ". . . Hymenaeus and Alexander, whom I have handed over to Satan that they may learn not to

---

51. Please note, many "alternative" healers are not occult at all; many are just quacks.
52. See the extensive literature references in Ouweneel (2004).
53. E.g., Mayhue (1999, 157-61).

blaspheme" (1 Tim. 1:20).

The potential overseer "must be well thought of by outsiders, so that he may not fall into disgrace, into a snare of the devil" (1 Tim. 3:7). "Now the Spirit expressly says that in later times some will depart from the faith by devoting themselves to deceitful spirits and teachings of demons" (1 Tim. 4:1-2); "some [confessing Christians] have already strayed after Satan" (1 Tim. 5:15); "they [i.e., certain heretics] may come to their senses and escape from the snare of the devil, after being captured by him to do his will" (2 Tim. 2:26); "... bitter jealousy and selfish ambition ... is earthly, unspiritual, demonic" (James 3:14-15). "Be sober-minded; be watchful. Your adversary the devil prowls around like a roaring lion, seeking someone to devour" (1 Pet. 5:8).

The second error is the claim that believers, since they live in a broken world, must acquiesce to the curses and demonic bonds that may still rest upon their lives. Lord's Day 10 of the Heidelberg Catechism has sometimes played a negative role here, as if believers must accept all the miseries in their lives as coming from God's "fatherly hand," so that they would not be allowed to fight them.[54] Instead, when Satan harasses believers, they should plead with the Lord about it (2 Cor. 12:7-8). Many believers could receive healing or deliverance if they would sincerely implore the Lord (James 4:2-3), or would make use of the ministry of healing and deliverance. There is a path to liberation in the name of Jesus Christ, in the power of the Holy Spirit.

The third error is that Christians go to the other extreme, and believe that each childhood trauma, every sin, each—especially mental—ailment, and every adversity in their lives go back to demonic bonds. The ministry of deliverance is no panacea against mental problems in general. Ministers would embarrass themselves if they tried to cast out demons that are not present in

---

54. Cf. Ouweneel (2016, 80-84).

the first place. I believe this is one of the meanings of the charisma of the "discerning of spirits" (1 Cor. 12:10 KJV): the minister of deliverance needs this charisma to be able to tell whether a person needs the ministry of deliverance, or ordinary pastoral counseling. For a mental ailment a person needs healing; for a demonic bond they need deliverance.

14.7 Boundness and Possession
14.7.1 Demonic Influences

A classic distinction that has been made in church exorcism (i.e., casting out demons), and that still appears to be a useful starting point, is based upon three expressions that have been derived from Latin noun *sessio*, "the sitting" (cf. "session"), which is derived from the Latin verb *sedere*, "to sit":[55]

(a) *Circumsessio*, literally "sitting around": the powers are sitting, so to speak, around the person and oppress them; the city is surrounded, beleaguered, but is itself still free of the hostile powers (cf. Ps. 118:5, 10–12).

(b) *Obsessio*, "coercion, compulsion (cf. obsession, although its meaning has shifted)": the powers have penetrated the city, have taken hold of certain parts of it, but the city's heart is still free.

(c) *Possessio*, this is possession in the actual sense of the term (the person is "possessed"): the powers have taken the entire city, and have even taken possession of its heart: the city hall; the owners or leaders of the city no longer have any authority over the city.

It is my conviction and that of many others that demonic possession cannot occur in a true Christian; no born again Christian can be in the condition described in Luke 8:29. This is because the heart of the Christian's "city" is in the possession of Christ, or of the Holy Spirit. God has sent the Spirit of his Son into the believer's

---

55. See Van Dam (1970, 151–52).

heart (Gal. 4:6), and it is through the Spirit that Christ dwells in their heart (Eph. 3:16–17). Here, Satan cannot penetrate. However, the *circumsessio* and the *obsessio* can certainly occur among Christians. If Paul says, "[D]o not give the devil a foothold" (Eph. 4:27 NIV, Gk. *topos*; others: "place, room, opportunity"), this ties in entirely with the images mentioned. To give the devil a foothold is a form of *obsessio*: he has gotten a foot inside the door, though he may not have conquered entire streets and houses.

In James 1:8 and 4:8 we find the remarkable Greek term *dipsuchos*, "double-minded." We are dealing here with a "divided" person, a person with literally two souls.[56] The normal situation for a Christian is that the believer has "one soul," which is entirely beset with ("baptized" into) the Holy Spirit. If the believer has "two souls," this means that a part of their being is under the influence of the Holy Spirit, but another part is beset with carnal doubt (James 1:6–8), or even demonic pseudo-wisdom (James 3:15), or even devilish impurity and self-conceitedness (James 4:7-10). A notion such as "double-mindedness" may help us gain insight into how a believer can still be exposed to demonic influences in their life, mind, and body. The Holy Spirit does dwell in such a believer, but has not received the opportunity to bring that *entire* person under his beneficial influence. Parts of the believer's soul have become the possession of the enemy, who will not easily let go.

14.7.2 Symptoms

What cases involve parts of a believer's soul being possessed by the devil? How do we assess that, and what do we do about it? It is important to determine the presence of demons, but as I said, it is equally important to not declare the presence of demons that are not there. A well-known minister of healing and deliverance, J. Wim-

---

56. *TDNT* 9:665; *DNTT* 3:686–87; cf. Ouweneel (2004, 189–90).

ber, warned that Christians often wrongly diagnose certain mental disorders as the result of demon activity. Wimber said that he himself never called anything a demon until he had actually spoken with such a being (cf. Mark 5:9). He used various criteria to establish whether he spoke with a demon. For instance, persons affected by demon activity undergo strong personality changes when the demon speaks through them (Mark 5:1–5 reports a very powerful example).[57] Such changes include flickering eyes, eye pupils rolling back, a covering of the eyes with a kind of film, distended nostrils, contracted lips, and swollen throat (cf. Mark 9:26). Some people fall to the ground, squirming and hissing like snakes, or make other animal sounds.

Of course, such phenomena can occur in cases of insanity as well, which does not imply that they involve demon activity. Though many people have equated insanity and demon possession, today we rightly assume that such a connection is incorrect in certain cases. However, we should not fall into the other extreme by assuming that such a connection *never* exists. On the contrary, we expect to encounter the activity of evil powers especially in the field of psychiatry and psychotherapy (mental disorders). Regrettably, numerous Christian psychiatrists and psychotherapists place the activity of demonic powers entirely beyond their horizon. For example, Christian physician G. Lindeboom claimed that the demonological view of illness had to be rejected entirely and unconditionally.[58] Christian psychotherapist A. Hegger claimed that he had never encountered demonic phenomena in his practice;[59] in my view, this says more about his scientific lens than about the facts. Psychiatrists and psychotherapists will

---

57. Wimber and Springer (1986, 240).
58. Lindeboom (1953, 7).
59. See the double interview in *CV Koers*, May 2008, with the revealing headline, "I prefer to keep my job free of superstition."

"see" the demonic only if they are open to it—both medically and theologically—in their thinking.

Over against this, others fall into the exactly opposite extreme of demonizing all mental disorders: they attribute certain mental disorders like epilepsy and schizophrenia entirely and unconditionally to demons, and reject any pathological mode of explanation. In between these two extremes, some Christian scholars like K. E. Koch[60] wish to understand mental disorders first in a natural scientific way, and only where this is impossible, introduce a demonological explanation. In Koch's view, especially in idiopathic epilepsy, which is not caused by brain damage but by mental conditions, demonic influence must be seriously considered.[61]

We do have to take care, though, as K. J. Kraan argued, that we do not divide the attribution of causes so rigidly that we adopt the unbiblical distinction (if not separation) between "nature" and "supernature,"[62] "where the supernature becomes relevant only at the point that natural explanations fail."[63] Indeed, in my view it is more correct to assume demonic influences in certain specific cases, even in mental and somatic disorders that seem to be entirely explicable in scientific terms. Just as a believer always attributes to God all healings, including those that are entirely scientifically explicable, so too, conversely, an entirely scientifically explicable disorder may be the effect of demonic influence (cf. the next section).

Every miracle of healing or deliverance, whether it is explained in a "natural" or a "supernatural" way—in itself a risky distinction[64]—is a step forward toward the ultimate salvation that will be realized in the Messianic

---

60. Koch (1972a; 1972b).
61. Cf. Van Dam (1985, 16).
62. Cf. Ouweneel (2004, §6.2.2).
63. Kraan (1974, 166).
64. Cf. Ouweneel (1995a, 70–71).

kingdom and on the new earth. All of redemptive history is a confrontation between God and the evil powers. In this history, every action of God in Christ is a *miracle*, that is, a partial victory over the evil powers, a further step toward the ultimate great salvation. Modern investigators may desire to explain various examples of "demon possession" in the New Testament in psychological and medical terms, and to a certain extent there may be truth in their findings. But whether or not they are right in this respect, in each deliverance of a human being manifests a measure of *salvation*: people

> came to Jesus and found the man from whom the demons had gone, sitting at the feet of Jesus, clothed and in his right mind, and they were afraid. And those who had seen it told them how the demon-possessed man [Gk. *ho daimonistheis*] had been healed [or saved, Gk. *esōthē*] (Luke 8:35-36).

He had been "healed" from his demons, and in this way the power of the kingdom of God became somewhat visible (Matt. 12:18).

14.8 A Way of Deliverance
14.8.1 Causes of Demonic Bondage

Experienced ministers of deliverance mention a great number of possible causes of demonic bondage. I do take this very seriously,[65] but in a theological work like this one I am limiting myself to causes that can be derived directly or indirectly from Scripture. Identifying such causes can be very important in the ministry of deliverance because only then can they be eliminated.

(a) *Contacts with occultists* (occult healers, Spiritists, and the like), Satanists, idolaters. Since idolatry in its

---
65. See Ouweneel (2004, 181-88); important examples include Koch (1972a; 1972b); Van Dam (1970; 1985; 1993); Subritzky (1985, 1991); Horrobin (2003); and Van de Kamp (2012).

essence is demon worship (see §14.6.2), idolatry entails explicitly opening oneself to the influence of demonic powers. Idolatry and the concomitant sexual immorality and rebellion can bring God's people under the power of Satan (1 Cor. 10:1–13, 20–21; cf. 5:10–11; 6:10; 10:7–8; Rev. 2:20–21, 24). The consequences of idolatry can have effects later in the third and the fourth generations (Deut. 5:7–9; cf. Exod. 20:5; 34:7; Num. 14:18). There are also curses that have effects in subsequent generations (Gen. 9:24–25; Deut. 28:41–46; Josh. 6:26; 9:23; 2 Sam. 3:28–29). Suffering such effects in subsequent generations does not mean that children are being *punished* for the sins of their ancestors—on the contrary, see Ezekiel 18:20—but it does mean that they experience the *damage* of their ancestors' sins, for instance, because ancestors had allowed themselves to be influenced by occult phenomena.

(b) *Pernicious addictions* imply that people have surrendered "into captivity" under the evil powers: "orgies and drunkenness, . . . sexual immorality and sensuality" are "works of darkness" (Rom. 13:12–13), that is, the domain of Satan (Acts 26:18). This means that addiction to nicotine, alcohol, and other drugs (substance addictions), but also to pornography, gambling, food, games, and so on (process addictions), always entails surrendering a certain measure of self-control, a control that then easily can pass into the hands of Satan and his consorts.

(c) *"Legitimate rights"*: Ephesians 4:22–27 shows us an important principle, which has been described as a "legitimate right" that people give to demons in their own lives. "Legitimate" does not mean that demons obtain from God the right to take possession of people, but it means that such people themselves have allowed them in, consciously or unconsciously. Through bitterness, licentiousness, strife, and jealousy (cf. Gal. 5:19–21), "room" (or a "foothold") is given to the devil (Eph. 4:27, see §14.7.1). He enters through the gateway of sin, and in the ministry of deliverance he can be cast out only through the gatewat of the *confession* of sin. In James 3:14-15, jealousy, selfish ambition, boasting, and falsehood are called "earthly, unspiritual [Gk. *psychikē*] and demonic [Gk. *daimoniōdēs*]."

(d) Diseases are not in all cases due to demonic bondage, yet disease and demon possession are related perhaps more often than some Christians think. In the New Testament, we find the case of the woman who "was bent over and could not fully straighten herself" (Luke 13:11). This seemed to be a purely physical condition (*spondylitis deformans?*), which today can be easily explained. Yet, the text clearly says that this condition was due to a "spirit of infirmity" (KJV; AMP: "an illness caused by a spirit (demon)"), and that she had been "bound" by Satan (v. 16). We also hear of "mute" and/or "deaf spirits," that is, apparently, demons who make their victims mute and/or deaf (Matt. 9:32-33; Mark 9:25; Luke 11:14). Further we learn about people "afflicted with unclean spirits" or "oppressed by the devil" who were "healed" (Acts 5:16; 10:38), and about "evil spirits" coming out of the sick (Acts 19:12).

14.8.2 Renouncement

The person in demonic bondage must renounce every curse, every bond with Satanic or occult phenomena with which they have come into contact, whether consciously or unconsciously.[66] Counselors can assist such a person in researching the past to find such demonic influences (this is the importance of §14.8.1). Christian living is totally incompatible with such bonds, as we learn from 2 Corinthians 6:14-16:

> Do not be unequally yoked with unbelievers. For what partnership has righteousness with lawlessness? Or what fellowship has light with darkness? What accord has

---

66. See extensively, Ouweneel (2004, chapter 6).

Christ with Belial [i.e., Satan]? Or what portion does a believer share with an unbeliever? What agreement has the temple of God with idols [which represent demonic powers, Deut. 32:17; 1 Cor. 9:19-20; Rev. 9:20]?

First, the person who is in bondage must sincerely and extensively confess their contacts with demonic powers—with all their devastating consequences—even if these contacts were unconscious, and even others, especially parents, had brought them into contact with such evil powers. They will then renounce the consequences of the contacts with such powers. A suggestion for a possible prayer could be:

In the name of the Lord Jesus Christ I renounce every contact with anything that is occult or demonic, and everything that stands under a curse. If I still possess occult objects, I promise to destroy them. I renounce any claim that Satan and his demons might still have on me, or assert having on me (cf. Acts 19:18-19).

Knowing what glorious work Jesus has accomplished, the person concerned may be convinced that each curse on their life will be broken, and that they may proclaim their freedom from every evil, sinful, or Satanic bond. Thus, they will experience the truth of Paul's statement: "Christ redeemed us from the *curse* of the law by becoming a curse for us—for it is written, 'Cursed is everyone who is hanged on a tree' [Deut. 21:23]—so that in Christ Jesus the blessing of Abraham might come to the Gentiles" (Gal. 3:13-14). To underscore this, the person concerned may pray something like this: "Lord Jesus, I wholeheartedly believe that, on the cross, you have taken upon you every curse that might come over me. Therefore, I pray you that you now release me from every curse on my life—in your name, Lord Jesus Christ! And in faith I now receive my deliverance, and I thank you for it. Give me the power of the Holy Spirit to live a true life of gratitude and of dedication to you, so that

Satan will never again have any grip on me."[67]

14.9 Final Remarks
14.9.1 Various Metaphors

Healing and deliverance belong to the wonderful results of Christ's work on the cross. They form some of the important proofs that this work involves much more than merely solving the problem of sin. The minister can speak with authority because of Christ's finished work, as did, for instance, Paul in the case of the girl with the spirit of divination; he told the spirit: "I command you in the name of Jesus Christ to come out of her" (Acts 16:18). Jesus' ministers do not "pray" for those circumsessed, obsessed, or possessed, but they command the evil powers to leave the person involved, as did Jesus himself (e.g., Mark 1:25; 5:8; 9:25; Luke 8:29; cf. 4:36).

The metaphor involves a person living in a house, as we read explicitly in Matthew 12:44. If a person has no right, or no longer has any right, to live there, another person with the appropriate divine authority can call upon him with mere words, in order to get him out of the house. This is like Jesus calling with a loud voice to Lazarus when he was still in his grave: "Lazarus, come out" (John 11:43). Often, the demons come out with a loud voice, too (Mark 1:26; 5:7; Acts 8:7). Such accompanying phenomena (cf. Mark 9:25-27) should not disturb the bystanders; they did not disturb Jesus and his servants either. Such phenomena are part of the struggle being waged, in which the power of Jesus Christ must always prevail.

Let us briefly look again at some of the metaphors mentioned in §8.1, to get a clearer picture of this.

(a) *Rural life*. In the ministry of healing and deliverance we are dealing with "weak, sick, injured, strayed" sheep. Jesus has laid down his life for his people in or-

---

67. Cf. ibid., 175-76.

der to save his miserable sheep from the claws of the lion and the bear, the thieves and the robbers (cf. 1 Sam. 17:34–37; John 10:8–10): "He will tend his flock like a shepherd; he will gather the lambs in his arms; he will carry them in his bosom, and gently lead those that are with young" (Isa. 40:11). In the ministry of healing and deliverance, the love and care of Christ come to light in a touching way.

(b) *Medical care.* Sin is often compared to illness, for instance, cancer (2 Tim. 2:17) or leprosy (see §5.6): "From the sole of the foot even to the head, there is no soundness in it [i.e., Israel], but bruises and sores and raw wounds; they are not pressed out or bound up or softened with oil" (Isa. 1:6). Forgiveness and atonement are compared to healing: "By his wounds you have been healed" (1 Pet. 2:24, quotation from Isa. 53:5). In previous sections, we have seen that Scripture establishes a close connection between literal medical care (healing of diseases) and spiritual medical care ("healing" of sins).

14.9.2 Other Metaphors

(c) *Social-societal life.* Originally, the term "reconciliation" belonged to the social-societal sphere, and referred to the restoration of the right relationship between two parties. Family members who oppose each other with a hostile and estranged attitude (cf. Isa. 59:2) must be reconciled to each other in order to be able to live together in a workable way. In a similar manner, people must be reconciled to God: "[I]f while we were enemies we were reconciled to God by the death of his Son, much more, now that we are reconciled, shall we be saved by his life" (Rom. 5:10). For many people, demonic bondage stands in the way of a new, intimate relationship with God; demons attempt to maintain as large a gap as possible between the believing soul and its God. Therefore, the ministry of deliverance is desperately needed.

(d) *The legal order.* Christ's work on the cross has also clearly judicial aspects. There is guilt, there are debts, in the form of trespasses of God's law, that must be paid: ". . . Jesus our Lord, who was delivered up for our trespasses and raised for our justification" (Rom. 4:24–25). This judicial element comes to light also in the "legitimate" rights that demons claim to have over their victims, and that must be broken in the name of Jesus. If the demons "legitimately" entered their victim because of the latter's sins, they must leave their victim as soon as the latter breaks these rights through the confession of their sins and through renouncing the former bonds.

(e) *Marriage.* Christ has acquired his church as Bride by surrendering himself for her unto death (Eph. 5:25–27). Ultimately, this will be consummated in the wedding of the Lamb:

> "[T]he marriage of the Lamb has come, and his Bride has made herself ready; it was granted her to clothe herself with fine linen, bright and pure"—for the fine linen is the righteous deeds of the saints. And the angel said to me, "Write this: Blessed are those who are invited to the marriage supper of the Lamb" (Rev. 19:7–9).

Perhaps this is a metaphor that seems to have the fewest connections with the ministry of deliverance. However, this ministry can play a concrete role in removing various "spots and wrinkles" that, unfortunately, still afflict the bride (Eph. 5:27; cf. Ezek. 16:1–14).

(f) *Commerce.* Once, believers were slaves of sin, death and devil, but Christ ransomed them from their power with the price of his own life: "[Y]ou were bought with a price. So glorify God in your body" (1 Cor. 6:20). However, in the ministry of deliverance we are confronted with the fact that regenerated people, too, can still be bound in various ways. The work of Christ is sufficient not only to redeem us from the *kingdom* of Satan (Matt.

12:25-28) but also from various *bonds* that may still surround the redeemed person. It is like a chained man who is redeemed from prison and enters his freedom—but still must be freed from his chains (cf. again John 11:44).

(g) *Military service.* Christ's work on the cross was not only an atoning sacrifice to God, but also a battle, a war, in which Christ gained the victory over sin, death, and especially Satan and his powers: God "disarmed the rulers and authorities and put them to open shame, by triumphing over them in him [i.e., Christ; or, through it, i.e., the cross]" (Col. 2:15). Jesus came in order "that through death he might destroy the one who has the power of death, that is, the devil" (Heb. 2:14). "The reason the Son of God appeared was to destroy the works of the devil" (1 John 3:8). However, the battle that Christ fought *for* believers on the cross against Satan must be distinguished from the battle that *they themselves* must still fight against Satan in their walk of faith, in the power of the Holy Spirit. In this battle, specific struggles may play a role that can be overcome through the ministry of deliverance.

14.9.3 Closure

Christians cannot avoid all warfare against Satan and his powers during their walk of faith—on the contrary, such warfare is an essential part of their Christian life (e.g., Eph. 6:11-12; Phil 1:27-28; Col. 1:29-2:1; 1 John 2:13). However, the ministry of deliverance has been granted to them in order that they can be delivered from *some* forms of warfare. We thank God for all these glorious consequences of Christ's atoning sacrifice. One day, in the consummation of the ages, these results will fully come to light. But we praise God also for all the glorious effects that believers, already today, may experience in their earthly walk of faith.

Some Christians exhibit the tendency to postpone

these results to the end of the ages, today here on earth they lead a "poor sinner's" life (this is especially the hyper-Calvinist attitude). Other Christians do the opposite: they claim all the results of Christ's atoning sacrifice already today, as if the consummation of the ages were already a full spiritual reality in the here and now (this is especially the Pentecostal and Charismatic tendency). As so often happens, the truth lies in the middle; we still live in the tension between the "already" and the "not yet," between D-day and V-day (see §8.7.2).

As long as this is the case, theologians will continue to wrestle over precisely what of the "already" has been realized, and precisely what of the "not yet" we must await. The same is true with respect to the believer's justification and sanctification:[68] believers have been justified and sanctified, but they must learn to live the life of the just and of the saints. The same principle is encountered in other experiential aspects of salvation, as we hope to see in the next volume in this series.

---

68. See Ouweneel (*RT* III/2).

Bibliography

Aalders, G. C. 1923. *De profeet Jeremia.* KV. Kampen: J.H. Kok.

Abdolah, K. 2008. *De Koran: Een vertaling.* Breda: De Geus.

Adeyemo, T., ed. 2006. *Africa Bible Commentary: A One-Volume Commentary.* Grand Rapids, MI: Zondervan.

À Kempis, T. 2007. *The Imitation of Christ.* Minneapolis, MN: Filiquarian.

Alexander, J. A. 1953. *The Prophecies of Isaiah.* Grand Rapids, MI: Zonder.

Alexander, R. H. 1986. *Ezekiel.* EBC 6. Grand Rapids, MI: Zondervan.

Allen, R. B. 1990. *Numbers.* EBC 2. Grand Rapids, MI: Zondervan.

Allis, O. T. 1970. *Leviticus.* New Bible Commentary. Grand Rapids, MI: Eerdmans.

Allport, G. W. and J. M. Ross. 1967. "Personal Religious Orientation and Prejudice." *Journal of personality and social psychology* 5 (1967): 432-43.

Althaus, P. 1949. *Der Brief an die Römer.* 6th ed. Göttingen: Vandenhoeck & Ruprecht.

_____. 1952. *Die christliche Wahrheit: Lehrbuch der Dogmatik.* 3rd ed. Gütersloh: Bertelsmann.

Altizer, T. J. J. and W. Hamilton. 1966. *Radical Theology and the Death of God*. Indianapolis: Bobbs-Merrill.

_____. 1996. *Freedom from Addiction: Breaking the Bondage of Addiction and Finding Freedom in Christ*. Ventura, CA: Regal Books. *Op weg naar vrijheid in Christus: Stappen naar bevrijding zonde en gebondenheid*. Heverlee: Centrum Pastorale Counseling.

Ashley, T. R. 1993. *The Book of Numbers*. NICOT. Grand Rapids, MI: Eerdmans.

Aulén, G. 1931. "Die drei Haupttypen des christlichen Versöhnungsgedankens." *Zeitschrift für systematische Theologie* 8:501–38.

_____. 1951. *Christus Victor: An Historical Study of the Three Main Types of the Idea of Atonement*. Translated by A. G. Hebert. New York, NY: Macmillan.

Baarlink, H. 1998. *Het evangelie de verzoening*. Kampen: J.H. Kok.

Baker, M. D., ed. 2006. *Proclaiming the Scandal of the Cross: Contemporary Images of the Atonement*. Grand Rapids, MI: Baker Academic.

Barclay, R. 1827. *An Apology for the True Christian Divinity: Being an Explanation and Vindication of the Principles and Doctrines of the People Called Quakers*. 8th ed. New York: Samuel Wood & Sons.

Barker, G. W. 1981. *1, 2, 3 John*. EBC 12. Grand Rapids, MI: Zondervan.

Barrett, C. K. 1957. *A Commentary on the Epistle to the Romans*. Black's New Testament Commentary. New York: Harper & Row.

Barth, K. 2009. *Church Dogmatics. Study Edition*. Translated by G. W. Bromiley et al. Vols. I/1–IV/1. New York, NY: T&T Clark. (Editor's Note: The original fourteen volumes have been published in the *Study Edition* as thirty-one volumes. For citation purposes, the original volume enumeration is followed by the number of the equivalent new volume: e.g.,

III/3=18. The sections [§] are identical in both editions. The final number[s] refer[s] to the page[s] in the new *Study Edition*. Sample citation convention: *CD* III/3=18, §51.2:130.)

_____. 1976 (repr. 1933). *The Epistle to the Romans*. Trans. by E. C. Hoskyns. Oxford: Oxford University Press.

Bartlett, A. W. 2001. *Cross Purposes: The Violent Grammar of Christian Atonement*. Harrisburg, PA: Trinity Press International.

Bavinck, H. 2002–2008. *Reformed Dogmatics*. Edited by John Bolt. Translated by J. Vriend. 4 vols. Grand Rapids, MI: Baker Academic. 1928^4. *Gereformeerde dogmatiek*, dl. 1-4. Kampen: Kok (abbrev.: GD).

Berger, K. 2004. *Jesus*. München: Pattloch.

Berkhof, H. 1986. *Christian Faith: An Introduction to the Study of the Faith*. Translated by S. Woudstra. Rev. ed. Grand Rapids, MI: Wm. B. Eerdmans. 1990^6. *Christelijk geloof: Een inleiding tot de geloofsleer*. Nijkerk: Callenbach.

Berkhof, L. 1981. *Systematic Theology*. 4th rev. and enlarged ed. Grand Rapids, MI: Eerdmans. 1949^4. *Systematic Theology*. Grand Rapids, MI: Eerdmans.

Berkouwer, G. C. 1952. *Faith and Sanctification*. Translated by J. Vriend. Studies in Dogmatics. Grand Rapids, MI: Eerdmans.

_____. 1954a. *Faith and Justification*. Translated by L. B. Smedes. Studies in Dogmatics. Grand Rapids, MI: Eerdmans.

_____. 1954b. *The Person of Christ*. Translated by J. Vriend. Studies in Dogmatics. Grand Rapids, MI: Eerdmans.

_____. 1958. *Faith and Perseverance*. Translated by R. D. Knudsen. Studies in Dogmatics. Grand Rapids, MI: Eerdmans.

_____. 1960. *Divine Election*. Translated by H. Bekker.

Studies in Dogmatics. Grand Rapids, MI: Eerdmans.

———. 1965. *The Work of Christ*. Translated by C. Lambregtse. Studies in Dogmatics. Grand Rapids, MI: Eerdmans.

———. 1971. *Sin*. Translated by P. C. Holtrop. Studies in Dogmatics. Grand Rapids, MI: Eerdmans.

Bernard, J. H. 1979. *The Second Epistle to the Corinthians*. EGT 3. Grand Rapids, MI: Eerdmans.

Bleek, F. 1840. *Der Brief an die Hebräer*. Vol. 3. Berlin: Dümmler.

Bloesch, D. G. 1978–1979. *Essentials of Evangelical Theology*. 2 vols. New York: Harper & Row.

———. 1997. *Jesus Christ: Saviour and Lord*. Carlisle: Paternoster.

Blum, E. A. 1981. *1, 2 Peter, Jude*. EBC 12. Grand Rapids, MI: Zondervan.

Böhl, F. M. T. 1923. *Genesis*. Vol. 1. Tekst & Uitleg. Groningen: J.B. Wolters.

Bolkestein, M. H. 1945. *De verzoening*. Nijkerk: Callenbach.

Bonhoeffer, D. 2001. *Discipleship*. Minneapolis, MN: Fortress Press.

Borger-Koetsier, G. H. 2006. *Verzoening tussen God en mens in Christus*. Zoetermeer: Boekencentrum.

Bos, F. L. 1932. *Johann Piscator: Ein Beitrag zur Geschichte der reformierten Theologie*. Kampen: J.H. Kok.

Bosworth, F. F. 2000. *Christ the Healer*. New Kensington, PA: Whitaker House.

Bouma, C. 1927. *Het evangelie naar Johannes*. KV. Kampen: J.H. Kok.

———. 1937. *De brieven van den apostel Paulus aan Timotheus en Titus*. KV. Kampen: J.H. Kok.

Brom, L. J. van den et al. 1998. *Verzoening of koninkrijk: Over de prioriteit in de verkondiging*. Nijkerk: Callenbach.

Bromiley, G. W., ed. 1953. *Zwingli and Bullinger.* Library of Christian Classics 24. Philadelphia: Westminster Press.

———. 1985. *Theological Dictionary of the New Testament: Abridged in One Volume.* Grand Rapids, MI: Eerdmans.

Brown, C., ed. 1992. *The New International Dictionary of New Testament Theology.* 4 vols. Carlisle: Paternoster.

Bruce, A. B. 1979. *The Synoptic Gospels.* EGT 1. Grand Rapids, MI: Eerdmans.

Bruce, F. F. 1964. *The Epistle to the Hebrews.* NICNT. Grand Rapids, MI: Eerdmans.

———. 1984. *The Epistles to the Colossians, to Philemon, and to the Ephesians.* NICNT. Grand Rapids, MI: Eerdmans.

———. 1988. *The Book of the Acts.* NICNT. Grand Rapids, MI: Eerdmans.

Brümmer, V. 2005. *Ultiem geluk: Een nieuwe kijk op Jezus, verzoening en Drie-eenheid.* Kampen: J.H. Kok.

Brunner, E. 1934. *The Mediator: A Study of the Central Doctrine of the Christian Faith.* London: Lutterworth Press.

———. 1950. *Dogmatics.* Tranlated by O. Wyon. Vol. 1: *The Christian Doctrine of God.* Philadelphia, PA: Westminster Press.

Budiman, R. 1971. *De realisering der verzoening in het menselijk bestaan: Een onderzoek naar Paulus' opvatting van de gemeenschap van Christus' lijden als een integrerend deel der verzoening.* Delft: Meinema.

Bultema, H. 1981. *Commentary on Isaiah.* Grand Rapids, MI: Kregel.

Burger, H. and R. Sonneveld, eds. 2014. *Cruciaal: De verrassende betekenis van Jezus' kruisiging.* Amsterdam: Buijten & Schipperheijn.

Burnaby, J. 1959. *The Belief of Christendom: A Commen-

tary on the Nicene Creed. London: SPCK.

Calvin, J. 1960. *Institutes of the Christian Religion.* Translated by F. L. Battles. The Library of Christian Classics. 2 vols. Louisville, KY: Westminster John Knox Press.

Campbell, J. M. 1996. *The Nature of the Atonement.* Edinburgh: Handsel Press.

Carson, D. A. 1984. *Matthew.* EBC 8. Grand Rapids, MI: Zondervan.

Chafer, L. S. 1983. *Systematic Theology.* 15th ed. 8 vols. Dallas, TX: Dallas Seminary Press.

Chambers, L. T. 1958. *Tabernacle Studies.* Kilmarnock: John Ritchie.

Charnock, S. 2002. *Christ Crucified: A Puritan's View of the Atonement.* Fearn: Christian Focus.

Clarke, A. G. 1949. *Analytical Studies in the Psalms.* Kilmarnock: Jon Ritchie.

Coates, C. A. 1911. *An Outline of the Book of Numbers.* Kingston-on-Thames: Stow Hill Bible & Tract Depot.

———. 1922. *An Outline of the Book of Genesis.* Kingston-on-Thames: Stow Hill Bible & Tract Depot.

———. 1927. *An Outline of the Epistle to the Romans.* Newport: Stow Hill Bible Depot/London: G. Morrish.

———. 1930. *An Outline of the Book of Exodus.* Kingston-on-Thames: Stow Hill Bible & Tract Depot.

———. 2007. *An Outline of the Book of Leviticus.* Pomona, CA: Pomona Press.

———. n.d. *Spiritual Blessings.* Kingston-on-Thames: Stow Hill Bible & Tract Depot.

Cohen, A., ed. 1983. *The Soncino Chumash.* Soncino Books of the Bible. London: Soncino.

Cole, R. A. 1965. *The Epistle of Paul to the Galatians.* Tyndale New Testament Commentary. Grand Rapids, MI: Eerdmans.

Craigie, P. C. 1976. *The Book of Deuteronomy*. NICOT. Grand Rapids, MI: Eerdmans.

Cullmann, O. 1962. *Christ and Time: The Primitive Christian Conception of Time and History*. London: SCM.

Danker, F. W. 2000. *A Greek-English Lexicon of the New Testament and Other Early Christian Literature*. 3rd ed. Revised and edited by Frederick W. Danker. Chicago: University of Chicago Press.

Darby, J. N. n.d.-a. *The Collected Writings of J. N. Darby*. Kingston-on-Thames: Stow Hill Bible and Tract Depot.

———. n.d.-b. *Synopsis of the Book of the Bible*. 8 vols. Available at http://www.sacred-texts.com/bib/cmt/darby/index.htm.

Davids, P. H. 1990. *The First Epistle of Peter*. NICNT. Grand Rapids, MI: Eerdmans.

De Graaff, F. 1987. *Jezus de Verborgene: Een voorbereiding tot inwijding in de mysteriën van het evangelie*. Kampen: J.H. Kok.

De Groot, D. J. 1952. *De wedergeboorte*. Kampen: J.H. Kok.

De Gruchy, J. W. 2002. *Reconciliation: Restoring justice*. London: SCM.

De Kruijff, G. G. 1998. *Het diepste woord: Theologie na Golgotha*. Baarn: Ten Have.

Demarest, B. 1997. *The Cross and Salvation: The Doctrine of Salvation*. Wheaton, IL: Crossway Books.

Denham Smith, J. n.d. *The Prophet of Glory, or, Zechariah's Visions of the Coming and Kingdom of Christ*. London: James E. Hawkins.

Den Heyer, C. J. 1997. *Verzoening: Bijbelse noties bij een omstreden thema*. Kampen: J.H. J.H. Kok.

Dennett, E. 1888. *Zechariah the Prophet*. London: W.H. Broom & Rouse.

Denney, J. 1979. *St. Paul's Epistle to the Romans*. EGT 2. Grand Rapids, MI: Eerdmans.

Dennison, J. T., Jr., ed. 2008-2014. *Reformed Confessions of the 16th and 17th Centuries in English Translation*. 4 vols. Grand Rapids, MI: Reformation Heritage Books.

De Vaux, R. 1964. *Studies in Old Testament Sacrifice*. Cardiff: University of Wales.

De Wilde, A. 1981. *Das Buch Hiob*. Leiden: Brill.

Diestel, L. 1859. "Über die Heiligkeit Gottes." *Jahrbücher für deutsche Theologie* 1859:3-62.

Dodd, C. H. 1935. *The Bible and the Greeks*. London: Hodder & Stoughton.

Dods, M. 1979. *The Epistle to the Hebrews*. EGT 4. Grand Rapids, MI: Eerdmans.

Duffield, G. P. and N. M. Van Cleave. 1996. *Woord en Geest: Hoofdlijnen van de theologie van de Pinksterbeweging*. Kampen: Kok/Rafaël Nederland.

Ebeling, G. 1979. *Dogmatik des christlichen Glaubens*. Vol 1. Tübingen: Mohr (Siebeck).

Eddy, P. R., ed. 2006. *The Nature of the Atonement: Four Views*. Downers Grove, IL: IVP Academic.

Edwards, J. 2003. *A History of the Work of Redemption*. Edinburgh: Banner of Truth Trust.

Elsinga, C. B., ed. 1998. *Om het hart van het evangelie: Een boek voor de gemeente over verzoening*. [Middelburg]: CeGe Boek.

Erickson, M. J. 1998. *Christian Theology*. Vol. 1. Grand Rapids, MI: Baker Book House.

Eveson, P. H. 1996. *The Great Exchange: Justification by Faith Alone in the Light of Recent Thought*. Bromley: Day One Publishers.

Fackre, G. J., R. H. Nash, and J. Sanders. 1995. *What About Those Who Have Never Heard?: Three Views on the Destiny of the Unevangelized*. Downers Grove, IL:

InterVarsity Press.

Fee, G. D. 1987. *The First Epistle to the Corinthians*. NICNT. Grand Rapids, MI: Eerdmans.

Feinberg, C. L. 1986. *Jeremiah*. EBC 6. Grand Rapids, MI: Zondervan.

Finlan, S. 2005. *Problems with Atonement: The Origins of, and Controversy about, the Atonement Doctrine*. Collegeville, MN: Liturgical Press.

Fromm, E. 1967. *You Shall Be as Gods: A Radical Interpretation of the Old Testament and Its Tradition*. New York: Holt, Rinehart & Winston.

Frost, S. B. 1971. "The Book of Jeremiah." In *The Interpreter's One-Volume Commentary on the Bible*. Edited by C. M. Laymon. 372–404. Nashville: Abingdon.

Gaebelein, A. C. 1965. *The Book of Psalms: A Devotional and Prophetic Commentary*. Neptune, NJ: Loizeaux Brothers.

———. 1972. *The Prophet Ezekiel: An Analytical Exposition*. Neptune, NJ: Loizeaux Brothers.

Gall, A. von. 1900. *Die Herrlichkeit Gottes: Eine biblisch-theogische Untersuchung*. Giessen: Ricker.

Geisler, N. L. 2011. *Systematic Theology*. Minneapolis, MN: Bethany House.

Geldenhuys, N. 1983. *Commentary on the Gospel of Luke*. NICNT. Grand Rapids, MI: Eerdmans.

Generale Synode van de Gereformeerde Kerken. 1977. *Verzoening met God en met mensen*. 3rd ed. Kampen: J.H. Kok.

Gispen, W. H. 1982. *Exodus*. Translated by Ed van der Maas. Grand Rapids, MI: Zondervan. 1939. *Het boek Exodus*. KV. Kampen: J.H. Kok.

———. 1950. *Het boek Leviticus*. COT. Kampen: J.H. Kok.

———. 1954. *De Spreuken van Salomo*. Vol. 2. KV. Kampen: J.H. Kok.

———. 1959–1964. *Het boek Numeri*. 2 vols. COT. Kampen: J.H. Kok.

Graafland, C. 2000. "Van de Beeks oordeel over de klassiek gereformeerde theologie." *Wapenveld* 50/2:13–16.

Grant, F. W. 1890. *The Numerical Bible: The Pentateuch*. New York: Loizeaux Brothers.

———. 1902. *The Numerical Bible: Hebrews to Revelation*. New York: Loizeaux Brothers.

———. 1956. *Atonement in Type, Prophecy and Accomplishment*. 8th ed. New York: Loizeaux Brothers.

———. 2013. *Genesis in the Light of the New Testament*. New York: Loizeaux Brothers (repr.: Amazon Digital Services).

——— and J. Bloore. 1931. *The Numerical Bible: Ezekiel*. New York: Loizeaux Brothers.

Grau, M. 2004. *Of Divine Economy: Refinancing Redemption*. New York: T. & T. Clark International.

Greijdanus, S. 1925. *De brief van den apostel Paulus aan de Epheziërs*. KV. Kampen: J.H. Kok.

———. 1931. *De eerste/tweede brief van den apostel Petrus*. KV. Kampen: J.H. Kok.

———. 1955, 1941. *Het evangelie naar Lucas*. 2 vols. 2nd ed. KV. Kampen: J.H. Kok.

Grogan, G.W. 1986. *Isaiah*. EBC 6. Grand Rapids, MI: Zondervan.

Grosheide, F. W. 1954. *Het heilig evangelie volgens Mattheüs*. 2nd ed. CNT. Kampen: J.H. Kok.

———. 1955. *De brief aan de Hebreeën en de brief van Jakobus*. CNT. Kampen: J.H. Kok.

———. 1957. *De eerste brief aan de kerk te Korinthe*. CNT. Kampen: J.H. Kok.

———. 1959. *De tweede brief van Paulus aan de kerk te Korinthe*. CNT. Kampen: J.H. Kok.

———. 1960. *De brief van Paulus aan de Efeziërs*. CNT.

Kampen: J.H. Kok.

Grudem, W. 1988. *The First Epistle of Peter.* TNTC. Leicester: InterVarsity.

———. 1994. *Systematic Theology: An Introduction to Biblical Doctrine.* Grand Rapids, MI: Zondervan.

Gulley, P. and J. Mulholland. 2003. *If Grace Is True: Why God Will Save Every Person.* New York: HarperSanFrancisco.

Gysseling, M. 1980. *Corpus van Middelnederlandse teksten (tot en met het jaar 1300),* II.1: *Fragmenten.* 's-Gravenhage: Martinus Nijhoff.

Haak, T. 1918. *The Dutch Annotations Upon the Whole Bible.* London: Henry Hills.

Hamilton, V. P. 1990. *The Book of Genesis Chapters 1-17.* NICOT. Grand Rapids, MI: Eerdmans.

Harless, A. G. C. 1834. *Commentar über den Brief Pauli an die Epheser.* Stuttgart: Liesching.

Harris, M. J. 1976. *2 Corinthians.* EBC 10. Grand Rapids, MI: Zondervan.

Harris, R. L. 1990. *Leviticus.* EBC 2. Grand Rapids, MI: Zondervan.

Harrison, E. F. 1976. *Romans.* EBC 10. Grand Rapids, MI: Zondervan.

Hartley, J. E. 1988. *The Book of Job.* NICOT. Grand Rapids, MI: Eerdmans.

Heering, G. J. 1937. *Geloof en openbaring.* Vol. 2: *Richtlijnen voor een dogmatiek op den grondslag van evangelie en reformatie.* Arnhem: Van Loghum Slaterus.

Heijkoop, H. L. 1977. *Het offer: De geestelijke betekenis van de offers in het Oude Testament.* Winschoten: Uit het Woord der Waarheid.

Hengstenberg, E. W. 1829-1835. *Christologie des Alten Testaments.* 2 vols. Berlin: Ludwig Oehmigke.

Hertz, J. H. 1932. *Leviticus.* The Pentateuch and Haftorahs. London: Oxford University Press.

Heyns, J. A. 1988. *Dogmatiek*. Pretoria: NG Kerkboekhandel.

Hill, D. 1967. *Greek Words and Hebrew Meanings*. Cambridge: University Press.

Hines, S. G. and C. P. DeYoung. 2000. *Beyond Rhetoric: Reconciliation As a Way of Life*. Valley Forge, PA: Judson Press.

Hodges, H. A. 1955. *The Pattern of Atonement*. London: SCM.

Hoek, J. 1988. *Zonde: Opstand tegen de genade*. Kampen: J.H. Kok.

———. 1998. *Verzoening: daar draait het om*. Zoetermeer: Boekencentrum.

Holmes, A. F. 1977. *All Truth Is God's Truth*. Grand Rapids, MI: Eerdmans.

Horrobin, P. J. 2003. *Healing through Deliverance*. 2 vols. Tonbridge: Sovereign World.

Hughes, P. E. 1962. *Paul's Second Epistle to the Corinthians*. NICNT. Grand Rapids, MI: Eerdmans.

Ironside, H. A. 1907. *Notes on the Book of Proverbs*. Neptune, NJ: Loizeaux Brothers.

Jacob, B. 1974. *The First Book of the Bible: Genesis*. New York: KTAV Publishing House.

Jukes, A. 1976. *The Law of the Offerings (Leviticus i-viii)*. Grand Rapids, MN: Kregel Classics.

Jüngel, E. 1977. *Gott als Geheimnis der Welt*. Tübingen: Mohr (Siebeck).

Kähler, M. 1898. *Zur Lehre von der Versöhnung*. Leipzig: Deichert.

Kaiser, W. C. 1990. *Exodus*. EBC 2. Grand Rapids, MI: Zondervan.

Kamphuis, J. 1982. *Aantekeningen bij J. A. Heyns' Dogmatiek*. Kampen: Van den Berg.

Keil, C. F. 1887. *Manual of Biblical Archaeology*. Vol. 1. Edinburgh: Clark.

Keil, C. F. and F. Delitzsch. 1976-1977. *Commentary on the Old Testament.* 10 vols. Grand Rapids, MI: Eerdmans.

Kelly, J. N. D. 2003. *Early Christian Doctrines.* Peabody, MA: Prince Press.

Kelly, W., ed. 1856-1920. *Bible Treasury: A Monthly Review of Prophetic and Practical Subjects.* Available at https://bibletruthpublishers.com/bible-treasury/lpvl22465.

―――. 1870. *Lectures Introductory to the Study of the Acts, the Catholic Epistles, and the Revelation.* London: W.H. Broom.

―――. 1896/1897. "The Offerings of Leviticus." *BT* N1-2.

―――. 1923. *The Epistles of Peter.* London: C.A. Hammond.

―――. 1927. *Selected Passages from the Writings of the Late William Kelly.* Edited by W. J. Hocking. London: C.A. Hammond.

―――. 1952. *An Exposition of the Acts of the Apostles.* 3rd ed. London: C.A. Hammond.

―――. 1966. *An Exposition of the Gospel of John.* London: C.A. Hammond.

―――. 1970. *Lectures Introductory to the Study of the Pentateuch.* Winschoten: H.L. Heijkoop.

Kidner, F. D. 1970. "Isaiah." In *The New Bible Commentary Revisited.* Edited by D. Guthrie and J. A. Motyer. 588-625. Grand Rapids, MI: Eerdmans.

Kittel, G. et al., eds. 1964-1976. *Theological Dictionary of the New Testament.* Translated by G. W. Bromiley. 10 vols. Grand Rapids, MI: Eerdmans.

Kiuchi, N. 1987. The Purification Offering in the Priestly Literature. *Journal for the Study of OT Suppl.* 56.

Knevel, A. G. and M. J. Paul, eds. 1995. *Verkenningen in de oudtestamentische messiasverwachting.* Kampen:

Kok Voorhoeve/Hilversum: Evangelische Omroep.

Knowling, R. J. 1979. *The Acts of the Apostles*. EGT 2. Grand Rapids, MI: Eerdmans.

Koch, K .E. 1972a. *Occult Bondage and Deliverance: Counseling the Occultly Oppressed*. Grand Rapids, MI: Kregel.

_____. 1972b. *Christian Counseling and Occultism: A Complete Guidebook to Occult Oppression and Deliverance*. Grand Rapids, MI: Kregel.

Koehler, L. and W. Baumgartner. 1953. *Lexicon in Veteris Testamenti Libros*. Leiden: E.J. Brill.

König, A. 2006. *Die Groot Geloofswoordeboek*. Vereeniging: Christelike Uitgewersmaatskappy.

König, E. 1927. *Die Psalmen eingeleitet, übersetzt und erklärt*. Gütersloh: C. Bertelsmann.

Korff, F. W. A. 1942. *Christologie: De leer van het komen Gods*. 2 vols. Nijkerk: Callenbach.

Kraan K. J. 1974. *"Opdat u genezing ontvangt": Handboek voor de dienst der genezing*. 3rd ed. Hoornaar: Gideon.

Kroeze, J. H. 1960. *Het boek Job*. KV. Kampen: J.H. Kok.

_____. 1961. *Het boek Job*. COT. Kampen: J.H. Kok.

Küng, H. 1976. *On Being a Christian*. Translated by E. Quinn. Garden City, NY: Doubleday. Küng, H. 1971. *Christen zijn*. Hilversum: Gooi & Sticht.

Landmann, S. 1962. *Joodse humor*. Amsterdam: Van Ditmar.

Lane, W. L. 1974. *The Gospel According to Mark*. NICNT. Grand Rapids, MI: Eerdmans.

Lanooy, R., ed. 1994. *For Us and for Our Salvation: Seven Perspectives on Christian Soteriology*. Utrecht/Leiden: Interuniversitair Instituut voor Missiologie en Oecumenica.

Lekkerkerker, A. F. N. 1949. *Gesprek over de verzoening*. Amsterdam: Holland Uitgeversmaatschappij.

Levine, B. A. 1974. *In the Presence of the Lord*. Leiden: Brill.

———. 1989. *Leviticus*. Torah Commentary. Philadelphia: Jewish Publication Society.

Lewis, C. S. 1944. *Beyond Personality: The Christian Idea of God*. London: Geoffrey Bles.

———. 1956. *The Last Battle*. Harmondsworth: Puffin Books.

———. 1971. *The Four Loves*. Fort Washington, PA: Harvest Books.

Liefeld, W. L. 1984. *Luke*. EBC 8. Grand Rapids, MI: Zondervan.

Lightfoot, J. B. 1895. *Notes on the Epistles of St. Paul*. London: Macmillan.

Lindeboom, G. A. 1953. *Gebedsgenezing*. Assen: G.F. van Hummelen.

Lundius, J. 1726. *Heiligdommen, godsdiensten, en gewoontens der oude Jooden, voorgesteldt in eene uytvoerige verhandeling van het Levitische priesterdom*. Amsterdam: Schoonenburg & ten Hoorn.

Luther, M. 1883. *Luthers Werke*. Vol. 1. Weimar: Hermann Böhlau.

———. 1892. *Luthers Werke*. Vol. 5. Weimar: Hermann Böhlau.

McCrossan, T. J. 1982. *Healing and the Atonement*. Tulsa, OK: Kenneth Hagin Ministries.

McGrath, A. 2007. *Christian Theology: An Introduction*. Maiden, MA: Blackwell.

Mabie, H. C. 1906. *The Meaning and Message of the Cross: A Contribution to Missionary Apologetics*. New York: Revell.

MacCullough, J. A. 1930. *The Harrowing of Hell: A Comparative Study of an Early Christian Doctrine*. London: T. & T. Clark.

Mackintosh, C. H. 1972. *Genesis to Deuteronomy: Notes*

on the Pentateuch. Neptune, NJ: Loizeaux Brothers.

Marshall, I. H. 1978. *The Epistles of John.* NICNT. Grand Rapids, MI: Eerdmans.

Mayhue, R. 1999. *De belofte van genezing: Is genezing altijd de wil van God?* Vaassen: Medema.

Meinardus, O. F. A. 1989. *Monks and Monasteries of the Egyptian Deserts.* 2nd ed. Cairo/New York: American University in Cairo Press.

Metzger, B. M. 1975. *A Textual Commentary on the Greek New Testament.* 2nd ed. London/New York: United Bible Societies.

Milgrom, J. 1970. *Studies in Levitical Terminology.* Berkeley: University of California.

_____. 1976. *Cult and Conscience.* Leiden: Brill.

_____. 1983. *Studies in Cultic Theology and Terminology.* Leiden: Brill.

_____. 1991. *Leviticus 1-16.* Anchor Bible Commentary. Garden City, NY: Doubleday.

Migne, J.-P. 1879. *Patrologiae Latina.* Vols. 17. Available at https://archive.org/details/ patrologiaecurs131migngoog/page/n4/mode/2up.

Moerkerken, A. 2004. *Ons troostboek: Verklaring van de Heidelbergse Catechismus.* Houten: Den Hertog.

Moffatt, J. 1979. *The First and Second Epistle to the Thessalonians.* EGT 4. Grand Rapids, MI: Eerdmans.

Moltmann, J. 1973. *The Crucified God: The Cross of Christ As the Foundation and Criticism of Christian Theology.* London: SCM.

_____. 1990. *The Way of Jesus Christ.* London: SCM.

Moody, D. 1970. *Romans.* Broadman Bible Comm. London: Marshall, Morgan & Scott.

Morphew, D. 1998. *Breakthrough: Discovering the Kingdom.* Capetown: Vineyard International Publications.

Morris, H. M. 1976. *The Genesis Record: A Scientific and*

Devotional Commentary on the Book of Beginnings. San Diego, CA: Creation-Life Publishers.

Morris, L. 1955. *The Apostolic Preaching of the Cross.* London: Tyndale Press.

_____. 1971. *The Gospel According to John.* NICNT. Grand Rapids, MI: Eerdmans.

_____. 1981. *Hebrews.* EBC 12. Grand Rapids, MI: Zondervan.

Müller, K. W. and T. Schirrmacher, eds. 1998. *Werden alle gerettet?: Moderner Heilsuniversalismus als Infragestellung der christlichen Mission: Referate der afem-Jahrestagung 1998.* Bonn: Verlag für Kultur und Wissenschaft.

Murray, J. 1955. *Redemption: Accomplished and Applied.* Grand Rapids, MI: Eerdmans.

_____. 1968. *The Epistle to the Romans.* NICNT. Grand Rapids, MI: Eerdmans.

Nathan, R. and K. Wilson. 1995. *Empowered Evangelicals: Bringing Together the Best of the Evangelical and Charismatic Worlds.* Ann Arbor, MI: Servant Publications.

Nee, Watchman 1968. *Spiritual Man.* Richmond, VA: Christian Fellowship Publishers.

Nee, Watchman 1977. *The Normal Christian Life.* Carol Stream, IL: Tyndale House Publishers.

Nettles, T. J. 1986. *By His Grace and for His Glory.* Grand Rapids, MI: Baker.

A New Catechism: Catholic Faith for Adults. 1967. Translated by K. Smyth. New York, NY: Herder & Herder.

Newberry, T. 2014. *Types of the Levitical Offerings.* Chattanooga, TN: AMG Publishers.

Noordtzij, A. 1982. *Leviticus.* Translated by R. Togtman. Bible Student's Commentary. Grand Rapids, MI: Zondervan. 1940. *Het boek Levitikus.* KV. Kampen: J.H. Kok.

———. 1983. *Numbers*. Translated by E. van der Maas. Bible Student's Commentary. Grand Rapids, MI: Zondervan. 1957. *Het boek Numeri*. KV. Kampen: J.H. Kok.

North, R. 1954. *Sociology of the Biblical Jubilee*. Rome: Pontifical Biblical Institute.

Nygren, A. 1930–1937. *Eros und Agape: Gestaltwandlungen der christlichen Liebe*, Bd. I,II. Gütersloh: C. Bertelsmann.

Okholm, D. L. and T. R. Phillips, eds. 1995. *Four Views on Salvation in a Pluralistic World*. Grand Rapids, MI: Zondervan.

Olivier, D. 1984. "Der verborgene und gekreuzigte Gott: Das epistemologische Grundgesetz der Theologie nach Luther." *Lutherische Kirche in der Welt: Jahrbuch des Martin-Luther-Bundes* 31:55–60.

Otto, R. 1958. *The Idea of the Holy: An Inquiry into the Non-Rational Factor in the Idea of the Divine and Its Relation to the Rational*. Translated by J. W. Harvey. New York, NY: Oxford University Press.

Ouweneel, W. J. 1973. *Het Hooglied van Salomo*. Winschoten: Uit het Woord der Waarheid.

———. 1976. *De ark in de branding*. Amsterdam: Buijten & Schipperheijn.

———. 1978. *Het domein van de slang: Christelijk handboek over occultisme en mysticisme*. Amsterdam: Buijten & Schipperheijn.

———. 1982. *"Wij zien Jezus": Bijbelstudies over de brief aan de Hebreeën*. 2 vols. Vaassen: Medema.

———. 1988/1990. *De Openbaring van Jezus Christus: Bijbelstudies over het boek Openbaring*. 2 vols. Vaassen: Medema.

———. 1991. *Israël en de Kerk, oftewel: Eén of twee volken van God?: Confrontatie van de verbondsleer en de bedelingenleer*. Vaassen: Medema.

———. 1993. *A Critical Analysis of the Internal and Ex-*

ternal Prolegomena of Systematic Theology. Theological dissertation. Bloemfontein: Universiteit van die Oranje-Vrystaat.

_____. 1994. *Godsverlichting: De evocatie van de verduisterde God: Een weg tot spiritualiteit en gemeenteopbouw.* Amsterdam: Buijten & Schipperheijn.

_____. 1995. *Alverzoening,* Vaassen: Medema.

_____. 1997. *De vrijheid van de Geest: Bijbelstudies bij de Brief van Paulus aan de Galaten.* Vaassen: Medema.

_____. 1998. *De zevende koningin: Het eeuwig vrouwelijke en de raad van God.* Metahistorische triologie. Vol. 2. Heerenveen: Barnabas.

_____. 1999. *Neemt, eet: De maaltijd van de Heer.* Vaassen: Medema.

_____. 2000a. *Het Jobslijden van Israël: Israëls lijden oplichtend uit het boek Job.* Vaassen: Medema.

_____. 2000b. *De zesde kanteling: Christus en 5000 jaar denkgeschiedenis: Religie en metafysica in het jaar 2000* (Metahistorische trilogie, dl. 3). Heerenveen: Barnabas.

_____. 2001. *Hoogtijden voor Hem: De bijbelse feesten en hun betekenis voor Joden en christenen.* Vaassen: Medema.

_____. 2004. *Geneest de zieken! Over de bijbelse leer van ziekte, genezing en bevrijding.* 4th ed. Vaassen: Medema.

_____. 2007a. *De Geest van God: Ontwerp van een pneumatologie.* EDR 1. Vaassen: Medema.

_____. 2007b. *De Christus van God: Ontwerp van een christologie.* EDR 2. Vaassen: Medema.

_____. 2007c. "Theologische vragen rond ziekte en genezing." *Bulletin voor Charismatische Theologie* 59.1:2-13.

_____. 2008a. *De schepping van God: Ontwerp van een schepping-, mens- en zondeleer.* EDR 3, Vaassen: Medema.

———. 2008b. *Het plan van God: Ontwerp van een voorbeschikkingsleer. EDR* 4. Vaassen: Medema.

———. 2010a. *De kerk van God I: Ontwerp van een elementaire ecclesiologie.* Heerenveen: Medema.

———. 2010b. *De kerk van God II: Ontwerp van een historische en praktische ecclesiologie.* Heerenveen: Medema.

———. 2012a. *De toekomst van God: Ontwerp van een eschatologie.* Heerenveen: Medema.

———. 2014. *Wisdom for Thinkers: An Introduction to Christian Philosophy.* Jordan Station, ON: Paideia Press.

———. 2015. *Een dubbelsnoer van licht: honderd grootse joodse en christelijke godsmannen door de geschiedenis heen, en hun moeizame relaties.* Soesterberg: Aspekt.

———. 2016. *The Heidelberg Diary: Daily Devotions on the Heidelberg Catechism.* Edited by N. D. Kloosterman. Jordan Station, ON: Paideia Press.

———. 2017. *The World Is Christ's: A Defense of Christian One-Kingdom Thinking.* Edited by N. D. Kloosterman. Jordan Station, ON: Paideia Press.

———. Forthcoming. *An Evangelical Introduction to Reformational Theology.* Edited by N. D. Kloosterman. 13 vols. Jordan Station, ON: Paideia Press.

———. Forthcoming-a. *The Ninth King: The Last of the Celestial Empires: The Triumph of Christ over the Powers.* Edited by N. D. Kloosterman. Jordan Station, ON: Paideia Press.

Pannenberg, W. 1991. *Systematic Theology.* Translated by G. W. Bromiley. 3 vols. Grand Rapids, MI: Eerdmans.

Parry, R. A. and C. H. Partridge. 2003. *Universal Salvation?: The Current Debate.* Glasgow: Paternoster.

Pawson, D. and R. T. Forster. 1996. *Once Saved, Always*

Saved?: A Study in Perseverance and Inheritance. London: Hodder & Stoughton.

Peake, A. S. 1979. *The Epistle to the Colossians*. EGT 3. Grand Rapids, MI: Eerdmans.

Philippi, F. A. 1878. *Commentary on St. Paul's Epistle to the Romans*. Edinburgh: T. & T. Clark.

Pinnock, C. 1996. *Flame of Love: A Theology of the Holy Spirit*. Downers Grove, IL: InterVarsity Press.

Piper, J. 2004. *Waarom moest Jezus sterven?* Utrecht: De Banier.

Pollock, A. J. 2009. *The Tabernacle's Typical Teaching*. Fincastle, VA: Scripture Truth Publications.

Poortvliet, R. 1974. *Hij was een van ons*. Bussum: Van Holkema & Warendorf.

Pop, F. J. 1999. *Bijbelse woorden en hun geheim*. 10th ed. Zoetermeer: Boekencentrum.

Prince, D. 2000. *Atonement: Your Appointment With God*. DPM USA.

_____. 2004. *Overwinning over de dood: De geweldige, hoopvolle betekenis van de opstanding*. Heemskerk: DPM Nederland.

Race, A. 1993. *Christians and Religious Pluralism: Patterns in the Christian Theology of Religions*. 2nd ed. London: SCM.

Rad, G. von. 1975. *Old Testament Theology*. Translated by D. M. G. Stalker. Vol. 1: *The Theology of Israel's Historical Traditions*. London: SCM Press.

Rahner, K. 1965. "Die anonymen Christen" *Schriften zur Theologie*. Vol. 6. 545–54. Einsiedeln: Benziger.

Rahner, K. 1971. *Ik geloof in Jezus Christus*. Brugge: Desclée De Brouwer.

Ratzinger, J. 2007. *Jesus of Nazareth: From the Baptism in the Jordan to the Transfiguration*. Translated by A. J. Walker. New York, NY: Doubleday.

Reichert, V. E. 1985. *Job*. Soncino Books of the Bible.

London: Soncino.

Richardson, D. 1981. *Eternity in Their Hearts*. Ventura, CA: Regal Books.

Ridderbos, H. 1959. *Aan de Romeinen*. CNT. Kampen: J.H. Kok.

———. 1960. *Aan de Kolossenzen*. CNT. Kampen: J.H. Kok.

———. 1967. *De pastorale brieven*. CNT. Kampen: J.H. Kok.

———. 1975. *Paul: An Outline of His Theology*. Translated by J. R. DeWitt. Grand Rapids, MI: Eerdmans.

———. 1987. *Matthew*. Translated by Ray Togtman. Bible Student's Commentary. Regency Reference Library. Grand Rapids, MI: Zondervan Publishing House.

Ridderbos, J. 1955. *De psalmen*. Vol. 1: *Psalm 1–41*. COT. Kampen: J.H. Kok.

———. 1985. *Isaiah*. Translated by J. Vriend. Bible Student's Commentary. Grand Rapids, MI: Zondervan. 1934.

Ritschl, A. 1966. *The Christian Doctrine of Justification and Reconciliation: The Positive Development of the Doctrine*. Vol. 3 of *Christliche Lehre von der Rechtfertigung und Versöhnung*. Translated by H. R. Mackintosh and A. B. Macaulay. Library of Religious and Philiosophical Thought. Clifton, NJ: Reference Book Publishers.

Roscam Abbing, P. J. 1950. *Diakonia: Een studie over het begrip dienst in dogmatiek en practische theologie*. 's-Gravenhage: Boekencentrum.

Ross, A. P. 1991. *Proverbs*. EBC 5. Grand Rapids, MI: Zondervan.

Sabourin, L. and S. Lyonnet. 1970. *Sin, Redemption, and Sacrifice*. Rome: Pontifical Biblical Institute.

Salmond, S. D. F. 1979. *The Epistle to the Ephesians*. EGT

3. Grand Rapids, MI: Eerdmans.

Sanday, W. and A. C. Headlam. 1950 (repr. 1902). *A Critical and Exegetical Commentary on the Epistle to the Romans*. International Critical Commentary. Edinburgh: T. & T. Clark.

Sanders, E. P. 1977. *Paul and Palestinian Judaism: A Comparison of Patterns of Religion*. Philadelphia: Fortress Press.

Sanders, J. 1992. *No Other Name: An Investigation into the Destiny of the Unevangelized*. Grand Rapids, MI: Eerdmans.

Schaeffer, F. A. 1982. *The Complete Works: A Christian Worldview*, Vol. 2: *A Christian View of the Bible As Truth*. Westchester, IL: Crossway Books.

Schilder, K. 1940. *Christ Crucified*. Translated by H. Zylstra. Vol. 3 of *Christ In His Suffering*. Grand Rapids, MI: Eerdmans.

_____. 1950. *Christ In His Suffering*. Translated by H. Zylstra. 4th ed. Vol. 1 of *Christ In His Suffering*. Grand Rapids, MI: Eerdmans.

Schlatter, A. 1961. *Die Evangelien nach Markus und Lukas*. Stuttgart: Calwer Verlag.

Schlatter, A. 1963. *Die Briefe an die Galater, Epheser, Kolosser und Philemon*. Stuttgart: Calwer Verlag.

Schlink, E. 1986. "Trinität. IV. Dogmatisch." In *Die Religion in Geschichte und Gegenwart: Handwörterbuch für Theologie und Religionswissenschaft*. Edited by K. Galling. Vol. 6. 1032–38. Stuttgart: UTB.

Sevenster, G. 1946. *De Christologie van het Nieuwe Testament*. Amsterdam: Holland.

Shelton, R.L. 2006. *Cross and Covenant: Interpreting the Atonement for 21st Century Mission*. Milton Keynes: Paternoster.

Sherman, R.J. 2004. *King, Priest, and Prophet: A Trinitarian Theology of Atonement*. New York: T. & T. Clark International.

Simpson, A.B. 1880. *The Gospel of Healing.* New York: Christian Alliance.

Smith, D. 1979. *The Epistles of John.* EGT 5. Grand Rapids, MI: Eerdmans.

Smits, P. 1959. "Waarvóór stierf Jezus?" *Kerk en Wereld* 51/7:1ff.

Smouter, W. and C. Blom, eds. 2001. *Vergeef me... Verzoening tussen mensen en God.* Zoetermeer: Boekencentrum.

Sölle, D. 1967. *Christ the Representative: An Essay in Theology After the 'Death of God',* London: SCM.

Spurrell, J. M. 1966. "An Interpretation of 'I Thirst'." *Church Quarterly Review* 167:12-18.

Stauffer, E. 1948. *Die Theologie des Neuen Testaments.* 4th ed. Stuttgart: Kohlhammer.

Stern, D. 1992. *Jewish New Testament Commentary.* Clarksville, MD: Jewish New Testament Publications.

Strack, H. L. 1894. *Die Bücher Exodus, Leviticus, Numeri übersetzt und ausgelegt.* München: Beck.

Strange, D. 2001. *The Possibility of Salvation among the Unevangelised: An Analysis of Inclusivism in Recent Evangelical Theology.* Carlisle: Paternoster.

Strong, A. H. 1907. *Systematic Theology.* Valley Forge, PA: Judson.

Stuart, C. E. n.d. *Thoughts on Sacrifices.* London: G. Morrish.

Subritzky, B. 1985. *Demons Defeated.* Tonbridge: Sovereign World.

_____. 1991. *How to Cast Out Demons and Break Curses.* Auckland: Dove Ministries.

Tasker, R. V. G. 1963. *The Epistle of Paul to the Romans.* Tyndale NT Comm. Grand Rapids, MI: Eerdmans.

Taylor, J. V. 1972. *The Go-Between God: The Holy Spirit and the Christian Mission.* London: SCM.

Tenney, M. C. 1981. *The Gospel of John.* EBC 9. Grand Rapids, MI: Zondervan.

Ter Schegget, G. H. 1999. *De menslievendheid van God: Gedachten over de verzoening.* Baarn: Ten Have.

Thiselton, A. C. 2015. *Systematic Theology.* Grand Rapids, MI: Eerdmans.

Thompson, J. A. 1980. *The Book of Jeremiah.* NICOT. Grand Rapids, MI: Eerdmans.

Trench, R. C. 1953. *Synonyms of the New Testament: Studies in the Greek New Testament.* 9th ed. Grand Rapids, MI: Eerdmans.

Trevethan, T. L. 1995. *The Beauty of God's Holiness.* Downers Grove, IL: InterVarsity Press.

Unger, M. F. 1971. *Demons in the World Today.* Wheaton, IL: Tyndale.

Van Dam, W. C. 1970. *Dämonen und Besessene: Die Dämonen in Geschichte und Gegenwart und ihre Austreibung.* Aschaffenburg: Pattloch.

_____. 1985. *Mensen worden bevrijd.* Kampen: J.H. Kok.

_____. 1993. *Wezens uit onzichtbare werelden.* Kampen: J.H. Kok.

Van de Beek, A. 1998. *Jezus Kurios: De Christologie als hart van de theologie.* 2nd ed. Kampen: J.H. Kok.

_____. 2000. *Gespannen liefde: De relatie van God en mens.* Kampen: J.H. Kok.

_____. 2002. *De kring om de Messias: Israël als volk van de lijdende Heer.* Zoetermeer: Meinema.

_____. 2008. *God doet recht: Eschatologie als christologie.* Zoetermeer: Meinema.

Van de Kamp, W. 2005. *Het wonder van het kruis: De laatste achttien uur voor Jezus' sterven.* Doetinchem: CrossLight Media.

_____. 2012. *Geboren om vrij te zijn: Handboek voor bevrijdingspastoraat.* 2nd ed. Aalten: Crosslight Media.

Van den Brom, L. J. et al. 1998. *Verzoening of koninkrijk:*

Over de prioriteit in de verkondiging. Nijkerk: Callenbach.

Van der Voet, N. 1996. *Altijd vergeven? Over schuld en vergeving tussen mensen.* Zoetermeer: Boekencentrum.

Van der Waal, C. 1990. *The Covenantal Gospel.* Neerlandia, AB: Inheritance Publications.

Van der Wal, C. 1973. "De rechtvaardiging." In *De religie van het belijden.* Edited by H. Goedhart et al. 65–78. Kampen: J.H. Kok.

Van Egmond, A. 2001. *Heilzaam geloof: Verzamelde artikelen.* Edited by D. van Keulen and C. van der Kooi. Kampen: J.H. Kok.

Van Gemeren, W. A. 1991. *Psalms.* EBC 5. Grand Rapids, MI: Zondervan.

———, ed. 1996. *The New International Dictionary of Old Testament Theology and Exegesis.* 4 vols. Carlisle: Paternoster.

Van Genderen, J. and W. H. Velema. 2008. *Concise Reformed Dogmatics.* Translated by G. Bilkes and E. M. van der Maas. Phillipsburg, NJ: Presbyterian and Reformed Publishing Company.

Van Leeuwen, J. A. C. 1928. *Het evangelie naar Markus.* KV. Kampen: J.H. Kok.

——— and D. Jacobs. 1952. *De brief aan de Romeinen.* 3rd ed. KV. Kampen: J.H. Kok.

Van Veluw, A. H. 2002. *De straf die ons de vrede aanbrengt: Over God, kruis, straf en de slachtoffers van deze wereld in de christelijke verzoeningsleer.* Zoetermeer: Boekencentrum.

Vaughan, C. 1978. *Colossians.* EBC 11. Grand Rapids, MI: Zondervan.

Verkuyl, J. 1992. *De kern van het christelijk geloof.* Kampen: J.H. Kok.

Vine, W. E. 1985. *The Collected Writings.* Vols. 1–4.

Glasgow: Gospel Tract Publications.

Vonk, C. Forthcoming. *Numbers*. Translated by N. D. Kloosterman. Opening the Scriptures. Jordan Station, ON: Paideia Press.

Vos, J. 2005. *De betekenis van de dood van Jezus: Tussen seculiere exegese en christelijke dogmatiek*. Zoetermeer: Meinema.

Warfield, B. B. 1970. *Selected Shorter Writings of Benjamin B. Warfield*. Edited by J. E. Meeter. 2 vols. Nutley, NJ: Presbyterian and Reformed Publishing House.

Weaver, J. D. 2001. *The Nonviolent Atonement*. Grand Rapids, MI: Eerdmans.

Weber, O. 1981. *Foundations of Dogmatics*. Translated by D. L. Guder. Vol. 1. Grand Rapids, MI: Eerdmans. 1955/1962. *Grundlagen der Dogmatik*, Bd. I, II. Neukirchen: Verlag der Buchhandlung des Erziehungsvereins.

Wenham, G. J. 1979. *The Book of Leviticus*. NICOT. Grand Rapids, MI: Eerdmans.

Wentsel, B. 1987. *Dogmatiek*. Vol. 3a: *God en mens verzoend: Godsleer, mensleer en zondeleer*. Kampen: J.H. Kok.

———. 1991. *Dogmatiek*. Vol. 3b: *God en mens verzoend: Incarnatie, verzoening, Koninkrijk van God*. Kampen: J.H. Kok.

Westcott, B. F. 1883. *The Johannine Epistles*. London: Macmillan.

Whybray, R. N. 1972. *The Book of Proverbs*. Cambridge Bible Commentary. Cambridge: Cambridge University Press.

Wiersinga, H. 1971. *De verzoening in de theologische diskussie*. Kampen: J.H. Kok.

———. 1972. *Verzoening als verandering: Een gegeven voor menselijk handelen*. Baarn: Bosch & Keuning.

Wigram, G. V. 1970. *The Blood, the Cross and the Death of*

Jesus Christ. . . . 5th ed. Bible Truth Publishers.

Wiles, M. 1974. *The Remaking of Christian Doctrine.* London: SCM.

Wimber, J. and K. Springer. 1986. *Power Healing.* London: Hodder & Stoughton.

Wood, A. S. 1978. *Ephesians.* EBC 11. Grand Rapids, MI: Zondervan.

Wuest, K. S. 1977a. *Ephesians and Colossians in the Greek New Testament.* Grand Rapids, MI: Eerdmans.

_____. 1977b. *First Peter in the Greek New Testament.* Grand Rapids, MI: Eerdmans.

Young, E. J. 1972. *The Book of Isaiah.* Vol. 3: *Chapters 40-66.* Grand Rapids, MI: Eerdmans.

Scripture Index

OLD TESTAMENT

Genesis
1	327	6:14	151, 162	18:19	273, 343
1:2	601	7:1	343	21:6	68
1:22	97	7:2-3	269	22	271, 305, 359
1:28	96, 97	8:20	167, 168, 170, 267	22:2	168, 270, 271
2:17	415	8:20-21	269	22:2-3	167
3	26, 75, 266	8:21	227, 269, 270	22:6-8	167, 413, 514
3:1-6	213	9	156	22:6	406
3:8-9	97, 101	9:6	156, 157	22:7	266
3:22-24	138	9:9-17	97	22:7-8	270, 406
3:15	265, 267, 367	9:21	270	22:7-13	204
		9:24-25	658	22:8	270, 392, 406
3:17-18	268	9:26	129		
3:21	64, 265, 266, 268	11:1-9	586	22:9	412
		12:17	503	22:13	167, 266
		13:10	110	22:14	406, 514
4:1-17	447	13:15	436	22:16	271
4:4-5	267	14:4	632	23:13-14	264
4:3-5	16, 266	14:18-19	252	24:27	122
4:4	170, 266	14:19-20	29	26:10	189
4:18	125	14:19	99	27:1	632
5:22	44	15	97, 272	28:20-21	179
5:24	44	15:6	271, 272	30:27	113
6:1-4	213, 643	15:9	270, 272	31:35	229
6:3	644	16	599	31:54	178
6:5	269	17	97	32:5	113
6:6	403	17:1	273	32.20	152, 158
6:9	44	17:10-14	272	35	97

41	599		202	23:15	199
41:1-7	580	12:24	200	24:1-8	97
46	97	12:26	200	24:3-9	181
47:29	113	12:27	201, 202	24:8	161
48:1	632	12:29	200, 201	24:10-11	140
48:16	244	12:42	199	24:15-16	136
49:9	367	12:43	201	25:8	98
49:18	318	12:46	203	25:1-9	99
		12:48	201	25:10	135
Exodus		13:1-2	200	25:17-22	161
2:2	135	13:3-4	199	25:21-22	98
2:16	599	13:8	200	26:19-21	264
2:17	50	13:8-9	199	26:25	264
2:18	599	13:11-15	200	28	211
3:5	117	13:12-15	200	28:4	214
3:6	139	13:14	199	28:38	385
3:8	100	13:16	199	28:41	225
3:14-15	98	14	98	28:43	385
4:22-23	393	14:13	47, 48, 165	29:1	205
4:22	242	14:14	377	29:9	202, 225
4:32	165	14:30	48	29:14	170
6:1-13	97	15	99	29:20	226
6:6	165, 242, 243	15:1	56, 57	29:22	225, 226
		15:2	48	29:22-23	225
9:17	135	15:11	56	29:26-27	225
10:25	176	15:13	99, 242, 243	29:26-28	226
11:4	201			29:27-28	191
12	198, 203, 204, 207	15:17	98	29:29	225
		15:26	623	29:31	225
12:1	199	17:16	377	29:32-33	167
12:3-6	266	18:12	176	29:33-34	225
12:3-14	165	18:21	122	29:33	225
12:3	491	19:5	97	29:35	225
12:5	199, 205	19:15	229	29:39	202
12:6	202, 491	19:16	136	29:36	161
12:7	200	19:56	203	29:38-41	266
12:8	199	20:5	658	29:38-42	163, 165, 204
12:11	201	29:4	615		
12:12	56, 377	20:32-33	176	29:38-46	194
12:13	24, 92, 159, 197, 202	21:1-6	239	29:40-41	167
		21:24	509	29:41	165
12:17	199	21:30	259	29:42-43	150
12:21	201	22:2	271	29:42-45	165
12:22	200, 326	22:7-9	192	29:42-46	98, 99
12:23	60, 200, 201,	22:16	271	30:10	159, 161

Scripture Index

30:11-16	262, 263	1:11	187	4:22-27	187
30:12	259, 262	1:13	170	4:22	182, 189
30:16	161	1:1-17	162	4:23	205
30:17-21	233, 234	1:17	170	4:24	171
30:18-21	615-616	2	174	4:25	184
30:28	168	2:1-16	162	4:26	167, 176
32:10	158, 161	2:1	163, 266	4:27-35	184
32:15	454	2:2	175	4:27	182, 189
32:20	153	2:3	175, 191	4:28	205
32:29	225, 454	2:9	175	4:29	171
32:30	158	2:10	175, 191	4:30	184
32:31-34	452	3	177, 178	4:31	174, 184, 211
32:34	59	3:1-17	162		
32:35	158	3:1	205	4:32	205
33:2	59	3:2	171, 187	4:33	171
33:11	44, 141	3:5	176	4:35	167, 176
33:14-15	59	3:6	204, 205	4:1-5:13	162
33:18	32	3:8	171, 187	5	316
33:18-19	135	3:11	177	5:1-4	183, 187
33:20	139	3:13	171, 187	5:1	385
33:23	140	3:16	177	5:2-5	189
34:6-7	158, 550	3:19-21	266	5:5	159, 278
34:6	111	4	183, 232, 316	5:6	204
34:7	281, 658			5:6-6:7	189
34:9	281	4:1	174	5:14-6:7	162
34:18	199	4:2	182, 187	5:15	182, 191, 204, 205
34:25	199, 201	4:3-12	184		
37:6-9	161	4:3	185, 189, 205	5:15-16	190, 191
39:2-14	14			5:17	189, 191
40:1-38	174	4:4	171	5:17-19	194
40:31-32	616	4-6	163	5:18	182, 190, 204, 205
40:34	96	4:6	184		
40:34-35	138	4:7	184	5:19	189, 192
		4:10	184	6:2-3	182, 192
Leviticus		4:12	174, 184	6:4	189
1	168, 174			6:6	190, 204, 205
1-3	183	4:12-13	190		
1-7	162, 272	4:13	182, 187, 189, 211	6:7	189
1:2	163			6:8-13	162
1:3	168, 205	4:13-21	184	6:9	164
1:4	165, 169, 171	4:15	171	6:10	191
		4:17	184	6:11	174
1:5	187	4:18	184	6:12-13	164
1:9	170	4:21	174, 184	6:14-18	175
1:10	204, 205	4:22-26	184	6:14-23	162

6:16	178	9:15	182	15:30	163
6:17	189	9:17	225	15:31	185, 228, 229
6:18	178, 191	9:24	164	16	194, 206, 207, 212, 213, 618
6:22	191	10:1	164		
6:22-29	184	10:1-2	220		
6:24-30	162	10:10	190		
6:26	178, 182	10:12	191	16:1-2	220
6:27	188	10:14-15	191	16:2	186, 219
6:29-30	178	10:17	191	16:3	163, 214
6:30	149, 184, 386	12:4-5	227	16:4	208
		12:6-8	226	16:5-10	208
7:1-7	189	12:6	228	16:5	163, 386
7:1-10	162	12:7	227	16:6	220
7:1	191	12:8	204, 228	16:8	212, 609
7:3-5	190	12-15	187, 188	16:10	212, 609
7:6-7	178	14	222	16:11	208, 220
7:6	191	14:3	222	16:12	219
7:7	190	14:4-7	221-222	16:12-13	209
7:11-21	162	14:4	200, 326	16:13-15	162, 219, 388
7:12	178	14:6	200, 326		
7:12-15	256	14:10-20	224	16:14	209
7:15-16	177	14:10	204	16:14-15	186
7:16-17	176	14:12-14	194	16:15	219
7:16	163, 178	14:12	222	16:15-16	217
7:18-19	177	14:13	191	16:16	188
7:18	176, 385	14:14	188	16:16-19	210
7:26-36	162	14:14-18	223	16:17-21	210, 609
7:31-36	191	14:19	162, 386	16:18-19	209
7:32-36	177	14:20	170	16:18-20	217
7:37	386	14:21	222	16:20	149
8:6	256, 615	14:22	162	16:20-22	384
8-9	163, 177, 188	14:31	162	16:20-23	210, 609
		14:49-53	221-222	16:21	171, 217, 278, 553
8:14	225	14:49	200		
8:15	149, 182	14:51-52	200	16:22	60, 212, 216, 624
8:18	225	15	227, 228		
8:22	225	15:2-12	228	16:23-24	211
8:23-24	188, 226	15:12	188	16:24	214, 220
8:25	226	15:14-15	230	16:25	211
8:27-28	225	15:15	163	16:26	211, 212
8:28-29	225	15:16-17	229	16:27	211
8:28	226	15:18	229	16:28	188
8:29-31	226	15:19-23	229	16:29	220, 610
8:31	225	15:25-27	229	16:29-32	207
8:33	225	15:29-30	230	16:31	610

Scripture Index

16:32	220	23:28-32	207	8:10	171
16:33	188	23:37	176	8:12	188
16:34	220	24:9	191	9:2-14	201
17:3-6	178	24:17	157	9:3	202
17:7	213	24:20	509	9:13	385
17:8	176	25	243	10:32	110
17:11	24, 70, 147, 155, 159, 439, 505	25:8-34	210	12:8	141
		25:9	161	12:10	222, 623
		25:10	248	12:10-15	194
		25:23	107, 239	13:7	241
17:14	439	25:23-37	239	14-16	230
17:16	385	25:30	239	14:18	111, 658
18:9	191	25:42	240	14:19-20	281
19:2	118	25:47-54	239	14:19	557
19:5	176	25:55	240	14:20	505
19:7	176	26:13	240	14:33	385
19:8	385	26:16	623	14:34	385
19:18	103, 107	26:25	623	15:3	176
19:20-22	195	26:40-46	505	15:5	176
19:21-22	190	26:40	278	15:8	176
19:22	155	26:41	272-273	15:22-29	316
19:34	103	27	239	15:27-28	182
20:3	117			15:30	182, 316
20:20	385	**Numbers**		15:32-35	182
21:22	191	3:13	200	16:46-48	209
22:2	117	3:40-51	262	18:1	385
22:9	385	3:44-51	200	18:12-18	191
22:14	191	3:40-51	171	18:15-18	200
22:16	189	5:2	229	19	230, 231, 232, 233, 234, 616, 617, 618
22:18	163	5:3	229		
22:19	204	5:7-8	189		
22:21	163, 178, 20	5:8	161, 239		
		5:31	385	19:2	231, 617
22:28	204	6-7	177	19:3	232
22:29	256	6:12	65, 190, 195	19:6	200, 326
23	163, 194			19:9	230, 232, 616, 617
23:4-43	163	6:14	163		
23:5	201, 202	6:16-17	163	19:8-9	188
23:7-11	206	6:20	191	19:13	230
23:19	177, 194	7:15-17	163	19:17	232
23:20	191	7:21-23	163	19:18	200
23:27	206, 610	7:89	98, 141, 150	19:19	182
23:27-28	161			19:20-21	230
23:27-32	206	8:16-18	200	19:21	188
23:28	161	8:8	188	20:12-13	117

20:25-28   231
21:29   59
25:16-18   263
27:18   171
27:23   171
28-29   194
28:3-8   204
28:3-10   163
28:5-8   167
28:11-15   163
28:16   201
29:39   163
29:7-11   206
29:8-9   214
29:8-11   215
29:11   161
31   263
31:22-23   188
31:50   263
31:54   263
32   239
32:21   55
33:3   201
33:4   56, 377
35   156
35:12   240, 241
35:13-15   156
35:19-27   240
35:16-21   182
35:22-25   241
35:25   156
35:28   156
35:31-32   259
35:33   156, 393

Deuteronomy
1:31   106
4:15-16   403
4:19   58
4:20   100
4:37   104
5:5   454
5:7-9   658
6:5   103, 107
6:13   118
7:6-16   107
7:7-8   104
7:9   121
7:13   104, 107
7:23   639
7:25-26   639
9:15   454
10:1   454
10:15   104
10:16   272-273
10:18   105
10:20   118
12:6   176, 177
12:7   178
12:11   176, 177
12:23   155, 439
12:27   176, 177
13:3   103
14:1   242
15:12-18   239
15:15   240
16   163
16:1-2   201
16:1-8   203
16:1   199
16:3   199
16:5-6   201
16:6   199, 202
16:12   199
19:4-7   241
19:6   240
19:12   240
19:21   509
21:2   486
21:8   154
21:22-23   500
21:23   324, 500, 627, 660
23:5   104
23:18   117
25:5-10   240
27:1-8   81
27:7   178
28:21-22   623, 626
28:35   623, 626
28:41-46   658
28:60   623, 626
28:68   240
29:26   58
29:29   281
30:1-11   53
30:6   272, 273
32:4   121
32:6   241
32:17   55, 213, 649, 659, 660
32:18   58
32:27   403
32:43   154, 246
33:12   105
33:16   100
33:29   537
34:7   632
34:9   171
34:10   141

Joshua
2   599
4   599
5:15   117
6:17   343
6:26   658
7:19   179
9:23   658
10:14   378
10:42   378
13   239
14:11   632
20:2-3   241
20:3   240
20:5   240, 241
20:9   240, 241
22:26-28   176, 177
22:27   177
22:29   176
23:9-10   378

Scripture Index

Judges
2:1   48
2:18   48
3:9   48
3:15   48
3:31   48
4:4   49
5:4-5 136
5:12   646
5:18   49
6:14-15 48
6:22-23 139
6:26   9
6:36-37 48
10:1   48
10:2-3 49
1010-16 51
11:24 59
12:7-14 49
13:5   49
13:16 49
13:22 139
13:23 49
15:2   135
15:20 49
16:30 376
16:31 49
17:5   225
17:12 225
20:26 49
21:4   49

Ruth
1   599
2:20   240
3:9-13 240
4:1-8 240
4:5   240
4:14   240

1 Samuel
1:2   67
1:3-4 179
1:9-11 179
3:4-9 141
3:14   155
4:4   98
5:3-4 376
6:3-4 189
6:8   189
6:17   189
7:2-14 49
7:9   168, 389
9:16   49
11:13 49
12:3   259
12:22 109
13:12 273
15:22 273
16:2-5 178
16:12 135
17:34-37 335, 662
17:43 377
17:45-47 377
17:47 49
19:5   49
21:4-5 229
24:16 49
30:26 55

2 Samuel
4:4   202
3:28-29 658
5:4   632
6:2   98
6   372
7   97
7:28   122
11:4   229
11:9-13 229
12:13 301, 505
12:14 55
12:24-25 105
14:4   50
14:11 240
14:13 189
18:19 49
18:3   49
19:2   49
19:34-35 631, 632
20:14-22 261
21:3   153
23:10 49
23:12 49
23:36 241
24:1-17 262
24:9   263
24:10 556
24:15-17 201
24:25 170

1 Kings
1:1   632
1:6   135
2:11   632
8:10-11 138
8:26   122
8:51   100
8:30-39 281
8:35-36 57
8:46-50 557
8:59-63 181
8:63-64 177
13:33 225
16:11 240
18:3   167
18:21 202
18:26 202
18:29 167
18:42-44 628
19:11-12 137
21:3   239
21:27-29 552

2 Kings
3:20   167
5   599, 635
5:1   49
5:10-14 635
5:25-27 194
5:26-27 222
5:27   623
6:15-17 377
6:26   50
9:7   246

13:5	49, 50	30:22	177	13:18	246-247
13:14	627, 628	31:2	177	13:23	246-247
13:17	49	33:16	177, 256	14:4	227
16:15	167	35	201	15:14	227
19:15	98			16:19-21	246-247

Ezra

17:3 246-247

1 Chronicles

3:22	241	4:17	20	17:13	644
12:18	20	5:7	20	17:14	644
13	372	7:10	27	19:25	241, 246
13:6	98	9:4-5	167	19:26-27	247
16:10	17	9:15	206	22:29-30	51
16:34	110	10:11	179	23:3-7	246-247
16:35	117	10:19	195	23:10-12	246-247
17:23-24	122			24:1-12	246-247

Nehemiah

18:8	616	7:22	122	24:19-20	644
21:1	262	9:17	110, 281	25:5-6	227
21:3	263	9:27	49	29:4	44, 583
21:5	263	9:33	121	31:37	246-247
21:14-18	201	11:1	117	33:6	340
21:26	170	11:18	117	33:23	260, 451
28:11	161	13:26	105	33:23-24	246-247
28:9	596			33:23-26	260
29:5	225	**Esther**		33:24	261
29:21-22	178	1:14	39	36:18	260
29:3	117	2:17	113	37:2-5	136
		5:8	113	38:1	136
2 Chronicles		10:3	20, 379	40:15	56
1:9	122			42:8	170
2:11	104	**Job**		**Psalms**	
5:13	110	1:5	170	1:1	129
6:17	122	1:21	599	1:2	27
7:1	164	3:5	238	2:1	397
7:7	177	7:1	546	2:2	36
11:15	213	9:19	246	2:9	340
13:9	225	9:33-35	246	3:8	47, 78, 92
16:19	602	9:33	451	5:5	383
20:7	45	10:2	246	5:7	117
26:16-21	194	10:7	246	5:10	189
26:19-21	222	10:9	340	7:9	49
26:19	623	10:17	246-247	9:10	306, 322
29:7-8	170	10:21-22	644	9:12	246
29:24	182	13:3	246-247	10:18	49
30	201	13:8	246-247	11:5	508
30:18-20	257	13:15	246	13:5	52

Scripture Index

14:2-3	227, 599	26:1	49	45:7	508
16	643	25:8	110	48:1	117
16:1	330	25:11	281, 557	49:7-8	80, 452, 509
16:8-11	330	25:14	44		
16:10-11	354	25:18	281, 557	49:7-9	14, 259, 83
16:10	330, 642	26:1	49	50:23	92
16:13	242	27:4	135	50:13	256
18:4-5	617	29	136	50:14	178, 256
18:7-9	138	31:5	121, 329, 330	50:23	256
18:43-45	538			51	572, 611
19:1	141, 584	32:1-2	281	51:2	160
19:4	587	32:3-5	554	51:4	19
19:12	556	32:4	628, 623	51:5	227
19:14	244	32:5	281, 301, 505, 557	51:7	200, 160, 326
19:9	122				
22	306, 308, 322, 323, 501	33:4	121, 122	51:9	182
		33:21	117	51:16-17	269
		34:8	110	51:17	556, 557, 604
22:1	306, 322, 353, 358, 473, 477, 487, 501	34:21-22	189		
		35:24	49	51:16-19	279
		36:5-6	540	53:2-3	227, 599
		37:11	127	54:6	110
22:2	487	37:20	55	55:4	617
22:3	324	37:25	306, 322	55:12-14	447
22:4	358	37:28	306	55:14	45
22:5-6	358	37:39-40	52	56:12-13	178
22:7-8	322, 353	40	217, 308	57:3	122
22:7-21	358	40:6	176, 312	58:3	227
22:8	306	40:6-8	217, 252, 279, 392	61:7	122
22:13	322				
22:14	306	40:6-10	55	65:3	155
22:15	306, 325, 496	40:7-8	312	65:5	52
		40:7-9	354	66:3	538
22:16	306, 322	40:10	53	66:10	340
22:18	306, 322, 353	40:12	354	65:11	110
		40:13-15	358	66:13	274
22:21	487	40:13	169	66:15	274
22:22	255, 322, 353	41:9	447	66:18	274
		42:5	52	68:21	189
22:24	322	43:1	49	68	645, 646
22:27	322	44	354	68:1	55, 446
22:31	327	45	106	68:6	321
23:4	100	45:2	66	68:18	372, 641, 645, 646
25:5	52	45:3-4	367		
25:10	122	45:4	122, 357	68:21	55, 446

69	217, 308, 353, 354, 358	87:4	56	110:4	252
		88	354, 358	111:7	122
		89:10	55, 56, 446	111:9	116
69:4	193, 325, 353	89:14	122	115:16	434
		88:15	617	116:15	353, 364
69:4-5	308	89:28	122	116:17	256
69:5	217, 354	89:51	55, 446	116:17-19	179
69:9	217, 325, 353	90:2-3	613	118:1	110
		90:17	135	118:5	653
69:16	110	92:9	446	118:10-12	653
69:18	244	94	136	118:22-23	497
69:21	325, 353	94:14	306, 322	118:24-26	55
71:15	53	96:10	296	118:25	50
71:19	327	98:2	53	118:29	110
72	247	99:1	98, 161	119:65	126
72:13-14	247	99:8	281	119:68	110
72:14	353	100	178	119:86	122
72:7	127	100:5	110	119:97	27
73:1	110	102	354, 358, 612	119:123	53
73:24	318			119:142	122
74	354	102:1-11	354	119:151	122
74:2	242	102:15	136	119:154	241
74:13	56	102:23-24	354	122:6	126
77:7-9	169	102:24-27	612	126:1-3	68
77:15	244	102:24	635	127:2	105
78:8	502	103:1	117	130:3-4	281
78:35	242	130:3-4	550	131:2	106
78:38	155	103:3	281, 559, 623	132:9	310
78:40	403			132:13-14	107
78:49	201	103:4	244	132:16	310
78:51	200	103:8	111	132:16-17	55
78:68	107	103:12	559	133	308, 310
79:1	117	103:13	106	135:3	110
79:6	588	104:1-2	139	135:8	200
79:9	52, 157	104:30	601	136:1	110
80:1	98, 219	105:42	117	136:10	200
81:15	538	106:1	1	136:29	200
85:1	169	106:10	244	138:2	117
85:8	124	106:37	55	139:23	596
86:2	52	107:1	110	141:2	167, 209
86:5	110, 159, 281, 550	107:2	244	145:8	111
		107:22	256	145:9	110
86:15	111	107:21-22	178	146:8	105
87	575	109:21	110		
87:2	107	110:1	252		

Proverbs
1:8	261
3:12	443
3:32	45
6:16-19	508
3:19	606
6:35	259
8:1-4	607
8:31	607
9:1-6	607
9:10-11	607
9:13	607
18:32-36	607
13:8	259
14:9	274-275
15:8	274-275
15:9	105
16:6	258
16.14	152, 158
20:6	121
21:1	541
21:3	274, 274, 275
21:18	261
21:27	274, 275
23:10-11	241
25:4-5	340
28:10	261
28:13	278, 301, 505, 554, 559, 639
28:18	51
30:10	189
31:6	326

Ecclesiastes
1:14	161
2:5	6
4:13	161
5:1	274
7:6	68
7:11	161
11:8	644
12:1-7	632
12:14	591

Song of Solomon
4:13	6
6:13	96
8:6-7	106

Isaiah
1:5-6	335
1:6	662
1:9	612
1:14	403, 508
1:16-18	339
1:17	49
1:18	559
1:24	446
1:27	52, 408
1:11-15	274
1:15-17	274-275
2:1-5	577
2:3-4	126
2:10	134
2:19	134
2:21	134
5:2	403
5:16	117
6	144
6:1	140
6:3	115, 117
6:5	139
6:3-4	138
6:7	258
7:14	99
8:8	99
8:10	99
9:6	125
9:7	125, 127
10:20-21	354, 612
10:20-22	612
11:9	117
11:11	354, 612
11:16	354, 612
12	386
13:13	377
13:21	213
14:9-11	644
14:12-15	57
25:7-9	54
25:8	373
26:3	128
26:12	124, 128
26:13	55, 56
26:19	608
27:9	157, 247
28:5	354
28:18	152, 153, 634
29:16	340
30:1-11	613
30:7	56
30:15	52
31:1	202
31:3	202
31:5	202
32:15-18	42-43
32:17-18	127
32:18	127
33:20	621
33:22	621
33:24	281, 621, 629, 634
34:14	213
35:2	138
35:4-10	54
35:5-6	634
35:8-10	242
35:9	242, 243
35:10	244
37:4	354, 612
37:16	98
37:31-32	354
37:32	612
38:10	635
38:17	160, 559
40:11	389, 662
40-66	242, 247, 249
40-54	53
41:1	54
41:2	54
41:8	44
41:14	244

41:25	54, 340	48:17	244		625, 626
41:14	52	48:18	126	53:5-6	193, 612
42:1-4	629	48:20	243	53:5	76, 167,
42:1-7	352	48:22	126		293, 291,
42:1	271	49:1-7	247, 352		335, 411,
42:7	634	49:3	352		491, 539,
42:13	446	49:6	55, 247		662, 625
42:18-19	634	49:7	121, 244,	53:6	520
43:1	244		247	53:7	165, 167,
43:2	100	49:15	106		204, 205,
43:3	52, 244,	49:21	245		353, 367
	259, 568	49:26	246, 568	53:8-10	483
43:4	104	50:1	245	53:8	14, 282,
43:8	634	50:1-2	106		381
43:11	52, 568	50:4-11	352	53:9	167, 205,
43:14	52, 244	51:9	55, 58,		293
43:16-21	242		377	53:10	167, 189,
43:25	53, 394,	51:9-11	242		193, 365,
	559	51:10-11	243		440, 476,
44:6	52, 244	51:11	244		477, 491,
44:22	53, 160,	52:3	244		496, 624
	559	52:7	125	53:11-12	485, 532,
44:22-23	244	52:9	242		626
44:24	52, 244	52:9-10	31	53:12	167, 367,
44:28	54	52:1	117		486, 613
45:1	54	52:13-		54:1	245
45:9	340	53:11	352	54:1-8	242
45:20	613	53	204, 205,	54:5-8	106, 245,
45:25	344		352, 388,		337
45:13-14	244-245		389, 572,	54:8	237
45:14-15	568		612, 624,	54:10	128
45:17	53		625, 625,	55:1	519, 536
45:20	52		626, 626,	55:7	281
45:21	568		629	55:12	128
46:1	58	53:2-3	476	56:1	53
46:3	354, 612	53:2	175	56:6-7	576
46:11	54	53:3-5	14, 625,	56:7	117
46:13	31		626	56:10	634
47:1-4	246	53:3	167, 352,	57:15	279, 556,
47:4	244		495		557, 604
47:11	153	53:4-5	282, 381	57:17-18	634
47:13	52	53:4-6	503	57:19	128
48:2	117	53:4	293, 167,	57:21	126
48:10	340		485, 503,	58	210
48:14	105		622, 624,	58:3-10	274-275

58:6-11	30	
58:8	137	
58:14	246	
59:1-2	53	
59:2	102, 324, 336, 662	
59:11-12	53	
59:16	52, 136	
59:17	246	
59:18	446	
59:20	242, 247	
60:1-2	137	
60:4	246	
60:10-12	577	
60:15-16	63, 64	
60:16	244, 568	
60:17-22	42-43	
60:21-22	613	
60:21	344	
61	211	
61:1	338, 622	
61:1-2	247, 629	
61:2	248	
61:8	508	
61:10	106	
62:12	242, 244	
62:4-5	106	
63:1	52	
63:3-4	378	
63:3	368	
63:4	246	
63:5	52	
63:8	568	
63:9	100, 104, 120, 132, 246, 355	
63:10	444	
63:11-14	355	
63:16	241, 242	
63:18	242	
64:8	241, 340	
64:10	117	
64:11	116	
65:2	446	
65:9-10	242	
65:17-25	249	
65:25	389	
66:2	556, 557	
66:3	55	
66:6	55, 446	
66:12	125	
66:13	106	
66:14	55, 446	

Jeremiah

2:27-28	52	
3:6-13	106	
3:22	634	
4:4	272-273	
4:14	52	
6:20	275	
7:22-23	277	
8:20	211	
8:21-22	634	
8:22	335	
10:10	121	
10:25	588	
11:4	100	
11:12	52	
12:8	444	
14:12	275	
17:10	596	
17:26	277	
18:3-6	340	
18:4	340	
18-19	340	
18:23	258	
19:1	340	
19:11	340	
23:5-6	54	
23:9	117	
29:11	124	
30:12-15	335	
30:14	444	
31:3	104	
31:11	244	
31:20	103, 112, 132	
31:31-34	462	
31:33	462	
31:34	160, 247, 281, 394, 462, 560	
32:7-8	239	
32:10-12	248	
33:6	124	
33:11	110	
33:18	277	
33:15-16	54	
34:8-10	248	
	38, 599	
	44:4 508	
46:11	335	
50:20	505	
50:33-34	241, 244	
51:5	189	
51:34	55	
51:44	55	
51:34	57	
51:44	57	
53:10	347	
53:12	347	

Lamentations

2:4-5	444
3:22-23	121
3:25	110
3:26	92
3:33	159
3:58	244
4:2	340
5:7	385

Ezekiel

1:26	144
1:28	144
1:26-28	136, 140
4:5-6	385
10:4	136
10:18	136
11:15	243
11:22-23	136
16:1-14	663
16:8	106
16:42	158

16:63	154, 157	7:9	140, 145	2:12-17	610, 611
18:20	658	7:13	144	2:13	111
20:41	117	7:13-14	317		
28:22	117	7:21-22	145	**Amos**	
28:25	117	9:9	281, 505	2:6-8	276-277
29:3	56	9:17-19	557	3:7	45
31:14	617	9:21	167, 205	4:1	276-277
33:11	159, 520	9:24	117, 154, 211, 393, 609	4:2	118
34:3-4	335			4:4-5	275
34:4	335			4:5	256
34:16	335	9:27	216	5:10-12	276-277
34:22-24	54	10:13	55, 58	5:12	259
36:20-21	117	10:20-21	58	5:15	104
36:23	117	11:35	340	5:21-24	275-276
37:12-14	608	12:2	608	5:21	508
37:23-24	54	12:10	340	6:8	118, 403, 508
37:26	128				
38:16	117	**Hosea**		7:2	557
39:27	117	1-3	337	8:4-6	276, 277
40:34-35	136	3:2	337	9:7	586
41:22	178	2:1-12	106		
43:2-5	136	2:15	106	**Jonah**	
43-44	616	2:18-19	106	2	505
43:20	182	3:1	106	2:9	92
43:22-23	182	5:6	275	4:12	111
43:26	225	5:9	122		
43:27	177	6:1	634	**Micah**	
44:10	385	6:2	608	2:1-2	276-277
44:16	178	6:6	275	4:10	244
45:15	167, 176	8:13	275	5:5	125
45:17	167, 176	10:2	189	5:8-9	41
45:18	182	11:1	104	6:6-8	276
46:12	179	11:1-4	106	6:8	592
46:17	248	11:8	111, 132	7:6	447
		11:9	117	7:18	281
Daniel		12:8	393	7:19	160
1:4	135	13:10	52		
2:31-35	580	13:14	244, 373	**Nahum**	
3:5	100	14:2	256, 557	1:2	55, 446
4:10-18	580	14:4	634	1:3	111
4:13	213	14:2-3	52	1:7	110
4:17	213	14:5	104	1:8	55, 446
4:23	213				
4:37	122	**Joel**		**Habakkuk**	
7	144	1:12	339	1:13	324, 473,

Scripture Index

	488, 501, 552

Zephaniah
3	41
3:14-16	41
3:17-20	42
3:17	52, 105, 403
3.19	41

Haggai
2:6	377

Zechariah
4:6	601
4:10	601
6:8	158
6:12-15	619
6:13	126
6:15	577
7:2	401
7:10	276-277
8:17	508
8:22	401
8:23	577
9:9	54
9:10	128
9:16	54
12	572
12:4-9	615
12:10-13:1	614
12:10-11	211, 617
12:10	618
12:11	615
13:1	615, 616, 617
13:4	625
13:7	307, 365, 440, 496, 625
13:9	340
14:3-4	615
14:16-21	577
14:20-21	616

Malachi
1:2-3	105
1:6	241
1:7	178
1:12	178
2:10-16	107
3:3	340
3:5	276, 277
3:17	393
4:2	137
7:18	110
7:20	110

NEW TESTAMENT

Matthew
1:21	36, 47, 62, 173, 189, 271, 307, 323, 519, 568
1:23	99
1:28	536
2:22	390
2:28	441
3:7	398
3:8	559
3:10	335
3:15	483
3:17	104, 393, 486
5:23-24	455, 459
4:3	265
4:5	117
4:23	36
5:3-11	129
5:8	33, 138
5:10	364
5:20	526
5:31-46	29, 85
5:38	509
5:43-45	447
5:44	445
5:45	540
3:38	390
6:9	117
6:12	336, 556, 560
6:13	60, 565, 566
6:14-15	507
7:16-20	335
7:22-23	605
7:22	606
8	625, 626
8:2	222
8:5-13	637
8:8	559
8:9	536
8:10	637
8:16-17	622, 624, 625, 626, 629
8:17	167, 625, 626
8:25	62
8:31-32	214
9:2	623, 628, 637
9:6-7	637
9:13	275
9:21-22	633
9:22	19, 62, 336, 568, 637
9:28-29	637
9:32-33	659
9:34	78
9:35	36
10:7-8	650
10:8	630
10:22	299
10:24-25	337
10:25	37
10:28	478, 641
10:34-36	447
10:38	362, 545, 546
11:5	222

11:28	519, 536, 580	
12:7	275	
12:17-21	629	
12:18	657	
12:24	60, 78, 375	
12:25-28	649, 664	
12:29	376, 642, 643	
14:30	62, 568	
12:18	486	
12:31-32	507	
12:32	182	
12:33	335	
12:40	642	
12:43-45	640	
12:43	214	
12:44	661	
13:58	628	
14:36	61, 633	
15:28	319, 637	
16:18	36	
16:21	357, 409, 490, 509	
16:22	386	
16:24	362, 363, 545, 546	
16:25	547	
16:27	534, 591	
17:5	104, 137, 173, 189, 393, 486	
17:13	137	
17:24	328, 414	
18:10	44	
18:22-24	554	
18:23-35	554	
18:26-27	549	
18:27	418, 553	
18:32	553	
18:34	383, 509, 551	
18:35	560	
19:17	110	
20:18-19	358	
20:22-23	502	
20:23	252	
20:28	13, 62, 73, 160, 237, 259, 289, 304, 307, 323, 337, 341, 387, 390, 441, 507, 532, 533	
21:9	50	
22:7	316	
22:15	490	
22:44	252	
22:15-22	66	
22:36-40	39	
22:30	44	
23:10	250	
23:24	66	
24:14	36, 587	
24:15-31	598	
24:22	299	
24:29	367	
24:30	144, 615	
25	39	
25:11-12	605	
25:31-46	591	
25:34-40	355-356	
25:34	541	
25:40	605	
25:41	539, 541, 641	
25:46	411, 539, 541	
26:10	605	
26:18	490	
26:27-28	507	
26:28	70, 71, 160, 186, 303, 308, 323, 337, 387, 463, 532, 551	
26:31	496	
26:54	357, 410, 490, 509	
26:56	476, 490	
26:64	144	
27	307	
27:4	353, 476	
27:19	38	
27:24	38	
27:26-50	476	
27:26	440, 497, 625	
27:29-30	440	
27:32	545	
27:34	193, 217, 325, 326	
27:35	440	
27:39-44	499	
27:39	322, 353	
27:40-41	317	
27:42	368	
27:45-46	205	
27:43	306, 322, 353, 566	
27:44	317	
27:45-54	323	
27:46	202, 306, 322, 358, 412, 473, 476, 477, 501, 515	
27:48	193, 217, 325	
27:50	329, 347	
27:51	220	
27:52-53	642	
27:52	374	
27:53	117	
27:54	498	
28:18	435	
28:19	586	

Mark

1:20	321
1:24	118

Scripture Index

1:25	661	11:25	560	1:74	36, 41, 338, 566
1:26	661	12:6	104		
2:5	507	12:33	275	1:77	568
3:5	445	12:34	596	1:79	309
3:21	77	13:10	586	2:1	60
3:27	338, 376, 643	13:26	144	2:7	476
		14:24	71	2:9	134
4:35-41	100	14:27	362	2:11	50, 64, 568
5:1-5	655	14:36	500		
5:7	661	14:62	144	2:14	309
5:8	661	15	307	2:21	479
5:9	655	15:23	326	2:22-24	181, 228
5:23	633	15:24	473	2:22-38	311
5:28	633	15:33-34	205	2:24	128
5:34	633	15:33-39	323	2:29	309
5:39-42	638	15:34	202, 306, 322, 353, 358, 473, 501	2:35	319
5:41	389			2:36	67
6:5-6	628, 638			2:38	567
6:13	630			2:41-51	311
6:20	116	15:36	325	3:7	398
6:56	633	15:37	329	4:16-22	211
7:32-34	638	15:40	320	4:17-21	629
8:31	410, 509	16:1	320	4:18-19	247
8:34	362, 363, 545	16:9-20	647	4:18	338, 525, 622
		16:15	586		
9:12	167	16:16	587	4:19	553
9:19	490	16:17-18	631	4:26	278
9:23	362, 363, 637	16:17	630, 647, 650, 651	4:27	222
				4:34	118
9:25-27	661	16:18	630	4:44	525
9:25	659, 661	16:20	630	5:29	309
9:26	655			6:27	447
9:37	278	**Luke**		6:35	447
10:14	343	1:3	350	7:3	61, 633
10:23-25	62	1:6	27, 38, 591, 594, 596	7:19	560
10:26	62			7:36	309, 661
10:29-30	321			7:47-48	507
10:45	13, 62, 73, 259, 304, 307, 337, 341, 390, 507, 532	1:22	310	7:48-50	560
		1:35	118, 175	7:47	292, 348
		1:47	64, 568	7:50	309, 633
		1:68-77	61	8:29	653, 661
		1:68	390, 567	8:35-36	657
10:52	19, 62, 336, 637	1:69	568	8:36	568, 633
		1:71	36, 62, 338, 647	8:43	195
11:23	9			8:48	309, 633

8:50	568, 633, 637	15:21	554	23:12	446
		15:23	310	23:26	362
9:12-17	309	16	643	23:33	314
9:22	409, 490, 509	16:11	120	23:34	183, 306, 307, 314, 498, 500
		16:19-31	582		
9:23	545, 546	16:22	642, 643, 645	23:36	325
9:25-27	661				
9:35	271	16:23	643	23:39-43	309
10:5-6	309	16:22-23	641	23:40-43	555
10:9	630	17:8	310	23:42-43	316
10:21	488	17:7-10	38	23:43	6, 23, 642, 643, 645,
10:27	103	17:14	222		
10:31	311	17:17	222	23:44-48	323
10:33-35	25	17:15-18	639	23:44	202, 205
11:2	117	17:15-19	558	23:40-42	85
11:4	556,	17:19	19, 62, 336, 633, 637	23:46	307, 329, 500
11:11	390				
11:14	659			24:21	61, 390, 567
11:15	78, 375	17:25	409, 490, 509		
11:21-22	376			24:26-27	586
11:24	214	18:9-14	459	24:26	357, 410, 490, 509
11:37	309	18:11-12	459		
12:47-48	8	18:13	385, 395, 506, 459	24:27-31	315
12:51	309			24:29-30	310
13:11	634, 659	18:14	385	24:36	309
13:16	634, 659	18:17	111	24:39	403
13:8-9	315	18:25	68	24:41-43	310
13:12	319	19:10	62	24:44	410, 509
13:24-27	605	19:38	128, 309	24:46-47	315
13:25	606	19:42	309, 315	24:46	410, 509
13:26	606	20:13	512	24:52-53	311
13:34	106, 445, 536, 627	20:36	44	46-47	310
		21:27	144		
14:1	309	21:28	62, 567	**John**	
14:12-13	309	22:14-23	310	1:1	100, 145
14:12-24	25	22:15	490	1:1-3	15
14:16-17	309	22:19	469	1:4-5	134
14:26	278	22:20	24, 387, 453	1:9	583, 584
14:27	545, 546			1:12	312
15	21	22:37	167, 410, 509	1:13	15
15:11-24	554			1:14	15, 100, 134, 251, 351
15:11-25	25	22:44	369, 476, 499, 501		
15:11-32	336, 458				
15:17-24	348	22:53	367, 497	1:15-17	15
15:20	458, 549	23	307	1:18	140

Scripture Index

1:19-22	15		403, 587	8:10	319
1:29	15, 165,	4:42	520	8:11	559
	203, 218,	4:34	312, 328,	8:24	494
	271, 303,		412, 486	8:29	412, 487
	245, 369,	4:42	31, 50, 64,	8:34	337
	389, 414,		345, 580	8:44	268
	520, 580	5:13	639	8:48	77
1:35	15	5:14	559, 623,	8:49	407
1:36	165, 203,		628, 639	8:52	77
	303	5:20	108	9	635, 636
2:4	319, 497	5:24	382,	9:31	582, 593
2:17	193, 217,	5:26-29	541	9:35-38	636, 639
	325, 353	5:28-29	538	9:41	494
2:19	251	5:29	382, 591	10	22
2:19-21	100	5:30	312, 486	10:8-10	662
2:21	251	5:34	63	10:8	335
3:1-10	342	5:36	328	10:9	63
3:2	559	6:6	273	10:10-17	335
3:5	22, 233,	6:29	328	10:11	110, 303,
	339, 602	6:37	87		339, 347,
3:6	227	6:38	312		495, 507,
3:7	563	6:31-33	175		519
3:8	601	6:32-69	463	10:13-15	347
3:14-15	357, 410,	6:35	587	10:14	110
	490, 509	6:38	486	10:15-18	507
3:14-16	507	6:39-40	428	10:15	303, 339,
3:15-16	587	6:40	587		340, 495,
3:16	14, 22, 105,	6:44	22, 87, 428,		519
	271, 272,		602	10:16	335
	291, 292,	6:46	140	10:17-18	347, 491,
	303, 346,	6:47	587		439, 495
	403, 405,	6:49-51	175	10:17	174
	416, 420,	6:51	345	10:18	477
	510, 512,	6:53-56	70	10:20	77
	520, 523,	6:53-58	303	10:26-27	519
	531	6:54	303, 428	10:27-29	335
3:17	31, 63, 345	6:57-58	175	10:28	303
3:18	587	6:57	428	10:34-35	563
3:19-20	584	6:69	118	10:38	328
3:36	23, 87, 398,	7:5	320, 498	11	628
	402, 587	7:17	627	11:4	141
4:10	326	7:18	486	11:11	374
4:13-14	326	7:20	77	11:12	19, 62
4:21	319	7:24	104	11:14	374
4:24	115-16,	7:38-39	326, 433	11:24	319

11:25-26 587	375	312, 523
11:26 374	14:31 104	17:22-26 131
11:42 487	14:32 105	17:23 105
11:43 661	15:1-8 335	17:24 32, 132,
11:44 649, 664	15:8 312	134, 138,
11:49-52 507	15:9-10 104	143, 312
11:50 339, 389,	15:12 28, 39	523
390	15:13-14 340	17:25 116
11:51 390	15:13 303, 391,	18:4 325
12:27-28 311	519	18:9 327
12:27 62	15:14 28	18:11 497
12:31 345, 369,	15:20 337, 357,	18:16 321
375	654, 547	18:32 327
12:32 580	5:22 494	19 307
12:38 327	15:25 353	19:3 19
12:46 587	15:26 434	19:4 217
12:47 63	16:7 433	19:5 325, 351
12:31 60	16:9 494	19:11 497
12:41 144	16:11 60, 345,	19:17 325, 347,
12:47 31	375	547
13:1-15 234	16:14 434	19:18 322
13:8 233	16:27 399	19:24 306, 322,
13:10 233, 339	16:32 412, 487	327, 353
13:14-15 349	16:33 338	19:26 320
13:16 337	15:25 325, 327	19:26-27 319
13:18 327, 447	16:27 105, 106,	19:27 321
13:23 320	108, 312	19:28-29 217
13:31 290, 311,	16:32 323, 514	19:28-30 353
412	16:33 126, 128	19:28 306, 324,
13:31-32 329	17:1-2 541	326
13:34 28, 39	17:2 522-523	19:29 325
14:2 433	17:3 75, 133,	19:30 326, 327,
14:1-3 312	328, 478	347, 414,
14:6 579, 581,	17:4-5 329, 434	425
599	17:4 203, 290,	19:34-37 618
14:9 142	311, 327,	19:34-35 440
14:12 630	328, 412,	19:34 476, 618
14:13 311	414, 425	19:36 203, 327
14:15 28, 38	17:6 523	20:2 320
14:16 433	17:9 519, 523	20:9 410, 509
14:19 428	17:11 116, 118	20:13 319
14:21 28, 38	17:12 327	20:15 319
14:26 434	17:21-23 32, 94	20:17 322, 433,
14:27 125	17:21 294	488
14:30 60, 345,	17:22 143, 143,	20:21 477

20:23	311, 327, 414	3:19-21	221, 504	8:6-7	650
		3:19	301, 315	8:7	630, 661
20:25	322	3:21	248, 461	8:14	593
20:27	322	4:3	476	8:32	167
21:7	320	4:9	19, 62	8:32-35	204
21:11	215	4:10	301, 358, 503	9:3	139
21:20	320			9:4	356, 498
		4:11-12	504	9:8-9	139
Acts		4:12	1, 63, 79, 529, 579, 581, 600	9:10	651
1:1	350			9:12	630
1:8	586			9:17	630, 651
1:10-11	615	4:26	36	9:34	630
1:24	596	4:27	118	9:37	374
2:4	26	4:29-30	630	10:2	167, 591
2:23-32	301	4:29	337	10:3	206
2:24	14, 24	4:30	118	10:2-3	205
2:27	642, 643	4:31	26	10:34-35	582, 591
2:23	356, 495, 503, 495, 496	5:16	630, 650, 659	10:35	409, 593
				10:38	223, 310, 659
		5:26	455		
2:24-27	476	5:30-31	302	10:39	358
2:24	374, 567	5:30	301, 358, 495, 503	10:43	301
2:25-28	354			11:1	593
2:31	330, 476	5:31	50, 301	11:14	63, 343
2:33	330, 433, 434	5:34-39	596	11:28	60
		6:8	630	12:15	44
2:34	252	7:2	137	13:10	409
2:36	333, 358, 435, 495, 503	7:23	316	13:18	316
		7:25	62	13:21	316
		7:30	316	13:23	50, 64
2:38	301, 504	7:35	62, 390, 567	13:26	568-569
2:39	343			13:28	503
2:40	63	7:42	316	13:27-39	302
2:47	63	7:50-56	78	13:35	354
3	635	7:51	272	13:36	374
3:1	167, 202, 205, 206	7:52	38, 301, 358, 409, 503	13:37-39	428
				13:38-39	302, 504
3:6	264, 630			13:39	409
		7:55	134, 137, 140, 221	13:47	568
				13:48	87
3:14	38, 116, 118, 409	7:58	498	13:52	26
		7:59	329	14:1	88
3:15	301, 315, 358, 495, 503	7:60	316, 374	14:8-10	630
		8:1	498	14:9-10	637
3:16	630, 636	8:4-5	651	14:9	19, 62, 633
3:17	183, 315				

14:11	403	20:24	36		589
14:15	403	20:25	586	1:20	82, 140, 141, 584, 590
14:17	110, 540, 586	20:28	14, 186, 302, 464, 512, 519	1:24	458
14:19	78				
14:22	365	21:20	316	1:26	458
15	478	22:3	596	1:28-29	588
15:1	63	22:7	356	1:28	458, 588
15:5	596	22:11	137	1:32	408
15:10-11	83	22:14	38, 409	2	589, 593, 603
15:11	63, 344	22:20	594		
15:31	64	22:21-22	78	2:1	590
16:7	354, 569	23:1	594	2:2-5	382
16:14	596	23:4-5	632	2:4	110, 111, 558, 590, 604
16:16-23	78	23:24	61		
16:17	63, 337	24:5	60		
16:19	64	24:15	409, 538	2:4-8	627
16:30-31	63	24:25	382, 409	2:5	227, 398
16:31	343	26:4-5	594	2:6-7	582
16:34	343	26:13	137	2:6-10	538
17:2-9	78	26:14	356	2:6-11	589
17:3	357, 410, 490, 509	26:18	61, 74, 78, 338, 649, 658	2:6-13	601
				2:6	85, 535
17:6	60			2:7	601
17:11	593	26:20	559	2:8-16	582
17:13	78	27:20	62	2:8	389, 402
17:18	10	27:31	62	2:12-16	590
17:26-28	592	27:34	62, 568	2:13	27, 84
17:27	601	27:44	62	2:14-15	571
17:30-33	78	28:8	630	2:14-16	584, 585
17:30	586	28:22	597	3:23-24	580, 585
17:31	409	28:25-27	144	2:23	290, 336, 407
17:31-32	68				
18:8	343	**Romans**		3:11	599
18:12-17	78	1	593, 603	3:24-25	508
19:12	659	1:1	92, 337, 512	3:25	280, 303
19:11-12	650			2:29	272
19:13-16	651	1:5	113, 127	3:3-4	119
19:18-19	660	1:14	512	3:4	121
19:19	639	1:17	409, 416, 417	3:5	398, 473
19:27	60			3:7	121
19:21-41	78	1:18	398, 405, 443, 458, 588	3:20	83
19:32-41	628			3:22	460
20	303			3:23-24	478, 519
20:9-10	628	1:19-21	585, 588,	3:23	134

Scripture Index

3:24-22	417		252	7:6	338, 480
3:24-25	387	5:10	36, 150,	7:12	116
3:24-26	401, 409,		395, 397,	7:18	273
	417		426, 446,	7:24-25	565, 595
3:24	62, 87, 567		449, 450,	7:24	566
3:25	71, 149		456, 457,	8	105
	187, 388,		467, 483,	8:2	338
	395, 528		662	8:3	188, 271,
3:26	121	5:11	148		303, 336,
3:28	83	5:13	124		411, 473
4:3	271	5:15-18	336	8:4	84, 28, 38,
4:6	83	5:18-19	532		408
4:9	271	5:18	460, 520,	8:7	397, 446,
4:15	398		532, 580,		450
4:17	127		585	8:9	354
4:18	271	5:19-21	471	8:11	426, 427,
4:19-25	271, 272,	5:19	414, 532		428, 430
	272	5:20	397	8:17	134, 360
4:22	271	5:21	478	8:18-24	43, 44
4:24-5:2	428, 429	6:3-4	426, 467	8:20-21	218
4:24-25	663	6:3-6	303	8:20-23	629
4:25	167, 223,	6:4	330, 427,	8:21	64, 338,
	292, 329,		429		345
	336, 426,	6:5	335, 467	8:23	62, 566,
	427	6:6	287, 362,		567, 633
5	80		368, 369,	8:23-24	63
5:1	42, 150,		466, 543,	8:27	596
	166, 180,		563	8:28-33	519
	566	6:7-8	478	8:28	350, 457
5:2	134, 138	6:8	32	8:29	120, 147,
5:5	30, 39, 105,	6:9-11	426		143
	457	6:10	466	8:30	134
5:6	449	6:11	467, 544	8:31-32	292
5:6-11	449	6:13	467	8:32	22, 121,
5:6-8	389	6:16-17	337		271, 272,
5:7-8	510	6:18	64, 338		346, 389,
5:8-9	23	6:18-19	337		392, 393,
5:8	105, 386,	6:20	337		414, 420,
	449	6:21-22	64		496, 512
5:9-10	34, 298,	6:22	64, 337,	8:34	254, 430,
	303, 445,		338		431, 433,
	565	6:23	373		436
5:9	398, 441,	7:2-3	338	8:38-39	367
	463, 448	7:3-4	64	8:38	59
5:10-11	423, 456,	7:4	426, 429	8:39	105

717

9:21-23	340	12:20	446	4:20	31
9:21	290	13:1	59	4:33	124, 126
9:22	111, 398, 402	13:11	34, 63	5:5	63, 651
		13:8-10	28	5:7	203, 388
10:2	595	13:9-10	39	5:7-8	197
10:9-10	79	15:3	180, 193, 217, 353	5:10-11	658
10:9	426			6:10	658
10:18	587	15:18-19	630	6:11	160, 233, 298, 339, 566, 602, 618
10:19	398	15:21	217		
10:21	446	15:22	193		
11	607	15:30	133		
11:6	87	15:31	566	6:14	430
11:12	572	15:33	124	6:20	260, 264, 337, 663
11:14	568	16:13	321		
11:15	456, 460, 520, 572, 580, 608	16:20	124, 370	7:5	229
		26:18	375	7:11	336, 455, 457
11:16-24	575	**1 Corinthians**		7:14	343
11:16	575	1:8	591	7:16	319, 568
11:17	335	1:16	343	7:22	337
11:21	575	1:17-18	465	7:23	260, 264
11:22	110	1:18	69, 285, 287, 538, 544	8:3	350, 457
11:24	575			8:5	55
11:25-27	247, 598			8:11	522
11:26	344, 567	1:21	568	9:19-20	659-660
11:28	109, 446, 448, 449, 450	1:30	62	10:1-13	658
		1:18-24	86	10:1-5	354
		1:23-24	69	10:7-8	658
11:32	580	2:2	85, 287, 361, 465	10:10	200
12:1	166, 173, 257			10:16-17	467
		2:1-5	69	10:16	71, 464
12:6-8	66	2:5-8	375	10:18-21	166, 180
13:6	328, 414	2:7-8	315	10:19-20	55
13:8	84	2:14	79, 593	10:20-21	658
13:10	84	2:6-8	375	10:20	649
13:11	565, 568	2:6	60	10:21	178
13:12-13	658	2:8	60, 375, 496	10:32	575
14:8	93	2:13	77	11:1	469
14:10-12	85	2:14	65, 77	11:24-25	469
14:15	522	3:6	335	11:25	71, 453
14:17	31	3:12-15	591	11:26	467
14:18	173	3:15	63	11:29-30	628
14:19	180	3:16	101, 576	12:8-10	66
11:26	50, 60, 62	4:4-5	591	12:10	651, 653
12:2	38	4:14-15	321	12:13	25, 37

Scripture Index

13:2	9	3:9	462		420, 427,
13:12	33	3:11	180		473, 487,
13:8-10	30	3:16	598, 608,		624, 501
13:12	138		598	6:2	569
14:16	121	3:18	38	6:11	651
14:24	651	4:4	91, 92, 134	6:14-16	659
15:2	63	4:6	91, 92, 134,	6:16	101
15:3-4	476		414	6:19-20	460
15:3	303, 389	4:7	340	7:10	556
15:6	374	4:9	306	7:15	593
15:7	320	4:14	430	8:5	349
15:12-23	430	4:17	134	8:9	346
15:12-19	329	4:18	539	9:15	292
15:12	427	5	462	10:1	110
15:15	427	5:3	425	10:11	650
15:17	425, 427	5:5	433	10:18-21	180
15:18	374	5:9	173	11:2	250
15:20	374	5:10	85, 535,	12:1	38
15:21-22	426		591	12:2	140
15:26	369, 373	5:14-15	349, 424	12:3	32, 643
15:28	145	5:15-17	429	12:7-8	652
15:45	532	5:15	93, 389,	12:7	632, 651
15:50-55	428		426, 526,	12:8-10	632, 633
15:51-57	254		531	12:9	66
15:54-55	427	5:17	345	12:13	6
15:54-57	373	5:18	462	12:15	349
15:56	373	5:19	512, 572,	13:4	368, 465
16:15	343		580	13:11	124
		5:18-20	397, 457		
2 Corinthians		5:18-21	217, 303,	**Galatians**	
1:3	129		420, 424	1:4	22, 254,
1:6	34	5:19-20	405		272, 302,
1:3	129	5:19	150, 287,		346, 391
1:10	63, 289,		336, 460,	1:6	36
	565, 566		520, 524,	1:10	337
1:19-20	271		526	1:14	594
1:20	272, 414	5:20	396, 445,	2:4	64
2:10	651		536	2:16	83
2:11	374	5:21	188, 217,	2:20	254, 287,
2:15	173, 538		294, 307,		302, 346,
2:14-16	371		324, 324,		362, 389,
3:3	462		339, 365,		391, 464,
3:4	62		369, 389,		475, 543
3:6	462		392, 404,	2:24	287
3:8	462		405, 412,	3:1	464

3:5	630	6:12	464, 544	2:11-22	455
3:6	271	6:14	69, 85, 285,	2:13-16	303
3:7	575		287, 302,	2:13	386, 574
3:10	395		465, 544	2:14-16	455
3:11	83	6:15	345	2:14-22	344
3:13-14	500, 660	6:16	180, 574	2:14	166, 577
3:13	64, 324,	6:17	360	2:15	575
	336, 337,			2:15-16	571
	390, 395,	**Ephesians**		2:16	287, 397,
	405, 418,	1:3	129, 355		446, 465,
	476, 486,	1:5-6	554		542, 573,
	500, 510,	1:5-7	549		576
	626, 627	1:6	166, 189	2:17	463
3:19-20	450	1:7	62, 71, 187,	3:17	335
3:19	454		204, 303,	3:17-19	347
3:28	455		336, 386,	2:18	138
3:29	575		440, 463,	2:19-22	372
4:4-5	479, 480		510, 554	2:19	208, 573,
4:4	476, 477	1:10	290		574, 574,
4:5	64	1:11-22	573		576
4:6	354, 654	1:13	63, 566,	1:20-21	59
4:8	588		569	2:20-22	574
4:14	593	1:14	62, 566,	2:20	576
4:15	632		567	2:22	576
4:16	446	1:15	25, 93	2:2	60
4:19	37, 321	1:19-22	372	2:4	125
4:23	271	1:20-22	435, 646	2:5	34, 63, 87
5:1	338	1:20	330, 430,	2:7	110
5:6	84		431, 435	2:8	34, 63, 87
5:11	287, 464,	1:21	367	2:8-9	65, 83
	544	2	574, 575	2:20-22	101
5:14	30, 39	2:1-5	36	3:3	575
5:16	30, 38	2:1-6	430	3:5	575
5:17	38	2:1	336	3:6	573, 574,
5:18	38	2:2	338, 375,		575
5:19-21	658		367	3:7	36
5:20	446	2:3	227, 398	3:9	575
5:22	111, 180	2:4-6	431, 435	3:10	36, 59, 367
5:22-23	111	2:5-6	432	3:12	138
5:24	362, 465,	2:5	336, 427,	3:14-19	45
	466, 543,		565	3:15	321
	546	2:6	426, 433	3:16-17	654
6:2	28, 39	2:8-9	555	3:18	25, 82, 576
6:5	80	2:8	555, 565,	3:19	138, 141
6:7-10	591		576	4	645

Scripture Index

4:8-10	372, 645, 646	6:11	374		126, 127, 141, 180
4:8	641, 642	6:12	60, 341, 355, 367, 542	4:8	135
4:9-10	294			4:9	124
4:9	641	6:17	569		
4:13	37	6:18	628	**Colossians**	
4:18	588	6:23	125, 180	1:4	25, 204
4:22-27	658			1:10	173
4:22	543	**Philippians**		1:12-14	550
4:24	38, 575	1:1	337	1:13-14	554
4:27	654, 658	1:9	63	1:13	367, 375, 512, 566, 649
4:30	62, 566, 567	1:19	354, 565		
		1:23	32, 319, 374	1:14	463
4:32	549, 560	1:27-28	664	1:16	367
5:1	469	1:28	568	1:19-20	512
5:2	493, 495, 510	2:1	349	1:19-22	460
5:1-2	226, 257	2:5-8	349, 465	1:20-21	397
5:2	39, 166, 173, 189, 211, 254, 272, 303, 347, 349, 356, 391	2:6-7	512	1:20	435, 464, 465, 525, 537, 542, 573
		2:6-8	466		
		2:6	558		
		2:7	346, 351		
		2:8-9	434		
		2:8	285, 414, 476	1:21	397, 420, 446, 449, 450, 456, 537
5:5	589				
5:6	398, 402, 473	2:9	346, 372		
		2:12	34		
5:10	173	2:10-11	537	1:22	467
5:18	26, 264, 566, 640	2:12-13	87	1:29-2:1	664
		2:12	565	1:24	364
5:18-20	225	2:25-27	627	2:10	372
5:22-32	250	3:4-6	594	2:11	272
5:23	64, 344	3:6	594	2:12	426, 429
5:25-27	344, 663	3:7-11	594	2:14-15	464
5:25-26	339	3:9	478	2:15	646, 664
5:25	106, 254, 303, 340, 347, 391, 519	3:10-11	360, 428, 467	2:12-13	550
		3:10	364, 426	1:13	31, 60, 338,
		3:15	38	1:14	62, 303
5:26-27	93, 337	3:18	69, 287, 464, 544	1:15	74, 140
5:26	618			1:16	59
5:27	663	3:20	50, 64	1:19-20	333
6:8	591	3:20-21	63, 428	1:19	145
6:6	337	3:21	143, 254	1:20	68, 71, 187, 287, 303, 309
6:11-12	664	4:7	42, 124,		
				1:16-20	13

ETERNAL SALVATION

1:21-23	299	2:13	593		585-586, 627
1:22	303	2:14-15	358		
1:23	586, 587	2:16	398	2:3-6	517, 520
1:26	575	3:3-4	365	2:3	64
1:28	38	3:5	265	2:4-6	460
2:7	335	3:13	591	2:4	536
2:9	142, 145	4:5	588	2:5	14
2:13-14	370	4:13-15	374	2:5-6	161, 450, 600
2:13	336	4:14	430		
2:14-15	303, 542	4:17	32	2:6	73, 254, 260, 337, 341, 346, 390, 475, 533
2:14	337, 549, 564	5:8-9	34, 63, 565, 566		
2:15	338, 367, 370, 371, 435, 564	5:8	569		
		5:9	398, 402		
		5:10	374	3:7	652
3:1-4	427	5:23	591	3:15	101, 208
3:1-3	430, 436, 565	5:16-19	558	3:16	330, 435
		5:23	124	4:1-2	652
3:1	426, 433			4:10	533, 540
3:4	143	**2 Thessalonians**		4:16	63, 565
3:5	543	1:6-9	391	4:21	119
3:5-6	473	1:7-10	538	5:15	652
3:6	398, 402	1:8	587, 588	5:23	628
3:9	543	1:9	137, 411, 539	6:15	13, 21, 132
3:10	38			6:16	138, 139, 142, 290, 295, 406
3:11	455	1:10	143		
3:12	116	1:11	173		
3:13	560	2:10	593		
3:15	42, 125, 126, 558	2:13	105	**2 Timothy**	
		2:16	105	1:2	125, 321
3:17	558	3:16	125, 180	1:9	63, 83, 112, 565
3:23-24	591				
4:2	628	**1 Timothy**		1:10	50, 64, 368, 374, 563
4:12	337	1:1	64		
		1:2	125, 321	2:6	62
1 Thessalonians		1:11	91, 92, 130, 132	2:12-13	119
1:6	469, 593			2:12	360
1:9	342	1:13	183, 315, 498	2:13	122, 409
1:10	60, 398, 402, 429, 567			2:17	335, 662
		1:15-16	560	2:20-21	101, 340
		1:15	568, 594	2:20	290
2:7	321	1:16	111	2:22	566
2:8	349	1:17	140, 290	2:24	337
1:9	649	1:20	651-652	2:26	652
2:11	321	2:3-4	540, 580,	3:1-5	119

Scripture Index

3:12	365, 547	1:3	137, 221,		399, 430,
3:15	63		387, 426,		436
3:16	644		431, 435	4:15-16	254
4:17-18	567	1:10-12	354, 612	4:15	352
4:18	63, 566	1:13	252, 432	4:16	219
4:20	628	1:14	63, 566	5:1-10	220, 253
		2:3	63	5:1	256, 387
Titus		2:5	127	5:3	387
1:1	337	2:9	303, 389,	5:6	251
1:3	64		415, 460,	5:7	62, 322
1:4	50, 64,		466, 520,	5:8	510
	321		521, 580,	5:10	219, 251
1:7	208		586	6:2	382
1:10	466	2:10	510, 569	6:5	127, 635
2:10	64	2:12	255, 322,	6:9	63, 253
2:11-12	64		353, 436	6:16-17	253
2:11	64, 87, 460,	2:13	330	6:17	450
	520, 568,	2:14-15	368, 374,	6:19-20	218, 219
	580, 586		565	6:20	214, 219,
2:13-14	13	2:14	74, 351,		251, 431
2:13	50, 64, 131,		274, 374,	7:1-10	253
	568		368, 467,	7:2	125
2:14	61, 254,		563, 643,	7:3	125
	337, 338,		664	7:11	251
	344, 346,	2:15	64	7:13-14	252
	390, 391,	2:17	148, 149,	7:17	251
	565, 567		208, 209,	7:18-19	253
3:1	59		219, 251,	7:19	253
3:3	446, 449,		384, 387,	7:20-21	253
	599		388, 395,	7:22	327, 416
3:4	64, 108,		442, 453,	7:23-28	220
	110		618	7:24-25	214
3:5	63, 83, 233,	2:18	214, 254,	7:25-26	352
	339, 565,		352, 399	7:25-28	251
	602	3:3	253	7:25	63, 93, 254,
3:6	50, 64	3:6	101, 208,		255, 399,
			224, 299		430, 436,
Philemon		3:7-4:13	354		566
1:5	25	3:14	299, 406	7:26	118, 218,
1:10	321	3:15	374		431
4:18	173	4:9	127	7:27	209, 219,
		4:14	186, 218,		256, 356,
Hebrews			219, 431,		387
1:1-3	15		618	7:28	253
1:2	345	4:14-16	214, 251,	8:1	219

8:1-2	214, 218, 219, 221, 251, 255, 432, 436		505, 512, 551	10:14	219	
		9:23	254, 256, 509	10:15-16	153	
				10:19-20	218, 219	
8:2	255	9:23-24	219	10:19-22	214, 220, 233, 255, 256,	
8:3	256	9:23-28	209, 254			
8:6	253, 450	9:24	209, 221, 431	10:19	71, 464	
8:8	453			10:20	219, 220	
8:12	386	9:25-26	463	10:21	101, 208, 224, 618	
8:26-27	219	9:26	495			
8:27	220	9:27	582	10:25	63	
9:14	356	9:28	566, 568, 618	10:26-29	182	
9:5	161, 264, 387			10:26	256, 387	
		9:29	303	10:27	382	
9:6-12	218, 219, 220	9:25-28	220, 251	10:29	386, 411, 453, 522	
		9:26	166, 219, 256, 356			
9:7	209, 387			10:34	253	
9:9	256	9:27	382	11:3	345	
9:11	219, 254	9:28	166, 219, 221, 356, 389	11:4	254, 256, 268	
9:11-12	186					
9:12	390, 424, 431, 437, 438, 463			11:6	557, 602	
		10:1	127, 256	11:7	62, 343	
		10:1-13	220	11:16	254	
9:11-14	219, 254	10:1-14	209	11:17-19	271	
9:11-15	214	10:1-18	254	11:27	140	
9:12	71, 197, 209, 218, 223, 303, 567	10:4-10	392	11:28	200	
		10:4-14	251	11:31	592	
		10:4	153, 280	11:35	62, 254	
		10:5-6	391, 392	11:40	254	
9:13-14	251, 232	10:5-7	354	12:1-2	355, 432, 465	
9:14	22, 160, 166, 187, 205, 209, 222, 272, 303, 356, 386, 463	10:5-10	217			
		10:5	256	12:2-4	360	
		10:6	386	12:2	92, 221, 333, 341, 346, 425, 432, 476	
		10:7	312, 392			
		10:8-10	280			
		10:8	256, 386			
	9:15 450, 451, 453, 467, 567	10:9	312, 393	12:6	443	
		10:10	153, 219	12:14	33, 566	
		10:11-13	221	12:23	476	
9:16-17	451	10:11	256	12:24-25	463	
9:18-22	452	10:12	217, 219, 356, 387, 426, 432, 435, 495	12:24	450, 453, 463	
9:20	453					
9:22-24	218			12:28	127, 173	
9:22	24, 70, 72, 147, 187,			13:11-12	174	
		10:13	209	13:12	303, 464	

13:14	127	5:14-16	628	2:21-23	293
13:15	165, 224, 225, 255, 256, 436	5:14	630	2:21-24	293, 360
		5:6	38, 365	2:22-24	205, 364, 491
		5:15	19, 62		
13:20	124, 453	5:16	554	2:22	167, 217, 294
13:21	173	5:20	568		
				2:24	80, 167, 188, 217, 290, 293, 335, 369, 383, 389, 392, 418, 440, 411, 473, 474, 480, 485, 491, 501, 624, 625, 662

James

1 Peter

1:1	337	1:1	13, 66		
1:2-3	364	1:2	186, 303, 463		
1:6-8	654				
1:8	654	1:3-4	427		
1:12	350	1:3	129, 426, 565		
1:19	111				
1:25	27, 38	1:5	34, 63		
1:27	276-277, 350	1:7	340		
		1:18-19	386, 390, 463		
2	84				
2:5	350	1:9	63	3:7	66
2:8	39	1:10	66	3:14	357, 364
2:10	336	1:11	354	3:15	117
2:12	27, 38	1:10-11	303	3:17	364
2:13	382	1:13	66	3:18-4:6	580, 581
2:14-16	276, 277, 350	1:15-16	118	3:18	23, 38, 99, 100, 145, 339, 365, 387, 389, 426, 451, 474, 475, 501
		1:17	535		
2:14	84	1:18-19	61, 71, 165, 187, 204, 264, 337, 366, 567		
2:17	84				
2:22	84				
2:23	45, 271				
2:24	84, 624, 625, 662	1:18	73-74, 337, 338		
				3:19	643
3:1	382	1:19	260, 303	3:20	111
3:14-15	652, 659	1:21	426, 427	3:21-22	435
3:15	654	2:2	34, 63, 566	3:21	63, 429
3:19	643	2:4	475, 484, 496	3:22	59, 367, 372, 646
3:22	646				
4:2-3	628, 652	2:5	101, 165, 208, 220, 224, 225, 257	4:18	566
4:4	397, 446, 450			4:1-2	464
				4:10	66
4:7-10	654			4:13	360, 364
4:8	654	2:7	497	4:17	101, 208, 382
5:1-6	276-277, 350	2:9	224, 225, 375		
				4:18	34, 63, 299
5:8	652	2:16	337	5:5	66
5:14-15	623	2:19-20	66, 364	5:8	322, 369,

	374, 652	2:1-2	399	4:10	148, 150, 167, 386, 388, 395, 414, 420
5:10	66	2:1	38, 254, 321, 433, 436		
5:13	321				
5:14	125, 180				
		2:2	148, 167, 219, 366, 386, 388, 395, 396, 414, 477, 520, 523, 524, 526, 528, 529, 560, 580, 586	4:11-12	350
2 Peter				4:12	139, 140
1:1	50, 337, 522, 568			4:14	64, 271, 292, 520, 580
1:4	75, 563				
1:7	137			3:14-15	350
1:11	50, 64			4:9-10	512
2:1	541			4:16	102, 104, 109, 115, 292
2:4	644				
2:9	60, 382, 411, 567				
		2:5	38	4:20-21	457
2:20-22	640	2:11	350	4:20	140, 277, 350
2:20	50, 64	2:13	38, 664		
3:2	50, 64	2:14	38	4:21	39, 350
3:7	382	2:15-17	345	5	370
3:9	520, 536, 558, 580, 586, 627	2:17	31, 369	5:1-2	350
		2:20	118	5:1	277
		3:1	399	5:2	457
3:13	345	3:2	142, 143	5:6-8	463
3:15	111	3:5	217, 294, 369	5:6	71, 618
3:18	50, 64			5:11-12	579
3:18	37	3:8	74, 338, 366, 368, 664	5:19	31, 369
				5:20	75, 478
1 John				5:21	589
1:1	94	3:10-12	350		
1:2	14, 75	3:12	268, 447	**2 John**	
1:3	32, 94, 131	3:14-15	350	1:3	125, 180
1:1-4	478	3:16-18	350, 350	1:10	20
1:5	115, 134, 139	3:16	349, 349, 393	**3 John**	
1:6-10	603	3:17	277	1:4	321
1:7-9	560	3:21	370	1:15	125
1:7	71, 160, 187, 204, 222, 303, 339, 366, 386	3:22	173		
		3:23	350	**Jude**	
		4:7	350	1:1	337
		4:8-10	292, 406, 412	1:2	180
				1:7	411
1:9	386, 409, 417, 464, 550, 554, 557, 603	4:8	102, 104, 109, 115, 350	1:15	382, 411
				1:25	64
		4:9-10	105, 271		

Scripture Index

Revelation
1:1	337
1:4	66
1:5	61, 160, 166, 187, 204, 248, 303, 339, 386, 440, 445, 463, 567
1:5-6	249
1:6	220, 224
1:7	614, 615
1:16	137
1:14-15	145
1:18	643
1:23	596
2-3	119
2:7	6, 32, 643
2:16	556
2:20-21	658
2:20	337
2:23	85
2:24	658
3:2	488
3:7	118
3:8	38
3:9	445
3:12	488
3:19	445
4:2-3	140
4:8	114
4:9	290
4:11	290, 35, 248, 248, 249, 562
5:1-13	469
5:2	248
5:3	249
5:5	367, 370
5:6-22:33	204
5:6	493, 601
5:9	74, 166, 187, 249, 264, 303, 337, 386, 463, 493, 615
5:10	220, 224
5:12-13	290
5:12	20, 493
6:9	250
6:10	116, 250
6:16-17	398
6:16	402, 445
7:1-8	598
7:3	337
7:4	615
7:9	615
7:10	20, 63, 469
7:12	20, 290
7:14	160, 166, 187, 339, 386
9:2	138
9:20	55, 649, 659-660
10:7	337
11:2	117, 615
11:8	615
11:18	337, 398
12:3	56
12:9	59, 249, 265, 367, 370
12:10	63
12:11	303, 386, 464
13	59
13:4	370
13:7	615
13:8	493
14:3-4	249
14:6	615
14:10	398, 402, 403
14:11	138, 539
15:4	118, 322
15:8	137
16:5	118
16:12-16	63
16:19	398, 403
17:12-14	63
17:14	338, 370, 469
18:2	213
19:1	63
19:2	337
19:3	539
19:5	337
19:7-9	663
19:7	250
19:11-21	63
19:15	398, 496
19:20	641
20:2	59, 249, 265,
20:6	220, 224
20:7-10	338
20:9	107
20:10	250, 369, 539
20:13	535
20:11-15	85
20:6	116
20:9	615
20:14	369
21	461
21:1	345, 461, 117
21:2	250, 367, 370
21:3	101, 150
21:5	461, 537
21:1-8	249
21:5-8	345
21:8	461, 537
21:9	250
21:9	134, 134
21:10	117
21:11	134
21:12	615
21:23	137, 138
22:3	142, 337
22:5	138

ETERNAL SALVATION

22:6   337
22:3-4   33, 38
22:12   535
22:17   250, 536,
          627
22:21   64

Subject Index

A
Aaron 159, 175, 176, 217, 220, 225, 226, 231, 238, 252, 253, 310, 385, 553, 615, 616
Abel 16, 170, 238, 254, 266, 267, 268, 269, 271, 378, 447
Abraham 16, 17, 25, 44, 84, 98, 99, 108, 120, 213, 241, 252, 253, 270, 271, 273, 343, 412, 514, 642, 643, 645, 660
Abraham's bosom 642

Adam 97, 99, 112, 113, 118, 238, 264, 265, 266, 290, 294, 426, 478, 525, 532, 564
Ahab 552
Ahijah 632
Ancient of Days 144, 145, 348, 407, 442, 479, 505, 563
Apollos 335
Areopagus 78, 592
Arminians 87, 523
Asceticism 9
Asia Minor 639
Athanasian Creed 72, 73, 563
Athens 69, 78, 85

Atonement ix, 15, 22, 23, 70, 72, 73, 76, 77, 80, 81, 88, 147, 148, 149, 150, 151, 152, 153, 154, 155, 156, 157, 158, 159, 160, 161, 162, 167, 168, 169, 171, 176, 180, 185, 192, 198, 205, 207, 210, 216, 220, 228, 229, 230, 232, 233, 234, 238, 257, 258, 259, 262, 263, 264, 265, 278, 281,

ETERNAL SALVATION

288, 289,
291, 292,
295, 296,
297, 301,
310, 311,
314, 335,
336, 342,
356, 357,
366, 367,
381, 382,
383, 385,
386, 388,
390, 392,
395, 396,
399, 404,
405, 407,
411, 414,
416, 420,
421, 431,
439, 441,
442, 443,
455, 459,
460, 463,
472, 474,
479, 480,
481, 482,
492, 494,
499, 508,
510, 511,
517, 518,
521, 523,
524, 527,
528, 529,
530, 533,
535, 536,
543, 548,
562, 572,
609, 617,
622, 623,
626, 627,
629, 630,
633, 635,
646, 649,
662
Atoning Sacrifice
 ix, 88,
148, 154,
155, 173,
180, 182,
192, 203,
221, 229,
251, 257,
258, 269,
304, 338,
342, 351,
364, 384,
386, 393,
394, 397,
399, 402,
410, 425,
450, 457,
459, 474,
486, 505,
506, 507,
511, 522,
528, 529,
532, 540,
547, 551,
553, 561,
578, 600,
603, 604,
618, 624,
664, 665
Attributes of God
 93, 115
Augustine, St.
 75, 76,
110, 133,
135, 290,
338, 373,
555, 561,
563, 579,
644

B
Babylon 47, 48,
53, 56, 57,
58, 213,
242, 243,
244, 246,
612
Babylonian Exile
 53, 245
Baptism 25, 37,
343, 426,
429, 467,
483, 488,
507, 649
Belgic Confession
 25, 76, 82,
193, 344,
396, 398,
414, 482,
501, 502
Berea 78
Bethlehem
 178, 309
Bible i, x, xii,
xiii, xiv,
xv, 4, 6,
15, 18, 24,
27, 32, 35,
67, 71, 80,
86, 100,
101, 106,
110, 114,
115, 119,
120, 127,
131, 143,
152, 201,
222, 234,
258, 288,
289, 290,
291, 292,
293, 323,
340, 342,
343, 349,
362, 393,
394, 396,
397, 412,
439, 444,
463, 474,
476, 477,
485, 486,
511, 519,

Subject Index

521, 527,
531, 536,
539, 548,
553, 556,
565, 578,
579, 580,
581, 591,
593, 599,
623, 626,
631, 632,
647, 666,
671, 672,
673, 674,
675, 676,
677, 678,
681, 682,
683, 686,
687, 688,
692, 693

Blood of Christ
47, 71, 72,
160, 165,
166, 187,
204, 209,
218, 222,
232, 251,
264, 302,
386, 417,
453, 463,
464, 465,
467, 468,
479, 567,
572, 573,
617

Body of Christ
25, 35, 37,
66, 374,
429, 455,
461, 573,
575, 576,
577

Burnt Offering 99,
148, 162,
163, 164,
165, 166,

167, 168,
169, 170,
171, 172,
173, 174,
175, 176,
177, 178,
180, 181,
184, 187,
188, 189,
190, 194,
198, 202,
204, 205,
208, 209,
211, 214,
215, 217,
218, 225,
226, 228,
230, 231,
232, 257,
266, 269,
270, 271,
275, 279,
286, 308,
311, 312,
328, 359,
392, 406,
412, 484,
489

C
Caiaphas 389, 418
491, 494
499, 507
Cain 266, 267,
268, 378,
447, 494
Calvary 21, 254,
306, 307,
347, 359,
499, 501,
515, 609
Calvinists 7, 8, 87,
540
Calvin, John 287,
395, 405,

419, 483,
545, 579

Canons of Dordt
396, 415,
529
Christ   iv, v,
vi, viii,
ix, 1, 4, 7,
11, 12, 13,
14, 15, 16,
17, 18, 21,
22, 23, 24,
25, 27, 28,
29, 30, 32,
35, 36, 37,
38, 39, 40,
45, 47, 49,
64, 66, 68,
69, 71, 72,
73, 74, 75,
76, 77, 78,
79, 83, 85,
86, 87, 88,
91, 92, 93,
94, 100,
101, 106,
110, 112,
118, 120,
121, 125,
126, 128,
131, 134,
137, 138,
141, 142,
144, 145,
147, 148,
149, 150,
151, 152,
153, 154,
160, 161,
164, 165,
166, 167,
172, 173,
174, 175,
180, 186,

ETERNAL SALVATION

187,188,
189,193,
197,202,
203,204,
205,206,
207,208,
209,211,
214,216,
217,218,
219,220,
221,222,
224,225,
226,228,
230,232,
233,234,
237,238,
247,248,
250, 251,
252, 253,
254,255,
256,257,
259,260,
261,264,
268,269,
270,271,
272,278,
280,281,
285,286,
287,289,
290,291,
292,293,
294,295,
296,297,
298,299,
301,302,
303,304,
305,307,
309,311,
313,314,
317,319,
321,323,
325,327,
329,331,
333,334,
336,337,

338,339,
341,342,
343,344,
345,346,
347,348,
349,350,
351,352,
353,354,
355,356,
357,360,
362,363,
364,365,
366,367,
368,370,
371,372,
373,374,
376,377,
378,383,
384,386,
387,388,
389,390,
391,392,
395,396,
397,399,
400,401,
403,404,
405,406,
409,410,
411,413,
414,415,
416,417,
418,419,
421,423,
424,425,
426,427,
428,429,
430,431,
432,433,
434,435,
436,437,
438,439,
440,441,
446,447,
448,449,
450,451,

452,453,
454,455,
456,457,
458,459,
460,461,
462,463,
464,465,
466,467,
468,469,
471,473,
474, 476,
477,478,
479,480,
481,482,
484,485,
486,489,
490,491,
493,494,
495,496,
498,500,
501,504,
509,511,
512,513,
514,515,
517,518,
519,520,
521,522,
523,524,
525,526,
527,528,
529,530,
531,532,
533,535,
536,537,
538,539,
540,541,
542,543,
544,545,
546,547,
548,549,
550,551,
553,554,
558,560,
561,562,
563,564,

Subject Index

565, 567, 568, 572, 573, 574, 575, 576, 577, 578, 579, 580, 581, 582, 584, 585, 586, 587, 590, 595, 596, 597, 598, 599, 600, 603, 604, 605, 606, 611, 614, 615, 617, 618, 621, 622, 623, 624, 625, 626, 627, 629, 630, 631, 632, 633, 634, 635, 637, 639, 640, 641, 643, 644, 645, 646, 647, 648, 649, 650, 651, 652, 653, 654, 655, 657, 659, 660, 661, 662, 663, 664, 665, 666, 667, 668, 669, 671, 672, 681, 685, 688, 689, 693

Christianity 2, 3, 4, 8, 9, 11, 17, 32, 342, 367, 374, 434, 561, 563, 564, 580, 596, 597, 598

Christology viii, 11, 14, 72, 151, 286

Church v, viii, 3, 4, 8, 9, 13, 24, 25, 26, 28, 31, 32, 33, 36, 40, 72, 73, 75, 76, 78, 82, 93, 96, 101, 128, 172, 173, 186, 201, 203, 208, 209, 216, 224, 228, 250, 255, 264, 289, 302, 304, 305, 322, 327, 336, 337, 339, 342, 343, 344, 347, 354, 359, 364, 367, 435, 454, 464, 465, 475, 512, 513, 561, 562, 563, 565, 572, 573, 574, 575, 576, 584, 597, 601, 623, 640, 649, 650, 653, 663

Church Fathers 32, 73, 75, 76, 128, 289, 322, 367, 454, 561, 584, 640

Conversion viii, 15, 16, 17, 37, 63, 70, 225, 301, 342, 343, 348, 362, 409, 463, 464, 467, 506, 542, 555, 594, 608

Cosmos 10, 60, 140, 218, 345, 369, 461, 517, 525, 526, 583

Council of Nicaea 72, 597

Covenant viii, ix, 16, 19, 49, 70, 71, 91, 97, 98, 128, 152, 160, 161, 164, 181, 183, 186, 209, 219, 247, 253, 272, 300, 302, 308, 343, 372, 376, 387, 416, 450, 451, 452, 453, 454,

Creation 462, 463, 507, 522, 575, 579
Creation 21, 26, 43, 82, 93, 106, 139, 141, 218, 248, 249, 254, 290, 297, 345, 429, 460, 461, 525, 573, 574, 579, 585, 588, 589, 590, 593, 600, 629
Creator 92, 408, 563, 593, 602, 603
Cross of Christ 69, 218, 287, 301, 303, 341, 356, 362, 363, 455, 464, 465, 466, 467, 541, 542, 544, 545, 546, 572
Cross Theology 71

D

Day of Atonement 151, 152, 153, 161, 162, 163, 171, 186, 188, 194, 198, 206, 207, 208, 209, 210, 211, 214, 215, 216, 219, 220, 222, 251, 258, 382, 384, 388, 439, 506, 508, 522, 524, 572, 609, 610, 618

Day of Pentecost 27, 101, 302, 434

Death 8, 16, 21, 24, 34, 35, 36, 47, 50, 54, 62, 63, 64, 68, 75, 78, 88, 100, 120, 131, 152, 156, 157, 159, 166, 167, 173, 175, 187, 194, 203, 205, 206, 207, 208, 216, 218, 222, 223, 230, 231, 232, 233, 241, 247, 254, 259, 260, 261, 262, 265, 266, 268, 271, 285, 293, 295, 298, 299, 300, 302, 303, 304, 305, 310, 313, 315, 316, 317, 318, 320, 324, 328, 330, 334, 335, 336, 338, 339, 341, 342, 343, 345, 347, 349, 350, 351, 353, 356, 357, 358, 360, 361, 363, 364, 366, 367, 368, 369, 371, 373, 374, 375, 376, 382, 384, 387, 388, 390, 395, 397, 406, 410, 411, 412, 415, 418, 420, 423, 425, 426, 427, 428, 434, 437, 438, 439, 440, 441, 446, 449, 451, 452, 456, 461, 463, 465, 466, 467, 468, 469, 471, 473, 475, 476, 477, 479, 481, 483, 489, 490, 491, 492, 493, 496, 497, 498, 500, 503, 505, 509,

510, 511, 517, 518, 520, 521, 523, 524, 529, 531, 537, 540, 541, 543, 547, 548, 561, 562, 563, 564, 565, 566, 567, 568, 579, 580, 581, 582, 585, 586, 595, 607, 615, 616, 617, 626, 627, 629, 631, 640, 641, 642, 643, 644, 645, 646, 662, 663, 664

Deity of Christ 23, 72

Demons 2, 55, 60, 78, 213, 214, 375, 376, 605, 621, 624, 631, 634, 639, 646, 647, 648, 649, 650, 651, 652, 653, 654, 656, 657, 658, 659, 660, 661, 662, 663

E

Early Church 72, 73, 76, 304, 649

Ecclesiology ix, 224, 577

Egyptians 48, 51, 199, 200, 242, 623

Eli 141, 155, 322

Elijah 33, 205, 552, 628

Elisha 627, 628, 635

Elizabeth 27, 591, 594, 596

Enlightenment 2

Enoch 44, 99, 212

Ephesus 78

Ephraim 103, 112

Epicureans 69, 86

Eschatology 21, 63, 345, 577, 581

Eternal Life viii, 16, 23, 29, 62, 70, 75, 87, 133, 259, 303, 321, 328, 350, 410, 463, 471, 478, 509, 520, 523, 531, 538, 539, 541, 579, 582, 587, 589, 590, 591

Eternity 53, 94, 95, 104, 105, 106, 142, 150, 279, 327, 398, 539, 551, 565

Ethical Model 286, 291, 297

Evangelical ix, xv, 4, 24, 26, 542, 640, 669, 682, 685, 689

Eve 213, 264, 265, 266, 564

Evil Spirits 78, 650, 659

Exclusivism iv, 579, 585

Exegesis 70, 82, 151, 232, 322, 450, 521, 524

Ezra 20, 27, 156, 167, 178, 179, 195, 205, 206, 210, 212, 260, 267

F

Faith vi, 3, 9, 13, 18, 22, 24, 35, 37, 42, 45, 61, 62, 65, 66, 69, 71, 72, 79, 83, 84, 85, 87, 120, 121, 122, 126, 138, 166, 173, 179, 180, 186, 190, 192, 224, 225, 255, 268, 271, 272,

ETERNAL SALVATION

273, 275,
298, 299,
302, 303,
311, 333,
338, 342,
343, 344,
348, 350,
360, 362,
363, 365,
383, 387,
388, 401,
402, 409,
416, 417,
418, 425,
427, 428,
429, 430,
432, 446,
457, 460,
463, 465,
467, 478,
482, 494,
498, 519,
524, 526,
528, 529,
531, 532,
543, 550,
555, 557,
558, 566,
574, 580,
582, 594,
595, 602,
606, 622,
623, 627,
628, 630,
631, 633,
635, 636,
637, 638,
639, 647,
652, 660,
664

Faithfulness
93, 95, 98,
106, 110,
111, 118,
119, 120,

121, 122,
123, 124,
158, 258,
259, 275,
388, 550

Family 17, 191,
199, 208,
224, 238,
239, 241,
243, 252,
314, 321,
336, 342,
343, 429,
532, 576,
578, 614

Fellowship
10, 93, 96,
330, 682

Flood 97,
213, 269,
270, 585,
643, 644

Forgiveness
23, 24, 61,
70, 72, 88,
113, 147,
154, 155,
159, 160,
186, 187,
218, 257,
263, 280,
281, 286,
296, 301,
302, 303,
305, 308,
310, 311,
314, 315,
316, 319,
330, 338,
343, 387,
400, 410,
414, 418,
428, 439,
440, 450,
456, 458,

459, 463,
465, 467,
504, 505,
506, 507,
508, 512,
518, 523,
549, 550,
551, 552,
553, 554,
556, 557,
558, 559,
560, 561,
564, 586,
603, 604,
623, 631,
633, 636,
638

Freewill Offerings
163, 165,
178, 183

G
Garden of Eden
112
Gentiles 24, 28, 61,
69, 78, 86,
206, 211,
287, 304,
315, 342,
344, 358,
361, 446,
448, 455,
456, 463,
465, 478,
542, 571,
572, 573,
574, 575,
576, 577,
578, 586,
587, 588,
589, 590,
591, 592,
593, 598,
599, 601,
603, 608,

Subject Index

	630, 660	586, 587,	408, 409,
Gethsemane		588, 589,	414, 437,
	439, 476,	590, 594,	438, 439,
	492, 497,	595, 596,	441, 442,
	499, 500,	597, 598,	443, 448,
	502	599, 600,	451, 454,
Godhead	14, 95,	601, 602,	459, 462,
	142, 144,	603, 606,	485, 486,
	145, 406,	607, 644,	501, 513,
	513	648	525, 526,
Go'el	15,	Grace 9, 10, 11,	539, 561,
	237, 238,	64, 66,	562, 563,
	241, 247,	112, 113,	566, 567,
	248	676, 682	568, 574,
Good Shepherd		Grain Offering	584, 589,
	507	148, 162,	633, 641,
Good Works 8, 13,		167, 174,	654, 672,
	84, 85,	175, 176,	677, 681,
	258, 344,	178, 266,	690, 693
	565, 591,	275, 312,	Guilt Offering
	595, 601,	484, 489	148, 155,
	605	Greece 3, 11, 58	162, 165,
Gospel	v, 10, 17,	Greek xv, 3, 6,	167, 178,
	18, 30, 33,	11, 19, 20,	182, 189,
	36, 39, 65,	35, 44, 50,	190, 191,
	66, 70, 78,	58, 60, 61,	192, 193,
	91, 92, 93,	62, 63, 64,	194, 195,
	129, 130,	67, 85, 91,	222, 286,
	134, 206,	92, 95, 96,	308, 312,
	217, 287,	103, 107,	483
	321, 349,	108, 110,	
	361, 368,	111, 112,	**H**
	388, 391,	118, 120,	Hades 374, 641,
	409, 411,	122, 129,	642, 643,
	416, 417,	130, 137,	644, 645
	443, 447,	153, 161,	Heavenly Sanctuary
	448, 460,	213, 255,	71, 209,
	466, 482,	278, 280,	210, 218,
	524, 529,	317, 319,	220, 221,
	534, 538,	327, 328,	424, 436,
	540, 569,	335, 345,	438, 439,
	572, 573,	368, 371,	441, 463,
	578, 579,	385, 386,	464, 609,
	580, 581,	387, 390,	618
	582, 585,	393, 401,	Hebrew 6, 35, 42,

45, 48, 49, 50, 52, 66, 98, 103, 108, 110, 111, 112, 117, 118, 121, 122, 125, 128, 129, 135, 136, 151, 153, 155, 161, 167, 168, 179, 182, 188, 189, 198, 200, 201, 202, 238, 240, 243, 248, 257, 259, 270, 278, 322, 385, 387, 393, 439, 462, 485, 486, 598, 613, 616, 624, 626, 633, 644, 677

Heidelberg Catechism 13, 18, 76, 83, 366, 415, 424, 427, 432, 474, 475, 492, 500, 652, 685

Hell 8, 18, 36, 374, 501, 539, 640, 641, 644, 646

Herod 220, 304, 446, 499

Hezekiah 177, 257

High Priest 143, 149, 156, 157, 162, 171, 174, 186, 208, 209, 210, 211, 214, 215, 217, 219, 220, 224, 231, 238, 250, 251, 254, 255, 310, 321, 352, 384, 388, 431, 432, 436, 441, 453, 454, 507, 609, 618

Holiness 33, 38, 61, 8, 93, 103, 109, 114, 115, 116, 117, 118, 119, 122, 123, 124, 185, 216, 258, 410, 524, 553, 566

Holy Land 107, 242, 245

Holy Spirit viii, ix, 19, 22, 26, 27, 30, 37, 38, 39, 70, 72, 76, 77, 79, 86, 99, 106, 115, 127, 144, 145, 175, 182, 205, 207, 223, 301, 303, 310, 317, 326, 339, 354, 360, 368, 405, 433, 434, 444, 447, 457, 488, 494, 530, 559, 566, 572, 576, 585, 586, 600, 601, 602, 603, 604, 605, 606, 607, 639, 652, 653, 654, 660, 664, 686, 689

Humanity 6, 12, 14, 23, 24, 26, 71, 74, 75, 76, 94, 95, 97, 100, 101, 105, 113, 119, 123, 132, 175, 193, 216, 218, 269, 270, 288, 290, 292, 295, 315, 334, 341, 351, 356, 357, 359, 382, 396, 397, 400, 404, 405, 407, 408, 420, 424, 434, 442, 443, 445, 446, 448, 449,

Subject Index

  450, 451,
  453, 454,
  458, 466,
  468, 480,
  481, 483,
  494, 497,
  506, 508,
  548, 549,
  553, 562,
  564, 573,
  593, 601,
  642
Hyper-Calvinists
  7, 8, 540

I
Inclusivism
  580, 585,
  689
Intercession
  251, 254,
  255, 311,
  352, 430,
  436
Irenaeus 73, 75,
  320, 601
Islam 3, 8, 12,
  32, 213,
  342
Israel iv, 11, 20,
  27, 31, 41,
  48, 49, 50,
  51, 52, 53,
  54, 55, 56,
  57, 58, 60,
  61, 63, 68,
  78, 97, 98,
  99, 100,
  104, 107,
  117, 128,
  135, 140,
  153, 154,
  171, 172,
  181, 184,
  185, 188,
  198, 199,
  200, 203,
  204, 205,
  206, 207,
  208, 209,
  210, 211,
  214, 216,
  221, 228,
  230, 239,
  241, 242,
  243, 244,
  245, 246,
  247, 257,
  262, 263,
  277, 290,
  302, 304,
  309, 317,
  333, 337,
  341, 342,
  343, 344,
  352, 353,
  354, 358,
  377, 378,
  385, 393,
  435, 444,
  454, 456,
  478, 491,
  495, 503,
  520, 550,
  553, 557,
  567, 571,
  572, 573,
  574, 575,
  576, 577,
  579, 581,
  583, 585,
  586, 587,
  589, 591,
  593, 595,
  596, 597,
  599, 600,
  601, 603,
  605, 607,
  608, 609,
  610, 611,
  612, 613,
  614, 615,
  616, 617,
  618, 619,
  623, 637,
  662, 686

J
Jacob 41, 54, 60,
  64, 97, 98,
  99, 107,
  113, 120,
  152, 157,
  190, 241,
  243, 244,
  246, 247,
  318, 504,
  579, 632,
  677
Jerusalem 3,
  31, 33, 41,
  52, 78,
  117, 125,
  126, 134,
  137, 202,
  205, 208,
  243, 250,
  279, 309,
  310, 315,
  316, 321,
  401, 409,
  503, 509,
  537, 586,
  606, 609,
  611, 614,
  615, 616,
  617, 621,
  631, 642,
  650
Jesus Christ
  iv, v, 11,
  13, 21, 37,
  49, 64, 69,
  74, 79, 85,
  86, 91, 92,

ETERNAL SALVATION

	93, 94,		202, 203,		434, 594,
	100, 118,		204, 207,		596, 597,
	131, 134,		215, 242		598, 688
	142, 144,	Job	44, 51, 56,	Judgment	24, 29,
	145, 148,		136, 170,		49, 85,
	160, 166,		227, 238,		117, 123,
	175, 180,		241, 246,		138, 144,
	204, 208,		247, 260,		158, 174,
	252, 254,		261, 340,		183, 194,
	257, 280,		451, 546,		216, 217,
	285, 287,		583, 592,		242, 249,
	289, 290,		599, 644,		261, 263,
	292, 298,		676, 679,		272, 282,
	302, 304,		684, 686		316, 323,
	323, 328,	John, The Apostle			340, 359,
	339, 344,		140, 144,		381, 382,
	346, 365,		204, 550		383, 391,
	366, 372,	John the Baptist			399, 400,
	373, 392,		33, 61,		404, 411,
	396, 397,		165, 203,		420, 444,
	399, 405,		204, 303,		448, 458,
	413, 417,		506, 507,		463, 464,
	418, 423,		559		465, 473,
	426, 428,	Jonah	92,		474, 481,
	429, 431,		111, 339,		485, 492,
	435, 436,		505		494, 497,
	451, 456,	Joseph	99,		501, 502,
	460, 463,		113, 228,		503, 534,
	465, 471,		299, 320,		535, 538,
	477, 480,		474, 482,		539, 541,
	482, 504,		642		543, 582,
	512, 513,	Josephus, Flavius			585, 586,
	515, 523,		137, 267,		587, 590,
	537, 544,		401		606, 611,
	549, 562,	Joshua	50,		628
	565, 568,		171, 273,	Justification	viii, ix,
	587, 595,		354, 355,		15, 16, 19,
	603, 606,		378		34, 84, 88,
	618, 630,	Josiah	77		93, 126,
	652, 660,	Judah	52, 243,		223, 233,
	661, 669,		245, 252,		268, 272,
	681, 693		318, 367,		298, 336,
Jethro	592, 599		370, 444,		343, 385,
Jewish Tradition			616		386, 409,
	44,	Judaism	8, 342,		426, 428,

740

Subject Index

456,459,
463,465,
467,520,
532,555,
564,565,
585, 602,
610,663,
665

K
King Agrippa 78
Kingdom of God
 viii, 19,
 36, 62, 68,
 127, 131,
 286, 314,
 330, 342,
 343, 363,
 365, 506,
 554, 596,
 649, 657

L
Lamb of God
 5,165,
 203, 204,
 218, 303,
 389, 414,
 520, 562
Law ix, 8, 9,
 15, 27, 28,
 30,38,64,
 7,84,126,
 147,183,
 190,198,
 218,222,
 231,238,
 240,253,
 258,262,
 263,268,
 279,280,
 290,302,
 311,312,
 327,336,
 338,361,
 365,373,
 390,392,
 407,408,
 411,414,
 417,425,
 428,429,
 446,447,
 462,471,
 476,477,
 478,479,
 480,481,
 482,500,
 504,551,
 571,577,
 590,594,
 596, 599,
 617,627,
 630, 660,
 663
Lawgiver 408
Lawlessness 13,
 338, 344,
 346, 349,
 567, 605,
 659
Lazarus 1, 41,
 628, 643,
 645,649,
 661
Legalism 27,
 38,64, 85
Legalism 8
Leprosy 40,
 194, 198,
 222, 230,
 335, 425,
 558, 623,
 662
Lewis, C.S. 580, 604
Liberal 30, 70,
 81, 88,
 553
Liberty 27,38,64,
 248, 338,
 463, 553,
 622
Logos 11, 12, 15,
 75,100,
 145, 583,
 584
Lord's Supper 8,
 25, 70, 71,
 166, 180,
 308, 390,
 467, 469,
 475, 477
Love iv, v, 5,
 15, 17, 19,
 21, 23, 27,
 28, 29, 30,
 31, 38, 39,
 40, 42, 45,
 58, 84, 88,
 91, 93, 94,
 95, 99,
 100, 102,
 103, 104,
 105, 106,
 107, 108,
 109, 110,
 111, 112,
 113, 114,
 115, 116,
 121, 123,
 124, 126,
 128, 131,
 132, 133,
 135, 138,
 141, 158,
 159, 166,
 173, 189,
 217, 226,
 237, 238,
 242, 245,
 246, 257,
 258, 259,
 262, 270,
 271, 275,
 276, 278,
 281, 288

291, 292,
293, 304,
320, 334,
335, 337,
341, 342,
345, 346,
347, 348,
349, 350,
355, 382,
383, 393,
397, 399,
402, 403,
405, 406,
409, 410,
412, 413,
414, 416,
417, 418,
420, 423,
430, 443,
445, 447,
449, 457,
458, 466,
472, 498,
510, 512,
520, 522,
549, 550,
592, 607,
610, 611,
614, 634,
662

Luther, Martin
20, 84, 86,
109, 129,
131, 140,
288, 367,
403, 409,
419, 562,
680, 683

Lystra 78

M

Marriage 336, 663
Martyrdom
18, 356
Marxist 6

Mediator 20, 14
397, 450,
670
Melchizedek
125, 251,
252, 253,
396, 592,
599
Mercy Seat 98, 149,
161, 216,
219, 221,
264, 387,
388, 395
Messiah 5, 34, 50,
61, 78,
125, 193,
204, 205,
210, 211,
247, 252,
268, 282,
306, 308,
309, 312,
314, 317,
318, 324,
342, 352,
353, 354,
355, 356,
358, 361,
367, 385,
410, 440,
483, 496,
503, 509,
574, 596,
597, 598,
608, 609,
612, 613,
624
Messianic kingdom
28, 29, 31,
54, 63,
127, 128,
248, 318,
319, 555,
577, 609,
613, 616,

617, 629,
635, 656
Messianic Psalms
308, 358
Micah 41, 110,
125, 160,
244, 276,
277, 281,
447, 560,
592
Middle Ages 73
Midianites
263, 378
Miracle 131, 206,
606, 656,
657
Monasticism 33
Moralism 8, 595
Moses 11, 29, 32,
44, 48, 50,
97, 98, 99,
100, 140,
158, 171,
174, 183,
199, 262,
302, 316,
354, 355,
377, 378,
409, 428,
450, 451,
452, 454,
455, 504,
509, 550,
567, 599,
616, 632
Most High God
242, 252
Most Holy Place
98, 209,
216, 220,
223
Mount Sinai 99,
377, 550
Mount Zion
107, 372,

Subject Index

642
Mystical Aspect
  8, 32
Mystical Model
  286, 294,
  297
Mysticism 9

N

Naaman 592, 599,
  635
Nazareth 474, 628,
  686
Netherlands 3, 7,
  55, 228,
  297, 479,
  534
New Covenant
  71, 97,
  161, 416,
  450, 452,
  453, 454,
  462, 463
New Creation
  345, 429,
  574
New Testament
  x, xiv, xv,
  xvi, 6, 13,
  19, 34, 36,
  43, 59, 61,
  62, 64, 66,
  71, 74, 87,
  100, 101,
  106, 108,
  109, 110,
  118, 119,
  124, 129,
  130, 131,
  137, 150,
  151, 153,
  165, 166,
  167, 172,
  175, 180,
  182, 183,
  186, 198,
  201, 203,
  204, 208,
  219, 220,
  223, 224,
  238, 255,
  256, 263,
  269, 271,
  277, 278,
  290, 296,
  297, 303,
  305, 318,
  321, 322,
  324, 336,
  344, 346,
  350, 353,
  354, 355,
  357, 359,
  367, 368,
  378, 384,
  385, 388,
  389, 397,
  398, 399,
  400, 401,
  411, 416,
  425, 443,
  444, 446,
  448, 450,
  454, 462,
  465, 468,
  469, 478,
  481, 483,
  484, 488,
  489, 581,
  584, 623,
  628, 641,
  657, 659,
  667, 670,
  671, 672,
  675, 678,
  681, 689,
  690, 693
Nicene Creed
  72,
  305, 492,
  671
Nicodemus
  342, 596
Noah 44, 97, 99,
  170, 238,
  267, 269,
  270, 343,
  429, 585,
  593, 643,
  644
Nomological Aspect
  8, 27

O

Offering 12, 13, 15,
  16, 17,
  167, 169,
  175, 182,
  189, 250,
  272, 273,
  307, 309,
  311, 482,
  678
Old Testament ix,
  xiv, xv,
  29, 31, 38,
  47, 48, 55,
  61, 101,
  106, 110,
  113, 117,
  118, 121,
  128, 136,
  137, 143,
  144, 147,
  148, 149,
  150, 151,
  153, 154,
  155, 157,
  158, 159,
  161, 163,
  164, 165,
  166, 167,
  169, 171,
  173, 175,
  177, 179,

ETERNAL SALVATION

180, 181,
182, 183,
185, 187,
189, 191,
193, 195,
198, 204,
206, 221,
223, 224,
225, 234,
237, 238,
239, 241,
250, 251,
256, 259,
264, 265,
268, 272,
278, 279,
280, 281,
297, 301,
303, 314,
318, 354,
359, 374,
376, 377,
378, 383,
384, 388,
400, 425,
432, 444,
446, 462,
465, 468,
469, 485,
493, 505,
508, 511,
608, 609,
610, 622,
640, 644,
645, 646,
673, 674,
678, 686,
691

Origen 73,
290, 361,
373

P

Paganism 2,
158, 442,
649

Paradise 3, 5, 6, 7,
21, 23, 32,
113, 138,
319, 554,
642, 643,
644, 645,
646

Paul, the Apostle
27, 33, 61,
63, 71, 82,
189, 298,
309, 315,
347, 428,
456, 459,
524, 596,
628

Pascal, Blaise
120, 598

Paschal Lamb
76, 469

Passover Festival
199, 200,
201

Passover Lamb
164, 490

Passover Meal
310, 490

Patristic 75

Peace Offering
148, 162,
163, 166,
167, 175,
176, 177,
178, 179,
180, 181,
194, 226,
286, 308,
309, 310,
312

Pentecost 27, 86,
101, 163,
194, 205,
206, 207,
302, 434,
575 665

Periodic Offerings
163

Pesach 13,
163, 198,
201, 202,
203, 207,
323, 326,
469

Peter, the Apostle
13,
315, 358,
364, 503,
583,

Pharaoh 56, 59,
113, 503,
580, 592

Pharisees 67,
309, 342,
596

Philippi 78,
591, 686

Placationism 19,
400, 406

Politeia 574, 576

Pontius Pilate 72,
304, 351,
492

Predestination
viii, ix,
15, 19,
460, 518,
521, 522,
532, 534,
535, 579

Prodigal Son
22, 25,
310, 336,
348, 458,
459, 506,
507, 549,
554

Promised Land 99,
107, 203,

Subject Index

354, 378
Propitiation ix, 71,
147, 148,
149, 150,
158, 166,
167, 193,
208, 219,
251, 382,
384, 386,
387, 393,
394, 395,
396, 399,
400, 401,
402, 405,
406, 407,
409, 414,
417, 420,
441, 442,
460, 462,
472, 489,
512, 520,
526, 527,
528, 531,
561, 586,
614
Protestant 3, 8,
67, 82, 83,
84, 86,
114, 115,
224, 228,
291, 344,
366, 649
Purification 14,
226, 228,
230, 616,
678

R
Rahab 56,
343, 377,
592, 599
Ransom-to-Satan
Model 10, 73
Reconciliation
ix, 16, 40,

147, 148,
149, 150,
216, 287,
311, 336,
348, 395,
398, 399,
400, 402,
404, 405,
413, 414,
423, 424,
425, 441,
442, 443,
444, 445,
448, 450,
451, 455,
456, 457,
458, 459,
460, 461,
462, 464,
465, 489,
511, 512,
518, 520,
523, 524,
525, 526,
542, 561,
572, 573,
577, 578,
608, 614,
662
Redeemed
viii, 16,
21, 27, 31,
48, 52, 53,
61, 93, 98,
99, 100,
124, 125,
134, 154,
164, 205,
237, 242,
243, 244,
245, 246,
249, 250,
329, 330,
337, 345,
355, 366,

378, 390,
408, 411,
467, 468,
500, 554,
567, 627,
633, 644,
645, 660,
664
Redemption
viii, 1, 5,
14, 15, 19,
21, 22, 26,
32, 35, 44,
49, 53, 61,
62, 71, 75,
87, 113,
117, 118,
123, 187,
197, 205,
211, 218,
220, 223,
239, 240,
242, 243,
246, 247,
248, 249,
262, 264,
296, 297,
299, 318,
327, 328,
329, 334,
335, 343,
374, 378,
383, 386,
387, 388,
390, 391,
400, 408,
413, 424,
425, 431,
434, 437,
438, 439,
440, 463,
469, 479,
483, 489,
523, 549,
550, 561,

562, 564,
565, 566,
567, 585,
629, 649

Reformational
Theology 16
Reformed
Theology 80, 107
Reformers 76,
290, 291
Regeneration
viii, 16,
17, 34, 35,
37, 39, 63,
70, 88,
299, 301,
339, 342,
348, 360,
439, 602
Religion 4, 8, 9,
10, 11, 12,
268, 342,
544, 550,
581, 593,
595, 597
Repentance
12, 15, 52,
192, 207,
211, 238,
275, 302,
310, 314,
315, 409,
458, 494,
506, 520,
552, 553,
555, 556,
557, 558,
559, 572,
585, 586,
590, 602,
603, 604,
613
Restrictivism
579

Resurrection
15, 16, 86,
141, 207,
221, 222,
247, 254,
302, 304,
305, 309,
310, 314,
315, 318,
329, 330,
335, 359,
360, 363,
374, 424,
425, 426,
427, 428,
429, 431,
438, 466,
467, 469,
483, 487,
510, 531,
538, 541,
562, 608,
622, 629,
635, 641,
642, 643,
644, 645
Righteousness
5, 13, 14,
19, 30, 31,
32, 38, 42,
43, 44, 47,
51, 52, 53,
61, 65, 66,
77, 83, 93,
94, 95,
105, 114,
116, 120,
121, 123,
124, 125,
126, 127,
188, 210,
211, 216,
244, 260,
261, 271,
272, 273,

274, 275,
276, 290,
291, 292,
293, 319,
327, 334,
337, 340,
357, 360,
364, 365,
366, 367,
382, 389,
396, 401,
406, 408,
409, 410,
415, 416,
417, 418,
419, 420,
424, 425,
427, 428,
460, 462,
467, 471,
472, 477,
478, 482,
483, 484,
489, 494,
520, 524,
526, 532,
553, 566,
585, 594,
596, 598,
602, 609,
625, 629,
659
Righteous One
116, 261,
365, 389,
490
Ritualism 7
Romans 23, 30, 80,
120, 148,
149, 180,
188, 280,
291, 302,
321, 357,
359, 371,
387, 388,

S

Sabbath 127, 182, 207, 274

Sacrifice ix, 3, 24, 9, 77, 78 88, 99, 119, 147, 148, 154, 155, 157, 158, 159, 160, 165, 166, 167, 168, 169, 171, 173, 174, 176, 178, 180, 182, 183, 189, 192, 201, 203, 205, 208, 209, 212, 213, 214, 215, 216, 217, 219, 220, 221, 222, 224, 226, 229, 231, 232, 251, 252, 254, 255, 256, 257, 258, 264, 266, 267, 268, 269, 270, 272, 273, 274, 275, 278, 279, 286, 290, 296, 297, 299, 300, 304, 305, 309, 311, 312, 315, 316, 334, 338, 339, 341, 342, 347, 349, 351, 356, 359, 364, 382, 384, 385, 386, 387, 392, 393, 394, 395, 397, 398, 399, 400, 402, 410, 411, 415, 425, 426, 432, 435, 436, 439, 451, 457, 459, 468, 472, 474, 484, 485, 486, 489, 493, 494, 495, 497, 505, 506, 395, 401, 416, 423, 445, 449, 450, 456, 457, 458, 460, 471, 473, 493, 495, 503, 504, 528, 571, 572, 575, 580, 584, 588, 589, 590, 593, 601, 603, 607, 667, 668, 671, 673, 676, 681, 682, 686, 688, 689

507, 508, 510, 511, 512, 513, 522, 527, 528, 529, 532, 533, 540, 541, 547, 548, 551, 553, 561, 562, 577, 578, 600, 603, 604, 616, 617, 618, 624, 649, 664, 665

Sacrificial Substitution Model 76

Salvation 1, 2, 7, 8, 9, 11, 18, 20, 21, 23, 32, 33, 35, 43, 47, 48, 49, 51, 52, 53, 55, 57, 59, 61, 63, 64, 65, 67, 69, 71, 72, 73, 75, 77, 79, 81, 83, 85, 87, 91, 92, 93, 95, 97, 99, 101, 102, 103, 105, 107, 109, 111, 113, 115, 117, 119, 121, 123, 125, 127, 129, 131, 133, 135, 137, 138, 139,

141, 143,
145, 298,
342, 343,
347, 489,
531, 532,
633, 672,
679, 683,
685, 689
Salvational
Aspect 49
Samuel 49, 50,
141, 153,
168, 170,
178, 261,
273, 667
Sanctification
viii, 15,
16, 88,
118, 119,
164, 298,
343, 386,
565, 665
Sarah 68, 271
Satan 10, 18, 21,
35, 36, 48,
59, 60, 61,
62, 63, 64,
73, 74, 78,
154, 213,
249, 250,
262, 265,
286, 287,
289, 293,
297, 334,
338, 341,
363, 366,
368, 370,
372, 374,
375, 376,
502, 518,
541, 547,
561, 562,
564, 646,
649, 650,
651, 654,

658, 659,
660, 661,
664
Satisfaction 13, 76,
81, 83, 88,
153, 159,
192, 198,
216, 219,
222, 223,
286, 287,
288, 289,
290, 291,
292, 293,
295, 296,
297, 301,
348, 366,
382, 393,
394, 395,
396, 400,
402, 406,
407, 411,
415, 417,
418, 420,
421, 443,
472, 479,
505, 511,
522, 524,
529, 533,
548, 551,
561
Saul of Tarsus
356, 498,
594, 595
Scapegoat 171, 208,
212, 213,
214, 216,
219, 220,
524
Sectarianism 9
Septuagint 108,
118, 131,
149, 153,
162, 168,
179, 201,
212, 256,

Sin
327, 385,
386, 400,
401, 566,
624, 625
1, 14,
15, 23, 24,
26, 35, 36,
47, 50, 51,
52, 53, 54,
61, 62, 63,
64, 66, 71,
74, 75, 78,
112, 113,
118, 119,
132, 148,
149, 152,
153, 154,
155, 156,
157, 158,
159, 160,
161, 162,
163, 164,
165, 166,
169, 170,
171, 172,
173, 174,
176, 177,
178, 179,
180, 181,
182, 183,
184, 185,
186, 187,
188, 189,
190, 191,
192, 193,
194, 198,
203, 205,
207, 208,
211, 214,
215, 216,
217, 218,
222, 224,
225, 226,
227, 228,
230, 231,

Subject Index

232, 233, 244, 251, 252, 253, 254, 257, 258, 265, 266, 275, 276, 279, 280, 281, 286, 290, 292, 293, 294, 296, 299, 303, 307, 308, 312, 314, 316, 324, 328, 335, 337, 338, 339, 341, 343, 345, 347, 352, 356, 360, 363, 365, 366, 367, 368, 369, 373, 382, 384, 385, 386, 387, 388, 389, 392, 393, 399, 400, 401, 402, 404, 405, 406, 411, 412, 414, 415, 418, 424, 425, 426, 436, 443, 447, 456, 462, 466, 467, 471, 473, 474, 476, 483, 484, 485, 487, 488, 490, 494, 495, 498, 500, 501, 506, 507, 508, 509, 510, 511, 512, 520, 521, 527, 528, 529, 534, 535, 541, 543, 544, 550, 551, 556, 557, 559, 561, 562, 563, 564, 577, 585, 609, 610, 611, 612, 614, 615, 616, 617, 618, 622, 623, 624, 625, 626, 633, 635, 639, 642, 649, 652, 658, 659, 661, 663, 664

Sinaitic Law 177, 478, 484

Sinner 4, 18, 22, 24, 76, 92, 93, 120, 121, 149, 154, 156, 167, 169, 172, 173, 174, 185, 209, 222, 278, 311, 335, 385, 386, 395, 396, 401, 402, 405, 406, 411, 416, 417, 442, 444, 457, 458, 459, 481, 506, 511, 552, 553, 555, 594, 665

Sin Offering 148, 153, 154, 159, 161, 162, 165, 166, 169, 170, 171, 172, 173, 174, 176, 180, 181, 182, 183, 184, 185, 186, 187, 188, 189, 190, 193, 194, 198, 207, 208, 214, 215, 225, 226, 227, 228, 230, 231, 232, 233, 258, 275, 279, 286, 292, 307, 308, 312, 314, 316, 328, 382, 386, 387, 389, 473, 483, 490, 507, 509, 512, 618

Socialism 6

749

Sola Cruce 10, 85
Sola Fide 83, 85, 348
Sola Gratia 10, 87
Sola Scriptura 10, 81
Solomon 105, 107, 164, 177, 220, 247, 274, 278, 355, 557, 607
Son of Man 13, 70, 144, 145, 160, 237, 259, 290, 304, 311, 317, 329, 357, 358, 390, 409, 441, 490, 496, 507, 509, 513, 532, 538, 636
Soteriology viii, 1, 11, 15, 18, 63, 74, 81, 83, 92, 134, 148, 150, 289, 518, 561, 562, 563, 565, 568
Spiritism 648
Spirit of God 65, 79, 326, 630
Stephen 76, 78, 140, 221, 301, 316, 329, 455, 498, 503
Stoics 69, 86
Sublapsariaism 518, 519, 523, 535
Substitution 48, 76, 79, 88, 193, 198, 216, 222, 292, 293, 295, 296, 297, 299, 300, 301, 336, 348, 366, 381, 382, 383, 384, 385, 389, 390, 391, 393, 412, 418, 489, 510, 511, 522, 524, 533, 535, 536, 561
Suffering 18, 361, 364, 658
Synod of Dordt 87, 479
Synoptic Gopels 205, 304
Systematic Theology viii, 2, 23, 413

T

Tabernacle 99, 101, 138, 149, 163, 174, 184, 185, 206, 210, 217, 218, 219, 220, 228, 229, 233, 250, 264, 432, 436, 438, 509
Talmud xiii, 156, 202, 207, 208, 210, 583
Tent of Meeting 99, 150, 228, 230, 231, 233, 262, 263, 615, 616
Tertullian 220, 290
Theopaschitic Model 286, 294, 297
Theopaschitism 19, 400, 402, 406
Theotic Category 9, 36
Torah iv, viii, ix, 19, 27, 38, 39, 103, 120, 125, 151, 227, 240, 266, 273, 316, 452, 453, 454, 478, 551, 577, 581, 583, 584, 589, 590, 591, 592, 593, 594, 597, 598, 605, 680
Trinitarian 11, 72, 73, 93, 95,

Subject Index

Trinity 8, 12, 21, 72, 94, 96, 104, 105, 105, 133, 133, 142, 143, 144, 305, 323, 412, 597, 366, 407, 668
413, 688

Typology 221, 224, 251, 305, 439, 484

U

United States 5, 3

Universalism 460, 461, 517, 518, 533, 534, 536, 539, 581

Unrighteouness 120, 127, 274, 278, 386, 409, 417, 458, 467, 472, 538, 550, 557, 588, 589, 603, 606

Utopia 6

Uzziah 222, 623

V

Vicarious Model 286, 290 293

Vulgate 84, 129, 201, 212, 219, 395, 526

W

Wisdom 20, 36, 66, 67, 69, 77, 86, 114, 315, 375, 606, 607, 654

Word of God 79, 489, 513, 539

World 2, 5, 6, 7, 10, 12, 13, 15, 31, 36, 40, 41, 47, 58, 59, 60, 64, 65, 66, 68, 69, 70, 71, 76, 85, 86, 94, 95, 104, 105, 107, 108, 119, 125, 126, 127, 133, 141, 150, 165, 167, 180, 203, 208, 218, 219, 249, 251, 285, 287, 290, 302, 303, 314, 327, 329, 334, 345, 350, 355, 361, 364, 369, 370, 371, 375, 389, 398, 399, 405, 406, 414, 416, 424, 434, 435, 442, 443, 445, 446, 456, 457, 460, 463, 464, 465, 474, 475, 476, 483, 494, 501, 505, 512, 519, 520, 521, 523, 524, 525, 526, 527, 528, 529, 531, 541, 544, 550, 559, 561, 571, 572, 574, 581, 583, 584, 586, 587, 588, 597, 598, 604, 607, 608, 634, 643, 646, 652

Y

Year of Jubilee 210, 239, 243, 248

Yom Kippur 151, 161, 163, 198, 206, 207, 607, 609, 610

Z

Zebedee 320, 321

Zechariah 27, 61, 135, 309, 310, 496, 591, 594, 596, 601,

	614, 615, 616, 617, 618, 647, 672
Zion	31, 41, 52, 60, 68
	107, 243, 247, 279, 310, 372, 408, 444, 567, 610, 611, 612, 621, 642
Zwingli, Ulrich	604

www.ingramcontent.com/pod-product-compliance
Lightning Source LLC
Chambersburg PA
CBHW071400160426
42811CB00115B/2438/J